THE COMPANION GUIDE TO

EAST ANGLIA

THE COMPANION GUIDES

GENERAL EDITOR: VINCENT CRONIN

*It is the aim of these guides to provide a companion,
in the person of the author, who knows intimately
the places and people of whom he writes, and is able to
communicate this knowledge and affection to his readers.
It is hoped that the text and pictures will aid them
in their preparations and in their travels, and will
help them remember on their return.*

LONDON · NORTHUMBRIA
THE WEST HIGHLANDS OF SCOTLAND · IRELAND
THE SOUTH OF FRANCE · THE COUNTRY ROUND PARIS
NORMANDY · THE LOIRE · PARIS
FLORENCE · VENICE · ROME · NEW YORK
MAINLAND GREECE · THE GREEK ISLANDS
TURKEY · JUGOSLAVIA · MADRID AND CENTRAL SPAIN

In preparation
THE SOVIET UNION · THE LAKE DISTRICT · JAPAN
KENT AND SUSSEX · THE WELSH BORDERS
UMBRIA · GASCONY AND THE DORDOGNE

THE COMPANION GUIDE TO

East Anglia

JOHN SEYMOUR

Revised and with a new chapter by
JOHN BURKE

COLLINS
8 Grafton Street, London W1

William Collins Sons and Co. Ltd
London · Glasgow · Sydney · Auckland
Toronto · Johannesburg

First published 1970
Revised (third) edition 1988
Reprinted 1990

BRITISH LIBRARY CATALOGUING IN PUBLICATION DATA

Seymour, John, *1914*–
The companion guide to East Anglia.–
3rd ed. – (The Companion guides)
1. East Anglia (England) – Description
and travel – Guide-books
I. Title   II. Burke, John
914.26′04858   DA670.E13

ISBN 0 00 217861 3

Maps by Leslie Robinson

Photoset in Linotron Times by
Rowland Phototypesetting Ltd
Bury St Edmunds, Suffolk
Made and printed in Great Britain by
Hartnolls Limited, Bodmin, Cornwall

Contents

Preface   *page* 9
Preface to revised edition   13

 1 Woodbridge to Aldeburgh   15
 2 Woodbridge to Southwold   36
 3 Woodbridge to Eye   51
 4 Ipswich, Stowmarket   68
 5 Norwich   91
 6 The Yare   111
 7 The Waveney   130
 8 The Bure and the Coast to Mundesley   145
 9 Aylsham, Cromer, East Dereham   161
10 Norwich to Wymondham   182
11 King's Lynn and the Great Ouse   196
12 King's Lynn to Houghton Hall   210
13 King's Lynn to Fakenham   228
14 King's Lynn to Swaffham   248
15 Marshland and Fenland   268
16 The Brecklands   289
17 Bury St Edmunds to Ickworth   309
18 North of Bury St Edmunds   325
19 South-west Suffolk   339
20 The West Suffolk Wool Villages   352
21 From Sudbury to Woolpit   368
22 Cambridge: the Colleges   381
23 Cambridge: University and Town   425
24 North East Cambridgeshire   433

25 Ely   445
26 North West Cambridgeshire   461
27 South West Cambridgeshire   472
28 Huntingdonshire and Peterborough   491
29 The East Anglian Voyage   511

The East Anglian Dialect   526
Bird Watching   537
Index   546

KEY TO SYMBOLS USED ON THE MAPS

- ✗ Windmill
- ⚲ Watermill
- ⌂ Outstanding house
- ∴ Ancient monument
- ♠♣ Woodland
- ♜ Castle
- ✛ Church, cathedral or monastery

Illustrations

Castle Rising *(Aerofilms)*   *facing page* 32
Orford Castle *(Aerofilms)*
Framlingham Castle *(Aerofilms)*
Caister Castle *(Edwin Smith)*

Cratfield *(Edwin Smith)*   33

Retable of Thornham Parva *(Edwin Smith)*   64

East Anglian Boats *(John Seymour)*   65

Norwich Street: Elm Hill *(Edwin Smith)*   96
Norwich Keep *(A. F. Kersting)*
Norwich Cathedral *(Paul Popper)*

Pargetting at Clare *(Edwin Smith)*   97
Bishop Bonner's Cottages at East Dereham
    (Edwin Smith)
Willie Lott's Cottage *(Noel Habgood)*

The Norfolk Broads with Herringfleet Mill
    (Sport and General Press Agency Ltd)   128
Yachting on the River Bure *(G. Douglas Bolton)*

King's Lynn: Custom House *(Kenneth Scowen)*   129
King's Lynn: Clifton House *(W. R. Bawden)*
Wisbech: North Brink *(A. F. Kersting)*

Castle Acre Priory *(Aerofilms)*   224
Castle Acre: Prior's Solar *(Edwin Smith)*
Castle Acre West Front *(Edwin Smith)*

Denver Mill *(Noel Habgood)*   225
Cley Mill *(Noel Habgood)*
Thurne Mill *(A. Sinclair)*
Saxted Green Mill *(Noel Habgood)*

Maps

Woodbridge - Southwold   19
Diss - Ipswich   53   Ipswich   69
Ipswich - Felixstowe   77   Norwich   93
Norwich - Lowestoft   112   Norwich - Gt Yarmouth 147
Norwich - Cromer   163   Norwich - Diss   183
King's Lynn   199   King's Lynn - Fakenham 212

Mildenhall *(Edwin Smith)*   256
Blythburgh *(Edwin Smith)*
Neston *(Edwin Smith)*
March *(Edwin Smith)*

Breckland *(Edwin Smith)*   257
Fenland *(Noel Habgood)*

Blickling Hall *(Noel Habgood)*   416
Holkham Hall *(Guy Gravett)*

Melford Hall *(Edwin Smith)*   417
Oxburgh Hall *(Edwin Smith)*
Hengrave Hall *(A. F. Kersting)*

Ely Cathedral *(Edwin Smith)*   448

Great Court, Trinity College, Cambridge *(BTA/ETB)*   449
Peterborough Cathedral *(Peter Burton)*

Maps (cont)

King Lynn - Downham Mkt 251
King Lynn - Chatteris 271   Thetford Area 291
Bury St Edmunds 311   Newmarket-Beary 326
Bury - Sudbury 355   Cambridge 383
Ely - Cambridge 435   Cambridge-Huntingdon
               - March 463

Newmarket - Royston 474
Peterborough - Huntingdon 493
East Coast 515   North coast 520
Nene - Ouse - Cam 522

Preface

East Anglia is flat, and it is no use anybody saying anything else. Strangers to it often express wonder as to what we see in the place. And not only is it flat, they say, but large acres of it are treeless, and there are a lot of very muddy fields: why, then, do East Anglians so passionately defend it? It is my hope that this book will give at least part of the answer.

In spite of being so near to London East Anglia is still very much a country place. This fact has often been put down to the dreadful service of the old L.N.E.R. and the utter inadequacy of the A12, but I would say that it is more probably because East Anglia is not a *pretty* place. Surrey, Sussex, Kent and Hampshire have wooded hills and valleys and picturesque little villages (the latter almost entirely inhabited by people who are either retired from – or commute to – London). And further, in the winter time, over East Anglia a cold wind blows: some people say it comes straight from Siberia. True, we have rather more sun than anywhere else in England, and our summers are lovely. And our villages are not yet inhabited by commuters, but, for the most part, by true East Anglian country people. We have our weekenders, and we have our retired people, and they are accepted and welcomed into the community; but they do not overwhelm it as they tend to do south of London. East Anglia is a large lump of England, and our culture is very distinctive and very strong: until the Fens were drained, and the Essex forests cut down and made passable, East Anglia was very much cut off from the rest of England. The first time I took my wife, who is Australian, into a Suffolk pub, she came out after a long evening, and said: 'Thank God nobody asked me a question – I couldn't understand a word anybody said!'

But what has this flat and supposedly featureless country got to offer to the tourist?

In the first place it has a greater wealth of magnificent medieval building than any other area of the same size in the world.

Apart from Ely Cathedral, and Norwich, and King's College Chapel, there is such a plethora of superb medieval churches that, after making the East Anglian tour the traveller is bound to be disappointed in what he finds of this sort in any other part of the British Isles; and to the East Anglian a visit to some locally famous church in any other part of England is almost always a disappointment: he is apt to think: 'What is all the fuss about?' But the tourist from the south often gets no farther than the famous West Suffolk 'wool country': Lavenham, Long Melford, and Bury St Edmunds. I would urge him to go farther north – to such unheard-of places as Sall, Cawston, Ranworth, Trunch, and then west to that medieval merchant-adventurers' lair of King's Lynn, and farther west into the Norfolk Marshland country, where he will find a series of churches of such diversity and curious interest, with such a wealth of medieval art, that will make the churches of the Suffolk 'wool villages', in all their perpendicular magnificence, seem stereotyped by comparison. Certainly to the lover of English Gothic architecture East Anglia is the most important place in the world.

But there is plenty in East Anglia besides churches.

There is perhaps a greater wealth of good Tudor domestic building than anywhere else. There are said to be five hundred timber-framed Tudor farmhouses in Suffolk alone and they are beautiful beyond belief. There are a hundred beautiful villages: little places no outsider has ever heard about: Coddenham, Somersham, East Harling, Old Buckenham. There are splendid little market towns in which hardly a building offends and most are lovely: Woodbridge, Eye, Wymondham, North Walsham: a score of others.

And for the lover of scenery, if his taste is subtle and mature enough, East Anglia offers enormous charm and great diversity. The *valleys*, gentle declivities though they may be, are always charming: much of the scenic charm of both Suffolk and Norfolk lies in their valleys. In Suffolk there are miles and miles of deserted coast: very difficult to attain by road and therefore still unspoilt. There is the Sandling country behind this coast: miles of wild heathland and big old light-land farms. On the other side of the county is Breckland: one of the biggest areas of wild country in England, wherein roam uncounted deer: red, fallow and roe and, quite wild, the golden pheasant. In North Norfolk, and in Suffolk too, there are miles of that lovely material: *mud*. Muddy tidal estuaries, miles of saltings, where loneliness and wildfowl rule the world. And Broadland, which people who don't know imagine to be nothing but motor boats and transistor radios is, for the most of its miles, a haven of watery, willowy, bird-haunted peace.

Of great houses East Anglia has more than its fair share: Ickworth, Holkham, Wimpole, Oxburgh, Blickling, Heveningham and Raynham are but a few. Cambridge is a cultural world of its own, and the student of English architecture need go no farther: for here are to be found fine examples of every style from Saxon to Concrete Brutalism. For little unspoiled country towns Suffolk and Norfolk cannot be beaten. We got over our industrial revolution in medieval times, and our lack of water power and coal saved us from the degradation and ugliness that followed in other places.

So to the tourist I would say: if what you are looking for is English countryside, English architecture, and English culture at its very best, come to East Anglia. If it's mountains you are looking for, or goats, then you would do better to go somewhere else.

As for the question 'What is East Anglia?', my answer has been: Suffolk, Norfolk, Cambridgeshire and the Isle of Ely. Historically the East Anglian kingdom did not extend south of the Stour into Essex, nor west of the Cam. I have respected the southern frontier but not the western, for I have included the whole of Cambridgeshire (though the western part in rather less detail) in the book. This is, I believe, the generally accepted definition of East Anglia among East Anglians today.

Preface to revised edition

Since the first publication of this book a great many changes have taken place in East Anglia, not least in the road system so scornfully (and rightly) condemned in the original Preface. The A12 is no longer utterly inadequate: there is in fact dual carriageway from west of Brentwood as far as Ipswich, and the tangle of Ipswich itself is now bypassed by the splendid Orwell Bridge. Beyond that the road reverts to its older status, but recent stretches of dual carriageway bypass Wickham Market, to the benefit of its residents if not of its shops and public houses, Martlesham and Saxmundham. The M11 motorway now simplifies the journey from London to Cambridge, where it joins the widened A45 across country; and the A45 itself, east to west across central Suffolk and Cambridgeshire and on into the Midlands, now skirts Stowmarket, Bury St Edmunds, Newmarket and Cambridge, and also links with the dual carriageway A604 to Huntingdon and a junction with the A1.

Two neighbours have been incorporated into our region in recent years. Boundary changes of 1974 decreed that the county of Huntingdon and Peterborough (itself created only in 1965 by amalgamating Huntingdonshire and the Soke of Peterborough) should henceforth be a part of Greater Cambridgeshire. In the Spring of 1986 traditionalists won a great victory in having the name 'Huntingdonshire' officially restored to the district within the old boundaries. Although the purist may object that this does not strictly belong to East Anglia, much of its fenland nature has a family resemblance, and it would in any case be rather absurd to write about present-day Cambridgeshire while arbitrarily excluding what is now an administrative part of it. An extra chapter has therefore been added to cover these thoroughly delightful additions – a bonus rather than an excrescence.

It has been considered advisable to remove references to specific entrance fees to great houses and similar properties. One may grow wistful over the thought of paying three and six ('children two shillings') to visit Holkham Hall, or staying at Seckford Hall for 42s 6d a night; but shillings and pence are no longer with us in that form, and our decimalized prices change so rapidly nowadays that there is little practical value in the inclusion of details which will be out of date before any further edition of this book can be published.

Similarly, the names of many of the author's friends and acquaintances have had to be taken out. Several have left this region or, sadly, this world. And in view of the swift turnover of pub landlords and shopkeepers, and the demise of once sturdy family businesses in face of competition from chain stores and fast-moving entrepreneurs, no attempt has been made to replace the departed with their contemporary – and probably temporary – replacements.

It is hoped that new entries and the expansion of older entries in line with current conditions will make up for these omissions. There will never be a shortage of fine things to see and hear in East Anglia, of great characters to talk to and listen to, or of wonderful air, wonderful waterways, and wonderful skies.

CHAPTER 1

Woodbridge to Aldeburgh

Ideally **Woodbridge** should be approached from the sea, as the first East Anglians approached it, up the beautiful Deben Estuary. Then the traveller may see the red-brick town below its church and (if his keel be not grabbed by the mud of Upper Troublesome Reach first!) be greeted by a small spinney of yacht masts growing before the big gaunt tide mill so beloved by artists who painted the pictures one used to see in railway carriages. The first record of the mill, powered by estuary waters through a big tidal pound, is in 1176. Its successor in our own times was clad in corrugated iron and in danger of rusting and crumbling away until bought by the enlightened Mrs Rodney Gardner and put in the hands of a preservation trust. Restored in 1982 with fully operational machinery, historic photographs and working drawings, it is open Easter and Spring Bank Holidays, June and October weekends, and daily from early July to the end of September. The tidal pound has now been dug out and turned into a yacht basin.

The railway station is within pea-shooter range of the quay, so train traveller and seafarer disembark at nearly the same spot, graced recently by the conversion of an old cinema into the bright Riverside Theatre. As for the motorist along the A12 bypass, he is offered a selection of turnoffs from a sequence of roundabouts. Whatever the approach, the visitor is immediately refreshed by the charm of this splendid little Georgian country town.

Woodbridge (Anglo-Saxon *Udebryge*) is an old place, having been granted, together with the nearby royal manor of Kingston, to the monks of Ely by Edgar the Peaceable in AD 920. As the effective head of navigation on the Deben it must early have become a port. In medieval times Goseford, a now extinct town which was farther down the estuary, was the main port and shipping centre: in 1338 Goseford sent fifteen ships and 538 men and eleven boys to France in the king's name. It sent thirteen ships to the siege of Calais, but only three to meet the Armada, so by Tudor times Goseford was fading away. Woodbridge itself, being farther inland and therefore nearer to the dwindling oak forests of High Suffolk, took its place as the ship-building port and also – as the river below it was better trained and the draught of water increased – a big timber exporting town.

By the mid-seventeenth century 350 ships were registered at Woodbridge. Then the fate befell the port that has befallen all other ports in similar situations; that caused grass to grow in the streets of Amsterdam (until the invention of the steam dredger saved that place). It was not that the rivers silted up, as is generally supposed. It was that ships became larger, and of deeper draught. Fifty years ago only sailing barges came into Woodbridge (and an occasional schooner on high spring tides). The former great ship-building industry died away; but never completely – a spark remained which has now been blown again into a flourishing yacht-building industry.

The quay area still has charm, but the Victorians mauled it with their gas-works and their railway, and later people have carried on the bad work with a horrible concrete 'prom'. But as we progress up into the town we find very little that is displeasing. The town was lucky – as were so many East Anglian towns – in having had great prosperity in periods of good taste, and it has a wealth of fine eighteenth-century buildings, with a smattering of Tudor. The more immediately noticeable buildings in the latter style are the King's Head, on the Market Square, with its corbels carved as faces (and a superb room upstairs for assemblies) and the Bell and Steelyard just down New Street. The steelyard, which hangs outside the latter, with new rope rove through its blocks as though ready to hoist up and weigh the passing motor cars, took part in a 'London Street' exhibit in the 'Victorian Era Exhibition' in London in 1897, and a model of it can be seen in the Science Museum at South Kensington to this day.

The Crown is an ancient hotel. John Fox was born there in 1528. He was appointed gunner in the *Three and a Half Moons*, a merchant ship bound for Spain with a crew of thirty-eight men. The ship was attacked by eight galleys of Sultan Murad's Turkish fleet and taken, the crew sold into the galleys, and Fox pulled an oar for fourteen years, at the end of this time being the only survivor from the crew of his old ship. One winter, when the galleys were laid up in Alexandria and the slaves kept ashore under guard, Fox led a rebellion of 268 men, only two others besides himself of whom were British (William Wickney of Portsmouth and Robert Moore of Harwich) and they overpowered the guard, seized a galley and oars and escaped to sea. There eight men died of starvation but the ship eventually reached Candia in Crete where the monks welcomed them and hung Fox's rusty sword up in their church as a relic. Fox was rewarded by the Pope, and sent by him to Philip of Spain who made him Master Gunner of Valencia with a salary of £2 10s a month. In two years he returned to England, was pensioned by Queen Elizabeth, returned to Aldeburgh to command an old ship of his, the *Mary Fortune*, and he served aboard her under Admiral Lord Seymour against the Armada. After this he continued quietly trading between Blythburgh and London, and when he died in 1594 he left £10 to the poor of Woodbridge.

Peter Pett, a Commissioner to the Admiralty in Pepys's time, sailed into Woodbridge, married the daughter of the Crown Inn, one Margaret Cole, and set up a ship-building yard in the town. He built two royal warships there in 1650. The Bull Hotel, up the road, has great associations with Edward Fitzgerald, who used to put his friends up there, including Alfred Lord Tennyson. A generation back blood horses were bred in the hotel stables. When Fitzgerald was explaining to the landlord what a famous poet Tennyson was, the landlord replied: 'Well he may be a fine poet but he doesn't know a damn' thing about horses!' Tennyson was most annoyed when 'Fitz' left him to pay the hotel bill.

The church, although not one of the great Suffolk churches, is good enough. Look at the fine flint and stone flush-work around the north porch and at the base of the tower. This flush-work building with alternate knapped flint and freestone is an East Anglian speciality. The tower is 108 feet high, and as the church stands on a hill it offers a fine view over the red pantiles of the town, and also of one of the beauties of Woodbridge normally hidden from visitors, the gardens lying behind the Georgian façades of the streets.

Inside, the church has a grand airy spaciousness. There is an air of wealthy urban sumptuousness about it, conferred by present and recent parishioners. The gilded, green, blue and scarlet font cover may be recent, but it is magnificent nevertheless, and so are the polished brass candelabra, reminiscent of those found in Danish and Swedish churches. The monument (in the chancel on the north side) to Thomas Seckford is interesting because Seckford had so much to do with Woodbridge that he can practically be said to have created it as it is today. He was Master of the Court Rolls in Elizabeth I's day, and his ghost may be seen by ghost-lovers at Seckford Hall in high hat and splendid period costume, carrying his wand of office, bemoaning the fact that most of the money he left for the poor has in fact been appropriated by the rich. The three-storied monument in the south chapel depicts, in a life-like way, Jeoffrey Pitman, his two wives, and his two sons.

The churchyard is an oasis of bosky charm. The Market Hall has hardly a jarring note to it. The Shire Hall, which is said to have been built by Thomas Seckford in 1570, once had its lower floor open to the wind to be used as a market. This floor was bricked in in Regency times and converted to a corn exchange, and now the buildings are used as a court room. The English word 'tawdry' is said to come from the old fair which used to be held in Woodbridge market on Saint Audrey's Day, 23rd October. The goods sold there were describable by our present word 'tawdry', a corruption of the name of the blessed saint.

Outside the town **Seckford Hall** is worth visiting. Its beautiful Tudor façade was built in about 1530 by Thomas Seckford's father, and there is talk of Thomas's ghost wandering about the place from time to time. Well nigh derelict just after the Second World War, it was fortunately converted into a most desirable hotel with a reputation for good food in a setting furnished with antiques and surrounded by attractive gardens.

Set against the generosity of Thomas was the misconduct of his brother Henry, a notorious pirate whose exploits were not too severely frowned on by Elizabeth I until he misguidedly seized a

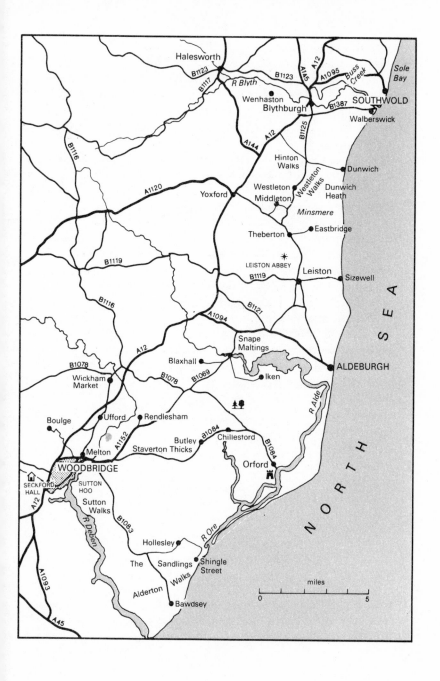

Venetian ship 'by mistake'. Such behaviour must have endeared his memory to a later Woodbridge seafarer, Edward Fitzgerald.

   Fitzgerald, who leapt to fame with the sudden popularity of his translation of *The Rubaiyat of Omar Khayyám*, was a splendid Victorian eccentric, who sailed the seas in small and somewhat scruffy yachts, dressed in a top hat which he tied on in gales with a scarf which went under his chin, and making huge friends with Suffolk sailors and fishermen, until he was even able to write a book on their *Suffolk Sea Phrases*. Although of Irish blood he loved his Suffolk, and was seldom able to tear himself away from it for long. He once sailed to the Maas in his little yacht intending to see some paintings at Rotterdam, but on a fair wind springing up from home he immediately gave orders to his skipper to sail home again, back to the Deben Estuary, and he never clapped eyes on canvas (excepting that over his head). Tales about him are endless, and of the 'Woodbridge Wits', the small coterie of civilized people with whom Fitzgerald associated. His admirers may wish to make a small pilgrimage to Boulge churchyard, but a couple of miles to the north, where 'Fitz' lies buried below a rose whose ancestor came here as a clipping from the rose on Omar Khayyám's grave at Naishapur. It was his own wish that the epitaph should read: 'It is He that hath made us and not we ourselves.' But less humble, more typical:

> *By heaven! the bold sun*
>   *Is with me in the room*
>   *Shining, shining!*
> *Then the clouds part,*
>   *Swallows soaring between;*
> *The spring is alive,*
>   *And the meadows are green!*
> *I jump up like mad,*
>   *Break the old pipe in twain,*
> *And away to the meadows,*
>   *The meadows again!*

One of Fitzgerald's closest associates – in fact his father-in-law, for 'Fitz' married this man's daughter in a misguided fit of sentimentalism and the marriage only really lasted one night if it can be said to have lasted that – Bernard Barton, was a Quaker bank clerk and a minor poet. He was beloved of everybody in Woodbridge, and so much so that the Woodbridge ship owners named a ship after him. He remarked, on hearing that he had been thus honoured: 'If my Bardship never gets me on the muster-roll of Parnassus, it will get me into the Shipping List.'

Thomas Churchyard was a solicitor of the town, a collector of early English landscapes, and a not-negligible painter in his own right. He was much influenced by Constable but carried impressionism somewhat further. He painted with great gusto and a very sure eye. There is a good collection of his watercolours in Christchurch Mansion, Ipswich. He died in 1865, and a contemporary wrote of him: 'His manner was polished and gentlemanly in the extreme, his conversation full of wit and anecdote to overflow; while his varied information, especially on matters connected with art, made his company at all times amusing and delightful.'

Melton's ugly new church has an old and beautiful sacrament font in it.

A short excursion should be made from Woodbridge to **Ufford**, which has the finest font cover in England. When 'Smasher' Dowsing, the Cromwellians' church-basher, came to Ufford to do his hatchet-work, he was forcibly kept out of the church by the church wardens, and thus the latter saved this cover, and probably at the risk of their lives. Apart from this treasure the little church is interesting. There are good fifteenth-century bench-ends. Local benefactors give money to have some of the hideous Victorian glass in the windows removed from time to time, and their excellent actions are commemorated by glass engravings on the new clear glass executed by an Ipswich engraver, Mrs Sheila Elmhurst. The north wall of the nave has herring-bone and stratified masonry of the eleventh century. The old stocks by the churchyard are no longer needed in such a respectable community. The village is a little showplace now, with most of its houses restored by wealthy Woodbridge people, but its name carries ancient echoes: it derives from the Uffingas or Wuffingas, the royal line which we shall encounter more than once in the neighbourhood. The searcher for the real beginnings of East Anglia must be drawn inevitably towards the sea; and on his way will pass by the very cradle of this ancient kingdom.

It is known from the writings of Bede that the first kings of all East Anglia, the members of the Wuffinga dynasty, had their Great Hall at **Rendlesham**, a tiny village north-east of Woodbridge, dominated nowadays by an American-occupied aerodrome. There is little to see there now, save a great park and woods and peace (the latter only when the planes are grounded), and the winding Deben valley, and nobody knows where the Great Hall was, although various 'Saxon' remains have been dug up. But certainly some kings (such of them as died at home) were buried at **Sutton Hoo**, which is, by the way, now a hot rival to Hoxne as a candidate for the probable site of St Edmund's martyrdom.

A track which leads straight off to the right from the junctions of the Hollesley and Shottisham roads on Sutton Common leads straight to the eleven barrows of Sutton Hoo. Four barrows have been excavated.

All you see there is the sandy ridge on which you stand and the wood in front of you which cuts off your view of the Deben Estuary. Before this wood grew up there must have been a fine view, for the ridge is a hundred feet above the mud and salt water of the estuary. Here, over thirteen hundred years ago, a ship eighty-nine feet long (as long as an East Coast sailing barge) was carried or dragged on skids up the hill, a treasure chamber was built in her and filled with a priceless treasure, and she was buried deep in the sand. In *Beowulf* is described just such a ship burial; and the treasure is still there for all to see, in its golden splendour, but safe inside the King Edward VII gallery at the British Museum.

Mr Basil Brown, then a young man on the staff of Ipswich Museum, was given the task of opening some of the barrows in 1938. He started on the smaller mounds. The first had some bones in it. The second some bones, some pieces of bronze, some pottery, and a Frankish throwing axe. The third contained a boat. Not much of a boat, and not much left of it.

Next year, in April, Brown attacked the biggest of the barrows, and thereafter he went from excitement to excitement until he realized that he was the discoverer of the greatest archaeological find that has ever been made in England or is ever likely to be made. On the 8th of June the Office of Works took over the responsibility for the dig and put Mr C. W. Phillips in charge. Mr

Basil Brown went on working under him. Mrs E. M. Pretty, the owner of the land, generously gave what was found to the nation.

The great ship, with holes for thirty-eight oars, was laid bare. Little was left of the wood of her, except its perfect imprint in the sand, and nearly all her iron rivets and roves. Of human remains there was no sign.

There were some large, lavishly ornamented but inferior pieces of silver from Mediterranean lands (one huge bowl had the stamp of the Emperor Anastasius on it), a helmet and shield of Swedish design, some Celtic hanging-bowls with the Christian fish symbol, a bewildering mass of Anglo-Saxon jewellery – most of it gold set with garnets and worked with intricate designs. There was a gold-mouthed purse filled with Merovingian gold coins, there were buckles and mounts, all bullion, a great sword with scabbard and harness, a shield, an iron battle standard, a ceremonial whetstone (symbol of the king – the Swordgiver of his people? Recently pottery sherds were unearthed at the site of Ipswich Co-operative Society with heads on them *exactly* like the strange pear-shaped heads of the great whetstone). There were angons, spear heads, the mountings of a great drinking-horn. There was a gold-mounted harp, and one can look at it and hear the author of *Beowulf* sing:

> . . . the harp music, and the clear voice of the poet, singing
> how Man was made long ago, and how God made the world
> a bright sea-enriched plain, made the sun and moon to light
> its inhabitants, clothed the earth with leaves and branches,
> gave life to all moving things.

But the digging up of history was interrupted by history in the making. Once more East Anglia was threatened by Germanic invasion. The great dig was completed a few days before World War Two broke out, and it was not until after the war that the finds could be properly evaluated. Models and details of recent excavations are displayed in Woodbridge Museum.

Dating can be done fairly accurately from coins and other arte-facts, and this places the burial in the middle of the seventh century. Which king was it who had this mighty funeral in his honour? Wehha, Wuffa, Tyttla, Raedwald were all too early. (It was Raed-wald (died AD 624) who – converted to Christianity in AD 619 –

23

prudently installed two altars in his church at Rendlesham – one pagan and one Christian.) Great research has gone on, and so far Aethelhere, who died in battle on the Winwaed (AD 654) fighting in the Mercian army against the King of Northumbria, is considered most likely. The fact that he died far from home would account for his body not having been found in his burial ship. The site was re-excavated in 1966–7.

All this country between the A12 road and the sea is marvellous walking country. It is called the **Sandlings**, by reason of its being light and sandy. Here are great open sandy heaths with a blaze of yellow gorse and broom blossom in summer (and gorse blooms all the year, of course – when gorse is in bloom kissing's in season. There's a Suffolk saying about what to do with a reluctant maiden: 'Git her up agin' a whin bush bor! She 'on't back away then!'). There is heather and ling. Nowadays great acres of former heath-land have been ploughed up and they grow fair crops of rye, poor crops of barley, and acres and acres of carrots. Large stretches are under the Forestry Commission, and planted with Scots and Corsican pine: the great stretches of the Rendlesham and Tunstall Forests put one in mind of Siberia and packs of wolves. One can walk or ride a horse through these forests, which after all belong to the people of Britain; but the fire peril is intense. A cigarette-end can destroy a million trees.

It is not quite a flat country. It is a low table-land cut into by river valleys and estuaries. Seabirds wheel and shout over saltings and marshes. It is a sparse, little inhabited, country. Farms are few and huge. It is not a country of fine buildings: most farmhouses and cottages seem to have been built in the last couple of centuries, of brick, and to a nondescript architecture. Here is little timber framing – there never was much timber. The churches are of flint (as they are all over Suffolk) and some of the cottages near the sea are of beach pebble.

This coast is much the same from the Orwell Estuary, in the south, to Lowestoft and the Norfolk border in the north where it comes to an end. The country being treeless by nature, and well drained, it was a natural habitation for Stone Age people, and worked flints are everywhere. The Romans looked upon it as a barren coastline to be defended against the Saxons, under the command of the 'Count of the Saxon Shore'. When the Romans left, the first East Anglians seem to have sailed for the Wash, and left their boats, and moved inland to settle as farmers in scattered communities. It was not until Raedwald and his kin arrived, and settled near the Deben Estuary, and retained their ships and their command of the sea, that East Anglia was united and began to take on a name and character of its own. These Anglo-Saxons, like the Stone Age people, found the Sandlings easy to farm: but they slowly hacked their way into the great elm and oak forests of High Suffolk, with its heavy, intractable, but exceedingly fertile, land.

In the Middle Ages the Sandlings were given over to the sheep. You will see the word 'walks' all over the map: Sutton Walks, Alderton Walks, Hinton Walks, Westleton Walks. This means sheep walks, large areas of uncultivated ground supporting sheep and wandering shepherds.

Then, late in the eighteenth century, began the pheasant craze. Rich men from the cities bought up vast tracts of the Sandlings, great estates were formed, and the whole country given over to the cult of the pheasant. The inhabitants had either to become gamekeepers or other estate servants or get out. Pheasants were bred, pheasants were preserved, and pheasants were shot in vast numbers. The pheasant cult reached its peak in Edward VII's reign: but still you will see more pheasants in the Sandlings than anywhere else in England – the Brecklands not excepted.

Hitler's war brought about the next change in the Sandlings country: it introduced arable farming. New methods of cultivation and artificial fertilizers, and now more and more piped irrigation, are making these sandy acres profitable to plough, but wind erosion is becoming severe, and in a dry spring roads are blocked with sand that has blown off the arid fields.

Ramsholt is a good little place to go to see the Deben Estuary. You climb the red crag hill there, over the road from the pub, and get a fine view down to the south of the river, and can imagine the Wuffing king and his seafarers sounding their way in over the bar to reach the shelter of the estuary and found a kingdom.

Farther downstream **Bawdsey** is given over to the Royal Air Force, who play with radar in the great manor house on the cliff. The first coastal warning station was established here in 1936

25

after transfer of the original research centre from Orford Ness. A weekend ferry service crosses the river to Felixstowe Ferry from May until late July, then weekdays also until early September.

North is **Hollesley** (we say 'Hozeley') with its huge open Borstal prison, in a superb position overlooking the mouth of the Ore. It was founded early in this century as a Labour Colony for the unemployed, and dubbed the 'Colonial College'. Canada, Australia and New Zealand are filled with descendants of men who trained there before going overseas.

Follow the road over the marshes and you will come suddenly to **Shingle Street**. This is well named, excepting that there is no 'street' in the accepted modern sense. But there is plenty of shingle – in fact little else. There is a row of cottages built along the top of a shingle bank, with the sea down the slope in front of them and the wide marshes at their back. I can only think of one other place in England so uncompromisingly spare and bleak, and that is Boulmer, in Northumberland, but there each little cottage has a fishing coble drawn up in front of it. At Shingle Street you will see a few fishing boats: not cobles but the famous 'punt' of this coastline, and anything less like a punt would be hard to imagine. These boats are beamy, full-bilged, clinker-built, transom-sterned, always white-painted, and they are built to come through the breakers to the shore bow-on (unlike cobles which come through stern-on). They are then hauled up the steep shingle beach on skids with a windlass. But these boats belong to part-time fishermen. More and more of the houses at Shingle Street belong to week-enders, but Norman Scarfe, the scholarly author of the *Shell Guide to Suffolk* (the best of the series so far) lives in one of them.

It is fun to walk along the beach, northwards, to the mouth of the Ore, which is there a great flood, and very swift. At low tide steep-sided islands are revealed in the mouth, showing how easily the navigator may come to grief when trying to enter this difficult river.

To avoid further confusion let it here be said that the Ore is the same river as the Alde. The lower reaches are called the Ore, as is that branch of the headwaters which runs by Framlingham. The rest of it is called the Alde. It is as improbable that the men of Orford would submit to calling *their* river the Alde as it is that the men of Aldeburgh should call *theirs* the Ore, so it has to go by both names.

The coast here has the loneliness and desolation of a desert shore: the yellow horned poppy, the sea bindweed and maritime thistle among the sparse flora. You can, if you like, walk right along the river wall to Chillesford, and for a naturalist, or a lover of lonely places, what a superb walk.

If you are travelling by car though, go back to Hollesley and turn right through Boyton (simply to see the fine brick almshouses, the central range built in 1736) and then through a lovely land of ridges and marshy valleys to **Butley**. If you pass Butley Church note the fine roof of 'Norfolk' reed thatch, in fact very Suffolk reed, because it was cut within sight – almost spitting-distance – of the church. Every thatcher has his own trade mark in the pattern of the roof ridge 'frieze'. This one is that of the Chilvers family.

Then you must go to look at the gatehouse of Butley Abbey.

The gatehouse is now a private residence, but if you can get permission to see the outside of it do so, for here is one of the best pieces of flush-work in East Anglia, which means in the world, for this is very much an East Anglian art. And here it is seen in splendid exuberance: a great many marvellously done heraldic shields, which indicate a date of the early fourteenth century making this one of the earliest examples of flush-work in the country, besides one of the best. The freestone, as opposed to the flint, was brought from France, and the track of a canal has been traced leading to the priory from the Butley River (just as a canal was dug from the Wensum to Norwich Cathedral). This stone is said to have come from the valley of the Yonne, a tributary of the Seine. Much stone in East Anglian buildings came from Caen in Normandy, but as you get into Norfolk more and more Northamptonshire stone is found, particularly of course in that part of the country drained by the rivers which run into the Wash.

More fascinating perhaps than this gatehouse – the poor remains of a great religious house – is the 'Register or Chronicle of Buttley Priory, Suffolk, 1510 to 1535', which has been edited by A. G. Dickens and turned into understandable English (there is a copy at the Seckford Library, Woodbridge). This gives a splendid look at the everyday life of a religious house just before the Dissolution.

It is mundane and intimate. The writer shows humane concern when a hard winter kills off birds and rabbits, pleasure when a good herring harvest fills the poor people's bellies. He enjoys recounting how Mary, Queen Dowager of France, and her husband Charles Brandon, Duke of Suffolk, used the priory rather like a hunting box, following the hounds in nearby Staverton Forest, or picnicking in Brother Nicholas's garden only to be driven indoors – into the church – by a scatter of rain. The list of servants at the priory is fascinating. Cooks, pantrymen, launderers, dairy maids, bakers and maltsters, warreners, a cooper, a slaughterman, ploughwrights and cartwrights, shepherds and carters and many others, including a 'keeper of swannys and pulleyn'. The continuity of life in England is nicely illustrated by the fact that a great modern farmhouse now straddles the site of the old priory, and the lands which once supported a great religious community now support the family of a modern farmer, who owns an uncounted number of combine harvesters. There is a local legend that a silver coffin is hidden somewhere at Butley containing the remains of Michael de la Pole, killed at Agincourt.

Turn sharp left past the priory and you will come to Staverton Thicks, a dense and ancient wood of oak and holly, the oaks stunted by the poorness of the land. Some say it was planted by the Druids, others that it was planted by Butley monks who – having been given permission to take *one crop* off the land – planted oaks! There is a pleasant book about this haunted ancient forest: *The Cottage in the Forest* by Hugh Farmar (Hutchinson).

The pub at Butley is a favourite of mine for it is still completely unspoilt. Nowadays one lives in terror of fine country pubs being 'tarted up', but the Oyster has not had a penny mis-spent on it, either by the brewers or the landlady. The company to be found in it are foresters and farm workers, and here you will hear the purest coastal Suffolk, the sweetest English, and far closer to the language of Chaucer than any English you will find in a town. If the seeker wishes to find the heart of East Anglia he must learn to know East Anglian countrymen, learn to appreciate the richness of their dialect and understand their wry humour.

On a fine summer's evening the old game of quoits was regularly played here. The throwing of heavy metal rings long distances into a pad of clay produced a fine thirst, catered for here by the near-immortal Vera Noble, ruling spirit of these premises for a good half century – and her family for untold years before her.

A little farther along the road, the lane to Butley Mill, is Mounts Field – just an ordinary field, but from it a Neolithic village of the 'Beaker' period has been dug up, Bronze Age axes have been found, Iron Age material, Roman material, and the foundations of a 'Saxon' house. What more can you ask of one field?

Chillesford is a tiny hamlet but a name familiar to geologists because here can be seen the Chillesford Beds and the Coralline Crag. In the latter (a Pleistocene deposit until recently thought Pliocene) can be found four hundred different species of mollusc shell, 142 of which are extinct. They were laid down in a warm sea, some 2,000,000 years ago, in between forty and fifty fathoms of water. The much thinner Chillesford Beds consist of fine micaceous sands and clays containing estuarine fauna. The thirty-one-foot long vertebral column of a whale was found in the old brick-works just along from the church (the last brick-maker, Mr Chittleburgh, died only a few years ago). There is a crag quarry just in front of the church, but the Coralline Crag can be seen without looking into it, for the tower of the church is built of it (as is the tower of the eleventh-century church of Wantisden, now lost to an airfield).

It is now but a short walk to **Orford**. The walker should go by Friar's Walk, a lane that takes off just beyond the Mill Lane junction and leads past Sudbourne Hall. Within living memory Sudbourne Hall employed twenty-two gamekeepers and a tailor to make green liveries for them to wear. Within living memory a whole row of cottages was pulled down in Orford because the doctor complained to the squire that the inhabitants made too much noise near his house. Within living memory it was usual for six thousand pheasants to be shot here in one day. The estate is partially broken up now though, and the great house pulled down.

Orford is a curious little town. The Market Square (no longer a market) is attractive, but for one hideous modern house. Quay Street is a quite charming village street, with a long strung-out green. The church is noble, and could house all Orford's inhabitants and the people for miles around. The castle really does 'stand sentinel', as so many castles have stood in so many guide books throughout the ages. Climb to the top of it (for a small fee) and you have a great view of the strange geographical phenomenon of the Ore and Alde River, with its narrow ten miles long shingle bank which separates it from the sea. The army used the castle as an observation post during the last two wars, and no doubt its military uses are not over yet, despite its eight hundred years.

Alas, only the keep remains, the great tower that was the heart and citadel of the castle. But this is in fine order, one of the finest keeps in England. A drawing done of the castle in 1601 by John Norden shows its former huge ramifications. The mystery to me is where all this stone has gone to. You don't see much stone in the buildings round about, and most of what you do see came from the old Austin Friary, fragments of which can be seen next door to Chantry Farm.

The castle was built for Henry II in 1165 and onwards, the work supervised by the then equivalent of the Ministry of Works: a gentleman named Alnoth. The keep was revolutionary in its day, being the first in England built polygonal in shape, not square. This was to counter the nasty habit of attackers of undermining the corner of a square thus causing it to collapse: it was later that round keeps came into vogue, better still. Orford also has pointed windows instead of Norman round ones, showing the influence of the new Gothic ideas. Inside is a chapel, and garderobes, and a great hall, and a cellar below with a well in it. We are told (by Ralph of Coggeshall) in *Chronicon Anglicanum*, fifteenth century, and quoted by Camden, that a Wild Man was held in the dungeon. He was taken in nets from the sea by fishermen, and was half man, half fish, but although put to torments he could not be made to talk like a Christian, and finally he escaped to the sea again. A modern portrait of him can be seen over the justly popular smoked fish and wine restaurant in the square. Hubert de Burgh, of 'Heat me these irons hot' fame in Shakespeare's *King John*, was a warden in Orford Castle, and it seems just possible that the 'Room in a Castle' in which poor little Arthur was immured was here.

The stone that the keep is built of is interesting: much of it septaria, dredged out of the sea off Felixstowe and Harwich. Orford has been patched up recently with ugly sandstone: ignore that.

The church has a ruined Norman chancel standing to the east of it, with splendid twirly and dog-tooth decoration on the forlornly standing piers. The existing nave, aisles and west tower are Decorated of the finest, and the church has a wide, grand air. Several of Benjamin Britten's works have had their first-ever performance here, and every year during the Aldeburgh Festival some work of his is performed. The tower was repaired recently (the top fell off in 1830) and is unfinished. There are many fine brasses, all of about 1500.

At the bottom of Quay Street the Jolly Sailor beckons – one of the finest of old waterside pubs. The front bar, opening off the street, has a huge table on which the locals play cribbage by the hour. A brass marker by the fireplace shows the level which the sea reached in the 1953 flood, when the then landlord nobly dived into the cellar to rescue the beer, the customers meanwhile sitting on the table with their legs up secure in the knowledge that licensing laws were unlikely to be enforced that night. When the roof was lifted off the pub by a local whirlwind in 1963, one customer was heard to enquire: 'What the hell is a 'gooin' to happen in 1973 – an aarthquake?' But somehow the supply of beer never fails in these disasters.

Within a glass case are three 'muff dogs', little larger than hamsters, brought back from China by some seafarer long ago and preserved by an expert taxidermist. Numerous secret cupboards hint at past smuggling activities, and tradition has it that it was in the tiny 'Captain's Room' at the north end of the building that the body of Will Laud the smuggler was laid after he had been shot by Preventive men on Orford beach. This is all part of the local romantic tale of Margaret Catchpole, a serving girl who fell in love with Will Laud and in due course was apprehended, tried, and transported to Australia. The Jolly Sailor for long had a copy of the handbill offering a reward for her capture. There is still a facsimile on the premises, but the original is in Christchurch Mansion Museum, Ipswich. The Reverend James Cobbold's novel, *Margaret Catchpole, a Suffolk Lass*, recounts all these doings, and there is hardly an inlet along this coast or up the rivers Deben and Orwell which does not claim some part in the legend.

The quay was once busy with traffic to and from the Secret Weapons Research Establishment on 'The Island' over the river.

The Ness is in fact not an island, being connected by shingle to the mainland at Slaughden, but it was kept firmly and secretively isolated until most of the mysterious activities were wound up in the 1970s.

Orford was a great port in Elizabethan times and thereafter until the seventeenth century. She sent wool to the Continent. The port decayed when ships became of deeper draught; but old men can still tell of times when Orford had her own fleet of schooners, ketches and boomy barges, her brewery, her bakers and butchers, blacksmiths and wheelwrights, tailors, carpenters, millers and builders.

The magnificent Town Regalia is unique in England. There are miniature oars made of silver, once carried by the Portmen who enforced the rights of Orford over the fisheries in the River Ore. The Town Charter, too, is famous, and has been much pored over by students of constitutional matters from afar.

The road north to **Iken** gives grand views of the River Alde. The river turns inland (if you are following it upstream) at Aldeburgh and widens out there so that at high tide it resembles a beautiful wide lake. The late Julian Tennyson wrote of Iken in his book *Suffolk Scene*: 'Everyone wants to lie in his own country: this is mine. I shall feel safe if I have the scream of the birds and the moan of the wind and the lapping of the water all round me, and the lonely woods and marshes I love so well.' He lies, though, not at Iken but in the Burma jungle, having been killed there during the war against Japan.

Blaxhall, a few miles inland, is an untouched and remote village scattered about former common land. George Ewart Evans's book about it, *Ask the Fellows who cut the Hay*, is an enthralling record of the early memories of old local men and women, fit to rank with Ronald Blythe's evocation of the Charsfield district a few miles to the west in *Akenfield*.

Snape Maltings, beside the bridge over the Alde, are a happy amalgam of several periods of good industrial building, now well covered with virginia creeper. They worked as maltings until 1965 when the firm succumbed to the pressure of giant monopolies. The following year the premises were taken on by the Aldeburgh Festival organizers, Benjamin Britten and Peter Pears, and in 1967

EAST ANGLIAN CASTLES. *Above left*, Castle Rising (p.210), a Norman keep within earthworks that are said to be Roman. *Right*, Orford, of which only the Keep remains, was built for Henry II as a counter to Framlingham (*below left*), which was the stronghold of turbulent barons; the Bigods, Mowbrays and Howards, Framlingham is an example of a castle influenced by returned crusaders; with a huge curtain-wall. *Right*, Caister Castle, built by Sir John Fastolf in the 1440's.

Cratfield, Suffolk.

Queen Elizabeth II opened a new concert hall there. On the opening night of the 1969 season an electrical fault led to the whole interior being burnt out. Within twelve months it was restored, and the Queen returned to reopen it. Today there are concerts during the Festival season and at special weekends. Classes in the School for Advanced Musical Studies are open to the general public on prior application, as full-time observers or just sitting in on classes in which they are particularly interested. The complex also includes a piano workshop, art gallery, shops, coffee and wine bars; beside the quay is a craft centre, and river trips are offered during the summer.

There is a 'Sailor's Walk' along the north bank of the Alde from Snape to Aldeburgh, though incursions of salt water make it hazardous at certain times of year. The Plough and Sail inn takes its name from the combination of barley farming and seaborne transport which once flourished here. Departing seamen used to drop barley seeds into cracks in the bar tables and return to find them sprouting. The Crown inn, a short distance along the road, was much used by smugglers, with peepholes to watch over the river and countryside, and a windowless upstairs room for use as a hidey-hole in times of danger from pursuers.

At the top of the hill stands a truncated windmill, converted into living quarters by Britten just before the Second World War, looking down on the Maltings in which so much of his music was later to be heard. Beyond it, well away from the village, stands the rather stark church; and half a mile to the east of that church an Anglian ship was dug up in 1862: the burial has been dated between AD 635 and 650. No treasure was found, but in the heathland all around there was discovered a cemetery of burial urns, now cut through by the A1094 to Aldeburgh.

Aldeburgh can hardly fail to please. Now a holiday and residential town for people with money and good taste, it was an ancient port which rivalled Orford. One enters past the church, a large and interesting one (the south porch is pierced to allow ceremonial circumambulation without stepping on unhallowed ground). Straight down to the sea you come to the Moot Hall, which is splendid and early sixteenth century: now right on the sea, it was once in the centre of the town. The rest of Aldeburgh has

33

gone – having been devoured by the sea, including all of Roman Aldeburgh.

The beach has many boats, or 'punts' and a strong force of professional fishermen. It is famous for its 'long-shore' herring, and for the best sprats in England in November and December. The lifeboat stands poised like a fish eagle – ready to swoop down into the breakers if there is need. Even in days of oar and sail the lifeboat never failed to launch when called – in spite of the terrific seas which hit this beach in easterly gales. On one occasion she launched, was overturned, and every member of the crew was drowned. The two towers on the beach are the watch towers of the now-extinct 'beach companies', salvage companies that pre-dated the Royal National Lifeboat Institution. Watch was kept from them for wrecks in bad weather, and boats stood ready to crash the breakers and put to sea. Walk south until you come to the place where the River Alde nearly meets the sea, where there is a yacht club, and the most northerly of all Martello Towers in East Anglia.

Benjamin Britten (a Lowestoft man) collaborated with friends to found the Aldeburgh Festival of Music and the Arts in 1948, with little more than the tiny Jubilee Hall and local churches at their disposal. The town had already inspired him to compose the most important English opera for centuries: *Peter Grimes*, based on one of George Crabbe's dour poems. Its first performance marked the reopening of Sadler's Wells after the Second World War. The presence of Lord Britten, as he eventually became, is sorely missed by all who had the privilege of seeing and hearing him play, conduct, and devotedly watch over everything that went on in 'the Borough' and at the Maltings. In 1986 his inseparable creative companion Sir Peter Pears followed him into the haven of Aldeburgh churchyard.

When we observe the teeming music lovers, all looking very fashionable and metropolitan in this rustic setting, the women in the very latest and least practical of hats, and the least sensible of shoes, hastening between concerts, exhibitions, wine tastings and plays, or savouring briefly the sea breezes along the Crag Path by the shingly beach, we may feel that it is a far cry from the Aldeburgh depicted by George Crabbe, inhabited by:

> *. . . a wild amphibious race,*
> *With sullen woe displayed in every face;*
> *Who far from civil arts and social fly,*
> *And scowl at strangers with suspicious eye.*

Crabbe, born in Aldeburgh the son of a salt tax collector, sailed away from the place (aboard a fish carrier) to London to become a poet. Before this he had unsuccessfully tried to become a doctor. His verse, and Burke, got him preferment in the Church, and it is strange that he had been exiled from Aldeburgh (a place which he believed he hated) for twenty-eight years before he began to write his poetry about it. None of the other places which he professed to like inspired him so well as the memories of the place which he didn't like. I don't believe 'the Borough' was ever as bad as he made it out to be.

CHAPTER 2

Woodbridge to Southwold

A diversion from the A12 north of Woodbridge takes you through **Wickham Market**, with a picturesque watermill astride the river Deben. Another watermill not far away, off the road to Needham Market at Letheringham, is set in a lovely surround of lawns, gardens and water meadows, open to the public Sunday and bank holiday afternoons from Easter to the end of September, plus Wednesday afternoons from June to September. Its near neighbour is Easton Farm Park, with a nature trail and picnic areas, a pets' corner, and working animals including Suffolk horses and more than a hundred cows whose modern milking routine can be inspected from an overhead gallery, contrasted with the Victorian dairy on the premises. The farm is open daily from Easter until the end of September.

Strike north-east for **Leiston**, where in 1728 a Mr Garrett, the local blacksmith, set up a plant for making blades and agricultural implements. The factory grew, producing steam-rollers and fire engines in peacetime, tanks and shells during the wars. It was a later Garrett who built Snape Maltings (see p. 32) and whose daughter Elizabeth Garrett Anderson became England's first woman doctor and, in 1908, first Lady Mayor – of Aldeburgh. The Leiston Works have now been pulled down, but the Long Shop of 1853 is preserved as a museum showing one of the first 'assembly lines' for producing steam engines, along with other relics of Garrett enterprises. The museum is open weekdays from April to September. Another survivor is Summerhill, just across the old railway line, the school where the late A. S. Neill practised his ideas of progressive education.

North of Leiston you will see, standing up out of the open fields on your left, the romantic ruins of **Leiston Abbey**. Enough remains of this Premonstratensian abbey for it to be well worth going off the road for. The Lady Chapel is the only complete building left of the grand church, having been preserved because it was useful as a granary after the Dissolution. It was restored in 1920 as a chapel, and was restored again, and more elaborately, after being used as a furniture store for displaced persons during the Hitler war. It is now a place of peace and great beauty, open to all, and Holy Communion is celebrated there every Wednesday morning at 8.30 in the winter and 8 in the summer. An altar has been built over the site of the original high altar of the abbey, now under the sky amid the ruins, and Holy Communion is celebrated there on the last Saturday of every May.

The great barn belonging to the abbey is a thing worth visiting for itself. The dwelling house, too, which was built after the Dissolution, encroaches on the abbey buildings, and is built partly of the material of the ravaged church. It is beautiful and interesting, dating from 1536, with a large Georgian addition and not altogether happy twentieth-century alterations. For some time used as an Anglican Conference and Retreat House, it has since 1977 been administered as a music-making centre by the Pro Corda Trustees of the National Association of Young String Players. Upstairs in this grand old farmhouse, you can see the hanging knees of ancient ships, broken out of some wreck of long ago and incorporated into a new roof. The abbey was founded in 1182, but was then down at Minsmere, on the coast, now a bird sanctuary belonging to the Royal Society for the Protection of Birds. It was moved to its present place 'from its swampy site near the sea' in 1365, burned down about 1380 and rebuilt on a grander scale. It flourished until the Dissolution when it was quarried for its stone, and such buildings as were left standing were used for cow houses, stables and granaries by the adjoining farm.

Not three miles away, on the coast at **Sizewell** is an atomic power station whose now ordained expansion was the cause of bitter controversy for several years. It channels electrical power to the Midlands along monstrous cables and pylons, and raises the temperature of the sea water in its vicinity by ten degrees. From late 1987 onwards the locality has been invaded by heavy lorries rattling supplies to Sizewell B station. Not far from Leiston, too, if you can find it by careful map-reading, is the pleasant little Eel's Foot public house in the hamlet of **Eastbridge**, made famous years ago by broadcasts of folk singing put out by the BBC. It is a good departure point for a walk around the perimeter of Minsmere. Although the bird reserve itself is open only by permit, the path across the neighbouring marshes to the sea is a very fine one, and on the seaward rim there is a hide for public use. Beyond, the path climbs steeply up to the airy expanse of Dunwich Heath, cared for by the National Trust, with wide views across the bird sanctuary towards the hulk of Sizewell. Or perhaps one should do the journey in reverse, leaving the car on the heath and skirting Minsmere to finish up gratefully at the Eel's Foot!

But back to the main road which runs north from Leiston, and we come to the three villages of Theberton, Middleton and Westleton. All three are delightful – their houses scattered as if they were built haphazard on common land years ago, and then strung together by roads. **Theberton** has the prettiest little church, from the outside, that you could find in England: thatched roof, round tower with an octagonal top to it. A piece of shot-down Zeppelin is kept in a glass case by the font; and in the new graveyard is a board commemorating the fact that sixteen German airmen were buried there, after their airship had been shot down by a fighter in June 1917. They were recently moved to where they must lie in some gigantic war cemetery, anonymous and forgotten. While they laid at Theberton their graves were decorated with flowers once a year, at dead of night, by some undiscovered person, and on their common headstone was written: 'Who art thou that judgest another man's servant? To his own master he standeth or falleth.'

At Theberton Hall, in 1843, Charles Montagu Doughty was born. He wrote *Travels in Arabia Deserta*, which some think the best travel book that has ever been written. He developed a new language, almost, to write it, a compound of the English of the Revised Version, Arabic, and – I like to think – Suffolk. It is a superb prose – rich and powerful, and once you attune your ear to it it will carry you along through some of the strangest and most desperate adventures ever man had. A thing which sets him high above most other travellers is the instant sympathy he seems to have felt for everyone he met – whether king or camel driver.

Westleton is a big and fine village standing about a fine green, with a horse pond now commandeered by greedy ducks continually seeking scraps from the back door of the White Horse pub. Its once famous windmill has now, alas, been demolished. Still Westleton can boast of its repeated successes as 'Best Kept Village in East Suffolk', due in no small measure to the local enthusiasm of the world's leading clematis specialist, Mr James Fiske. A local boy, he started work in big nurseries in other places, fell in love with clematis, started growing them on his own at home and now grows a hundred and fifty different varieties and sends them to all parts of the world, making his remote and otherwise little-known village, to clematis lovers at least, world famous. Another, older, source of fame is the witch's stone near the priest door of the huge thatched barn-like church, over which no grass will ever grow, and if you put your handkerchief in the grating of the wall and run eastwards, northwards, and back again by the west end of the church (circumambulating widdershins) you will be vouchsafed the sound of the Devil clanking his chains below the grating. The present writer has not tried it.

A short road through the lonely Sandlings (where there are notices which say: 'Beware of Adders') takes you to **Dunwich**. Here is little to see, but much to think about. Nearly all of the Dunwich that mattered has been swallowed up by the sea. Even when Domesday was written the sea had carried away (*mare abstulit*) one of the three carucates of cultivated land there. Domesday records 236 burgesses in Dunwich, making it a far bigger town than Ipswich with 110. It also records twenty-four Frenchmen, 178 poor men, and eighty mere men. At that time the town rendered 68,000 herrings a year as tax. But it was in the Middle Ages that Dunwich grew to what was then a great city.

The visitor will now find a tiny hamlet behind the cliffs of the seashore. On the top of the cliffs at one point is a walled quadrangle now used as a smallholding: once the wall of a priory. If he explores the foot of the cliffs below where All Saints Church used to be, before it totally disappeared from view, he will find human bones in plenty: local children were fond of digging these up to embellish their bedrooms. This is now forbidden: a family was buried alive – and unburied dead – some few years ago. They were sitting in a cave at the bottom of the steep crumbling cliff. Better to leave the remains of our ancestors in peace.

Nowhere else in England has so great a place come to so little. It was at Dunwich that Christianity came finally to rest in East Anglia. The Burgundian missionary, Saint Felix, may have been bishop there, and there he crowned Sigebert, half brother to Eorpwald, son of Raedwald of Rendlesham, King of East Anglia. Sigebert built his palace at Dunwich in AD 630 to 631. Later there was a monastery of Dominicans and another of Friars Minor. There was a lazar-house and a Maison Dieu hospital, a church of the Knights Templar, three other chapels and a cell of Eye Priory. At one time there were nine churches in Dunwich, and it was a great port owning – in the thirteenth century – eighty 'great ships'.

Of all this greatness and beauty what is left? There is the Norman apse of the Lazar Hospital moved to a new position inland and with an ugly vault built next to it and the curtain wall of Grey Friars which was used as an anti-aircraft gun site during the Second Great War. The church is new. The tower of the last of the nine churches fell into the sea in 1918 (there are photographs of this in a tiny museum).

Dunwich has a tenuous link with New York. John Daye, the printer, was born there, and the modern publishing firm, John Day of New York, was named after him. The first John Daye invented Saxon type-face, and printed Foxe's *Book of Martyrs* and other religious works. Edward Fitzgerald loved Dunwich, where he was wont to visit the artist Edwin Edwards, who had a house there, and in this house Charles Keane of *Punch* taught him to play Spanish Dominoes. Dunwich is nowadays a place of Roman Catholic pilgrimage, and the sea is blessed there every September.

But what can we do there now? There is a good pub which serves good meals. There are Westleton Walks to the southward, marshes and pine woods to the north. There is a fine sweeping view on a clear day across Sole Bay to Southwold. You can stand on the cliffs and gaze down into the sea and imagine streets and houses, and harbour works, and those nine churches and an unrecorded number of pubs. You can imagine you hear, as fishermen coming home in their boats at night have imagined they have heard, the sound of bells coming up from the waters.

There must at one time have been a capacious natural harbour at Dunwich: now there is no trace of a coastal formation which could have been a harbour at all. But not many hundreds of years ago there was a natural inlet of the sea. Defoe records that in his day Dunwich was still exporting butter, cheese and corn, and that a local rhyme had it:

> *Swoul, and Dunwich, and Walberswick*
> *All go in at one lousie creek.*

Swoul meant – and still means locally – Southwold. The creek was 'lousie' presumably because the sand bar which strangled Dunwich was already forming across its entrance.

A walk of three miles along the beach northwards brings us to **Walberswick**, or Walhbert's village, the habitation of the Walberswig Whisperers, men noted for their loud voices, which could be heard across the river and the marshes in Southwold.

Many people are rude about Walberswick, lamenting the fact that what was once a fine little fishing village is now a kind of seaside Hampstead Garden Suburb. It is, indeed, the haunt of ex-theatrical folk and lady water-colourists, but it is very attractive nevertheless. An attractive position, with its small sandy beach, Sole Bay on one side and the rushing tidal River Blyth on the other, full of fishing boats, marshes to the south, heathland to the west. The church has a noble tower, built in 1426 by Richard Russel of Dunwich, and Adam Powle of Blythburgh, masons. The contract of these two men can be seen in Gardner's *Dunwich*. It specifies that the 'steeple' should be like that of Tunstall, the west door like that of Halesworth, likewise the windows. The two masons were to find all material, and were to be paid forty shillings and a case of herrings every year. One imagines that they did not become rich men. In Cromwell's time 'Smasher' Dowsing did a thorough job here – destroying forty windows and defacing all the tombs, thus earning a different sort of immortality from that of Messrs Russel and Powle. The tower, the south aisle, and the porch are all that are left of this once mighty church, besides the ruins of the rest of it.

The village is the remains of a much bigger place. There are lovely greens, big houses – many of them old and beautiful, some, on the outskirts, modern and bogus-timbered. There is a fine eighteenth-century building near the middle which is now one of the best contemporary pottery shops in the country. Walberswick is a paradise for children who do not yearn for the pin-tables and jangling juke-boxes, but can find their fun on the sands, the marshes, the river and the sea.

Sometimes a ferryman will row you across the mouth of the Blyth. If not there is a Bailey footbridge a mile upstream. This was once the bridge of the now-defunct light railway between Southwold and Halesworth, a railway locally famous because the carriages for it had been manufactured for the Emperor of China. They were not delivered, owing to some war or financial difficulty, but were sent to the Halesworth-Southwold Railway instead, and it is said that the imperial dragons could sometimes be seen under the paintwork. A collection of comical cartoons concerning this railway can be seen in the Sailor's Reading Room in Southwold, about which more later; and meanwhile the walk along the old railway track from Southwold to Halesworth is a delightful experience. It takes you up the lovely Blyth valley, and through **Wenhaston**, the church of which is famous for its Doom: a quite marvellous panel.

But just over the Bailey bridge is the Harbour Inn: one of the very finest of Suffolk's several fine waterside inns. It stands on the river wall, with marshes close behind it and the strongly tidal river in front. The scene is very Dutch, and the town of Southwold, just under a mile away over the flat marshes, looks like a town of Zeeland. These marshes were flooded in 1953 and many people drowned. The river is furnished on both banks with wooden stages, at the ends of which lie fishing boats. Many of these belong to weekenders, working men or farmers who fish in their spare time, trawling or drifting in professional fashion, but about ten are manned by full-time fishermen, who make a living at the job. But we will deal with Southwold Harbour (it is Southwold Harbour although it is much nearer to Walberswick than it is to Southwold) when we come to Southwold itself.

The road to Blythburgh skirts a nature reserve accessible by a number of public footpaths, and near the A12 pass the hillocks of Toby's Walks, a delightful parking area and wild playground.

Blythburgh is a strange and interesting little village on the edge of marshes, and the tidal waters from the sea come right up to it. It is the remains of a much bigger place: indeed a place that centuries ago was of some importance. Besides the cluster of fine old village houses, the magnificent White Hart Inn, with its 'Dutch' gables and moulded and carved ceilings that was once a court house, the scant remains of an Augustinian priory in somebody's garden, there is a church of a size suitable for a place perhaps a hundred times as large. The church is best first seen from across the marshes from the north. It stands there barnlike and huge, very graceful, but with its tower out of proportion to the rest of it, for the church is 128 feet long and the tower but 83 feet high. It is a fine church whichever way you look at it, but seen from the distance from far away across the marshes it is one of the grandest sights in Suffolk.

Entering the church one is struck by its lightness and whiteness and emptiness and grand proportions. There is the air of a Continental church about it, with large areas of uncluttered stone-flagged floor. Simply to wander in, and savour the sense of space, of light, of simplicity and massiveness, is an experience; but do not miss the backless benches with their carvings of Deadly Sins, such as Gluttony, Drunkenness (very rightly in the stocks to sober up), Sloth (in bed), Hypocrisy (praying with eyes open), Avarice (sitting on a chest), and one particularly deadly sin which some prude has censored with a hammer. There are fifteenth-century poppy heads, and in the south aisle are the Seasons, including a very large man in a very small boat. Outside are carved dripstones, including a very amiable chained bear. The painted roof is very noteworthy, and the carved angels, their wings much shot away by Cromwell's enthusiasts but replaced by the generosity of some Americans. The font, according to legend, was shattered by the Devil.

On Sunday the 4th of August 1577, while the minister was reading the second lesson, a 'strange and terrible tempest' 'strake' down through the wall of the church, toppled the spire down through the roof so that it shattered the font, tumbled the bells and the Jack o' the Clock (he was repaired, and is still there), killed a man and a boy and scorched many members of the congregation. It was known that this visitation was of the Devil, because as he fled out of the north door on his way to Bungay his fingermarks were revealed, and the truth of the legend verified. If you search in the choir, near the organ, you will find the carved signature of Dirck Lowensen van Stockholm, aged twelve, AD 1665. Dirck was one of the children of a Dutch community imported from Holland to reclaim marshes in the Blyth and correct the course of the river. In the seventeenth century as in the twentieth, wherever in Northern Europe there was a difficult drainage or sea defence job to be done, there were Dutchmen there to do it. Over the South Porch is a small oratory, or priest's room.

A king was killed near Blythburgh, and buried in the church. According to the *Liber Eliensis* (Ely Chronicle) King Anna and his son were slain at the battle of Bulcamp Hill (where now stands an eighteenth-century workhouse converted to a hospital) and their bodies brought to Blythburgh Church and buried. King Anna's remains were later removed to Bury St Edmunds, and after that to Ely, where his daughter Aethelthryth or Etheldreda (wife of the King of Northumbria) had founded a convent.

Anna, we are told by Bede, was a good man and had good and pious offspring. He founded Blythburgh monastery, and embellished the monastery founded by the Irish monk Fursey at Burgh Castle. His eldest daughter, Sexburgh, became Queen of Kent and later Abbess of Ely in succession to her sister Aethelthryth. Another daughter, Aethelberg, became Abbess of Brie, in France, so Anna had no reason to complain of the lack of piety of his daughters. Anna himself was son of Eni, and Eni was brother to the famous King Redwald or Raewald, who had the prudence to install both pagan and Christian altars in his temple of Rendlesham. Anna was brother to the Aethelhere whose death is thought to have been commemorated in the Sutton Hoo ship burial. Anna was killed here at Blythburgh fighting against Penda, King of Mercia, who was a pagan and a tireless warrior. The battle took place in AD 654 and in that same year Anna's brother Aethelhere was slain fighting beside Penda against the Northumbrians at the Battle of the Winwaed.

Blythburgh was more important, once, than it is today – a mere hamlet on the A12 road. It suffered the fate of most early ports. As ships became too deep draughted to reach its docksides the latter decayed, and trade was removed from it to places with deeper water. (Boston, Lincs, too, nearly died from the same cause.)

Blythburgh now is one of the purest of places, but according to an ancient rhyme this was not always so:

> *Beccles for a Puritan,*
> *Bungay for the Poor;*
> *Halesworth for a Drunkard,*
> *And Bliborough for a Whore.*

A road follows the north bank of the Blyth to **Southwold**: which is built on an island. Buss Creek cuts it off from the mainland to the north-east (*buss* was a square-rigged herring smack) as the Town Marshes and the Blyth do from the south-west, and the sea completes the triangle.

I cannot think of anything bad to say about Southwold. It is a real town, with good shops and good hotels. It is all that a small seaside resort should be. It has fine cliffs, a long sandy beach, a little harbour in the mouth of the Blyth, and a wealth of good houses, many of them Georgian.

The church is one of the great ones, even for Suffolk. The Victorian glass was all blown out in World War Two (except the west window), and now light floods into the superb Perpendicular-style building. Take note of the splendid flush-work and freestone work of the exterior, particularly the south porch, the loftiness and fine proportions of the nave roof and clerestory, the slenderness of the pillars. The pulpit is magnificent, a most rare fifteenth-century one, brightly painted. The organ case is exuberant Victorian work. The early sixteenth-century screen is one of the finest painted screens there is, even if the angels and blessed saints were touched up in Victorian times, making them, it is said, resemble the members of the Town Council. Reading from the north on this fine screen there are visible:

Angel with Trinity Shield.

Gabriel with sceptre of authority as God's messenger.

Archangel with sword and scales.

Potestates, with scourge and chained dragon.

45

St Andrew with saltire cross.
St Peter with keys.
St Paul with sword.
St John with poisoned chalice.
St James the Great, with a scallop shell on his pilgrim boat.
St Bartholomew with book and knife.
St Jude with boat.
St Simon with oar.

As in Blythburgh Church, there is a splendid Jack o' the Clock – a little wooden man in armour who strikes the bell on the hours. The church is filled with good wood carving. The hammerbeam roof is new, but fine nevertheless, there are two Brasyer bells, there is a door at the top of the stairs leading to the chamber over the porch which has a secret latch and a wealth of other interesting detail; but this church is a fine bright jewel without, and is flooded with light and magnificence within.

There is a broken tombstone without, to Samuel Charles May, who died in 1923. On it is inscribed:

> *His Anchor was the Holy Word,*
> *His Rudder Blooming Hope,*
> *The Love of God his Maintops'l*
> *And Faith his Sailing Rope.*

There is a small museum in Southwold, well worth seeing if you can ever find it open, but the nicest place for me is the Sailor's Reading Room.

This is open to all; but there is a box there for the landlubber to drop in small contributions for the upkeep of the place. In the winter there is a good coal fire, and generally some retired fisherman, or non-retired ones waiting for the weather to improve. (There is a local legend that – in sailing days – a fisherman would pop a candle out of his bedroom window when he woke up in the morning. If there was enough wind to blow the candle out – it was too rough to venture forth. If not enough wind – then not enough wind to sail. In either case the fisherman went back to bed. There is even a song about it, the refrain of which is: 'So I open the pane and pop out the flame, to see how the wind do blow!')

But the walls of the Reading Room are covered thick with

paintings and prints and photographs, and the tables with models. There is a fine scale-model of the yawl *Bittern*, a most famous rowing and sailing boat.

The 'beach yawls' were built in some numbers around the coasts of East Anglia for the purpose of taking men out to ships in the North Sea to put pilots aboard them, or assist them when in trouble, or rescue the men in them when the ships were *in extremis*. The yawls were the property of the 'beach companies', the members of which kept watch in foul weather, and vied with each other in launching their open boats to row or sail them to the scene of wrecks or ships in trouble. They were the precursors of the modern lifeboat. Their function was not solely humanitarian: salvage was their mainstay. They would carry an anchor off for a ship aground on the sands so that she would winch herself off – but not for nothing of course. Hundreds of lives were saved by the beach yawls before the days of steam and radar, for it is a poor seaman who will not drop everything else if another man's life is at stake. The *Bittern* was said to be the fastest of these boats, whether under sail or oar. She was 49 feet long, and built in 1890, one of the last. Her crew challenged the schooner *America*, of America's Cup fame, to a race, but the captain of the latter would not accept the challenge except for a prohibitive stake. The yawls carried shifting ballast in the form of bags of shingle which could be shifted by the large crew up to windward, and it is probable that – in hard weather – the *Bittern* would have left the *America* standing. Her lines were very close to those of the Viking ships.

Up on Gun Cliff, on one of Southwold's beautiful greens, stand six eighteen-pounder guns with the emblems of the Tudor Rose and Crown on them. These are rare pieces in that they were very large for their early period. They are said to have been captured by Prince Charles Edward from Edinburgh, recaptured by the Duke of Cumberland at Culloden and later presented by him to Southwold. They had to be buried in the 1914–18 war, because the Germans bombarded Southwold from the sea on their account, claiming that it was a fortified place.

Southwold was early renowned for its fishery. Domesday records an annual rent of 25,000 herrings a year, and that it had a *sea-weir*. (A weir was a wicker fence built out at sea to entrap fish, and generally paid a rent to the lord of the manor. A local song, which describes which fish are taken on the days of the week, has a line: 'Weir-fish for Wednesday, swell the net full!' This was because on Wednesday you got 'Wind from the northard – wind from the east' and therefore no fish could be caught at sea, so the weir was resorted to. There are no fish weirs left in East Anglia – on the other side of the North Sea there are hundreds.) But it was in the sixteenth century that Southwold rose to great importance as a port. In 1750 the Free British Fishery was created, in an attempt to seize back the herring fishing monopoly from the Dutch. This had its headquarters in Buss Creek, and at its zenith there were fifty great 'busses', or square-rigged herring vessels. The company came to grief, however, in 1792, and the fishermen returned to fishing from their small beach punts again. In 1757 the River Blyth Navigation Act was passed, part of the great spate of canal-fever legislation all over England, and the river was canalized and locked as far as Halesworth, to which inland town wherries could then sail. The harbour failed, however, when the saltings up-river were enclosed by landowners, which reduced the scouring action of the tides.

In 1898 the harbour was vested in Southwold Corporation, the Government voted £21,500 to improve it, in 1908 herring curing began again; seventy big Scottish drifters used the port and Southwold was full of Scottish fisher girls. The little railway reached the harbour in 1880, and then there was a great hope of Southwold becoming a rival to Harwich as a port for the Continent. None of the hopes were fulfilled, however. The herring industry went back to Lowestoft and Great Yarmouth, the railway is closed down, and a merciless gravel bar comes and goes over the harbour mouth, often practically bottling it up altogether. A couple of dozen small motor fishing boats still use it, though, and there is a good little yacht club; and ever and anon a new scheme is propounded for improving the harbour entrance and making Southwold a port again. Other less desirable schemes have also been mooted. In 1987 the district council misguidedly announced the development of a marina scheme, complete with houses, shops, a tourist hotel and other splendours. Fortunately the wrath of the townspeople was so great that, after a lot of acrimonious argument, the whole idea was dropped.

But Southwold's greatest excitement was the Battle of Sole Bay.

At Whitsun, 1672, a British fleet of seventy-one ships, mounting 4,000 guns, and manned by 23,500 men, lay at anchor just off Southwold, together with the allied French fleet. As it was Whitsun many of the English sailors were ashore getting drunk. Prince James, Duke of York, was aboard his flagship and in command of the Red, and the Earl of Sandwich (who lived at Shrubland Park, near Ipswich) commanded the Blue. Nobody had any expectation of the enemy, but at 2.30 on the morning of the 28th of March a French frigate sailed in with news that the Dutch were advancing from the south.

Great confusion immediately prevailed among the Allied fleets. The French ships slipped their cables, sailed away to the northward, and did not return. The British were left to face the Dutch fleet of sixty-one ships, commanded by de Ruyter, aboard his *Seven Provinces*.

The Dutch sailed right in among the British fleet and a battle ensued, the noise of which could be heard for many miles inland. The people of Southwold lined the cliff tops watching the carnage, and the commander of the town ordered that the bridge over Buss Creek should be destroyed to prevent people from leaving, so that, in the event of disaster, there should be English manpower enough to defend the town.

The *Great Holland*, of 62 guns, was pressed by the tide against the still-anchored *Royal James*, which had the Earl of Sandwich aboard. Sandwich ordered a boarding party away but three more Dutch ships drove in to help the *Great Holland*, the *Royal James* was set on fire, and later Sandwich's body was washed up on Clacton beach, and recognized by a ring that he was wearing. Van Ghent, the commander of the *Great Holland*, was also killed. One British ship was taken by the Dutch and the remnants of the crew battened down under hatches as prisoners, but one man – seeing that his Dutch captors were hard-pressed on deck – led his fellow prisoners to arise and together they overpowered the Dutch and took back the ship.

Altogether it was a most terrible and bloody battle: 800 wounded men were carried into Southwold, thousands were killed, great destruction was wrought to both fleets, and nobody really won.

49

Ten years later England had a Dutch king, and Great Britain and Holland were happily engaged in waging war against the French.

Adnam's beer is brewed in Southwold, long recognized as the best real ale in England. Deliveries to the pubs and hotels within the town itself are made by horse-drawn drays, which is good for the trade of dealers in cameras and film: holidaymakers are forever trying to find new angles on the horses and their cargoes against a backdrop of this pub or that. The inns themselves are a distinguished lot. The Red Lion on South Green is one of the few survivors of the terrible fire which swept through the town in 1659, after which the lovely, spacious greens were developed as firebreaks against any future catastrophe. The Lord Nelson, once called the Raven until Nelson-worship swept the country, has a small window in the seaward side of one of its dormer windows, from which – as from so many similar establishments along this coast – signals could be flashed to smugglers coming in below the cliff; and there are tales of blocked-up underground passages which once led from the cliff into the cellars. Certainly there are still some inexplicable passages, now choked with rubble, leading away from the cellars of the Sole Bay inn, much photographed because of its picturesque proximity to the lighthouse.

CHAPTER 3

Woodbridge to Eye

Strike north from Woodbridge and you come quickly into one of the remote back-blocks of Suffolk, where no tourist ever goes and where the villages have names like Dallinghoo, Monewden, Cretingham, Kettleburgh and even Hoo. The charm of this sort of country lies in its utter unselfconsciousness. Such villages are not subject to guide book treatment. Most of them have pretty little churches, all have fine farmhouses (estimates of the number of Tudor or earlier farmhouses in Suffolk vary between five and six hundred); they all bear quiet exploration, on foot, on wheels, or on horseback, by the stranger looking for unexpected beauty that does not depend upon dramatic effect or over-statement. Most of such villages have good little pubs. This is heavy-land arable country I must add, and for the most part the traveller is confined to the tarred roads.

At **Brandeston** is one of the flourishing vineyards which have made such wonderful progress in East Anglia in the latter half of this century; there is another a few miles north-east at **Bruisyard**. Both welcome visitors for tours and tastings from May to October.

Framlingham, beyond this back-block, is a little town of the first interest and importance. Most visitors head straight for the castle, but I would suggest a walk round the town first, and then the church, with the castle to round the day off.

Clustered on its little hill, with the tiny River Ore flowing through the marshes beside it, Framlingham still has something of the air of a fortified town; although there was never a town wall: the place was surrounded by a ditch. But there is a compactness, a jumbling of the streets, an antiquity. Taken together with its castle and its church it is clear that this was once a splendid place, where knights and squires rode in fine array, where armies gathered – a centre of power. Now, however, we have a charming little country town, with good shops, at least one excellent hotel, and the best agricultural hardwear supplier for many miles around. There is a book shop of real distinction, ranking with those of Southwold and Woodbridge, and plenty of good, ancient pubs: the Crown goes back many centuries and is still a good place to stay. Nearby on Market Hill is the elegant sixteenth-century Mansion House, later faced with mathematical tiles, like its neighbour. The lane called Queen's Head Passage leading off the hill is named after Mary Tudor, whom we shall meet again in the castle on the crest of the slope.

The nave of the big church is somewhat bleak to my taste, although there is a fine chestnut roof with hammerbeams concealed under fan vaulting (as at St Peter Mancroft, Norwich). But the chancel is amazing to behold. For it is crammed full of great monuments to the illustrious departed.

And before we go any further here, to describe these tombs and adumbrate their occupants, it will be convenient to list the owners of Framlingham from the earliest that we know down to the present day.

There was an important fortified dwelling here in East Anglian times: recently Anglian graves have been dug up near the moat. Hinvar and Ubba, the wild sons of old Lothbroc (Leather-breeches) are said to have captured the place when they raided England with some twenty thousand other Scandinavians in 865, entering the castle by a secret passage revealed to them by a prisoner. King Edmund is said to have hidden here during his celebrated flight from the Danes, before he fled north to Hoxne, but the evidence for this story appears to be pretty slight – if indeed existent.

After the Conquest Henry I granted whatever there was of Framlingham to Roger Bigod, and it remained in the turbulent hands of the Bigod family until the last one died out and Edward II gave it to his half-brother Thomas de Brotherton. It went to the latter's widow, thence to her aunt, thence to the aunt's daughter, and thence to the latter's husband John Mowbray. John died in 1368 and it remained with the Mowbray family (with occasional seizures by various kings) until the line died out in 1476 when it passed by marriage to the Howards, Dukes of Norfolk. These kept

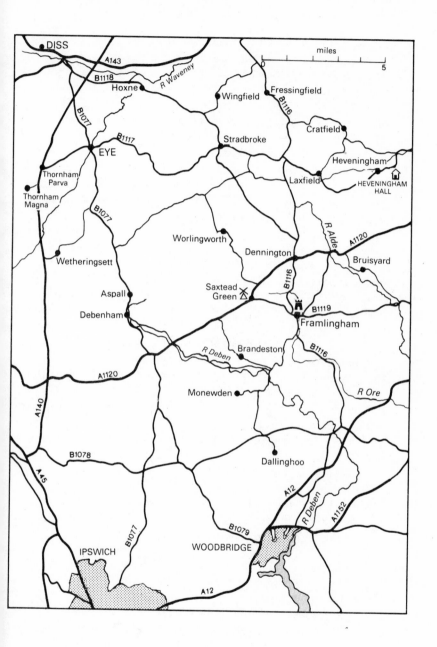

DISS

A143

B1118

R Waveney

Hoxne

Wingfield

Fressingfield

B1116

B1077

Cratfield

B1117

Stradbroke

EYE

Heveningham

Thornham
Parva

Laxfield

HEVENINGHAM
HALL

Thornham
Magna

B1077

R Alde

A1120

Worlingworth

Dennington

Bruisyard

Wetheringsett

B1116

Saxtead
Green

Aspall

B1119

Debenham

Framlingham

B1116

R Deben

Brandeston

A1120

Monewden

R Ore

A140

Dallinghoo

B1078

A45

A12

R Deben

A1152

B1077

B1079

WOODBRIDGE

IPSWICH

A12

miles

0   5

it (also with occasional surrenders to the Crown) until 14th May 1635, when Theophilus Howard sold it, and its estates, for £14,000, to a lawyer named Sir Robert Hitches, who could think of nothing better to do with it but try to pull it down. The great curtain wall was too much for his resources, however, and still stands. When he died he bequeathed the carcase to Pembroke College, Cambridge, and, in the ripeness of time, this body handed it over to the Ministry of Works.

So let us return to the church with its chancel full of monuments.

The chancel was rebuilt in mid-sixteenth century, much larger than it had been before and in fact out of proportion with the rest of the church. It is actually wider than the nave. It was built in the time of the Howards – by Thomas Howard, 3rd Duke of Norfolk. Thomas Howard is buried under the great block of stone to the south of the altar. This man only escaped having his head cut off by order of Henry VIII because the monarch died the night before it was due to happen, and thus on the collar of his effigy is written: 'By the Grace of God I am what I am.' Above his monument may be seen, hung high up on the wall, the helmet worn by the 2nd Duke at the Battle of Flodden, where the 2nd Duke successfully commanded the English. It is said that a rector tried to sell it once to an American for £500, but that the present Duke of Norfolk prevented him.

The 3rd Duke's son was not so lucky as his father for, imprisoned at the same time, his head fell the day before Henry VIII all too tardily died and England lost a good poet, and, from all that we hear of him, a civilized man. It will be seen that his coronet is carved lying beside the head of his effigy on the monument, in significance of the fact that he was beheaded.

Poor Henry Howard, Earl of Surrey, the beheaded poet, was imprisoned at Windsor, before his death, and he had known Windsor in happier circumstances in his gilded youth:

> *So Cruell prison how could betide, alas,*
> *As proude Windsor? where I in lust and joy,*
> *With a kinges sonne, my childishe yeres did passe,*
> *In greater feast than Priams sonnes of Troy:*
> *Where eche swete place returns a taste full sower,*

> *The large grene courtes, where we were wont to hove,*
> *With eyes cast up into the maydens tower.*

But being now imprisoned and ill-treated in this place of his former happiness:

> *Thus I alone, where all my fredome grewe,*
> *In prison pyne, with bondage and restrainte,*
> *And with remembrance of the greater greefe,*
> *To banish the less, I find my chief releefe.*

His body was brought from the Tower, and it lies at Framlingham next to the body of his countess, Frances de Vere.

The 4th Duke of Norfolk also had the misfortune to be beheaded, this time by order of Elizabeth I. The tomb in the north chancel aisle is for his two wives: Lady Mary, daughter of Fitz-Alan, Earl of Arundel (her effigy is the one with its head on a horse couchant and its feet on a hart at layes), and Lady Margaret, daughter of Thomas Lord Audley, Baron of Walden and Lord Chancellor of England. The head of her effigy is on a tiger collared and chained, and there is a wivern, or dragon, at her feet.

It may be noticed that there is a space between the effigies of these two ladies. It is said that this was intended for no less a person than Mary, Queen of Scots. The 4th Duke had the intention of marrying her, and then overthrowing Elizabeth and putting his new wife on the throne instead. It was this duke's marriage, incidentally, to the daughter of Arundel that brought Arundel Castle into the ownership of the Norfolk family, and the present Duke of Norfolk still lives at Arundel. There is a large and ornate tomb chest with shields round it, stories from Genesis, and four charming guardian angels. It is for Henry Fitzroy, Duke of Richmond, son of Henry VIII by Lady Elizabeth Mount, or Talbois, who was Maid of Honour to Henry's Queen Catharine of Aragon. Henry Fitzroy was the 'King's sonne' in Surrey's poem, childhood friend and confidant to the Earl of Surrey and also half brother-in-law, for Henry married Surrey's sister Lady Mary Howard, who is buried beside him at Framlingham. In his life he lived at Blackwell in Essex and Henry VIII 'loved him like his own soule' and made him Knight of the Garter, Duke of Richmond and of Somerset, and, then having no legitimate male offspring, obviously intended him for the throne. When the lad died, however, at the age of seventeen, he was already out of favour with his father and was buried at Framlingham with no pomp or ceremony.

This is an astonishing collection of fine Renaissance stone carving to find in a tiny and remote English township. Only at Fotheringhay, in Northamptonshire, can we see anything comparable. The church still has its eighteenth-century reredos – a rare survival.

The castle is best seen for the first time from a distance, preferably from the Dennington Road, across the flat vale of the Ore. It stands proudly on its hill, one of the most impressive military buildings in England, and certainly the most impressive in East Anglia.

Alas, when you get inside there is not much there. There is the 'Poor House', built up against the great shell of the castle on the west side. This is a fine enough hall, the south wing of it 1636 and the centre early eighteenth century. Three of the west windows are left from the medieval hall on the site of which the Poor House was built. The hall has been partially restored by the Department of the Environment. There are traces, and traces only, up against the inside of the east curtain wall, of the Bigods' hall and their chapel (although what such hell-raking fellows as the Bigods wanted with a chapel is hard to see – their *prison* still exists, stuck outside the castle on a limb to the west, well out of earshot of the noble owners). But the great curtain wall with its thirteen towers is most of what there is to see.

Framlingham was one of the first fortresses in England built thus as a curtain wall, instead of with a predominant keep, as at Orford. The tower-studded curtain wall idea came to England with the returning Crusaders, copied from the castles of the Saracens. One must imagine the castle extending southwards with an inner bailey (a pond, on which swim muscovy ducks of a piercing ugliness, opposite the Castle Inn, may be where the moat once was), and an outer bailey comprising most of what is now the town of Framlingham. It was a tremendous fortification, one of the strongest in Europe.

We may wonder where all this enormous quantity of stone came from, in this stoneless country. The answer is it all came up the Ore in boats (anchors have been dug out of the mud beside the now-tiny trickle of a stream), and it came from Barnack in Northamptonshire. It is oolitic limestone, of the sort that made houses from the Cotswolds to Lincolnshire, and it all came by sea.

The most rewarding thing to do is to climb up to the 'wall walk', which runs right round the curtain wall, and admire the view. From here you can gaze over the little red-roofed town to the southward, and the elm and oak hedged fields of heavy-land Suffolk in other directions. It is not difficult, while standing up there in the wind, to imagine Suffolk as it was when the castle was first built: a great forest in which men were only beginning to hack for themselves clearings to live in.

It would not be too absurd to say that the history of Framlingham reflects every stage of the history of England, at least up until the Industrial Revolution which one must admit has not impinged upon it much, except by bringing a railway which has now disappeared again.

The first post-Conquest owners, the Bigods, were a desperate lot of fellows. We get the impression that their contract with the English people around them was very simple: 'If you give us what we want we won't beat you up!' After some attempts to enlist the help of their old enemies, the Danes, against these new predators, the Anglo-Saxons knuckled under and established what relationships they could with their overlords. As for the Bigods' relations with their kings, these left a lot to be desired.

The second Bigod (his elder brother was drowned in the White Ship) was created Earl of Norfolk or of the East Angles by the king, presumably to keep him quiet. But he helped Stephen usurp the crown from the Princess Maud, or Matilda, then spent much of his life intriguing against Stephen. He supported Henry II against Stephen, then rebelled against Henry II. He harboured Robert de Beaumont, Earl of Leicester, and his Flemish troops, when these landed on the East Anglian coast, helped them to attack Orford (unsuccessfully), and when Leicester was captured Bigod took refuge in Framlingham, defended it against the king, but finally had to surrender it. It was then that, according to William Camden (b.1551), he shouted down from the castle wall: 'Were I in my castle of Bungay, upon the waters of Waveneye, I would ne care for the King of Cockneye!'

But he wasn't, and he had to care, and his castle was dismantled by Alnoth the Engineer (the man who built Orford Castle), at the cost of £14 15s 11d. What is surprising is that Henry did not have Bigod dismantled too.

Hugh died in 1178, and his son Roger re-fortified the castle. He entertained King John in it, but later was prominent among the barons in forcing the king to sign Magna Carta. Afterwards, however, the king had his revenge by attacking Framlingham, in 1215, and reducing it once more.

Roger, the 4th Earl, defied Henry III and actually challenged him to try and take Framlingham but the king declined. The 5th Earl, also a Roger (and the nephew of the 4th Earl) was ordered by Edward I to serve with his army abroad. It is recorded that the king said to him: 'By the eternal God you shall march or be hanged!' to which he answered: 'By the eternal God I shall neither march nor be hanged!' And he neither marched nor was hanged. But he was the last of a turbulent race: he died without heir and left the castle to the king (it has been said merely to prevent his own brother from getting it).

The Mowbrays were also a turbulent lot. The first (1st Duke of Norfolk) died in exile, the third was beheaded, together with Richard Scrope, Archbishop of York, for intriguing against the king. The fourth left the castle to Lady Anne Mowbray, who was married, at the tender age of *three* (some say four), to the five (some say four-and-a-half-) year old Duke of York, who was later one of the princes to be murdered in the Tower. Little Anne died in 1481 when she was eleven: her husband was murdered a few years later. In January 1965 a small lead coffin was dug up from a building site in Stepney and was found to contain her remains. The site was once occupied by a nunnery of the Order of St Clare (the Minories), and Anne's coffin had been moved to there from Westminster Abbey to make way for the Henry VII Chapel. She was returned to her former grave in the Abbey (after her bones had been examined by radiologists, osteologists and dentists).

Of the Howard family, John was killed at Bosworth Field, Thomas, as we have seen, led the English at Flodden, the 3rd Duke gave his niece (Catherine Howard) in marriage to Henry VIII. She was executed and he would have been executed himself, as we have also seen, had the king not died the day before this was due to happen.

Queen Mary came to Framlingham after the death of her brother Edward VI and raised her standard against the supporters of Lady Jane Grey, and to her came a great army from the countryside: 13,000 armed men. It was then that she was said to have kept a look-out across the forests to Orford Castle, so as to be informed about shipping, not knowing whether she was to keep her crown or have to flee the country. Unfortunately for nearly everybody she became queen (the Earl of Arundel came riding up to the castle gate to inform her that her rights as Queen of England were established) and she set about exterminating as many as she could of the people who did not agree with her. There was a nasty rumour (put about by Protestants?) that, while waiting in the castle, she gave birth to a baby, but that it was a monster, and she killed it by bashing out its brains against the castle walls.

Thomas, the son of the poet Earl of Surrey, was also executed – but this time by Elizabeth I. His son, too, Philip, Earl of Arundel, was sentenced to death for praying for the success of the Armada, and he died in the Tower.

After this Framlingham retired from its turbulent place on the stage of history. In Elizabeth's reign it was used as a prison for recusants, and when Sir Robert the lawyer left it to Pembroke College he did so on condition that they built a Poor House in it, and we have seen that this still exists.

Perhaps it is fitting that the last use of this mighty building should have been that of sheltering the poor. For centuries it sheltered people who tyrannized the poor. And perhaps, as we stand on its walls, we should shift our thoughts from the nobles who postured and intrigued and glorified themselves within the gates, and think of the real East Anglians without, who were busy through the centuries hacking their way into the forests with their soft iron axes, pit-sawing the hard oak to build houses and ships, ploughing the land which is the support of all human life.

Let us go north to **Dennington**, which must have been something of a suburb to the metropolitan grandeur of Framlingham.

This church is supposed to have been erected on the site of a 'Druidical Temple' on an ancient Way that ran north and south through the forests. Whether or no, it is a superb church, with some of the finest wood carving in the country: the bench-ends are justly famous, there is a seventeenth-century three-decker pulpit, a pyx canopy over the altar (made of one piece of wood in the early sixteenth century), superb parclose screens forming the south and north chapels – these are infinitely worth looking at. The south chapel is the Bardolph Chapel, or chantry. Here is Lord Bardolph's tomb (which was cleaned not long ago and revealed to be of alabaster: it had been painted to make it look like stone). The sarcophagus and effigies are very beautiful: the latter more so, perhaps, than any of the effigies of Framlingham. Lord Bardolph was one of the 'happy few' who fought with Henry V at Agincourt. There is a sciapod carved on a bench-end in this church (south side of centre aisle) said to be the only one in England. The sciapod had one great foot which it held over its head for shade against the African sun. Pliny records that these creatures were 'great leapers'.

But no list of contents can give any idea of the gracious beauty of this church, when you enter it, and of its lightness and sense of well enclosed and well formed space. This is one of the churches that even the architecturally incurious should not miss.

Saxtead Green, west of Framlingham, has a beautifully restored eighteenth-century post windmill in fine working order with great white sweeps, a fantail, and a three-storey roundhouse, in the care of English Heritage. It is open to the public on weekdays from early May to the end of September.

North of Dennington Laxfield, Heveningham and Cratfield are well worth visiting. At **Laxfield** a 'simple unlearned man', a shoe-maker named John Noyes, was burned at the stake in Bloody Mary's reign. He was taken before the Bishop of Norwich, refused to recant, taken back to Laxfield and there burnt. His neighbours, on the day, doused all their household fires, save one man, and his door was burst open and fire obtained. Noyes kissed the burning faggot before it was applied to the heap of incendiary material among which he stood, and his last words to his neighbours were: 'They say they can make God of a piece of bread – believe them not!'

As much to Laxfield's discredit as Noyes was to its credit was that other native son, 'Smasher' Dowsing. William Dowsing was employed under the egregious Earl of Manchester, during the Commonwealth, 'for the defacing, demolishing, and quite taking away of all images, altars, or tables turned altar-wise, crucifixes, superstitious pictures, monuments, and reliques of idolatry, out of all churches and chapels'. He is damned by his diaries, for he left copious accounts of his works of vandalism: hardly a church in Suffolk but suffered at his hands, and acres of medieval stained glass ('superstitious pictures') are lost to us for ever. There was a Dowsing among the men who burned John Noyes: was he an ancestor of William? There is still a Dowsings' Farm in the parish.

But before we condemn such men outright we should remember that they were activated, not by mere lust for destruction, but by intense religious fervour. To us the stone carving and the stained glass would have been priceless and irreplaceable works of art: to Dowsing and his friends they were works of idolatry that stood between Man and God. Dowsing went to work with his hammer in the spirit of those other East Anglians who charged the enemy at Marston Moor and at Naseby with the psalm rolling from their lips.

Heveningham Hall, open to the public during recent decades and often providing the setting for delightful chamber concerts, was built by Sir Gerald Vanneck to replace a Queen Anne house already existing on the site. Sir Robert Taylor, King George III's architect, designed it in a magnificient Palladian style; James Wyatt did the interior, and 'Capability' Brown landscaped the gardens in 1781–2. It still makes an imposing sight from the road, across the lake, though the interior has suffered a number of misfortunes: the dining-room was burnt out in 1949, but faithfully restored from the original plans; and then some of the finest features suffered in an even worse fire in the 1980s. At the time of writing there is no indication of possible reopening.

Cratfield is interesting in that its parish accounts are very complete and in a fine state of preservation for as far back as 1490. Religion was apparently a much merrier affair in those days: frequent mention is made of 'church ales', or *potationes ecclesiasticae*. Such days occurred on Passion Sunday, Pentecost, All Saints' Day, Plough Monday and the Fourth Sunday in Lent, which still is sometimes called 'Refreshment Sunday'. On top of this,

61

numerous legacies made provision for the purchase of ale for 'church ales' on other, non-official days. Seven and sixpence seems to have been a fairly usual sum for the provision of a 'church ale', and we can suppose that in those days that would have bought a very decent amount of beer. For the 10th of October 1553 expenses are listed for providing one soldier to help guard Princess Mary at Framlingham Castle, and most of the expenses for this come under the heading of 'Drinke', although there was also a firkin of butter which cost a shilling. At Armada time 23s 7d is charged for the expenses of 'trayned sougers'.

The now drowsy village of **Stradbroke** was once larger and busier. The name of its Hempsheaf inn derived from the crop used locally during the late sixteenth century for weaving sacking and sailcloth in attempts to offset the decline of the wool trade; but now even the inn is deceased.

Fressingfield is the place to eat if you like superb food and can pay for it. The Fox and Goose Inn, to the south of the church, is famous over England among gourmets, but it pays to book a day or two ahead, and specify what you want to eat. People come from as far as Yorkshire to Fressingfield – just for the *eating*. The inn building was the old guildhall, and has fine timbering. The church is one of the finest-looking small churches in Suffolk, both within and without. There is an array of superb fifteenth-century bench-ends – perhaps the best collection in England – all unstained oak, and the marvellous hammerbeam roof is of unstained oak too. Look in the eastern arch of the south arcade for the remains of the block and girder of the *rotula*, a ring of light which used to hang before the Rood. The initials 'A.P.' on a bench are those of Alice de la Pole, grand-daughter of the poet Chaucer. Prince Edward, later King Edward I, came hunting here once and fell in love with one 'Fair Margaret'. He left her in the tender care of the Earl of Lincoln, who cared for her so well that he married her himself.

At **Worlingworth** is a great font cover, which was formerly in the Abbey Church of Bury St Edmunds, before this was pulled down.

At **Hoxne** (pronounced *hoxen*) legend stubbornly holds that King Edmund was slaughtered by the Danes. There is still a plaque at one end of Goldbrook Bridge, which conveys the information that Edmund was discovered hiding beneath the bridge (presumably not the ugly structure we have here now) – given away by a pair of lovers who saw the glint of his golden spurs. The best account of this tale that will ever be is recorded in his book *Suffolk Scene*, by the late Julian Tennyson as from the mouth of a Hoxne roadman; but readings from the Anglo-Saxon Chronicle, Abbot of Fleury, and other sources, convey the following story, less colourful than the roadman's although no less packed with action:

In AD 869 and 870 Hinvar and Ubba and twenty thousand Danes laid waste Bardney, Crowland, Thorney, Peterborough, Ramsey, Eky, Stuntney and Thetford. Hinvar sent a message to the young King Edmund telling him to submit but Edmund refused to do so, in spite of the advice of his Bishop Humbert. The Danes attacked, Edmund fled, was eventually found hiding under a bridge given away by his spurs, was offered his life if he renounced Christianity, refused, and was killed. Days later a voice was heard coming from his dismembered head crying: 'Here! Here! Here!' A friendly wolf was found guarding the head, which was retrieved, and became the chief relic of Bury Abbey. For half a century following this East Anglia was completely under the heel of the Danes, and not until 918 did Edward the Elder (King Alfred's son) drive them out.

Hoxne Church, incidentally, is dedicated to St Aethelbert, as is Hereford Cathedral. Aethelbert was an East Anglian prince who was murdered in Herefordshire when he went there with the intention of marrying Offa's daughter. The pleasantest thing now about Hoxne is its churchyard, a deliciously unkempt jungle of huge cedars, yews, and other trees and shrubs, some of them overturning with their roots the Victorian tombstones. Inside the church are old bench-ends, one of them St Edmund's head being carried by the wolf, and there are interesting murals of the Seven Deadly Sins with the sinners, nicely labelled, being eaten by dragons growing out of a tree; and of the Works of Mercy: clothing the naked, giving drink to the thirsty, visiting prisoners, feeding the hungry, visiting the sick and burying the dead. The tower of the church is very grand. In 1797 John Frere discovered Acheulian hand axes in this parish.

Wingfield should be walked to, from Hoxne, for this is a most delicious walk and it is a crime to travel the distance in a motor car. Its castle presents a ravishing picture of moated stone walls with a timber-framed Tudor manor house forming one wing and sheltering beautiful gardens. Still privately inhabited, the castle changed hands in 1987, and public access remains uncertain at the time of going to press.

William atte Pool founded the city of Kingston upon Hull (where he set up as a merchant) in the reign of Edward I. He is thought not to have been of Norman stock, but he came from the Continent. His grandson, Michael, came to Suffolk and married Katherine Wingfield of Wingfield. The Wingfields were an Anglian family:

> *Wynkefelde the Saxon held Honor and Fee*
> *Ere William the Norman came over the sea.*

Michael was created Earl of Suffolk in 1385. His grandson, also Michael, fell at Agincourt, as Shakespeare observes:

> *Where is the number of our English dead?*
> *Edward the Duke of York, the Earl of Suffolk,*
> *Sir Richard Ketly, David Gam, esquire;*
> *None else of name; and of all other men*
> *But five and twenty.*

and rumour has it that he lies buried in a silver coffin at Butley. This Michael's brother married Alice, daughter of Thomas Chaucer and widow of the Earl of Salisbury.

The de la Poles were a boisterous lot, rather like the Bigods. Michael, the First Earl, who built the castle, had to flee to Paris on one occasion disguised as a poulterer, Michael the second died of a fever at Harfleur, and his eldest son fell at Agincourt. William led the English against Joan of Arc at Orléans and then came very near to having supreme power in England. He did this by arranging the marriage of Henry VI to Margaret of Anjou, having captured that lady at Orléans. Then, with the help of the queen (who was almost certainly his mistress) he became the power behind a very weak throne. Shakespeare makes him say (in *Henry VI*):

> *Margaret shall now be queen, and rule the King;*
> *But I will rule both her, and King, and realm.*

He overreached himself, principally by arranging for the murder of the virtuous Duke of Gloucester near Bury while Parliament

Part of the great 14th-century retable in the tiny thatched church of
Thornham Parva, which stands apparently lost in the muddy fields.

Above left, a "Boston Prawner" – one of the fleet which fishes in the Wash for pink shrimps. *Right*, one of the fleet of "pair fishing" boats working out of Wells. *Below left*, a King's Lynn cockling smack aground in the Wash several miles from land. The crew are waiting for the tide to turn and float her again. *Right*, a Wells whelker – built to go 30 miles out to sea and then carry a ton of whelks over the shallow Wells Bar.

was meeting there, and he was impeached and banished to France. While on his way there his boat was arrested at Dover, and he was taken ashore and beheaded over the gunwale of a boat. Shakespeare makes the sea-captain who commanded his death say:

> *Pole! Sir Pole! Lord!*
> *Ay, kennel, puddle, sink; whose filth and dirt*
> *Troubles the silver spring where England drinks.*
> *Now will I dam up this thy yawning mouth*
> *For swallowing the treasure of the realm:*
> *Thy lips, that kiss'd the queen, shall sweep the ground . . .*

All of which seems a long way from the sleepy village of Wingfield today.

Fourteenth-century Wingfield College, with its sumptuously timbered Great Hall, was hidden for two centuries behind a neo-classical façade until rediscovered and restored between 1971 and 1981. Now it is the setting for collections of prints, textiles and fabrics, a working printing press, and regular concerts and recitals, within a surround of walled gardens with inventive topiary. Quite apart from these special events and exhibitions, the college is open Saturday, Sunday and Bank Holiday afternoons from early April until the end of September.

The collegiate church has a mounting-block before it and a parson's shelter within, to shield the incumbent from the elements at a funeral while his flock endured whatever weather was ordained for them. In the north chapel is a monument to Sir John Wingfield, the founder of the college; in the south chapel, one to Michael, the 2nd Earl. Note among the decorations the punning *wings* of the Wingfields, the *leopard heads* of the de la Poles, and the *knots* of the Staffords, to whom the family was joined by marriage.

Eye is an absolutely lovely little town. Pevsner calls the tower of the church 'one of the wonders of Suffolk', and so it is, 101 feet of marvellous flush-work. Approach from the Stradbroke direction and you get a shock of surprise and beauty as you suddenly see the church, and the Norman castle on its high steep little hill beyond it, and then discover the early sixteenth-century guildhall. Then you come into the fine little town with its ancient houses and maze of streets, its Victorian town hall (really a corker!) and its ancient pubs. Remains of a priory can be seen in a farmyard not far from the church. The castle was built by William Mallet of Graville, Normandy, one of the Conqueror's trustiest men at Hastings. He died later fighting against Hereward the Wake. Go inside the church and see the rood screen with its triple cornice. The loft and rood are 1925: the screen is medieval and has, reading from the north, St Paul, St Helen, St Edmund, St Ursula concealing virgins under her cloak, Henry VI, St Dorothy with roses, St Barbara with tower, St Agnes with sword at throat and lamb, Edward the Confessor, St John, Catherine and wheel, William of Norwich with cross and nails (but read *A Saint at Stake* by M. D. Anderson, which is about this doubtful martyr), St Lucy with eyes on book, St Blaise (patron saint of wool combers), St Cecilia with sword in throat and roses at waist, and an effaced saint thought to be Peter. In the porch of the church, south wall, is a dole table, on which loans of money were made, and a nice verse of 1601 of advice to lenders.

In a number of corners of Eye there are stretches of brickwork in a style peculiar to Suffolk. Built in wavy corrugations, they are sometimes known as ribbon or serpentine walls, but are referred to locally as 'crinkle-crankle' walls.

The White Lion, still proclaiming itself a 'posting house', has a barn-like ballroom in its old stable yard, with a musician's gallery. Today the most commonly heard music is trad jazz. Over a century ago it was a very jolly and inexpensive place. The *Suffolk Chronicle* reported an inspection of the County Yeomanry after which 'a retreat was made to the "White Lion" where dinner was provided at 2s 6d a head, including as much wine and punch as each man could swallow.'

Out in the woolly back-block to the west are the Thornhams, Magna and Parva.

In **Thornham Magna** were the Killigrews. James was a sea-captain, and killed in an engagement with the French off Sardinia. Thomas was in exile with Charles II and was ordered to leave Venice because he was too debauched even for that place. After the Restoration he founded Drury Lane Theatre and wrote indecent plays while Lady Shannon, née Killigrew, bore Charles II

66

a child. At Thornham Magna Church Peals of Minor on six bells of 10,080 changes were rung in 1928.

Thornham Parva has a most famous retable in its church. The latter is a tiny thatched building standing out in the middle of a field, and it is often locked to protect its most valuable content.

The retable is of *circa* 1300 in framing of the same date. The figures on it are said by Munro Cautley to be, from the north: St Dominic, St Catherine, St John the Baptist, St Peter, the Crucifixion with the Blessed Virgin Mary on the left of the Cross and St John the Evangelist on the right, St Paul, St Edmund, St Margaret of Antioch and St Peter Martyr in the robes of a Dominican and with his scimitar lodged in his throat. But the painting, against good gesso work, is superb, the figures all slender and willowy and with graceful drapery – inspired by the very spirit of the Middle Ages. It is an astonishing experience to come across this great work of art out in the middle of a muddy Suffolk field. The retable was discovered, incidentally, in the stable of Lord Henniker among a load of junk which he had just bought from Rookery Farm, Stradbroke, a farm which had for long been occupied by Catholics. It still has an auctioneer's label stuck on it which reads *Second Day Lot* 171. This church also has wall paintings and is well worth going to see.

Wetheringsett, south-east across the Norwich–Ipswich Road, is notable for two of its past parsons.

One was Richard Hakluyt, who was Rector from 1590 to 1616, and he wrote *Principall Navigations, Voiages, Traffiques and Discoveries of the English Nation*, a book of endless fascination.

The other was not really a parson at all. He was George Wilfrid Ellis, first a tailor of Brighton, then butler to a bishop, and then bogus clerk in holy orders and incumbent of Wetheringsett from 1858 to 1883. He was industrious and very popular, but alas he was unmasked. A special Act of Parliament had to be passed to validate the marriages that he had solemnized for many were the respectable citizens of Wetheringsett who discovered that they had, all unknowingly, been born 'the wrong side of the blanket'.

CHAPTER 4

Ipswich, Stowmarket

Ipswich is a town of great antiquity and historic interest, but, alas, practically nothing remains to show for either. The Ipswichians seem to have made a decision in the past, and to have kept to it most assiduously, to erase every building of antique beauty and interest, and to turn Ipswich into, at every succeeding period, a 'modern' town. Unfortunately the search for 'modernity' is ever doomed to failure, for what is modern in one decade is horribly dated in the next. Thus Cornhill, the heart of the town, is a hugger-mugger of derivative styles, all started in 1812 when the ancient Moot Hall and the two hundred year old Market Cross were pulled down. There are mock-Gothic, mock-Renaissance, mock-Italianate, mock-Classical. At least now Ipswich seems to have turned its back on these imitations of former glories and much resolutely 'contemporary' building is going up. The new Civic College, in the old demolished Rope Walk (which used to be a slum area of wonderful liveliness) is a fine slab of glass and concrete. The Ipswich Hospital, at the top of Berner Street, is itself not a building of notable beauty but the new boiler house and cooler tower designed by Peter Barefoot are very spirited, and deservedly won the RIBA's bronze medal for 1960–63. Fison's office building, down by the station, is something of a *tour de force*: its occupants sit up in a great glass case on show like canaries and so slender are the concrete Vs which hold it up that one wonders why the whole edifice does not collapse at the first puff of wind. The glass engravings by John Hutton on the downstairs walls are very effective.

Another new building is the office of the *East Anglian Daily Times* in Lower Brook Street, which is decorated with terra-cotta arabesques. (This might be the place to say that East Anglia is better served than any other rural area in England with provincial

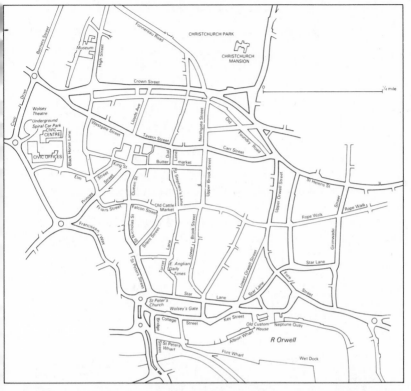

newspapers: both the *East Anglian Daily Times* of Ipswich, and the *Eastern Daily Press* of Norwich, are models of regional journalism; together they help greatly to create a climate of cultural autonomy in East Anglia.)

Much new building, too, has gone up in the large area of slum clearance decreed south-east of Cornhill – in particular the Underground Spiral Car Park, which is a gigantic affair and should be visited by all car park lovers. This was the first of its kind in this country, 180 feet in diameter and 46 feet deep with an entirely new method of concrete construction. Hard by is the new Civic Centre, and the Civic Drive.

But of ancient buildings in Ipswich, of the tiny scattering that there are left it can only be said that they are still there because nobody has yet got round to the business of pulling them down. As late as 1960 the old Half Moon Inn, which had a marvellous

69

carved corner-post depicting a friar in fox's clothing preaching to geese, and which itself was a pre-Elizabethan building and of great beauty, was ruthlessly bull-dozed. It was not in the way and has been replaced by no worthy substitute. It was old, that is all.

Ipswich is situated at a point which could not help but be the site of an important settlement, in very early times as at the present day. The River Orwell, which leads up to it, is the one easily navigable river in Suffolk: ships can enter or leave at any state of the tide or set of the wind. The site of Ipswich is at the limit of navigability of this river, and also at the lowest possible ford. Thus any road going from the south to the east of East Anglia perforce went through Ipswich, and any merchandise bound in or out of the hinterland could more conveniently be embarked or disembarked at Ipswich than at any other place: here sea-borne vessels were able to penetrate deep inland.

The Vikings found the place of great use to them. In 991 Olaf landed at Ipswich from ninety-three ships, overran the town, and then went off to fight and win the famous Battle of Maldon. In 1010, according to the Anglo-Saxon Chronicle:

> . . . the army (Danes) came to East Anglia after Easter and landed at Ipswich, and went straightway to where they had heard that Ulfcetel was with his army. That was on Ascension Day and at once the East Angles fled. The men of Cambridge-shire stood firm against them. The king's son Athelstan was killed there, and Oswig and his son, and Wulfric, Leofrine's son, and Eadwig, Aefic's brother, and many other good thegns and a countless number of the people . . . The Danes had control of the field, and they were provided with horses and afterwards had control of East Anglia, and ravaged and burnt the country for three months and even went into the wild fens; and there they burnt down Thetford and Cambridge.

The place where the battle was fought on Ascension Day was Ringmere Heath, over in the Breckland country.

By Domesday there were 110 burgesses and a hundred 'poor men' in Ipswich, and in the Middle Ages a great area of woollen industry around Lavenham. By Henry VIII's reign it was a very important town, and would have become more important still had it not been for the downfall of Wolsey.

Wolsey was an Ipswich man, and he spent his boyhood next door to where now stands that seedy-looking building, the old Hippodrome, now given over to Bingo. His father was a butcher, grazier and cloth merchant, and he owned an inn and was fined for allowing it to become a resort of 'friars and women of loose character' and also for selling beer at excessive prices. He was, nonetheless, a churchwarden.

Wolsey, in his hour of greatness, planned a great college at Ipswich, a College of Secular Canons. He began the buildings in Black Friar's Street, and incorporated the already existing Ipswich School. On his downfall the college crashed too, and all that is left of it is a brick gateway; but the school was re-incorporated by Henry VIII, ratified by Elizabeth I, and is now up in Henley Road, in a vast brick building put up in Victorian times but Elizabethan regardless.

Henry VIII once stayed in Ipswich, as the guest of a nobleman in Silent Street, and he attended Mass at the Our Lady of Grace Chapel in what is still called Lady Lane. This was a place of national pilgrimage, but at the Dissolution Henry VIII had it pulled down, and the effigy was burnt in London.

After Elizabeth, Ipswich waxed strong as a shipping town, and by the seventeenth century had captured most of the coal trade between the north and London. Defoe, in his *Particular and Diverting Account of whatever is Curious and worthy Observation*, says that Ipswich-built colliers were 'so prodigious strong that they would reign forty or fifty years or more'. These ships were laid up all winter in Defoe's time, their topmasts struck, and they lay at moorings in the Orwell: 'as safe as in a wet dock, and it was a very agreeable sight to see perhaps 200 sail of ships of all sizes lie in that posture every winter. All this while . . . the masters lived calm and secure with their families in Ipswich, and enjoying plentifully what in the summer they had got laboriously at sea, and this made the town of Ipswich a very populous place in the winter, for as the masters so most of the men, especially their mates, boatswains, carpenters, etc., were of the same place and lived in their proportions, just as the masters did, so that in the winter there might

71

be perhaps a thousand men in the town more than in the summer, and perhaps a greater number.' But by 1720 Defoe saw a great falling-away: 'It was melancholy to hear that there were now scarce 40 sail of good colliers that belonged to the whole town.'

It was Dutch ships that were, then as now, helping to knock out native English coastal shipping. As you roam around Ipswich docks now you will see Dutch, German and Belgian ships aplenty, and but a few English ones. The Wet Dock was built in 1839–42 by seventy-two gentlemen who constituted themselves as the River Commissioners, and was, when it was built, quite revolutionary and the biggest wet dock in the country. If you walk farther down the river you will come to berths for much bigger ships, unloading at Fison's big fertilizer factory, or the big modern power station. For the Port of Ipswich is expanding by building more tidal berths for bigger ships outside the old Wet Dock area.

Ipswich lost the coastal coal trade completely, to the rising County Durham and Northumberland ship-owning interests, but in the times of the big sailing ships it became an important port of entry for these, the very biggest having to lie at Butterman's Bay, down the river, and lighter themselves into sailing barges before proceeding up to the Wet Dock. Ipswich also became one of the biggest of the sailing barge ports, the big mills, Cranfields and Pauls, owning large fleets. The Industrial Revolution brought heavy industry, in the form of engineering works, boiler-makers, plough-makers and agricultural machinery makers: the name of Ransome and Rapier is still honoured on the town's industrial estate. You will see the name of Ipswich on the sluice gates of the mile-long Lloyd Barrage over the Indus in Pakistan, and on many other hydraulic works under a foreign sun. The first lawn mower was made at Ipswich (this would be disputed by the citizens of Stroud, Gloucestershire), printing started in 1548 (with John Bale's *Summary of the Illustrious Writers of Great Britain*) and W. S. Cowell Ltd. still carry on printing just off the Buttermarket, though more limited than of yore.

As for what there is to see today in Ipswich for the sightseer the story is soon told.

Old Ipswich was a timber-built town, but very few good timber-frame houses remain today. In Oak Lane, north of Tavern Street, is the old Royal Oak Inn, now offices, which has fine timber framing and Renaissance carving on its angle-posts – one of them depicting a smith at his anvil. South of this is the Great White Horse, in which Mr Pickwick had many of his adventures, and it is still a very good inn, and so is the Crown and Anchor in Westgate Street. The latter has an undistinguished modern front but old building of some charm inside.

The **Ancient House**, in the Buttermarket, is the pride of Ipswich. This was the home of the Sparrowe family for 200 years: merchants and grocers. They were staunch Royalists in the Civil War period (unusual for East Anglians) and there is a yarn, which must be quite untrue, of course, that Charles II slept in the Ancient House. Charles II certainly hid around, as Elizabeth I slept, but he certainly did not hide here, although recently a secret chamber was discovered upstairs.

This house is fifteenth century, but the amazing pargetting, or plaster moulding, on the exterior is Restoration. This pargetting symbolizes the four continents (the others had not been discovered at that time) and at one corner is depicted a scene from the 1st Eclogue of Virgil: the shepherd Tityrus sleeping under a tree. This is a building of great interest and beauty, which has had a vast and hideous red-brick cinema built right up against it. The Ancient House now houses a good bookshop, and one is allowed to inspect the building. There is a great Elizabethan picture of Hercules on the staircase.

Skirting **the docks** are still some old buildings: warehouse-cum-dwelling houses, such as No. 80 Fore Street and the nearby Old Neptune Inn (an inn no longer). These buildings had their backs to the river, for the unloading of merchandise, had store rooms and also living accommodation within (accommodation for apprentices as well as the master and his family) and withal a shop in front on the street. These merchants engaged in all forms of trade, importing goods from other countries in bulk, and selling it in pennyworths over the counter in the shop. It is interesting to compare these warehouses with those at King's Lynn.

Fore Street, in fact, has a busy, lorry-bustling charm. College Street, near it, still has Cardinal Wolsey's gate: Tudor brick on which the arms of Henry VIII can be seen. The Customs House, by the Wet Dock, is famous. It is of 1843–4, designed by J. M. Clark, a local man.

Of churches, Ipswich is in a county of fine churches (probably we can say *the* county) but itself has little of interest to offer. St Margaret's is Decorated and very beautiful; St Mary-le-Tower, the civic church, was hideously restored in 1860, nay rebuilt; St Mary at the Elms has a Norman south doorway and an early Tudor brick tower and has charm.

Perhaps the most interesting and unusual place of worship in Ipswich is the **Old Meeting House** in Friar's Street. This was built in 1699 by Joseph Clarke, who was a house carpenter, and is of wood. Without windows and inside furnishings the building cost £257, which also had to pay for 'four barrels of good small beers for to drink while imployed in said building', those early Presbyterians evidently not objecting to liquor – at least for their workmen. At the end of the eighteenth century the congregation turned to Unitarianism and the Meeting House became Unitarian, which it still is. Inside are four great wooden pillars always said to have been ships' masts, a candelabrum, thought to be Dutch and seventeenth century, which weighs 200 pounds, very fine and solid box pews, all original, with some 'wig pews' .in the galleries. There is a spy-hole in the door facing St Nicholas Street through which a watch could be kept for the Trinitarian mob in troubled times, and there is a sumptuous pulpit carved – if not by Grinling Gibbons himself – at least by his pupils. Defoe praised the building in 1720.

There are two museums in Ipswich. One in a Victorian brick building at the top of High Street, the **Ipswich Museum**, and it has the best collection in the world of fossils from the Crag (which it should have, for this deposit is a Suffolk speciality), very sound archaeological collections, and is one of the best museums for Early Paleolithic material in England. Much important research has been carried out by the staff of the museum (Basil Brown, of Sutton Hoo fame, worked here until his retirement). Replicas of Sutton Hoo finds are on display, together with replicas of Mildenhall Treasure items and gold torcs, or Iron Age collars, unearthed by a mechanical digger on Belstead Hills Estate in 1968.

A former curator was notable for the fact that he used to keep his bottled beer in the belly of the stuffed rhino.

The other museum is **Christchurch Mansion**, in the middle of a beautiful park. It has thirty-six rooms, all full of interest.

The house is on the site of an Augustinian priory. The latter was suppressed in 1537; the king had the lead taken off the roof and sold the house to a man named Sir Thomas Pope; this man sold it at a profit to a London merchant, Paul Withipoll, who wanted it for his son Edmund, who was having to get out of his house in Walthamstow because he had killed a French man-servant in a brawl. Edmund built the beginnings of the present house. Queen Elizabeth visited him twice.

In 1642 the house passed by marriage to the Hereford family and belonged to the Herefords until sold to Zachary Fonnereau, a Huguenot refugee. The Fonneraus built many more rooms on to it. In 1892 they sold it and (this being Ipswich) it was immediately proposed to pull it down and to turn the surrounding parkland (one of the most beautiful parks in the country) into a housing estate. However, in the nick of time one of the brewing Cobbold family intervened, bought it, and most magnificently gave the money to start the present excellent collection. It is perhaps the one thing that really makes the visit to Ipswich worth while.

The museum contains good collections of domestic furniture of various periods: the kitchen is particularly interesting. There is much carved woodwork from the many ancient houses that have been pulled down recently in Ipswich, and a most rare twelfth-century font of black Tournai marble. Two fine brasses from the bombed-out church of St Mary-at-the-Quay are noteworthy (particularly the brass to Thomas Pounder and his family), there are Fitzgerald relics, and a most interesting collection of Margaret Catchpole relics – including handbills for her recapture after she had escaped from prison, letters home (very illiterate and not at all like the letters made up by the Reverend Cobbold in his book about her) and the *stuffed lyre bird* that she sent home to her old mistress, Mrs Cobbold, from Van Diemen's Land. There is the sword of Tippoo Sultan captured by the Suffolks when they stormed the fort of Seringapatam in 1799, to rescue British officers immured there, and some fine ship models – including those beautiful ones made of bone by French prisoners of war in Napoleonic times. There is a panelled and painted room, Elizabethan, from Hawstead

Place. There are many Elizabethan wall paintings, and a most interesting panorama of Ipswich, with giant cabbages in the foreground, in the eighteenth century, by James Cleverly.

Most early writers praised Ipswich. Tusser likened it to Paradise, no less. Cobbett said: 'Fine, populous, beautiful, substantially built, well paved, everything good and solid, no wretched buildings to be seen on its outskirts.' From one point near it he could see the spinning sails of seventeen windmills. He noted that in 1830 wheat was 6s a quarter more in Ipswich than it was in Norwich, simply because Ipswich was a safe sail in any weather away from London and therefore it was cheaper to carry wheat there. Now Ipswich, this capital of England's chief wheat-growing area, imports more wheat than she exports. Great energy and prosperity in Victorian times wiped away old Ipswich, and today it is largely a mixture of Victorian and modern.

One of its most recent acquisitions is the Orwell Bridge – and very beautiful it is. The through traveller can now avoid both the congested centre of the town and the awful old ring road with its interminable succession of roundabouts, and sweep round to the south over this superb soaring highway. The side cuts off the view downstream, but approaching from either the Copdock or the Martlesham turnoff one catches tantalizing glimpses of craft on the Orwell, little inlets, and the gentle rise of the banks. Seen from below, the bridge itself is just as fine a sight.

It is well worth going down the left bank of the Orwell to Nacton and Levington. At **Nacton** is Orwell Park, now a boys' preparatory school, in the old home of Admiral Vernon, who captured Portobello for George II with six ships and the loss of but seven men, but who failed, alas, to capture Cartagena: episodes described in *Roderick Random*. Vernon was known as 'Old Grog' from his habit of wearing grogram breeches, and when he introduced the watering down of the Navy rum ration this was named *grog* after him. He died in 1775 and is buried in Nacton churchyard.

Broke Hall, farther down the river, still a private house, was the home of another seafaring gentleman, Sir Philip Broke. He commanded HMS *Shannon* when she captured the United States frigate *Chesapeake* on the 1st June 1813 within easy sight of Boston. The *Shannon* (39 guns) issued a personal challenge to the

76

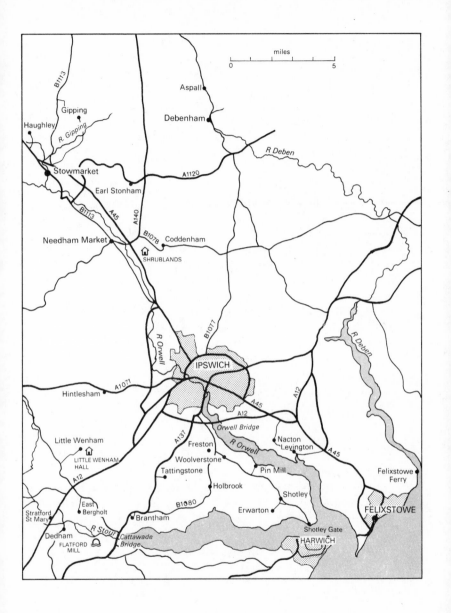

Chesapeake (44 guns) which was then lying in Boston harbour. The latter accepted the challenge and sailed out to battle, a battle which was watched by the entire population of Boston.

During a very short engagement 62 men were killed and 83 wounded aboard the *Chesapeake*, her captain, James Lawrence, falling in the first broadside, and the *Shannon* lost 43 killed and 39 wounded. The *Chesapeake* struck her colours and was taken. Even the boys in both ships, some mere children, climbed the rigging and slaughtered each other with pistols.

Levington is a charming little village, with lovely views of the estuary, and with the unspoilt Ship Inn near its church.

Farther on comes **Felixstowe**, an excellent seaside resort, very Edwardian in flavour, with a fine south-facing beach and a Fun Fair. It has little of the charm of Southwold or Aldeburgh, being a different sort of place, but in its way none the worse for that. Aqualung divers can visit the Roman fort at Walton Castle, for this is now under the sea and a couple of hundred yards from the shore. Landguard Fort, hard by, is a strange piece of military architecture, which has been adapted anew for each war, including the last one. The Dutch, under de Ruyter, attacked it in 1665, and made a landing; but withdrew to their ships before the Ipswich Militia could come at them.

During the 1970s the small harbour and docks enjoyed a vigorous expansion in the container trade, helped by the strangulation of the Port of London by restrictive practices. It is also busy with day trips to the supermarkets of Dutch and Belgian ports and with other regular services across the North Sea; and there is a ferry across the estuary to and from Harwich on the Essex bank.

To the other side of Felixstowe the land comes to a halt again at **Felixstowe Ferry**, a hamlet of shingly charm, with some lobster fishing boats, a small ferry running to Bawdsey on the other side (p. 25), the swiftly tidal and beautifully clean River Deben running out to sea over its sand bar. A place which combines very well the interest of sea and tidal river. There is a good anchorage here, west of the Horse Sand, for small yachts, and a good steep dry landing at all states of the tides on the shingle bank. Entering or leaving the river, though, requires local knowledge.

But to see the best of the Orwell, including the new bridge, follow the right bank down from Ipswich. A marvellous walk is to be had from Ipswich right down to Shotley along the shore, but even from a motor car fine views can be obtained of what is one of the most beautiful estuaries in England. The Orwell compares very well with anything that Devon or Cornwall have to offer.

Shortly after leaving the industrial area of Ipswich by crossing the Bourne Bridge we come to a stretch of road from which we obtain incomparable views over the water. The road then leaves the river to climb **Freston Hill**, so if we wish to follow the river from here we have to walk. The tower in Freston Park was built in the 1550s supposedly by a member of the Latimer family (some say the Goodings). The Latimers left shields in the windows of Freston Church. One story is that it was a watch tower, for looking out for ships inward bound up the estuary. The other that a father built it as a school for his daughter. She studied different subjects on each floor – ending up with astronomy on the roof. What she studied in the basement is not recorded. **Woolverstone Hall** was built in 1776, and was the seat of the Berners family before it became what it is now, a school. The Royal Harwich Yacht Club has its headquarters in the grounds, there is a boat yard, and the *cat house*. This latter is a little Gothic cottage, built 1793, with a white cat painted in the window which overlooks the Orwell. The legend is that the silhouette of a cat was placed there in times gone by to show approaching smugglers that the coast was clear. The legend is firmly believed throughout Suffolk, and there is no reason that I know of to suppose that it isn't true. It is pleasant that the tradition of the cat is still maintained by the present owners.

Following downstream through the magnificent park one comes to **Pin Mill**. This hamlet has had the misfortune to become known as a 'beauty spot' (which indeed it used to be), and on fine weekends in summer, when there is a line of parked cars and charabancs standing half a mile up the lane, the place has all the beauty of the North Circular Road. But in off-seasons it is still pretty, with charming old terraced cottages down in a dell, a tiny group of single cottages clustered together on the 'Grindle' (a tiny sparkling stream), a rough common dotted with stranded boats, the Butt and Oyster – a noble waterside pub (one can sail a boat up to it at high water springs and buy a pint through the window). The anchorage in the estuary is very crowded these days, and most inconvenient. There is half a mile of soft mud at low water, traversed by a rough 'hard', and the shore-going yachtsman develops a sixth sense which tells him – as he comes ashore in the afternoon – just where the water will be lapping at pub closing-time, and there he leaves his dinghy.

Old sailing barges pulled up on the mud house a number of folk, including a tattoo artist. The Webb family, bargewrights of long tradition, remember when Pin Mill was all barge folk: skippers and mates and barge repairers. Now most of the cottages have been bought up by weekenders and retired people. Once a great gang of dockers worked from Pin Mill, for the sailing ships from the Americas and the Continent were unable to get right up to Ipswich and so used to lie at Butterman's Bay, just below Pin Mill, and discharge their cargoes into sailing barges for the last stage of the journey. There was also a great fleet of *stone drudgers*. These were heavy fishing smacks which used to *drudge* (dredge in received English) the stone called septaria for the manufacture of 'Roman cement', which antedated Portland.

We can walk on downstream, first along a steep wooded cliff, at the foot of which great trees lie felled by tidal erosion, to a river wall, with marshes behind it, and along this to **Shotley**.

The old village of Shotley is set well away from the Shotley Road, on a hill overlooking the marshes and the mouth of the estuary.

> *Shotley Church – no steeple,*
> *Dirty Parson – wicked people!*

– no longer holds true, if it ever did, except in its description of the church. Shotley Church is a romantic place, set up on this lonely marsh-bound hill, among old brick cottages, not yet 'discovered' by anybody, and with a rare view out to the North Sea. The church is a strange building, with a Georgian chancel. Many hundreds of sailors are buried in the churchyard, including the entire ship's company of HMS *Gypsy*, which struck a magnetic mine in the Orwell, almost within a stone's throw of where the men are now buried.

Shotley Gate on the Stour estuary – just a few hundred yards from Bloody Point where the Stour joins the Orwell – is a modern village dominated by what was once HMS *Ganges*, a shore-based naval training station. The original HMS *Ganges* was an actual ship, built of teak in India in 1821, mounting 84 guns, the fourth ship to bear the name and the last sailing ship in the Royal Navy to fly an admiral's flag. In 1898 she was berthed off Shotley and used as a training ship, but in 1905 the shore station was commissioned under the same name, the real *Ganges* was towed away to Chatham, and the boy sailors moved on to dry land. Until recent times up to 1,600 lads would be trained each year for the Royal Navy, and one could watch them rowing races in cutters and whalers in the two rivers, or clambering up the dizzying mast which still soars above the old parade ground, with the 'button boy' perching perilously on the very top.

Now the institution has changed its name and purpose. Known as the Eurosports Village, it offers residential sports and leisure facilities over more than 150 acres including grass playing fields, tennis, squash and netball courts, swimming pool, and a range of conference and lecture rooms. Sailing activities are arranged in conjunction with local clubs.

To cater even further for sailors, ambitious plans are in hand for the development of Shotley Point Marina along the strip of old *Ganges* terrain forming the western boundary of Harwich harbour. Over a hundred holiday homes are to be set below a landmark known to ferry crews and passengers almost as well as the tall mast: a water tower built upon one of the Martello towers installed to fight off a Napoleonic invasion. There should eventually be more than 300 berths for yachts and dinghies in a locked basin. One can only hope that this increase in leisure craft will not give the captains of the busy European ferries entering and leaving the estuary too many grey hairs!

Not far away is the tiny village of **Erwarton**, where the winding road takes a sudden sharp twist to the left and reveals the lodge gateway of Erwarton Hall, arched and pinnacled in deep red brick. Behind it stands the sixteenth-century hall itself, with a front also of glowing brick, laid in the old English bond. This was once used as the private residence of the captain of HMS *Ganges*, the gardens being kept up by working parties from there.

81

The church of Erwarton is of that strange rock dredged out of the sea, septaria, like much of Orford Castle. It is said that the heart of Anne Boleyn was buried in this church. Her aunt, Amata Boleyn, married a Calthorpe at the Hall and Anne spent much of her childhood there. Henry VIII is supposed to have visited her, during their courtship, by yacht.

Bearing westward, one used to pass a picturesque watermill. Rescued before a new reservoir flooded the valley, it is now in the museum at Stowmarket. Beyond its lost site we come to the village of **Holbrook**, home of the Royal Hospital School.

The latter was founded at Greenwich in 1715, but transferred to Holbrook in 1933. Admission to the school is restricted to sons of officers and men of the Royal Navy, Royal Marines, Mercantile Marine and Lifeboat Service. A man named Gifford Sherman Reade, of Holbrook, gave land and money for the new school, and the architects were H. T. Buckland and W. Hayward. The architecture has been described as 'neo-Wren'. It is vast, sprawling, symmetrical, bright red brick faced in places with stone, with concrete cupolas here and there, and a huge cold-looking chapel with murals by Eric Gill. Whatever else one sees about the vast buildings, in term time or vacation, one never sees a boy, and one draws the impression that, if A. S. Neill's Summerhill School at Leiston is at one extreme end of the disciplinary spectrum, Holbrook is at the very extremity of the other. Superb views are to be had from the school over the mile-wide Stour Estuary.

If you do happen to diverge to **Tattingstone**, and see a row of cottages with one end built to look like a ruined church, this is the 'Tattingstone Wonder'. It was built by a squire because he said his neighbours were always wondering at nothing so he would give them something to wonder at.

Farther west the **Brantham** Bull is a noble pub, and down the hill by the river one comes to the 85-acre B.X. Plastic Works, perhaps the most severely functional set of buildings in England. The place looks like nothing so much as 85 acres of tortured, writhing steel pipes. It is built on the marshes, and protected from a return of the 1953 floods by a high wall. Uncompromising though it may be in appearance it is historically interesting. In 1876 British Xylonite made Celluloid in London: the first 'plastics industry'.

The firm moved to Brantham in 1887, and until recently the factory was supplied with raw materials by sailing barge. Even now a few little motor coasters unload chemicals there. Two thousand people are employed, and the factory makes a very wide range of plastic raw material. Thomas Tusser farmed at Brantham Hall, where he wrote, four hundred years ago, his *100 Points of Good Husbandry.*

Cattawade Bridge, which leads out of the ancient kingdom of East Anglia into Essex, is a fine old brick arch over the Stour. Just upstream is an ancient tidal mill, perhaps the last to work in England, after the last war a spice mill and now a factory for the manufacture of plastic-covered wire rope. The great tidal water wheel will, alas, turn no longer.

We are now on what has become hallowed ground, for this is John Constable's country. When the artist himself was travelling to it once in a carriage, a fellow-traveller who did not know him tapped him on the knee and said: 'Look out of the window, Sir – this is Constable's country!'

Constable wrote: 'I love every stile and stump and lane in the village; as long as I am able to hold a brush I shall never cease to paint them . . . The beauty of the surrounding country, its luxuriant meadow flats sprinkled with flocks and herds, its well cultivated uplands, its woods and rivers, with numerous scattered villages and churches, farms and picturesque cottages, all impart to this particular spot an amenity and elegance hardly anywhere else to be found.'

The village is **East Bergholt**. If you can get there, through the summer columns of charabancs and cars, you will find many fine Georgian houses and a most unusual church, with its broken remains of an unfinished tower and its bells housed in the wooden sixteenth-century bell house next door. The story is that every time the builders built more on to the tower during the day the Devil came along and cast it down at night. Another story, less pictur-esque, is that Wolsey was financing the building of the tower, and when he crashed the tower had to be abandoned. Anyway, the incomplete tower is most romantic, and the bell house quite unique. The bells (a very fine peal) are rung by hand, with the aid of ropes, and the bell-ringers must be nearly deafened. Stour Gardens, once the home of the late Randolph Churchill, has fine lawns and gardens open daily all year round, overlooking the river valley.

The little lane down to **Flatford Mill** is so thronged with traffic in the summer that I would not recommend it. But in off-seasons Flatford Mill is charming, although no more so than a score of other old watermills in Norfolk and Suffolk. On the way down, if you are very clever, you may be able to spot the place on which Constable stood to paint 'The Cornfield'. In the mill-house itself he was born, in 1776. His father, Golding Constable, owned two watermills on the river, besides East Bergholt windmill. The little group of buildings comprise the mill, mill-house, Willy Lott's cottage, and Valley Farm, all much painted by the artist, and painted so many times since by amateurs that it is a wonder they have not all been painted right away. The buildings stand unaltered: one sees them with a jolt of recognition if one is used to looking at the paintings. They now belong to the National Trust, and are rented to the Council for the Promotion of Field Studies (Flatford Mill Field Centre). There is hostel accommodation for fifty students. There is a vast car park and a thronged café. If Constable came back and saw it all on a fine Sunday afternoon it would be interesting to hear what he would say.

A popular game is trying to spot the places where the artist sat or stood to paint his famous pictures, and then see what the scene is like today. This is rendered difficult by the artist's readiness to shift, say, Dedham Church a half a mile or so if it suited his composition. But the country has altered little over the years. Fewer trees, more houses, more wire (or at least wire where there was no wire).

Constable fell in love with Maria Bicknell, grand-daughter of the Rector of East Bergholt, one Dr Rhudde. They wished to marry in 1800, but Rhudde persistently opposed their marriage, and they did not reach the altar until 1816, when Constable was forty. Maria died in 1829, leaving John the rest of his life to regret the sixteen years of happiness they might have had together had it not been for the stupidity of his grandfather-in-law.

Stratford Saint Mary some years ago had a by-pass road made round it, and not before time; for this nice little Tudor village was being choked by the roaring traffic of the A12. It has long been partially spoiled by a Water Board pumping station of such revolting aspect that, fascinated, one cannot wrest one's eyes off it to look at the beautiful Weaver's House and other buildings. The embattled Perpendicular church looks like a wedding cake: note the fine flush-work alphabet around its walls, and the arms of Chaucer quartered with those of de la Pole. The first Duke of Suffolk, a de la Pole, married Geoffrey Chaucer's grand-daughter. There is a headstone in the graveyard of Anne Richardson, who died in 1803 aged sixty-six. She was the last daughter of Samuel Richardson, the father of the English novel (*Pamela*). There are still several Richardsons living about Stratford St Mary. Stratford St Mary was a staging place in Roman times, on Route 9 of Antonine's 'Itinerary'.

Proceeding Ipswichwards again we can make a detour off the A12 to look at **Little Wenham** Hall. This solid little castle (it is a fortified house actually, but it looks like a castle to me) is of great interest because it was one of the first buildings in post-Roman times to have been built of brick (but compare Polstead Church). It was built at the latter end of the thirteenth century, and looks today quite unchanged. There is a great hall in it, kept furnished by the present owner, a chapel and a spiral staircase, and a fine view from the battlemented roof. One can stand there and imagine this very level country as it was when it was all one great hard-wood forest. There is a fine sixteenth-century tithe barn nearby, with brick nogging (an in-filling of bricks set at an angle to the horizontal) in timber framing and a thatched roof. But there are hundreds of such barns in East Anglia, great timber-framed barns are so common as to be commonplace. Many have been converted to twentieth-century uses, and serve as well now as they did when they were built. It's worth looking into the church just to see the early fourteenth-century wall paintings.

We might now work northwards, and circumnavigate Ipswich to the west and north.

Hintlesham used to be famous for its festivals which occurred every year for most of July. Mr Anthony Stokes, who owned the hall and was the prime mover, alas died in 1970. Mr Stokes was one of the passing breed of English eccentrics, and the festivals were a great asset to the locality. They were joyous occasions and did not take themselves too seriously. There was the occasion when

85

a ballet dancer fell through the stage in an excess of enthusiasm, and the other occasion when Mr Stokes opened a parcel solemnly presented to him after his closing speech and found that it contained a live frog. The village is charming and tree-shaded, the Hall magnificent. In the very pretty little country church is a memorial to Captayne John Timperley made of black stone inlaid with white stone to resemble a brass. It is floridly ornamented, with a Roundhead helmet and other warlike regalia. On the corbels 'in the way of' (as a sailor would say) the rood screen there are fine grotesque heads – one pulling his mouth open in a rude gesture. The Timperleys built the Hall in Elizabeth's time (they were recusants and had to flee the country), but a Georgian façade has been built in front of the old Tudor one, thus making a corridor immediately inside the front door ideal for exhibitions of paintings. For a while the celebrated chef Robert Carrier ran the premises as a luxurious restaurant and, although he has gone, the house, now an hotel, maintains the gourmet tradition.

Northward brings you over the chalk uplands, with many exceedingly pretty villages, to the valley of the Gipping, the river that turns into the Orwell at Ipswich. The Gipping valley started on the road to industrialism when the river was canalized in 1793, and horse barges, followed by steam ones, connected Stowmarket and other places cheaply to Ipswich Docks. The East Union Railway killed this goose in 1847 (you will still see the picturesquely decaying lock gates even from the road) but Stowmarket has now got a large chemical factory, besides several other works. The valley is much dominated by the A45, which runs from Felixstowe to Birmingham.

Needham Market has a roof in its church which Cautley in his *Suffolk Churches* calls 'the culmination of the English carpenter'. It is worth spending some time looking at this roof from the inside, working out how the various pieces are put together and how the thrusts are taken. A carved wood covering conceals the arch braces which support the hammerbeams, as at Framlingham, St Peter Mancroft, Norwich, and Ringstead, Norfolk. The church was originally fifteenth century. Much of the timber of the roof is Victorian, although no doubt a close copy of the original.

Stowmarket, a busy little market town, is the home of the Museum of East Anglian Life, a 30-acre riverside site with buildings collected from all over the region and re-erected here, including a wind pump and Alton watermill. Traction engines are often in steam, and there are various rural displays and special events at weekends. The museum is open daily from early April until late October. At **Shelland**, in the Church of King Charles the Martyr, is a barrel organ which is played at services. It was made in 1800 and plays thirty-six hymn tunes, which have not been changed since it was made. At **Gipping** stands the private chapel of the Tyrrell family, by the site of their now vanished mansion. Sir James confessed himself to have been the murderer of the Princes in the Tower (the bride of one of whom we discussed at Framlingham), and his ancestor, Sir Walter, is said to have shot the arrow into the heart of William Rufus while the two were hunting in the New Forest. Sir James built the beautiful little private chapel, one of the most perfect Perpendicular buildings in the country, but this did not prevent him from being executed by Henry VII.

At **Haughley** is a motte and bailey castle (Haughley is an attractive village with cottages amid the apple trees) and the experimental station of the Soil Association at New Bells Farm. New Bells Farm may be regarded as the pioneering centre of what became known as the Organic Movement, and has been visited by organic farming enthusiasts from all over the world. Recorded comparisons were made over several decades between food and livestock raised on artificially fertilized land, and food and livestock from a 75-acre section which, by a happy freak of agricultural history, had never been treated with synthetic fertilizers or sprays. The object was to establish how seriously modern farming practices might be damaging soil fertility and structure: how much contamination can we inflict on our environment without doing irreparable damage; and if there is a limit, how close are we to it? Activities at Haughley continue, but on a much reduced scale: a large part of the research has been been transferred to Bristol.

Earl Stonham church is a stunningly beautiful little country church: inside and out it has the utmost grace and elegance. Tiny although it is, it is cruciform, and has a clerestory. The roof is breathtaking – a single hammerbeam roof of sumptuously carved chestnut dating from the mid-fifteenth century. There are angels alternating with carved pendant bosses, and it has a massive solidity about the roof: it is built like a ship. The choir stalls are interesting, there is a triple hourglass in the south transept and there are remains of ancient wall paintings.

Aspall is a straggling little lost village in this moated country. Its old Hall is a typical completely moated fine Tudor house, and it still has its stew ponds and pigeon loft – and kept in use, too. It has for long been the house of the Chevallier family. Anne Francis Chevallier was the mother of Lord Kitchener. The family came to England as Huguenot refugees and became famous farmers. The farming writer Arthur Young praised their husbandry, and a variety of barley they bred, 'Chevallier', is known to every farmer in the land and has only recently been superseded. When the family came from Normandy they brought their cider mill with them – a granite trough around which rolls a huge stone wheel and is thought to date from the time of the Conquest. This mill is still there, and people intent on buying cider may see it, but the apples are nowadays crushed by a small motor-driven crusher. Aspall Cider is still made, and is for sale, and is some of the best cider in the country.

I call this heavy-land country between the A45 and the A12 the 'moated country' because so many of its farmhouses are surrounded by deep moats. These have been explained in various ways. One is drainage: every field hereabouts is surrounded by a deep ditch, which must be kept constantly cleaned out, otherwise cultivation becomes impossible. The siting of the homestead on an island of land isolated by a deep moat kept it well drained. Another is defence, perhaps in the times of the Danish invasions. Another is as stew ponds. Certainly carp and other fish were bred in them for the table. It is easy to see that this country was once all hard-wood forest – oak and elm. Indeed even today, looking over the fields, one gets the impression of fields in a forest, so many hedges have big elm or oak trees growing in them.

Crow's Hall, **Debenham**, is a magnificent example of these moated mansions, although grander than most of them. Built about 1508 of brick (more typical is timber framing and lath and plaster), it has a wide and deep moat on which the owner's children and their friends skate in the winter, inside is a great wealth of wonderful old oak – a great staircase every step of which is an oak beam, oak panelling everywhere and enormous panelled oak doors. The marvellous range of farm buildings before you come to the Hall are known as 'the Barracks', and the place was a Cavalier stronghold in the Civil War. It is now a private house, and the centre of a bunch of farms and a pedigree Jersey herd. Debenham is as beautiful a little Suffolk town as you will find: completely free from tourists although far more picturesque than plenty of tourist-ridden places farther south. The church is beautifully placed, nestling among the ancient houses, but over-restored within. It has, though, a massive rood beam, and a monument to a very pious-looking double-chinned gentleman named John Sheppard flanked by two very well-fed urchins old beyond their years. On the 18th October 1890, we are told, a peal of 5040 Bob Triples was rung at Debenham, and on 3rd December 5056 changes of Superlative Surprise were rung in three hours and two minutes. The fine bells, cast in 1761, were re-hung on ball bearings in 1932 and are famous among bell-ringers. There are two incontestably Anglo-Saxon windows on the south of the tower. There is a butcher's shop in Debenham, 'F. E. Neave', with a most colourful and beautiful sign; and the Debenham Rush Weavers turn out rush table mats, carpets, baskets, and other rush materials at the other end of the town.

Shrublands is a great mansion in a great garden, the latter one of the grandest in East Anglia. The hall was built, or rebuilt, in Elizabeth I's reign by Edward Bacon, the brother of the famous Francis, who had married into the property. Beyond a window and a few details little of this remains. The last of the Bacons, the Reverend Nicholas, who died in 1795, commissioned James Paine to build a new house between 1770 and 1772. In 1830 William Fowle Middleton, the then owner, added two wings, a terrace and a conservatory, designed by J. P. Gandy Deering. In 1848, having made the Grand Tour (which went to his head as it did to the heads of so many English magnates) he commissioned Sir Charles Barry to Italianate the whole thing up. The park and gardens were turned into an Englishman's idea of Italy or a copy of the gardens of the Villa d'Este. The gardens were extensively remodelled, and simplified, by William Robinson in 1888.

They are still very fine. There is a sumptuous staircase leading down from a terrace to a fountain and parterre, and thence a vista to an ornate loggia. There are fine vistas and fine trees, and Italianate gatehouses around the walls. Six Roman roads are said to meet in the park, and they have been retained in the form of tree-lined avenues.

As for the house today, it is a health clinic, where you may undergo Kneipp Water Therapy (wherein you are subjected to water from high-pressure hoses), sauna baths, colonic irrigation, fasting and dieting, and chiropractic manipulation.

Barham Manor, over the road, is Elizabethan, but much more modest than Shrublands. The Barham Sorrel Horse is an inn which has done well out of refugees from Shrublands cheating on their dietary régime by quaffing pints.

Coddenham's one street, up the hill, is like a fairy-tale village: it is a place with hardly a jarring note in it. Starting at the bottom of the hill Gryffon House was until recently the Crown Inn – alas strangled by licensing laws like many another fine country inn. According to story it was once the house of an archer named Wodehouse, knighted by Henry V after the Battle of Agincourt. Certainly it looks ancient enough for this to have been true. Up the street there are several oversailing half-timbered houses, with pargetted walls: the pink-washed post office, which is in Lodge House, was once a pub called the Live and Let Live, and above it is the one pub still open, the Duke's Head.

CHAPTER 5

Norwich

'A fine old city, truly, is that, view it from whatever side you will; but it shows best from the east, where the ground, bold and elevated, overlooks the fair and fertile valley in which it stands. Gazing from those heights, the eye beholds a scene which cannot fail to awaken, even in the least sensitive bosom, feelings of pleasure and admiration.' Thus George Borrow, in *Lavengro*. '. . . the fine old city, perhaps the most curious specimen at present extant of the genuine old English town.'

And he could say the same today. In spite of the sad if necessary removal of the cattle market from the Castle Bailey to the suburbs, and the building in the last year or two of vast skyscrapers containing a myriad of insurance workers, and the throwing up of that – to me – hideous city hall (many good judges like it – I think it looks like a gigantic public convenience, which I suppose is what it is), Norwich is still a fine city, and an ancient one, and bids fair to become a great centre of provincial culture, a bastion against the overwhelming and deadening metropolitanism that afflicts this land. For many centuries it was the second city of England, and although now far overtaken in size by the midland and northern parvenus it is still one of the finest and withal the most lovable. To a miraculous degree it has retained its ancient charm while adapting itself to the exigencies of the twentieth century.

Yes, there it spreads from north to south, with its venerable houses, its numerous gardens, its thrice twelve churches, its mighty mound, which, if tradition speaks true, was raised by human hands to serve as a grave-heap of an old heathen king, who sits deep within it, with his sword in his hand, and his gold and silver treasures about him. There is a grey old castle upon the top of that mighty mound . . .

There still is, and it contains probably the best provincial museum in England.

> . . . and yonder, rising three hundred feet above the soil, from among those noble forest trees, behold that old Norman masterwork, that cloud-encircled cathedral spire, around which a garrulous army of rooks and choughs continually wheel their flight.

Behold it still.

Norwich owes its individual character to the fact that it has always been an isolated city, cut off from the Midlands by the Wash and the Fens (almost unpassable until the nineteenth century) and a long way from London. It is a port, moreover, with close connections with the Continent. Until the railway age it would have been quicker for a Norwich man to have gone to Antwerp or Rotterdam than to any English city. Thus there is an isolationist feeling about the place, and a strong Continental influence. Isolation makes for self-sufficiency; and Norwich has always had a great variety of industry, made necessary by remoteness. As a shopping and marketing centre it is excellent, by reason of the fact that it serves a vast hinterland, and is the only first-class shopping centre for fifty miles.

I love to wander round the streets of Norwich, penetrating the jumble of medieval streets in the old walled city, looking into the occasional deserted church (there are far too many churches for the inhabitants), looking also into the seldom deserted pubs. When I was a boy it was said that you could go to a different church every Sunday of the year in Norwich, and a different pub every night. And I know of no city in England with better pubs. Not the grand pubs, or the pretentious ones, but the little back-street pubs and the working men's pubs (and working women's too, for there are very few traditionally men-only pubs in Norwich – the women earn with the men, in the many industries that employ them). There are pubs full of jolly old factory women who love 'a laugh and a joke', and don't care very much what the joke is about. There are pubs full of market stall-holders, pubs full of settled 'Travellers', or Gypsies, for there is a strong community of this brotherhood in Norwich – descendants, certainly some of them, of George

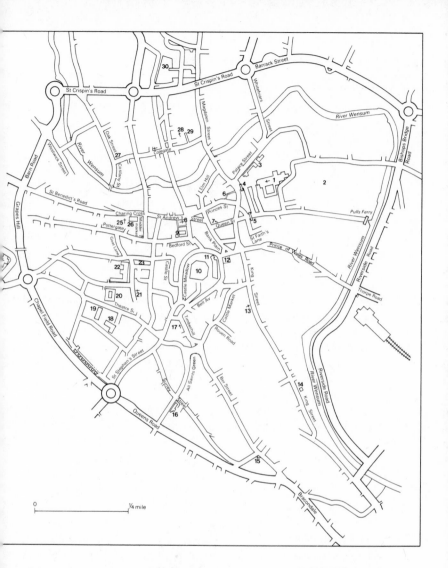

1 Cathedral
2 Cathedral Close
3 Edward VI School
4 Erpingham Gate
5 St Ethelbert's Gate
6 Tombland Alley
7 St Michael at Plea
8 St Andrew
9 Bridewell Alley
10 Castle and Castle Museum

11 Shire Hall
12 Anglia Television
13 St Peter Permountergate
14 Music House
15 St John de Sepulchre
16 BBC Television
17 St John the Baptist
18 Assembly House
19 Theatre Royal
20 County Library

21 St Peter Mancroft
22 City Hall
23 Guildhall
24 R. C. Cathedral
25 St Gregory
26 Strangers Hall
27 St Michael at Coslany
28 Octagon Chapel
29 Old Meeting House
30 Anglia Square

Borrow's Petulengro – pubs full of the sailors who come up the Yare, pubs where the most unusually jolly ladies of joy await their gentlemen friends (Norwich has the jolliest harlots of any city I know – most of the sisterhood are woefully dull), pubs full of lorry drivers, pubs full of rich farmers in from the Norfolk countryside, pubs full of burglars.

A burglar told me, in one of the latter, how, when robbing a warehouse, he had had a vision of God. He couldn't remember the exact words that the Deity spoke to him, but gathered that the meaning of them was: 'Lay off the stuff!' However, my friend heeded not the words, and pinched a carpet (more or less out of habit) and the police were waiting for him outside in the street and he got eighteen months.

Still a great deal of the social life of Norwich centres round its pubs, and always did so. Old Crome, the father of the Norwich School of Painting '. . . was a simple man, of genial company. To the end of his life he used to go of an evening to a public-house as to an informal club. In the privileged bar-parlour, behind the taps and glasses, he sat with his friends and the shop-keepers, talking of local things.' (The Rifleman, Colegate, was where he sat. Alas, it is closed now.) But before we lose ourselves completely in the pubs, let us go and look at **the Castle**.

The East Angles certainly had a fortified place at Norwich (though the Danes twice burned it down). At the time of the Conquest Gyrth Godwinsson, brother of King Harold, was Earl of the East Angles, and probably lived there. He was killed at Hastings, and the year after the battle the Normans pulled down a hundred houses in Norwich and built an earth and wood castle using the forced labour of the inhabitants.

Early in the twelfth century the wooden castle was replaced by the present stone structure. This looks, today, brand new; the reason being that it was refaced with Bath stone in 1834, by Salvin. But even before that date it must have been well preserved. The new keep was more than just a last-ditch refuge, but was the main residential part of the castle, and the fifth largest keep in England.

The first Norman to control it, under the king, was William Fitzosbern. A few years later Ralph Guader, Earl of Norfolk and Suffolk, was the Constable but plotted with other barons at his wedding feast to overthrow King William ('That Wedding Ale, Was many Man's Bale'), and was forced to flee to Brittany, leaving his wife in charge of the castle. This lady for three months withstood the king's forces so valiantly that she was granted a free pardon and allowed to join her husband in exile.

The Bigods (see Framlingham, p. 51) then became constables of the castle for the king, and kept the job, in spite of many intrigues, until they displeased King John by plotting against him, and were replaced by Hubert de Burgh (see Orford, p. 29), of 'heat me these irons hot' fame. The castle was attacked and taken by Hugh Bigod and his Flemish allies in 1174, but later re-taken by the king. In 1220 it was demilitarized and turned into the county jail, which it remained right up until 1887 after which it was transformed into a museum.

In Norman times the castle and the area around it were completely outside the jurisdiction of the city, and there was much friction between the Norman garrison within and the East Anglians without. The castle formed a foreign enclave within the city, and the cathedral and priory another. It was not until 1345 that Edward III consented to the citizens of Norwich renting land inside the castle fee, and thus one of the foreign enclaves was dissolved.

Whatever else you miss in the castle, do not miss the doorway leading to the outer building known as the Bigod Tower from the main body of the keep. Around this is superb Norman carving. This door was once the only way into the keep. Have patience, too, to wait for the time of day when you can join a guided party to the castle ramparts, if only for the fine views over the great city, and the strong sense of a romantic past.

As might be expected in the bird-rich county of Norfolk **the museum** in the castle has a fine collection of stuffed birds, including such rarities as the last of Norfolk's Greater Bustards (would that they had been left flying around) and a Greater Spotted Cuckoo. But the stuffed-bird-lover will discover such delights for himself. The 'Norfolk Room' is a triumph of museummanship, with magnificent dioramas of various types of Norfolk countryside: Broadland, Breckland, and the ordinary indiscriminate countryside in between. These six great displays are really excellent of their kind.

There are ten galleries of paintings, most of them, quite rightly, filled with the products of the Norwich School. There is a Crome Gallery and a Cotman Gallery. John Crome ('Old Crome') was born in 1768, the son of a weaver. At twelve he became an errand boy to a doctor, then an apprentice to a painter of coaches and of inn signs, and in this employment he learnt to grind and use colours. He met another apprentice, a boy named Ladbrooke, who supplemented his income by painting portraits of people for five shillings a head. Crome was thus encouraged to paint, and began doing landscapes at thirty shillings each. Ladbrooke and Crome married a pair of sisters, and remained close friends. Crome did his seven years as an apprentice, started the 'Norwich Society of Artists', in 1803, and founded the Norwich school of painting which in its time was famous throughout Europe and for a time was in the van of European landscape art. Crome and Cotman to a certain extent anticipated the Impressionists. Both were among the first to get away from a photographic reproduction of every leaf and twig, and to come close to catching the essence they were striving to depict. Cotman, perhaps more than Crome, seems surprisingly modern even when we see his work today.

But it was Crome who captured the feeling of Norfolk as no other artist has, and who realized – like John Constable – that it is the working and homely things making up our old countryside that are beautiful: the old mills and cottages, the work boats and working horses, the nature, water and the trees. Crome could never make a living by his painting alone, but was forced all his life to teach, to support his large family, including his son John ('Young Crome') who also became a painter.

John Sell Cotman was fourteen years younger than Crome, the son of a silk mercer. He went to London to paint at an early age, nearly starved, but was appointed, in the nick of time, Professor of Drawing at London University, and thus survived. He was a superb draughtsman, particularly of buildings; and his *Specimens of Architectural Remains* are unsurpassed. Cotman's house can be seen at St Martin's-at-Palace Plain, next door to the White Lion. It was here in 1824 that he opened his 'School of Drawing and Painting in Water Colour'. Tuition fees were one guinea and a half per quarter. His son, J. J. Cotman, was another good artist.

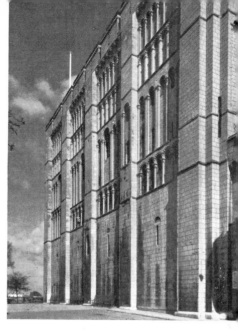

NORWICH. *Above left,* Elm Hill; *right,* the Keep. *Below,* the Cathedral nave.

East Anglian Cottage Architecture. *Above left*, pargetting at Clare; *right*, Bishop Bonner's Cottages, East Dereham. *Below*, Willie Lott's Cottage, Flatford Mill. John Constable lived next door and painted the cottage often.

There is still a lively Norwich Art Circle. Their work is often exhibited in the beautiful Assembly House, in Theatre Street (built 1754 by Thomas Ivory), where incidentally the most excellent cold collations can be had at lunch time on weekdays, not expensive.

For the rest there is much in this museum to instruct and amuse, including dioramas of what Norfolk may (or may not) have looked like during Mesolithic times and later, 'Snap', the ceremonial dragon such as that used by the St George's Guild (which was established in the fourteenth century and extinguished in 1732), the 'Parliament Chair', carved with cherubs, in which the newly elected Member was wont to be carried through the streets of Norwich, and flung painfully and perilously into the air at intervals, Lord Nelson's hat, some Lowestoft porcelain and much else.

While on museums, go, by all means, to the **Strangers' Hall**, in Norwich's Charing Cross. This contains furniture and domestic utensils of many different periods, and if the lover of Victoriana wishes to know just where his *outré* tastes may lead him, if he indulges them in full, let him take a look at the three Victorian rooms here. I always leave with a conviction that the art of living has steadily retrogressed since Tudor times. It is important not to become so engrossed in the fine exhibits as to ignore the house itself, a marvellously preserved medieval mansion. The undercroft is early fourteenth century, the Great Hall (the splendid open crown-post roof was added in the sixteenth century) mid-fifteenth.

The Hall has been inhabited by a succession of rich merchants (note the Grocers' Arms on the screen near the door – put there for Nicholas Sotherton, who moved in about 1525). Roman Catholic priests inhabited the place during much of the nineteenth century, then a private family, and it was presented to Norwich in 1922.

The other museum which the stranger should not miss is the **Bridewell**. The north wall of this is an example of squared flint at its perfection (a rather black and sombre perfection perhaps) put up in the, fourteenth century. The museum has local industries and crafts. Particularly interesting are examples of old building methods, brick making, the first wire-netting machine (Norwich led the world in making this useful stuff – it is difficult to see how people kept chickens without it), a Jacquard machine on a loom of amazing complexity, a beautiful wooden aeroplane propeller

97

(that high summit of the wood-worker's art), fine models of wind-mills and a Norfolk wherry. These are the things that catch my eye there – there is very much more. And not least, contained in the Bridewell, is the secret of the Norwich canary.

Norwich has for long been so famous for canaries that the very word canary has become to mean a Norwich man. The Norwich City football team (which so often wins its matches) is called 'The Canaries'. For many years canary fanciers up and down the land were yellow with envy at the *colour* of the Norwich breeders' canaries, which was yellow of the very yellowest. Then, in the year 1875, one W. Blackston let the cat, if not the bird, out of the bag. He published the secret of the Norwich canary fanciers to the astonished world. It was simply that they fed their canaries on cayenne. (They now feed them on Spanish red pepper, or *Capsicum annum*.) Thus the Norwich fanciers lost their great advantage over all others, although not their supremacy; and still, for many, the annual canary show at Norwich is the highlight of the year. I once asked a Norwich man in a pub which party was going to win the General Election. 'Election?' he said. 'What election? It's the Canary Show I'm worried about.'

Another musuem is in the old church of **St Peter Hungate**, which contains examples of ecclesiastical art, including weird and wonderful musical instruments, and much else of interest including part of a manuscript of a 'Wycliffe' Bible.

As for the churches of Norwich, if you try to see all of them you will suffer from a severe surfeit of ecclesiastical architecture.

But **St Peter Mancroft**, up in the Market Place, must be in-spected, for it is one of the great buildings of East Anglia. The finest Perpendicular, this church is noble and stately, in a perfect position dominating the lovely market place (dominating it in spite of the much bigger modern City Hall), set off wonderfully by gaily painted old houses that cluster around its foot. Inside you see a timber roof like that of Framlingham (but much bigger), a hammerbeam roof with the hammerbeams concealed by fan vault-ing. There is a rare timber baptistry, one of only three in England (one is at Trunch, where we shall go). The bottom part of this is fifteenth century, but the upper part was restored (well) in the nineteenth. The High Altar was made at Exeter in 1885, but the lower part, with Christ in Glory and Saints Alban, Augustine, Columba and Felix – the first to try to convert the heathen English – was built to the design of Sir Ninian Comper in 1930, to mark the church's five-hundredth birthday.

Sir Thomas Browne (1605–82 – *Religio Medici* and *Urn Burial*) has two tablets let into the wall south of the altar: one put there by his wife, when he was buried in the chancel, and the other in 1922 after his skull was decently re-buried after having been dug up by grave diggers in 1840, hawked around as a curio, and finally put in a medical museum. Sir Thomas's statue, with him depicted as contemplating a piece of urn, is just south of the church.

But it is the building itself that is noteworthy. Particularly look at the tower arch, as you stand in the nave and look west. It is a miracle of strength with economy. And the clerestory is lovely, whether viewed from within or without. The church plate is as good as there is, and there are Browne relics. The church's near neighbour is a fine, rambling, colour-washed inn.

To describe all the other churches in this city would be for another book, and another writer. Among things which have pleased me has been the painting of St George clad as a medieval knight on the west wall of the north aisle of **St Gregory's, Pottergate.** (Pottergate is a nice street to wander in anyway, and Old 'Snap', the dragon like the one in the Castle Museum, used to be kept in St Gregory's, for it was here that the St George Society used to hold their revels. There is a fine eagle lectern, too, dated variously 1493 or 1496.) Then there is the ancient glass in **St Andrew's Hall** in the north side, and particularly the bishop dancing with Death at the west end of the south aisle of St Andrew's church. St Andrew's Hall is a fine building, splendid Perpendicular, with portraits in it, including the last one made of Nelson and one by Gainsborough. This is now used for concerts and flower shows and such like; would that more redundant churches were. It was once part of the church of the 'Sackites' (called so because they used to dress up in old sacks), or Friars of the Penance of Jesus Christ. When these mendicants were suppressed in 1307 their convent was granted to the Dominicans, and they in their turn were suppressed in 1538. At one time the always separated choir of their church (called Blackfriars' Hall) was used by the Dutch community in

Norwich, and a Dutch service was held there once a year until recently. (It was in 1336 that Edward III, with his Dutch wife, brought the first parcel of Hollanders to England, in an attempt to turn the country from a wool exporting country into a cloth exporting one, for the Dutch were ahead of the English in fine weaving.) These two halls are among the very few friars' buildings left in England.

I like the arms of Good Old Sir Thomas Erpingham in the clerestory of **St John the Baptist**, **Timberhill**, for Sir Thomas fought at Agincourt (his tomb is in the cathedral). I also like a brass in **St Andrew's Church** commemorating the thrifty Alderman Gardiner, who departed this life in 1508. But before he went he sent a priest to Rome with instructions to obtain a Bull granting three hundred days' indulgence to anyone who would pray for him by his tomb – *provided the Bull could be obtained for not more than a fiver!*

I like the *names* of:

St Peter Permountergate, King Street (it has old wooden stalls).
St John de Sepulchre, Ber Street (good font).
St Michael-at-Coslany, Colegate (marvellous panelled flint work).
St Michael-at-Plea, Bank Plain (it had fine fourteenth-century panel paintings of the Resurrection, but these are now an altarpiece in the chapel at the east end of Norwich Cathedral).
St Michael-at-Thorn (bombed).

Nor are the Nonconformists to be ignored. Norwich was a 'hotbed' of Nonconformity, and still is. The Unitarian **Octagon Chapel**, off Colegate Street (a very interesting old industrial street over the river) is unique besides being octagonal, and was designed by Thomas Ivory, the local architect who also did that marvellous Georgian building, the Assembly House. It was built by the Presbyterians in 1756 but became Unitarian. The famous John Taylor preached there (causing it to be called 'a cucumber house for the forcing of Nonconformists'), and Harriet Martineau, the writer, was of the congregation. The **Old Meeting House**, just round the corner, is to my mind far more attractive. This was built in 1693, by the early Congregationalists. These had fled from persecution to Holland (many others went to America, and founded Norwich, Connecticut, there) but returned when they could, after the Act of Toleration, to build the Dutch-looking Old Meeting House, up an alley so that it could be defended against rioters. This is one of the very early Nonconformist chapels.

The first Quaker meeting house to be built in Norwich was in 1679, in Goat Lane. The famous Gurney family attended here. The Gurneys are a Norman family, still with a branch in Normandy. A present-day Gurney owns Walsingham Abbey. They were great bankers, and a highly talented and intellectual family. Elizabeth Fry, the prison reformer, was née Gurney, and one of seven lovely and spirited sisters. Harriet Martineau wrote of them: 'They were then a set of dashing young people dressed in gay riding habits and scarlet boots, as Mrs Fry told us afterwards, and riding about the country to balls and gaieties of all sorts.' The modern University of East Anglia is centred on the Gurneys' old home, Earlham Hall: most fitting, for Earlham Hall was a centre for lively and progressive ideas, a centre in the fight against the slave trade, and a resort of Wilberforce. In the grounds is the Sainsbury Centre for Visual Arts, housing collections of modern and ethnographic art, with temporary exhibitions at various times throughout the year, and a pleasant buffet and restaurant for the visitor. Open Tuesday to Sunday afternoons, closed Mondays and Bank Holidays.

While on the subject of Nonconformity, the site of Lollard's Pit may still be seen, next to Bishop's Bridge, marked today by a plate on a cottage; and I must quote George Borrow in *Lavengro* again: '. . . we are not far from hallowed ground. Observe ye not yon chalky precipice, to the right of the Norman bridge? On this side the stream, upon its brow, is a piece of ruined wall, the last relic of what was of old a stately pile, whilst at its foot is a place called Lollard's Hole; and with good reason, for many a saint of God has breathed his last beneath that white precipice, bearing witness against popish idolatry, midst flame and pitch; many a grisly procession has advanced along that suburb, across the old bridge, towards the Lollard's Hole: furious priests in front, a calm, pale martyr in the midst, a pitying multitude behind. It has had its martyrs, the venerable old town!'

At the junction of Earlham Road and Unthank Road is a vast

piece of Victorian Gothic, the Roman Catholic **Pro-Cathedral of St John the Baptist**, a riot of buttresses, gables and gargoyles; only not a cathedral because not the seat of a bishop.

And at last we must come to the glory of Norwich, and in the eyes of an East Anglian a glory of England too: the **Cathedral Church** of the most Holy and Undivided Trinity.

To enter this building and look along **the nave** and up at the glory of the stone vaulted roof is to feel dumbfounded at the skill, daring, and inspiration of the men who built it. One tends to be so overwhelmed by the grandeur of the interior that it is hard to give much attention to the marvellous details: the 1200 carved illustrative stone bosses in the cathedral and cloisters (328 in the nave alone), the sixty fine carved misericords in the choir and the canopies over the choir stalls, the marvellous fifteenth-century glass. The bosses in the nave (set up there by Bishops Lyhart and Nix in the fifteenth and sixteenth centuries) illustrate the entire Bible story, but you would need a powerful telescope or helicopter to see them properly, for they are seventy feet above your head.

You could spend a day looking at the wood carving in the choir alone. The carvings on the misericords represent commonplace life as it was lived in the reign of the Tudors as seen through the eyes of honest craftsmen.

The walls of the nave rise up in three tiers of the finest Norman stone, massive, solid and beautiful. The bishop's throne, in the Norman apse behind the High Altar, is, in part, the original one built by Bishop de Losinga when the foundations of the cathedral were laid. It is the only bishop's throne of its kind north of the Alps.

Bishop de Losinga started the building in 1096, by order of the Pope, as a penance because he had committed the sign of simony: he had paid William Rufus £1900 to make him a bishop. Before this he had been Abbot of Ramsey, in the Fens. Rufus made him Bishop of Thetford, he went and confessed to the Pope, and the Pope ordered him to move the seat of the see to Norwich and build a cathedral there, and also to build churches at King's Lynn and Yarmouth, which he did. In his life he completed the presbytery, with its apse and ambulatory, the beginnings at least of the central tower, the transepts, and part of the nave. The rest was completed after his death. A spire was built in the thirteenth century, but

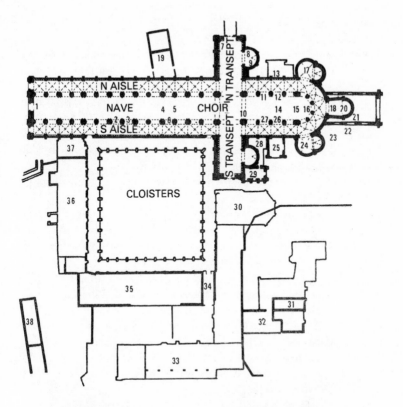

1 West Doorway 1430
2 Chancellor Spencer
3 Bishop Wykke's Chantry 1535
4 Nave Altar
5 Pulpitum 1465
6 William Ingott, Organist 1621
7 Bishop Bathurst 1837
8 St Andrew's Chapel
9 Canon Green Memorial
  Madonna by John Skelton 1960
10 Lectern 14th century
11 Sir Thomas Erpingham Chantry
12 John de Berney Chantry
13 Reliquary Arch & Treasury 1424
14 Bishop Herbert de Losinga's Tomb 1119
15 High Altar
16 Bishop's Throne 1105 and 1959
17 Jesus Chapel 1096
18 Saxon Chapel foundations 1050
19 Cellarer's Office 1370
20 St Saviour's Chapel foundations 1096

21 St Saviour's Chapel 1930
   World War I Memorial Chapel
   Norfolk Regiment Chapel
22 Lady Chapel ruins 1250
23 Nurse Cavell 1915
24 St Luke's Chapel 1096
25 Bauchon Chapel 1330
26 Bishop Overall 1669
27 Bishop Goldwell 1499
28 Chapter Room 1961
29 Vestry
30 Site of Chapter House, Parlour,
   Dormitory (now road)
31 Prior's Lodge, now Deanery
32 Reredorter foundations
33 Infirmary Pillars 1180
34 Dark Entry 1125
35 Refectory ruins 1125
36 Guest House 1275
37 Locutory 1275
38 Bishop de Losinga's Palace 1104

collapsed in 1362: the present spire is fifteenth century, the second highest in England (after Salisbury), and the golden weathercock is 315 feet from the ground!

The fire of 1509 that burnt the timber roofs saved the cathedral in June 1942, for the timber was replaced by stone and German incendiaries failed to ignite it.

The dull (in my opinion) Perpendicular west window was put in by Bishop Alnwich in the fifteenth century. The famous flying buttresses were set up to hold the high vaulted roof of the presbytery, which is one of the architectural wonders of this world. This cathedral manages to get the best of all the worlds: it combines the clean massive simplicity of the Norman with the springing elegance and daring of later ages.

Outside, **the cloister** is the biggest in England, and it is interesting to notice the transition of styles in its building, with a long break for the Black Death. The east walk is fourteenth century and Decorated: the north walk is Perpendicular built after 1430. Over the cloister is housed the cathedral library, one of the most notable libraries in Britain with seven thousand rare and old books including some of the earliest printed in England.

At the east end of the cathedral, outside the new chapel built as a memorial to the men who were killed in the First World War, is the grave of a Norfolk girl, Nurse Edith Cavell.

Daughter of the Rector of **Swardeston** (a small village south-west of Norwich on the New Buckenham road where are Cavell relics and a window) she was born on the 4th December 1865, reared on the strictest of Victorian lines, became a nurse at twenty-two, at forty-one became matron at a clinic in Belgium, was suffered to remain there by the Germans when they occupied the country in 1914, but was arrested 5th August 1915 and charged with aiding Allied soldiers to escape to Holland. She was shot by orders of the German High Command on 12th October 1915, and before her death she said to the Reverend Stirling Gahan, the English Chaplain in Brussels: 'I know that patriotism is not enough. I must have no hatred or bitterness towards anyone.' After the war her body was brought home and given a funeral service of almost royal proportions in Westminster Abbey and then actually buried under the walls of Norwich Cathedral, on the plot of land known as Life's

Green. There is a dreadfully ugly statue of her in front of the Maid's Head Hotel.

The route of a canal can be traced, leading to the cathedral from the River Wensum. Up this the thousands of tons of stone were shipped from France, without which it would have been impossible for such a vast building to have been built in a stoneless region.

The **cathedral close** offers a rewarding stroll to the old watergate and much-photographed house of Pull's Ferry. Beside the close is the old chapel of the **Edward the Sixth School**, originally the chantry chapel of St John, with a statue of Nelson looking at it (he attended there for a short time, and it seems unfair to have his statue eternally gazing at his erstwhile prison). The school is no parvenu, having been founded as Carnary College, with its chapel, in 1316 and made into a school by Edward VI. George Borrow went there and was soundly whacked (he ran away once but was dragged back), so did Lord Justice Coke (see Holkham p. 217), so did the Rajah of Sarawak (he ran away too – and stayed away) and two botanists, Sir William Jackson Hooker and John Lindley.

These last two were concerned with the farcical business of the naming of the giant water lily (*Victoria amazonica*) about which a comic opera could well be written. The business split the nation in half: even the Cabinet was involved; and there was a chase across Europe by no less than four Victorian gentlemen, sponsored by various warring scientific societies, the gentlemen all in deep disguise, to seek out an old German who was found sitting in his garden next to a pool containing a vast, and flowering, *amazonica*, which had been there for years while scientists were battling through the jungles of the Amazon looking for what was half believed to be a myth. A good account of this can be read in *Some Ancient Gentlemen*, by Tyler Whittle.

John Lindley was the son of a market gardener and nurseryman of Catton, just by Norwich. He was born 5th February 1799, was the first Professor of Botany at London University and was mainly instrumental in getting Kew Gardens opened to the public. He arranged for his old school-fellow Hooker to be made the first director. Hooker, son of a Norwich merchant, botanized in wild Scotland and was arrested there as a spy, botanized in Iceland and was shipwrecked on his return (his luggage, when it was rescued, was found to contain nothing but his journals and an Icelandic girl's wedding garments), was Professor of Botany at Glasgow, and was made a Knight of Hanover for his services to botany. Norwich was once rich in botanists: Clarke Abel, a Norwich surgeon, went with Lord Amherst's embassy to China in 1816 and was also shipwrecked on his return and all his specimens were lost. Sir James Edward Smith, born and buried in Norwich, founded the Linnaean Society of London. And of course Sir Thomas Browne was one of the first of botanists, and is buried at St Peter Mancroft.

The gates to the cathedral close are most noteworthy. There is St Martin's, or Bishop Alnwick's, round the corner, but the best ones are, first, **St Ethelbert's Gate**, which has an unsuitable flush-work gable plonked on top of its fourteenth-century self, and was built by the townspeople as a penance, some years after one of their periodic attacks on the monks. On this occasion they had set fire to the cathedral, in a small way.

The other is **Erpingham Gate**, a memorial to Sir Thomas, who lived near St Martin-at-Palace. This is said to be one of the finest Perpendicular monuments in England. In deep moulding are the twelve apostles, the twelve virgin saints to keep them company, and Sir Thomas in the niche above:

'Good morrow, old Sir Thomas Erpingham:
a good soft pillow for that good white head
Were better than the churlish turf of France.'
'Not so, my liege: this lodging likes me better,
Since I may say, "Now lie I like a king".'

Tucked away in a side street behind the cathedral is the Adam and Eve Inn, a splendid little ancient place to go and quench one's thirst after gazing up at all those bosses.

For other noteworthy inns, the Maid's Head, in **Tombland**, is famous although the exterior has been horribly and badly modernized. But inside is still fine. Queen Elizabeth slept there in 1578 (she was half an East Anglian: her grandfather, Sir William Boleyn, is buried in the cathedral); Sir John Paston mentioned the inn in one of the famous Paston Letters in 1472. The Bell, on Castle Meadow, is a fine old coaching inn. Norwich has been restrained about pulling down good old buildings, but I can never forgive it for bulldozing the Buff Coat, on Market Hill. It was a place where some of the spirit of Merry England still survived, and I once stabled my horse there.

Magdalen Street is a thoroughfare of old buildings incorporating many new shops. In 1958 it was the first street to be redecorated by the Civic Trust. A gay and harmonious colour scheme designed by good architects encouraged the shopkeepers to conform. The bright harmony of the scheme has unfortunately since been broken by the introduction of a lumpish flyover and the modern brick shopping precinct of Anglia Square. Facilities here, including parking, are admittedly excellent; but the immediate impression is far from alluring, and too many unpretentious little residential side streets have been truncated into stubby dead ends.

King Street is also historic and interesting, though a deplorable number of its once-loved features have been eroded. Bought up by one of the faceless (and tasteless) monsters, the brewery no longer brews. The Old Barge, a superb inn with a groined cellar from the twelfth century, a fourteenth-century floor, fifteenth-century superstructure and sixteenth-century oak screens, closed long ago. The Ship was bought by the Council and converted into flats. But the Ferry, a favourite with the crews of small freighters unloading corn for the nearby mills on the Wensum, has been worthily refurbished and commands a stimulating prospect of the river.

At the end of King Street the **Carrow Works** makes Colman's Mustard. It was built where it is to make use of the river for its traffic, on the site of a Benedictine nunnery, which probably contained the cell of Saint Julian, or Mother Juliana, a fourteenth-century mystic who wrote *XVI Revelations of Divine Love*. Colman's offices are now in what was the old Colman home, part of which was the Prioress's residence, built in the sixteenth century. Mother Juliana's shrine is the rebuilt (after bombing) church of St Julian, where she spent most of her life as anchoress, up the street.

The **'Music House'**, once called the 'Jew's House', is in King Street, and perhaps the oldest private dwelling house in England. Behind the stone façade of the early seventeenth century most of the remains are twelfth century, but the magnificent timbered roof in the great hall was put there by Sir John Paston (probably) and

107

he bought the house in 1487. Sir Edward Coke (pronounced *cook*), Lord Chief Justice under James I, married Bridget Paston, and thus came to live there. In Queen Elizabeth's time the City Waits used to meet there, hence the new name. 'Jew's House' is older. (There is an item of city expenditure for fitting out the City Waits to sail round the world with Sir Francis Drake.)

Elm Hill, off Tombland, is one street preserved out of hundreds without much alteration, and is cobbled and now lined with antique dealers. Near the top, the Briton's Arms with its mighty thatch and timbered oversailing upper storey was once an inn, now turned into a coffee house and restaurant. Across the street is an entrance to another place of refreshment – a snack bar in a vaulted crypt which leads on to cloisters housing antique and craft markets. Set back from the corner is an ugly Victorian building which was once the domicile of that strange prophet Father Ignatius, who made Norwich too hot for himself and took his community off to live in the Black Mountains at Llantony. The Paston family appear once more: their fifteenth-century home stands a little way down the slope, rebuilt after a devastating fire in 1507. Behind the teetering row of old buildings on the same side are Elm Hill Riverside Gardens, offering fascinating glimpses of jumbled brickwork, timber and plaster on the rear of those houses.

The **Maddermarket Theatre** between Charing Cross and Pottergate is one of the most famous and thriving amateur theatres in the world. It was the first to go back to an Elizabethan apron stage, and has a tradition of anonymity among its actors, who are generally admitted to be the best amateur company in the country. It owes its success to the inspiration of the late Nugent Monk.

Up on the **Market Place**, and Gentleman's Walk, are the various market stalls, with their awnings of various colours: certainly the most picturesque market place in England and one of the most ancient. Originally the market was in Tombland, but was moved to its present position when the Normans came. The cattle market was hard by the castle, but it was moved into the suburbs in 1960 and is said to be the most modern and up-to-date cattle market in the world: the sales rings look like astronomical observatories and cattle go through them thousands a day, many to be sent to the Continent for beef. Norwich has always had one of the greatest cattle markets of the country, for here was the centre for the distribution of all the store (i.e. unfatted) cattle that were brought in from Ireland and Wales, and down from the North of England and Scotland, for East Anglia, and subsequently the gathering place for the cattle newly fattened in the yards of the great arable farms and on the lush marshes. The Clerk of the Markets in Norwich can claim to be the holder of the oldest municipal office in England. There are continuous records of his office going back to 1456, though it may be considerably older.

The Guildhall is a perfect little Gothic building somewhat restored but the lovely east end, completed in 1535, is older. There is a magnificent sword inside. It belonged to the Spanish admiral Winthuysen, but was captured by Nelson at the Battle of St Vincent, and presented to Norwich. The Guildhall was built in the first half of the fifteenth century; in 1511 the roof fell in, in 1634 the place was nearly undermined by saltpetre diggers, in 1861 Thomas Barry, the City Architect (who built the controversial porch on St Andrew's Hall) clapped a police station on the south side of it, and in 1908 it was proposed to pull it down! You can go inside it at times specified on a noticeboard.

The vast modern **City Hall** is an unhappy amalgam of brick and stone: some of the bricks having been carted all the way from Buckinghamshire (though there was a perfectly good yard making hand-made bricks just outside Norwich). The roof, we are told, is of concrete and asbestos, supported on steel beams. The design is said to have been inspired by Ostberg's Stockholm Town Hall. Heraldic lions are stuck on the walls, outside, looking less East Anglian than Babylonian. There is a fine collection of civic plate inside. The City Hall was opened in 1938 and looks it.

The new **City Library**, next door, is an example of good, unobtrusive, modern architecture, and it seems that modern architecture to be good must be unobtrusive, for this age cannot carry off the grand statement. They have gone to the trouble of panelling the outer walls with flint, the traditional East Anglian material, and the result is very pleasing. The building includes the American Memorial Library, given by the 2nd Air Division, USAAF, in memory of their men who died serving from East Anglia in the Second World War.

109

Norwich is a thriving and striving modern industrial city, although most of its industries have at least their roots far back in the past. The boot and shoe industry was old in Norwich in the Conqueror's time, it suffered some eclipse during the great days of the cloth industry, but came into its own again when the cloth industry fled to the North of England in search of coal. Then the thousands of skilled hands in Norwich, bereft of employment, turned to boot making. I asked an official of Norvic's factory how long he had been in the industry, and he said: 'Well, I know my great-grandfather was a garret-master.' Until recent years garret-masters organized the work of shoe workers who worked at home, but now all the work is done in factories.

There is heavy engineering and light, electric motors, chocolate biscuits, insurance, and a factory which did the metal work for the airship R101. The BBC has a studio in All Saints' Green, in a fine Georgian house.

If you want a good view over the city go up on **Mousehold Heath**. This, like Lollard's Pit, is holy ground to lovers of liberty, for here Sir Roger Bacon and Geoffrey Lister stood up for the freedom of Englishmen in 1381, and Robert Kett and his men for the same cause in 1549 (see North Walsham and Wymondham, pages 158 and 190).

CHAPTER 6

The Yare

Broadland is basically three main rivers: Waveney in the south, forming the border between Norfolk and Suffolk, Yare in the middle, forming the sea water route between Norwich and the sea, and Bure in the north. Bure ('the North River' to all Broadsmen) is the most characteristic of the three, winds the most, connects with most 'broads', and has most tributaries.

The way to see Broadland is by boat and there's an end to it. Roads avoid the waters. The rivers wind, and are cut off from dry land by miles of soggy marshes, alder carrs and reed beds. Norwich itself is a Broadland city, and Broads pleasure boats come up Yare and Wensum to within a quarter of a mile of the cathedral.

At **Thorpe St Andrew**, John Sell Cotman, one of the fathers of English landscape painting, was born in 1782. Thorpe has been called the Norfolk Richmond, and indeed this riverside suburb has an urbanity and some good eighteenth-century dwelling houses, and modern flat buildings, but is spoiled rather by being cut off from the water by an urgent motor road. The river is placid and tree-flanked, and on it float motor yachts of the plushier kind. Joseph Stannard's painting 'Thorpe Water Frolic', in Norwich Castle Museum, depicts the place in lustier days.

Brundall, farther downstream and also on the north bank, is also a place of select riverside residence, with an Edwardian air and plenty of very typical Broadland marshes and reed beds to the south of it. There is a tradition that the Romans had a shipyard here.

Strumpshaw, besides having a comic little hill from which you can see both Norwich and the German Ocean, has a church with a good fifteenth-century screen.

111

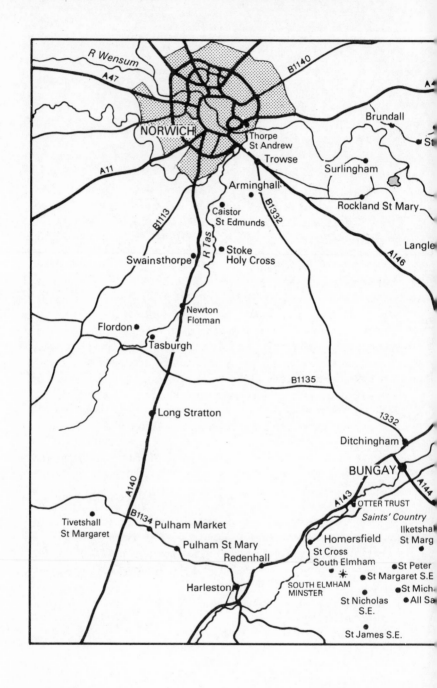

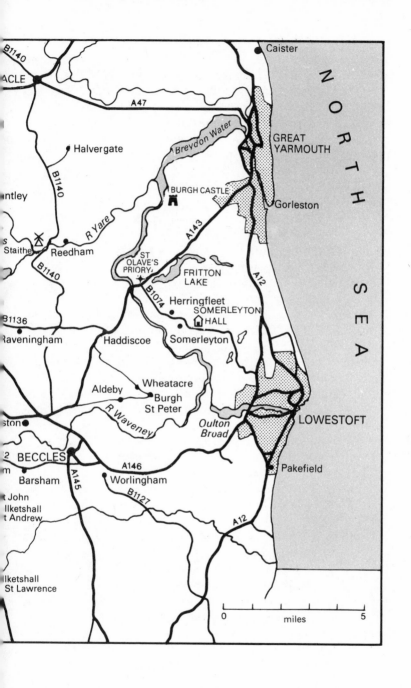

B1140

ACLE

Caister

A47

N O R T H

Halvergate

Brevdon Water

GREAT YARMOUTH

B1140

ntley

BURGH CASTLE

Gorleston

R Yare

A143

s Staithe

Reedham

ST OLAVE'S PRIORY

FRITTON LAKE

A12

B1140

B1074

Herringfleet

SOMERLEYTON HALL

B1136

Raveningham

Haddiscoe

Somerleyton

S E A

Wheatacre

Aldeby

Burgh St Peter

R Waveney

Oulton Broad

LOWESTOFT

ston

BECCLES

A146

Pakefield

2

Barsham

A145

Worlingham

t John

llketshall

B1127

A12

t Andrew

lketshall

St Lawrence

0   miles   5

Cantley is blessed with a sugar beet factory, the smoke of which can be seen during the autumn and winter 'sugar campaign' from many miles up and down the Yare and, indeed, all over the Broadland. The factory was built where it is so that beet could be transported to it by water, but alas, short-sighted counsels have prevailed, and the factory now uses only road and rail, and the narrow winding Broadland lanes are now made perilous by lurching sugar beet lorries.

The traveller will before this have noted that the sugar beet is one of East Anglia's chief crops, generally the only 'root break' among the constant succession of white straw crops, chiefly barley. Sugar beet is a laborious crop to grow. After the seed has been drilled in early spring the little plants must be singled out, and this is still generally done with the hand hoe at a big cost to the farmer. Tractor hoeing is then necessary at least once, and a second hoeing by hand, and then the beet must be lifted, either with an expensive machine which often breaks down, or by hand. When harvested by hand the operation is known as 'knocking and topping', for two beet are knocked together to shake off the mud, and subsequently topped with the topping knife. In the autumn, and right through until after Christmas, much of the rural population of East Anglia is out in the fields 'knocking and topping'. Factories such as the one at Cantley then extract the sugar, and the remaining waste material is bagged as 'pulp' and returned to the farmers to make a very good cattle feed.

A 'Blytheburghes boat' foundered in the river at Cantley in 1343. She was laden with sea-coal, salt, iron, Baltic timber, onions, and salt herring and, of course, was bound for Norwich.

Norton Staithe has a fine drainage windmill, restored in 1962 by the Norfolk County Council and now looked after by the National Trust.

Reedham is a most excellent place. It spreads along the broad river (big steamers come past for Norwich or the sea), and seen from the water it is one of the most attractive water fronts you could find. There are several good pubs, and an hotel, and another very good pub too down at Reedham Ferry, and even if you never wish to cross the river there make an excuse to do so, for the voyage in the chain ferry is an experience not to be missed, and the only way you can get a car across the Yare between Norwich and Yarmouth. Reedham is supposed to have been a seat of East Anglian kings, and it is here that Lothbroc, old Leather-breeches and a Danish prince, is supposed to have been murdered by the English king's falconer, but this story has been told once and for all time by the road-mender in Julian Tennyson's *Suffolk Scene* and I will not repeat it here (see Hoxne, p. 62).

Acle has a flourishing market with a long reputation among local breeders of store pigs because of the good prices fetched there. St Edmund's church is thatched and has a Norman tower crowned with fifteenth-century battlements. Inside are a fine tall screen and a font of 1410 with lions and woodwoses, or wild men.

Halvergate village is the starting point for a marshland walk taking in the Stracey Arms wind pump, with contains an exhibition of photographs dealing with Broadland drainage, and also Berney Arms windmill, restored into working order and housing its own exhibition on windmills. The marshland, reclaimed from the sea, is cut up by dykes. Much of its grazing has by custom been owned by the parish and auctioned off to graziers on a yearly basis. Frequent controversy over 'enclosures' or grazing areas was made worse in the 1980s by schemes to plough up considerable tracts and endanger their wild life. Fine fattening cattle are still to be seen by the three Broads rivers every summer, but in the winter the whole unpopulated area is given over to the snipe and wild duck, the curlew and the heron. The fattening of cattle on these Norfolk marshes is an age-old pursuit. A hundred years ago kilted Highlanders used to walk down from their fastnesses driving skinny cattle, to be sold in Norwich market for fattening. Norwich market has waxed fat on 'store' cattle (thin cattle ready for fattening) to be sold to the graziers, and then again from the very same cattle, duly fattened, brought in to be sold to the butchers. In 1723 Daniel Defoe wrote:

These Scots runts, so they call them, coming out of the cold and barren mountains of the Highlands of Scotland feed so eagerly on the rich pasture in these marshes, that they thrive in an unusual manner, and grow monstrously fat; and the beef is so delicious for taste, that the inhabitants prefer 'em

115

to the English cattle, which are much larger and fairer to look at. Some have told me there are above 40,000 of these Scots cattle fed in this country every year, and most of them in the said marshes between Norwich, Beccles and Yarmouth.

Breydon Water is a large stretch of tidal salt water or of mud, depending on the time of the day. It is a desolate place in winter, with cormorants sitting on the big posts planted in the mud which mark the narrow channel for the big ships. Many and many a Broads hire cruiser goes ignominiously on to the mud here, in the passage from the 'North River' to the Waveney or the Yare.

Its outlet (or inlet, according to which way the tide is running) connects with Great Yarmouth harbour. To alleviate the grounding or bogging-down of road traffic in that town, a new bypass bridge was opened over Breydon Water in March 1986, on a day so windy that police warned the official party not to cross it after the Transport Minister had cut the tape. In the end the occupants of the double-decker buses provided for the occasion packed themselves in downstairs to keep the vehicles steady; and the formal inauguration went off gustily but without mishap.

This might be the place to discuss the Norfolk Wherry, for at one time big fleets of these vessels used to race each other across Breydon Water on their way up from the ships in Yarmouth harbour to the quayside of Norwich, or back again with Norwich goods for export. Of all the sailing vessels evolved by use and time for a highly specialized purpose, the Norfolk Wherry was perhaps the most famous. She had to be capable of sailing very close to the wind (for it is difficult to 'tack' in very narrow rivers), of being brought about single handed and with great ease, of navigating very shallow broads and rivers, of dropping her mast with great facility to shoot the many bridges, of being propelled by man-power when the wind failed or was a dead header down a narrow reach, of pushing through reeds, and of carrying a good weight of cargo.

The Broadland rivers form a close network of water roads in a highly populated and very productive country, and thus a big fleet of these cargo vessels came into being and there was strong competition to evolve the most efficient form. The end result was a vessel some 58 feet long by 14 feet beam and 4 feet draught, with a soft-chined hull, a long straight keel (which in some cases could be dropped on the river bottom so that the boat could penetrate a very shallow creek, to be picked up again on coming out), with sweet lines, a mast 40 feet high but quite unstayed except for the heavy fore-stay used for lowering the mast down and hauling it up. Owing to its being unstayed the mast had to be strong, and was some 12 to 15 inches in diameter. So that it could be lowered it was in a tabernacle, and had three-quarters of a ton or more of iron or lead at its heel to act as a counter-weight. A child could raise or lower this enormous spar with his hand. A big wherry would carry 40 tons.

The sail plan was simple: one large, black, high-peaked mainsail, bent to a long gaff but boomless, and nothing else. The height of the sail made it efficient for catching the breeze over high trees (very necessary in Broadland), the shape made it efficient for sailing into the wind. The shape of the hull, particularly the bow section, gave the wherry the extraordinary power of 'shouldering' along a lee bank, when sailing near the wind, pushing a cushion of water between herself and the bank as she sailed. A wherry could sail straight for a bridge – drop mast and sail all standing – shoot through – and have her mast and sail up again, sail drawing, losing hardly any speed. When wind failed, the wherrymen supplied a 'shoulder breeze', punting with long poles called 'quants' (they are called 'spreets' in the Fenland waterways), shoved from the shoulder as the wherrymen walked from forward to aft along the deck. The men were a race apart. They lived in their little warm cabins, drove their craft into every nook and cranny of their maze of rivers, got their food off land and water as they could, formed a floating community of their own. Now there is one sailing wherry left, the 'Albion', kept by the Norfolk Wherry Trust at Ludham. Many an old wherryman is still alive, though, and willing to tell the stranger, in the pubs of Broadland, of the days and the life that are gone. Most of their sons have become lorry drivers.

The A47 runs straight as a ruler across the flat marshes to **Great Yarmouth**. Yarmouth is supposed by many people to be nothing but fat cockney women in funny paper hats jostling each other along the crowded prom. It is that, but many other things too. To the sailor it is an exciting harbour entrance, and many a good ship

117

has smashed herself against the South Pier, or missed the harbour and rammed the beach to north or to south of it, or – in sailing-ship days – been forced to beach herself on the 'spending ground' round the bend of the harbour in desperation. To the Broads pleasure sailor Yarmouth is a long 'marina' where the Bure meets the Yare, where he can tie up preparatory to making the (to him) perilous crossing of Breydon Water. To the lover of ancient places it is a big town of narrow streets and 'rows', old buildings, and much history – which is nearly all connected with herrings.

In Roman times the site of Yarmouth may not have existed, or at best was a sand-bank surrounded by sea. The Romans had their town to the north of it, at Caister, and their great fort and naval base at the top of Breydon Water at Burgh Castle. What is now Broadland was then under a tidal sea, and Norwich was practically a seaside town.

In Anglo-Saxon times Yarmouth was a scattering of huts on a sand-bank, occupied by migratory fishermen. In Norman times, and just before, the fishermen of Rye and Dover and the other Cinque Ports used to come there in force every year for the 'herring voyage', and Edward the Confessor granted rights to the Barons of Hastings to control the annual 'Herring Fair' to which buyers came from far and wide to buy salt herrings. For six hundred years the 'Portsmen', or bailiffs of the Cinque Ports, came to Yarmouth to control the Herring Fair and protect their fellow citizens. As time went on, and Yarmouth became an important place in its own right, their arrival led to friction and resentment, and silly arguments as to who should sit in the front pew in church; but in the seventeenth century the thing was settled amicably and the institution lapsed. The banner that the Portsmen were wont to have borne before them is still preserved at Dover, though, and the brazen horn with which their heralds announced their presence is at New Romney.

To the rest of England, and indeed northern Europe, Yarmouth meant herrings. Henry appointed a Provost who received an annual rent of 10,000 of these fish. In 1238 there was a disastrous drop in price because the Swedish buyers were prevented from coming to the Fair – by the fact that the Tartars were at Sweden's gates. In 1357 the Statute of Herrings was enacted, which defined a 'last' as

10,000, a 'hundred' as 6 score, which fixed maximum prices, enforced a free market and made it compulsory for boats to moor inside the harbour before discharging their herrings, thus ensuring Yarmouth's monopoly.

But in the sixteenth century Yarmouth was falling upon hard times. She was forced to sell the church plate, also the bells and vestments, in order to pay for yet another attempt to keep the harbour mouth open. The common mouth of the three rivers was always trying to break through in another place, and the old channel was often silting up: Yarmouth was for ever fighting for its very existence to keep the channel clear. Further, there was stiff competition from the Netherlands. Dutch 'busses', or herring ships, sailed into Yarmouth with their catches, and undersold the English, and when denied the use of Yarmouth as a base they salted their herrings at sea (as indeed they still do) and took them straight back to Europe to undermine the Yarmouth export trade. For ever since the herrings mysteriously departed from the Baltic in the early Middle Ages, northern Europe had become used to buying this important fish from Yarmouth. Charles I ordered that the Dutch fishermen should be driven from our waters; Cromwell carried on this policy, and so did Charles II.

In October 1797 the men of Yarmouth watched Admiral Duncan and Onslow bring in the captured Dutch ships of the line after Camperdown, and after that Dutch power in the North Sea began to decline and Yarmouth had a revival. The Sunday nearest Michaelmas was for years celebrated after this as 'Dutch Sunday', a fair was held on the South Denes, and the ceremony of 'wetting the nets' performed there.

In the nineteenth century the Dutch boats were seen no longer in Yarmouth, but Scots ones came instead. Every year a huge fleet of 'Scafies' and 'Zulus' sailed from the north, then came steam drifters, and later motor boats, many of them 'pair fishermen'. 1913 was the heyday, with a thousand vessels fishing the Yarmouth herring voyage, Scots and English, and thousands of Scots fisher girls gutting the herrings on the South Denes.

But with modern gear, notably 'mid-water trawlers' from Continental countries, principally Russia, the fishermen have become too good for the fish. The North Sea shoals of herring have

119

dwindled to very nearly nothing. The mid-water trawl, unlike the drift net, takes spawn and immature fish. The North Sea has become fished out. EEC regulations have sought to restrict herring fishing so that new generations will have time to spawn and restock these waters, but such orders are all too often flouted. For a while Yarmouth's trawler fleet was outpaced by Lowestoft; but that, too, had fallen on bad times by the mid-1970s, and there seems little likelihood of restoring the fortunes of either.

But Yarmouth still flourishes as a trading port. Ships from all the Baltic countries, from London, and from the North of England, lie along her long straight quays. However she is no longer the great ship-owning port that she was. In 1702 no less than 211 colliers were registered in Yarmouth – all carrying coal from the north: more colliers than had any other port including London. In 1776 Parson Woodforde wrote in his Diary (he was Rector of Weston Longville near East Dereham):

> Nothing can beat what we saw today – immense sea room, ships and boats passing and re-passing – the wind being rather high, the waves being like mountains into the shore . . .
> In the evening we took a walk on the quay – as fine a one as ever was seen . . . we got on board an English vessel and were treated with wine, gin, etc. The sailors behaved very civil to us; had a difficult matter to make them take anything. She was a collier, and soon going back to Sunderland.

Major E. R. Cooper wrote that in October 1838:

> . . . there were nearly 2,000 vessels lying wind-bound in Yarmouth Roads. They got underway on November 1, and were followed by another 1,000 from the southward; all 3,000 sail went through the Roads in five hours, so that the sea could hardly be seen for ships.

Yarmouth's livelihood in more recent years was owed mainly to the North Sea oil and gas boom. Supply ships bustled to and from the rigs. Strange new technical names appeared on warehouses along the quays. Even though a large part of the supply industry moved eventually to Aberdeen, Yarmouth managed to retain some services, later threatened in turn by collapsing world oil prices and curtailment of exploration.

The town was badly battered in the World Wars, particularly by bombing and shelling in the second one, and many of the famous 'Rows' were destroyed. These were very narrow alleyways running at right angles to the harbour, once requiring special handcarts to carry goods down them. The market place in Yarmouth is great fun: bustling, hospitable, and happily permeated with a smell of chips from a number of stalls. The fourteenth-century Tolhouse, once a court-house and gaol, should be visited: one of the oldest municipal houses in England, it has a fine timbered roof to its main hall, dungeons below, exhibits of local industry, and a brass rubbing centre. It is open from June to September every day except Saturdays. The Old Merchant's House at Row 111 on South Quay, cared for by English Heritage, has two rooms restored to their original beauty, with ornate plaster ceilings: open Monday to Friday, April to September. Also on South Quay is the Elizabeth House Museum, dating from 1596 but specializing in displays of nineteenth-century domestic life, and Lowestoft porcelain. This is open daily, except Saturdays, from June to September, and Mondays to Fridays from October to May.

The Priory and Parish Church of **St Nicholas** was founded by Bishop de Losinga as one of his penances for the sin of simony. Alas, it was bombed in the Second World War, but has been rebuilt within the remains of its old walls in a lavish way. The church-knower may or may not like it; but should certainly go and see it. It is one of England's numerous 'largest parish churches in England', and certainly it has wide aisles, an enormously wide nave, and a floor area of 23,000 square feet. The modern electric lighting is one of its best features: the fittings are well designed and meet for their job and not made to look like anything but electric light fittings, and seen in depth across that vast expanse they look impressive. There is some modern glass by Mr Brian Thomas and five noteworthy and very spiky modern wall paintings by Meneer Ru van Rossem, done while he was teaching at Yarmouth Art School. The patron saint, St Nicholas, is patron also of seafarers, children and pawnbrokers (who all have in common innocence of heart, perhaps?), there are Tufa stones from the Rhine in the Norman tower brought hither as ballast in Norman ships, and the word 'holy-stones' used by sailors for the rough stones with which they scrub the decks is supposed to derive from stones from the fabric of St Nicholas, and therefore holy as well as good for scouring. In the churchyard there is an interesting tombstone commemorating the loss of life when a new suspension bridge over the Yare collapsed in 1840. The Eye of God can be seen in the relief looking down at the disaster in some surprise.

For better or for worse Anna Sewell, author of *Black Beauty*, was born in Great Yarmouth, and Sarah Martin is locally revered because she used to read the Prayer Book to the inmates of the dungeons in the Tolhouse jail. Dickens, of course, wrote marvellously of Great Yarmouth in *David Copperfield*. His description of a gale there is superb.

Apart from its garish sea-front Yarmouth is still a town full of character and worthy of exploration. And even the sea-front has its compensations. The Maritime Museum has imaginative displays of East Anglian coastal history, including the story of the fisheries, Captain Manby's life-saving inventions, and toys and ornaments made by seamen in their spare time. It is open daily throughout the year, except on Saturdays and Sundays between October and May, for a very small entrance fee.

For those wanting to escape the huge Marina Centre and pier entertainments, there are boat trips to the seals of Scobie Sands and up the Broadland rivers from the Marina and Yacht Station.

And I cannot resist quoting from the works of that dissolute Elizabethan Thomas Nashe, although he was a Lowestoft man, on the chief product of Yarmouth. It was in an orgy with Nashe, incidentally, of Rhenish wine and pickled herrings, that a Yarmouth man called Robert Greene overreached himself and died of over-indulgence. But thus Nashe:

> The puissant red herring, the golden *Herperides* red herring, the red herring of Red Herrings Hal, every pregnant peculiar of whose resplendent laude and honour to delineate and adumbrate to the ample life were a woorke that would drinke drie fourscour and eighteene Castalian fountaines of eloquence, consume another *Athens* of facunditie, and abate the haughtiest poetical fury twixt this and the burning Zone and the tropike of Cancer . . . But no more winde will I speed on

it but this: Saint Denis for Fraunce, Saint Iames for Spaine, Saint Patrike for Ireland, Saint George for England, and the red Herring for Yarmouth.

Gorleston, over the Yare and down near the mouth of it, has some very interesting old streets and still some of the atmosphere of an old seaport, and it has a lifeboat station with a tradition of heroic rescues. Whether rightfully or not Gorleston men are called 'Kill-Jews' by some of their less reverent neighbours: in recognition of the fact that they are supposed to be very thrifty. It is implied that even a member of a mercantile race would find it impossible to get a living among them. The *Gorleston Psalter*, a lovely early fourteenth-century illuminated manuscript, is now in the British Museum.

Three miles inland (once in Suffolk, now Norfolk) is **Burgh Castle**, with the Roman fort of Gariannonum, once one of the chief naval bases of the *Comes Litoris Saxonici*, the Count of the Saxon Shore. We know that the Emperor Carausius once held this title, and that a Provost's command of African cavalry was stationed at Burgh Castle. They must have found the east wind a bit raw.

The fort was complementary to Caister, which was a Roman town and port northwards over the great estuary which has now dwindled to Breydon Water. A contour map will enable one to imagine this country in Roman times, when all that is now sea-level marsh was then sea, and the sand-bank on which Yarmouth now stands was only then being formed. Burgh Castle was thus on a wide arm of the sea. All there is now is a quadrangular field surrounded on three sides by walls and open on the other. The flint rubble has eroded badly, leaving the harder, or better bonded, tile upper courses to stand out, and thus many fragments of the wall stand up like so many vast mushrooms. It is difficult to imagine what the fort must have been like, beyond that it was large (620 feet by 383 feet), but it is fascinating to stand there and try to fill in the details of this great fortress looking over miles of shallow water to the low wooded hills of Norfolk, with fleets of war galleys at anchor, and Gallic trading ships sailing in, bound upstream to yet another Roman Caister, or Caistor – that near Norwich.

Besides plenty of Roman coins and pottery, Saxon relics have been found; and Burgh is supposed to have been the site of the Cnobheresburg mentioned by Bede, where the Irish missionary St Fursey settled and founded a monastery, in the reign of Sigebert, about AD 640. St Fursey later became an anchorite, sensibly removed to France to get away from pagan invasion from Scandinavia, founded a monastery at Lagny, near Paris, and his body is at Peronne, where it is said to have defied corruption, and is still an object of reverence and pilgrimage.

St Olave's Priory, near the bridge across the Waveney, was founded by Roger Fitz Osbert in Henry III's time for the Austin canons. Its early fourteenth-century undercroft with a brick vaulted ceiling, unusual at so early a period, is open free all year round. One Sirek was the ferryman at St Olave's in Edward I's time, a job made redundant by the bridge built in the fifteenth century by the wife of Chief Justice Hobart of London. Beside it, the Bell inn is a fine mixture of timber and red brick. A short distance along the river bank stands a slender trestle windpump in working order, open daily all year round; and there is another more substantial smock drainage windmill on the levels below neighbouring **Herringfleet**, preserved as an example of the hundreds of windmills which once pumped water up from the low marshes into the high wall-enclosed rivers of the Broads country. Now this work is done by oil and electricity. Strangers sometimes express wonder why, if so many pumping windmills were necessary (and still survive in ruin) in Broadland, there are no such windmills in the far greater area of the Fens, where the water has to be lifted from the low land to the high rivers in just the same manner. The explanation of this is that in Broadland the mills could be put on hard foundations, and therefore were substantially built of brick. In Fenland they had to be built on peat, and the level of the peat was constantly altering. Consequently it was the fashion to build them of temporary wooden framework so that they could be easily moved. Hence none survive. At Manor Farm, Herringfleet, is a superb great thatched barn with Tudor flint and brickwork, and the church has a tower which looks Saxon but which is said to be in fact early Norman, and some colourful German glass.

Fritton is famous for its Decoy, a beautiful tree-surrounded lake with gardens, a play area and woodland walks, open April to

September. The practice of duck-decoying, still practised in one or two places but no longer at Fritton, involves luring wild duck down from the sky by feeding barley and also by keeping a flock of tame duck. The tame duck are trained (by feeding) to swim into a large netting funnel, on the signal of a whistle from the operator and (surprisingly) the appearance of a small white dog. The wild duck swim after the tame, the entrance of the funnel is closed, and the wild duck have their necks wrung and are sent off to city markets.

Fritton has a queer asymmetrical thatched church, with a low and dark semi-circular Norman chancel, a Saxon base to the tower and Roman bricks. Still to be seen are the iron rings, 700 years old, between nave and chancel on which the Lenten Veil was once hung. Here one can still imagine something of the ancient rites and mysteries of the early Church, when religion was a magical affair.

Somerleyton has a vast neo-Elizabethan hall, built on the shell of a genuinely Elizabethan one by Samuel Peto, a man who had a hand in building Lowestoft Harbour. He also transformed the village into a cluster of ornamental cottages with school and station to match. The house has lush gardens, a maze and miniature railway, open Easter and May Day holiday weekend afternoons, and Thursday, Sunday and Bank Holiday Monday afternoons late May to late September.

Haddiscoe (we are back over the Waveney in Norfolk now) is known to sailors for its Cut: a straight artificial canal joining the Yare with the Waveney and cutting off some miles of navigation including Breydon Water. This canal was made in Victorian times by the men of Lowestoft, who were busy trying to cut Yarmouth's throat by forcing through an entrance to the sea for Norwich at Lowestoft instead of at Yarmouth. They succeeded physically in making their channel but financially the thing was never a success. It came to little, and recently even the lock between Lake Lothing and Oulton Broad, a vital link in the waterway, collapsed, and was only repaired after a great fight to save it from being filled in. Haddiscoe Church is famous for its round Saxon tower, good Norman south doorway (note figure over it) and a floorstone in the nave for Jan Piers, a Dutch dikemaster who drained many of the surrounding marshes.

125

We might make a detour through Wheatacre and Burgh St Peter and Aldeby, for this is a remote countryside, much cut-off from the world by being in a loop of the River Waveney. **Burgh St Peter** has a church a long way from the village, remarkable for its strange brick tower which is shaped like a square telescope, and is a great landmark to sailors on the Waveney. Beside it is an hotel, in a fine position and with a jetty into the river. Sailing up the river here very early in the morning I once saw many score of coypu. These still exist in Broadland, in spite of the cold winter of 1962–63 which killed most of them off. They are rodents, as large as spaniels, at home in the water as on land, rat-like in appearance but with the extraordinary feature that the teats of the females are along their backs and the young ones cling on to these when the mothers are swimming and thus are dragged along the top of the water.

Aldeby was Aldeburgh in Domesday, and thus is Anglo-Saxon, not Norse. There was a priory there, founded by Ralph de Beaufon immediately after the Conquest, and a tablet in the wall of the church commemorating one Will Slater, a coach driver, in these terms:

> *True to his business and his trust,*
> *Always punctual, always just.*
> *His horses could they speak, would tell*
> *They loved their good old master well.*
> *His up-hill work is chiefly done;*
> *His stage is ended – race is run.*
> *One journey is remaining still, –*
> *To climb up Zion's holy hill.*
> *And now his faults are all forgiv'n*
> *Elijah-like drives up to heav'n;*
> *Takes the reward for all his pains,*
> *And leaves to other hands the reins.*

Raveningham has a fine Georgian hall with Cotman and Turner watercolours inside it, and paintings by Constable and Gainsborough.

Loddon is a delightful old East Anglian town, once a Broads port, with a watermill even now on the River Chet which connects with the Yare. There are pleasure boat yards, and the staithes of an agreeable little marina. The church is large and fine and fifteenth century, standing grandly in a vast graveyard, and has a painted screen unusual in that it depicts scenes instead of just people. It has a representation of St William of Norwich, bound saltire-wise to stakes, with Jews catching the blood which is gushing from his side in a basin. Anti-racialists will be glad to know that recent historical research has completely discredited this gory legend. These screen panels may have come from the older Norman church, and have been moved to the present building when it was built, which was between 1480 and 1490. (Dr Tudor-Craig says they are not pre-1480.) A relic of an even earlier church – the Anglo-Saxon one – is the alms box on the pillar facing the door. This is hewn of one piece of oak, like a dug-out canoe; and is supposed to be one of the oldest in England. It may well be old, for there is a legend that Loddon Church was founded in AD 630 by St Felix himself, the East Anglian apostle.

When the present Perpendicular church was built it was paid for by Sir James Hobart, Attorney-General to Henry VII and ancestor of the man who built Blickling. This man has his altar tomb in the sanctuary, and in the south aisle, near the door, his portrait is painted on a panel with that of his wife, Francis. Loddon Church and St Olave's Bridge are depicted with them: he paid for the church and she for the bridge.

For those who admire the constructions of the eighteenth and early nineteenth centuries Loddon is a gem of a little town. How nice to have seen it when the stately sailing wherries reached up the little River Chet, and lay and loaded and unloaded at the old wharfs. But for people interested in our present age Loddon is important too. This century has seen our country defaced from one end to the other with ugly, boring, tasteless council houses. The ones built since Hitler's war are not quite so crassly hideous as the ones built before, but they are bad enough. But at Loddon, and in the area controlled by Loddon RDC, the recent council housing has been designed by a firm of Lowestoft architects, Taylor and Green, and it is (or should be) a model for council housing for the world. Keeping well within the financial limits set by the council housing, obeying even the ludicrous laws of proportion (which legislate for a race of giants, or giraffes) these architects have

127

managed to design homes which blend in beautifully with their surroundings, which continue in the tradition of East Anglia without slavishly aping the past, which do not strive ridiculously into a space-age future, which have unity and yet diversity, which in every case are pleasing to the eye, and which are said by the inmates to be pleasant to live in. It is well worth seeking out these little estates wherever they are to be found, and every architect in the country should be made to go and look at them.

At **Langley** are the flint remains of a Premonstratensian abbey. At **Rockland St Mary** is the New Inn, well known to Broads sailors who venture into Rockland Broad. Rockland is a perfect little broad, reed and tree-surrounded, connected to the Yare by a long narrow shallow channel along which, at one place, a line of old wooden sailing wherries have been sunk to form a bank. One can look down into the water-filled cabins and think of the bright coal fires that once burned in the stoves and of the life that was once lived there.

In winter the river here provides plentiful supplies of reeds, sometimes still carried in the traditional Broads reed punt. They are cut in standing water – at this point the Yare is still slightly tidal – and often in snow and ice (ice makes it easier, for the reed beds then are firmer walking). The reeds in winter are thick and brown and shoulder-high – one can easily cut oneself on them, and the clothes of the reed-cutters last but a short time. The reeds are tied into bundles, brought by punt to dry land, and sold to thatchers at prices which become higher and higher every year and make thatching with Norfolk reed a very expensive business, even for the smallest buildings. But a Norfolk reed roof should last seventy years, except for the ridge, which is generally done in the more flexible wheat straw and which needs renewing every twelve years. A kind of sedge grows in Broadland, however, which is sometimes used for ridging, and which will last nearly as long as the reed itself. An extensive example of this latter can be see in the big shooting lodge on Hickling Broad. Hardly anyone now remembers that the downy tops of the reeds were at one time stripped off as 'fledge', and used to stuff cushions, horse collars, and other things that needed stuffing.

Surlingham has a nature reserve under the control of the Norfolk

THE NORFOLK BROADS. *Above*, Herringfleet Mill, with the bird-haunted solitude of the remoter broads. *Below*, boats running before the wind down the River Bure.

Above, KING'S LYNN. *Left*, Low tide at the Customs House, originally a Merchants' Exchange. *Right*, Clifton House is one of the splendid merchants' combined houses and warehouses that back on to the Great Ouse. *Below*, WISBECH. The north "Brink" of the river Nene.

Naturalists' Trust, displaying Broadland life in its fullness and perfection within a wide area of protected land and water. It owes much to the loving care over many years of the great Norfolk naturalist, writer and broadcaster, the late E. A. Ellis – 'Ted' to everyone who knew him, including thousands of television viewers.

CHAPTER 7

The Waveney

From Norwich one might advantageously begin the journey to the Waveney by going down the valley of the River Tas.

Arminghall, just south-west of **Trowse**, is the site of a large Neolithic temple, discovered from the air in 1929, excavated in 1935, and consisting of significant depressions in the ground best seen from a flying machine. It was a sort of wooden Stonehenge, 270 feet in diameter, and late Neolithic: dated *c.* 2500 BC.

Venta Icenorum was the Roman town at present-day **Caistor St Edmunds**, or Caistor-by-Norwich. This is well seen from an aeroplane too, for from above the complete street-plan of the Roman town can be descried – public baths, forum and all.

From the air it can be seen that the streets of the Roman town extend beyond the walls, as though they were built before the walls and the latter were superimposed on them. Roman occupation is supposed to have begun about AD 70 (mid-first-century pottery has been found), and then streets were laid out on the grid-iron pattern. It can be imagined (from the name as much as anything) that Venta was at first simply a trading station in the country of the Iceni tribe, probably much like a nineteenth-century Red Indian trading station. About AD 100 public buildings of more durable material were built: forum, basilica (Town Hall) and public baths with water brought from the Tas by wooden pipes. The walls were built about AD 200. These were substantial: an outer ditch some 80 to 100 feet wide crossed by wooden bridges at the gates, a wall 11 feet thick and 20 feet high, with towers at intervals, backed by a thick earthen rampart, and built of flint rubble faced with brick and dressed flint. There was a gate in each of the four walls. In the third century two temples were built near the forum: in 270 the forum and basilica

130

were rebuilt, but smaller, on the old foundations. About AD 300 glass making started in Caistor, and there was a pottery. After 360 the town began to decline, and the presence of a large Anglian cemetery outside the east gate has given rise to the belief that Anglian mercenaries were brought in to defend the town against Saxon pirates. Evidence indicates that the Romans, or Romano-British, lingered on until the early fifth century. For most of the above information I am indebted to Miss Barbara Green, of Norwich Museum.

What we see at Caistor now is romantic in the extreme. There is a farouche little church crouching down low behind the huge grass-grown east wall of the Roman town, far from any village and only just holding its own, one feels, against the pagan ghosts that beleaguer it. The path into the church passes through what was the east gate of the Roman town, and there are blocked Saxon windows in the south wall of the nave and a fine fifteenth-century Four Evangelists font. On this are the arms of Edward the Confessor, (probably thought up posthumously since Saxons didn't have arms) and it is thought that there was a west gallery in the church built about 1050 for no less a person than the king himself: for the church was in his gift before he gave it to Bury St Edmunds' Abbey. The inside of the church is simple and has an indefinable air of great antiquity. The scrubbed quarry-tile floor is pleasant, and so are the white high plain walls – but ruined by the *scandalous* electric heaters slung up on both sides.

Much of the charm of East Anglia lies in its valleys, and the valley of the Tas is no exception. The Tas villages are as charming as their names: Stoke Holy Cross, Swainsthorpe, Newton Flotman, Flordon and Tasburgh. At **Newton Flotman** is a medieval bridge, and a monument in the church to his forebears put up by Thomas Blandevyle in 1571. Blandevyle was famous in his day as a writer on such diverse subjects as astronomy, navigation, logic and horse-manship.

Long Stratton is a pretty village and the church is the only church in England save Yaxley in Suffolk to have a sexton's wheel. This is in fact two wheels which counter-rotate. The upper had strings attached to it – one string for every day of the year sacred to the Virgin Mary. A person wishing to keep a Lady Fast, or

Madonna's Fast, would ask the sexton to spin the wheels, and the string of the upper wheel which caught in the lower wheel indicated on which of the six possible days the supplicant might propitiously keep the fast.

Tivetshall St Margaret has a monstrous Royal Arms of Elizabeth I over the chancel arch – a truly spectacular piece of work. **Pulham St Mary** is notable for its double-storied porch, said by some to have been built by William of Wykeham and others by John Morton, Archbishop of Canterbury, Lord Chancellor of England, and Cardinal of Rome in Henry VII's reign. The porch has carved pinnacles, traceried stone between bands of quatrefoils, small windows in front, niches under canopies, angels, and embattled beams in the roof. It is a gem of stone work, and well worth going off the road to see. There is an Early English piscina in the church, like three intersecting stone rainbows.

Pulham Market is a charming little place, in post-war years boasting a vineyard which has won prizes in competition with the most distinguished French and German viticulturists.

Harleston (Saxon *Herolfston*) is one of Norfolk's many good, small, predominantly eighteenth-century towns which suffered cruel pressure from through traffic until bypassed. Today there are much more agreeable conditions for appreciating its little closes with names like Keeling's Yard and Shipp's Close which one should look into, and a minaret over the Midland Bank from which, momently, one expects to see the manager lean forth and utter the Call to Prayer. Harleston church is Victorian, but the dressed flint is worth looking at, for it belies the contention that men have lost the art of working in dressed flint. It is very good. (Whether men could do it *now* though is open to question.)

The Swan Inn is Georgian, and mellow, and pleasant to go into.

Redenhall (Saxon *Radahalla*) has an old church, and a very fine one: the Norfolk historian Blomefield described its fifteenth- to sixteenth-century tower as 'The finest tower of any country parish church in the country'. Certainly its proportions are beautiful, and the relationship of tower to nave. If you went to Wingfield, over the river, you would recognize the leopards carved on the base of the tower, for these are the de la Pole emblem. The roses with them are for Brotherton. If you clamber up the tower you will get

132

a fine view of the Waveney Valley, and also see the rebus of a former rector, carved on the south-east pinnacle, a shell and a tun, for his name was Shelton. The modern crossword addict had his counterpart in the sixteenth century. The west door has horseshoes, farrier's pincers and a hammer carved on it, and a bullet-hole by a man who was very rightly transported to Australia for this peccadillo. The double eagle lectern is fine, and about 1500, and you should not miss the fifteenth-century Venetian vestment chest, which has paintings of a square rigger and galleys inside the lid. It is a noble church altogether, but as there is an excellent little guide book (obtainable in St John's at Harleston if not here) I shall say no more about it.

From here on, downstream, the **Waveney Valley** is extremely beautiful. If John Constable had been born at Harleston, instead of at East Bergholt, we would have processions of motor coaches along the Waveney instead of along the Stour. As it is, the Waveney is frequented only by people who have business there, or the rare few who know of its beauty and go for pleasure. But certainly Constable's Stour has nothing the Waveney has not got, except Constable.

Behind the hospitable Buck inn at **Flixton** on the B1062 is the Norfolk and Suffolk Aviation Museum, with a collection of historic aircraft, flying relics, models, and paintings. Admission free on Sundays and Bank Holidays from Easter until the end of October, plus Sunday, Tuesday and Wednesday evenings from the beginning of June until the end of August. The Waveney hereabouts is a coarse fisherman's paradise. But for a world more mysterious than any waterway or skyway, one must strike south into 'The Saints'.

The **Saints' Country** is real back-block of East Anglia, a hillbilly land into which nobody penetrates unless he has good business, and that is always connected with agriculture. The reason why it is called Saints is that it contains the following parishes: St Mary South Elmham, St Cross South Elmham, St Margaret South Elmham, St Nicholas South Elmham, St James South Elmham, St Michael South Elmham, St Peter South Elmham, All Saints South Elmham, Ilketshall St Margaret, Ilketshall St John, Ilketshall St Andrew, Ilketshall St Lawrence, and All Saints Mettingham. So beware of getting lost: it is really not much good asking anyone

133

the way. There are purists who will tell you that the Saints' Country only includes the South Elmhams and not the Ilketshalls, and that the latter are part of the 'Seven Parishes' and include All Saints Mettingham and the two parishes of Bungay. But actually, to most local people it is all 'Saints'. The South Elmhams were a deanery, in the manor of Almar Bishop of East Anglia. The Ilketshalls belonged once to Ulfketle, Earl of East Anglia in the eleventh century.

But, apart from perhaps liking to see a very remote and lost (if not particularly beautiful) farming country we go to the Saints to see **South Elmham Minster**.

There is an Elmham in Norfolk and, as we have seen, a whole rash of them in Suffolk; and the men of both counties have long been eager to claim for *their* Elmhams the honour of being the seat of the second East Anglian bishopric (Dunwich being the first). Alas for Suffolk: research indicates that North Elmham probably wins the day. But, whatever South Elmham Minster was, and whatever it was used for, it is a most romantic place to go to and should not be missed. Renewed excavations may yet yield up a surprise.

One proceeds from Homersfield to Elmham St Cross, keeps straight on through the little village, and on to Hall Farm. Here one must ask permission to go farther, for the holy place is on private ground; but the farmer can usually be persuaded to admit the truly interested. The Hall itself is a good sixteenth-century house with a stepped gable and several older stone arches inside: built originally, it is said, by de Losinga to be a summer palace for the Bishops of Norwich. There is a stone building in the garden (by the moat) called the chapel, although whether it was one or not none can say: certainly there are no specific ecclesiastical features.

From the Hall it is expedient to *walk* – south across the fields – and you will come to the Minster surrounded by high and beautiful trees, elms and hornbeams, around which, in the nesting season, rooks wheel and shout. The situation is lonely and romantic. Inside the square of trees, growing from a deep ditch and bank, stand the ruins of an ecclesiastical building nearly, if not quite, a thousand years old. There are no declamatory sign-boards, litter baskets, nor indeed litter, and you are unlucky indeed if you find anyone else there. The ruin is just over a hundred feet long. It was long thought to be seventh century, very early Anglian; but excavations carried out by Ipswich Museum in 1964 date it as eleventh century (although a ninth-century gravestone was found under the foundations). Still to be seen are the remains of a semi-circular apse, a short, aisleless nave and a third division of the church, either the sub-structure of a tower or a narthex. This latter was an anti-nave used in early Christian churches for lesser breeds such as catechumens, penitents, and the excommunicated. Such an arrangement can be seen today in the Syrian Christian churches of the Nestorians or Thomists in southern India.

It would be hard to go to South Elmham Minster, alone, and not feel a sense of mystery and awe: and what of a night vigil at the time of the full moon! This was a holy place very far back in our East Anglian history, and its complete desolation today makes it the more impressive.

Bungay is the most interesting town in the Waveney Valley, and one of the most beautiful in East Anglia.

One theory of the derivation of its name is that it comes from *Bon Eye* – good island; but Professor Schram says that it derives, in fact, from *Bun-incga-haye*, meaning the Enclosure of the Tribe of Bonns. The town still retains, and has done certainly for a thousand years, a Town Reeve and Feoffees. Town Reeve is a much older title than the upstart Mayor, which only came in with the Normans.

But Bungay is certainly a long-inhabited place (apart from the fact that the skull of a hairy rhinoceros was dug up nearby). Before the sea receded from Broadland it must have been open to navigation – probably at the head of navigation on the river, and also it was on an easily defensible island. The fosse to the west of the castle is supposed to be Ancient British. Bungay was an important river crossing for the Romans (whose Stone Street ran through it to Venta), when the Normans came there was already a castle and an important settlement, and the Normans quickly made it a very strong place.

The first Norman owner was William de Noyers who had it from the Conqueror in 1070. In 1103 it went to our old friend Roger

135

Bigod (see Framlingham, p. 51) and Hugh, Roger's son, built a keep with walls 18 feet thick and probably 90 feet high in 1165. When Hugh rebelled against Henry II in 1174 the latter ordered his castle at Bungay to be dismantled, but Bigod paid a fine (the old ballad has it of 'three score sacks of gold', but the history books say 1000 marks). Henry forbore and the castle was spared. Sir Hugh's defiance lingers on in song and story in Suffolk and Norfolk, and until recently – and who knows, perhaps even still? – children sang rhymes about it:

> *When the Bailey had ridden to Bramfield Oak,*
> *Sir Hugh was at Ilketshall Bower*
> *When the Bailey had ridden to Halesworth Cross*
> *He was singing in Bungay Tower:*
> *'Now that I am in my castle of Bungay*
> *Upon the river of Waveney*
> *I will ne care for the King of Cockney.'*

Another rhyme has it, though, that he was actually in his castle of Framlingham when forced to surrender to 'the King's Bailey' and shouted down from the walls:

> *Were I in my castle of Bungay . . .*
> *I would ne care for the King of Cockney.*

The visitor can see, under the south-west corner of the ruins of the keep, a mine-gallery: indeed he can creep through it if he likes. This small tunnel goes from the west side diagonally across to the forebuilding on the south side, and in the middle of it are two small cross-cuts (as a miner would say) running north-east and south-west into the masonry. This could be nothing else but an unfinished sapper's tunnel driven with the intention of causing that corner of the castle to collapse. The practice was to drive such a tunnel, shoring perforce with timber as you went, and then, at the appropriate moment, set fire to the timber and wait for the whole thing to come down. It is supposed that this sap was driven by Henry II's engineers (could it be supervised by Alnoth – the builder of Orford Castle and the dismantler of Bigod's other castle at Framlingham?), but discontinued when the ransom was paid up. It is also recorded that King Stephen attacked and captured *Castellum de Bunie* at Whitsuntide 1140.

Roger Bigod (another Roger) completely rebuilt the castle in 1294 (in 1281 Edward had given him 'the right to crenellate') as a big curtain wall in the Near-eastern style brought back by the Crusaders, much like Framlingham. In 1483 the castle, by then long abandoned, passed to the Howards, Dukes of Norfolk, in whose possession it still is. The vast extent of the defended works is indicated by 'Castle Hills'; some earthworks which can still be seen (rather mixed up with a bus depot and other things) to the southward. These marked part of the wall of the outer bailey. Beyond them, too, is the Town Ditch which was certainly Anglo-Saxon if not, indeed, Celtic.

It is a sad fact that in stoneless East Anglia castles do not last long. When they become redundant they are too often quarried for their stone; and this is what has happened to Bungay. All that is left of that massive keep of the Bigods are the stumps of a couple of towers and a few banks and foundations. As at Orford one is puzzled as to where all that stone has gone to. We know that Bungay was thoroughly quarried in the eighteenth century (when so much quarrying was done) by a local builder named Mickle-burgh, and that after this a folly cottage was built between the two towers by a romantic lady named Mrs Bonhote who wrote a novel called *Bungay Castle*, but the cottage has since been pulled down. The two existing towers were each side of the bridge pit, and the latter has recesses meant to accommodate a drawbridge (there is now a modern wooden bridge there). Beyond the towers can be seen the foundations of the two-chambered keep, the fore-gallery and a mine gallery. The ruin stands in a small green, and a signboard gives addresses of nearby shops from which the key may be obtained. A couple of hundred yards down the lane are a public open space and children's playground on the ramparts of Castle Hills.

Bungay is a famous printing town. There have been times when 80,000 books have come off the presses there in a week. In 1795 John Brightly, a school master, set up a wooden press. A grocer's assistant from Norwich, J. R. Childs, joined him, and drove all over England with a tandem and cart selling the books published by Brightly. Childs consolidated his position by marrying Brightly's daughter, and subsequently the firm became John and R. Childs. Childs became, locally, a great man. George Borrow and Edward

137

Fitzgerald used to go all the way to Bungay to dine with him.

In 1837 Childs, a strict Nonconformist, was sent to prison for refusing to pay the church rates, but released after a great liberal agitation to return in triumph to Bungay. Because of his immurement the church rate was abolished. In 1866 the firm printed the second edition of *Alice in Wonderland*. Ten years later another distinguished printer's name made its appearance when Richard Clay took over the business, still surviving today in spite of threats of impersonal takeovers in the 1980s.

There is a fine Butter Cross in the centre of Bungay, a domed octagonal shelter surmounted by a lead figure of Justice. This was built to replace an earlier market cross after the fire which consumed the town in 1688. There are no butter-wives regularly selling their wares on the spot now, but a jolly little market is still held every Thursday. In 1964 the local council tried to move one of the regulars, a fishmonger, in order to make room for a bus stop; but he pleaded that a market and fair had been established in Bungay in 1199 by Hugh Bigod, waved his arm above his head at the figure of Justice, and won the day.

Near the Butter Cross is an electric light standard with the Black Dog of Bungay depicted on it, on a leaden panel (the lead was part of the now defunct Corn Cross). A bronze plate at the base of the standard quotes these words:

> *All down the Church in midst of fire*
> *The hellish monster flew;*
> *And passing onwards to the Quire*
> *He many people slew.*

This is in memory of that Sunday in August, 1577, when Old Shuck or Black Shuck, the terrible Black Dog of East Anglia, appeared in the church during a thunderstorm (the same one in which the Devil left his mark in Blythburgh Church), and wrought great havoc. Sightings of Shuck are common in East Anglia, nowadays as in the past.

The chief, and very grand, church in Bungay is St Mary's, and it was the church of the Benedictine nunnery founded by Gundreda, wife of Roger de Glanville, in the middle of the twelfth century. Ruins of the nunnery can still be seen to the east of it. The lower

138

part of the great tower (which has been compared to Redenhall) was built about 1450, the upper part after the great fire of Bungay of 1688.

St Edmund's, just down the road, is red brick and stone, 1892, Roman Catholic, and covered all over with statuary inside and out. It is nothing if not lavish. Holy Trinity, the other parish church, south-east of St Mary's, had a very early round tower with some Saxon work in it. Both Anglican churches have interesting church-warden's books: that of St Mary's dating from 1523, excellently preserved, and written in the greatest detail. It is a mine for local historians. There is a Druid's Stone to the west of St Mary's and if you dance round it, on the right night and in the right frame of mind, you will raise the Devil.

Modern Bungay is dated by the 1688 fire, for then Tudor Bungay was wiped out, with the exception of the odd house like the one in St Mary's Street which has Samson and Delilah carved on the window sill, and which is early sixteenth century. The other big factor in the building of modern Bungay was the rendering of the Waveney navigable, after the Navigation Act of 1670. The lock was built at Geldeston, the river canalized, and wherries came up in their hundreds. Many fortunes were made in Bungay water-borne trade. Bungay was a weaving place until as late as 1855: hemp was grown in the locality, many houses had hand looms in them, and 'Bungay Canvas' was famous for sails.

A Bungay industry is the working of leather. The firm of Nursey and Son Ltd was started in 1790, and is still in the hands of Nurseys. It processes sheep skins and turns them into wind-defying coats, slippers, hats, gloves, mittens and much else. Some work is done in the factory with modern machinery, but over 200 people are employed in the countryside round about hand-stitching skins in their own homes: the sort of local industry that does nothing but good to the countryside. Headquarters and a large shop are to be found in Upper Olland Street.

Châteaubriand, known locally as 'Monsieur Shatterbrain', spent part of his exile from France at the house of the Ives family in Bridge Street, where he fell in love with beautiful Charlotte Ives. George Crabbe went to school in Bungay, hated it, and got his own back with some condemnatory passages in *The Borough*.

Bungay has its share of good pubs, though it has lost its once cheerful Falcon on the riverside. Just across the river in **Ditchingham**, where we enter Norfolk once more, is the Triple Plea with an inn sign depicting three men arguing over a woman's body while the Devil looks on. The men are a lawyer, a doctor, and a divine. The origin of the picture lies in a piece of verse which starts in a sort of lively calypso style:

> *Law, Physic and Divinity,*
> *Being in dispute could not agree*
> *To settle which among them three*
> *Should have the superiority.*

And it ends:

> *But if men fools and knaves will be*
> *They'll be ass-ridden by all three.*
> *Now if these three cannot agree*
> *The Devil shall ride them three times three.*

About a mile west of Bungay is the Otter Trust, where species of otter are exhibited in conditions as close as possible to their natural environment. There are also lakes of wildfowl, riverside walks, and woodland with deer. The otters' antics can be hilarious, and the surroundings are delightful. Open daily April to October.

The Bungay-Beccles road south of the river takes you to **Mettingham**, where there is an old castle. A gatehouse remains, with two towers, and traces of a barbican. This was a house fortified by Sir John de Norwich, when he was licensed to crenellate in 1342 as a reward for having commanded the English forces at the Battle of Sluys. For this service he was also made a baron. He was one of England's first great sea commanders, saw service against the Spanish as well as the French, was Admiral of the Northern Fleet and Bailiff of Yarmouth.

From Mettingham perhaps it would be best to go north except that it would be a pity to miss **Barsham**, with its round-towered church and seventeenth-century parsonage forming a lovely group set back amid tall trees. A rector of Barsham was the grandfather of Horatio Nelson. In 1806 a dreadful thunderstorm broke above the church and lightning struck through the east window, smashing the mullions and the mensa of the altar. Repairs were made, and at the same time the chantry chapel was restored and re-dedicated. In our own time there was a worse disaster, when the thatched roof of the nave caught fire and the interior was severely damaged. The roof has been re-thatched and a great deal of work done within; but at the time of writing – 1986 – there remains a lot more to be healed.

Now cut back and cross the river by Ellingham bridge, with its watermill as pretty as any Constable ever painted; and then find the muddy marsh track to the superbly sited pub at **Geldeston Lock**, where the beer once had to be brought by boat, and patrons had also to come by boat or trudge across the field to gain entrance . . . and then, according to the whim of the eccentric landlady, be served or told to go back the way they had come. Nowadays the brewery can deliver by road and customers are not summarily dismissed; but the downright cussed charm of the place remains.

Beccles has a solidly comfortable waterfront which smacks to me of Edwardian gentlemen in white flannel trousers, blue jackets with brass buttons, and blue peaked yachting-caps. Nice gardens run down to the private staithes at which the smart varnished motor launches are tied up. The houses at the tops of the gardens are not Edwardian though, but solidly Georgian as are those at Bungay and for the same reason. Beccles also was burnt out – by a number of fires – and there is little of Tudor Beccles left. Beccles also had its heyday in the great days of the Norfolk Wherry, and was then a most flourishing port. The last 'billyboy', one of the bluff-bowed sailing ships from Yorkshire which used to trade to every hole and corner of the East Coast, put in there in 1924. There is no lock between Beccles and the sea, and Beccles could be a seaport again if conditions could be manipulated in her favour. As it is, Broadland cruisers lie tied up along the staithes, sometimes in serried ranks, and the waterside pubs enjoy visitations from holiday sailors who enjoy – as do the locals – the gardens and greens and the seats from which to look at other people making a mess of their mooring procedures.

Beccles church is impressive, standing on an eminence commanding the surrounding levels, its bell tower a wonderful vision for anyone approaching by boat from Geldeston Lock. The south porch is worth going to East Anglia to see – double-storied, mid-fifteenth century, marvellously detailed. Inside the door the church is dull, but it has its memories: here in 1749 Catherine Suckling came from nearby Roos Hall to marry the Reverend Edward Nelson, giving birth nine years later to Horatio Nelson, an earlier son of that name having died in infancy. The massive Perpendicular campanile is separate from the main body of the church: a mighty pile of stone.

Beccles – now bigger than Bungay – was once much smaller, but the place is no parvenu. Domesday records that it rendered 10,000 herrings a year to the Abbey of St Edmunds. This reminds us that at that time it was almost a seaport, for Broadland was still flooded. One notices again and again in East Anglia that only the places that are near navigable water have great churches, with vast amounts of imported freestone in them, such as Beccles. It was easier to sail a freight of stone from Normandy to the heart of East Anglia up one of her rivers, than it was to move it a few miles overland. The native flint – and later brick – was everywhere available, 'freestone' from France or Northamptonshire became more expensive every mile it had to be dragged from the nearest staithe.

One could spend some time wandering around Beccles, absorbing the urbane atmosphere of its eighteenth-century buildings. Like Bungay, it was once cursed with through traffic, and the late Adrian Bell's attractive book, *A Street in Suffolk*, complained of the heavy traffic shaking the old houses of Northgate to their foundations. He did not live to see the saving bypass.

Beccles is a growing small industrial town, with a printer, a factory that makes winches for trawlers and another which makes machinery. But you might live in Beccles and not know that there was a factory there.

Worlingham has a hall built early in the nineteenth century by Francis Sandys, of Ickworth fame, described by Norman Scarfe as 'perhaps the most beautiful house of manageable size in Suffolk', but the inside is far more beautiful than the outside. It is in a nice situation, with parkland and woodland going down to the Waveney marshes. (Map, p. 112–113).

Oulton Broad is a great place for small boat sailing, but made hideous from time to time (too often) by screeching speed boats.

Sir John Fastolfe's funerary brass used to be in the church, but was robbed by a scrap-metal dealer in 1857.

George Borrow lived on an estate by Oulton Broad for the latter part of his life, and there he wrote some of his few books. He welcomed Gypsies to stay on his land, a fact which enraged his landed neighbours, who showed Christian charity by persecuting these people as so many land-owners do today. Borrow was grandly eccentric at Oulton, striding about in a splendid cloak, leaping fully clothed into the Broad when he felt like it and swimming across it: joining in great parties with his Romany friends, quarrelling with his neighbours, being rude to poor Agnes Strickland when she tried to present him with her 'Queens of England' ('for God's sake don't, Madam. I should not know where to put them or what to do with them') and fighting (unsuccessfully) the railway company when they wanted to build their railway across his estate. Nothing remains of his house now. (Map, pp. 112–113).

Lowestoft, like Yarmouth, is a great mixture. It has its big seaside resort element, more solid and 'respectable' than that of Yarmouth where the comic paper hat tends to be the order of the day. There are large and (to me) rather forbidding hotels and boarding-houses along the front at South Town. But the fishing harbour is the heart of Lowestoft.

On the opening-up of the Dogger Bank as a trawling ground, and especially with the discovery of the fantastically sole-rich 'Silver Pit', the big West Country trawling fleets moved round to the East Coast. The arrival of the railway in Lowestoft (unprevented by George Borrow) soon knocked out the great London trawling fleet based on Barking; for it was quicker to sail fish from the Dogger to Lowestoft and rail it to Billingsgate than to sail it all the way there. (Hull and Grimsby benefited by the same factors.) From the pattern of the famous West Country 'Brixham Trawler' was evolved the equally famous 'Lowestoft Trawler', a heavy and powerful vessel, with a 'cod-fish bow and mackerel stern', ketch-rigged, often equipped with a steam winch for hauling the trawl, capable of holding the sea in any weather at all. It was almost never that a Lowestoft trawler was overwhelmed by weather alone, and they ranged all over the North Sea. As 'fleet fishing' was developed (the practice of letting the trawlers stay out on the grounds for months

143

at a time, while 'fleet carriers' ferried the fish to market) the sailing smacks never saw port for months together, nor did the men.

There are no sailing trawlers left now and, as we have seen at Great Yarmouth, even the most modern powered fleets have fallen on hard times. At this moment of writing in 1987 there is still a splendid fish smokehouse in Raglan Street supplying the finest kippers and other delicacies the heart (or palate) could desire; but ten years from now – or even by the time these pages are in print – can we be sure it will still exist? Its devotees hope so.

Of Lowestoft's other industries, shipbuilding prospered from the time when Tudor monarchs subsidized the construction of naval defence vessels up to our own century and the yards of Brooke Marine. Lowestoft has also claimed a small share in oil-rig construction and maintenance.

Less rugged, but manufactured with equal craftsmanship, was Lowestoft porcelain, whose production lasted for no more than 45 years after the discovery in 1756 of fine clay on the Gunton estate of Hewlin Luson; but this very limitation has meant that the products now fetch high prices from connoisseurs.

Between Gunton Hall and Corton cliffs today is East Anglia's first American-style 'Theme Park' at Pleasurewood Hills, with boating lakes, scenic railway, and enough amusements to occupy energetic children (if not their exhausted parents) for a full day at a time. It is open daily, in an attractive heathland setting above the sea, from early May until late September.

Lowestoft Ness is the most easterly point in the British Isles, and on a day of wind straight from Siberia it can feel like it. But it is a welcoming place, and all the bombing and shelling of two World Wars has not destroyed its gritty individuality.

Pakefield men were once known as the 'Roaring Boys', and were notable smugglers. The Reverend Francis Cunningham, one of their vicars, is said to have read the burial service over a coffin filled with contraband lace under the eye of the revenue men. The coffin was interred, but later dug up and the lace distributed. Another parson, evidently not so accommodating to the Free Trade, is said to have been buried alive by his parishioners. Nowadays the people of Pakefield are much more settled.

CHAPTER 8

The Bure and the Coast to Mundesley

Wroxham is the capital of **the Broads**. Here both banks of the Bure are deeply indented with artificial basins, in which – all winter – hundreds if not thousands of Broads boats lie waiting for their season of usefulness. Roys – the 'biggest village store in the world' – throngs all summer with people buying tinned food and woolly hats (indeed you can buy practically anything there), and the boatyards hum the year through with band-saw and planing machine as more and yet more Broads hire craft come off the production lines. And – every Saturday morning throughout the summer – a great army of strong-armed cleaning women descends upon the place, to clean the returning hire craft, swab them, scour them, turn them upside down and inside out and get them ready for the afternoon's new lot.

Horning, just down the river, on the north bank, with a ferry, is another great Broadland place but less resolutely commercial and it has more substantial Edwardian-type river-lodges with green lawns coming to the water's edge and thatched boat-houses. In its way it is a pleasant place – given over to the charm of lapping water.

It would be as well to warn here – if you love peace and solitude do not go cruising on the Broads in July and August. The ratio of motor boat to sail has, alas, altered very much for the worse in recent years, and the Bure can have all the quietness and solitude of the Southend Road on a bank holiday. I do not say that you *cannot* get away from the motorized and transistorized rabble, for there are plenty of quiet corners on the hundred odd miles of waterways of the Broads (Broads promoters always say there are two hundred, but I think there are only that if you go all the way and back!). And the two South Rivers are relatively unfrequented: most of the ordinary hirers start on the North River and cannot bring themselves to face the terrors of Breydon Water.

For years the origin of the Broads, these strange shallow lakes, or meres, which lie along the sides of the Broadland rivers and offer such marvellous opportunities for small boat sailing, bird-watching, and pike fishing, remained a mystery. One would have thought that the first Dutchman who clapped eyes on them (particularly if he came from that part of his country known as Randstad Holland) would not have been in a moment's doubt; for his part of Holland has exactly the same kind of meres, but on a much larger scale, and it has always been known how *they* were formed. Indeed they are still being formed. But various and ingenious were the explanations – geological, hydraulical, and plain mystical – until somebody came up with the theory that they were just dug.

They were peat diggings. Then evidence flooded in. The comparison with Holland was at last made, a great amount of historical evidence was brought forward to show that the digging of peat was a great industry in late Saxon and early Norman times (until in fact the shipping of 'sea coal' from the North of England supplanted it), and soundings were taken that proved conclusively that the Broads were artificial. And indeed the merest glance at a map would indicate that they were. No natural movement of water, or anything else not man-aided, could have formed those basins of regular depth, each one connected by a straight artificial cut to the nearest river, obviously with the purpose of shipping the peat out. And I would here advance a further theory. For many centuries Great Yarmouth supplied the whole of Northern Europe with salt herring. Where did the salt come from? Certainly not all the way from the Cheshire salt measures. It must have come from the sea, and what more likely than that peat, so easily available and so conveniently connected to Yarmouth by water, was used to fire the brine pans?

It would be hard to describe to the uninitiated the abiding *charm* of the Broads. In a land where the difference in level between land and water is often only a few inches, where 'land' tends to consist

146

of flooded reed beds or alder swamps so that it is difficult to say where water ends and land begins, where mysterious little channels open off the rivers and widen out into tree-surrounded lakes, where, in other places, the rivers run for miles between banks so that the sailor looks down on the backs of grazing cattle, and where the little villages are almost without exception beautiful: in such a land you must travel yourself, and by water, to find the meaning of this particular kind of charm. It is a new experience, and only to be equalled by sailing the rivers and meres of Friesland, the Malabar backwaters of South India, or other rare places, and somehow even these, though they may be fascinating, do not quite capture the subtle quality of the Norfolk Broads.

Some of this quality can be studied and analysed at **Ranworth**, where the Broadland Conservation Centre has an exhibition of the regional ecology. There is a birdwatching gallery equipped with binoculars and telescopes.

And where but in East Anglia could one expect to find, in such a tiny village, such a masterpiece as the church's medieval screen? It is complicated with two projecting wings which serve as retables for two nave altars and two wings east and west to form the sides of these two chapels. The painting is in oils, and is said to show Spanish influence. The various figures on it have been identified thus:

North Retable: Saints Etheldreda, Agnes (with lamb), John the Baptist, Barbara.

Centre: Simon (with fish), Thomas, Bartholomew, James the Less, Jude (with boat), Matthew.

South Wing: Two small figures, Lawrence, Thomas, Michael (with feathered body).

South Retable: Mary with her two children James and John, the Virgin and Child, Mary of Cleophas with her two children (one of them is Jude, holding a boat), Margaret.

The faces, alas, are defaced; but nothing can convey the delicacy of the painting which remains: the red and green and gold of the flowers on their white ground, the hunting scenes – dogs and swans and ducks and lions. The whole thing was covered over at some time with whitewash, and discovered and cleaned in the last century.

Then, there is the *Sarum Antiphoner*: a sheepskin book written and illuminated by the monks of Langley Abbey in the fourteenth century, and a fine example of East Anglian illumination. It was lost in the reign of Edward VI, discovered by a Victorian collector, sold to a bookseller who offered it to Ranworth – whence it had come – for fifty guineas. This was raised by public subscription. The illuminations, of vegetable dyes and burnished gold, are as brilliant now as when they were first laid on. It is said that the gold leaf was burnished by rubbing it with agates.

Notice, too, the fifteenth-century oak lectern, which was probably used up on the rood loft before the Reformation put a stop to all that. One of its two desks has the plainsong notation of the Gloria painted on it, the other the eagle of St John. And climb up the tower for a magnificent aerial view of the North Broads. The church is now in good repair; not long ago umbrellas had to be used, inside, by the congregation.

Half a mile along the lane one comes to **South Walsham Broad**, beautifully tree-surrounded. South Walsham itself is a lovely little village. **Upton** is a scattered, lost place near an amphibious never-never land called, lugubriously, The Doles. It has a fine church with a marvellous fourteenth- or fifteenth-century font with dogs fighting, lions twisting their tails together, a dragon, and a man with a branch in his mouth. How it makes one wish to meet the artist! Acle we have seen, but north-east is **Acle Bridge**, where Broads sailing boats must lower their masts, and good sport is provided on windy days leaning over the bridge rail watching them do it. It is surprising what entertainment is provided. **Filby** and **Ormesby Broads** are not accessible by water from the Broads system, Muck Fleet, which ought to make them so, being silted up. They make together a great and beautiful stretch of water, and being crossed by two motor roads on causeways are easily seen by the motorist. Filby is another place with a good screen in its church: lions, birds, dogs and a hare being stooped at by a falcon adorn the gorgeous robes of fifteenth-century saints. (The upper carved part is nineteenth century, just in case anybody should be led to enthuse too loudly about it.)

And so we come to the coast again and Caister, Caister-on-Sea.

As one may infer by its name this was another Roman station: a very important naval base of the Count of the Saxon Shore. It once stood on the north side of the great sea-inlet which ran into Broadland from where Yarmouth now stands. The remains of the Roman town have been excavated, and can be seen; although as with most Roman remains, there is little enough to see.

Caister Castle (a mile inland) is all muddled up with Sir John Fastolf, or Fastolfe, Sir John Falstaff, and the Paston Letters (see p. 156).

Sir John Fastolf came back from fighting in the French wars, in the 1440s, having made a very good thing out of them. He led the English archers at Agincourt, helped to besiege Caen and Rouen, fought against Joan of Arc, took a big part in the political settlement after these events, and accumulated a lot of gold. With this he built Caister Castle, in which he spent the rest of his life in peace. He had made a great many enemies, but was a friend and helper to the Pastons, and this has ensured his immortality, for he is mentioned again and again in the famous Letters.

Another oblique sort of immortality was given him by Shakespeare, who modelled his Falstaff partly on Fastolf. (The latter even owned a pub in Eastcheap called The Boar's Head.)

On Fastolf's death his castle went to the Pastons (the will was in doubt, as John Paston was the executor of it). Ten years after, the Duke of Norfolk, who apparently hadn't got enough castles of his own, laid claim to Caister, and – after a year's siege in which he had to bring up eventually three thousand men – he took it, and kept it until his death, when it was re-occupied by the Pastons. They kept it until the seventeenth century when they sold it to a London businessman. Even he would be surprised by its present juxtaposition of moated remains, veteran and vintage car museum, and the Festival of Britain Tree Walks removed from Battersea Park. They are all open daily except Saturday from mid-May until late September.

Caister is notable for its lifeboat, and the vigorous long-shore fishing community that centres around it. The Ship is a delightful pub, much frequented by this nautical community, and there are medals in it which were presented to the men of Caister by the Tsar of Russia, for saving men off Russian ships. As at nearly every lifeboat station on the East Anglian coast there have been frightful disasters: the mortality figures of lifeboating make it, far and away, the most dangerous occupation in the world. In 1885 at Caister a 'beach yawl' (the precursor of the modern lifeboat) went down with all hands, and the RNLI lifeboat overturned in the surf in 1901. There is a lady in Caister today who will tell you how – when she was seven years old – she was sent off early in the morning to fetch the milk. When she got back her aunt (her mother was dead) said to her: 'Your father was drowned last night.' She ran down to the boat-house, looked inside, and saw nine figures lying under blankets. Her father was one and her two uncles others. The boat had put out the night before into an impossible on-shore gale, been driven some miles down the coast and overturned in the breakers. In the morning the watchers on the shore had managed to drag out the bodies. When, at the enquiry afterwards, the chairman of the Board asked one of the three survivors why, on seeing the impossible nature of the gale, the boat had not turned back, the man addressed said the words which have become the motto of Caister fishermen: '*Caister men never turn back!*'

At **Hemsby Gap** there is Bingo.

Winterton is a wind-swept little place of much character. The Fisherman's Return is a fine pub, marred only by a juke box, and again there is a fine community of fishermen. Winterton men have, for years, gone away to sea in Yarmouth trawlers or drifters, or else fished off their own beach in little boats. There is an old rhyme in Winterton which I don't think does the place justice:

> *Pakefield for Poverty*
> *Lowestoft for Poor,*
> *Gorleston for Pretty Girls*
> *Yarmouth for Whores,*
> *Caister for Water Dogs*
> *California for Pluck:*
> *Beggar old Winterton –*
> *How Black she do look!*

There are several old men in Winterton who remember the sailing trawler days (the most famous was Mr Sam Larner, who knew a thousand songs and broadcast some of them frequently on the wireless. Alas, he died in 1965). They will tell you of the days when the smacks sailed out of Yarmouth northward-bound, and raced each other to the South Shields fishing grounds:

> *First the Dudgeon,*
> *Then the Spurn.*
> *Flamberry Head*
> *Come next in turn.*
> *Scarboro' Castle*
> *Standing high*
> *Whitby Rocks*
> *Lie Northerlie!*
> *Sunderland*
> *Lay in a Bight*
> *Canny ol' Shields*
> *Afore Dark that Night!*

If they had a fair fresh of wind on their beam or abaft of it the great smacks would 'sail like the Devil' and leave steamers far behind.

Defoe went to Winterton, and wrote that half the village was built from the timbers of wrecked ships, and that 200 coal ships were lost off it one winter's nights, and thousands of lives. Before the RNLI station was closed down the boat, in its short career, had saved 500 lives.

The church is splendid: on a height, and its great tower (127 feet) is a famous landmark for sailors (as is Caister water tower). The church has a fine stone porch, and an anchorite's cell in the wall. The names of many perished fishermen are written up in the church.

Horsey stands where the Broads come to within a couple of miles of the sea, on what must at one time have been a very narrow, low, and apparently sea-threatened strip of land – a neck providing land communication to Roman Caister. Roman coins have been dug up there, and there is Saxon work in the church. One can sail into Horsey Mere with a Broads boat, and take a short walk to the beach and have a bathe in the North Sea. It is here that at very high tides the sea has broken into the Broads and flooded thousands of acres.

Happisburgh is pronounced 'Haisboro', and gives its name to the dreaded sand-bank a dozen miles out, which stretches parallel with the Norfolk coast. There is a lonely lighthouse on a cliff, and the beautifully proportioned fifteenth-century church tower is no less than 110 feet high. Probably, like other coastal church towers, it was built high to be both watch tower and landmark for sailors. Lights were often put in church towers before the days of Trinity House. There is a beautiful octagonal font.

In the churchyard are buried 32 men of HMS *Peggy* which went on the sand in 1770, 119 men of HMS *Invincible*, wrecked 1801, all hands of HMS *Hunter*, wrecked 1804, twelve men of the barque *Young England*, wrecked 1876, and three German airmen from Hitler's war.

The coast makes its transition about here from being low-lying and protected by sand-dunes only (compare the Netherlands) to high ground with cliffs.

Instead of following the coast north of Winterton it might be desired to strike inland to **Potter Heigham**. Here is a famous medieval bridge, again a marvellous place for the land-lubber to lean on the parapet and watch the Broads sailor making a fool of himself below, for here the latter must lower his mast and negotiate the old road bridge, which is villainously low, and also the railway one. There were generally some real working wherries to be seen lying at Potter Heigham, their huge masts recumbent and their sails all removed. A few are motorized now, and used mostly for carrying mud. The old village of Potter Heigham is a mile north of the bridges and the growing Broads settlement by them, and was the site of a Roman pottery. Great piles of wood ashes from the kilns have been found. The church has a beautiful roof, with embattled hammerbeams, a rather defaced fifteenth-century screen, and some interesting wall paintings. Harry Cox, a long-lived farmworker who contributed so much to the revival and recording of authentic folk music, lived in retirement at Potter Heigham until his death in 1971.

Ludham, more inland, has a church that – anywhere but in East Anglia – would be famous. Ludham is beautifully situated on high ground between the Rivers Thurne, Bure, and Ant. Womack Water connects it to the Thurne, and Ludham Bridge is over the Ant. On the Bure are the remains of St Benet's Abbey, which must indeed have been in a swamp. One imagines that the monks

153

must have suffered terribly from the rheumatism, if not indeed from the shaking ague. There is little to see there now, although every Broads sailor is familiar with the stump of a windmill growing out of the remains of the Abbey gate right by the water's edge, with cattle grazing the lush pastures around it. Because at the Dissolution the reigning Abbot became Bishop of Norwich, and surrendered the cathedral estates to the Crown while retaining those of the Abbey, the Bishop of Norwich still draws his revenues from the old estates of the Abbey, and is still the Abbot: the only mitred Abbot in the House of Lords. Consequently, once a year, on the first Sunday of August, the Bishop visits the ruined Abbey by water (it is difficult to get there by land) and holds a service. It is worth going there, in a boat, to watch him.

Hickling has a famous broad and gave its name to a punt designed for wildfowling. However the broad is now owned by the Norfolk Naturalists' Trust and is a National Nature Reserve. It is a great pike-fishing water. Down the lane which goes to the White Slea (a division of the broad – a sort of Sea of Okhotsk) is the famous 'Royal Shooting Lodge', built almost in the water, and beautifully thatched with Norfolk reed and ridged with sedge grass. Inside the lodge are many paintings by local bird artists and the place has a marvellous period atmosphere. The Pleasure Boat at Hickling Staithe, at the other end of the Broad, is a fine inn and a good place to sail to, or to get to in any other way. Mr Edwin Vincent, known as king of the Hickling pike fishermen, once caught a 31-pounder.

Barton Broad is a beautiful reed-ringed broad on the River Ant, almost unapproachable by land. West of it is the tiny village – so small that it doesn't really exist – of Barton Turf, in the church whereof is perhaps the second best rood screen in England. Here there is a fine set of the orders of angels fourteenth century:

Potestates: armed, with a devil on a chain and a scourge.
Vertutes: 4 winged, with cap, sceptre, and feathered body.
Dominaciones: 4 winged, triple-crowned and with chasuble.
Seraphim: 6 winged, feathered body, fire girdle, censer.
Cherubim: 6 winged, many-eyed, feathered, girdled, with outspread hands.
Principatus: 4 winged, belt with bells, vial and palm.

Troni: 6 winged, long-sleeved robe, holding a church and a pair of scales.

Archangeli: in alb, alms box at girdle, spear, 2 naked souls a'praying.

The angels are beautifully painted, and really most alluring.

There is a later, fifteenth-century section of the screen with Henry VI, King Edmund, Edward the Confessor, and a Dane with a battle axe and two loaves of bread.

Stalham, connected by a dike to the river Ant, once had a public house (now private) named after its still working windmill. Here Peter Warlock and E. J. Moeran collected local folk songs, and Moeran was inspired to compose his evocative pieces *Stalham River*, *Lonely Waters*, and *Windmills*.

A country road due north brings us to **Bacton**. From its flinty surroundings have sprouted brick buildings, huddled below tall, incongruous steel masts, all seemingly enmeshed in a web of piping. This is Bacton Gas Terminal fed by pipelines from North Sea rigs: the first to be laid, the 34-mile Shell/Esso line, cost about a quarter of a million pounds a mile. By day it is pretty stark; by night its lights sparkle like a funfair.

Dwarfed by this intruder, **Bromholm Priory** was in the Middle Ages one of the holy places of Europe. There remain a gateway and ruins of a choir and conventual buildings, now forming part of a farmstead as Mother Shipton prophesied they would. Some of the ruins were turned into a fortification in Hitler's war, and there are loopholes and bits of concrete.

Bromholm is mentioned at least twice in *Canterbury Tales* and once in *Piers Plowman*. 'By the Holy Rood of Bromholm!' was a binding medieval oath. Originally a small and very poor Cluniac House, founded in 1113, it was visited early in the thirteenth century by a wandering priest, who had a portion of the True Cross. He had been chaplain to Baldwin of Constantinople, had filched this relic (it was carved into the form of a double crucifix) and had hawked it all round Europe but found nobody who would pay his price. The monks of Bromholm would though, and promptly raised no fewer than thirty-nine people from the dead with it, and cured blindness, leprosy, possession by the Devil, and many lesser evils. Pilgrims began to stream in (among them Henry

155

III) and the priory became enormously rich, and for a time rivalled even Walsingham.

Paston is a tiny hamlet, where the famous Paston family lived, before they moved to Oxnead, Norwich, Caister, and other places. The most notable sight there is the famous Paston Barn, built in Elizabethan times of flint and thatch and with an alternate hammerbeam and tie-beam roof. In the church is a Paston monument, said to be that of the John Paston who was the executor of Sir John Fastolf's will. He was supposed to have been buried in the priory, but was removed to Paston at the Dissolution.

At this point we will mention the Paston Letters. The most extraordinary collection of intimate, private writing from the Middle Ages, these letters tell us not only a great deal about East Anglia but also much about the history of England.

The Paston men spent much of their time in London going to law, or else at home defending their enlarging properties from various attackers. The lawlessness of the times (fifteenth century) is shown by such passages as this, in a letter from Margaret Paston to her husband John in London – a passage thrown in among demands for groceries and cloth at 44d the yard – '. . . Pray you to get some crossbows and windacs to bind them with, and quarrels; for your houses here be so low that there may none man shoot out with no long bow, though we have never so much need.' And she goes on to ask for short pole-axes and jacks. (Jacks were armoured jackets, quarrels were the bolts to be fired from crossbows.)

John Paston sent a petition to the king, saying that Lord Moleyns had seized his manor of Gresham, storming it with a thousand men 'arrayed in manner of war, with cuirasses, briganders, jacks, sallets, glaives, bows, arrows, pavises, guns, pans with fire and teynes burning therein, long cromes to draw down houses, ladders, picks with which they mined the walls, and long trees with which they broke up gates and doors'.

The men may have been, nay were, hard and worldly; probably they had to be to exist: but one is struck again and again by the gentleness, high education and good common sense of the women.

What could be more tender than this, from a wife to a husband? From Margaret to John her husband, who was then ill and Mayor of Norwich:

By my troth, I had never so heavy a sickness till I wist of your sickness til I wist of your amending . . . if I might have had my will, I should have seen you ere this time: I would ye were at home lever than a gown, though it were of scarlet.

(*Lever* is still a common East Anglian word.) And what husband would not be moved to forgiveness by this:

Right worshipful husband, I recommend me to you, beseeching you that ye be not displeased with me, though my simpleness caused for you to be displeased with me. By my troth, it is not my will neither to do nor say that should cause for you to be displeased; and if I have done, I am sorry therefore, and will amend it. Wherefore I beseech you to forgive me, for your displeasance should be to heavy for me to endure with.

(She then goes on that she wishes him to send her some herrings and eels.)

Probably the most famous love letter ever written was by a Paston girl to her father's farm bailiff with whom she had fallen in love. But there are plenty of references to weightier matters, such as the detailed account by one Wm. Lomner to John Paston about the cutting off of the Duke of Suffolk's head with a rusty axe at Dover (see Wingfield, p. 65).

Paston Windmill has been repaired by the County Council.

Mundesley is a good solid respectable seaside town, and that is all there is to say about that. **Knapton** church has the best double hammerbeam roof in Norfolk.

Trunch is a little inland village worth seeing for at least one thing: the magnificent four-poster font cover, or baptistry. I will not describe it, but merely advise the reader to go and see it, for it is a marvel of medieval wood working. Again much of its impact rests on the apparent remoteness from 'civilization' of its setting.

Trunch also has a noteworthy group of farm buildings, with flint walls patterned with brick. We are really drawing into the flint country here, and there are few sights more solidly satisfying than a good group of farm buildings: farm house, bullock yards, stables, piggery, implement shed and mighty barn: all built of the grey flint,

157

and standing grouped together like a medieval fortress. At Trunch lived a famous builder of organs, just as at Cley, farther along the coast, lived one of violins (the making of which he doubled with boat-building).

North Walsham, yet farther inland, was pretty well wiped away in the great fire of 1600 (how much of Tudor East Anglia went up in flames!) and what is there now is a little town replete with Georgian prosperity. Much of the latter was due to the digging of the North Walsham and Dilham Canal, which connected the town with the River Ant and the Broads and thus with world commerce. But North Walsham was prosperous before Tudor times too, and was a famous wool weaving town: hence the great empty church, with its ruined tower 150 feet high, and all that stone from Barnack near Stamford. It is an interesting and beautiful little town today, completely unselfconscious and unspoiled, with little winding alley-ways to explore. The Market Cross was put there by a Bishop of Norwich in 1550. The arms of Edward III and John of Gaunt are carved in the pinnacled porch of the church, and there is a good fifteenth-century font cover with a pelican feeding her young at the top of it, and the ghost of a fifteenth-century screen. There is Sir William Paston's tomb, for this is Paston country. But the most notable aspect of the church is the fine uncluttered vista inside that huge nave and chancel.

Sir William Paston founded the Paston Grammar School in 1606, and it is still working, although rebuilt in 1765. Nelson went to it, from the age of ten to when he went away to sea in the *Raisonnable*, with an uncle. North Walsham must have had a lot to do with the forming of his character.

There are several crosses about the country near North Walsham, and one about a mile south of the town is known as the monument to the Peasants' Revolt of 1381. The Black Death led to a shortage of labourers, thence to the Statute of Labourers which was to make labourers labour, thence to the 1379 Poll Tax, thence to unrest and Wat Tyler and – in East Anglia – Sir Roger Bacon and Geoffrey Lister. On 17th of June 1381 a mob met on Mousehold Heath, marched on Norwich, and killed the commander of that city, Sir Robert de Salle. They were counter-attacked by Henry Despencer, the Bishop of Norwich, at the head of a strong force. The Bishop drove them from the city, attacked their main body on North Walsham Heath, and defeated them. Geoffrey Lister fled to the sanctuary of North Walsham Church. The Bishop had him dragged from the altar and drawn and quartered, but first was as good as to grant him absolution.

The village of **Worstead** has given its name to a cloth. At the beginning of the fifteenth century William Paston wrote to a cousin: 'I pray you will send me hither two ells of Worsted for doublets, to happen this cold winter, and that ye enquire when William Paston bought his tippet of fine worsted cloth, which is almost like silk, and if that be much finer than that ye should buy me after seven or eight shillings, then buy me a quarter and a nail thereof for collars, though it be dearer than the others, for I shall have my doublets all Worsted, for the glory of Norfolk.'

Worstead was known for cloth before Edward III brought his Flemings over to 'exercise their mysteries' and to teach Englishmen how to make fine cloth; but it is probable that worsted cloth was made by the Flemings from the first, for there was some immigration right from the time of the Conquest. Worstead was undoubtedly a town before it was a village, and had two churches. With the passing of the woollen trades to the North of England it dwindled away; but there are still weavers' houses to be seen there, with tall ceilings to take the looms, and cellars to store the wool.

The present church is one of the grand ones of Norfolk. The tower is 109 feet high, with elegant detail: the Victorian pinnacles were happily struck by lightning and removed. Note the vault in the lower story of the porch, with the Coronation of the Virgin in the centre boss and the symbols of the evangelists around it. The lovely flowing tracery of the east window is late fourteenth century: the chancel clerestory and the two chapels perhaps a century later. The chancel screen dates itself as 1512. The lettering which names the painted figures is Victorian and possibly inaccurate, but certainly the southernmost figure is that stubborn virgin St Uncumber, who miraculously grew a beard to stop her father from marrying her off, whereat he, reprehensibly if perhaps with some justification, crucified her. She is the patron saint of beards. William of Norwich stands – with his pair of nails and a dagger – beside her, beatified in the cause of anti-semitism; and twelve other figures probably

159

represent the Apostles. At the west end is a ringers' gallery, but the screen below it is much repainted by the Victorians. The font cover, fine if nearly rebuilt in 1954.

Coltishall is a little place of simple enchantment, and near it there is magnificent coarse fishing in the River Bure.

Frettenham is remarkable for the enlightened and, so far as I know unique, action of a Victorian squire who gave half an acre of land to every householder on his estate, thus anticipating Sri Vinobe Bhave: the Indian apostle of land reform.

CHAPTER 9

Aylsham,
Cromer, East Dereham

There are two rules to follow in East Anglia to ensure the pleasantest travelling: one is to stay in the river valleys, the other is to avoid main roads. From Norwich to Aylsham we might follow the former rule by going back along the Coltishall road as far as Horstead and then travelling up the Bure. This will take us through the village of **Buxton** where Thomas Cubitt was born, the man who, some might think for worse, built more of nineteenth-century London than anybody else. The other rule would take us out of Norwich through Drayton and Reepham.

Drayton has its Old Lodge, built by the redoubtable Sir John Fastolf, left, like Caister, to the Pastons and attacked while in their hands by the greedy Duke of Suffolk and therefore mentioned in the Letters.

Reepham is another of the scores of good little eighteenth-century towns in Norfolk and Suffolk. It has two churches and the remains of a third, for the parishes of Hackford and Whitwell had their churches in the same churchyard as Reepham. Hackford's was burnt down in 1543, Whitwell's is still there and has a good Jacobean pulpit. Reepham's is a fine building, with an altar-tomb to Sir Roger de Kerdiston who died in 1337. This is a beautiful piece of carving, exquisite in detail, and has fine moustaches. There are good bench-ends too, which should not be missed. The village square is dominated by the fine red-brick Old Brewery House, known locally as Dial House because of its lovingly painted and preserved sundial.

This is a good day for the church-hound, for just east of Reepham is **Cawston** which I think is my favourite church of all. It has a superb tower all faced with freestone. Whence all that stone so far from a navigable river? The cost of over-land haulage must have been immense. But the story is that it came from Normandy, up the Bure to Coltishall, and then each parish through which it had to go over-land did the cartage free. It has a beautiful wodewose (wild man) and a dragon carved over the west door, there is a good screen with saints galore (St Peter is a splendid old gentleman!) and no-one less than Sir Gilbert Scott said that the hammerbeam roof of the nave was the finest in England. As if all this were not enough there is a Plough Gallery in the west arch. The gallery was placed there by the Ploughman's Guild. There is still a fine plough in the church underneath it, the kind of heavy wheel plough that came to England from Holland in the sixteenth century. In old days the Ploughman's Guild would drag a plough around the village on Plough Monday (the Twelfth Day of Christmas) and collect 'largesse' (their word for contributions) from the householders, who gave it freely, realizing as they did that their very lives depended on the plough.

That Bread may not be wanting
Behold the Painful Plough!

The money thus gained would be spent, in an appropriate fashion, at the nearby Plough Inn, and on the following day the ploughmen would go to work again for the first time after the twelve days' rest of the Christmas Holiday. The Plough Inn at Sygate in Cawston was, unfortunately, closed down in May 1950 (the old inn sign still hangs in the church under the Plough Gallery) but this used to be called, it is said, the Plough Lights Inn – the lights referred to being the ones kept burning by the ploughmen in their Plough Gallery in the church.

Ask to see the stamped leather Chalice case, which is very beautiful, and fourteenth century like the chancel of the church. The church was paid for largely by Michael de la Pole the 1st Earl of Suffolk (see Wingfield, p. 64), and his picture is on the wall of the transept, dedicating the church to St Agnes. The arms of the de la Pole family are displayed over the west doorway: besides de la Pole, Morely, Wingfield, Stafford and Brotherton. Most of the

162

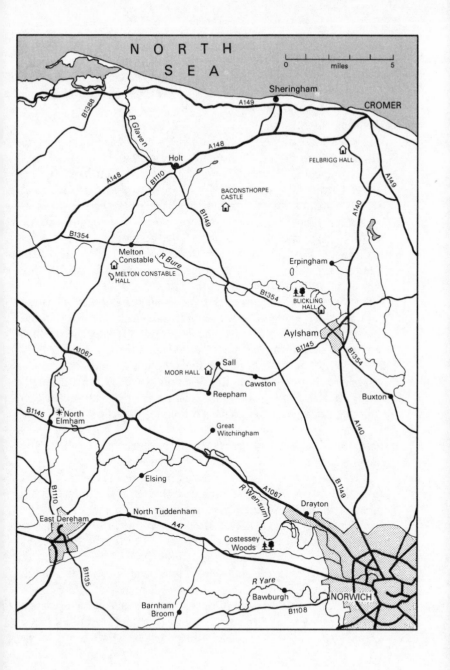

church is fifteenth century. It must not be forgotten, while seeing these mighty churches in what are now small villages, that this was Norfolk's wool country. The lightish land of North Norfolk was sheep country *par excellence*, the little villages grew into weaving centres, and the great churches of the Perpendicular period were paid for by wool.

Just outside Cawston is a stone which marks a duel fought on Cawston Heath in 1698 between Sir Henry Hobart of Blickling, 4th Baronet, and Oliver le Neve. Le Neve was left-handed, and ran the baronet through the body, whereat he died. Sir Henry had served on King William's staff at the Battle of the Boyne.

Lest you should think that Cawston church is the final word for Norfolk village churches pass on to **Sall** or Salle, a couple of miles to the west. For here is a church even grander than Cawston's, grander than many cathedrals in fact, although Sall is such a tiny village that it can hardly be said to exist.

This time the stone is from Barnack, that same oolitic limestone from which Cotswold villages are built and which runs in a slanting line right across England; but the soaring tower is partly of flint, and not all of freestone as the tower of Cawston. Three immensely wealthy families contributed to the building of Sall church: the Briggs, the Fountaines, and the Boleyns. Anne Boleyn, Elizabeth I's mother, is said by some people to have been buried in Sall Church; although a more general opinion is that she was buried in the Tower of London, and that her exhumed body there was identified by having six fingers on one hand, a peculiarity taken by enemies in her lifetime to indicate that she was a witch.

There are two lovely scaly angels swinging censers over the west door, and as you walk inside the church your eye is immediately taken by the marvellous upward-striving lines of the seven sacrament font and its cover, the latter most beautiful in spite of the fact that the Puritans ripped all the carvings out of it. The sacraments depicted are: Holy Communion, Holy Orders, Holy Baptism, Confirmation, Penance, Holy Matrimony, Unction, and the eighth panel, on which all the carving is defaced, represented the Crucifixion. These seven sacrament fonts are very much an East Anglian speciality; only two of the thirty-nine which are said to exist are not in Norfolk or Suffolk. Below the panels on Sall font are angels holding symbols of the particular sacrament above, and round the base of the font the four evangelists once sat on chairs, with their symbols: one can still make out the extremities of Mark's lion and Luke's ox. It is interesting to compare these symbols with the vehicles, also animals, of the members of the Hindu pantheon.

The nave arcade is famous, with its lofty slender piers and great dimensions. The roof is a marvel of engineering. The arch braces of this very wide and lofty roof come down to rest on corbel brackets which are themselves the ends of the rafters of the aisles – brought through the nave walls for the purpose. Thus the outward thrust of the mighty nave roof is taken partly by the walls of the aisles, an ingenious idea and one that works.

There is a powerful feeling of lofty dusty emptiness and lack of use about the interior: how could there not be inside such a great building in a tiny, almost non-existent parish? But there are great artistic riches for the seeking out. Down the centre of the nave are good brasses: the most westerly is to William and Margaret Fountaine, died 1505 and 1519, the fifth from the west end is to a Boleyn, one Simon, who was a priest and whose will is still in existence showing that he left money for the light of the three guilds, the light of the Holy Cross on the rood, to each Virgin's light and to each plough light. Simon, who died in 1482, also left his black cloak to the parish clerk 'if he pays what he owes me; otherwise not'.

The Boleyns were small farmers until one of them, Geoffrey, went to London, made money, became Lord Mayor, and was knighted in 1457. It was he who bought the Blickling estate from Sir John Fastolf. Sir Geoffrey's grandson, Thomas, was created Earl of Wiltshire and Viscount Rochford by Henry VIII when the monarch was courting his unfortunate daughter.

The pulpit is interesting: fifteenth-century 'wine glass' pulpit which was 'rose up' (heightened) in the seventeenth century into a three-decker, at the expense of Thomas Knyvett, who was one of the men who unmasked Guy Fawkes when the immortal man was intent upon blowing up the Houses of Parliament.

The north transept of the church was restored by Sir Alfred Jodrell after 1910, and contains the Jodrell vault. The glass in the windows is by Mr H. Bryans of London, with traces of old glass incorporated in the new designs. The north window of the transept was blocked up to provide a site for a monument to Edward Hase in 1801, and this led to a lawsuit because Hase's heirs had no legal right to place the monument there without permission of the rector or the bishop. However, it is still there right or wrong. There is a most amusing brass to Thomas Rose, his wife Katrina, and children no less than a round dozen, being eight tiny boys grouped by their father and four slightly larger girls grouped by their mother. Rose paid for the chapel in this transept and it was known as Rose's Chapel. We know where at least some of the money came from, for Rose was censured in the Cawston Court Roll in 1425 for 'grazing 500 sheep on Causton Common where he ought not to graze more than 200'. This is just an illustration of the fact that Sall Church was built upon the fleeces of sheep, not on weaving as were the great West Suffolk churches, but upon grazing and shearing. Rose lived before the height of the Enclosures that turned North Norfolk from a populous arable country into a depopulated sheep-run, but the process was even then being well advanced.

The Lady Chapel over the north porch should be seen, with its fine ceiling, and massive oak bar to secure the door.

The south transept was added by Thomas Brigg, who died in 1444. The timber roof is beautiful, and so is the empty niche in the west corner. The base of the chancel screen has paintings of those learned Latin doctors, viz: Saints Thomas, James, Gregory, Jerome, Augustine, Ambrose, Philip and Bartholomew. The top of this screen was sawn off in the sixteenth century. The chancel is magnificent, with the original fifteenth-century stalls and miserere seats, and nine scenes from the life of Jesus carved on the bosses of the roof: the Annunciation, Nativity, Circumcision, Epiphany, Entry into Jerusalem, Last Supper, Crucifixion, Resurrection, Ascension. The mighty east window has some patches of old glass in it.

Nobody should contemplate going to Norfolk without seeing Sall church. It is perhaps the almost total depopulation of the countryside in which it was built that gives it its immense austerity and dusty dignity. There it is – a vast, cathedral-like building – standing forlorn and empty among the deserted fields. There is a rusty wheel-plough standing in the porch, which ought to be better looked after.

Moor Hall, on the Reepham Road, is medieval although very much altered to turn it into a shooting box in later times. It has good flint walls (cracking in places), a fine gloomy staircase and a spacious Gothic downstairs W.C. Bees are apt to hive in a cavity over the front door.

Animal-lovers should not miss **Great Witchingham**, for here lives Philip Wayre with his Norfolk Wildlife Park and Ornamental Pheasant Trust. Here he and his family and staff keep and observe and train such things as pheasants threatened with extinction in their own lands, eagles, otters, badgers, foxes, deer, barbary sheep, coypu, and a Malayan sun bear which once chased, and flung to earth, a producer of the BBC. There are many other, animals besides, teas and light lunches are provided, and the Park is open all the year round.

Aylsham provision market is a charming place, with old buildings of brick with Dutch gables. It is said that wherries came to Aylsham, up the Bure (they certainly could not in these days), and if so that would account for the town's former prosperity. In the Middle Ages it was noted for worsted cloth and for linen. At Burgh-next-Aylsham, just down the river, is a most splendid watermill.

According to Domesday 'Elesham' was held by Guert (a Dane) in the reign of the Confessor, as sixteen ploughlands (a ploughland was land that could be ploughed by a team of eight oxen) and had woodland for 300 pigs (at about two acres per pig). At Guert's time there were twenty villeins, at the time of Domesday eleven. There were formerly eight-eight bordars, later sixty-five, then two serfs and at Domesday three, and there were two mills.

Guert may have been 'Gurth', Earl of East Anglia and younger brother of King Harold (who lived very near at Blickling: according to Domesday he held that manor). Gurth was killed at Hastings, and the manor of Aylsham bestowed on Ralph Guader, Earl of Norfolk. This man rebelled in 1075, and the king kept the manor.

Later it went to John of Gaunt, who may or may not have spent part of his time there, and who is supposed to have founded the church, in about 1380. The church is subtantially unaltered since Gaunt's day. The wonderful font is fairly undamaged, there is a copy of the 'Breeches Bible' (in this 1611 edition of the Geneva Bible is written, in Genesis III 7: 'they sewed fig leaves together and made themselves breeches'). Humphry Repton (1752–1818), famous landscape gardener, architect and partner of John Nash, is buried under his own epitaph, and roses are still grown on his grave.

> *Not like Egyptian tyrants consecrate*
> *Unmixed with others shall my dust remain.*
> *But mold'ring, blending, melting into earth*
> *Mine shall give form and colour to the Rose,*
> *And while its vivid blossoms cheer Mankind,*
> *Its perfumed odours shall ascend to Heaven.*

Fanny Burney's younger sister Charlotte lived in Aylsham, with her husband Clement Francis, surgeon and ex-secretary to Warren Hastings. Clement Francis read Fanny's first novel, *Evelina*, in India, fell in love with the authoress *in absentia*, and hastened home to introduce himself to Dr Burney at King's Lynn and woo his daughter. But, arriving there, he fell in love with Charlotte instead, married her, and set up as a practising doctor in Aylsham. Fanny stayed with them on 8th November 1792, just after Charlotte had had a son. There is a mural tablet to Dr Francis in the south transept of the church, by John Ivory of Norwich.

It is but a short way to **Blickling Hall**. One can scarcely see Blickling in less than a full afternoon. The house and garden, belonging to the National Trust, are open each afternoon except Mondays, Thursdays and Good Friday (but open Bank Holiday Mondays) from the end of March to the end of October. There is a picnic area, and refreshments are served throughout the season.

The first glimpse of Blickling is a great *coup d'œil*. The little tree-bordered lane from Aylsham is apparently leading you into one of those uninhabited deserts of barley and sugar beet of North Norfolk – about as far from civilization as you can get – when, without warning, Blickling appears: a church, an iron railing, behind it perfect lawns and – symmetrically flanked by two wings of out-buildings – the great begabled and bepinnacled hall of the reddest brick only spoiled, for me at least, by a quite incongruous white clock tower in the middle, looking like a howdah on an elephant's back. This wooden tower, erected early in the nineteenth century, sprang serious leaks in the second half of our own, but was restored by the National Trust for the pleasure of other folk who do not agree with my doubts.

This great façade, impressive though it be, gives no impression of the size of the house; for Blickling is long and deep and the front is narrow. This shape was imposed upon the Jacobean building by the moat of its medieval predecessor.

As we saw while discussing Aylsham, Blickling Manor belonged to King Harold – the last of the true English kings and a true East Anglian. William the Conqueror bestowed it on a chaplain whom he created Bishop of Thetford, and thus it became a home of the bishops of East Anglia. Herbert de Losinga, when he moved the See to Norwich, frequently resorted to Blickling. Bishop Everard, de Losinga's successor, bestowed the southern half of the manor to a soldier, John FitzRobert. It passed to Sir Nicholas Dagworth who was Captain of Aquitaine under Richard II and he built a hall which was probably on the site of the present mansion. Sir Thomas Erpingham, whom Shakespeare immortalized if Sir Thomas didn't do it for himself, and whom we have met with his great gate and tomb in Norwich, had the house at the beginning of the fifteenth century, and he sold the place to Sir John Fastolf, whom we noticed while discussing Caister (p. 150). Geoffrey Boleyn, whom as we have seen lived at Sall, went to London rather as Dick Whittington did and became Lord Mayor (helped, it is believed, by Sir John Fastolf whose favourite he was) and bought the house from Sir John. Three generations of Boleyns lived there until after Anne's barbarous execution by Henry VIII; the house then passed to the Clere family of Ormesby by marriage, and was then sold to Sir Henry Hobart about 1616.

Sir Henry was Lord Chief Justice, and baroneted by James I when that monarch founded his new order of baronets. Sir Henry's portrait, painted by Daniel Mytens, hangs over the fireplace in the State Bedroom; it shows a man of apparently great strength of character, thoughtful and not unkindly, with slender sensitive hands: the portrait either flatters the man or he was a fine fellow. He died in 1625, but not before he had begun the building of the present Blickling Hall. His son Sir John, the 2nd baronet, finished the building, but died with no heir, and so the place went to a grandson of the 1st Baronet, another John, who was an eager parliamentarian in Cromwell's Upper House but found that his conscience could encompass his turning an equally eager royalist at the Restoration. He even entertained Charles II and Queen Catherine at Blickling in 1671. Sir Henry, his son, was the man slain in a duel on Cawston Common. Sir Henry's son, John, was given the Earldom of Buckinghamshire by George II: it is said not for his own talents, but for those of his attractive sister, Henrietta Howard and later Countess of Suffolk. This lady was a noted wit and intellectual, well known to Pope and Swift, and generally thought to have been the king's mistress.

The 2nd Earl of Buckinghamshire, John, was described by Horace Walpole as: 'The Clearcake. Fat, Fair, sweet, and seen through in a moment.' Hardly the man, one would have thought, to have been sent Ambassador to Catherine of Russia, but sent he was. He brought back the greatest treasure of Blickling from this appointment: the splendid tapestry (described below) that hangs in the Peter the Great Room and which was presented to him by the Empress. The Hobarts had a habit of marrying well, and the 2nd Earl married a lady who died at the age of twenty-nine leaving him £50,000.

His lordship died twenty-four years later (of the gout), leaving a bevy of four daughters. The first one ran away from her husband, and so the second inherited Blickling. She had no issue, so the property went to her great-nephew who happened to be the 8th Marquis of Lothian. This was 1850. There is an effigy of the 8th Marquis by G. F. Watts in Blickling Church, which is well worth going to see for lovers of Victorian sculpture. Lady Lothian lived on until 1901, long after her husband's death. The family moved away from Blickling until Philip Kerr, the 11th Marquis, returned to it, in the intervals of his being such things as the Ambassador to the United States (which he was when he died in 1940). There is a most charming hidden garden made by him, which few visitors find, with a summerhouse, where he used to sit at peace with his Foreign Office dispatches, or, one likes to think, occasionally without them.

Lord Lothian left the Hall to the National Trust, who not only maintain it for the delectation of the public but also use it to house their Textile Conservation Workshop, repairing material from their properties all over the region. The workshop can usually be visited between 2 pm and 4 pm, Tuesday and Wednesday in the season.

As for the architecture of the house, careful detective work has shown that it was probably designed by Robert Lyminge, who was largely responsible for designing Lord Salisbury's Hatfield House. Much of the detail of the two houses is very similar. Unlike Hatfield, Blickling lacks a great hall, which was a feature of most big houses put up in its time; but a splendid staircase occupies the position that a Great Hall would normally have occupied. The present staircase is not all Lyminge's work, but probably added to in the eighteenth century by Thomas Ivory, the Norwich architect who designed the Norwich Assembly Rooms and many other buildings.

One enters the rooms that are open to the public by the south-east turret, which gives way into the **south drawing room**.

This was once the 'Eating Room', and, one imagines, simpler and more down-to-earth. It was redecorated by the 2nd Earl about 1765, but he left the amazing ceiling with its pendants hanging down like fruity stalactites. The pictures are mostly portraits of members of the family, or of other great Norfolk families: there is one of Sir Robert Walpole, 1st Earl of Orford (1676–1745); another, Henrietta Howard, Countess of Suffolk, whose father was the man killed in a duel on Cawston Common. Henrietta was the lady who is supposed to have been the mistress of George II, and the portrait indicates that she was indeed a lady of intellect and character, as all who described her averred. The lady and her daughter in another picture are thought to be of Mary Anne, 2nd Countess of Buckinghamshire, the heiress who brought £50,000 into Blickling and died so young. The picture is attributed to Francis Coates.

From here one passes into the **ante-room**, which has a most interesting ceiling of moulded plasterwork. Constantly, at Blickling, one is forced to admire the work of the plasterer, whose art was at its zenith when most of the house was decorated or redecorated, and whose art looks very much, in these days, like dying out. The **grand staircase** must be looked at, particularly the newel figures. The two bearded men on the bottom flight among the newel figures are said to be originals – the rest were added by the 2nd Earl of Buckinghamshire: the Ambassador to Russia. He also installed the wooden carvings of Anne Boleyn and her daughter, Elizabeth I. Poor Anne is dressed in eighteenth-century clothes, and has the information written underneath her that she was born here. It is the fashion now to say that Anne Boleyn was not born at Blickling, but I cannot think where else she is likely to have been born, since her mother and father certainly lived there. Not in the present house, of course, but on its present site. The pictures again give us an insight into the former occupants of the great house: there is poor Sir Henry who was killed in a duel, by Kneller; there is Sir James Hobart, whose portrait and whose altar-tomb we saw in Loddon Church – as the Blickling portrait shows him in the seventeenth-century clothing and he was a fifteenth-century man one must suppose that the Loddon portrait is more likely to be a true resemblance. Then there are two really superb portraits: one of Elizabeth I in full finery, and one of Sir Philip Sidney, looking gallant and grand.

Back through the ante-room we come into the **long gallery**, which is the *pièce de résistance* of the house. It runs the whole length of the east front from the ante-room onwards, and is 120 feet long. Alas, the whole west wall was covered, in Victorian times, with bookcases surmounted by weird painted patterns: a Ruskinesque delving into some age of chivalry which certainly never existed; but the ceiling – the ceiling! – must be one of the grandest stretches of moulded plasterwork in the world! I can never contemplate it without thinking with awe of the neck-breaking labour of putting it all up there. So beautiful was it (it was made early seventeenth century) that even those dreadful Victorians kept their hands and hammers off it, although it accords so ill with their pseudo-medieval caperings of the west wall that the juxtaposition looks absurd. On the Victorian shelves are several thousand venerable and valuable books, some Anglo-Saxon. There is the state chair sat on by James II in Dublin, and brought back as a relic by the 2nd Earl of Buckinghamshire after he had been Lord Lieutenant of Ireland, which he was after his mission to Catherine the Great. Jacob, the smooth man, and Esau, the hairy man and mighty hunter before the Lord, meet on a seventeenth-century Brussels tapestry over the fireplace (the latter is a modern fireplace put there to replace the mock Gothic monster that the Victorians put up in place of the earlier marble fireplace).

Turning left along the north end of the house brings us into the **Peter the Great Room**, with its splendid and spirited tapestry of the Tsar prancing along on his horse, under his eagle, with the slaughter and carnage of Poltawa going on well in the background. There is a big Gainsborough each side of the beautiful marble fireplace, one of the 2nd Earl, and the other of his second wife, Caroline Conolly, whom the earl married but eight months after the death of his first, who left him so much money. There is some notable eighteenth-century furniture.

Straight through is the **state bedroom**, with the noble and most striking portrait of the founder of present-day Blickling Hall: Sir Henry Hobart, painted by Daniel Mytens.

The **gardens** are beautiful, but certainly there is not the space to describe them fully here. I would urge the visitor not to miss the Orangery (probably by William Ivory – son of Thomas) with its statue of Hercules which was brought from the Pastons' seat, Oxnead Hall, by the 2nd Earl, likewise the fountain just east of the house which also came from Oxnead. There is also a lovely clump of oriental plane trees, looking strange and exotic north-east of the house, there are the marvellous crossing and radiating rides and avenues – each planted with a different species of tree (in two places you can stand at the intersection of eight roads), the Temple, which cuts off the view down the magnificent vista which looks from the house east-south-east: a vista bordered most beautifully by azaleas and rhododendrons. North-west of the Hall is a pyramidal mausoleum, designed by Joseph Bonomi, in which the remains of the 2nd Earl lie with his two wives in marble sarcophagi. The loveliest thing in the grounds is the large lake, which winds away out of sight so that one can imagine it much bigger than it is, with great beech trees growing on the high ground beyond it.

Blickling is the halfway mark on a recreational route for walkers and cyclists between Stalham and Cromer. It is known as the Weavers' Way in commemoration of the historic importance of the weaving industry in Norfolk. There are several car parks along the trail, including the Blickling Hall one, and longer or shorter stretches can be walked at will. A section rich in shrubs and wild flowers was once the track of the Midland & Great Northern Railway, familiarly known as the Muddle & Go Nowhere.

Close to the route skirting Thwaite Common is **Erpingham**, a feudal-looking small village with a mighty church tower built by Sir Thomas of Shakespeare's *Henry V* fame. There is a very good military brass inside the church, but it is to Sir John, Sir Thomas's father, who died in 1370.

Sir Thomas Erpingham was a knight whose story might appeal to anybody. He went to France to join the exiled Bolingbroke – after the latter's father John of Gaunt had died – came back to land at Ravenspur ('the baked shore at Ranspurg' – it was somewhere near Spurn Head) and helped to wrest the crown from the head of the effete Richard II. Later he fought at the battle to such effect that Henry said to him (according to Shakespeare): 'God-a-mercy, old heart, thou speakest cheerfully.' Besides the tower of Erpingham Church he built the famous Erpingham Gate at Norwich Cathedral.

Felbrigg Hall is another National Trust gem, for 300 years the home of the Windham family and its successors. The seventeenth-century exterior remains unaltered, and the spacious park has fine trees and lakeside walks. House and grounds are open in the afternoons, except Tuesday and Friday, from April to late October.

And so we come to the sea again, at **Cromer**, a medium-sized compact, predominantly railway-age seaside resort surrounding an ancient fishing village which sits within it like a pearl within an oyster. It has a simply grand Perpendicular church with one of the highest towers in Norfolk (160 feet) which served as the lighthouse before the real one was built. The church is a great building from the outside, but over-restored within: it had fallen into complete decay in the eighteenth century, so this was inevitable. There is some corking modern and recent glass: the east window of the south aisle is after Burne-Jones.

The little streets that radiate out from the church square are pretty if hellish for the motorist. The sea-front is most impressive, being backed by high, hotel-crowned cliffs, surmountable by stone steps, and very reminiscent of the Tower of Babel.

Cromer's glory is her record of lifeboat gallantry, and her hero the late Henry Blogg. About the latter a book has been written, he has been painted by an RA, and there are memorials to him both inside and outside the church. He was the most decorated of any lifeboatman in the British Isles, being awarded the 'Lifeboatman's Victoria Cross' (the RNLI's Gold Medal) no less than three times, the George Cross once, and the British Empire Medal. Most of the rescues he carried out were away on the Haisboro' Sands, and the tales of his daring as a coxswain are hair-raising. On one occasion – the wreck of the sailing barge *Sepoy* – he drove the lifeboat – in a breaking surf – right over the barge's deck on an enormous wave – thus giving the barge's crew time to jump from the rigging in which they were clinging to safety onto the lifeboat's deck. He would drive the lifeboat right into the crashing surf on the Haisboro', or on the 'Main' (mainland) until his crew wondered if they were afloat or already on the bottom. He carried this on right up to his death in 1954, thus demonstrating that a tough old 'un is as good as a tough young 'un. His nephew, Henry Davies, 'Shrimp' to his friends, became coxswain, and his family still carries on the great tradition.

Except for the paid full-time mechanic, all the lifeboatmen are part-time volunteers (Spurn Head has the only full-time lifeboat crew on the East Coast): during most of their lives they are fishermen, and at Cromer the fish they catch are chiefly crabs.

Cromer crabs are famous among all crab-lovers, and are undisputedly the best in England (with them I would include Sheringham ones, which are just the same). The little boats that catch them are worth examining – indeed cadging a trip in – for they are unique.

The Sheringham and Cromer crab boat is a very small, double-ended, clinker-built boat, with a straight keel, great beam, and very full bilges. She is lightly constructed ('like a basket') with numerous but very light frames. Her lines undoubtedly descend from those of Shetland boats which used to come down after the herring. So suitable is she for beach work that her lines have been sent to such far places as West Africa and the Falkland Islands to be copied by native fishermen.

The technique of crab fishing is to shoot long lines – called 'shanks' – of baited pots made of tarred string whipped round iron frames out on the rocky ground off-shore, pick them up next day, remove the crabs, and re-bait. The fishermen haul the shanks by

175

hand using the technique known as 'overrunning' – or letting the boat drive down over the shank carried by the swift tide. This calls for great skill and strength, and it is quite true that nobody can do it unless they are used to it. The line-hauler must haul like a madman to keep up with the pace of the tide; and the man who removes the crabs, and the baiter, must work like lightning otherwise the pot is snatched out of their grasp by the relentless progress of the boat. The pots, having been shot one day, *must* be looked at the next – even if a gale is raging. Collectively they are worth hundreds of pounds, and cannot be left out on the bed of the ocean at risk. Whatever the weather, practically, the men go to sea off their harbourless beach, and to watch them do it – or come running in afterwards – in a strong onshore wind, is breathtaking. Returning they run straight for the beach, the helmsman gives the boat a sheer just before she strikes, the crew fling their weights to the inshore side of the boat just in time – thus throwing her over and allowing the waves to bash (it is hoped) harmlessly up against her bottom. Meanwhile men ashore get a hook on from the tractor and drag the boat out of harm's way. Naturally there are accidents. 'Shrimp' Davies lost two brothers when their boat overturned shortly before the last war.

For people seeking a quiet seaside holiday of the traditional kind, I cannot think of a better place than Cromer – unless it be Sheringham. They both have the pleasantest atmosphere, impressive cliffs, good beaches, modest amusements such as repertory theatre and concerts, good friendly Norfolk inhabitants, and crab salads.

Sheringham, four miles west of Cromer, is much like it. It too has a fossilized flint-built fishing village inside the growing brick shell of the railway-age seaside resort, it too has a lifeboat and vigorous crabbing community. Its most celebrated railway today is the preserved 'Poppy Line' to Weybourne, with trains hauled by steam engines every Sunday and on many advertised days during the summer season. There is a collection of historic locomotives and rolling stock, and a model railway display.

It is said that Sheringham fishermen incline to Salvationism while those of Cromer favour – shall we say – more secular pursuits. Most celebrated of this century's mariners was 'Downtide' West, who as well as going to sea ran a fish restaurant in the High Street and a crab potting factory behind it. His father was given the title 'Downtide' after he had, as a little boy, gone long-lining with *his* father. One of the hooks of a line caught in the father's hand, and he shouted to the boy at the oars: 'Turn her uptide!' The boy turned the boat downtide instead, thus dragging the hook deeper into his father's hand and earning himself his hereditary title. There are so many Wests among Sheringham fishermen that everyone has to have a nickname for identification.

The Sheringham and Cromer crabbers were for long sworn enemies; and their meetings at such places as Aldborough horse fair always led to a fight – nor were they above occasionally cutting each other's shank ropes at sea. The Cromer men contemptuously used to refer to the Sheringhamers as 'Shaddocks'. But in 1928 a Sheringham boat (out whelking) was caught in a gale, the Cromer lifeboat went out to her (for Sheringham at that time did not possess a motor lifeboat) and just as she got alongside a great wave came and 'pitchpoled' the Sheringham boat – flinging her right over – stern over bows. Jack Davies, from the Cromer lifeboat, jumped overboard and got a line round two of the three Sheringhamers and these were saved, since when the two communities have (generally) been friends.

Sheringham, too, has fine cliffs (many fossils of large animals have been dug out of Sheringham and Cromer cliffs), and behind the cliffs is high ground which for Norfolk is extremely well wooded. Indeed the country there is very un-East-Anglia-like, more like the North Downs of Kent. The road that goes to Holt passes through lovely country: a picnicker's paradise. The un-East Anglian character of this ridge of hills is explained by the fact that it is not East Anglian. It is a series of moraines left by the glaciers which advanced across what is now the North Sea from the north. It contains rocks from as far away as Scandinavia, although in fact most of its substance derives from what has now become north-east England and the bed of the North Sea. Near Holt are masses of chalk: not laid down where it still is as in other parts of England, but dragged there by the bellies of great glaciers. It is this moraine which gives the Cromer Cliffs their great variety of rock and structure. The ridge is being attacked savagely by the sea, and the cliffs are crumbling away perhaps faster than any other stretch of the English coast, with the possible exception of Holderness. It is the destruction of these cliffs that releases the great masses of shingle which – dragged south by the scour of the tide – collect to form the shingle banks such as Orford Ness. Sheringham Park has a Humphry-Repton-designed landscape garden with fine rhododendrons.

Holt is a lovely little town. It was one of the first places to apply the technique first developed along Norwich's Magdalen Street of persuading householders to beautify their frontages according to a unified colour scheme, at the same time removing the uglier of the town furniture and replacing it with better designed. The result is a little town of clean gay colours, which blend well together and with a wall here and there that has been left grey flint. Holt is well known for Gresham's School, founded by Sir John Gresham in 1555 when he was Lord Mayor of London, and administered by the Fishmongers' Company. It is now a public school and one of the most progressive and enlightened in the country.

Castle-lovers might make the journey to **Baconsthorpe Castle**, three miles south-east of Holt. The road goes by a superb watermill, and then along a rather muddy but quite reasonably surfaced farm lane to a small car park by one of the finest aspects of the ruins, with a bridge leading on across a tranquil moat. Sir Henry Heydon built his fortified manor house in 1486. Two great gatehouses remain, with curtain walls, some remnants of a dwelling hall of the seventeenth century, and an eighteenth-century Gothic mansion consisting largely of stone taken from the original castle. The site is open daily.

Melton Constable has another of the great halls of North Norfolk, built (financially) on sheep and wool. The Astley family enclosed the park by charter in 1290; there are a lake, deer, and a mansion of 1670 long described by conservationists as 'the finest empty country house in England'. After years of neglect, apart from a brief spell as the setting for the film *The Go-Between*, it was put up for sale by its former owner in 1986. The church is full of Astleys. It was an Astley who prayed before the battle of Edgehill: 'Lord Thou Knowest how busy I must be this day – if I forget Thee do not Thou forget me!'

Farther south is **North Elmham**, where there should be far more to see, considering that here was probably the East Anglian Cathedral. In pre-Danish days North Elmham became a bishopric, St Edmund may have been crowned king there, the Danes are supposed to have laid the place waste in 866, the see was re-established in 955 but after this was removed to Thetford, and thence de Losinga took it to Norwich, where it still is. There is a great earthwork north of the present church, and it is evident that this was a heavily fortified place. The existing earthworks are supposed to have been built in the fourteenth century by Bishop Despencer. The cathedral has recently been excavated to a depth of about eight feet and the foundations can be seen.

South again – **East Dereham** where George Borrow was born at Dumpling Green, just outside. Here are the first words of *Lavengro*:

> On the evening of July, in the year 18——, at East D——, a beautiful little town in a certain district of East Anglia, I first saw the light.
> I love to think on thee, pretty, quiet D——, thou pattern of an English market town, with thy clean but narrow streets branching out from thy modest market place, with thine old-fashioned houses, with here and there a roof of venerable thatch . . . Pretty quiet D—— with thy venerable church, in which moulder the mortal remains of England's sweetest and most pious bard.

Except for the motor cars Borrow would find it much the same today.

Borrow mentions: 'A mouldering edifice, inclosing a spring of sanatory waters'. This is Withburga's Well, in the churchyard.

Withburga was a daughter of King Anna (see Blythburgh, p. 43) – a monarch who had several sainted daughters, and who founded a convent at East Dereham. She was buried there, miracles were wrought at her shrine and the presence of her body would have assured great prosperity to Dereham. But alas in AD 984 the Abbot of Ely came, with his wily monks, on a visit to Dereham, managed to get the burghers of the town drunk (perhaps no difficult matter?) and made away with the body of the saint. The men of Dereham

179

pursued the monks and would have caught them, had the monks not reached the sanctuary of the waters of the Fens near Brandon, boarded a boat, and got away across the flood. The remains of Withburga were buried at Ely beside the remains of her sainted sister Aethelthryth, or Etheldreda, the founder of Ely monastery and, in her life, wife of the King of Northumbria. A spring burst out from the site of Withburga's desecrated grave.

The mortal remains of 'England's sweetest and most pious bard' are those of William Cowper, who died at East Dereham and is buried in the church. There is an unfortunate window to him, and a monument by Flaxman. The Congregational Chapel is built on the site of the house in which he died, and wood from the latter is incorporated in it. The story of Cowper's death at East Dereham is melancholy in the extreme, and Mary Unwin, the widow whom he would have married and who cared for him until she herself broke down, is buried at East Dereham too.

Dereham Church is enclosed nicely by the churchyard and has great mellowness and peace. There is a chest in the church which is supposed to have belonged to the Howards, Dukes of Norfolk. It resembles somewhat the tomb of Thomas, 3rd Duke and father of the poet, Surrey, but it is Flemish, and sixteenth century.

Most of Dereham was burned down in post-Tudor times, but the cottages near the church with pargetting, or moulded plaster-work, are early sixteenth century, and called 'Bonner's Cottages' because here Bishop Bonner lived when he was still a curate. He afterwards made a great reputation by sending so many Protestants to the burning pyres (see p. 377). The cottages now house a local archaeological museum. Two miles north of the town, in the village of Gressenhall, is the much larger Norfolk Rural Life Museum.

On his way Norwichwards the traveller might seek out **Elsing** to see, in the church, Sir Hugh Hastings' marvellous brass memorial, one of the most lavish and elaborate brasses in East Anglia. The little figures on either side of Sir Hugh depict his more aristocratic relations, including Edward III, Warwick, Lancaster, Pembroke, Stafford. Sir Hugh died in 1347. Elsing Hall is 1460–70, much restored, but still a very fine moated manor house with oriel windows in its great hall.

North Tuddenham has a lonely church, which has very good fifteenth-century glass in many of the windows. There are saints on the remnant of the screen – including St Geron, whose likeness is in only one other church in the country: Suffield, in Suffolk. Geron was murdered by the Danes while proselytizing in the Low Countries.

One might alternate between the rivers Tud and Yare, and certainly have a look at **Bawburgh**, which is a pretty little village indeed and which has everything a village should have including a patron saint. Farm workers will wish to strike north to **Costessey Woods** to find St Walstan's Well. For St Walstan is the patron saint of their profession. He is supposed to have been a prince among the Anglians, but he threw off his princely robes to become a farm worker. He labourered all his life at Taverham – just north across the Wissey – and was noted for his saintliness. In the year 1016, while he was mowing a hayfield, an angel appeared to him and announced to him the hour of his death. He went on quietly mowing until he died, and his body was placed on a bier drawn by his own yoke of oxen. The oxen walked down to the Wissey, crossed that river by walking on the water (their hoof marks could still be seen on the surface of the water up until the Reformation), walked into Costessey Woods and there rested, and where they rested up sprang this well of water. For centuries this was a place of pilgrimage for farm workers, and there have been suggestions quite recently of cleaning the place up and repairing the shrine.

If the traveller wishes to see what the saint looked like, let him go to **Barnham Broom** church, for there is a portrait of St Walstan on the fine screen.

CHAPTER 10

Norwich to Wymondham

Leaving Norwich on the New Buckenham Road one passes (or does not pass?) the **Swainsthorpe** Dun Cow, which is late seventeenth century and mellow brick. In a land stacked full of ancient inns I only mention this comparatively new one because it is particularly attractive. **Mulbarton** is one of the many villages that have 'the biggest village green in Norfolk', and in the church is a curious memorial put up by a former rector, Daniel Scargill, to his dead wife. It is in the form of a copper book which can be opened to reveal some seventeenth-century verse which, although perhaps stilted and artificial after the manner of the time, expresses very touchingly the bereavement and pious hope of the widower. Scargill was expelled from Cambridge for losing his faith, but he managed to find it again and became a parson (see map opposite).

Forncett St Peter has a church with a tower that is Anglo-Saxon right up to the top, with circular windows. Most of our Anglo-Saxon towers have had Norman or later tops added to them. There is a long and involved story about a John of Forncett who did – or did not, according to which theory you care to accept – compose *Sumer is i-cumen in* while he was a monk at Reading Abbey, early in the thirteenth century.

South Norfolk differs from the north of the county in that it is heavier land (like the heavy old Suffolk boulder clay) and therefore is not suitable for sheep farming, as is the north. This meant that the Enclosures were not so complete here, and many small farmers and owner-farmers survive and there are few great estates. Farming in the north to this day is mainly conducted on huge farms – getting huger and huger as amalgamation follows amalgamation. Here in the south the small yeoman still holds his own, giving a different

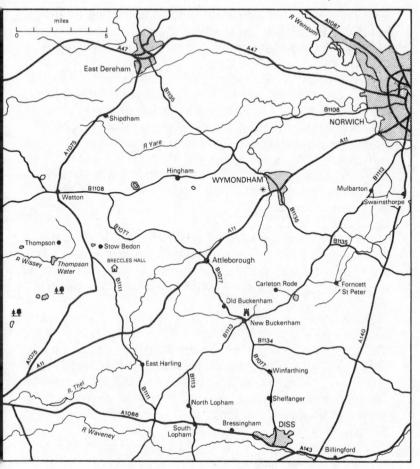

character to the landscape, and a feeling of much more independence to the people. Forelock-pulling is nothing like so common in the south as it is in the north.

I must mention the Farrier's Arms at **Carleton Rode**, simply because it is such an excellent little pub (it is called 'The Crow' by its habitués), has such a pleasant landlord and landlady, and such good and truly rural company.

New Buckenham may have been new in 1145, when the second

183

William d'Albini built a castle there, replacing the one he already had at Old Buckenham. At least, the situation is complicated; for 'New Buckenham Castle' is really within the parish boundary of Old Buckenham, so is New Buckenham cemetery, and the parson of New Buckenham is peculiar in that he sleeps with his head in one parish and his feet in the other. The town of New Buckenham grew up around the new castle, and it was actually laid out like any 'overswill' town in East Anglia today: the first recorded example of English town planning – fifteenth century in fact. The result is a very civilized village, and it does not rush headlong into the space age – the History School of the University of East Anglia has carried out research in the parish and, amongst other discoveries, has found 'an attitude to affairs which can only be described as eighteenth century'.

Of the castle only a moated mound remains, and the foundations of what is said to be the first circular keep in England. There are reasons for thinking that the Norman castle may have been antedated by a Roman one, or even an earlier. The main fabric was dismantled during the Civil War.

There is a seventeenth-century Market House in New Buckenham, its upper storey set high on stilts above the traders' floor, with a whipping-post inside and carved boards out. And John Eldred was born in New Buckenham. He went to Baghdad and came away from that place with 4,000 camels loaded with merchandise from the fabulous east, which he shipped home from Tripoli. The jaunt made him rich for life and he built 'Nutmeg Hall' at Saxham, in Suffolk.

In complete contrast to New is **Old Buckenham**, where nobody ever did any town planning. The village is a straggle of old houses and cottages, strung out around a rough old village green which is so large that you can hardly see across it and which makes it a long walk to visit your 'neighbour' over the road. As with many large villages Old Buckenham is divided into hamlets; and these are some of their names: Loss Wroo (Middle English for 'Lynx Corner'), Hog's Snout, Puddledock, Chattergate, Stacksford, Cake Street and Hungry Hill. Hungry Hill by the way is as flat as a pancake. At Hungry Hill is a ford through a tiny river – the grandmother of the Thet – where the ultra-protestant sect of

Sandemanians used to immerse each other totally, bestowing such names as Uzziah, Absalom and Karenhappuch, some of which still survive. Looking at the stream nowadays it is difficult to see how any but the most minute Sandemanian could be accommodated in it, but most East Anglian streams have shrunk during the last half century.

Old Buckenham church is thatched, and has a fine Norman north door with a 'consecration stone' beside it, carved with the crowned monogram of the Blessed Virgin. (There is one like it two piers from the west in the north aisle of Wymondham, but stuck in back to front.) The church has a polygonal tower and a well-kept churchyard with fine roses.

There is little to see of the first William d'Albini's castle except a mound and a scrap of ruin near Abbey Farm – all that remains of the Augustinian priory which was built from fragments of the old castle. The shape of the foundations of the latter has led people to believe that the Normans built on a Roman site. The d'Albini to whom the Conqueror granted the manor is said to have come over from France as the monarch's butler.

Old Buckenham Hall has a famous cricket pitch: the turf for it was brought by Lionel Robinson all the way from Australia, and Jack Hobbs used to say that it was his favourite ground. McLaren, the great cricketer, lived nearby at Warren Cottage.

We might strike south to **Winfarthing**, where there used to be a sword with two attributes: it could find lost horses; and if a wife burned a candle before it every Sunday of the year she would get rid of her husband. Just down the road, **Shelfanger** has an even stranger name. Winfarthing was shown in Domesday Book as **Wineferthinc**, meaning Wina's quarter part, or fourth part; and according to Eilert Ekwall, that great expert on English place names, Shelfanger comes from the Old English *scylf* (a hill) and *hangra* (a slope): though since there's little sign of a hill here, the first syllable may mean a plateau.

Diss is a splendid little town, so proud of itself that it managed to keep the railway station a good mile away from the centre, where it now stands by a busy, wide road steering motor traffic away also. Partly Tudor, Diss is built around a six-acre mere. The name Diss comes from Anglo-Saxon *dice*, meaning standing water, so the mere must be very old in spite of looking strangely artificial. (In East Anglia, as on Romney Marsh in Kent, a ditch is still commonly called a 'dick'.) There are many fine pubs in the town, notably the Greyhound and the Saracen's Head, from whose bar window one looks prophetically out across the churchyard.

John Skelton from Diss wrote his first verses on the death of Edward IV, became tutor to the Prince of Wales (later Henry VIII), and after taking holy orders was given the living of Diss. John Wilbye, the great madrigalist, was born here in 1574, though we associate him more with his long service at Hengrave Hall near Bury St Edmunds in Suffolk (see p. 337).

In the museum of Falsterbo in Sweden is an early seventeenth-century map of the Baltic countries and the North Atlantic, on which the British Isles are shown as a shapeless blob with three towns marked on it: one is Rochester, another Chatham, and the third is Diss.

Billingford has a splendid restored windmill with a five-storey red brick tower, white sails and fantail, open all year round: the keys are obtainable from the neighbouring Horseshoes inn.

Westward, **Bressingham** is of the very first interest to lovers of hardy perennials and steam engines. Gardens and nurseries have been carved out of a large parkland by the Bloom family, major producers of hardy perennials and Alpine plants – 5,000 species, all labelled and clear to see. Then there is the fine collection of old steam engines, stationary and locomotive, including the huge *Oliver Cromwell*, most appropriate in this East Anglian setting. On Sunday and Thursday afternoons in summer one can ride on a footplate, travel round the grounds on a number of narrow gauge railways, visit the museum of traction and other engines, enjoy a steam roundabout, or simply contemplate the lovely flowerbeds.

Farther west are the **Lophams**, **North** and **South**.

To see South Lopham church tower for the first time is to be carried back with something of a shock to the austere, military, and somehow terribly alien world of the Normans. It is very early twelfth century, logically proportioned, massive, powerful, and excellently preserved. It is said to have been put up by William Bigod. It is hard to believe that more than eight centuries have passed over it. More have passed over the little circular window in the nave west of the north door, for this is Anglo-Saxon. The chancel is Decorated, and the whole church unusual, interesting and extremely beautiful.

The weaving industry survived at North Lopham right into this century. At the Bridewell Museum, Norwich, is to be seen a Jacquard loom from Lopham of staggering complexity. The 'Jacquard', of course, was invented by a man of that name in Lyons in the early nineteen-hundreds to weave figured fabrics.

Just south of the Lophams are the headwaters of both the Little Ouse and the Waveney. Would that some mad millionaire would join these two headwaters (they are separated by the breadth of the road), lock the streams farther down, and thus join by water the important Broads system and the 2,000 miles of the waterways of England.

North of the Lophams stands **East Harling** which has a very fine church indeed, with a spire – which is unusual for Norfolk where spireless towers abound (it is a short lead spire similar in shape to St Peter Mancroft's, Norwich). There are two important fifteenth-century monuments: one to Sir Robert Harling and one to Sir Thomas Lovell. There is brilliant glass in the west window – put there by Sir Robert Wingfield and Sir William Chamberlain who can be seen at the foot of the window kneeling comfortably on cushions. These two knights were the husbands, one after the other, of Anne Harling, whose tomb (with Sir William) is in the church, much carved with shields and heraldry. The Harling Chapel was built by Anne's father, Sir Robert, who soldiered with Henry V and was thus probably one of the 'happy few' at Agincourt. But the way to see this church, and get the greatest impact from it, is to go down to the River Thet, nearby, climb down from the road, and look back through the trees.

We are on the eastern edge of the Brecklands now – about which more later. We can work our way northwards on the border of this sandy, empty quarter, to see **Stow Bedon** in the churchyard of which lies buried a man who died very recently. Until age seventy this man was a miller, until age 100 a very hard-working farmer, and at age 104 he died.

Near **Thompson** is Thompson Water, one of the Breckland meres and a fine coarse fishing ground – a forest-encircled lake. Thompson has a beautiful little thatched pub, set among woods. Most of this country belongs to Lord Walsingham, but much has been taken over by the army for use as a 'battle area'. Several villages have been evacuated and are in ruins, and you can only officially visit them if you are being buried there, and can prove that, in life, you were a local man. To visit them, in life, and unofficially, is frightfully melancholy, but beware of live mortar bombs (both lying on the ground and flying through the air), charging tanks, and parachutists falling from the skies.

Watton has a long and attractive village street. Wayland or Wailing Wood is nearby, in which the wicked uncle, of nearby Griston Hall, had the Babes in the Wood dumped. Their wails can still be heard at midnight by the faithful, and their grave can still be seen in the wood.

Shipdham church has the finest Tudor wooden lectern in the world and must be visited for that alone. There are said to be ancient books up over the porch.

South-east would bring us to **Hingham**, which is a very lovely large village around a spacious market square. The place is somehow rather lost and lonely, but full of fine Georgian and Queen Anne houses. Abraham Lincoln's ancestor, Samuel Lincoln, was a weaver at Hingham, and was baptized in the church in 1622. With many other Nonconformist Hingham weavers he fled across the Atlantic for freedom of conscience, and was followed by the parson, Robert Peck, who first destroyed the altar rail in Hingham church because he thought it was idolatrous.

There is a bust of Abraham Lincoln in the church, presented by Hingham Mass., and a mounting block in Hingham Mass., we are told, presented by Hingham, Norfolk. This is said to have an inscription on it which says that it 'was known to the Forefathers before the Migration'.

The church is Decorated, and fine, with soaring tower arch and arcades. It contains an enormous redstone monument to Lord Morley, Baron of Rye and Marshal of Ireland, who died in 1434, said to be one of the grandest monuments in England. It may have been designed by the same man who designed Erpingham Gate, in Norwich.

Attleborough is a small town notable for cider and turkeys. The former is made at Messrs Gaymers' works, though considerable contraction took place early in 1986. Until very recently there was a great annual turkey fair, at which one would see thousands of these birds and practically be deafened by their gobbling. They were carried in open trucks under wide-meshed nets, so that their heads stuck up through the latter and they surveyed the passing countryside in a most disconcerting manner.

In Defoe's day they travelled differently. Defoe was told by a man at Stratford St Mary, in Suffolk, that every year some 300 droves of Norfolk turkeys crossed the Stour with some 500 birds per drove, and that many more crossed at Clare and Sudbury. The birds started walking in August to get to London market in time for Christmas dinner, but they were fed and fattened on stubble fields all the way (one presumes with a small payment being made to the farmers). The story goes that these birds were made to walk over hot pitch occasionally, so as to coat the soles of their feet with this substance and thus harden them for the long walk. But change was creeping in in Defoe's day, and already birds were being carried Londonwards in wagons. The light land stretching from Attleborough to the Brecklands was turkey country in Defoe's day: it still is, although now turkeys and chickens are kept by the most modern methods. Tens of thousands of white ducks, too, may be seen crowded into vast concentration camps.

The great spectacle of Attleborough, which is otherwise not a very distinguished little place, is its church with a great screen and rood loft, the grandest and most complete rood loft in England, stretching as it does right across both nave and aisles. There are large and interesting wall paintings over the screen. The church is strangely cut off, because the Norman tower was once in the middle of a much larger building, and is now in the east end of what remains. The old choir, which was east of the Norman tower, belonged to the College of the Holy Cross, founded by Sir Robert Mortimer in the late fourteenth century and pulled down at the Dissolution.

Breccles Hall, west of Attleborough, is Tudor, with streams and water gardens.

If the stranger should ask me where he should go to see a Norfolk country town at its best, I should be tempted to say **Wymondham**.

189

Wymondham, pronounced 'Windam' by rich and poor alike, has so many fine houses in it that to mention them all would take many pages. There is the Guild Chapel dedicated to St Thomas à Becket, shortly after his murder, and rebuilt in the fourteenth century. Two monks were installed here to pray for the soul of the Earl of Arundel. It is now the County Library. Next door is the Green Dragon, famous with visiting Americans and defaced by a hideous petrol pump (I like the Cock much farther down on the road to Hingham), also a Market Cross, of 1617, and there is the **Abbey** – one of the great buildings of Norfolk and of England.

A Benedictine priory was founded at Wymondham by the William d'Albini who built the castle at Old Buckenham – the king's ex-butler. In 1834 lead coffins were excavated from close by the High Altar containing the remains of the founder's daughter-in-law, Maud, and her prematurely born baby. D'Albini intended that the church should serve both gown and town, but for some reason monks and townspeople could never agree very well, anywhere; and the history of this church was one long story of childish quarrelling. In 1249 the Pope, no less, had to be called upon to arbitrate, and he awarded the nave, north-west tower and north aisle to the people and the rest to the monks. This arrangement worked no better than the first. The monks walled off the nave from the choir of the church – denying thus the view that the people had formerly enjoyed of the great High Altar – and the people (after prolonged wrangling and litigation) built the present great west tower in 1445. The monks objected to the people having bells, because these disturbed their meditations. They built for themselves the lovely octagonal tower that survives now at the east end of the church, but originally in the middle, for the monks' choir, to the east of it, has all been pulled down. It was, incidentally, a direct descendant of William d'Albini, Sir Andrew Ogard, who, together with Sir John de Clifton who then lived in New Buckenham Castle, gave support to building the new west tower and managed to overcome the opposition of the monks to do so.

Not only could the monks not agree with the townspeople – they could not agree with their mother abbey either – St Albans. There were the most fascinating Trollopian intrigues as Wymondham sought to sever the connection and become an abbey in its own right, instead of a priory and a mere cell of an abbey. Then came the Dissolution, dissolved the whole lot of them, and the whole of the east end of the great church was pulled down but not, fortunately, the strangely lovely octagonal tower.

So the townspeople won in the end, and they still have this wonderful building, with its massively Norman nave, aisles and towers of the fifteenth century and later, and odd pieces of ruined monastic buildings outside. The present-day parishioners seem to be resolutely 'High Church', and the modern fittings are lavish. Sir Ninian Comper's screen is a many-splendoured thing. As there was no east window (the octagonal tower making such a window impossible) he was able really to go to town on it.

While at Wymondham Abbey we may well consider the brothers Kett, because one of them – William – was hanged alive in chains on one of the towers and there left to rot, while Robert, his brother, was similarly accommodated on the walls of Norwich Castle. They were Wymondham men, so here may be the place to review their triumph – and their downfall, and perhaps one cannot understand the present-day spirit of East Anglia without considering the brothers Kett.

On 20th June 1549 there was a riot at Attleborough, aimed against the new land enclosures, and fences were pulled down which had been illegally erected by one Squire Green on common land. On the 7th of July – a Sunday – fell the annual Feast at Wymondham, during which the old guild play of St Thomas was wont to be performed. A large crowd collected, speeches were made, and the next day a great body of people went and threw down fences which a man named Flowerdew had illegally erected round common land. (It was Flowerdew who had stolen most of the lead from the old Abbey of Wymondham.)

Kett came out, confronted the mob, and listened to their grievances. He was convinced by them, and according to Nevylle's *De Furoribus Norfolciensum*, written immediately after the time, he said: 'Whatsoever lands I have enclosed shall again be made common unto ye and all men, and my own hands shall first perform it.' He then led them in pulling down his own fences.

Without Kett the rising would quickly have been suppressed, like many in other parts of England; but Kett, believing that he

191

was fighting *for* the law, and not *against* it (for nearly all the enclosures and depopulations were illegal) proved to be a born leader.

A manifesto was drawn up (one would guess by Kett) which began:

The pride of great men is now intolerable, but our condition miserable.

These abound in delights; and compassed with the fullness of all things, and consumed with vain pleasures, thirst only after gain, inflamed with the burning delights of their desires.

But ourselves, almost killed with labour and watching, do nothing all our life but sweat, mourn, hunger, and thirst . . . The present condition of possessing land seemeth miserable and slavish – holding it all at the pleasure of great men; not freely, but by prescription, and, as it were, at the will and pleasure of the lord. For as soon as a man offend any of these gorgeous gentlemen he is put out, deprived, and thrust from all his goods . . . The lands which in the memory of our fathers were common, those are ditched and hedged and made several; the pastures are enclosed and we are shut out. Whatsoever fowls of the air or fishes of the water, and increase of the earth – all these do they devour, consume, and swallow up; yea, nature doth not suffice to satisfy their lusts, but they seek out new devices, and as it were, forms of pleasure to embalm and perfume themselves, to abound in pleasant smells, to pour sweet things to sweet things. Finally, they seek from all places all things for their desire and the provocation of lust. While we in the meantime eat herbs and roots, and languish with continual labour, and yet are envied that we live, breathe, and enjoy common air! Shall they, as they have brought hedges about common pastures, enclose with their intolerable lusts also all the commodities and pleasure of this life, which Nature, the parent of us all, would have common, and bringeth forth every day, for us, as well as for them? . . . Nature hath not envied us other things. While we have the same form, and the same condition of birth together with them, why should they have a life so unlike ours, and differ so much from us in calling?

The complete manifesto, in modern English, can be read in *The Rising in East Anglia in 1381* by Edgar Powell.

Kett led his men to Mousehold Heath, north-east of Norwich, where other rebels had been before him. There they made camp, and before long twenty thousand people had come to their standard. Twenty thousand men and women driven to such a state of desperation that they joined this assembly of outlaws knowing full well that by doing so they made it inevitable that they would be hanged if they were caught.

Under Robert Kett's leadership they were peaceable enough. True they sent foragers about the country to requisition food from big landowners, true that wherever they went they threw down illegal enclosures, and true they took some enclosing landlords prisoner. But they murdered nobody. They took no life except later on and in fair battle. Nobody remembered this when they were being slaughtered in their thousands in Norwich market place and outside the city.

The king sent a herald to Norwich to order them to surrender, and offering a free pardon if they did so. Kett answered him: 'Kings and Princes are wont to pardon wicked persons, not innocent and just men.' Kett insisted from first to last that he was there to uphold the law, not to break it.

The rebels by then had control of most of Norfolk, and also of Norwich. But after Kett's rebuffal of the King's herald, Thomas Cod, Mayor of Norwich, who had been on good terms with Kett, barred the city to him.

This angered the rebels and they stormed the walls. The citizens manned the defences and showered Kett's men with arrows, but 'vagabond boys, naked and unmarked, came among the thickest of the arrows, and gathered them up, and plucked out the very arrows that were sticking in their bodies, and gave them, all dripping with blood, to the rebels who were standing by, to fire again against the city.'

No fortress could withstand such spirit, the rebels swam the Wensum, stormed the walls, and took the city.

After this Mayor Cod was imprisoned, and Austen Steward (whose house we have noticed in Tombland in the chapter on Norwich) was made Mayor instead. He also managed to keep on fairly good terms with the rebels. Cod, though in their hands, was not harmed.

Even after this violence Kett's leadership was equal to restraining his followers, there was little looting, and no damage was done to the city. The rebels assumed that the city people would be with them, but by and large they were not.

On the return of York Herald to London the Marquis of Northampton set out with 1,500 soldiers to deal with the outbreak. This army occupied the city, the rebels attacked, Lord Sheffield was slain near the cathedral (a plaque still marks the spot), and the army fled back to London.

But the Government was gathering its powers. The Earl of Warwick was sent against Norwich with 12,000 trained troops, many of them German mercenaries with firearms. He arrived at Norwich – a herald was sent forward – and again rejected. The rebels told him that the pardon offered was nothing but 'barrels filled with ropes and halters'. Warwick occupied the city, and prepared to attack the rebel camp. His artillery train took a wrong turning and fell into the rebels' hands, but they did not know how to use it. Kett had one good gunner – Miles, who shot the king's master gunner and captured yet more of Warwick's artillery. In spite of the arquebuses of the Germans it looked as if the rebels would have the ascendancy.

But on Monday, 26th of August, 1,400 more Germans came to join Warwick, and it was on that day that Kett made his fatal mistake. Persuaded by some religious fanatics among his followers, who claimed that they had had visions, he burnt his camp on Mousehold, marched out of his strong defences there, and down to the low ground near the Wensum. There he took up a defensive position.

On the 27th Warwick attacked him. Miles, Kett's excellent gunner, managed with an iron ball to kill the king's standard-bearer. But then the mercenaries fired a terrific volley from their arquebuses, Warwick's cavalry charged, the rebels broke and fled and England was safe for the big landowners for another four hundred years.

Some of the rebels rallied and held their ground, were offered pardon, and knowing it to be worthless refused it and were killed fighting. They were the fortunate ones. The pursuit spread for miles. Kett fled with the others, and was found hiding in a barn at Swannington, eight miles from Norwich. The hangings started and went on for days. The enclosing landlords whom Kett had imprisoned (and not in one case physically harmed) clamoured for blood and more blood until even the bloodthirsty Warwick had to cry out: 'Is there no place for pardon? Shall we hold the plough ourselves, and harrow our own lands?'

Lest this should happen some labouring people had to be spared. William Kett, as we have seen, was hanged alive from one of the towers of Wymondham Abbey, and Robert from Norwich Castle walls until his body completely disintegrated from corruption. On Norwich Castle now hangs a plaque on which is written:

IN 1549 AD ROBERT KETT YEOMAN FARMER OF WYMONDHAM WAS
EXECUTED BY HANGING IN THIS CASTLE AFTER THE DEFEAT OF
THE NORFOLK REBELLION OF WHICH HE WAS THE LEADER. IN
1949 AD FOUR HUNDRED YEARS LATER THIS MEMORIAL WAS
PLACED HERE BY THE CITIZENS OF NORWICH IN REPARATION AND
HONOUR TO A NOTABLE AND COURAGEOUS LEADER IN THE LONG
STRUGGLE OF THE COMMON PEOPLE OF ENGLAND TO ESCAPE FROM
A SERVILE LIFE INTO THE FREEDOM OF JUST CONDITIONS.

A descendant of a Wymondham man, Samuel Huntington, signed the Declaration of Independence on behalf of the State of Connecticut. His ancestor, Simon, founded the towns of Windham and Norwich, in that state.

CHAPTER 11

King's Lynn
and the Great Ouse

One of the most romantic towns in England is **King's Lynn**.

Few towns have been as single-minded as Lynn, and Lynn's mind has always been firmly fixed on *trade*. What is surprising is that this commercial-mindedness has not led to the ruin of the old town, the pulling-down of everything not immediately profitable. Lynn has perhaps the finest collection of medieval merchants' combined houses and warehouses in England, still being used (although for other purposes than that for which they were built), still in good repair, and not too spoiled by being converted to modern employments. They remain, not because they have been consciously preserved by anyone (although the King's Lynn Preservation Trust does truly admirable work in this direction), but because they were so well built in the Middle Ages, so adequately maintained and discreetly altered in later centuries, that they are as useful as they were when they were first built.

Lynn still has the smell of Old England about it: and the smell, too, of voyages to Iceland, and the Baltic, and Italy, and Spain, the New World and the Low Countries and the Greenland whale fishery. It is in no way a 'show town' or tourist resort, trading consciously on its antique character. Its modern flavour is given it by the Wash fishermen who lived in its North End (but have now, alas, been planted out in council houses like cabbages, but are Wash fishermen still), by the farmers who throng its very large cattle market, by Fenland men and women who come in to spend money made ploughing and sowing and reaping in the richest fields on earth, by merchant sailors – British and foreign – who come roaming off the ships in its modern docks, and by merchants who are the very descendants of the ones who built so much of the Lynn we see, back in the Middle Ages.

In the very early Middle Ages Lynn and Boston (over the other side of the Wash) competed with each other for half the trade of England. The reason for the commercial ascendancy of the Wash ports was that they were the outlets to the sea of the richest hinterland of England: the cornlands of Marshland and Fenland, the Derbyshire lead mines, the Lincolnshire and Norfolk salternes, and above all the sheep and wool country of the East Midlands. The imports that came back from foreign countries were at first such exotic articles as furs from Novgorod (in 1245 the king's tailor went to Lynn and bought £174 17s 1d worth of 'greywork' from Edmund of Gothland; 'Greywork' was the fur of the Arctic squirrel, taken in winter), gerfalcons from Iceland, hawks and lesser falcons from Norway, wood and madder from Picardy, wine from Gascony, and the rarer Flemish and Italian cloths. Edward III banned the cloth, and instead imported Flemish weavers and got them to weave the cloth in England, and thus sprang up the great East Anglian weaving industry. After the ban on cloth-import, wool and woven woollen cloth became the biggest exports from Lynn. As time went on such aristocratic requirements as furs and gerfalcons declined, and articles of more mundane use came in: 'stockfish' (salt or dried cod) from Iceland, more and more wine, and the Baltic countries supplied ever-increasing quantities of forest products: rafters and deal boards, masts and spars for ships, furniture, wax, pitch, resin, tar and potash. This trade with the northern forests goes on to this day, as a stroll round Lynn docks will quickly show.

Like Felixstowe, Lynn as a port has profited from the partial seizing-up of the Port of London owing to poor labour relations, and although it no longer has its great medieval swagger it still handles grain and other commodities to feed its expanding local industries, and acts as a clearing-house for goods from Rotterdam destined for the Midlands. All the Baltic flags are to be seen in the docks and by the quays at one time and another, and German freighters continuing a tradition established in the thirteenth century by the trading towns of the Hanseatic League.

The proper way to approach a seaport is from the sea – in the case of Lynn, in from the Wash and up the Great Ouse. If the traveller does this the first opening into the land that he will see, on the Lynn side of the river, is a narrow creek that dries out to steep mud banks at low tide, called the **Fisher Fleet**. This, according to the Lynn fishermen, was presented to them for ever by King John. It is crowded with fishing boats, old and new; and should be visited even by the land-bound. There are virtually no fish in the Wash. The reason for this is that the Wash is a great breeding nursery for seals, and any finned fish that poked his nose into it would be snapped up immediately. So the Lynn fishermen go almost exclusively after shellfish: shrimps, cockles and mussels. The shrimps are boiled on board, as soon as they are caught: the mussels and cockles are raked up from the sand or mud by fishermen who have 'landed' on the sea-bottom from stranded boats. The smacks are anchored over the fishing grounds at high tide – far away in the Wash, miles from land – and the fishermen wait for the tide to go down. When it does they jump overboard on to the drying sand and rake out their cockles or harvest their mussels. Lynn fishermen still incline to such medieval-sounding names as Fyshe, Bun, Pegg, Rake, Benifer and Hornigold. They are an ancient race.

The Fisher Fleet was once twice the length that it is now, but in the 1880s it was cut in half to make the new Bentinck Dock. A boom was placed across the Fleet, and a fisherman died only a couple of decades ago who could tell of the scene when this was done, by a gang of men protected by policemen and councillors in tall hats; but the fishermen made at least a gesture of defiance – pitching the Chief Constable's hat into the water and covering some of the top-hatted gentlemen with mud.

There was a good little boat yard just south of the Fleet, where the Brothers Worfolk built wooden boats by traditional methods, but it has now been taken over by a larger firm. Just through the dock gates is the old fishermen's quarter that has recently been so ruthlessly pulled down to make room for worse things, but there is still the Tilden Smith, and the Fishermen's Arms, both good pubs (the Fishermen's Arms has been rebuilt, however). **St Nicholas Chapel**, in St Ann's Street, is in fact a large church

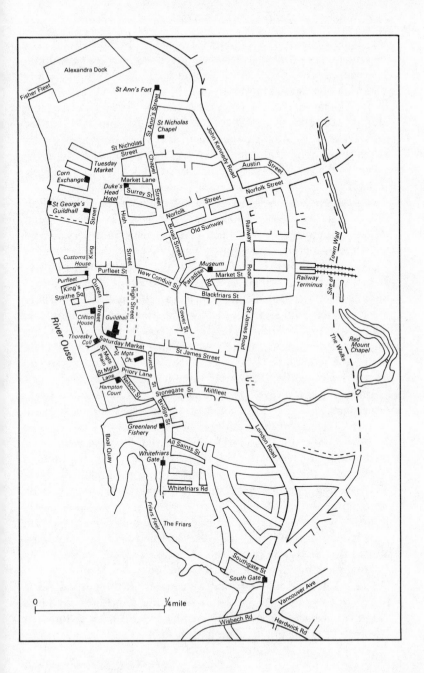

Alexandra Dock

Fisher Fleet

St Ann's Fort

St Ann's Street

St Nicholas Chapel

John Kennedy Road

St Nicholas Street

Austin Street

Tuesday Market

Chapel Street

Market Lane

Norfolk Street

Corn Exchange

Duke's Head Hotel

Surrey Street

St George's Guildhall

Norfolk Street

Old Sunway

King Street

High Street

Broad Street

Railway Road

Customs House

Purfleet St

New Conduit St

Museum

Paradise Rd

Market St

Railway Terminus

Site of Town Wall

Purfleet

King's Staithe Sq

Queen Street

Blackfriars St

Clifton House

Guildhall

High Street

Tower St

St James Road

Red Mount Chapel

Thoresby Coll

Saturday Market

St James Street

The Walks

River Ouse

St Mgts Plain

St Mgts Ch.

Church St

St Mgts Lane

Priory Lane

Hampton Court

Nelson St

Stonegate St

Millfleet

Boal Quay

Bridge St

Greenland Fishery

All Saints St

London Road

Whitefriars Gate

Whitefriars Rd

Friars Fleet

The Friars

Southgate St

South Gate

Vancouver Ave

0   ¼ mile

Wisbech Rd   Hardwick Rd

although officially it is a 'chapel of ease' to St Margaret's. The fishermen claim that this, too, was given to them by King John. The church is Perpendicular, with an Early English tower and a Victorian lead spire (the first one fell down); I find it grand but rather gloomy, but there is a bench-end that is well worth going there to see. On it is carved a fifteenth-century ship with a furled square mainsail and a furled lateen mizzen (a new-fangled invention at that time), one of the ships that was being built at Lynn in the 1400s (by the ancestors of the brothers Worfolk?) for the profitable Iceland trade.

Near St Nicholas is a modern ship's chandlers and a new Port Officials School in a very ancient building in St Ann's Street. Walking past the gate of the Austin Friary, past several very ancient half-timbered houses, and past a vast timber shed, you come to the **Tuesday Market**, as grand a non-collegiate urban open space as there is in East Anglia. Here is the exuberant corn exchange, built in 1854, and described by Pevsner as 'Jolly and vulgar'! There are plenty of good Georgian and Early Victorian buildings, and the big hotels. The Duke's Head is a fine place, put up in 1683 for the use of visitors to the new Merchants' Exchange by a Lynn vintner. The Maid's Head was much frequented by American airmen when nearby Sculthorpe was still a very big air base.

One should, wherever possible in Lynn, cut down to the River Great Ouse. Many streets lead down to the river but most of them come to a dead end there and one has to retrace one's steps. The reason for this is that it is down to the river that the great merchants' warehouses go. The pattern of these was a road running parallel to the river, the merchants' houses on this road, and at the back of the houses long narrow courtyards, flanked on either side by warehouses and cut off from the river by a further warehouse with its private wharf at which the goods, from the Baltic and elsewhere, were landed. It is these private wharves which still impede walking along the shore to the river. The great houses along the Strand in London once stood in a similar relationship to the Thames.

One of the first buildings that we come to in **King Street** (King Street was once called *Stockfishrow*) is the famous St George's Guildhall, which was a theatre in Shakespeare's time and it is known that his company once played there (and once again was paid by the corporation *not* to play there – in an outburst of beastly puritanism), and there is no reason to think that Shakespeare was not among them. Thus it is the only building in England in which it is possible – nay likely – that Shakespeare appeared upon the stage. After long use as a warehouse it is now a theatre again and the centre for the very lively annual King's Lynn Festival.

King Street has in it not a building but what is of interest and beauty. At the end of it is the Customs House. This was built in 1683 not as a Customs House but as the Merchants' Exchange by the same man who built the Duke's Head, and designed by Henry Bell, twice Mayor of Lynn and architect of many of its buildings. The lavish use of stone in it in this stoneless country was made possible by the fact that the stone could be shipped direct down the Nene, across the Middle Level Navigations, down the Great Ouse, and up Purfleet right to the very site of the building in Fen lighters. It is a very pretty building indeed and is adorned with a statue of Charles II.

Cut down riverwards to **King's Staithe Square** and its lane (*staithe* is Norfolk for wharf: thus there are staithes all over Broadland). Bank House, which has Charles I on top of it, is very fine. Samuel Cresswell, the grandson of Elizabeth Fry the prison reformer and one of the great Gurney family (see Norwich, p. 101) returned there to his home after a five-year voyage of exploration to discover if there was such a thing as the North-West Passage. There was. Farther on there are some more ancient warehouses.

Clifton House, in **Queen Street** (formerly called *Wyndgate*) is a splendid example. The dwelling house, on Queen Street, was rebuilt about 1708, but the splendid tower in the courtyard is Elizabethan, the warehouses that reach back to the river older, and the undercroft fifteenth century if not earlier. Recently a fourteenth-century pavement of Clare tiles has been uncovered in it: 'the most substantial secular pavement of this date preserved in position in England'. Thoresby College, farther south, was founded in 1502 by the Mayor, Thomas Thoresby, for training priests, but the house was turned into a merchant's house and warehouses at the Dissolution. What stands now is mostly seventeenth century, but in the great hall down by the river is a marvellous hammerbeam roof.

Continuing south are more merchants' houses, including the 'Steelyard', or 'Hanseatic Warehouse' opposite the church: here the dwelling house on the street (St Margaret's Plain) is eighteenth century, but the warehouses at the back much earlier; parts may go back to 1475 when the building was first put up. Hampton Court, farther south, is another great block of a merchant's house – counting-house, warehouses and apprentices' quarters. It has been restored by the King's Lynn Preservation Trust. Farther south, in Nelson Street (formerly *Lath Street*) are more of these superb domestic and industrial buildings. King Street, Queen Street, St Margaret's Plain and Nelson Street contain, between them, a great wealth of medieval industrial building, and it is most important that it should be preserved, for there is nothing else like it in England.

St Margaret's Church is of great interest to the architectural detective. Here again we see the result of good water-borne communication, for the very large building (what is left of it is over 230 feet long and it was built as a priory church and had more to it) is all limestone, brought from Northamptonshire. The church was founded by de Losinga over 800 years ago, as a part of his penance for the sin of simony (as were Great Yarmouth St Nicholas and Norwich Cathedral), but there is little Norman work left in it: some at the base of the south-west tower. There is a glorious early thirteenth-century chancel and an arcade and a fifteenth-century clerestory. The whole church is a cocktail of the work of different periods: from Norman down to Victorian Gothic – even Sir Gilbert Scott had a go at it. The south-west tower alone has in it, besides the Norman base already mentioned, some Transitional work, Early English, Decorated bell stage, eighteenth-century battlements. It has a clockwork moon dial of 1681. The north-west tower had to be rebuilt in Perpendicular times because it leaned. It now contains ten bells. By the west door are flood marks, the highest of them being that recording the flood of 1953.

Inside, the reason for the rebuilding of the north-west tower in the fifteenth century can be seen in the leaning of the Norman tower arch. The nave was rebuilt in 1745 after a spire had fallen through it in a gale in 1741. The arcade is very early Gothic revival. The organ is by Snetzler and its case of Grinling Gibbons-style wood carving. In the organ the dulciana stop is said to have been used for the first time. The chancel is fine Early English, there are the original stalls and good misericords. The pulpit is delicately inlaid and carved and most beautiful.

But the pride of the building, and the thing that makes it from one point of view pre-eminent, is the two great brasses: one to Adam de Walsokne and his wife Margaret (Adam died 1349) and the other to Robert Braunche and his two wives, Letitia and Margaret, who look so alike as to appear twins. Braunche died in 1364. Both brasses are nearly ten feet long, the figures are life-sized, and all the surrounding brass is filled with the most exquisite engraving. At the base of de Walsokne's is a scene of country life, with a vintage, and a man carrying corn to a windmill. At the base of Robert Braunche's is the picture that gives this brass the name of 'The Peacock Feast'. A banquet is depicted, at which a roast peacock features, and at which twelve guests are sitting down to a groaning table. The twelfth guest is in such a hurry to get at the victuals that he is depicted as leaping over the table. At the flanks stand musicians. It is known that Braunche, while Mayor, gave a mighty banquet to Edward III in 1349.

Lynn's mayor and corporation still give feasts and banquets: the last time I looked into the Guildhall there was a simply splendid affair going on. In 1215 King John was feasted at Lynn (it was known as Lynn Episcopi then – but by the locals no doubt as it is now – just plain Lynn) and again peacocks were featured in the menu. On the 12th October, after the banquet, the surfeited monarch left to cross the Fens. On the 13th his baggage train was overwhelmed by the tide – with a great treasure and his private shrine and all. People are still looking for it. John went on without his goods, reached Newark Castle, and there died, whether from over-eating at Lynn or from a broken heart one does not know.

The organ in St Margaret's is of interest to musical historians, for it was installed at the instigation of Charles Burney, then struggling for a living as organist and music tutor to children of the local gentry. He declared the original instrument 'Execrably bad . . . & the Ignorance of My Auditors must totally extinguish the Few Sparks of Genius for Composition I may have.' His *History of Music* became famous, though less so than the works of his daughter. Fanny was born at Lynn in 1762. When her novel *Evelina* eventually came out it was a *succès fou*: Dr Johnson roared over it, Jane Austen mentioned it with warm praise in *Northanger Abbey*, and Sir Joshua Reynolds had to be fed by attendants while he was reading it, because he could not put it down. Fanny, when she heard of its success, was so pleased that she danced round the mulberry tree. Fanny was afterwards introduced into society, was appointed Keeper of the Robes to Queen Charlotte but didn't like it and got ill, and then married a French refugee, General d'Arblay, and lived quietly until she died.

St Margaret's, like the rest of Lynn, was knocked about by Oliver Cromwell (in person almost for, as Colonel of Horse, he was for a time in command of the siege of the town). During the cannonade an eighteen-pound cannon ball came from the other side of the river and through the window over the west door of the church, smashed a pier, and scattered the congregation. Eighty lives were lost in the town during the bombardment. Oliver Cromwell moved off to other battles, leaving the Earl of Manchester finally to storm and reduce the town. Lynn was one of the very few places in East Anglia to stand for the king: Lowestoft was the only other of any size, and *she* went Royalist simply to annoy Great Yarmouth, for it was unthinkable that the two places could be on the same side. As one generally assumes that it was the trading and commercial classes that sided with Parliament it is strange that such a resolutely commercial place as Lynn should have sided with the king.

North of the church is the **Saturday Market**, which has been a market at least since de Losinga's time and still is one. A minute of the corporation records of 1427 rules that Jews should no longer be permitted to sell meat in Jew's Lane 'unless it be near the church' – in other words unless it be in the place where the church could draw revenue from the transaction. Jew's Lane is now Surrey Street. I have not seen it, but there is said to be a tiny Jewish cemetery near the old library. In the Middle Ages Lynn had a strong Jewish community.

Overlooking the Saturday Market is the famous **Guildhall**, one of the choicest municipal buildings in the country. The Guildhall itself was built for the Guild of Holy Trinity in 1421, in fine flint and freestone chequer-boarding. Behind it is a big Assembly Room, designed by William Tuck who was a carpenter and Thomas King who was a bricklayer in 1766 (thus proving that in an age of good taste the best buildings need not be architect-designed – what would we expect of a big public building designed by a carpenter and a bricklayer in this year of grace?), and on your left as you face the Guildhall is an Elizabethan addition which acts as the entrance hall and is a most jubilant building with no less than *two* great royal coats of arms up above the door (the upper of the two brought from St James's church when this was pulled down). Farther along Queen Street but adjoining is the Town Hall proper, built in 1895 but well in keeping with the rest.

The regalia kept inside the Guildhall is simply astonishing. London itself has nothing to beat the sumptuous gold and enamel 'King John's Cup' (not King John's because it dates from 1340). This has been said again and again to be the finest cup in the country. It speaks for the lightness with which people in places like King's Lynn bear the great weight of history that until recently this cup was commonly taken home by the reigning Mayor, for his personal use at his private parties. It is said that it was once sent along the street by a messenger to have some minor repairs carried out by a local jeweller. There is also 'King John's Sword' which may indeed have been given to the town by King John, when he gave Lynn its first charter in 1204. It is a little like Oliver Cromwell's Pipe though, in that it had a new silver ornamentation in the sixteenth century, and a new blade in the seventeenth. For three centuries the bishops of Norwich unrightfully kept it from Lynn, there were legal proceedings in 1520 to get it back, but it was not handed over (at the town bounds) until midsummer 1535. There is a complete set of charters down from John's time, and one of the time of Knut or Canute. There are town seals, chains of office, and maces. Most interesting of all there is the famous 'Red Book of Lynn'.

This records commercial activities with the Hansa towns and the Baltic ports, and squabbles between Lynn and Denmark and with Iceland: one of the latter caused by Lynn men having kidnapped '3 male and 2 female boys' and selling them into slavery. The complaint came from the Bishop of Iceland. There is an entry of 1394 which records that – ten years before that – citizens of Wismar and Rostock attacked the Lynn settlement in Bergen, and Henry IV had to pay 5,318 nobles to ransom the Lynn men. For centuries Lynn maintained factories or enclaves in Scandinavian and Hansa ports and there were foreign trading posts in Lynn.

Graphic displays of this fishing, trading and dock development history are housed in the Heritage Centre, the old gaol beside Holy Trinity Guildhall. In Lynn Museum near the main bus station at Old Market Street a church has been converted into an exhibition centre of natural and local history supplementing the Heritage Centre. In King Street a Museum of Social History in a finely proportioned town house features toys, dolls, maritime souvenirs and domestic articles over the centuries.

In Bridge Street there is a building still called the *Greenland Fishery*, originally a merchant's house, built by John Atkin in 1605, thereafter a pub, and now, alas, an office. The **South Gate** (early sixteenth century) through which the reader will probably have driven if he came overland in a carriage, is one of the few remaining parts of the town's walls. In the splendid public parks known as The Walk is **Red Mount Chapel**, built after 1485 (it is said by a man named Robert Corraunce). This contained a relic of the Virgin, and was taken in by pilgrims who had landed from ships at Lynn on the great pilgrimage to the Holy House at Walsingham, as a kind of spiritual *hors d'œuvre*. It is a building of the strangest shape, and has a perfectly lovely fan vaulted ceiling in the little chapel up above: the tracery of it has been compared with that of King's College Chapel, Cambridge.

Like so many towns, Lynn has now acquired its pedestrian shopping precinct at the expense of older thoroughfares, though at least here, as elsewhere in the town, attempts have been made to retain echoes of the past: many of the street signs carry the older name below the modern one, such as Burghards Lane allied with its successor, New Conduit Street.

Another noble gesture in favour of preservation was made in 1980 when CAMRA, the Campaign for Real Ale, wished to take over the fifteenth-century Lattice House, in danger of demolition. Local publicans tried to prevent this competition, but Judge David Moylan ruled that CAMRA should go ahead and 'fulfil an unsatisfied demand for a traditional old-fashioned English pub in the town'. The *Eastern Daily Press* applauded this call to resist the steady encroachment upon convivial pub life by 'an image and ethos more appropriate to Las Vegas'.

Little pieces of Lynn history that are of interest: In 1885 Frederick Savage of Lynn took out a patent for a machine called 'galloping horses' (the first roundabout): some gondolas are preserved at Thursford Steam Museum (see p. 247). In 1330 the first-ever voyage of exploration to the Arctic set out from Lynn. George Vancouver was born in the yard of the Quaker Meeting House. He sailed as a boy with Captain Cook and later commanded a ship of his own, made extensive discoveries along the south-west coast of Australia, in New Zealand, the Gulf of Georgia, mapped the coast north of San Francisco for the first time, and discovered Vancouver Island in Canada, returning to England in 1795. He got into trouble after all this for flogging poor Lórd Camelford and having him clapped in irons, but the boy was a midshipman and probably deserved it.

The first autobiography ever written was written by a Lynn woman, Margery Kempe, née Brunham. Daughter of a mayor of Lynn, she married a merchant, bore him fourteen children and after this went slightly strange in the head. She had visions, went on pilgrimages, but wherever she went she was avoided by fellow pilgrims on account of her intolerable habit of *weeping*. Her eyes gushed like the Great Ouse. She was born in 1364, but did not dictate her autobiography until after 1400. I have not read it, but am told that it casts fascinating light on the times.

Here we might consider the **Great Ouse** and the **Fen waterways**. King's Lynn owed its prominence as a seaport in the early Middle Ages, and its survival at all as one later, to the fact that it is at the mouth of a very extensive system of navigable waterways. The Great Ouse may not compare in size with the Amazon or the Mississippi, but it and its tributaries and connected waterways drain a country that has for a great many centuries been highly productive of the goods which men want, and also well to the forefront of civilization.

The Great Ouse itself was navigable as far as Bedford, taking in on the way Ely, St Ives, Huntingdon and St Neots, while Cambridge, and that older place Grantchester, are on a tributary and Bury St Edmunds and Thetford, the old capital of East Anglia, on others. Nor is this all. The Fen Middle Level Navigations not only covered the whole of the rich Fen country with water roads but they also provided a link with the River Nene which comes right down from the heart of the East Midlands. It is now possible (the author has done it) to travel by inland waterway from King's Lynn to Birmingham, Liverpool and London and, in fact, most other places of importance in the kingdom. In the Middle Ages it was possible too – but with short portages overland.

Boston vied with Lynn, but for part of the Middle Ages the Roman-dug Foss Dike Canal, which connects Boston's river to the Trent, was silted up, thus giving Lynn the advantage, for Lynn had the Nene.

This inland water traffic to Lynn survived until only a few decades ago, and even now the last of the Fen lighters – as grand a breed of boat in their way as the Norfolk wherry – lie rotting up by a quarry on the Nene.

The Fen lighter overcame the disability of having to be small (to pen through the tiny medieval locks of the Fens) by working in train, or 'gangs', of four or five boats each. The gang was pulled by a horse, which was trained to leap the fences that ran down to the water's edge (see Constable's painting 'The Leaping Horse', only that was on the Stour) and trained to jump aboard one of the lighters in order to be ferried across a river, or to be carried up or down one when the wind was fair and a sail could be set; or the gang could drive with the tide. The lighters were connected together by 'fest poles', which were short bowsprits held fast to the quarters of the barge in front by the 'fest ropes' – which had to be adjusted by the agile crew when the 'gang' was going round a corner. The gangs were, indeed, steered by these 'fest ropes', and had no rudders.

There is no longer any goods-carrying on the waterways (save one little tanker that carries diesel oil to the pumping stations) but, strangely, there is a kind of renaissance. Pleasure boating is causing the old waterways to be opened up again. In 1964 the Well Creek, from Salter's Lode into the Middle Level, was opened up again after years of disuse, and even now volunteers are working to make the Great Ouse navigable again as far as Bedford. And, in spite of weed and low bridges, it is still possible to penetrate to most parts of Fenland by the Navigations, and a fascinating experience it is too (although not as *pretty* as the Broads, by any means).

The Great Ouse at King's Lynn looks fairly uncompromising. The river is wide and artificially straight, and the water the colour of the worst kind of transport-café coffee. High banks wall the Ouse, as they do most of the Fenland rivers, and at high tide the water stands within them much higher than the surrounding countryside. The tidal range in the Wash is great (18 feet) and the speed of the tide is daunting: up to 7 knots. Until you gain Denver Sluice in fact, and non-tidal waters, the Great Ouse is not for the learner navigator.

A new phenomenon has grown up (or rather down) alongside the Great Ouse. In 1959 the Tail Sluices of the great new Relief Channel were opened. They stand up just south of King's Lynn looking colossal, which indeed they are: it has been said that they are the biggest drainage sluices in Europe. The mighty Cut-off Channel has since been dug, and was opened by the Duke of Edinburgh on the 19th September 1964. This runs parallel to the Great Ouse, to the east of it, starting near Mildenhall, and it thus cuts off all the water that drains down from the high land of Norfolk and Suffolk and prevents this from running either into the Great Ouse, or over it into the Fens. By ingenious inverted syphons the tributary rivers, Little Ouse, Lark and Wissey, run over the new channel regardless – the channel goes underneath them in concrete pipes – but in times of flood the tributaries can be diverted into the Cut-off Channel and thus prevented from joining their parent river. Thus it is hoped to avoid another disaster such as that of 1947, when 70,000 acres of Fenland was flooded by the Great Ouse breaking its banks, and Ely was temporarily made an island again. The Cut-off Channel is 27½ miles long and with its attendant works cost £3,000,000.

It protects from flooding half a million acres of land. It is hoped that it will prevent for all time that recurring terror of the Fens: burst banks and flooded country.

King's Lynn looks its best from out on the waters of the Great Ouse, when the sun is setting in Fenland splendour at your back. The town then resembles some splendid medieval city, or one of the ancient ports of the old Zuyder Zee: Enkhuizen or Stavoren, or Hoern the Golden.

209

CHAPTER 12

King's Lynn
to Houghton Hall

The country between King's Lynn and Hunstanton is some of the most distinctive and beautiful in East Anglia. The chalk uplands of north-west Norfolk here tumble down to the low marshlands by the Wash, giving way first to sandy, heathy country, and this heathland has been extensively afforested by wealthy landowners – not least among them the Queen and her royal forebears.

South Wootton, just out of Lynn, is a straggle of suburban houses about which it is hard to say anything nice except that they don't straggle far. But to the east of it, along a track, is **Reffley Wood**, in which there is said to be a temple built in 1789 by the members of a Royalist society. This society was founded in the secrecy of the wood during the Commonwealth time (in 1651 to be exact) and was limited to thirty members as this was the greatest number that it was lawful should meet together. The society still exists, there are still thirty members, they still meet in Reffley Wood, they still smoke churchwarden pipes, their chairman is still a direct descendant of the first chairman, and I have no doubt they are still Royalists.

At **North Wootton** is the Red Cat Inn, a fine place where one can put up for the night, and in the bar of which the Queen's Fishmonger has been known to hold forth.

And a couple of miles across Ling Common is **Castle Rising**, which is one of the most interesting places in England for lovers of that strange and foreign race, the Normans. The castle still stands massive and proud inside a giant earthwork, and the Norman church is one of the finest small Norman churches that there is.

The keep, or great tower, of the castle, stands in a high ring of earth, with the remains of a gatehouse and a bridge in front of it, and the foundations of a Saxon and Norman chapel partly buried in the earthwork to the north. The chapel was long suspected to be Saxon: recent excavations have proved that it is. The keep is wonderfully preserved, and second in size and importance as a Norman keep to Norwich Castle. It is wider than it is high – a 'hall keep', not a 'tower keep' – well built and lavishly decorated. A red-brick wall once surmounted the ramparts, shown on old engravings. The tops of the keep walls are too dangerous for public access, so one has to make do with the window embrasures for sweeping views across the marshes towards the Wash and the heathland in which stands Sandringham House. Stones from the castle's domestic buildings and outworks can be detected in many of the walls and houses of the village, but for some reason the keep itself escaped serious quarry and retains its two storeys of nine-feet thick walls; there is intersecting arcading in the forebuilding, a marvellous great staircase going under Norman arches (over it is an interesting passage-way to a sally-port), a vestibule at the top of the staircase with a vaulted ceiling and a fireplace that was once the main door into the Great Hall and is now backed with some rather nice medieval tiles, dug up nearby but nothing whatever to do with the castle. In the south-east corner upstairs are two smaller rooms – one an elegant chapel. There are three turrets, two of which are accessible. The south-west, one of the two that have staircases in them, is not open at the moment, but one wonders at the perfect condition of the winding steps in it after so many centuries. There is a fascinating gallery in the north wall.

The earthworks, round about, are supposed to have been originally Roman, and may even have started earlier. Rising is now a tiny place, and one may wonder at these signs of its great importance in time past; but for the geographical changes of the Wash shore Rising might have become the great port that Lynn became.

No doubt Roman and Norman ships came up the estuary of the Babingley Brook, and Rising was once very near the sea. Now the sea has receded – four or five miles away – but who can say, in the Wash, where land ends and sea begins? Whereas Lynn, by virtue of the Great Ouse, still has deep water access.

Little is known about Rising history until after the Normans came. The first owner recorded was Stigand, Archbishop of Canterbury. The Conqueror gave the manor (and the huge surrounding

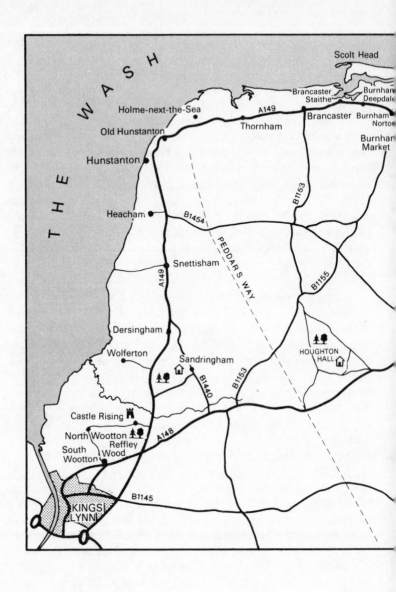

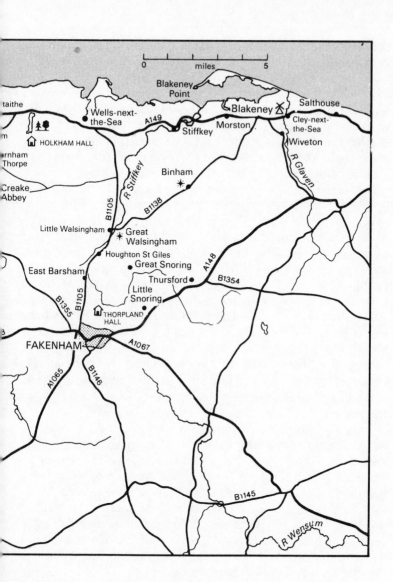

taithe

Wells-next-
the-Sea

A149

Blakeney
Point

Blakeney

Salthouse

Morston

Stiffkey

Cley-next-
the-Sea

Wiveton

HOLKHAM HALL

arnham
Thorpe

R Stiffkey

Binham

R Glaven

Creake
Abbey

B1105

B1138

Little Walsingham

Great
Walsingham

Houghton St Giles

East Barsham

Great Snoring

A148

B1354

Thursford

Little
Snoring

B1355

B1105

THORPLAND
HALL

FAKENHAM

A1067

A1065

B1146

B1145

R Wensum

0   miles   5

deer forest) to his brother-in-law, Odo, Bishop of Bayeux. When Odo rebelled William gave it to his butler, William d'Albini, who built Old Buckenham and married Matilda Bigod. D'Albini's son, also William, built the castle. This William married Queen Adeliza, widow of Henry I, and thus added Sussex to his titles and Arundel Castle to his properties. He built Rising about 1150. The fifth (and last) William d'Albini (or else his brother Hugh) obtained a charter for Rising at about the time when Lynn got its charter. Rising was a Rotten Borough until the Reform Bill, returning two members to Parliament. The corporation of this dwindled place was dissolved in 1838.

When Hugh, the last of the d'Albinis, died, the castle went to his sister who married Roger de Montalt. From the Montalts it went to the Crown. From 1331 to 1356 Queen Isabella was immured there, by her son Edward III, because he was angry with her for her suspected complicity in the murder of his father. It was a fairly liberal kind of open arrest, however, because Isabella (the 'She-wolf of France') moved around England fairly freely, and was visited by her son, and often received large sums of money from him. The Black Prince then held the castle, then Richard II, but he exchanged it in 1397 with John le Vaillant, or de Montford, Duke of Brittany, for the Duke's castle of Brest. No doubt le Vaillant used it as a hunting box, for this was one of the prime sporting estates of the realm.

After le Vaillant the castle was uninhabited and began to fall into decay. In 1544 it went back to a descendant, in the female line, of the founder: for Henry VIII exchanged it with his uncle, Thomas Howard, Duke of Norfolk, who could trace his ancestry back to the Conqueror's butler. The 7th Duke sold it, in 1695, to his cousin Thomas Howard (a nephew of the poet Dryden) and to this day it is in the Howard family, although looked after by English Heritage. The current Howard lives part of his time in a modest house in the village, and when he is in residence the Custodian flies the Howard flag from the top of the keep.

There is a lively account in the King's Lynn records of a Robert de Montalt, once an owner of the castle, going into Lynn to collect the revenues and tolls from the port and market of Lynn, to which the lords of Rising were legally entitled. But a man named Nicholas de Northampton and other Lynn worthies disputed this entitlement, and they advanced on de Montalt with 'banners unfurled and in a warlike manner'. They insulted de Montalt, nay drove him into his dwelling house in Lynn, broke down the doors, beat him and his men, carried away certain arms, swords, spurs, purses of money and jewels to the value of £40. They then bore him off to the house of Robert Costin and forced him to release all actions that he was taking against the Mayor and Commonalty of Lynn. All this, however, availed Lynn nothing; for in the subsequent legal action it was adjudged that Lynn must pay de Montalt £4000 damages, and he was still entitled to purloin the harbour and market tolls.

Lynn had its own back in the end though: if the courts favoured Rising, geography and history favoured Lynn:

> *Rising was a seaport when Lynn was but a marsh.*
> *Now Lynn it is a seaport town and Rising fares the worse.*

As for Rising church, a person in a hurry might look at two things: the west end and the font.

The west end is one of the finest pieces of Norman blind arcading in the country. The font is squat and primitive, and from its west side evil-looking faces leer out. This speaks a different language from any heard in the western world today. There is a noble Norman west tower arch, inside. Much of the church is Victorian.

Across the road from the church is the Hospital of the Holy and Undivided Trinity, or the Howard Bede House.

The Earl of Northampton founded it, the second son of the poet Surrey. It cost him £451 14s 2½d. This Howard was first educated by the Protestant Foxe, the Martyrologist, but then he came under the influence of the Bishop of Lincoln and he 'poped', or joined the Church of Rome. He fell out of favour with his cousin Queen Elizabeth, and intrigued against her in favour of James VI of Scotland, and when James came to the English throne found himself in favour again. He was said to have been treacherous and unscrupulous, but learned, artistic and charitable. His charities included the hospital at Rising, which he built in memory of his grandfather Thomas Howard 3rd Duke of Norfolk who had been imprisoned by Henry VIII (see Framlingham, p. 54); one at Clun in

215

the wilds of Shropshire, which was in memory of his brother, Thomas the 4th Duke, who was beheaded by Queen Elizabeth; one at Greenwich in memory of his father the Earl of Surrey, beheaded by Henry VIII; and one at Shotesham, in Norfolk, because that was where he was born – when his father and mother were unsuccessfully fleeing from the forces of the king.

The rules that he laid down for the hospital included provision that the Governess and eleven inmates should be of 'honest life and conversation, religious, grave and discreet, able to read if such a one may be had, single, 56 at least, no common beggar, harlot, scold, drunkard, haunter of taverns, inns or alehouses'. The place still functions as it did, and one of the sights of Rising is that of the twelve ladies (whom one is sure are all that the Founder said that they should be) walking across the road in procession to church dressed in their red cloaks with the Howard badge, and their steeple hats. They are impervious to being photographed, like the maids of Volendam. The hospital is old and attractive, and the original Jacobean furniture is still within.

For the rest – Rising has dwindled through the centuries, as the sea receded from its wharves and the great departed from its castle. Some of Kett's men gathered in what is still called 'Kett's Castle' – an earthwork in the fields – before they drew away to Watton and thence to Mousehold to join their leader. In 1643 the great deer chase had been practically denuded of timber, and the next year the deer were systematically killed off and the countryside 'deparked' and turned to agricultural uses. Now it is a country of huge estates, where the pheasant is king.

The nicest thing about **Wolferton** is its railway station. I should have mentioned before that the whole of this country is *Norfolk carr* country. The carr is a rusty-red ironstone, or sandstone containing iron, fairly hard and reasonable building material, the only example in East Anglia of a suitable native building stone with the exception of flint and – if you can consider it suitable – chalk. Wolferton railway station is Victorian-Gothic, as all good railway stations should be, and built of this warm, honey-coloured stone, but the special thing about it is that it is all done up for the Queen. The platform lamps are surmounted by crowns, and the whole place was specially decorated and kept in trim by British Rail against any visit to Sandringham by Her Majesty. Alas, she long since ceased to arrived by rail, preferring to travel by car; and, again alas, the whole delightful little line from King's Lynn to Hunstanton, along which engine drivers used to go through an elaborate ritual of exchanging large rings at intervals along the track, has been grubbed up. Mercifully, Wolferton station itself has been privately preserved in glowing splendour, with a museum of Victorian and Edwardian royal travel in the ornate retiring rooms designed originally for Edward and Alexandra when travelling to and from their much loved Sandringham. The museum is open daily, except Saturdays, from Easter until the end of September.

Sandringham hardly exists as a village, but it is a very large estate. The countryside for many miles around in fact belongs to the Queen. The estate was bought by Edward, Prince of Wales in 1861 (in preference to Houghton, which was offered to him as well) and the present Sandringham House built after 1870. It is very ugly – like a huge and grandiose Victorian seaside hotel, Jacobean in style, of red brick and stone. The gardens are fine, particularly the fruit and vegetable garden; and one can visit them most days in summer provided that no member of the Royal Family is in residence. There is a little church, set in the great parkland trees nearby, old but completely Victorianized, with much silver and gold in it, presented by a Mr Wanamaker who lived nearby, and an early Greek Christian font lying on the ground at its west end, the gift of one royal brother to another.

Whether the Queen is in residence or not the visitor is struck by the relaxed and informal atmosphere of the place. If there *are* any security police about – they are well hidden. People living in the locality preserve a tradition of leaving the Queen in peace, and she can ride about the country on one of her many horses with a scarf over her head just like any other horse-loving woman, and in winter the woods echo to the report of the Duke of Edinburgh's shotgun – as pheasant after pheasant bites the dust.

Dersingham is a large village, mostly of carr stone, and inhabited largely by wealthy retired people, some of whom, it is rumoured, settle there to be near the Queen. There are several large pubs which put people up, one of them entirely decked out with objects of the Horse Cult: not an image or a pattern or a gadget in the place but has some equine association.

Less reputable inhabitants favoured different pursuits, often in

217

defiance of Royalty and regulations. Within living memory the fishermen of the Wash turned to wildfowling in the winter, when ducks and geese were plentiful and fish were scarce, and there were plenty who trespassed on Crown land and made a living by fowling for as many months as they could and got whatever casual work there was in the summer. The chief methods of taking wildfowl were, firstly, *punting*. This involved going out on the sea in a tiny flat punt, pointed at both ends, painted grey for camouflage, with a huge gun – a cannon, no less – mounted on the foredeck. On sighting duck or geese the fowler would lie down flat behind his gun and propel the craft towards the quarry by short paddles or 'setting sticks'. When in range he would fire – and maybe kill a hundred birds, for his gun fired anything up to two pounds of shot! Much smaller shots were the rule, though, and if he got a shot in a week he was lucky, and this only after lying about night after night in freezing weather, and probably soaking wet. Secondly there was *flight-netting*. Anyone possessing such nets nowadays disguises their purpose by using them to cover up strawberry beds, since their use has been made illegal. The method was to set up nets, hundreds of yards long and made of fine cotton, along the tideline in time for the evening or morning flight when ducks and teal love to fly very fast and very low up and down the shore. The racing birds would fly into the nets and be trapped. Thirdly there was *swivel-gunning*, which involved the mounting of a huge gun like a punt gun on a swivel ashore and letting drive into the 'brown' of a big flight of duck or geese as they winged by.

Wildfowling is one of the most ancient activities of men in East Anglia, and up until the age of broiler chicks provided an important source of food for country people, and a livelihood for the men. There are still thousands of grey geese (mostly pink-foot) on the Wash every winter, and even more widgeon, teal, and mallard. 'Shore gunners' used to go after them in their hundreds, hiding behind the sea walls at flight time with small shoulder guns, but the number of birds they killed was negligible, because they were amateurs: wildfowling in the Wash has always been a business for cunning, well-versed experts. Today practically the whole coast and the banks of the Wash are National Bird Reserves, and to go shooting at all one has to be a member of a recognized wildfowling association.

In Dersingham Church is one of the most beautiful carved chests I know. **Snettisham** has a marvellous church – doubly marvellous (in Perpendicular East Anglia) because it is of the Decorated style. The tower, with its high stone spire (the latter unusual for East Anglia too – Northamptonshire is the 'county of squires and spires') was once a crossing tower, in the middle, but the old chancel, which was to the east of it, has been removed. The glory of the place is its west window: Decorated at its most free and exciting, lovely flowing tracery – lacework in stone!

Over fifty bronze, tin, and gold alloy Celtic torcs – heavy neck ornaments of one or more rods twisted into barley-sugar shapes with decorated ends – have been found near Snettisham; and in 1985 a hoard of jewellery was unearthed, perhaps the most important in quality and quantity ever rediscovered from the Roman Empire.

A road goes from Snettisham down to **the Wash**, and here might be a good place to go to contemplate this extraordinary arm of the sea. At Snettisham beach, if you are lucky, you may well see that strange phenomenon, horse-and-cart fishermen. People still drive out over the sands at low tide (they can easily go two or three miles there) in carts, rake cockles out of the sand, load them into the carts, and carry them back and sell them.

The sands of the Wash, at low tide, stretch for miles and miles: one could play a game of cricket on hard sand seven miles from the shore! But the *strand-looper* or sand roamer wants to know what he is doing, for the tide comes back again very very quickly and it is easy to get cut off. There are plenty of deeper guts and gullies in the sands, which one may cross without noting them when they are dry – only to find them racing water when one wishes to get back. The sands have ancient evocative names, like Pandora, Thief, Blackguard, Seal, the Westmark Knock and the Gat. To navigate a boat among these sands requires great skill, for when the water covers them you cannot see them, yet your keel feels them all too easily. Nor are they stable – they shift about. Two decades ago the deep-water channel to King's Lynn was five miles to the west of where it is now.

Nor must it be thought that the Wash is a calm, inland sea. A very common wind in these parts comes from the north-east, and when the wind blows north-east or northerly the Wash is anything but placid, but a raging ocean; not for nothing is the light-float in the middle of the Wash named 'the Roaring Middle'. But to people who know it the Wash is a sea of enchantment. On summer days it can be a place of mirage. Lines of houses and bunches of trees can be seen – apparently hovering above the horizon. On other, very clear days 'Boston Stump' – the tower of Boston parish church – can be seen from twenty miles away, sharp and clear, and so can Hunstanton's banded cliffs. In calm weather the water has a silky, oily sheen on it, and as the tide recedes from the sand-banks these become inhabited by hundreds of seals as they flounder up out of the water to lie and bask in the sunshine. And it is fine, when the northeaster is blowing, to bring your boat to anchor in the lee of some drying sand-bank and lie there in peace while the great waves crash to death just over on its windward edge. For the walker there are fifty miles of lonely and deserted shoreline round the Wash – certainly the longest unbuilt-over shoreline in England.

Alas – serious pollution threatens the shellfish industry of the Wash, and so the livelihood of local folk.

Heacham (it is a fine walk along the shore to it from Snettisham beach) is where a party of Royalists landed from sailing keels from the Humber, in the time of the Commonwealth. Sir Hamon Le Strange – the man who commanded King's Lynn for the Royalists before Manchester stormed it – took them home to his big house of Hunstanton Hall and gave them food and ale, and afterwards had to answer for it, for he had only been allowed to go free after King's Lynn on condition that he stayed out of politics. Another Le Strange, Sir Roger, made an attempt to take Lynn back from Parliament, failed and was sentenced to death, but fled to France. He came back at the Restoration, went to London, and became the most savage of the Restoration pamphleteers, making a bitter attack on Milton among other people. But he also translated into English, for the first time, Aesop's *Fables*. The town sign commemorates another distinguished resident, the Red Indian princess Pocahontas, who married John Rolfe at Heacham Hall in 1614, only to die three years later.

Caley Mill is at the heart of the local lavender fields, seen at their overpoweringly radiant best during July and early August, when the little lavender water distillery can be visited.

Hunstanton (pronounced Hunston by most of the people who live there) is a railway-age seaside resort, with some big hotels and many smaller ones, a pier, a view of the sunset over the sea (unusual for East Anglia, but Hunstanton is the only East Anglian resort that faces west across the sea) and it is far less unattractive than it might have been because many of its Victorian and Edwardian buildings are built of carr stone. Now, alas, the reach-me-down in the form of the universal Peterborough brick is creeping in: Hunstanton ought to ban it here and now. The place is famous for its triple-banded cliffs, made of successive layers of carr stone, red chalk and white chalk. East of a line drawn from Hunstanton to Stoke Ferry lie the chalk uplands of Norfolk – a continuation of the Chilterns and the Gog and Magog Hills. West of the line are older rocks: carr stone, red chalk, and gault clay.

Old Hunstanton, now overwhelmed by its full-blown daughter, has the ruins of a church which is said to have been built at the spot where St Edmund landed from over the sea in Schleswig Holstein to come and be king of the East Angles.

Holme-next-the-Sea is special in being the terminus of the Peddar's Way, and also of the Icknield Way. The latter is said to have been a Roman Road, and also a Pre-Roman road; and Holme to have been an especially holy place amongst the British. Certainly the Way is dead straight, after the manner of Roman roads, and peters out to the south somewhere in the Brecklands. Before it peters it gives the impression that it is heading in the direction of Colchester, or Camulodunum. But all is shrouded in the fog of conjecture. Was it indeed Roman – and why did it go to Holme? The Romans certainly had a biggish naval base and fort five miles to the eastward – why would they have a station at this place? One conjecture, as good as the next, is that the Romans had a ferry service from Holme across the mouth of the Wash to Lincolnshire. This would seem to be possible, if only because, in the days when much of Fenland was flooded, it would otherwise have been a very long way by land from Caistor-by-Norwich, or Brancaster for that matter, to Lincoln or even York.

Holme marks the end of the Wash coast, and the beginning of another shore of the greatest interest and charm.

In 1986 the Prince of Wales opened the 93-mile Norfolk Coastal

221

Path from its junction here with the Peddar's Way, including a ramblers' hostel on Lord Melchett's estate at Ringstead. From Holme to Cley the sea is separated from the dry land by wide, drying sands and by a series of natural bays, or harbours, protected from the sea by banks of sand-dunes and flanked by miles of saltings and salt marsh. This coast is the very paradise of bird lovers, of fishermen, of small boat sailors, and of lovers of wild places. Nowhere else in England is there a piece of coast remotely like it, and it has a broken, sandy, wind-swept beauty quite unsurpassed.

Thornham is the first of these natural harbours, a small one and less used and known than the others. The channel into the harbour, from seaward, is not well marked nor easy of entrance. The little village itself is built largely of chalk, both red and white (chalk for building is called *clunch* in Norfolk). Here and there is a little flint. But this is the transitional country between the carr stone, which occurs only in a narrow belt near the Wash and south through Downham Market, and the great flint area which stretches all the way along that coast as far as, perhaps, Mundesley.

Brancaster is the next of the harbour villages. It straggles now, with plenty of modern houses, many of them very ugly, for it has grown quickly as a golfing, sailing, and holiday centre. If you go into the Jolly Sailor (which serves marvellous food) you may hear one Norfolk voice among twenty Midlanders. There is a golf course out on the marshes next to the sea. **Brancaster Staithe** has a vigorous sailing club. The harbour is bigger than that of Thornham, and much more used: the entrance is well buoyed (but the channel inside terribly tortuous and confused by small buoys laid to mark mussel-laying), there are one or two professional whelking boats, and on fine weekends, when the tide is high, the wide natural harbour is busy with scores of racing boats performing their weird gyrations. Across the harbour is **Scolt Head**, a wild and lonely island belonging to the National Trust, a birdwatchers' and botanists' paradise but restricted as to landing.

Brancaster was the Branodunum of the Romans. On Rack Hill, between Brancaster and its staithe, is the site of the Roman fort, with practically nothing to see. It is interesting to speculate what the geography of the harbour was when it was built. Certainly this was a naval base, and a fort of the Saxon shore.

And so we come to the Burnhams, seven. About **Burnham Deepdale** there is little to say, except that its church has an Anglo-Saxon tower and perhaps the most interesting Norman font in England. The font, of Barnack stone (Barnack Church has a Saxon tower too) is decorated with the Months of the Year, and I know of no representation of this theme that I like better. In January a bearded man is about to drink from a horn; in February he warms himself in front of a fire, and if anybody has experienced a February south-easter at Burnham Deepdale he will know why; in March he digs his garden, in April he looks as if he is pruning – although I should have said much too late, he should have attended to that instead of doing all that quaffing and fire-warming. In May the books say he is beating the bounds, but I should say that was anybody's guess. At any rate he is doing something with a flag near a tree. In June he looks as if he is pulling out an enormous weed – probably fat-hen, I should imagine. In July he is mowing with what looks like a primitive scythe, though one is always taught that the scythe wasn't invented in those days. In August of course he is harvesting: in fact binding a sheaf of corn. In September he is into it straight away with his flail – no waiting months to thresh for better prices. In October he is probably grinding corn with his stone hand-mill, in November he is bringing in his pig for slaughter, and in December he is enjoying the fruit of all this labour: he is having himself a good feast. And what an amiable old fellow he looks too! Lions, or other wild beasts, creep about in the jungle over his head, perhaps symbolizing the perils and dangers that beset a man, unless kept at bay by steadfastness and vigilance.

Burnham Norton also has an Anglo-Saxon church tower and a Norman font. It has two pulpits – one Jacobean and used, the other fifteenth century with paintings of the Four Doctors of the Church and also the donors. To the east of Norton Church are some remains of a White Friary.

Burnham Overy is a most charming village, with a fine windmill and also a watermill over the River Burn. The latter, with its good adjoining buildings, is National Trust and very fitting and beautiful it is too. Overy was once called 'Overy Town' and was certainly much bigger than it is today. Probably it was a port, before the sea receded and Overy Staithe had to be built. The Burnhams were, collectively, a considerable port; but the coast has advanced hereabouts many miles, by reason of the tides bringing thousands of tons of sand and shingle from the Yorkshire coast and dumping it here. As the sea receded **Overy Staithe** was built, one of the prettiest little villages of all, with a fine range of granaries and maltings, also cared for by the National Trust. Plenty of barges, schooners and brigs and brigantines came into Overy Staithe until the railways came and knocked them out. Now there is small boat sailing. No commercial fishing, except for a few mussel layings. The late Captain Richard Woodget, Master of the *Cutty Sark*, lived at Overy Staithe. Overy Church is strange, with a squat Norman tower (once higher) and remains of north and south transepts. As population fell away, and the little seaport town became a tiny agricultural village, the church was truncated. The church still doesn't seem to be able to make up its mind which side of the tower it wants to be: it has had several goes at each. (Map, pp. 212–213).

Nearly everybody thinks that the name *Overy* comes from sheep. It is far more likely to come from the Anglo-Saxon *Offer*, meaning a river bank. The old spelling of Overy was *Offrey*.

Burnham Market is a most handsome little town, with a great wide main street that bifurcates and splendid Georgian houses. One fine inn, the Hoste Arms, is named after one of Lord Nelson's protégés who later became a great naval commander in his own right. Another is called the Lord Nelson; and two miles south brings us to **Burnham Thorpe** and the birthplace of the 'Norfolk Hero' himself.

The traveller will have noticed that he is in Nelson country, if only because for miles around the pub signs have all proclaimed such names as The Nelson, The Victory, The Trafalgar, The Hero, or The Norfolk Hero. Horatio Nelson was born in Burnham Thorpe Rectory, and has given rise to a small local literary industry given over to producing such suppositious statements as 'when he was a boy Horatio must have . . .' (wandered in these fields, climbed this tree, strolled along this footpath many times, etc.). He must have indeed.

But two things strike the curious traveller in Burnham Thorpe. One is the quiet, but very profound, pride of the ordinary working villager in the fact that Nelson was a local man. Nelson was the

Castle Acre Priory, the grandest monastic ruin in East Anglia. *Above*, seen from the air. *Below* (*right*) the great West Front, its Norman blind arcading broken into for the 15th-century window that gapes above the door. The Prior's Solar (*left*) was later still, Tudor, and a comfortable dwelling house.

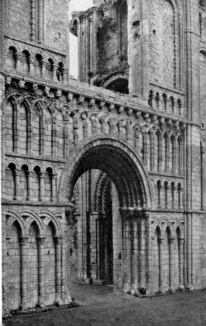

EAST ANGLIAN WINDMILLS. *Above*, grinding mills at Denver – the summit of the mill-wright's art – and at Cley-next-the-Sea. *Below left*, the pumping mill at Thurne, one of the greatest windmills that drained the Broads country. Saxtead Green mill (*right*), is a post mill; the whole body turns with the wind and all the grinding machinery with it.

only commander ever really to have captured the love of the ordinary working Englishman. The other is the absence of any brash 'Nelson Industry', other than the names of the Nelson Memorial Hall and the Trafalgar Stores. No 'Victory Café' sells Trafalgar buns to the curious – nowhere you can get a cup of tea, in fact. (This absence of public tea places is common to many East Anglian villages, and is in very great contrast to the conditions that prevail in, say, Devon.) There are no shops selling little china Horatios or prints of the Death of Nelson – no picture postcards even in Burnham Thorpe itself. As Nelson was, after Shakespeare, the greatest Englishman this is either very strange – or else a comment on the East Anglian character. Look what has happened to Shakespeare's birthplace! Instead, it is Burnham Market which thrives on Nelson souvenirs.

The pub ('Nelson used to sit on that bench over there') has a nice atmosphere in its tap room, with plenty of Trafalgar oleographs and other contemporary relics and except for these probably much the same as it was when Nelson drank beer in it. But the saloon bar – alas – this has recently broken out with a juke-box, hideous decorations – and a *dire* mural. One prays that this *décor* does not spread to the rest of the inn.

Next door to the pub there is a huge flint barn – and Nelson may well have been born in it, according to local legend, and not in the vicarage at all. The story is that his mother was taken short on a drive in a pony-cart and just didn't make it to home. But see the barn in any case: it is fine, with a great timber roof. The Burn, now a little stream, flows by it, but once was tidal and navigable for ships (or at least lighters) and it is likely that the great barn was a wharf-side warehouse.

At Nelson Hall, a house near the church, you can see many Nelson relics, and exhibitions are often arranged there. The church and Nelson Hall between them contain, of Nelsoniana: his medicine chest, his silver goblet, the crest of a modern HMS *Nelson*, a tattered White Ensign, one vast replica of the flag flown on *Victory* at Trafalgar (sometimes flown from the church tower), some Nelson letters, graves of members of his family, Nelson's signature in the marriage register witnessing the marriage of a friend (he spelt 'Horatio' wrong and was made to do it again) and the tree in the

225

churchyard up which the child Nelson is said to have climbed to show how brave he was. His birthplace has been pulled down – to make way for the present very undistinguished rectory (it is instructive to compare the latter with the pictures of the former to see how tastes have 'progressed'), but there is a pond in the lovely old vicarage garden said to have been dug by Nelson when he was home on half pay. As well as a commemorative plaque on the outer wall of the garden there is a signpost to catch the attention of the traveller beside the little river Burn, cheerfully alive with vociferous ducks. Lavender seedlings and yew cuttings from the old rectory flourish in the Maryland Naval Academy, USA. The rectory's incumbent who fathered such a splendid son is buried in the village church, with a bust of that son above his tomb.

Burnham Thorpe church is far from the village, incidentally (there is a perfectly lovely old farmhouse over the lane from it – the Norfolk farmhouse at its tenderly beautiful best) and the fields round about are hummocked with what are thought to be the remains of old cottages. It is believed that when the Black Death raged through the little place the inhabitants, in panic, fired their houses and fled to the site of the present-day village where they built new ones.

South a mile is **Creake Abbey**, which is a thirteenth-century ruin. Enough remains to make it worth going off the road to look at. Abbey Farmhouse, next to it, is all mixed up with the remains of the cloister and conventual buildings, and part of the choir and crossing of the abbey church remain.

The two Creakes are charming villages, strung out in the valley of the Burn. **North Creake** has a church with fine wall paintings and a hammerbeam roof with angels painted on the beams, together with a discreet modern chapel commemorating a young parishioner who died in 1978. A stone from Creake Abbey, close to which he lived, is incorporated in the altar. **South Creake** church is also graced with hammerbeams and carved angels up aloft. South Creake is largely a fifteenth-century building. The Creakes are a mixture of flint and chalk – the forge at North Creake for example is a chalk building. When the old people, locally, suffer from acid stomach some of them still gouge a piece from the wall of the nearest house and eat it.

On the way back to Lynn one might well look at **Houghton Hall**, whose state rooms and model soldier collection are open Thursdays, Sundays and Bank Holidays from Easter to late September, with an outdoor picnic area, children's playground, and stables with heavy horses and ponies. Home of the Walpole family for generations, and without doubt the largest, grandest country house in Norfolk, it was designed by Colin Campbell, a great student of the Palladian style. It contains a collection of paintings and tapestries and would contain more if the 3rd Earl of Orford hadn't sold so many to pay for his eccentricities. They went to the Czarina of Russia, so you must go to the Hermitage, in Moscow, if you wish to see them. Sir Robert Walpole, England's first Prime Minister, the longest to hold this office, and probably the most corrupt, had the place built. His son Horace, the epicure, letter-writer, and occasional novelist (*The Castle of Otranto*) preferred to live at Twickenham, where he built the delicious Strawberry Hill. When he did come to Houghton for a visit he wrote to a friend that he went to the church, where the congregation was divided with men one side, women the other. There was some talking, and when the parson glared a woman said: 'Sir – it is not among us!' 'So much the better,' said the parson. 'It will be the sooner over.'

Houghton Park is a product of the vast new wealth amassed by a few people early in the eighteenth century, and you either like it, or you don't.

Sir Robert, for aesthetic reasons, had the village of Houghton pulled down, and put up again somewhere else. It is said that the ruins of the old village inspired Goldsmith to write *The Deserted Village*. Sir Robert's attitude to the villagers on his estate when he pulled their village down about their ears and put it somewhere else, to improve his view, is very typical of the man and his times.

CHAPTER 13

King's Lynn to Fakenham

We should arrive at **Holkham Hall** on a Sunday, Monday or Thursday afternoon during June and September, with the choice also of Wednesday afternoons in July and August, or Spring and Summer Bank Holiday Mondays. There are refreshments and a free car park; and a pottery and garden centre.

Holkham Hall is the most perfect example of a great house built in the Palladian style as it returned to England after that Baroque period which followed the death of Inigo Jones. It stands there, massive, precise, severely classical, and almost exactly as it looked when it was finished in 1762. Considered by itself alone, divorced from its countryside, it is a work of art. Considered within its countryside, it is incongruous. There is nothing of Norfolk or East Anglia about it any more than there is about Houghton Hall, its earlier rival.

Holkham was the product of the great wealth of the Coke family, combined with the vast enthusiasm of the 1st Earl of Leicester, combined with the diligence and genius of William Kent, a coach-painter from Yorkshire. Kent had been sent to Italy to study art by a patron and had returned to work with Lord Burlington as an architect. He made an intensive study of Palladio's *Book of Architecture* and of the work of Inigo Jones, and developed a style which was the culmination of that style known as Palladian. The working plans and on-the-spot detailing were attended to by another architect, Matthew Brettingham.

The Coke (pronounced *cook*) family is an example of a family which rose to wealth and greatness during the upheaval which followed the Reformation. Edward Coke, the founder of the family's prosperity, was the son of a Norfolk barrister practising

228

in London: by his merits he became Speaker of the House of Commons, Solicitor General, and Attorney General, by his marriages (one to a Paston and the other to a Hatton) he acquired a huge holding in land. We may blame him for leading the prosecution of Sir Walter Raleigh, but we must praise him for opposing James I when that monarch tried repeatedly to set aside the law, and for his opposition to Charles I when he tried to do the same. James imprisoned him for a time in the Tower. Coke died before the Civil War, but his work was part of the movement that was leading towards it. He bought the Holkham Estate from the Armigers in 1610; one of many similar purchases.

The Coke family managed to stay afloat during both the Civil War and the Restoration. Thomas Coke succeeded to the estates in 1707 when he was ten years old, and shortly afterwards he set out on the Grand Tour, accompanied by his chaplain and a retinue of other officers. He encountered Lord Burlington in Italy and became fired with a great enthusiasm for Italian art and architecture. He made a great collection of paintings and sculptures, returned to England and devoted the rest of his life to the building of Holkham Hall.

He never lived to see the Hall completed. Whatever satisfaction he derived from it was in the building; and his enjoyment was girt with brick kilns and builders' rubble. His great collection of works of art remained wrapped up for most of his lifetime, for he had nowhere to put it. Holkham Hall was to become a museum to house his collection, and a library to house his great accumulation of books. Many of these have now been given to the University of East Anglia, Norwich. Thomas Coke died, and his widow completed the building of the house in 1762: it had taken twenty-eight years to build, and decades of thought, discussion, and research before that. Thomas Coke had first watched Burlington House go up, and he, Burlington, and William Kent had spent years in studying and discussing the architecture of the classical world, and of contemporary Italy.

So Coke died, the great house was completed, and 'Capability' Brown was called in to do the garden. Thomas Coke, who when he died was 1st Earl of Leicester, left no heir; but the estates were left to a nephew who took on the name of Coke. This man died in a year, leaving the place to his son, also Thomas Coke, who became famous in England as 'Coke of Norfolk'.

'Coke of Norfolk' was, off and on, a Member of Parliament for over fifty years, a Whig, and bitterly opposed to the war against the American colonies. Also he was one of the great 'improving landlords' of the eighteenth and early nineteenth centuries. It is often said that he invented the 'Norfolk four-course rotation'. This is not so ('Turnip' Townshend of Raynham Hall came nearer to it), but he applied it on his home farms and imposed it on the many tenants of his 50,000-acre estate. He managed during his life to raise the rent he extracted annually from his tenants from £2,000 a year to £20,000. He experimented with the newly emerging breeds of sheep, cattle and pigs (he imported Italian pigs as his great-uncle had imported Italian works of art), and in many ways he was an agricultural innovator. The marl pits which dot the North Norfolk plain are mostly due to him, for he caused his tenants to marl their light soil (that is apply dressings of clay mixed with chalk dug up from selected pits). He made them improve fertility by gradual increase of stocking rates, by the 'golden hoof' (the folding of sheep on arable land), by the adoption of rotation farming instead of the old wasteful method of bare fallowing.

By attending Court in country dress he led a revolution in dress style: the Regency 'dandies' who came after him copied his country Norfolk clothes. His agricultural ideas spread over England by means of the annual 'sheep-shearings' that he held in his barn (still standing), and that were attended by his tenantry, neighbours, and by agriculturists from all over Britain. It was on one of these occasions that one of his tenants got up and admonished the others: 'Do you do as his Lordship do you'll do better you do do!' The first of these Norfolk 'dos' can be translated as 'if' and the fourth and last as 'prosper'. The East Anglian 'do' (pronounced *dew*) can have many meanings.

When 'Coke of Norfolk' (now Lord Leicester of the second creation) died his neighbours erected, by subscription, the great column which stands to the north of the house and which has such peaceful emblems on it as a wheatsheaf at the top, and cows and sheep and other beasts of the field about the plinth.

The severity, not to say plainness, of the exterior of the house does not prepare you for the magnificence of the Marble Hall.

First you enter an **ante-hall**, which is embellished by busts of such illustrious departed as Homer, Alexander the Great, and the 2nd Earl of Leicester in terracotta, and four marble busts by Nollekins of, respectively, Francis Duke of Bedford, Charles James Fox, William Windham and the Marquis of Hastings. On the left is a Thomas Tompion clock, made in 1676 for Greenwich Observatory and wound up once a year.

Then you step into the vast colonnaded interior of the **great hall**, and great it certainly is, by any standards: 60 feet high. All seems to gleam with marble and alabaster and gold. Busts of various Earls of Leicester look down at you from on high: at the foot of the stairs is a bust of 'Coke of Norfolk' by his friend Sir Francis Chantrey and another of the 1st Earl, first creation, also by Chantrey but from a model by Roubilliac. The founder of the house is also represented by a bust by Roubilliac over the doorway, looking in. There is a bas-relief by Chantrey of William IV signing the Reform Bill, with Coke of Norfolk standing there to see that he does it, the Trial of Socrates by Westmacott, Death of Germanicus by T. Banks RA (a poignant spectacle indeed!) and the delivery-up of the gates of Florence to Cosmo the Great by Pietrino da Vinci, all bas-reliefs. And at the end of the gallery, round to the right, is a plaque, carved by Sir Francis Chantrey, of two woodcock – slain by Sir Francis Chantrey in one shot in 1829. Two woodcock killed in one shot is unusual to say the least of it – can it be that these birds were sent to their final rest at a moment of mutual tenderness?

The **north dining-room** is a perfect cube, with a ceiling from a design by Inigo Jones. There is a superb head of Aphrodite over one of the fireplaces said to have come out of the Parthenon, there is a huge bust of Lucius Verus discovered when clearing the harbour of Nettun, and there are classical busts of Geta and Marcus Aurelius, with marble drapery added to them in the seventeenth century. The carpet – probably an Axminster – echoes the Inigo Jones design of the ceiling.

The great **statue gallery** and **tribunes** (the three rooms are 105 feet long and cut across the house almost at its narrowest part, which gives some idea of the scale of the place) contain an astonishing collection of classical statuary: many a museum of world fame would find it hard to match. From the left, as you go into the North Tribune, are Athene, Thucydides (a copy of a bronze original which was described by Professor Poulson as the earliest individual portrait in Greek art; certainly looking at the bust we feel we know the man), Dionysius, Diana – said to have been owned by Cicero and bought by the 1st Earl in 1717 for which act he only just escaped imprisonment by the Italian authorities – Venus Genetrix, a bust of Apollo (over the fireplace), Lucius Verus over the niche and the Pythian Apollo in it, Meleager, a wonderful statue of Silenos, Poseidon, bust of a man called Sulla of Hadrian's reign, a brace of young satyrs, in uneasy juxtaposition with them a Roman lady of Hadrian's time, the head of an empress of the time of Elegabalus, a bust of Seneca, a bust of an old man and a statue of Ceres. The furniture is all contemporary with the house and was made by Goodison from designs of William Kent, the chief architect of the house.

To the right, from the South Tribune, are private apartments, for the 6th Earl lives in the house, although he does not now occupy the principal rooms. But to the left is the **drawing-room**, with a full-length portrait of Nell Gwynne by Kneller, four landscapes by Orizonti, Numbers 84 and 85 are emblematical representations of King William's wars by Hondecooter, there is a storm by Poussin, a Madonna *in Gloria* by Pietro da Pietri, Apollo flaying Marsyas by Claude le Lorrain, portrait of Henry Rich, Earl of Warwick, by Van Dyck.

Next the **saloon**, hung with the original Genoa velvet, and with two lovely mosaic tables found in Hadrian's villa near Tivoli. Furniture made to Kent's design and covered with Genoa velvet. Pictures are: The Artist's Daughter by Maratti, The Holy Family by Rubens, A Lady playing on a Spinet by Maratti, Coke of Norfolk, aged twenty-eight – wearing the famous country clothes that he wore when presenting the address to George III asking for the independence of the American colonies, the clothes which inspired the accepted regency style – by Gainsborough. Portrait of Fox by Opie – commissioned by Coke of Norfolk, William III by Kneller, Duc d'Arenberg by Van Dyck, Lord Chief Justice Coke by Cornelius Johnson.

The **south dining-room** is also hung with Genoa velvet, and the fireplace is from a design by Inigo Jones. Pictures from left to right: Sir Thomas More after Holbein, copy by Andrea del Sarto of the Raphael in the Uffizi Gallery of Pope Leo X, Cardinal Guilio de Medici and his nephew Cardinal de Rossi, A Venetian Lady by Titian, A Venus – said to be Princess d'Obilo – with a portrait of Philip of Spain after Titian, A Sunset by Swanavelt (copied from a Claude), a still life by Hondecooter, St John baptizing Christ by F. Bolognese, Archbishop Laud after Van Dyck, Joseph and Potiphar's Wife by Guido Reni, Sir A. Talmarsh by Sir Peter Lely. The blue porcelain is Sèvres, 1792–1804, chairs by Chippendale.

The **landscape room** contains a fine collection of Claude le Lorrains. Claude was said to have been the 1st Earl's favourite artist, and you would go far to find such a good collection of his work. There are also pictures by Nicholas and Gaspar Poussin.

The **green state bedroom** is hung with three panels of Brussels tapestry by Auwere, representing Europe, Africa and America, and a fourth panel, representing Asia, by Saunders of Soho. This room was slept in by Queen Victoria in 1835, and George V in 1912. Over the fireplace is the 1st Earl in the robes of the Bath, and over the door are the four seasons by Zucharelli.

In the **brown state dressing-room** is the only copy ever made of the cartoon which Michelangelo designed for one side of the hall of the Great Council of Florence, before it was maliciously destroyed by Baccio Baninelli. It is by Bastiano di San Gallo. There is also a fresco on stone by Annibale Caracci, and paintings by Maratti, Bassano and Giordano.

The **brown state bedroom** has velvet of 1910, Coke of Norfolk over the fireplace in fancy dress by Battoni and presented to Coke by Louise, wife of Charles Edward the Young Pretender. The fancy dress was worn at a ball given in honour of Charles Edward's marriage in Rome, painted by order of the bride (with whom Coke danced), and the statue in the background, of the lovelorn Ariadne, is said to be an actual likeness of Louise. There is James II by Lely and portraits of early Cokes.

The **state sitting-room** has Brussels tapestry, a ceiling designed by Lord Burlington (who took a great interest in the building of the house of course), portraits of the 1st Earl's great-grandparents, the Duke and Duchess of Leeds by Kneller.

Many large museums could envy the Holkham collection. Considered as a home, which is what it was designed for, I cannot think of anything more uncomfortable than Holkham Hall. Considered as a piece of East Anglia it is of course absurd, being a piece of Italy. But as one of the finest of the collections amassed by the English noblemen in their eighteenth-century raids on Italy and the classical word it is of the first interest.

The park at Holkham is one of the finest in the country: Canada and other wild and semi-wild geese flock on the big lake, deer graze within sight of the great house, and the collection of trees, which extends for miles, is most famous. Cuttings from the many fine ilex trees are sent to London to feed the giraffes at the zoo.

A number of features and activities have been added to the premises in recent decades. An attractive nineteenth-century building houses the 'Bygones' collection featured on Dick Joice's popular television series, including displays of fire engines, traction engines, old cars, a laundry, and an original nineteenth-century harness room. Craft demonstrations are held during the summer, and there are 'steam days' as announced at various times. In one wing of the hall is Holkham Pottery, established by the wife of the 5th Earl. This nobleman caused a stir in 1973 with a speech on the environment: it was the first time he had spoken during 22 years in the House of Lords. He commented that neither his father nor great-grandfather had, in 23 and 67 years respectively, spoken at all.

The road opposite the main gates leads to Holkham Gap, where there is a car park for the beach and for trails through a National Nature Reserve.

Wells-next-the-Sea is one of the most splendid little towns in England, but it carries its unawareness of its quality and uniqueness to the point where both are being damaged. Street after street of flint housing (and flint houses become rarer and rarer as more are pulled down every year and none are put up) have been bulldozed to clear land for 'development', and what the development is can too well be imagined. Characterless brick and concrete building that will eventually make Wells just another seaside town like a thousand others, and not the little flint jewel that it has been, and in part remains.

Wells has one of the most distinguished waterfronts in England. Great eighteenth- and nineteenth-century warehouses loom up over the waterfront road, and there is hardly an intrinsically ugly building along the whole front, although several have been *made* ugly, hideously so, by their owners trying to copy the lowest of the pin-table-and-Bingo culture. A fisherman once said to me, as we were coming up on the tide to the whelk boiling sheds: 'Blackpool has its "golden mile" – well Wells has its "golden hundred yards" anyway!' The marvel is that people who have good enough taste to want to go to Wells should want to see this fine waterfront cheapened and vulgarized.

Coasting shipping still comes up to the Wells Quay. Very often a small Dutch coaster can be seen discharging fertilizer, or cattle cake, or chemicals.

There are two little fishing fleets. One consists of a small fleet of tiny decked motor trawlers locally known as 'the spratters'. These belong to a firm of enthusiasts who originally started 'pair fishing' (dragging one net between two boats) for sprats from Whitstable, in Kent. They became migratory, following the fish wherever these were to be found, but now they seem to have settled in Wells. They still catch sprats when there are any, but more often these days 'roka', as skate are called in East Anglia (like many East Anglian words this is of Dutch, and Low German, derivation). They trawl for these with small orthodox otter trawls.

But the traditional Wells fleet consists of the 'Wells whelkers'. Most of these are open clinker-built boats built much on the lines of the Sheringham crabbers but twice as big. There are, too, a couple of ex-RNLI lifeboats (of the 'Liverpool' type), converted to the fishery.

A trip to sea in a whelker is a great experience, particularly if a nor'easter is blowing. The boats generally leave very early in the morning – any time after midnight. They get over the bar in the mouth of the Wells river as late as they dare on the ebb tide, and often they leave it a little fine and *bump* hard as they go across the drying sand and meet the breakers. Once out over that bar they have the scarcely comforting thought that they cannot get *back* again – come Hell or high water – until many hours later, for they must wait until the tide recedes, and returns, and covers the bar

235

with enough water to float them. They head straight out to sea, and may go anything up to thirty miles.

Here they sight their 'dan buoys', small sticks bobbing about on the waves with flags flying from them. Then comes the business of hauling the 'shanks' of whelk pots, which is much the same as hauling crab pots except that it is done with a power winch, and from much deeper water. Soon the man whose job it is to empty the pots is standing knee-deep in whelks and cannot move his feet. Another man works hard at rebaiting the pots with salt herring and flinging them overboard.

When all the pots have been handled and shot again – many hours of very hard work – the boats head for home. They all assemble outside Wells Bar, and bob about waiting for enough water. If a gale has blown up meanwhile they must just stay and face it – there is nowhere they can go for shelter. Finally one boat tries – bumps hard on the hard sand bar amid sheets of spray – gets over – the others cautiously follow – and they all go running up the calm river to the boiling sheds, where the whelks are unloaded and put straight into the coppers. Nearly all the whelks in England go over the Wells Bar. There is good money in it for fishermen, but it is hard and dangerous work, and each little family firm has thousands of pounds invested in boats and gear. A Russian trawler can come along (one often does) and roll up and completely destroy a whole shank of pots worth a couple of hundred pounds in a few minutes.

A local pub, rearing above the beach and much frequented by weekend sailors at their nearby moorings and by local fishermen, is the Shipwrights Arms. Among the most respected of those local families is that of the Coxes, who still go whelk fishing and who have produced one accomplished landscape and seascape painter, Jack Cox, and a very distinguished cox in another sense: David Cox, coxswain of the lifeboat.

Wells' lifeboat is stationed right out near the bar and is launched beyond it into the open sea. You get there by walking along a mile of straight river wall, or driving along the road behind it. At the beginning of the wall is a memorial to the eleven members of the crew of the boat when she capsized in 1880. There is a big caravan camp behind the wall, and a beautiful sandy beach backed by a belt of sand dunes planted with Corsican pines (by the 2nd Lord Leicester).

Another way of travelling along this stretch is by a miniature railway which operates daily from Easter until the end of September. During that same period there is also a narrow-gauge light railway running along four miles of the old Great Eastern track from Wells to Little Walsingham, through a landscape rich in wild flowers and butterflies.

Going east we come to **Stiffkey**, pronounced just as it is spelt and not, as journalists insisted in the great days of its notorious rector, *stukey* – although in William the Conqueror's time it was spelt Steuakai. Here all is flint, and the village's charm is tempered only by the fact that the A149 – curse of the North Norfolk coast – goes right through it.

Morston is the embarkation point for boats carrying passengers out to **Blakeney Point**, a National Trust nature reserve on salt marsh and sand-dunes. There are two observation hides, and a graphic display in the lifeboat house, which shelters the Warden during the nesting season. The Warden is also in charge of the motor boats for taking people out to it. People are welcomed there, as well as birds; and in the spring time the place is rowdy with dive-bombing terns, and oyster-catchers and other nesting waders. The point is wild and sandy, with high dunes covered with coarse grass and other flora, sea hammering it on one side and lost creeks and mud-flats on the other. Sunk down amid the sand-dunes is a weird old lifeboat house, now used as a hostel by various groups of people who go and camp there. The point is not an island, like Scolt Head, but one can walk there from Cley. Sometimes the birdwatchers outnumber the birds, and then the only thing to do is to watch the birdwatchers.

Blakeney is perhaps the most beautiful village in Norfolk. Its beauty is carefully preserved, though, by the wealthy people who have bought up nearly all the little cottages, and converted them either into holiday homes or else houses to retire to. This has happened all along this flint coast: the retired, commuters, and 'summer residents' have snapped up most of the old cottages and houses that once belonged to fishermen, seafarers and farm workers, and the latter classes have had to move off to council houses (like the ones in that vast estate that defaces Wells), or else to towns where there are cheaper houses and more work. Certainly no fisherman could afford to buy a 'fisherman's cottage' today. Cottages that would have been considered dear at £50 before the Second World War now fetch thousands. But the charm of this coast is that it was built up by farmers and their men, and by fishermen, sailors and wildfowlers.

Blakeney is now what is called 'select', meaning that many of its inhabitants have a lot of money. There is no 'pin-table-and-Bingo culture' there. And the wealthy inhabitants care for the flint cottages and houses excellently: had they not bought them most of them would have fallen down. There is a Blakeney Housing Trust that has bought up and repaired many of them – alas that there is not an equivalent in Wells.

Blakeney has a superb natural harbour, protected from the sea by Blakeney Point, with a perfectly sheltered deep-water anchorage called 'The Pit' about three miles downstream from Blakeney Quay. Blakeney is perhaps the best place of all from which to enjoy the unique mixture of open sea, and dunes, saltings, mud-flats, salt marshes and creeks of this fascinating coast. There can be few stretches of country anywhere which arouse such passionate love and enthusiasm in the people who know it and live there. A man could spend his life in getting to know it.

The quay is always so crowded with yachts and other craft that it is difficult for a stranger to find a berth. Most of the open motor boats used for taking passengers out to Blakeney Point were introduced by Mr Stratton Long, who also founded a well-stocked yacht chandler's in the great warehouse which reaches down to the quay. Mr Long founded his fortunes on the salvage of 'Queen Bee' target planes from the sea for the Americans. Blakeney's commercial greatness is remembered in the fourteenth-century Guildhall, open dawn to dusk. The church up on the hill is very fine, though much restored inside. Besides the high fifteenth-century west tower there is another, unique turret at the east end, with a staircase inside leading to a small room above the chancel.

On the slopes of **Wiveton Downs** behind, there are pathways over undisturbed countryside with views inland and along the coast. A car park beside the Wiveton Road gives immediate access to a

17-acre picnic site. The whole area is a showpiece for anyone with an interest in Ice Age formations and deposits.

East again, over the Glaveney River, is **Cley-next-the-Sea** (Cley is pronounced Cly). Another lovely flint village, smaller than Blakeney now but it was once, as Blakeney was, a thriving port and the eighteenth-century Custom House still stands at the east end of it. A Custom House of this size indicates a big trade with the Continent, and indeed Cley has a Low Country air about it, with Dutch gables over its hotel. Even allowing for the deeper draught of ships, the Glaven Estuary must have silted up seriously since that Custom House was built: certainly no coasting vessel could get up there now.

Cley church merits the epithet 'great'. It speaks of enormous prosperity in the fourteenth century when most of the church was rebuilt. Cley, then, was probably the exporting port for at least half of north Norfolk's sheep country: thousands of tons of wool must have gone out of it to be sailed away to Europe.

The nave is marvellous, and very grand. The chancel is much smaller: the building is commonly supposed to have been stopped by the Black Death. The projected great west tower never got built. I sometimes wonder if it was not only the Black Death that interfered with this: was it not also the importation of Flemish weavers by Edward III which changed the traffic from exporting raw wool to exporting finished cloth, and the source of the exports from the sheep country of north Norfolk to the weaving centres in south and east Norfolk and in Suffolk?

The fifteenth-century south porch is extremely beautiful. There is a nice arcade on the south of the nave with good carving under it, and there are some good bench-ends. It is a church not to be missed, standing as it does – a great work of art – on the edge of nowhere. There is a large and well preserved windmill at Cley, open some afternoons between Easter and the end of September.

Salthouse is yet another coastal flint village, also with a fine church. The village was much bashed by the 1953 tidal surge.

Cutting inland, and south-west, we cross the Glaven again and quickly climb up on to the high and windy chalk uplands and come to **Binham**. Binham is an example of the many little flint villages that back this wonderful coastline. These villages are generally compact, standing amid miles of empty country, and generally built around one or more huge farmsteads rather as villages tend to be in northern France. Everything is flint – even the massive barns and the cattle yards.

The cattle yards of these East Anglian farms were built to house fattening bullocks in the winter – bullocks fed on the straw and mangolds grown in the huge fields. Dairying is a new industry in East Anglia, introduced originally by Scots farmers who flooded in and bought up farms during the depression of the 1920s. The great barns were the temples of High Farming, the sort of farming Coke of Norfolk encouraged. All these great East Anglian barns are built upon the same plan, a huge rectangle with two opposing transepts in the middle, like the transepts of a church, each containing very large doors. The purpose of the opposing doors was to allow a through wind to winnow the grain after threshing. The threshing-floor was in the middle, at the crossing. Here men battered the sheaves, the winter through, with their flails (or 'frails' as East Anglians call them), and the flails – a long and short stick joined together – were joined together by eel skin, this being considered the toughest material for this exacting task. The eel catchers of East Anglia made more by selling their eel skins than they did from the eels inside them. The common way of catching eels along this coast was by *pritching*. The *pritch* is a barbed Neptune's trident, which is stabbed into the mud where the eels are hoped to lie. Another, rather barbarous, fishing engine exclusive to North Norfolk is the 'butt drag'. This is an iron bar set with big barbed cod hooks which is dragged through the mud so that the hooks impale the 'butts' as dabs are called in East Anglia.

But back to Binham. The priory church here is one of the most atmospheric buildings in Norfolk. The west end of it is Early English (not well represented in East Anglia) and the great (alas bricked-up) window has been described by Pevsner as 'the paradigm of Geometrical tracery at its purest'. The window is so large that there is hardly any wall. The splendid Norman triforium and clerestory have been described as surpassing even Norwich in excellence. The former aisles have been knocked off and the whole place truncated and mutilated, and it has obviously suffered – and no doubt still suffers – from a lack of money and attention: and how could such a fine great place not do so, supported as it is by a tiny population around two or three farms? The wonderful Early English west front was the work of Prior Richard de Parco, early thirteenth century. It is a premature example of 'geometrical' tracery.

De Parco was a good prior, and much given to building. A successor, William de Somerton, was the medieval equivalent of a horse-player: he was an alchemist, and he sold most of the priory's valuables to obtain money for his researches. He fled to Rome in the end, leaving the priory much in debt. But Binham would have gone down anyway: it had no relics to compete either with Bromholm with its Holy Rood, or Walsingham with its Holy House. It was a cell of St Albans, and like that other cell of St Albans, Wymondham Abbey, its history is one of constant bickering with its mother abbey. In fact one wonders how the monks ever found time for any prayer or meditation so constant was their quarrelling and their litigation. In 1212 or so, Robert Fitz Walter suddenly laid claim to the patronage of the place, and besieged it with troops. 'By God's Feet!' said King John. 'Either I or Fitz Walter must be King in England!' And he sent soldiers to chase Fitz Walter away.

The ruins of the priory buildings, and the great east end of the church pulled down at the Reformation, still have much old masonry to see, and the place should be visited, alone, on a fine night with a full moon. The experience is transporting.

From Binham it is but a short step to Walsingham, perhaps the most successful religious house of all. We come to **Great Walsingham** first, which has a beautiful fourteenth-century church with lovely window tracery. But it is **Little Walsingham** which is really the greater of the two.

> *As ye come from the holy land*
> *Of Walsingham,*
> *Met ye not with my true love*
> *By the way as ye came?*

In the reign of King Edward the Confessor the wife of Walsingham's lord of the manor, named Richeldis, dreamed that the Virgin Mary appeared to her and asked that a replica of the House of the Annunciation should be built in the village. The site of the shrine would be revealed by the appearance of a fresh spring of water. The Lady Richeldis awoke from her dream, found the new spring of water, and built over it a small and simple shrine. The fame of this rapidly spread, and the place came to be known as 'England's Nazareth', and so great were the numbers of pilgrims to it that the Milky Way in the heavens, with its myriad stars, became known as 'the Walsingham Way' and was said to point to Walsingham. For centuries it was the greatest goal for pilgrimage in England, not excluding even Canterbury. To visit it, indeed, was the equivalent of visiting the real Nazareth in the Holy Land. The Normans took the shrine over from the English, and every king from Richard I to Henry VIII made pilgrimage, the latter walking barefooted from Barsham Manor (as many pilgrims do today). The vast wealth of the shrine caught Henry VIII's eye, however, and at the Dissolution he sequestered all, and had the image of Our Lady of Walsingham (which had appeared miraculously in the original shrine) taken to London and burnt in Cromwell's London house at Chelsea, so that 'the people should use no more idolatrye unto it'.

> *In the wrackes of Walsingham*
>   *Whom should I chuse*
> *But the Queen of Walsingham*
>   *To be guide to my muse?*
>
> *Then thou Prince of Walsingham*
>   *Grant me to frame*
> *Bitter plaintes to rewe they wrong*
>   *Bitter wo for thy name.*
>
> *Bitter was it oh to see*
>   *The seely sheepe*
> *Murdered by the raveninge wolves*
>   *While the shepherds did sleep.*
>
> *Bitter was it oh to vewe*
>   *The sacred vyne*
> *While the gardiners plaied all close*
>   *Rooted up by the swine.*

Bitter, bitter oh to behould
  The grasse to growe
Where the walls of Walsingham
  So stately did shewe.

Such were the works of Walsingham
  Where she did stand
Such are the wrackes as nowe do shewe
  Of that holy land.

Levell levell with the ground
  The towres doe lye
Which with their golden, glittering tops
  Pearsed once to the sky.

Where weare gates no gates are nowe,
  The waies unknowen,
Where the press of peares did pass
  While her fame was far blowen.

Oules do scrike where the sweetest himnes
  Lately were songe,
Toades and serpents hold their dennes
  Where the palmers did throng.

Weepe, weepe O Walsingham,
  Whose dayes are nightes,
Blessings turned to blasphemies,
  Holy deeds to dispites.

Sinne is where our Ladie sate,
  Heaven turned is to hell,
Sathan sittes where our Lord did swaye,
  Walsingham oh farewell.

I make no apologies for printing these beautiful verses, for firstly they are the most moving expression of the intense horror which the Reformation caused to the faithful over all the land, and secondly they are supposed to have been written by an East Anglian, Philip Howard, Earl of Arundel.

It speaks for the thoroughness with which the Reformation was carried out that so very little of this 'Holy Land of Walsingham' remains. Once, besides the huge abbey church, there was a great complex of religious houses, hostels which could house thousands of pilgrims, hundreds of merchants and palmers and other commercial hangers-on selling holy relics and images to the devout.

For anything equivalent existing today one must go to Madura, or Ramaswaram, or Badrachalam, or other of the great shrines of South India, in their times of especial holiness: places thronged with people – people pious, merry, credulous or just commercial – people laughing, jostling, friendly, sometimes open-mouthed with religious wonder – but all enjoying every moment of their religious holiday. Nothing that we see at Walsingham today gives any hint that such things could have been. The pilgrimages have begun again, but they are very decorous and English affairs.

The Augustines founded their priory in 1149. All that remains of the great church is the fifteenth-century east window which still stands gaunt and impressive in the abbey gardens backed by great beech trees, and the gatehouse and fragments of the old monastic buildings incorporated in the big eighteenth-century house. There are two wishing wells associated with the foundations of the shrine. The grounds are open to the general public on Wednesday afternoons in April, plus Saturdays and Sundays from May to September, and daily except Tuesday and Thursday in August; also Bank Holidays from Easter to August.

There is a Slipper Chapel in the neighbouring parish of **Houghton St Giles**. Pilgrims on their way to the shrine used to leave their shoes in this little fourteenth-century grey stone building and walk the last mile barefoot. Today it is dwarfed by a huge modern building of red brick and tile, with stone panels, dedicated as the Roman Catholic Shrine of Our Lady and Chapel of Reconciliation, open daily all year round.

Anglicans have their own shrine in Little Walsingham. In 1931, the Rev. Hope Patten – the incumbent of the parish – started the building of a replica of the Walsingham Holy House, which was itself a replica of the Holy House of Nazareth. The original Holy House of Walsingham was visited by Erasmus, in 1511 (when he resided at Cambridge) and he describes it thus:

The original chapel is built of wood and pilgrims are admitted through a narrow door at each side. There is but little or no light but what proceeds from tapers yielding a most pleasant and odoriferous smell, but if you will look in you will say it is the seat of the gods, so bright and shining it is all over with jewels, gold and silver . . .

The new Holy House is of the same dimensions as the original, but is built of brick and not wood. The story of the selection of the site for it is that Hope Patten, together with a band of enthusiasts including the late Duke of Argyll, walked out of the parish church and knelt down in the main street of Little Walsingham to pray for a sign. No sign was forthcoming, but later Hope Patten sited the shrine on a convenient plot by the cross-roads, and as the foundations were being dug a filled-in well was found, and this is taken to be the original holy well of the Lady Richeldis.

Now, the new Holy House is enclosed within a large pilgrimage church, and the well is incorporated within the wall. A replica of the original Virgin of Walsingham (which had appeared miraculously) was made at Chelsea where the other was burnt, and installed within the shrine, and is the chief object of pilgrimage. In addition to the altar in the Holy House, and the High Altar, there are sixteen other altars in the church, most of them in small dimly lit shrines with round brick domes over them, and there is a chapel of the Eastern Orthodox Church in which Orthodox priests come to celebrate their liturgy. Within the church are two pieces of the True Cross, a relic of St Vincent and one of St Thomas, a statue of St Charles the Martyr (otherwise Charles I), numerous pieces of (very 1930s-looking) statuary, murals, and a great wealth of icons and reliquaries, and vestments. In the garden are the Stations of the Cross, and a replica of Christ's sepulchre.

It is unfortunate that the shrine church was built when it was, for this was not a peak of excellence in English architecture, and the plastered exterior has all the distinction of a hundred pre-1940 suburban churches and fits very ill in Little Walsingham which otherwise hasn't got an undistinguished building in it. The interior is more impressive, and probably very meet for its purpose. The whole inside is a complex of round brick arches, giving mysterious vistas in every direction, with many glimpses into dimly lit chapels – all very richly furnished. The Holy House itself is a strange building, its walls set with stones from other religious foundations in the British Isles and hung with petitions from the faithful and also thanks for material and spiritual benefits received. One can purchase bottles of the water from the well. A large addition is now planned for the church.

In the ancient and beautiful college buildings beside the new shrine three or four priests live, and there is a small nunnery. The nuns run a hostel for pilgrims, and also a shop selling religious objects. Pilgrims come in great numbers, at least 100,000 every year, and recently they included the Bishop of Southwark.

The Russian Orthodox church has its own shrine in the shrine church, and their Brotherhood of St Seraphim of Sarov has taken over Walsingham's abandoned railway station for a centre.

The parish church of Little Walsingham should not be missed in all this excitement, for it contains the finest 'seven sacrament' font in East Anglia, which is famous for this kind of font. It is richly carved but, alas, defaced. The church was gutted by fire in 1961 but admirably rebuilt, with a radiant stained glass window over the altar.

Great Snoring should be visited, not only because it has such an extraordinary name, but because it has a lovely late Tudor rectory and the Four Last Things (Heaven, Hell, Death and Judgement) on the commandment board in the church. **Little Snoring** has a wonderful Norman font and pre-Norman round tower.

East Barsham is famous for its manor house (with a nice pub opposite). This is one of the best examples there is of early Tudor carved and moulded brickwork and is really a most spectacular and theatrical building, lavishly decorated, said to have been built by Sir William Fermor in Henry VIII's reign. It looks superb from the top of the hill in the Fakenham direction, especially in winter when the hills are covered with snow. There is a free vigour about this highly decorative use of brick in late medieval and early Tudor times that we may well envy at this present day, when 'brick' is another word for dullness. East Barsham manor was inhabited by a member of the Hapsburg family up until the last war.

Thorpland Hall, just north of Fakenham on the River Stiffkey, is another typical North Norfolk wool king's mansion, also of Tudor brick with a pinnacled gatehouse, mullioned windows, and wonderful moulded chimneys.

Fakenham has some good brickwork too, including nice Victorian maltings and a big flour mill. There are good eighteenth-century brick houses too around the market place, and it is an attractive little country town, on the River Wensum. The church is large, very restored, but has a Decorated clerestory and beautiful Decorated east window tracery (with Victorian glass). The best things are the sedilia and piscina, late fourteenth century and extremely graceful.

North-east of Fakenham, off the road to Holt, is **Thursford**, with its huge collection of showmen's steam engines, ploughing engines, a narrow gauge steam railway, fairground organs, barrel organs, and one of the last of the mighty Wurlitzers which once thundered through our theatres and cinemas. The Thursford Collection is open every afternoon from Easter to the end of October, Sunday afternoons in March, April and November, and Good Friday and Easter Monday. There are special Christmas events in December, and then the grounds close during January and February.

CHAPTER 14

King's Lynn to Swaffham

The **River Nar**, which debouches into the Great Ouse at King's Lynn through a squalid creek, was once called Norfolk's 'Holy River': there were so many religious foundations along it. Near its mouth now lie the rotting remains of a Humber Keel: one of those highly specialized vessels of north-eastern waterways, reminding us of the once strong commercial ties between North Norfolk and the Humber area.

First upstream is Blackborough Priory, founded by the Benedictines but chivalrously handed over to nuns and with now practically nothing to see. **Narborough**, farther upstream, stands below the fifty-foot contour and may well have been the head of navigation of the river. John Braine, a monk of Thetford in Henry IV's time, wrote that Narborough was a city in the reign of the British king Uther Pendragon, in AD 500, but was captured by Waldy and razed to the ground. It was razed to the ground again quite recently, in an ill-advised 'improvement' move, which destroyed all the houses along the river, which had made it one of Norfolk's outstandingly beautiful villages, and erected a soulless housing estate instead.

From nearby starts Devil's Dyke, and as nobody knows anything about this we may as well leave it to the Devil. **West Acre** had a very large Augustinian priory, of which significant fragments lie each side of the river, most of them mixed up with a modern farmyard. The Stag Inn is a nice building, of a fine mixture of flint, carr stone and old brick, with a spirited inn sign depicting what looks more like a stag in rut rather than one at bay. Some of the older regulars can remember burning lime in the big lime-pits over the river. All Saints church is a mainly Perpendicular building, with an odd sculptured panel in the north porch showing a seated figure

– much earlier than the church and possibly taken from the priory.

Narborough Hall, just downstream of West Acre, is a vast hall with its villageless church standing in its park as though God were the personal property of the squire, and there are notable Scots pine plantations in the park. The Hall was built by the father of Sir Andrew Fountaine, who was knighted by William III and was Vice-Chamberlain to the Prince of Wales. Sir Andrew travelled in Europe and collected a great quantity of majolica ware. The whole village had been bought by the Fountaines at the end of the seventeenth century. They were an offshoot of the ffunteyns of Salle. There is a lake, trout, and wildfowl.

Castle Acre is the greatest place in East Anglia for ruin-lovers. This area of Norfolk, high on the chalk uplands, may strike the traveller as being desolate and depopulated. The country, with its light grey-looking chalky soil which blows away in such vast dust storms every spring, is given over to big farmers who have bulldozed away every hedge and spinney, leaving only the little clumps of beech trees that stand up on the rounded hills like scalp-locks on the shaven pates of Red Indians – and they have left those simply because they are growing on old marlpits which are unploughable. The practice of marling, now no longer in use, was the digging-out of mixed chalk and clay from pits and the spreading of this on the land. It was practised in Roman Britain, revived by eighteenth-century agriculturalists (notably Coke of Norfolk, who owned most of this land), condemned by the Suffolk farming writer Arthur Young as being useless, and thereafter discontinued.

There is something very medieval, yes and foreign, about Castle Acre. It reminds one of a big agricultural village in northern France. This is due to its compactness, lack of straggle, hill-top site. Instead of living in cottages scattered over the countryside as farm workers do in other parts of England, such of the inhabitants of this stretch of countryside as are still farm workers live in this town-like village and travel anything up to five miles to work. In the carrot-digging season, which lasts from late summer right through the winter, you will see large gangs of men and women strung out over the prairie-like fields, with cars parked in scores by the roadside.

Entering Castle Acre it is impossible to ignore the vast earthwork of the castle up on the hill. Although the castle itself was a

Norman foundation, archaeological investigations have shown that the earthen ramparts must have been there before the Normans, and may well date from the Iron Age. Castle Acre stands at the junction of the Peddar's Way, a Celtic and then Roman track, and another Roman road beginning at Water Newton west of Peterborough and probably finishing at Caister-by-Yarmouth on the east coast. The Normans added the mound, as they usually did on such eminently defensible sites. William de Warenne, 1st Earl of Surrey, who also founded the priory at Lewes, was the builder. The whole village of Castle Acre is the outer bailey of the castle, which is what gives it its fine fortified appearance: most of the houses have stones and flints filched from the ruined walls. In the middle of the village is a sturdy eleventh-century gateway to the outside world.

The priory, the finest ruin in East Anglia, lies low in green fields by the river Nar. In the care of English Heritage, it is closed all day Monday, and Tuesday mornings in winter.

William de Warenne, and his wife Gundreda who was a daughter of William the Conqueror, visited the great abbey at Cluny in Burgundy, and on coming to England established the Cluniac Priory of St Pancras at Lewes, where the de Warennes had their chief castle. The order spread over England from there, and houses were opened at Wenlock, Northampton, Bermondsey, Daventry, Pontefract and Thetford. Castle Acre was formed as a daughter priory of Lewes, and in her turn had four daughters: Bromholm (p. 155) with its relic of the True Cross, Normansburgh and Slevesholm in Norfolk, and Mendham in Suffolk, very little of which remain to be seen.

The 2nd Earl of Surrey richly endowed Castle Acre Priory: the churches of Acre, Methwold, Wickmere and Trunch were some of the East Anglian properties devoted to the priory, to say nothing of '15 acres of land and 2,000 eels' at Methwold, and a serf named Ulmar 'along with his garden'. For centuries there was an uneasy relationship between the English Cluniac houses and the Chapter-General in France. In 1283 one William of Shoreham actually fortified the monastery and refused to admit Benedict of Cluny, who had been appointed by Cluny prior in his place. There was friction between the foreign mother-house and the kings of England.

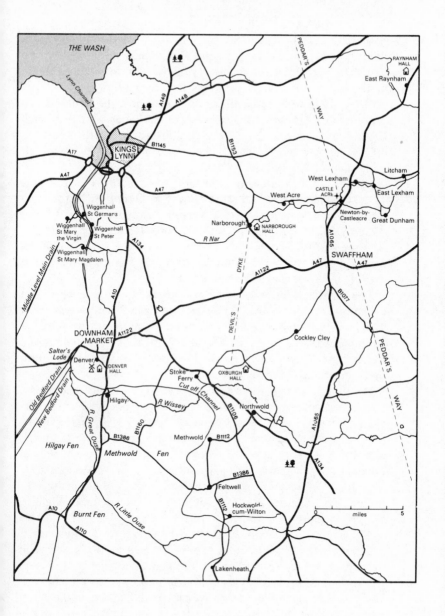

THE WASH

Lynn Channel

A17

A149
A148
B1145

KINGS LYNN

A47

A47

Wiggenhall St Germans
Wiggenhall St Mary the Virgin
Wiggenhall St Peter
Wiggenhall St Mary Magdalen

Middle Level Main Drain

A134

A10

A1122

DOWNHAM MARKET

Salter's Lode
Denver
DENVER HALL

Old Bedford Drain
New Bedford Drain

Hilgay

R Great Ouse

Hilgay Fen

B1386
B1160

R Wissey

Methwold Fen

Methwold

A10

Burnt Fen

A110

R Little Ouse

Stoke Ferry
Cut off Channel

B1106

Northwold

B1112

B1386

Feltwell

B1112

Hockwold-cum-Wilton

Lakenheath

B1153

R Nar

Narborough
NARBOROUGH HALL

West Acre

West Lexham
CASTLE ACRE

DEVIL'S DYKE

A1122

A47

Cockley Cley

OXBURGH HALL

A1065

A134

PEDDAR'S WAY

RAYNHAM HALL
East Raynham

Litcham

East Lexham

Newton-by-Castleacre
Great Dunham

SWAFFHAM
A47

B1077

A1065

PEDDAR'S WAY

0   miles   5

Edward I heavily taxed the 'alien priories', including Acre, as did Edward II and Edward III. In 1373 the priors were naturalized British by Letters Patent, thus severing connection with the foreign mother-house. In 1401 the monks bought an Indulgence of the Portiuncula from Pope Boniface IX, which brought penitents and presumably their money to the priory on the 1st and 2nd of August every year, on which dates this Indulgence was effective. The biggest draw the priory had, though, was the arm of St Philip; but even this, in 1533, only brought in ten shillings. And on 22nd November 1537 the Reformation came to Acre, and the last prior, Thomas Malling, signed the place away to Henry VIII, who gave it to Thomas Howard, Duke of Norfolk, from whom it was taken away by Elizabeth I and given to Thomas Gresham. Eventually, with the surrounding countryside for many miles it came into the hands of the Coke family, and the 5th Earl of Leicester handed it over to what was then the Ministry of Works.

The existing ruins are marvellous to behold, with the west front of the priory church standing up high and gaunt, and ornamented with the most elaborate Norman blind arcading anywhere to be seen: indeed some might think a superfluity of embellishment. The site, on green green lawns on the low riverine marshes away from the village, adds to the enchantment.

We enter through the fine early sixteenth-century gatehouse, which has two entrances, one for vehicles and one for foot passengers. Under what were the upper windows (big square Tudor-looking windows they must have been) are, from left to right, the arms of Fitzalan quartering Warenne (the Yorkshire family of Fitzalan was long connected with the priory), the Royal Arms, de Warenne, Maltravers, with the arms of the priory underneath over the pedestrian door. The arms, now very defaced, are thought to have been those of Mowbray.

The church was a copy of the second church of Cluny when it was built in the eleventh and twelfth centuries. It originally had five apses, for there was an apsidal chapel to the east of each transept, an apse to each chancel aisle, and one to the chancel. The foundations of these apses are clearly to be seen on the grass. In the fourteenth century the east end was pulled down and a square-ended presbytery built and a south chapel. In the fifteenth century the north chancel aisle was enlarged to make a big square-ended chapel.

But it is the wondrous west front that astonishes the beholder, and has something of the impact of Tintern Abbey when seen for the first time as one rounds the bend of the road. It is a classic example of how each age ruthlessly imposes its taste on the buildings of the past, and completely undervalues the achievement particularly of the immediately preceding age. Those two Early English pointed windows high up on the south side of the façade – surely any builder of sensibility would have retained the Anglo-Norman tradition in adding-on to that vast pile of round arches? But no. E.E. was the latest thing, and E.E. the windows had to be. And as for the huge Perpendicular west window: the whole fabric of the Norman work was torn asunder to insert that – and nobody can think that it looks anything but incongruous. In so many great buildings the builders 'got away with' such additions to older styles: triumphantly, for example, at Norwich. But at Acre their enthusiasm outran their taste.

The foundations of the priory have been well excavated and can easily be followed: the two vanished towers that were flush with the west front, the transepts with the early apsidal chapels already mentioned, the dormitory, with a vaulted undercroft, which runs south from the chapter house, the large and well-preserved *necessarium* to the south of it again – the size of it leading us to wonder whether all the monks used to want to employ it at once. The prior's house is still in perfect order, very pretty Tudor with a bay window and a gabled roof, more like the dwelling of a wealthy merchant than that of a religious. It has a private chapel upstairs, with the ghosts of wall paintings.

Do not neglect Castle Acre **parish church**. On the pulpit are representations of the Four Doctors – placed there from a screen over an aisle. They are: Augustine, Gregory, Jerome and Ambrose. Fragments of medieval glass in the windows of the south aisle, and painted decorations on the rood screen and the font cover show how colourful the whole interior must once have been. Over the north door are carved the shields of de Warenne and Fitzalan.

A Saxon burial ground was dug up at Acre, with over a hundred urns, and two great stone coffins were discovered in the Nar, in

253

Victorian times, when a new bridge was being built, and the parson ordered that they were to be carried up to the church. He did not provide the workmen with sufficient *beer* money, however, for such an exacting task, and they accordingly threw the coffins back again, where they rest today. Nobody has yet gone to the trouble of looking for them. It is possible that they were the coffins of William de Warenne and Gundreda. It was the custom for such grand people to keep coffins for themselves in all their various residences throughout the country in case death might come to them while they were in residence.

North-east, still voyaging up-Nar, we quickly come to **Newton-by-Castleacre**, which has a church with a very fine Saxon crossing tower with four Saxon-looking windows. It is strange that, in a land where there is very little Saxon work left, there is a little group here of four Anglo-Saxon churches: this one at Newton-by-Castleacre, **East Lexham** (read the brass plate west of the altar rail here), **West Lexham** (but a picture inside of 1891 shows the place completely in ruins, so it is a reconstruction) and **Great Dunham**. The latter (a couple of miles south of East Lexham) is most certainly worth going to see. Its church stands next to a lively school, it has plenty of Roman tiles in its arches, it has long-and-short work in its tower and naves and typically Saxon windows. It *looks* Anglo-Saxon and very ancient. Why this profusion, in this little group of villages, of Anglo-Saxon remains? This area must have escaped even Norman rebuilding: could it have been so unprosperous? Or was it because the great monastic house at Castle Acre overshadowed all else? Now the whole area is one of huge estates and practically depopulated, and so these tiny churches are more than adequate for the population.

Litcham is a fine little town, administrative centre for a district, and very attractive with much tarred flint. Priory Farm down by the river incorporates fragments of what used to be a medieval chapel and possibly a rest-house for pilgrims on their way to Walsingham. The church, mainly Perpendicular, has a fifteenth-century poor-box and an array of box pews, polished by age. In some of the windows there is seventeenth-century Flemish glass.

North, beyond the source of the Nar, are the **Raynhams**, where in Hall Farm's spacious buildings Dick Joice began assembling his incomparable collection of farming, forestry, warreners', poachers', keepers', mole-catchers' and country tradesmen's implements, pioneers of the 'Bygones' now housed at Holkham Hall (see p. 228). East Raynham church was rebuilt in the nineteenth century, but still has an elaborate Easter Sepulchre preserved from the earlier building, one of a number of monuments to the distinguished local family of the Townshends.

Raynham Hall is another of Norfolk's splendid seventeenth-century houses. The Hall, which is at East Raynham, was built by Sir Roger Townshend who started it in 1622. The house has given rise to much discussion as to who designed it, some plumping for Inigo Jones, others for Roger Platt, and yet others for Sir Roger himself, together with his master mason William Edge with whom Sir Roger had gone touring in the Low Countries. Certainly the great gables have a Netherlandish look, and seem scarcely a pure enough Palladian for Inigo Jones. Most of the interior of the house was done by William Kent, of Holkham fame. The house is a great block of brick and stone, standing amid flat lawns; and it looks as if it would be far more comfortable than either Holkham or Houghton: despite its size there is something homely and comely about it.

The Townshends were another family risen to wealth in the law courts. The first, Sir Roger, was a justice of the Court of Common Pleas and he has an exceedingly sumptuous monument in the form of that Easter Sepulchre in the church – he died very late fifteenth century. He was lawyer to the letter-writing Pastons and bought much land off them. A later Townshend, Charles, 2nd Viscount, married a sister of his illustrious neighbour Sir Robert Walpole and became politically prominent. More useful, he became agriculturally prominent, and played a great part in the introduction of the turnip into England – thus earning a title for himself much grander than that of Viscount: 'Turnip' Townshend. Turnip cultivation (followed by that of the mangel-wurzel or cattle-beet) took the place of the old wasteful bare fallow in the rotation of ploughlands. It was a cleaning crop (i.e. its cultivation eradicated weeds) and it allowed sheep and cattle to be kept, and even fattened, in the winter. It led the way to the 'Norfolk Four Course

Rotation' that spread all over England, and which itself gave rise to the great era of High Farming which only ended with the repeal of the Corn Laws.

'Turnip's' grandson, George, took over command from the dying Wolfe on the heights of Abraham and led his troops to victory. Later he became Lord Lieutenant of Ireland. In the First World War another Townshend, Sir Charles, led the defence of Kut in Mesopotamia. After a long siege by vastly superior Turkish forces he had to surrender, with 9,000 men.

South again: **Swaffham**. Here is a most elegant town, a little rural Paris, once called 'the Montpellier of England'. It was the product of more wealth, better horses and carriages, and better roads in the late eighteenth century and Regency times, all of which factors permitted the gentry to drive long distances to a social centre, to attend routs and balls, concerts and *soirées*, and to bring their daughters in for the season and to marry them off. Many elegant eighteenth- and early nineteenth-century houses remain, including the large Assembly Room (Hamond's Grammar School opposite) which must have been the hub of it all and was built in 1817. Swaffham is the finest predominantly Regency town in East Anglia. There was once a lively theatre there (W. B. Rix, in his book *Swaffham*, records that 'In 1806 Earl and Countess Nelson with their daughter, Lady Charlotte, Lady Bolton, Miss Horatio Nelson Thompson and Lady Hamilton stayed in Swaffham and bespoke the play "She Stoops to Conquer"'). Many county families took houses in Swaffham for 'the season', and many country clergy gathered there to live, so much so as to give rise to anxiety by the Bishop who maintained that they ought to live in their parishes. Some of them replied that – at any rate – they could *see* their parishes from the high ground of Swaffham!

A great activity of Swaffham in Regency times was hare coursing. In fact it was only the lack of hotels that prevented the town from becoming the venue for the Waterloo Cup. The Swaffham Club, which was a coursing association, was formed by Lord Orford in 1776, and it was on the heaths around Swaffham that his lordship coursed Czarina – the ancestor of every true-bred greyhound in the world today. He coursed Czarina forty-seven times and she was never once beaten. In her last match Lord Orford worked

Four of the marvellous roofs of East Anglian churches. *Above left*, spandrels at Mildenhall; *right*, one of the carved angels at Blythburgh. *Below left*, Neston; *right*, the "angel roof" at March.

Above, Breckland: that area of sandy heath country once called the 'desert of East Anglia' and now containing the second largest forest in Britain. *Below*, part of the Cambridgeshire Fens: the most fertile soil in Britain. Here Hereward the Wake defied the Normans, long before the land was drained and made habitable.

himself up into such a passion about it that he fell from his horse and died.

But Swaffham existed before the eighteenth century, as one can see from the church, which is fifteenth century and magnificent. The lavish use of Barnack stone in it tells of great wealth when it was built, for the stone must have been carried over-land for several miles from the River Nar. The particularly splendid north aisle, with its seven bays and its clerestory with thirteen Tudor-arched windows, is said to have been paid for by the Pedlar of Swaffham. This man (whose story is told in detail in *Folklore as an Historic Science* by Sir L. Gomme but is much repeated by the people of Swaffham) went to London and met a stranger on London Bridge (some versions have it that the Pedlar had gone to the bridge to throw himself off it). The man told him of a dream that he had had – that he had gone to a remote Norfolk town called Swaffham, and gone to a certain garden (and here he described the Pedlar's own) and dug in it and found a great treasure. The Pedlar kept his counsel, went straight home, dug in his garden – and hence the north aisle of Swaffham Church. There is a library over the vestry, with a fine fifteenth-century *Book of Hours*.

I was once travelling in remotest Yorkshire and I came to a village, called Gargrave. I went into a cobbler's to have a shoe mended. The cobbler spoke with a powerful Norfolk accent, and when I asked him (in a Suffolk one) whence he had come he said: 'I come from Swaaafham where they dew three daaays thraaashin' fer naaathin'' (where they do three days threshing for nothing). I was able to give him the correct reply: 'Well thass saaathin'!' (well that's something). Not since Stanley accosted Livingstone at Ujiji has there been such an encounter.

At **Cockley Cley**, south-west of Swaffham, an Iceni village has been reconstructed on the site of an original encampment, complete with towers and a drawbridge. Nearby are a local folk museum in an old forge cottage, and a fragment of a seventh-century Saxon church.

Continuing south-west we come to **Oxburgh Hall**, built by Sir Edmund Bedingfeld in 1482 (at least, that is when he received licence to crenellate), and Bedingfelds have lived in it ever since. Originally from Bedingfield in Suffolk, they came into the estate of Oxborough (note the difference in spelling between village and

257

hall) by marriage: one Edmund Bedingfeld married Margaret Tuddenham of the family then in possession. About 1460 Sir Thomas Tuddenham, brother of Margaret and the owner of Oxborough, was executed for being on the wrong side in the Wars of the Roses, but Margaret, having married a Yorkist, was allowed to inherit. On Margaret's death in 1474 Oxborough went to her grandson, Edmund, who, as we have seen, received licence to build a fortified house in 1482 from Edward IV, and he built Oxburgh Hall: in essence the same as we see it today although differing in many details: much of it was rebuilt in Victorian times. Henry VII slept in what is now called the King's Chamber over the gateway. Queen Elizabeth may or may not have slept in the room above: it is still called Queen's Chamber. Mary, Queen of Scots, certainly did.

The history of the Bedingfeld family has been one of consistent loyalty to two causes: that of Rome, and that of the Crown of England. The family rose to great favour with the Crown until the Reformation; but after that, remaining resolutely Catholic, led a precarious existence far from the paths of power. A Bedingfeld, Edmund, served Henry VIII in his wars, and was entrusted with the custody of Catherine of Aragon when that lady was divorced. Edmund's son, Henry, was entrusted by Catherine's daughter, Queen Mary, with the custody of the future Queen Elizabeth, when that princess was immured in the Tower and later at Woodstock. When Elizabeth became queen she quickly dismissed Sir Henry from his office – some writers record with a tart remark while others say that she bore him no grudge. As her reign went on, and Protestantism became more firmly established, families like that of Oxborough fell from prominence and power and were subject to penal laws.

The Civil War greatly damaged the family for of course it was Royalist: the Sir Henry of the time and three of his sons were captured, the fourth son was killed, and the Hall was occupied and severely damaged by the Roundheads. A Royalist family in the middle of Roundhead East Anglia was precariously placed. But the family clung on to its estates, became prosperous again at the Restoration, and in 1775 the Sir Richard of the day (a baronetcy had been bestowed on the family by Charles II) had enough money and enough time, alas and alas, to pull down what must have been the marvellous medieval Great Hall and Great Kitchen that formed the south side of the quadrangle of the Hall. The Sir Henry of the nineteenth century (who married one of the last of the Paston family) built the Roman Catholic chapel in front of the Hall in about 1835, also the tower at the south-east corner, the turreted kitchen-garden walls. The charming French *parterre* gardens were laid out about 1845, when also the delightful garden buildings were built.

Oxburgh is one of the most charming of the great country houses of England, and the little village that lies next to it is charming too. There is a feeling of great remoteness about the place, far from any important road, far from a town, near the Fens but not of them, near the desolate Brecklands but also not of them: a small corner of fertile English countryside hemmed in between Fen and Breck. The view through the gate in the great surrounding wall is breathtaking: the mighty mellow brick mass of the Hall with that marvellous fortified gatehouse across the moat; the gatehouse seven stories high and almost exactly as it was when it was built nearly five hundred years ago, when machicolations were carefully provided so that substances heavy and hot could be poured through them on to the heads of attackers. Pugin called this gatehouse 'one of the noblest specimens of the domestic architecture of the fifteenth century' and so it is, if indeed we do not classify it as military architecture. Transitional the Hall may have been between purely defensive building and the undefended domestic buildings of Tudor times, but Oxburgh was still meant to be defended, if never from full-scale siege at least from robbers or marauders or unfriendly neighbours. That wide moat was not just dug to keep fish in.

The bridge over the moat is eighteenth century, replacing a drawbridge. The finest thing inside the gatehouse is its brick stairway: a marvel of constructing in brick what is normally constructed in stone. The roofs of the gateway itself, and of the adjoining armoury, have fine brick vaulting. The brick fireplace of the King's Chamber, on the first floor, is noteworthy. The moulded beams and the panelling in this room are modern.

But it is the King's Chamber that contains the wonder of Oxburgh

– the famous Oxburgh Hangings, ranged around the bed. These, of green velvet, were made some time about 1570 as wall hangings, and they contain over a hundred panels of needlework executed by Mary, Queen of Scots, during her endless imprisonment, and also by Elizabeth, Countess of Shrewsbury, or 'Bess of Hardwick'. When Queen Mary was incarcerated in Tutbury Castle it was reported of her that all day she 'wrought with hir Nydill, and that the diversitie of the colors made the worke seme lesse tedius, and contynued so long at it till veray Payn made hir to give over'.The chief impression of the needlework panels is a powerful one of organic wholeness. The themes are animals and plants, mostly cribbed in fact from books of natural history, but the total effect is of the work of people in close sympathy with a world of life and living things: it is a humbling experience for a modern man to stand before it. *Virescit Vulnere Virtus*, stitched Mary: Virtue is strengthened by wounds. Certainly Mary's deep and bitter wounds strengthened her feeling for colour and form, and for life. The gatehouse is opened to the public at specified times between March and October, as are other rooms.

It is interesting to discover that the original township of Oxborough was situated, as one would have expected it to have been, at Oxborough Hythe, meaning the port of Oxborough, down on the River Wissey. There is nothing left of this at all, but when it existed it made Oxborough part of the world of the Fenland rivers: linking it closely with Cambridge and King's Lynn, and – with Cambridge – with metropolitan culture and civilization.

Oxborough's parish church is in ruins. Its tower, which was no less than 150 feet, fell on top of it in 1948 and wrecked it pretty thoroughly; but not, fortunately, the amazing Bedingfeld chapel, which is unfortunately kept locked at the time of writing, but one can see quite a lot through the windows if indeed one does not have time to seek out the vicar and ask for the key. The fame of this place are the two terracotta monuments, Italianate in style and most spirited. There are other Bedingfeld monuments in the chapel. The Roman Catholic chapel by Pugin, hard by the gate of the Hall, is 1835, and notable for the Flemish altar retable, early sixteenth century, various pieces of old stained glass, and two Bedingfeld monuments for lovers of Victoriana.

Continuing southwards we reach a strip of country that I always consider as an inland shore, for it runs along where the higher country of the Breckland ends, and the flat Fens begin. It is a coastline from which the waters have receded and left it high and dry. I here have to warn the reader to discount some of what I say in praise of the villages along this 'shore'. I think they are marvellous; but to many eyes they would no doubt appear to be just villages. They are by no means Lavenhams, but then in the summer their streets are not choked by charabancs.

Northwold is the most northerly village of this ancient shore, and like the others it is a fascinating mixture of chalk 'clunch', flint, carr stone and old brick. The church is Decorated and beautiful, with marvellous thirteenth-century piers, each looking almost like four pillars although in fact all of a piece, and with stiff-leaf capitals. The tower is Perpendicular, late fifteenth century. The great thing is the Easter Sepulchre, perhaps the best in East Anglia, with four Roman soldiers startled and disturbed among the olive trees. This lovely piece of sculpture makes you feel the spirit of the fourteenth century when it was made, and it is very hard to forgive Cromwell's zealots who so savagely defaced it.

Methwold is the next of the border villages, almost a small town in fact, with big farmsteads all mixed up in it: all chalk, carr stone, flint and brick again like Northwold. Unusually for Norfolk the church has a steeple, a most beautiful slender octagonal one. The east window is decorated with a sort of tracery which makes one wish that the Perpendicular style had never been invented. It was, though, and the rest of the church is in it. The brass inside to Sir Adam de Clifton (died 1367) is famous. It was sold to a tinker in 1860, broken into 130 pieces, but put together again in 1888. There is a sixteenth-century vicarage, with a chimney up the middle of its stepped gable. Methwold, like other of these border places, had its river port, Methwold Hythe. Fenland reclamation has cut this off from its navigation, it is now two miles from its river – the Wissey. It is a charming group of buildings, sited right between the flat Fens and the chalk upland. The great new Cut-off Channel runs hard by it, blue and cold. Down the lane to it a fine view can be had across Fenland. There is a fine farmstead there: the house green-washed and the buildings of clunch.

261

At Methwold started the East Anglian outbreak of the Peasant Rising that ended, as we have seen, in drawings and quarterings at North Walsham. It was at this time that Parson Ball composed the verse:

> *When Adam delved and Eve span*
> *Who was then the Gentleman?*

Methwold Manor, belonging then to the Duke of Lancaster, was invested by the rebels, Methwold Court Rolls were burnt, but otherwise no lives were lost or damage done.

There is the site of a Roman villa half a mile north-west of Methwold. The Romans, or Romano-Britons, undoubtedly conquered large areas of Fenland, which were left to go back to swamps and waters when the Romans retired.

Feltwell is much overwhelmed by an airbase. There are two churches: a big St Mary's with a splendid Perpendicular tower and much Decorated work, and a smaller St Nicholas which had a carr stone tower which was being repaired by workmen in 1898. The workmen went next door to the Chequers, for a well-earned pint or two, and while they were there the pub was shaken by a terrible rumbling – and when they they ran to the door and looked out the tower had crumbled into ruins. The pub, fortunately, still stands. St Nicholas is still used as a chapel, and has Norman elements. Not only has it lost its tower, but it has lost its chancel too, the latter having been pulled down by the Reverend Edward Bower Sparke in 1862, in order to use some of the material to build another aisle on to St Mary's. Sparke drew revenue from four fat livings, and so could afford to indulge in such activities.

Sparke's north aisle in St Mary's is lush indeed, and so are the windows he installed: much of the glass by Didron, of France, and in better taste than much glass of the period (certainly in better taste than the great spate of glass of the early twenties with all those knights in armour with Rupert Brooke's face). The benches are well worth looking at, and there are interesting brasses.

Apart from the great Perpendicular west tower, with its pinnacles and ornate parapet, most of this church is Decorated. And the question arises: why, in predominantly Perpendicular East Anglia, is there so much work of the Decorated style left in the churches of this ancient shore of the Fens? Can the reason be that these villages reached their prosperity in the great sheep-rearing period but *before* the great cloth weaving era initiated by the importation of Flemish weavers into East Anglia by Edward III? These villages were well placed to enjoy the wool-exporting boom; with access, as they had, to the sheep-walks of the Brecklands and also the lush meadows of the Fens, and with water connection from their hythes with King's Lynn, one of the greatest of English ports trading with the Continent. But the whole area, King's Lynn included, got left behind in the weaving boom of late medieval and Tudor times, when Lavenham and the villages about it, and Worstead and Norwich and the east Norfolk villages, boomed as weaving villages, and the estuaries and river ports of east Suffolk and Norfolk exported the finished cloth and outstripped King's Lynn as Continental ports. And then, when the Fens were effectively drained in the seventeenth century, it was done by Metropolitan financiers and Methwold and the other border villages did not share in this prosperity. Hence they remained as backwaters, and have so remained ever since; and their churches, built in the Decorated style popular in the days of the raw-wool boom, were never pulled about and rebuilt in the late middle ages as were the great Perpendicular churches of the weaving parts of East Anglia.

Hockwold cum Wilton has a Tudor hall built on the E plan of red brick, and **Wilton** Church has a stone spire, nice benches, and a monument to Cyril Wyche by John Ivory, of Norwich.

Just south of Hockwold the road crosses the great new Cut-off Channel (for details see p. 209) and here the interested traveller should turn left off the road (east) and follow the channel up-stream until he comes, after a short walk, to the inverted syphon by which the Channel is carried down under the River Little Ouse. The Little Ouse is allowed to flow on regardless (it can have no way of knowing that there is a Cut-off Channel there) until time of flood, when its waters can be diverted through a sluice into the Cut-off Channel and thus prevented from going on to join the already-swollen Great Ouse. The water of the Channel still has that cold, eerie, blue colour of water flowing over chalk. Nature has scarcely had time to assert herself in the form of water weed and many fish.

Just north of Lakenheath Station is an odd-looking factory with many chimneys. This is England's chicory factory. Chicory is grown about the Fens and brought to this place to be ground up and roasted to be put in coffee, mostly of the bottled essence variety. Chicory takes the place of sugar beet in places where eel-worm infestation makes the cultivation of the latter unprofitable.

North-west, towards King's Lynn again, **Stoke Ferry** is an old river port on the Wissey, an important trading centre in the days of the Fen Lighters, and still accessible by small boats. In 1985 a bypass relieved the twisting road through the village of heavy traffic, and at last the dust could be washed off house fronts.

At **Denver** George William Manby was born. He went to school with Nelson and later – after having stood on Yarmouth beach watching a great ship perishing in the surf with the loss of all hands – he invented first a mortar, and then a rocket life-saving apparatus, the latter, streamlined and modified, still in use today. By 1823 his apparatus had saved 229 lives and Parliament awarded him £2000. He is buried at the big river port of **Hilgay** nearby. Denver has a well-maintained grinding windmill – the finest for miles, also Denver Hall with its beautiful east gable which is early sixteenth century and pretty gatehouse of 1570.

It also has Denver Sluices, old and new. The Old Sluice was built by Vermuyden to limit the run of the sea tides up the Great Ouse. It was destroyed by the Fen Tigers – men who made a living from eeling and wildfowling and didn't want the Fens to be drained – and was opposed strongly by sailors and traders, one of whom pointed out that 'whereas of old ships from Newcastle were wont to make 18 voyages in the year to Cambridge with sea coal, now, since the blocking of the stream at Denver and the diversion of its waters at Earith, they can make but 10 or 12, whereby the price of fuel has increased by half.'

The sluice was 'blown up' again by a high tide in 1713, and there were loud rejoicings by its opponents. But it was rebuilt again, and then again – much bigger and stronger – by Sir John Rennie, who also built Old Waterloo Bridge. Since Rennie's time it has been remodelled and has had steel gates fitted. It will be noticed that it is a double lock – that is that at low tide a vessel passing through it goes downhill from south to north, but at high tide uphill. The tidal river, north of Denver, varies greatly in height with the tide, the fresh water south of it remains constant. Through this sluice the water draining from 800,000 acres of land used to pass: now that the Cut-off Channel has been opened this load is lightened. The New Denver Sluice was opened in 1959, and it either passes or restrains the waters of the Cut-off Channel.

Over the river, and just downstream (i.e. north) from the old Denver Sluice the New Bedford Drain, which is tidal, debouches into the Ouse. If you follow it upstream it rejoins the Ouse far up near Earith. Just downstream from its mouth is Salter's Lode, where a single sluice gate lets the Old Bedford Drain into the Ouse. All water traffic from the Great Ouse system bound for the rest of England must go through this gate, or else the other sluice gate of the recently repaired Well Creek just by it. These gates can only be used when there is 'a level', i.e. when the salt tidal water outside is level with the fresh non-tidal water inside. This condition is obtained only for a few moments twice a day.

At the north-east end of the Ouse Washes the Wildfowl Trust administers the 850 acres of **Welney** nature reserve. More than sixty species can be found nesting here in spring and summer, and winter counts show thousands of widgeon, pochard, teal, pintail, and Bewick's swans. A spacious observatory overlooks a swan lagoon – floodlit in winter – and there is screened access to a number of hides along the earth banks. The reserve is open daily all year except Christmas Eve and Christmas Day.

Downham Market is a great place for lovers of the Norfolk carr stone, for it is the most considerable town to be largely built of it. It has a charm and mellowness all of its own, a couple of fine old and comfortable hotels and big mills down by the railway, and streets relieved of traffic by a 1986 bypass. Downham was once a very big river port, but was first cut off from the river by the railway, and since that again by the Riley Channel, which carries the waters of the Cut-off Channel to the main river at King's Lynn. This has left a narrow strip of new grassland between the Channel and the Great Ouse, along which it is very pleasant to walk northwards to the Wiggenhalls, strolling now westwards to the ancient river, now eastwards to the new canal. For the naturalist it is interesting to see how life, vegetable and animal, is beginning to colonize the great new gash.

265

The Wiggenhalls are four villages of the Norfolk Marshlands. The **Marshlands** are not to be confused with the Fens. The Marshlands, nearer the sea than the Fens, are of slightly higher land, not so subject to flooding, and have been inhabited from the earliest times. In the true Fens, excepting on the 'islands' of high ground such as Ely, there is hardly an old building. In Marshland the villages are ancient, and of an ancient prosperity. The Wiggenhalls cluster along the Great Ouse, which has not changed its course thereabouts for many centuries, and they have a charm about them not to be found in the graceless villages of the raw Fen.

Wiggenhall St Mary Magdalen has a most distinguished church with fifteenth-century glass in the windows of its north aisle: a 'must' for the saint-knower, for in the long gallery of saints depicted are many uncommon ones. There is a fine old pub crouching under the river bank by the bridge. Here until recent years lived the Great Ouse's last remaining professional eel catcher. From a smack on the river he would set a 'stow-net' – a bag-net which hangs down from the boat while she is at anchor, so that fish are driven into it by the tide. With this the fisherman catches his bait and uses it in a great number of grigs, or eel-hives, which are traps with a one-way opening. Once upon a time many tons of eels went up to Billingsgate from hereabouts. There were also smelts, a delectable tiny fish which smell of cucumber when being fried. Unfortunately England's total consumption of these is about a hundredweight a week, so the market is restricted. They were historically a royal delicacy, and until recent years the kings of England arranged for a special supply from the Great Ouse. Now hardly anybody has heard of them, so most get thrown back.

There is a most pleasant walk (two miles) down the east bank of the river, past **Wiggenhall St Peter**, which has a church in fascinating ruin hard up against the high river bank, to **Wiggenhall St German**.

The latter is a most picturesque small Marshland village, with no less than three pubs: so many because at one time it was a great mooring-up place for Fen lightermen who were such thirsty fellows.

The church is strongly redolent of the spirit of the Middle Ages. No doubt there is much to see here beside the benches, but I can never see it for I cannot take my eyes off the superb wood carving of these.

They are fifteenth century, heavy and dark-looking, with intricate carving. The backs are carved, but it is the astonishing collection of bench-ends that makes such compulsive viewing. The aisle carvings are modern ones, and very good too; although they cannot, of course, quite capture that style and spirit that only comes from the Middle Ages. The nave bench-ends are an astonishing collection: sinners being swallowed by huge jaws, sinners committing away their sins, saints standing under their canopies straight from the age of faith and innocence, a monkey blowing a trumpet, weird beasts and animals.

The series of carvings in the north aisle depicting incidents of the life of St German is Victorian. He was, of course, the Duke of Burgundy, and a great hunter and he lived from AD 380 to 448. He hung trophies of the chase in a tree but a local bishop cut the tree down. The bishop then had a dream which caused him to entice the angry duke into his church and there he forcibly ordained him. Afterwards German was acclaimed bishop. He came to England twice in order to refute the Pelagian heresy (which denied the doctrine of Original Sin).

At **Wiggenhall St Mary the Virgin**, just over the river, is an even more complete and perfect collection of benches, and less restored. But somehow they don't give one quite that feeling of having dropped back five hundred years. There is also a fine brass lectern, 1518. The great Elizabethan hall in a muddy field just before you get to the church is in fact mid-nineteenth century, only the entrance and the stable block are original.

Between St German and St Mary the Virgin the biggest pumping station in England lifts water from the Middle Level Main Drain up into the Great Ouse.

CHAPTER 15

Marshland and Fenland

Perhaps the best thing about **West Lynn** is the view from it of East Lynn. Ferry Square has its own charm (and the above fine view), there is a vast canning factory, and the church has a good Decorated tower and a nice nave roof.

Terrington St Clement is a big, very ugly village north of the A17 (a trunk road between East Anglia and the Midlands and North and one of the most congested in the country: narrow, winding and crammed with heavy traffic) with hardly a nice-looking building. There is, however, a most gracious farmstead just south of the church.

And the church, the setting of Dorothy L. Sayers's *The Nine Tailors*, is magnificent even for East Anglia: it is often called 'The Cathedral of the Marshland'. The impression it conveys is one of width and massiveness, probably because of the depth given to it by its squat and heavy detached tower: Perpendicular and ashlar-faced and supported by heavy diminishing diagonal buttresses. This tower has had its uses: it served as a refuge both in 1613 and in 1670, when the sea broke through the dikes and came rolling over the Marshlands. The inhabitants of the parish had to remain in the tower and be fed from King's Lynn by boats.

The west front is very fine, with a great west window, niches to left and to right of it (and one above). There is a splendid clerestory, with flying buttresses – although obviously not as many as were intended. There are transepts, also not brought to completion and smaller than they were meant to be.

The later Perpendicular porch makes a fine entrance, with its sumptuous panelling. There is a sundial in it.

The interior of the church is very grand. Immediate view into the main body of the church is barred by a big eighteenth-century west screen, which once supported a musicians' loft. This may spoil the vista, but it also adds charm and intimacy. Through it the great crossing arches greet the eye. They were built to support the tower; but when it came to the point the nerve of the builders failed them and they decided to place the tower, campanile fashion, without the church. The quaking silt of the Marshland could not be trusted with such a weight.

Between the windows up in the clerestory are sea creatures and men and animals, and the string-course has heads and angels. The chancel has a clerestory too, only of brick. The great five-light east window has glass in it as a memorial to the hundred men who died in the 1914–18 war. There are four ancient and interesting altar-slabs in the chancel, an Early English door to the vestry, a lovely sixteenth-century font cover with windows that open to reveal the most delightful primitives of scenes from the life of Jesus. There are great Creed and Commandment boards (1635), a fine Early English graduated sedilia and a double piscina south of the sanctuary. There is part of a chancel screen still undefaced. Why did the Marshland churches escape so much of the attentions of the Cromwellian church-bashers? The Marshlands and Fens were solidly pro-Parliament (except the Royalists in King's Lynn and in Crowland Abbey), and even now they are staunchly Nonconformist – so far as those prosperous and materialistic areas are anything. Why did the churches of the area escape defacing?

The church is almost all of Barnack stone. Can it be that one reason for the grandeur of the Marshland churches, and their fine state of preservation, is the absence of flint in their locality? This cheap material could not be used, and so freestone had to be floated down the Nene from Northamptonshire, and with this more ambitious buildings could be attempted within a given budget. I am not decrying flint: the wonder of it is that, in the flinty parts of East Anglia, such magnificent buildings were constructed of what is, after all, a very difficult building material. As we range into Marshland, and south into Cambridgeshire, we shall find less flint and more dressed limestone. We shall miss perhaps the rough tweedy texture of the flint walls, and find the churches have more affinity with those of the southern Midlands than with those of the eastern parts of East Anglia.

The remains of a Roman sea-wall can be seen close to the north and east of Terrington St Clement, looking no different from any other sea-wall. There is a hamlet Orange Row north of the village, so named because the Prince of Orange stayed there, as a refugee from the French, with a countryman named Baron Feagle. They must have felt at home in this Dutch-type country. Another Hollander, Count Bentinck, saved the village in 1607 by building a bank – there is still a Bentinck's Farm north-east of the village, and Count Bentinck was a benefactor of the church until he died of Fen-fever. The reason that the altar of the church is raised up is that there is a Bentinck vault underneath it.

Terrington St Clement was founded on sheep, for at the time when that great tower was built, and most of what now stands of the church, the plough behind those old sea-walls had given way to grass and sheep grazed thick on the lush pastures. No good looking for sheep pastures now – the plough holds sway again over nearly every acre of Marshland as it does of Fenland, although there is a nice green meadow to the east of the great church on which fat Herefords graze all summer long.

To the south is Lovell's Hall, which is Early Tudor, and very impressive amid such uncompromising surroundings.

Sutton Bridge is in Lincolnshire, the home of the 'Yellowbellies' as Lincolnshire Fenmen have long been called on account of their alleged propensity to turn yellow with the quaking ague. There is now, fortunately, no such distemper left in the Fens: draining has put an end to it. We shall hardly venture to claim Lincolnshire as East Anglia: it certainly isn't linguistically; perhaps nowhere in England is there such a sharp division in the common speech of the people in such a short distance as there is between Sutton Bridge and King's Lynn: the inhabitants of the two places hardly speak the same language. The very distinctive and most mellifluous Norfolk dialect gives way quite abruptly to that extraordinary harsh Lincolnshire brogue with its strong affinity with the Midlands and North.

There are two good old Boston-built fishing smacks in Sutton Bridge, which both go down the fiercely tidal Nene to trawl for the little brown shrimps that are found in the Wash close in to the sandbanks. (The much larger, but less delicate, pink shrimps –

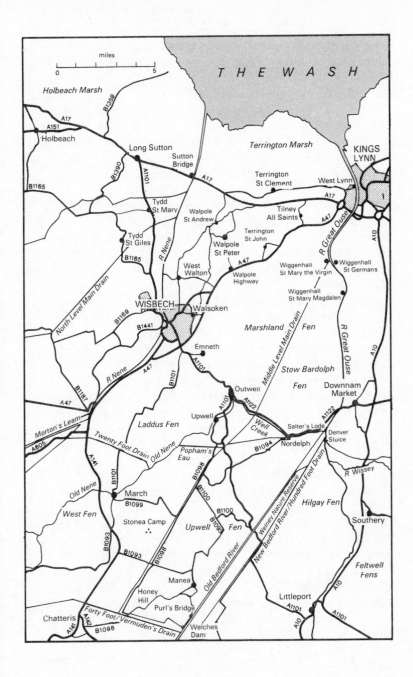

miles
0   5

Holbeach Marsh

THE WASH

A17
A151
Holbeach
B1359
B1390
Long Sutton
Sutton
Bridge
A17
A101
B1165

KINGS
LYNN
Terrington Marsh
Terrington
St Clement
West Lynn
A17
A447
A10

Tydd
St Mary
Walpole
St Andrew
Tilney
All Saints
Terrington
St John
Tydd
St Giles
B1165
Walpole
St Peter
A47
West
Walton
Walpole
Highway
Wiggenhall
St Mary the Virgin
Wiggenhall
St Germans
Wiggenhall
St Mary Magdalen

R Nene
North Level Main Drain
B1169
WISBECH
B1441
Walsoken
Marshland Fen
Middle Level Main Drain
R Great Ouse
A10

Emneth
Stow Bardolph Fen
Downnam
Market

R Nene
A47
B1101
A1101
Outwell
A1101
A1122
A47
A1187
Upwell
Well Creek
Salter's Lode
A1122
Denver
Sluice
Morton's Leam
A605
Twenty Foot Drain
Old Nene
Laddus Fen
Popham's Eau
B1094
Nordelph
R Wissey

A141
Old Nene
B1101
March
B1099
B1098
B1100
Welney Nature Reserve
New Bedford River/Hundred Foot Drain
Hilgay Fen
Southery
West Fen
Stonea Camp
B1100
B1098
Upwell Fen
Old Bedford River
Feltwell Fens
B1093
B1093
B1098
Manea
Honey
Hill
Purl's Bridge
Littleport
A1101
A10
A1101
Chatteris
A141
A142
B1098
Forty Foot/Vermuden's Drain
Welches
Dam
A10

locally miscalled 'prawns' – are found in the much deeper water in Lynn Deep, and are fished for by the more powerful smacks which operate from Boston.) The Lineham family, who have been here for generations, are ever ready to assist visiting boatmen, and there is hardly a nook or cranny of these labyrinthine channels which they do not know.

The region is also beloved by wildfowlers, and very good pink-foot shooting can be had in the wintertime. Local advice is not hard to come by. The Bridge Hotel is an excellent place offering good solid comfort, and the drive to the mouth of the Nene – along the east bank – here the Nene is a wide, straight, artificial river – is interesting if hardly picturesque. It has views over the Wash at the end, and there are two little lighthouses – never used for their proper purpose although Peter Scott learnt much of what he knows about birds while living in one of them, with Mackenzie Thorpe for his guide.

It is interesting to notice, as one drives down the Nene, how sea-wall after sea-wall has been built, to enclose yet another slice of the Wash. Looking out to sea from the last one ('to sea' may seem a euphemism, for unless it happens to be the top of a very big spring tide the sea will be nowhere in sight: it may well be three miles away), one realizes that this process of accretion may continue. Now the saltings are being heavily colonized by marram grass, introduced on purpose to hold the silt together and speed up the accretion of new dry land. Sir John Rennie, builder of Denver Sluice (No 2) and the old Waterloo Bridge (to say nothing of Plymouth Breakwater) proposed a scheme for uniting the mouths of the four Wash rivers out at Lynn Well, and reclaiming, or 'inning', all the sea-bed in between, thus acquiring 150,000 new acres. He even obtained Acts of Parliament to do it, but more is required to accomplish such work than Acts of Parliament. Recently the idea has been put forward of building a great dam right across the mouth of the Wash, thus turning the water of the Wash from salt to fresh and overcoming the growing water shortage of Eastern England. The Wash, by the supporters of this scheme, is often compared to the Zuider Zee. But the two seas are not really comparable. The Zuider Zee is protected from the fury of the North Sea by the Zeeland Islands and the sands of the Wadde: the

Wash is not. The Wash has a tidal range of 19 feet or so: the Zuider Zee, before it was inned, a mere three or four. Also the water in the mouth of the Wash is far deeper than that in the mouth of the Zuider Zee. It seems more likely that Sir John Rennie's scheme will be achieved by slow accretion over many years, and every few decades the inning of another few hundred acres, and one day the four rivers may indeed share a common outlet – out near the Roaring Middle. (Although when one considers the modern Dutch 'Delta Plan', the inning of the Zeeland estuaries, one wonders whether anything is impossible to engineers, particularly Dutch ones.)

Botanists will notice the increasing poverty of the flora as they pass towards the sea down successive sea-walls, due, of course, to the fact that terrestrial plants have not yet had time to colonize these areas won from the saltings.

If you go to Sutton Bridge in a boat, by the way, you had best tie up at the Linehams' jetty (with permission) for there is practically nowhere else, and there is a twenty-foot rise and fall of tide, which is formidable. Ashore, there is a golf course, and this is interesting because it is in the bottom of a large harbour basin. The harbour was built in the 1800s, and would have been a very large and elaborate wet dock had it ever been completed. Even now, the masonry of the quays, and of the great lock chamber in the entrance, gives an idea of the vast amount of labour that went into it all. If it had been completed it would certainly have killed Wisbech as a port, and probably taken a lot of trade from Boston and King's Lynn. As it was a spring of water under the foundations of the great lock chamber caused part of this to subside, the company ran out of money, and the whole thing came to nothing. In 1953 the great tidal surge came over the outer lock gates – and the road along the Nene – and flooded the dock again, incidentally carrying a big steel lighter right over the top and dumping her in the old dock, where she was to be seen until recently.

Back safely in Norfolk, and East Anglia proper, we may travel southward to the Walpoles.

Walpole St Andrew has a strange local industry: the searching for King John's treasure, for it is supposed that it is in this parish that King John's baggage train subsided into the raging waters of the incoming tide. Some years ago a professor from Nottingham University made test borings, and brought up some metal, but people engaged in this strange quest are reticent with information. Walpole St Andrew church has a hermit's cell in the base of its brick tower, and a mysterious chamber halfway up it.

At **Walpole St Peter** we are back among the very great churches of the Norfolk Marshlands. This is certainly a rival of Terrington St Clement, to many eyes far more stately and graceful: in fact it is one of the very beautiful parish churches of England. It is the Queen of the Marshland, and inside and out it is completely sumptuous: if the visitor to Marshland sees no other church – at least let him see this one.

The tower is about AD 1300 (which itself replaced a Saxon one) and was the first stage of the complete rebuilding of the Norman church. The nave was then constructed, and is very early Perpendicular: almost transitional in fact between Decorated and Perpendicular; this gives the arches inside a grace missing in later Perpendicular work, and the tracery of the aisle windows has a freedom and beauty not present in the later work -- for example in the big Perpendicular east window. The chancel is pure Perpendicular. The tower is not as sumptuous as the rest of the church, and too small for it. The rood turrets and the bell-cote on top of the east end of the nave make a fine group: the bell-cote still has its sanctus bell. Under the High Altar (which is literally high as a result) is a sort of tunnel, or passage, called 'the bolt-hole'. It is said to have been built in to the church to conserve an ancient right of way; but was more probably to allow ceremonial circumambulation on consecrated ground (compare the pierced porch of Aldeburgh church). It has some good carvings in it, and rings for tethering horses.

The south porch is richer than many an entire church: the bosses require an hour or more to study. There are sinners being swallowed, dog killing hare, fox and goose, pelican in her piety, sundry dragons, the Assumptions of Our Lady with God looking on, the Last Judgement in which the fate of sinners is made to look very dire. There is a Pietà in the north-west corner – rare in England: the Madonna holding the dead Christ.

Inside, the church is beautiful indeed. Partly this is because of the great clear windows, the large seventeenth-century brass chandelier and the six smaller Victorian ones, but mostly it is due to excellent proportions and the absolute perfection of the arcades and of the lofty clerestory. There is a fine Jacobean font cover, with doors that open to the font, the west screen is good, and about 1630, and there is some old carving in the pews of the nave. The lectern is early Tudor, in the shape of a very fierce eagle. Nowhere in this building does the eye alight without pleasure.

The Walpole family, from which came the first prime minister of England, left this village in the reign of King John. The village has its own saint, Godric, who must have been something of a big landowner in Anglo-Saxon times, for it is recorded of him that in AD 970 he gave Turingtonea (now Terrington) to the Abbey of Ramsey, and that he made a pilgrimage to the Holy Land. In the church is a statue possibly of Hickathrift, the giant of the Marshland, about whom tales are still told.

I must here ask the traveller to make a strange detour: to take the road to Walpole Highway out of Walpole St Peter – thence nearly into Wisbech – and then north again to **West Walton**. The reason for this diversion is that it is most important to approach West Walton from the south, for this gives the best view of the marvellous Early English tower standing up from its little clustering hamlet from the dead-flat fields of light-brown earth.

And here is yet *another* glorious church and for lovers of the Early English period one of the most important churches in all East Anglia.

The great detached tower is pure Early English, and a masterpiece. The west front of the church itself has had its polygonal Early English buttresses (which would have echoed the tower) pulled down and replaced by later ones and, alas, only one original aisle window remains – in the south-east of the church – all the rest have been replaced by Perpendicular (leading one to reflect that the 'restorers' of the Perpendicular age did as much harm, in their way, as those of the Victorian).

But inside much is original thirteenth century, and there is a fine, very ancient, feel about the building. The circular piers of the nave have four detached shafts each of Purbeck marble (in places replaced in a reach-me-down manner with wood), and the piers

275

have some of the finest stiff-leaf capitals in the country – very delicately done, and the arches above them are finely moulded. The clerestory, which is also original Early English, is unusual and noteworthy, and there are paintings between the windows – also mid-thirteenth century. Also below the clerestory are painted the emblems of the tribes of Israel: Dan, Gad, Asher, Naphtali and Joseph on the north side, and Issachar, Zebulun, Judah, Levi and Simeon on the south. These are seventeenth century – touched up in the nineteenth.

One of the most interesting things in the church is the 'Flood Board'. This records that on 1st November 1613 the sea overflowed all Marshland, on 23rd March 1614 'this Country was overflowed with the fresh', and on 12th and 13th September 1670 'againe overflowed by the Violence of the Sea'. But now:

> *Heavens face is clear, though the Bows appeare*
> *Reader nerefear, there is no Arrow neare.*

The 'fresh' of course refers to fresh water. Thus in 1953 part of Marshland was overflowed by the sea, but in 1947 very much of it – and Fenland too – was overflowed by 'the fresh' – the fresh water in the swollen rivers bursting the banks. There is also the verse:

> *Surely our Sinns were tinctured in graine,*
> *May not we say, the labour was in vaine*
> *Soe many Washings, still the Spotts remain.*

And so we go south to **Walsoken**, which according to Sir Nikolaus Pevsner had the grandest Norman church of Norfolk. We use the past tense because the village, now but a suburb of Wisbech, has been appropriated by Cambridgeshire.

The course that I should advise is to walk into the building and straight up to the splendid font. Spend some time contemplating this, and then set about looking at the rest of the church. Not that the latter is not noteworthy – simply that the font might get neglected for the church if a special move is not made to notice it.

The arcades, late Norman, are splendid, the piers slenderer than is found in earlier Norman work – their arches richly carved with zigzags. The capitals are varied and beautiful. The great chancel arch is interesting – a trifle later than the arcade arches – pointed and not round and yet in much the same style. Here Early English is separated from Norman by a hair's breadth. The tower (marvellous) is right into the Early English period. Inside the church there is fine carved timber up aloft, with paintings of angels. In both aisles there are carved screens, that in the south aisle having especially delicate tracery, and some first-rate wood carving on the bench-ends.

Terrington St John, not to be forgotten, has a beautiful church, with an interesting passage connecting the tower to the nave, and an unusual clerestory. **Tilney All Saints** is Norman and noteworthy. And that, finally and completely, is the end of my list of the great Marshland churches – unless the insatiable traveller wishes to include Tydd St Giles and Tydd St Mary.

The 'Marshland Series' is far less known than it deserves to be. For every person who makes the Marshland tour, a thousand probably make the tour of the West Suffolk wool villages. True we do not see in Marshland the absolute soaring perfection of the Perpendicular style, as we see at Long Melford or Lavenham, or in the tower arch of Stoke-by-Nayland; but here we have a great variety of medieval architectural styles including the earlier ones not otherwise well represented in East Anglia, a rich variety of building materials and an atmosphere and feeling of medievalism quite unique. If anyone can look at the bench carvings of Wiggenhall St German or Wiggenhall St Mary the Virgin and not come away with a greater awareness than he had had before of the mind of the medieval Englishman, then he had better address himself to the science side.

Wisbech claims to be the Capital of the Fens. Certainly it would be a good centre from which to see Fenland, and Marshland too; and it is a seaport, and a river port, and set amid orchards. Furthermore it is a most pleasant small town.

The comparatively roadless wedge of country, with its apex on Wisbech, seen on the map to the north of the town, was once an arm of the sea. That, in Wash terms, means that the sea used to overrun it at high water: at low it would have been sand-flats or quaking mud. Thus Wisbech was built as a seaport town, and a transhipment port into river lighters. The present course of the

277

River Nene is artificial (the old Nene ran miles to the east of it) and the process which is still going on – the embanking of the successive mouths of the Nene – has left Wisbech ten miles from the sea.

Ships still go to Wisbech, however, and the visitor can generally see some quite large coasters lying alongside the long quays which have been built each side of the river. The berths are very tidal and at low water, which appears to be most of the time, the ships are hard and fast aground on the mud. Russian timber ships seem to predominate, but there are Dutchmen (of course), Belgians and West German and sometimes even an English vessel. One of the most wonderful documentary photographic records of any English town is that made by Samuel Smith of Wisbech beween 1852 and 1862. His early camera preserved vistas of great sailing ships by the quays and warehouses, demolition of the old bridge, and street scenes which can be slotted into the present layout of the town. Most of the photographs are shared between the Wisbech and Fenland Museum near the church, and the Kodak Museum.

The important parts of Wisbech are solidly Georgian, and are centred on the river, and on the old Wisbech Canal which has been most foolishly and reprehensibly closed down and filled in. But it is obvious that most of what we see of Wisbech was paid for by shipping, and in the eighteenth and early nineteenth centuries. A very large fleet of coasters was based there then, mostly 'billyboys' of the Yorkshire type, and much of the trade was, indeed, with the North. When we admire the gracious Georgian buildings of Wisbech, or explore Peckover House, let us remember the old ships which paid for it all.

The two Brinks of Wisbech – North and South – are together one of the most perfect and beautiful Georgian ensembles in England. The River Nene has been used here as the Dutch use rivers: as the prime embellishment of the town, not something to be stuck away out of sight along the backs of slummy houses. The sober and stately mansions of the two Brinks gaze across the wide river at each other in mutual admiration. The North Brink is the finer of the two: possibly the wealthier of the citizens preferred their houses facing south.

Peckover House looks grander from the rear than from the front:

or perhaps one should say from the garden than from the street. The garden is Victorian, and very peaceful, and has a very big maidenhair tree in it. The house is the result of great wealth married to Quaker restraint and austerity in the early mid-eighteenth century. True, the restraint and austerity let go a little indoors, and there is a lavishness of carved wood and moulded plaster all in the very best of taste: the rococo wood carving over the fireplace in the drawing-room is superb. The house was built in 1722, and bought by Jonathan Peckover at the end of the century. He had come from Fakenham in 1777, and founded the local banking firm of Gurney, Birkbeck and Peckover (which merged with Barclay's in 1896). The house, in the care of the National Trust, opens its principal rooms and gardens every afternoon except Thursday and Friday from Easter until mid-October, with refreshments in the old kitchen.

William Godwin was a Wisbech man. The son of a Calvinist minister he at first preached hell-fire but then came to the conclusion that 'Not God himself has the right to be tyrant' and later became an atheist. He wrote *Political Justice* in which he extolled pacific anarchism and he said that 'generosity is a duty, not a virtue. It is impossible for me to confer a favour on any man. I can only do him a right,' and also that 'marriage is the most odious of all monopolies'. He enjoyed this monopoly though, marrying Mary Wollstonecraft after she had been deserted by her lover and left to support her daughter Fanny. Godwin's daughter by her, Mary, married Shelley. The poet's *Prometheus Unbound* owed much to Godwin's creed; Mary is remembered by her novel, *Frankenstein*.

And here, at the 'capital of the Fens', it would not be a bad time to discuss just what **the Fens** are. From Bedford to Hunstanton, from Lincoln to Cambridge, lies the Great Level, and on it is produced a quarter of the food grown in England. The Great Level is really a kind of multiple inland delta: the four Fenland rivers, Wissey, Welland, Nene and Great Ouse, all run down into it, and through it, depositing their silt as they sluggishly creep to the sea. Their exit into the Wash is complicated by the very high tidal range of that part of the ocean. At high tide the sea forces itself high up the rivers: in medieval times it went very much farther than it does now, for now it is limited by such flood-bars as Denver Sluice on

279

the Great Ouse. When the tide is high, and at springs, the fresh water running down the four rivers – which are the drains of a large part of England – cannot reach the sea, and it is then that they are inclined to burst their banks: as they did in 1947, when the great snow of that year melted, in 1953, when there was a phenomenal tidal surge, and more recently when Wisbech was waterlogged.

The Great Level is not, in fact, quite level; although you might think it is were you standing, say, on the high ground between Newmarket and Bury St Edmunds looking north-west – for it then looks as if the whole world is as flat as a billiard-table. But in fact the area nearest the sea – particularly in the east – is higher than the areas inland: the inland areas are below mean-sea-level, and this, of course, also leads to complications in draining. Formerly the Fens proper – the island areas – were a great swampy lake, here fresh water and there brackish, but with islands rising from it as at Ely, Thorney and Ramsey, where the monks took refuge and built their abbeys and cathedrals, and the *roddans*. The latter are interesting. They are winding banks of land slightly higher than the encompassing Fens, and often roads or villages are constructed on them. They are composed of a different soil from the Fen: the latter is the black peat, the roddans are riverine sands or gravel. In fact the roddans are the old beds of rivers, which were once lower than the surrounding Fen. Now the Fen has shrunk, with the decomposition of the peat, leaving the harder beds of the old rivers standing higher.

North of Southery **the Marshlands** begin. Here the land is above mean-sea-level, and not peat, as the Black Fens are, but a silty loam. This land was laid down under salt water, whereas the Fens were laid down by fresh. When Cobbett toured the Marshlands, early in the nineteenth century, 'the land was covered with beautiful grass, with sheep lying upon it as fat as hogs stretched out sleeping in a stye'. The Marshlands are now nearly all under the plough, for this land, although to a slightly lesser extent than Fenland, is pure gold.

The Marshlands have long been dry land (although always subject to occasional flooding by 'salt or fresh') and therefore they were inhabited from earliest times. The wonderful churches were the products of this habitation. The Black Fens, however, are new country, born in the seventeenth century and after, and except for their islands have no old buildings on them.

The Romans drained part of the Lincolnshire Fens, and the presence of the Roman villa we have seen at Methwold (p. 261) leads us to suspect that they at least started draining the Norfolk Fens; but in the Dark Ages all went back to swamp. To see what it was like (better than reading Kingsley's *Hereward the Wake*) we can go to the Biesbos area of southern Holland – though this too will soon all be 'inned' and drained by the indefatigable Dutch. But the Biesbos at the time of writing is almost certainly almost exactly as Fenland was in the Middle Ages. The men of the Fens (the 'Fen Tigers') were a semi-aquatic race (like the present-day '*Polderjongen*' of the Biesbos) who lived on low swampy islands and threaded the winding channels through the high reeds in flat-bottomed boats. In the Middle Ages the monks came to the larger islands and began the work of enclosing and draining on a small scale. But it was not until the seventeenth century, when the great wealth released by the Dissolution was causing an upsurge of capitalistic development all over England, that Dutchmen were imported from Holland with their skills of land reclamation and the task was tackled properly. Then the rivers were canalized – their windings straightened out – and often they were duplicated or even triplicated by great artificial drains like the Forty Foot (or Vermuyden's Drain), the Sixteen Foot, the Twenty Foot, Morton's Leam, the Old Bedford, the New Bedford, the Middle Level Main Drain. High banks were built along these artificial rivers and often the water in them runs high above the countryside and water has to be pumped up into them from the field drains. This was at first done by windmills – often several in series – each one raising the water a few feet. Then came steam, then diesel, and now electrical power.

Men with capital, then called 'adventurers' (there is still at least one 'Adventurers' Fen') sunk great fortunes, and men like Cornelius Vermuyden came from Holland to supervise the work. The Duke of Bedford and Charles II were two major capitalists. The 'Fen Tigers' bitterly resented the intrusion: they saw their old hunting and fishing grounds being destroyed and themselves being reduced to the status of landless labourers, and they made frequent attacks on the new works. The first time Vermuyden built Denver Sluice (p. 264) the Fenmen blew it up; but he built it again, and in time the wild tigers were tamed.

The land thus laid dry was rich beyond any other land in England, for it was pure peat – many yards deep. Without any fertilizer wheat grew as no wheat had ever grown before, and so did any other crop: it needed no manure because it *was* manure. But as the land was drained and ploughed and cropped it began to be noticed that it was sinking, it was getting lower in relation to mean-sea-level. The windmills that had to pump the water out of the fields up into the high embanked rivers had to pump higher and higher, and more and more windmills had to be placed in series to do it. We have already noticed, when discussing the Broads, that in the Fens none of these pumping windmills survives (other than the one preserved at Wicken Fen) because they were temporary structures, of wood and not of brick, so that they could be moved about as occasion demanded.

But the land sank until no combination of windmills could cope with the draining, and in the nineteenth century steam came in the nick of time to save the Fens. Then the Fen lighters had to thread every navigable ditch carrying coal to the new steam engines, and one by one the little brick buildings with the tall chimneys that still dot Fenland were built. Nowadays great pumps driven by diesel power or electricity spin night and day to pump the Fenlands dry.

In 1851 one of the iron columns that held up the Great Exhibition building was driven down through the peat of Holme Fen until its top was level with the surface of the ground, with the intention of measuring the shrinking and sinking of the peat. Now the top of the pillar is twelve feet from the surface of the ground: and it must be remembered that this is in woodland, which has never been ploughed: on ploughland the shrinkage has been much worse. This shrinkage is due to three things: the contraction of wet peat as it dries out, wind and water erosion of peat constantly being ploughed, and the actual *using up* of the peat, which is an organic substance, by its decay, and by its being taken up by growing plants. Every ton of wheat or sugar beet or carrots sent away out of Fenland takes with it a little topsoil.

Thus the task of the engineers grows harder, as the land sinks in relation to the sea. And thus the task of the farmer gets harder, as – now only here and there in places, but the places are increasing every year – the sterile yellow clay begins to show on the surface, as its layer of peat has been stripped away. The Fens are a wasting asset.

But meanwhile the Fen farmers get richer and richer, and any able-bodied man or woman can earn good money in Fenland; making enough in the summer to live out the winter at leisure. The Fenlands are one of the last refuges of the Travellers, or Gypsies, who go there in thousands, all motorized now and most with television sets in their smart trailer caravans. Most Fenland farmers are self-made, having worked their way up from labourers. Most labourers have an acre or two of land on which they can work in their spare time: and two acres of Fenland, one of sugar beet and one of strawberries, are traditionally said to give a man a living. The Fen people work as no other people in England work: just about all the time. They live for work.

You are often told by a Fenman: 'There are no gentlemen in the Fens.' Of course the truth of this depends on what you mean by 'gentlemen': rather I would say that *all* are gentlemen in the Fens. But certainly nobody ever went there to 'retire', or to set up a country seat. There is no 'county society' in the Fens, and 'ladies of the manor' are not encouraged. Who would go for pleasure to a country as flat as a board, nearly as treeless, over which for nine months of the year a wind from Siberia cuts like a knife?

I can see a strange desolate charm about the little brick farm-steads standing like ships out at sea in the miles and miles of dead-flat black Fenland, generally at the ends of long muddy tracks. But more and more Fenland farmers are deserting these and going to live in hideous modern villas in the towns, to farm their distant fields from afar like Punjabi peasants.

The Fenmen are fiercely independent – but also interdependent. Each farmer knows that only by the communal effort of keeping up the river banks and drainage channels can his fields be kept dry: and meanwhile the great River Boards, disposing of millions of pounds, fight their never-ceasing battle to get the inland waters safely across Fenland to the sea. As for independence, it is evident from the complete absence of 'forelock pulling': and did not Cromwell draw the best and most resolute of his Ironsides from the Great Level?

South-east of Wisbech **Emneth** is notable for me for its Swan Inn, which should be visited during the strawberry-picking season. It is one of the pubs among the orchards and fruitful fields of the Wisbech district with a long tradition of singing the old folk songs and dancing the old step-dance, often in competition and for wagers; though unfortunately too much of the folk singing has become contrived and 'folksy' rather than spontaneous.

That Emneth is in Marshland and not in Fenland is shown by the fact that it has an ancient church, mostly Perpendicular but with a twelfth-century Early English chancel. On the floor are two coffin lids from the thirteenth century, adding their evidence that Emneth has been above the waters for a long time. There are also some nicely lettered modern stones. The whole mixture of centuries and styles is held together by a chain girdle cemented into the thickness of the walls.

In 1774 Lord Orford sailed with a fleet of nine ships through Outwell and Upwell and described them as 'populous towns'. Presumably his Lordship took the course of the Old Nene. Now we can still sail through them, with a fleet of *boats* if not with one of ships, thanks to the exertions of the Fen Watermen's Association (headquarters in March) in opening up once again for navigation the Well Creek, which joins the Old Nene with the Great Ouse at Salter's Lode.

The Well Creek crosses the Middle Level Main Drain on an aqueduct, with sluices under it. The sluice-keeper supplements his income by catching eels, which he does by lowering 'hives' into the water – not the old-fashioned kind woven from withies, but wire netting over a framework.

A house in Cemetery Road, Outwell, has long been the home of the Doubleday family, one of them a skilled Middle Level pilot and another the champion long-distance skater of England and Chairman of the Fen Skating Association. This sport has a long tradition and is still very much alive – when the weather is right for such activity. In ancient times Fenmen made skates of bone, and freezing of the waters made travel easy for them where before it had been difficult. King Canute is supposed to have made a practice of skating to Ely, preceded by a very heavy man known as Pudding to test the ice for him. Now, as soon as the waters freeze up, many young farmers pull out their skates and cover long distances at great speeds from one town or village to another. The severe cold of January and February 1986, may have distressed many people, but it certainly suited these ice racers.

There is a big and very ancient drain just south of Upwell called Popham's Eau. There are several Eaus about Fenland. Eau is pronounced *ee* by the cognoscenti, and derived from Anglo-Saxon, not French as is commonly supposed.

Upwell and **Outwell** are in effect one community, and make what must be one of the longest villages in England. They are strung out along the Old Nene (here a stagnant ditch), the Wisbech Canal, and Well Creek: the streets and houses are arranged each side of the waterways with a very Dutch effect. Coal chutes and other unloading and loading gear may be seen decaying along the water-ways, and not-so-old men can remember the days when Fen Lighters brought all the bricks to build these villages from the Peterborough brick works, coal straight from the ships in Wisbech, fertilizer and animal feeding stuffs, and took away grain and other farm produce. The 'Fen Tramway' once clattered through the streets – a branch railway that ran along the open roads. Alas, it has gone the way of water navigation: into oblivion.

A light is thrown on the Fenland character by a farmer who lived in one of these two villages, Outwell, until he was murdered by burglars in 1967.

He was born a farm worker's son in a cottage with one room up and one room down. He lived at the end in a big old Tudor farmhouse, with a cluster of 'Traveller' caravans in the back yard all through the strawberry season, farming perhaps a thousand acres of Fen of which fifty were down to strawberries (average crop four tons per acre – average price to the jam factories £100 a ton). And he amassed what was almost certainly the best collection of Dresden china outside a museum in England, and one of the foremost collections in the world. To walk into the rooms in which this great collection was displayed was like walking into some fantastic cave of treasure.

March might be called the Crewe of the Fens, and truth to tell there are parts of it with about as much charm as the real Crewe. The railway traveller from East Anglia to the Midlands, if he has the great hardihood to go 'cross country' and not via London, is apt to find himself shivering for long periods on the open platforms of March as the unimpeded north-east wind howls at him over the flat Fen.

But the best way to go to March is by water, for the Old Nene runs right through it. From the deck of your boat you get a glimpse of the spire of the Town Hall, and if you climb up the bank to have a closer look at the latter you will find a Palladian building which might well have made Palladio turn in his grave when it was built in 1900. But March church must be visited, if only for its absolutely splendid double hammerbeam roof with a massed choir of wonderful carved angels with outspread wings. The effect is breath-taking. So too, but in a different way, is the cast-iron memorial fountain to George V's coronation at the top of Broad Street.

Three miles south-east of March is **Stonea Camp**, a very large and rambling Iron Age earthwork, right in the back of beyond. The imagination kindles at the idea of Bronze Age men living on what must have been a tiny island amid the reed swamps and quaking bogs. South of it, at **Honey Hill**, was a Roman encampment. This must have been one of the Empire's remotest trading posts, for – make no doubt of it – we are here in the deep black heart of Fenland. If the traveller wishes to plumb the very depths of it – let him go to Manea, Welches Dam, and Purl's Bridge.

Around **Manea** all through the autumn and winter you will see long lines of men, women and children, picking up carrots from the rich deep black peat soil. Most of these carrots, by the way, go to the jam factories, for carrots are an 'acceptable substitute' for fruit in factory-made jam. Standing on Manea station and looking along the line you can see the curvature of the earth. At **Welches Dam** is a staunch which could lift a boat from the Forty Foot (or Vermuyden's Drain) up into the higher Old Bedford River. 'Staunch' is the Fenman's word for a lock, as it also is on the Suffolk Stour, and 'slacker' is his word for a lock-paddle. Welches Dam transfer has been out of commission for some time now: the limit of navigation on the Old Bedford in the present day is Mepal Pumping Station, about 2½ miles south of the dam, and Vermuyden Drain is unnavigable west of it.

Along the high eastern bank of the Old Bedford stands a row of huts with a faint air of military guard-posts about them. They are in fact hides provided by the Royal Society for the Protection of Birds, who administer almost 2,000 acres of nature reserve between the Old and New Bedford. There is a visitor centre open at weekends, and the hides themselves are open at all times and available for use free of charge.

At **Purl's Bridge** on the west bank, the Ship inn looks isolated but is much visited by local connoisseurs and especially by bird-watchers. There is indeed a bridge, but a home-made one of planks on top of floating oil drums. (A 'purl' is a tiny stream.) When boats came regularly this way, the bridge had to be cast adrift and then made fast again after the craft had gone through. It links the west bank to the washland, an important feature of life in the Fens.

There are many washes, or washlands, in Fenland. They are areas of low country kept uninhabited, but down to grass and grazed by cattle and horses in the summer time, and in winter they are used as safety valves, or reserve buoyancy, for the Fens. When the pressure of water in the rivers becomes too great and the latter threaten to burst their banks, sluices are opened which allow some of the water to cascade into the empty washlands – thus relieving the pressure in the rivers. The wash between the two Bedford Rivers is apt to be flooded every year, and it is then that one can catch plump silver eels, as they work their way seawards – fattened on the millions of earthworms that come to the surface of the ground of the flooded lands – trying to find their way back to the Sargasso Sea to breed.

Nordelph is a little village which not only sounds Dutch but looks Dutch and probably once *was* Dutch, for this countryside was much populated by the *polderjongen* imported from his own country by Cornelius Vermuyden. Its attractive village sign manages to look both Dutch and local all at one go, depicting Fenland skating just as we have already encountered it around Outwell (see p. 285). Set trimly at the junction of the Well Creek and Popham's Eau, in the late nineteenth century it was the terminus of a packet service to Wisbech, for which the operator, a Mr Whybrow, charged a fare of twopence. The Chequers inn at the waterside has an attractive garden, and offers real ales, bar food, and a selection of pub games. From the undulating main road between here and Downham Bridge you get a good idea of the precariousness of Fenland, for the road runs many feet below the water in the rivers, particularly in the Great Ouse at high spring tide. There are little cottages crouching below the river wall that seem to have their roof-tops below the level of the water.

CHAPTER 16

The Brecklands

The Breckland country was once called the great East Anglian Desert. It is a stretch of country quite as distinctive in its way as the Fens are in theirs, or the Broadlands in theirs. It is an area of wind-blown sand covering the underlying chalk, sometimes with a layer of glacier-borne boulder clay in between, and the chalk is very rich in flints. In days gone by the sand blew with the wind, forming large moving sand-dunes, and in 1677 John Evelyn wrote: 'The Travelling Sands . . . that have so damaged the country, rouling from place to place, and like the Sands in the Deserts of Lybia, quite overwhelmed some gentlemen's whole estates.' He advocated the planting of trees to contain them.

But it was not always a desert. In Neolithic time areas of very light land with few trees, such as the Breckland, were the most sought after for farming; for this land could be easily worked without much tree-felling or draining, and with primitive ploughs. Thus Breckland was early a place of settlement. In Anglo-Saxon times, and later during the Dane-law, Thetford, capital of Breckland, was one of the very important places in England. It was the capital not only of East Anglia but at times of eastern England. It was then a great city, with palaces and many religious houses. Such a city could never have arisen in a desert, and there can be no doubt but at that time the sandy lands of Breckland were fertile and fruitful, as parts of them have been made again today. It was the sheep boom of the Middle Ages that destroyed Breckland. The hooves of the sheep, called 'golden hooves' when these animals are confined within hurdles on arable land for the great good that they do, were hooves of destruction when they were allowed to wander at large over a depopulated countryside, for the country had (with the rest of the lighter lands of Norfolk that were suitable for sheep grazing) been practically cleared of human beings. The vegetation – the comparatively fragile vegetation of arable land which had been allowed to tumble down into grass – was overgrazed by the sheep, and trodden out by their sheep hooves. The same process may be seen going on in a hundred countries in Africa and Asia today.

At the beginning of this present century life in Breckland was at a very low ebb. Villages had all but disappeared. Thetford was a small impoverished town and the countryside was given over entirely to the pheasant cult, a cult that was as destructive to the land and its inhabitants as the cult of grazing sheep had been, for the one thing the pheasant-preserver does not want is *people*.

Tenant farmers scrabbled for their rent in the interstices between the more desolate brecks – their cropping plan compulsorily decided for them by their landlords to suit, not good farming, but game preservation. The sparsely-covered open countryside moved and crept with rabbits, which were, in fact, the only profitable crop. (In 1922 the Forestry Commission had to kill 83,000 rabbits before they could plant trees in their first 6,000 acres.)

Where the gamekeepers would let them in it was a great place for naturalists. The great bustard lived here until 1838 when the last pair was shot, and the stone curlew, a lesser relative, still survives. There are still rare plants. The Spanish catchfly (*Silene otites*), the maiden pink (*Dianthus deltoides*), the field gentian (*Gentian campestris*) and the dwarf orchis (*Orchis ustulata*) are still to be found, and a friend of mine tells me that *Orchis militaris* is common in a certain wood but torture would not drag from him which one.

There are still corners of Breckland which convey an idea of what this countryside was like before the trees took over. Rolling, seldom quite flat but never hilly, with heather and ling and gorse and bracken and soft rabbit-cropped grass and sand-sedge; with occasional large fields of grey dusty soil planted with rye or perhaps with turnips or mangolds or nowadays sugar beet; with, on the better farms, sheep enclosed on turnips inside hurdles manuring the arable land and consolidating it beneficially with their hooves (in this case 'golden' ones); with tall grand Scots pines growing in

290

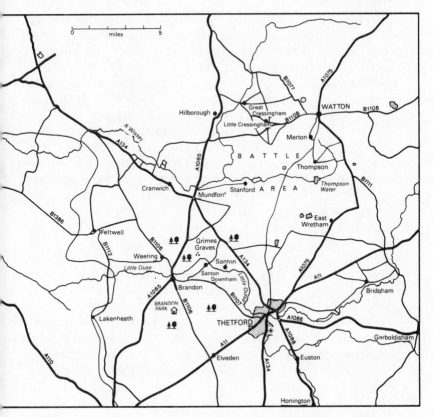

belts or else grandly alone with spreading branches warped by the wind; with lonely, often ugly and box-like, flint farmhouses or gamekeepers' or warreners' cottages. A desolate countryside, but a countryside fiercely loved by its few inhabitants.

Now nearly all of it is completely altered. The Forestry Commission has planted over fifty thousand acres with Scots and Corsican pine. This may not sound much, but if you stand on an eminence in Breckland (such as the top of one of the Commission's fire-watch towers) you look over an apparently limitless expanse of dark green tree tops, and you might well imagine yourself in the pine forests of Poland or Pomerania. Pine trees are what you see

291

and pine trees are *all* you can see for many a closely packed mile. Down below, though, you can walk along dark rides through the forest, except where areas are prohibited because of arboricultural necessity. Several picnic sites have been laid out with plenty of parking space, some clusters of tables and benches, and a number of waymarked trails of varying lengths. Two particularly spacious areas lie beside the A134 between Thetford and Mundford, and another above the deep, mysterious Devil's Punchbowl near Wretham. You may meet a roe deer, very likely a herd of red deer, which are common, and you may see some crossbills in the trees – large finches which have their bills crossed to make them useful for extracting the seeds from pine cones. The flora and fauna of the pine forests are not very rich: few animals or plants can survive in that darkened land where the ground is a thick carpet of sterile pine needles. The most beautiful thing in Breckland, indeed one of the most beautiful in the world, is the golden pheasant (*Chrysolophus pictus*). I have seen five cocks together, a most rare sight, for although these birds are common they are very retiring. In the forest dusk they seem to flame with a fantastical brilliance of vivid colour; their gold far outshines any precious metal.

The only way to see pristine pre-forest Breckland now is to brave the terrors of the **'Battle Area'**, west of East Wretham, although not legally, and not illegally either if the red flags and manned barriers show that the area is being used, for then we are likely to have a paratrooper land on our heads or – worse – a mortar bomb. Then there are also Thetford Heath south of Thetford, Lakenheath Warren, a beautiful but tiny area around Grime's Graves, apt to be invisible under sightseers in the summer time, and one or two other odd corners here and there. A fascinating feature are the meres. There is a scattering of these around the Wrethams, one at Stanford, one at Tottington, a fascinating little one at West Tofts (all in the Battle Area), lovely Thompson Water without it. The level of water in these is quite mysterious. Sometimes they are full – at other times a mere will quite suddenly empty. They seem to be governed by some unexplained movement of the water within the underlying chalk.

In the Battle Area are lost villages, empty and desolate and smashed by shell-fire. The only way you can visit them legally is to claim to be a native and die and be buried there. If the former inhabitants cannot return to them to live, at least they can go home after death, for funerals are allowed.

The great pine forest is broken here and there by rectangular clearings, generally some open land left around one of the far and few flint farmsteads. The Commission followed the enlightened practice of leaving such farms and smallholdings unplanted, and renting the houses and land to part-time forest workers who worked their holdings in their spare time. In spite of some failures there have been some successes; and scattered about the great forest are a number of successful and happy small farmers.

Thetford is a most fascinating small town, though in danger of being squeezed from all sides by large factories brought from London along with many of their workers, and steadily expanded since 1953. Memories of its older times are preserved in the Ancient House Museum in White Hart Street, restored from cottages presented to the town by that remarkable 'incomer' and benefactor, Prince Duleep Singh (see p. 307).

One of the oldest man-made erections in Thetford is the Castle. This is simply a mound but a big one (it *was* 100 feet high and 784 feet circumference at the base), there was once a parapet of clunch (chalk) round the top and wooden ramparts (now all gone); it *is* now a very steep hill up which children race and play, and it is crowned with great trees. A fairish view over Thetford and the forests may be had from the top of it.

Nobody knows the date of the castle, and modern research places the earliest occupation at Thetford in the 8th century. Camden identified Thetford as the Roman station of Sitomagus, but was almost certainly wrong: a fourth-century itinerary gives bearings which suggest a likelier site at Dunwich in Suffolk.

Being at the point where the Icknield Way crosses the Little Ouse, which was navigable to there, it is likely that Thetford was of early importance, and the fact that little in the way of Roman or pre-Roman remains have been found does not rule out the possibility that both the Romans and the Celts may have used this place. There is no evidence to show that the huge castle mound was not originally Iron Age (although indeed there is no evidence to show that it was).

293

Thereafter the Anglo-Saxon Chronicle is full of references to the town, mostly references to the sacking and burning of it by the Danes which at least indicates that there was something there to sack and burn.

In 838 the Danes attacked the town and failed. There are eight tumuli at a place called the Slough, between Thetford and Rushford, where, according to a folk tale, the dead from this battle are supposed to have been buried.

> *Hringmara heath*
> *Was a bed of death;*
> *Haarfager's heir*
> *Dealt slaughter there.*

Hringmara is modern Ringmere. In 866 the Anglo-Saxons foolishly allowed the Danes to winter in Thetford, but before that, in 820, the Danes under Ingua and Hubba had made their attack and defeated King Edmund at the battle of Euston: the seven tumuli on the high ground west of Snarehill are where the Danes are said to have buried their dead while the Angles buried theirs at Barnham Cross Common.

In 871 the Danes again sacked Thetford. It was rebuilt by the late Anglo-Saxons in 873 but the Danes, under Sweyne, burnt it again in 1004, and again in 1011, and by 1012 the Danes had command over the whole of East Anglia. Sweyne, who was King of all the Danes, made Thetford his capital, and died there in 1014. In 1015 Canute, or Knut, made it his capital, and in his reign there was peace. In 1020 the nunnery and monastery of St George was founded in the town of Urius – Camden claims to celebrate the battle in which King Edmund was beaten.

And then came the Conquest, and for centuries Thetford retained a certain amount of importance.

Arfast, the Conqueror's chaplain and chancellor, deposed the Saxon bishop of East Anglia (Egelmar who had his seat at North Elmham), and chose Thetford to be his bishopric: he enlarged the church of Great St Mary to be his cathedral. He schemed hard to add the great abbey of Bury St Edmunds to his possessions; it was still under Saxon control and he hoped that he could depose the abbot as easily as he had done Bishop Egelmar. But the Conqueror would not let him. If Arfast had succeeded it is probable that the face of East Anglia would now be very different: Thetford might well have remained the chief city, and the capital instead of Norwich.

Galgagus, raised by William I, succeeded Arfast (the chronicler says that he was 'learned and benevolent'), and was himself succeeded by de Losinga, who, as we have seen, committed the sin of simony to achieve the bishopric, went to Rome to confess, and was ordered by the Pope to remove his see to Norwich, build the cathedral there, and incidentally new churches at King's Lynn and Great Yarmouth.

This removal of the seat of the bishop might have been expected to have dealt a great blow to the town, but strangely it did not. For by then Roger Bigod had founded the great Priory of Our Lady.

In 1107 Henry I held his court in Thetford, and laid the foundation stone of the priory with great ceremony. Roger Bigod died soon after. He had willed his body to be buried in his new priory, but Bishop de Losinga forcibly moved it to Norwich and had it buried there.

The priory was manned by Cluniac monks from Lewes, as indeed was the Priory of Castle Acre (p. 249). At first they used the cathedral of Great St Mary, recently vacated by the bishop, but in 1114 they were ready to move into their new buildings. And Thetford continued to flourish as a religious centre: the list of the names of great men who were buried there gives some idea of its importance:

Roger Bigod, 2nd Earl of Norfolk, buried in 1218 but removed to Norwich.

Hugh, son of the above, died 1225.

Roger, the 2nd Earl's second son, killed by a tilting spear 1269.

Roger, last of the Bigods and Earl Marshal of England, died 1306.

John Lord Mowbray, Duke of Norfolk and his Duchess, 1460.

John Lord Mowbray, Earl Warren, died 1470.

Sir John Howard, created Duke of Norfolk by Richard III and killed at Bosworth Field 1485.

Henry Fitzroy, son of Henry VIII, died 1536.

Thomas Howard, died in the Tower 1537.

In 1540 Thomas Howard the Duke of Norfolk and his wife Agnes, their son Thomas, and Henry Fitzroy, were dug up and removed to Framlingham, where we have seen their tombs. Thetford's day was over, and even the dead were deserting it.

But Thetford had retained its importance right up until this time, the Dissolution. John o' Gaunt founded an Augustinian priory there, at what is now Ford Place. Henry VIII granted the town a charter in 1534, but in 1539 he struck the mortal blow: he dissolved the priory, along with the rest of the monastic houses in England, and sold the buildings to the Duke of Norfolk who promptly pulled some of them down. But even so, the town continued to prosper for a few years, for when Queen Elizabeth I made a state visit to it on 25th August 1578 it was reported that there were still forty butchers trading there.

The death of the priory, and the other religious foundations, would not have proved a death blow to the town had it still been the centre of fertile and prosperous countryside. But the great raw-wool boom had come and gone, the peasantry had been cleared away as the land had been enclosed for sheep, and the sheep had left the countryside a desert of drifting sand. Thetford never engaged in the great industry of weaving and finishing woollen cloth for export to the Continent: this trade went to Norwich and the East Suffolk towns: towns with a readier access to the ports from which ships sailed across the North Sea. Belatedly, in 1669, the Little Ouse was made reliably navigable to Thetford (it must have been navigable for shallow-draught at certain times before that) but by then King's Lynn, with which the town was thus connected, had declined as a Continental port though it was still busy as an entrepôt.

Thetford survived as a modest country town. There was a regular service of one train of Fen Lighters to King's Lynn once a week, and with the coming of the railways in 1845 (Thetford is on the Norwich–Peterborough line) more life returned to the place. In the early eighteen hundreds an attempt was made to turn it into a 'Chalybeate spa' and a book was written extolling the efficacy of the waters, but not much came of it.

What is there to see in Thetford today, of all the past grandeur and magnificence? Of the great Priory of Our Lady, to the north of the town, west of the railway station, once one of the 'most splendid specimens of Norman architecture this country could boast', little remains. Like the even greater abbey at Bury it was torn down after the Dissolution: after that event architecture was to glorify not God but rich men. The Holkhams and the Ickworths were to be the great buildings of the future.

We have already looked at the other Cluniac foundation at Castle Acre, and there were similarities between the two buildings. Both were derived, in plan, from the second abbey church of Cluny – the mother-house of the foundation. At Thetford was the same proliferation of blind arcading. The priory church, which was half as big as Norwich Cathedral (the nave was 121 feet long), has been excavated, and the foundations have been clearly revealed. As at the original Castle Acre church the chancel ended in a semi-circular apse, and there were chancel aisles each with apses too. But in the thirteenth century the chancel was lengthened eastward, thus eliminating the original apses (same story at Castle Acre only it happened there later) and a lady chapel was added – part of the window of which still remains. A chapel for the memorial to the 1st Duke of Norfolk was built on the north aisle in the fifteenth century and sacristies were erected late in the century. Outside the church a full range of monastic buildings was constructed, over many centuries.

Now only ragged-looking, at night rather ghostly, crags of flint remain, but to the imaginative they can convey something of the scale of what must have been a large and rich community. The remains are now cheek by jowl with a new bungalow estate, and to the west the forest presses in: only the fourteenth-century gatehouse, now mixed up with farm buildings, stands up high and proud.

Of other monastic remains in Thetford, at a place called the Canons, on the right of the road as you turn off to Brandon, stands what is left of the early twelfth-century Augustinian priory of St Sepulchre. There is a big flint barn not, however, part of the monastery, but few remains of the original work. What is left of John o' Gaunt's Nunnery and Monastery of St George is now a barn: there is still a fine arch, with Norman responds, so there was an older building there, with another blank arch in line with the east wall, and a large oblong building running north to south. It is all mixed up with a fine Tudor farmhouse. The Grammar School, a famous one, on the London Road, has at the back some Early English remains of a friary which was taken over by the Blackfriars in 1335.

The present town has charm, given it by plenty of flint building, also some good timber frame houses – the Bell Hotel is such, rambling and Tudor but recently much enlarged. The Ancient House, round the corner, is timber frame, now a museum, and it has in it one of the loveliest carved beam ceilings in existence. It is well worth going into the museum just to see this. Down by the river (or rivers, for here the Little Ouse is joined by the Thet) there is great charm, with a huge watermill of white brick, willow trees, swans and anglers. There is a pleasant no-man's-land between the two rivers.

There is a brilliant statue in front of King's House (behind which is a pleasant public garden) of Thetford's most brilliant son, Thomas Paine. It is given to few men to influence world history as much as this one did, by thinking, writing and talking. Paine was born at Thetford on the 29th January 1737, son of a Quaker staymaker, and was educated at the Free Grammar School. In 1774 he went to the American colonies at the suggestion of Benjamin Franklin, with whom he had been corresponding about scientific matters. It is inconceivable that a man such as Paine could have lived his life out under the Norfolk squirearchy: if America had not existed he would have had to invent it.

He became editor of the *Pennsylvania Gazette*, and he published a pamphlet called 'Common Sense' which advocated the complete independence of the American colonies and the formation of a North American republic. This is said to have had great influence in expediting the American Revolution. After independence had come, in fact, the States voted him £500 and a grant of 500 acres of good land and appointed him Clerk to the Committee for Foreign Affairs.

But in 1787 he went to France, and thence back to England. There he published *The Rights of Man* in answer to Burke's *Some*

Reflections on the French Revolution and to avoid subsequent action for sedition he had to go to France again.

He was met at Calais with great acclaim, and made a Citizen of the Republic. But he voted against the death sentence on the former French king, which annoyed the Jacobins so that in 1793 they immured him in the Luxembourg. After the fall of Robespierre he was released and published *The Age of Reason*, *Decline and Fall of the System of Finances in England* and *Agrarian Justice*, and his influence on France is said to have been as great as that on America. In 1802 he left France, as a protest at the Christian religion having been officially re-introduced, died in America, in 1809, and was buried on his own farm. William Cobbett, who much admired him, disinterred his remains and – at great trouble – brought them back to England to be buried here.

His statue, brilliant gilt, was done by Charles Wheeler, President of the Royal Academy, and presented to Thetford by the Thomas Paine Society of the United States. It says much for the broadmindedness of the burghers of Thetford that they have allowed it to be put there, though not without bitter controversy, for Paine was a Freethinker, and it can be said that to the Government of his country he was a traitor. But he was never a traitor to Humanity; and governments come and go. Thetford has given its name to a distinctive school of early medieval pottery: Thetford Ware.

A splendid long walk from Thetford is down the banks of the River Little Ouse to Brandon. Forests hem the little clear river and its narrow green valley in on both sides, the river is fine for canoeing, and there are ancient timber *staunches* at intervals: flash weirs of primitive design for taking the place of pound locks for navigation.

The river runs by **Santon** where – as often happens in Breckland – there is a church with no village. The church is Victorian, but built on an ancient site and it still has original Early English components. There is a permanent camping site there, and an isolated farmhouse.

Santon Downham, farther downstream, was another of the dead villages of the Breckland; but it has been revived by the Forestry Commission, which has built an entire new village there, mostly of timber houses prefabricated in Scandinavia. It is fitting that the

Commission should put up timber houses, but a little alarming that it should have to import them from Scandinavia. The old church is Norman, with two Saxon doorways, and if you approach the place not from the river but the road you find it deep in the forest, and down long avenues of marvellous old linden trees which clearly indicate that Breckland *can* grow other things besides Scots and Corsican pine!

Approached from the river, Santon Downham has the aspect of a river settlement in some wild and foreign land. There is a big seed extraction plant, where most of the conifer seeds used in England are extracted from their cones by being placed on wires over hot pipes. There is a big timber-treating plant, where poles and posts are pressure-treated with creosote. In the old block of estate buildings left are the headquarters of the Thetford Chase section of the Forestry Commission. From the car park a two-mile forest trail makes a leisurely, informative way through woods and glades, with seats at intervals for the weary. In 1969 distinguished visitors contributed oaks to a Jubilee Plantation commemorating 50 years of the Commission's work, together with pines from the US Air Force.

And here we might discuss the great new industry which has grown up in the Breck country. Planting was started by the Commission in 1922, at the beginning of the great agricultural depression. At that time it was impossible for any farmer to make a living in Breckland, particularly as nearly all the farmers were tenants and had to find their rent before they could think of anything else. Farmers and landowners were only too glad to sell their deserted fields to the Government.

Since that time new land has been taken over and planted up every year, first mostly with Scots pine but now more and more with Corsican which proves quicker growing in that climate. This Breckland climate has been described as Continental. The winters are very cold, the summers very hot, and the rainfall the lowest in England.

The forest is now over seventy square miles in extent, the second biggest in England, and an increasing harvest of timber is coming from it. The production is still mostly from thinnings, and goes for pit-props, fencing wood, pea-drying poles, or pulp wood; but already the first trees that were planted are over sixty years old and some timber big enough for the saw-bench is being produced. As time goes on a larger and larger proportion of the crop will go to the sawmills to be sawn into planks. Surprisingly at first glance the Commission is already clear-felling some of its forests in Breckland, although the trees are immature. Surprisingly, until one realizes that to 'farm' a forest economically it is necessary to have some blocks of forest at every stage of growth, so that ultimately every year some mature timber is clear-felled, and every year another block is planted.

The young trees are planted with the spade in shallow plough furrows at the rate of 2,150 an acre, and a good man will put in half an acre a day. In 1927 – the peak year – eight million trees were planted in Breckland. After twenty years the first thinnings must be taken; about 350 trees are cut out of each acre. Thereafter there is a thinning about every five years until the mature trees are clear-felled eighty years after they were planted. This at least is what will happen to most of the forest.

Fire, in this land of long dry springs, is a great danger; and in the war years and before, great acreages of forest were lost to this cause. Now fire-fighting is so well organized, there is such a good network of forest roads, and such good watch is kept from on top of the many watch towers, that the risk is much smaller. But people should not smoke in the forests, and there should be no open fires at all.

Farther downstream we come to **Brandon**, a pretty little Suffolk town, or big village, built largely of flint. Most of what is there now probably grew up about the river navigation, for until the Little Ouse was improved farther up, Brandon must have been the port of Thetford. Now it is the centre of the new forest products industry.

The Produce Depot at Brandon may be one of the biggest in the country: acres and acres of wood-piles. It had its own railway siding built to rail pit-props to the Midland coal fields, but unfortunately this is no longer used: such pit-props as go, now go by privately-owned road transport on the overcrowded roads. As the forest belongs to the Government, as do the Produce Depot, the railway and the coal mines, it is a little difficult to see why this should be so. Great quantities of pit-props still go, although unfortunately steel is taking the place of wood in many collieries, and this market for tree thinnings is smaller than it was. Most of the wood goes now for paper or chip-board or pulp – to places as far away as Sunbury-on-Thames: again, all of it by road.

South of Brandon is Brandon Park, wherein is a plantation of Scots pines 145 years old, which are a magnificent sight. They are busily and successfully regenerating themselves, and small trees are growing up among them.

But perhaps the most symbolic place in Brandon is an ugly pub called the Flint Knappers Arms in whose back yard was plied, until well into our own time, one of the oldest crafts in the world. Flints from Lingheath were brought here, and men in leather aprons would sit hitting the large chunks to strike off chippings for gun flints, or dressing the flints into blocks for building. Trade has dwindled, but there are still a few markets in Third World countries, and the renewed interest in flintlocks shown by the 2,000 'Old Gun Clubs' of the US has kept a handful of experts still chipping methodically away. Records from the eighteenth century into our own show the repeated names of certain specialist families – the Fields, Carters, Edwards and Snares – but also sadly show an incidence of silicosis known hereabouts as 'knappers' rot'.

At the time of Waterloo there were twelve knappers working at Brandon, and they were making a great deal of money, in fact they were bringing great prosperity to the little town. The Battle of Waterloo was won in the flint knapperies of Brandon rather than on the playing fields of Eton.

While concerned with flint we might go north-east to **Grime's Graves:** one of the most interesting places in England, and of the world. Grime's Graves are a series of shallow circular depressions in a 34-acre open space amid the pine forests, and why they are called Grime's Graves nobody knows. In 1869 the Reverend Canon Greenwell, of Durham, dug down in one of the depressions to a depth of thirty-two feet and found that it was an old mine shaft that had been filled in. Among the rubble he found some bones of *Bos longifrons*, bones of both roe and red deer, a bone pin and an artistically worked piece of chalk. He gave it as his opinion that he had re-opened an ancient flint mine.

Later more shafts were opened up, and it was found that the shafts had been sunk through the chalk to what is known as the 'floor stone', a layer of enormous and very hard flints at a depth underground of about twenty-six feet. From the bottoms of the shafts tunnels had been driven out radially, and these roads or tunnels had connected with those from other shafts thus providing better ventilation. Eventually the area had become pock-marked with shafts, and honeycombed by the interconnecting galleries down below. The chalk hanging-wall would not support itself in big spans, and pillars of floor stone had had to be left to support it: a miner might wonder how many Stone Age men were trapped underground by roof falls while trying too greedily to 'rob the pillars'.

In the bottom of one shaft (and it was a shaft in barren ground: the floor stone happened to be absent at that point) a little idol of a fertility goddess was found behind a rude underground altar. It is thought that the miners were sacrificing to the goddess of fertility to ask her to intercede for a better crop of flint. Red deer antlers are to be found in profusion, and sharpened bones for picks: in one mine alone 200 antler picks were found, their points worn out or broken, and on some of them the actual fingerprints of the miners could be observed, as fresh as those of last night's burglar. Drawings on flint, of elks and other animals, were found: one wonders what more lies underground in wait for people who have the time to excavate farther.

There were 366 of these mines: a considerable army of full-time professional miners must have been engaged at this skilled and specialized job. And all this up to the late Neolithic periods – radio-carbon tests indicate 2100 BC – when some of us might think of men as 'cave men', and hardly higher than the apes.

English Heritage now cares for the site, and two shafts are kept open for public inspection, one with a glass roof over it and an iron ladder down it to give access. It is a strange experience to climb down there, and see the apparently quite fresh marks of the antler-picks of the miners of four thousand years ago in the chalk, and crouch in the low galleries and imagine the Dawn Men, hacking away by the light of little lamps carved out of chalk, with animal fat for fuel. Surely it should be the aim of every miner to make the

303

pilgrimage to Grime's Graves, the very cradle of his craft.

Weeting, in which parish the mines are, has the ruins of a castle in it, moat-surrounded and rather beautiful in its lovely parkland, not far from the little Decorated church. There are round barrows here also.

North through the forest, **Mundford** is a large and attractive village, though now rather spoiled, and east of it, at Lynford Hall, the Forestry Commission runs a Forester Training School. **Cranwich**, to westward towards Northwold, has a quite genuine Anglo-Saxon round tower to its church with a circular window and circular sound holes, possibly Norman; it stands in the middle of a huge circular churchyard – unkempt and tree-begirt. There are lovely parklands all along the River Wissey, which runs through a most beautiful valley, well worth following up. You may thus walk to **Hilborough**, but you may have to argue yourself past gamekeepers. Hilborough has a fine church.

A pleasant circuit to the east might be made, skirting the wild and forbidden Battle Area, through the Cressinghams, Watton, Merton, and on south.

Great Cressingham has a fine church, with several details exactly the same as the ones at Hilborough. It also has some remains of a sumptuous brick house used as a priory. **Little Cressingham** has the romantic ruins of a church, and some barrows nearby in one of which an Early Bronze Age burial was unearthed complete with a crouching skeleton, a gold plaque, amber and gold beads, bronze knife and dagger.

Merton is the home of the de Grey family, with Lord Walsingham at its head. There is a good brass in the church to a William de Grey, either late fifteenth or early sixteenth century, depicting William as a young and handsome knight in armour with his two wives and two large families of long-haired children. The church has a round Norman tower, on possibly Saxon foundations, stands prettily in the great park, and has a beautiful fourteenth-century nave. For a stranger to enter it is rather like entering a private house: it feels so much the private property of this ancient family. A large part of the actual hall burned down in 1956. The nicest thing at Merton is the fine walled kitchen-garden, still worked by partially disabled ex-servicemen helped by a miniature tracked tractor.

Edward Fitzgerald died at Merton Rectory, while he was staying with his old friend George Crabbe, the grandson of the poet.

East Wretham is a farouche little village in wildest Breckland, with the very nice Dog and Partridge Inn, a large camp for soldiers training in the Battle Area, and one of the largest chicken factories in England. For those whose stomachs are strong enough to take it, to visit this is an extraordinary experience. There are huge open-air duck farms nearby, to the eastward, where ducks live bereft of water.

Bridgham is a charming tiny riverine village, and the woods to the south of it demonstrate that oaks and hard woods can, indeed, be grown on Breckland soil, for there are some fine stands of oak underplanted with beech.

Garboldisham is a lovely big village with an attractive church, and some of the cottages there are built of *clay lump*, a building material once very common in south Norfolk and north Suffolk, consisting of large blocks of unfired clay, such as are known in Southern Africa as 'Kimberley brick'. It will last for ever, but only if kept dry. A section of Devil's Ditch runs to the west of the village: another of the various works of the Devil in this part of the world, although a more recent theory has it as Anglo-Saxon, a frontier work between East Anglia and Mercia. There are several unopened tumuli nearby (map, p. 291).

Euston, across the Little Ouse and thus in Suffolk, is an example of a village built entirely for the comfort and aggrandizement of one family. The place is perfectly preserved, with much thatch, much 'estate Gothic', and no jarring note. The village was moved to where it is in the seventeenth century because it spoiled the view, and thus the church was left standing out alone in the great park. The church is very interesting, having been almost completely rebuilt from medieval beginnings of 1676 by an architect obviously conversant with the churches of Christopher Wren: William Bell? It has period fittings and copper gilt plate.

The Hall, once big enough to swallow up the entire village, and several neighbouring villages as well, but reduced in size in 1952, stands in its enormous park behind the River Black Bourn which has been canalized to form a wide and placid ornamental waterway. The park and gardens were designed by Kent, of Holkham fame, the trees planted under the direction of John Evelyn in 1671, who was here years before Kent.

Lord Arlington, a member of the notorious Cabal ministry (he paid the king £10,000 to make him Lord Chamberlain), had the Hall built in the 1660s, but it was enlarged and altered in the 1750s to bring it more into line with the Palladian tradition.

The Hall passed to Henry FitzRoy, son of Charles II and the Duchess of Cleveland, the king's mistress. Charles created FitzRoy 1st Baron of Sudbury, then Viscount of Ipswich, then Earl of Euston, and finally Duke of Grafton; but he was killed at the siege of Cork by a stray bullet in 1690.

In his life Grafton was a great hunting man, and kept one pack of hounds at Euston and another at Croydon so that he could hunt while he was living in London. To reach the latter he had to cross the Thames by ferry, and this so annoyed him that he pushed a bill through Parliament to allow Westminster Bridge to be built.

The French traveller de la Rochefoucauld dined at Euston in 1784, as he did in many other great houses through East Anglia, and he wrote thereafter: 'The sideboard is furnished with a number of chamber pots and it is common practice to relieve oneself whilst the rest are drinking; one has no kind of concealment and the practice strikes me as indecent.' The Hall is open to the public Thursday afternoons July to September.

Charles II used to stay at Euston, and his widow, Catherine of Braganza, lived there. Her confessor, Father Diaz, wrote: 'the place is very pretty, and has all the conveniences that we can desire, except that there are no cows.' Now there are cows.

Defoe said in 1722: 'a place capable of all that is pleasant and delightful in Nature, and improved by Art to every extreme that Nature is able to produce.'

Near Euston is **Honington**, now an airfield, and here was born Robert Bloomfield, the 'Suffolk Poet', on the 3rd December 1766. His father was the village tailor and his mother kept the dame's school. He wrote *The Farmer's Boy* and *The Horkey*, besides much other verse, and was kept alive by subscriptions from local gentry. *The Farmer's Boy* gives a good insight into Suffolk country life of this period. The church has a good font, and Norman south doorway.

We may round off our tour of Breckland by a visit to **Elveden**, surely one of the more exotic phenomena of East Anglia.

Admiral Lord Keppel, who died in 1786, lived in the house that stood on the site of the present Sikh palace, and it was he who planted the wind-driven countryside with a positive chequerboard of wind breaks of Scots pines. In 1801 Lord Albemarle was living there, and farming no less than 4,000 sandy acres; but he sold the estate in 1813. A subsequent owner was the king of the Sikh nation Maharajah Duleep Singh.

The Maharajah, banished from his court at Lahore and from India by Queen Victoria for his part in the Sikh wars, was allowed to live his life out at Elveden, where he consoled himself, aided by the enormous wealth of the Punjab, by setting out to out-squire the English. He once – *himself* – shot 789 partridges in a day – *partridges*, and again 2,350 of these elusive birds in nine days. In one year over 19,000 pheasants were slaughtered by the guns on his estate.

In the 1860s he employed the Victorian-Gothic architect John Norton to turn the original modest Georgian mansion into a vast oriental palace with a copper dome, richly scalloped onion-shaped arches within, ornamented ceiling vaults, beaten-copper-covered doors, and tons and tons of Carrara marble intricately carved by Italian craftsmen imported into Elveden for the purpose. In importing Italian craftsmen, he was being faithful to the tradition of his ancestors: most of the great North Indian palace builders imported Italians for stone carving and mosaic work. There were 350 men working full time for three years on the place. The effect is fantastic.

After the Maharajah's death the wealth of the Liffey replaced that of the Ravi. Elveden was bought by the family that owned Guinness's Brewery. The Lord Iveagh of the time employed William Young to enlarge the place yet again, giving it a new Italianate front of brick with stone dressings, three storeys high and with twenty-five bays, a massive domed portico, and yet more work inside, this time copied from the Taj Mahal!

As for the medieval parish church, the Maharajah, quite willing to flirt with Christianity, had already had a go at it, but Lord Iveagh really got down to the job. He employed the architect Caröe to add a north nave and chancel, and later a detached tower joined to the church by a roofed walk, or cloister. The tower has lavish flush-work – but every bit of the surface of the new work is so adorned with a lushness of completely unorthodox Neo-Gothic decoration that it looks like some fantastic film set. In fifty years' time it will no doubt be considered a gem.

The towering Corinthian column two miles down the Newmarket road is a war memorial to the men of the estate. It is 113 feet high and has 148 steps, no longer open to the public.

As for the present Lord and Lady Iveagh, they sensibly live in a modest and comfortable house and leave the Sikh-Irish palace to its strange memories. Lord Iveagh farms, with the help of a huge staff, some 10,000 acres, keeps more than 2,600 cattle, grows 700 acres or so of sugar beet and has proved that cattle and alfalfa, or lucerne, are of great value in the reclaiming of the wasted soils of Breckland. He is farming very profitably where, since the Middle Ages, nobody thought farming was possible.

CHAPTER 17

Bury St Edmunds to Ickworth

> To conclude an account of Suffolk, and not to sing the praises
> of Bury St Edmunds, would offend every creature of Suffolk
> birth; even at Ipswich, when I was praising that place, the
> very people of that town asked me if I did not think Bury St
> Edmunds the nicest town in the world.

As it was in Cobbett's day, it is now. **Bury St Edmunds** escaped
the fate of Ipswich by not rising to undue prosperity in Victorian
times. A wave of prosperity earlier, in the eighteenth century,
fronted most of the earlier timber and lath and plaster buildings
over with decent brick, or plaster inscribed to resemble stone; but
there was none of that wholesale sweeping away of everything
good, and replacing it with everything bad, that happened in the
capital of East Suffolk. The eighteenth century was a good time
for a town to be prosperous in: the nineteenth century, at least the
half of it, a bad. And what shall we say about the first half of the
twentieth century? As for the second half, Bury has, like so many
fine old places, acquired drab mile upon mile of suburban-type
dwellings, like a pearl in a bad oyster.

But Bury was great a very long time ago.

Sigebert, great-grandson of the pagan Wuffa – founder of the
great Wuffinga dynasty that gave us Sutton Hoo – started a small
monastery here in the seventh century. King Canute established a
community of Benedictines in 1020, and from then on, until the
Reformation, Bury was a town of the greatest importance.

It is strange that it was Canute, a Dane, who should have founded
a monastery in honour of St Edmund, an English leader who was
slain by the Danes. But then Canute was the first Dane who called

himself King of England; and what were the Danes but a later wave of the Angles and Saxons who invaded England after the going of the Romans? Wuffa, the first big-time English invader, after all came from Sweden, via Angeln in Denmark.

King Edmund, later a saint, may have been crowned at Bures on Christmas Day in about 850. He was influenced by the pacifism of early Christianity, but when the Danes landed and began to ravage his kingdom in that happy way they had he was at last, too late, persuaded to rally an army and go and fight them. The army was beaten, Edmund was captured, tortured and beheaded. Just why, out of all the English beaten and killed by the Danes, he should have been selected to be canonized remains something of a mystery. Brithnoth had a much more heroic record, but was perhaps not so saintly. But it is recorded, by the Abbot of Fleury, who heard the story from Dunstan, who heard it from the lips of Edmund's armour bearer who actually saw him die, that the king refused to renounce his faith, though scourged, shot full of arrows and finally beheaded; and that the story of the armour bearer moved King Aethelstan to tears.

Edmund was killed in 870, at a place called Haegelisdun. One school of thought places this at Hoxne, another at Halgeston which existed near Sutton Hoo (the burial place of the Wuffinga kings) and which was mentioned in Domesday but which no longer exists, and another at Hellesdon near Norwich. A writer of 1100 says that the body was buried at Suthtune, now identified (by the Halgeston-believers) with Sutton. Personally I favour Hoxne, not because there seems to be a shred of evidence to indicate that Edmund was killed there, but because Hoxne has so little else to give it fame – why deprive it of this? They even have a plaque there to say that Edmund was killed under Goldbrook Bridge. They will show us an old tree from which arrow-heads were removed. And is there not that marvellous description of Edmund's martyrdom by the road-mender of Hoxne in *Suffolk Scene* by Julian Tennyson? And as for Halgeston – it no longer exists.

Edmund's head and body were flung into a wood, and later a wolf miraculously led the bereaved English to the spot and was found holding Edmund's head: hence the numerous carvings of a wolf and a head in Bury St Edmunds and other places which

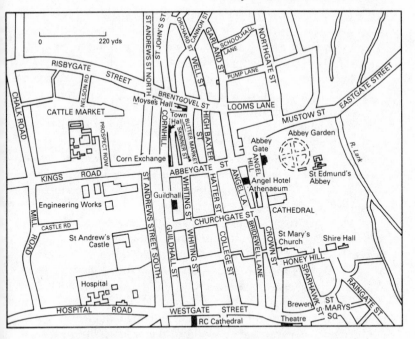

remember the saint (such as St Mary's, Hadleigh).

Thirty years after his death Edmund's remains were removed to what is now Bury St Edmunds but was then called Beodericsworth. Sweyn Forkbeard, Canute's father, was miracously struck dead by the spirit of St Edmund (no longer pacifist apparently) in 1014 because he would have rifled the shrine. But his son Canute, Christianized, gave a charter of liberties to the shrine, Edward the Confessor gave great possessions, and the abbey rose to be one of the greatest in the kingdom, a goal of pilgrimage to people from all over Europe, and the Abbey Church a very great building.

And now what is left? 'Alas, how like an old osseous fragment, a broken blackened shinbone of the old dead ages, this bleak ruin looks out. It is dead now and dumb; but once it was alive and spake.' Thus Thomas Carlyle.

The Abbey Church was something of the shape of Ely, but slightly shorter (it was 505 feet long, Ely is 537). There is a painting, belonging to the borough, painted by an architect in 1880, which

311

is supposed to show what the church looked like. Very possibly it does, more or less; although the artist's conception of the pre-Dissolution fields is far out: he has merely reproduced the post-Enclosure hedged fields that exist today (but which are rapidly being bull-dozed together to suit combine farming – we are going back to the 'open field' system with a vengeance). A reproduction of this painting hangs within the Abbey Gate.

The Normans, here as elsewhere, were forced to take over the English shrines and their saints, and they confirmed the liberty of the monks and did not even immediately replace the current abbot.

Abbot Baldwin, who died in 1097, built the eastern part of the church: the west end was completed under Abbot Samson in 1182.

Samson had a long struggle with King John, which the abbot won. In John's reign, or just after it, when the French Dauphin had landed in England to attempt to drive John off the throne, the sacred body of St Edmund was stolen, and taken to Toulouse, where it was recently unearthed – an entry in the Toulouse Abbey inventory giving away its whereabouts.

An intriguing situation has now arisen about this. Bones were discovered, and brought to England; but their authenticity was doubted and they were taken by the Duke of Norfolk to Arundel Castle and there they remain. In 1965 documents came to light indicating that they really were the bones of St Edmund. There are also some relics of St Edmund in the Roman Catholic Church.

The abbey was dissolved in 1538, and now little remains except some most romantic ruins in the midst of a pleasant public garden. Beside the little river Lark stand ragged turrets, lumps which look as old as Avebury, and grey pillars with only the sky as a roof. The despoilers made a thorough job, and the stones of the abbey are now to be found scattered about in domestic walls in Bury St Edmunds or, in greater quantity, buried in their foundations.

There have been recent excavations, and pointing of the un-covered stonework so as to preserve it, and the foundations of the monastic buildings can clearly be traced. There is a plaque, on the site of the High Altar, recording the fact that on 20th November 1214 the barons of England swore at this place that they would obtain from King John a ratification of Magna Carta. On 15th of June, the next year, they did so at Runnymede. The rose garden to the west of the cloisters was paid for from the proceeds of a book called *Suffolk Summer*, written by an American airman John Appleby of Arkansas. He achieved most notably that hard thing: an understanding of the East Anglian character by a foreigner. Or was he a foreigner? The great majority of early English settlers to North America were East Anglians: perhaps John Appleby was an East Anglian come home?

There is the Norman Gate, next to St James's Church, a splendid campanile built by Anselm after 1120; there is the abbey gate – a lovely and yet massive example of the work of the Decorated period; there are some dwelling houses built into large lumps of the ruined west front of the Abbey Church in the eighteenth-century 'Gothick' manner; there is the Abbot's Bridge, late twelfth century, over the Lark (or Linnet?).

The town itself was laid out by the Normans (under Abbot Baldwin), and is an example of early town planning as are New Buckenham in Norfolk and Ludlow in Shropshire. Like those other places (and New York) it is laid out on the grid system.

There are two great Perpendicular churches: St James and St Mary.

The latter is the finer of the two, although there is, indeed, a spacious magnificence about St James with its lovely arcades.

The nave of St James may well have been designed by John Wastell, who helped to complete King's College Chapel, Cambridge, and was a Bury man. The chancel was rebuilt by Scott in the 1860s. Both St James and St Mary are parish churches set in what was the perimeter of the old abbey. In 1914 a bishopric was created at Bury for the diocese of St Edmundsbury and Ipswich; and St James was designated the cathedral. After the Second World War, work started in earnest on extending the building with stone from Somerset and good Suffolk flint for ornamentation. The central tower still lacks its planned upper sections, but basic work was completed in time for a Festival in 1970, the 1100th anniversary of St Edmund's martyrdom. Painted armorial shields bearing the emblems of the Magna Carta barons were presented by an American society, the Dames of Magna Carta; and schools and parishes all over the county have contributed tapestry-covered hassocks with local emblems set in an agreed framework on a blue back-

313

ground. There is still controversy over the Gothic nature of the edifice – and even more over the retention of Victorian infillings in old walls of the precinct.

The first window from the west in the south aisle is worth seeking out. It is Flemish and early sixteenth century, and depicts a 'Tree of Jesse' – always an intriguing subject – and the Story of Susanna and the Elders. The rest of the glass is Victorian, but good of its kind.

St Mary, just along the street, is a lovely church – inside and out it is breath-takingly beautiful, and it is a blessing that it was St James, and not it, that was chosen to be embellished as a 'cathedral'.

The piers of the arcades are slender and perfect, the angel roof of the nave is superb and original, the roof of the chancel has a blue and gold 'wagon roof' with carved bosses on its panels – one of them depicting that favourite subject of the medieval satirist: a fox in the guise of a priest preaching to poultry.

To the left of the altar is the tomb of Mary Tudor, sister of Henry VIII, and Queen-Dowager of France.

She died in 1533 and was buried in the Abbey Church, but moved here after the Dissolution. We have seen her, and her husband Brandon, disporting themselves in the woods around Butley Priory. The east window of the south wall shows scenes from her life: it was presented by a distant relation, Queen Victoria.

The Suffolk Regimental Chapel, in St Mary's, is the best thing of its kind of England, and was designed by Sir Ninian Comper in 1935. The Suffolk regiment was raised in 1685 as the 12th of Foot, was centre of the Line at Dettingen in 1743 (the last battle in which an English king took part), stormed Seringapatam in 1799, and the Suffolks can wear the Minden Rose. Now, alas, the regiment is merged with the new Royal Anglian Regiment and so has lost its identity. The depot is on the Newmarket Road and looks rather like a Beau Geste fort.

The Notyngham Porch of St Mary's is noteworthy, halfway along the north side of the church. It was built mid-fifteenth century and paid for by John Notyngham, a local grocer (but a grocer in those days was more an importer of food-stuffs than just a shop-keeper). The porch has a beautiful ceiling of fan tracery.

There is a memorial in the church to those who lost their lives aboard HM Troopship *Birkenhead*. She struck a reef just west of Danger Point off South Africa and went down with several hundred men. The troops were paraded on deck when it was seen that none could be saved, and the one or two survivors reported that not a man broke ranks until the ship disappeared beneath the water. The bank that the ship struck is named after her, and is a famous place among Cape Town line fishermen for catching a kind of fish named the 'seventy-four' from its alleged resemblance to a 74-gun man-of-war (also kabeljau and steenbras).

In the churchyard, which is to my mind the most beautiful in any town of East Anglia, is a granite pillar commemorating the burning of fourteen Protestant martyrs.

In front of the Abbey Gate is Angel Hill, which would be a fine open space were it not for the fact that it has been turned into a vast car park.

The Angel Hotel, on the west side of the square, is a most splendid building, designed by Redgrave in 1779 but built on the site of an inn going back to 1452 for certain and probably far earlier, and named at different times the Castle, the Angel, and the Bear. The cellars of the building are very old indeed and have been well converted into a sort of crypt-restaurant, in which very good food and wine may be had.

The Athenaeum stands at the south end of the Hill, a rather plain Palladian building by Francis Sandys, that architect of another Palladian place – Ickworth. Plain it may be outside but it is sumptuous within; and nothing more incongruous can be imagined than an all-in wrestling match in the great Assembly Hall: sweat and bone crunching under the chandeliers. It was not always thus: we are told in Norman Scarfe's excellent guide that in 1818 great balls were held, attended by 'numbers of the first rank and fashion; but tradespeople, however respectable, are always rigorously excluded'. Balls are still held there – but more democratic.

At the other end of Angel Hill is a lovely Queen Anne house called Angel Corner, now used as a clock museum. Frederick Gershom Parkington left his collection of time measuring instruments, one of the best in the world, to Bury corporation as a memorial to his son who was killed in World War Two. There is a

315

great array here of instruments of many kinds, from a perfect Tompion bracket clock (note particularly the engraving on the back plate) to such esoteric devices as a 'nocturnal' inscribed 'For both Bears', meaning, not that this instrument is designed for the use of bears in telling the time at night, but that it is so constructed that the time can be told by it from sighting at the Great and Little Bear constellations of stars.

Walking south we come to Honey Hill, a most distinguished place, with the old town house of the Earls of Bristol (just why people living at Ickworth, in the suburbs almost of the town, should also need a town house in Bury, is hard to discover). Now this is offices. There are several good Georgian buildings and a modern library, and the police headquarters – brand new – are in what I for one think of as one of the most successful modern buildings about. Further down is St Mary's Square, elegantly Georgian and much happier now that the A45 no longer goes slap through it.

In Westgate Street the Theatre Royal is the only Regency theatre left in England, built in 1819 to the design of William Wilkins. Famous in its day, it was closed in 1925 and used as a brewers' warehouse, but restored in 1962 and put to use again as a theatre under the auspices of the National Trust. It has professional and efficient stage machinery behind the curtain, and elegant décor in front; and generates a great deal of enthusiasm among all its loyal audiences. In 1974 a 999-year lease was granted by the site owners – Greene, King & Sons, whose brewery towers above it on the other side of the road. This admirable company produces admirable beer, but its soaring metal chimneys, visible for miles away, are an incongruous eyesore.

Not far away is the Roman Catholic church, built 1837 and said to be one of the earliest buildings especially put up for this purpose in England since the Reformation. It is Grecian, all Grecian, and most elegant within. It is here that the bones of St Edmund will be lodged, if indeed they are not already so lodged.

The heart of Bury, the central grid laid out systematically by the Normans, is most attractive, with hardly a bad thing in it. The shop fronts are charming. Note the sixteenth-century posts carved as Henry VIII with a lady friend in the chemist's shop in Abbeygate Street, the frontage of the grocer's shop, and that of the seventeenth-century Cupola House. Chain stores have taken over a number of sites, but this is still a lovely town which refuses to be suffocated. Many old pubs remain unspoilt and and are frequented by farmers, malting men and true East Anglian country folk. The cramped little Nutshell claims to be the smallest pub in England: it is doubtful if a smaller one could serve enough customers at a time to make the place pay.

The grey Woolpit brick, cold as it may appear on some Victorian buildings, suits the urbanity of the late eighteenth century, and was used to clothe many old timber-framed houses, so that behind the civilized and precisely constructed fronts are a number of rough Tudor interiors, with great oak beams and tilting floors. The Town Hall, by Robert Adam, is famous; and for lovers of Renaissance building who do not mind the use of brick in what should so palpably be stone it is most satisfying. The Old Corn Exchange (now the Library) and the new, hard by it, are also classical. Boots the Chemists flanks a huge and grandiose Victorian-'Tudor' extravaganza, and just beyond it are some of the most vulgar modern buildings you could hope, or hope not, to find, and in a key position too.

Round the corner is Market Square, with a bronze wounded soldier of the Boer War (we may well wonder now what he was wounded for) surrounded by the stalls of higglers. And Moyse's Hall, a superb Norman dwelling house and now the Bury Museum.

In the other direction, down Guildhall Street, is the Guildhall, with a thirteenth-century door and a fifteenth-century porch.

Bury has a big cattle market, and the largest sugar factory in England. It also has the biggest factory for the manufacture of 'malt extract', the substance that much beer is made out of nowadays instead of the whole malt.

Bury, in its greatness, was a cultural centre and produced many works of art. The twelfth-century 'Bury Bible' is one of the first examples of English illuminated manuscripts. A volume of it is in Corpus Christi Library, Cambridge. In 1963 a dealer in Zurich produced a walrus-ivory cross, identified as that made in Bury in the twelfth century for Bishop Samson – exquisitely decorated with relief, but relief which among other things depicts, alas, the gory and unlikely tale of the martyrdom of William of Norwich. It was offered to the British Museum, who suspected it might be stolen property and puritanically turned it down. The Metropolitan Museum of New York promptly paid £80,000 for it.

At **Risby**, a little to the west of the town, is Highwayman's Vineyard, where estate-grown wines are bottled on a farm incorporating the original vineyard site of the abbots of Bury.

A mere three miles from Bury, south-west, is **Horringer**, where stand the gates of **Ickworth**. Ickworth is the eighteenth-century English equivalent of one of the pyramids of Egypt, a vast monumental edifice put up by a very rich man for his self-glorification. And besides being a very grand neo-classical building, it contains a considerable collection of works of art. It would have housed a much larger collection had not its builder been captured by the troops of Napoleon when that military man invaded Italy in 1798, and had all his artistic possessions taken away from him. As a place to live in – it hardly looks cosy; and the effort to *complete* it, to say nothing of having to maintain it, has been a drain on generation after generation of the Hervey family, and is now one on the National Trust (map, pp. 326–327).

The Hervey family came into the Manor of Ickworth by marriage in 1485, and were among the families which managed to weather the storms of Reformation, Counter-Reformation, Commonwealth, and Restoration: each time with their estates not only intact, but expanded. A Hervey was created Earl of Bristol in 1714 because he supported the Protestant Succession, and he married not one, but two wealthy heiresses. His son John married Molly Lepell, Queen Caroline's beautiful and witty Maid of Honour and became a great favourite with the queen herself (he wrote vivid memoirs about it all). He became Vice Chamberlain and later Lord Privy Seal to George II, and his son became Lord Privy Seal to George III and also Minister at Turin and Ambassador to Spain and absentee Viceroy of Ireland. Much of the famous family silver was collected by him. His brother, who succeeded him, was Vice-Admiral of the Blue and Viceroy of Ireland, and he also wrote memoirs of war afloat and love ashore, both of which activities he indulged in to the full. Yet a third brother succeeded him to the Earldom, Frederick Augustus; and it was this man who started the building of the present Hall in 1796.

Frederick Augustus Hervey, 4th Earl of Bristol, had received a bishopric or two in Ireland from the hands of his brother when the latter was Viceroy there, and had managed to extract no less than £20,000 a year out of the diocese of Derry. With this he was able to build a couple of grandiose houses in Ireland, both since pulled down, and travel extensively on the Continent. When his brother died and he came into the Earldom he added a further £20,000 to his annual income, was able to travel even more extensively (there are scores of 'Hotels Bristol' named after him in France and Italy), make his great collection of works of art which was confiscated by Napoleon, and build Ickworth Hall.

It was on a visit to his Suffolk estate in 1792 that the Earl-Bishop decided to build a mansion there, so he appointed an architect, Francis Sandys, and imported craftsmen from Italy.

He died in 1803, long before the mansion was completed, and he died not in one of his enormous houses but in the out-house of a wretched Italian peasant who would not admit the dying man into his dwelling because the latter was a heretic, and a bishop at that.

The 5th Earl was later created Marquess, grander yet; he completed the east wing of the house as a residence for himself, and he did enough to the great central Rotunda to make it suitable for entertaining. He thus reversed his father's plan, which was to live in the Rotunda, and use the wings as museums. The family moved into the house for the first time in 1830.

For over seventy years little further work was done to the enormous white elephant; but then the 4th Marquess married a railway heiress, Theodora Wythes, and she spent a great part of her fortune on trying to complete the house.

On the 4th Marquess's death, in 1956, the hall and park were taken over by the Government in lieu of death duties, and handed over to the National Trust with an endowment from the Marchioness. The formal gardens are a delight, and the Albana Walk leads into woodland rich with cedar, redwoods and evergreens. Indeed, the drive and parkland walks seem designed to deceive the visitor: the mansion itself (600 feet long and 104 feet high – Ely Cathedral is 537 feet long and 215 feet high) is so hidden by great belts of tall trees that we do not see it until very close by. It then suddenly

319

reveals its enormous bulk between the trees.

Entering the front door from the Ionic portico (itself bigger than many a house) we are treated to the sight of a man named Athamas engaged in throwing his children in the sea – their mother not unnaturally trying to restrain him. This is a group of statuary commissioned by the Earl-Bishop from Flaxman in 1790, in Rome, for 600 guineas. But before we go to look more closely at this we should observe the parallel scores on the end of the long table to the left on which guide books are sold. This table was brought up from the Servants' Hall in the basement, which now houses a tea-room, and the parallel scores are shove-ha'penny marks. It is interesting to compare the amenities below stairs with those of the lordly living quarters above.

Concerts and recitals are held on duly announced dates throughout the year in this rather echoing foyer.

On our left are the embroidered purses of the Privy Seal, which belonged to the two Herveys who held this office, and above them is a dashing portrait of John, Lord Hervey, father of the Earl-Bishop, depicted holding one of the privy-seal purses in his hand. Over the fireplace is the Earl-Bishop himself, by Angelica Kauffman, and other Herveys. High up above the stair-landing is St Jerome in the Last Communion by Ribera after Domenicino. There is a baby carriage, and two sedan chairs which have, inside, a pungent odour of the eighteenth century.

To the right is the Dining-Room, with Herveys all round the walls, including Theodora as a child in the 1880s between her two daughters at about the same age, and very fresh and charming they look too and the paintings are typical period-pieces. One can almost hear their nanny calling them in for nursery-tea. The chandelier, of about 1820, came from the Bristols' London house in St James's Square, and there is massive silver on the table. One of the candelabra was presented in 1840 to the Marquess of the day by his tenants for waiving their rents during the hungry 1830s when they could not have paid them anyway. Note the four magnificent soup tureens. Two are Italian, and two are in the same style by Frederick Kandler.

The next room – we are walking round the Rotunda, which is really an oval – is the Library.

The segmental shape of this room, made necessary by the shape of the building, is disguised in some parts by four great marble pillars: not marble really, but scagliola, from Coade's Ornamental Stone and Scagliola Works in Lambeth. They cost £216 18s 0d in 1822. The curtains are fine: three pairs from the early nineteenth century by the Gainsborough Silk Weaving Company and two pairs replaced by the same company in the first years of this century. All these curtains were dyed with vegetable dyes, and the replacements are indistinguishable from the originals. The chair covers on the other hand were replaced more recently by the same firm, and were aniline dyed, and the difference is lamentable.

Besides much splendid furniture there is a most charming hawk in the Library – Ch'ien Lung and porcelain; there is a sensuous chimney piece by the Italian, Canova; and of paintings there are a portrait of a son of Philip IV of Spain by Velasquez – a tubby little boy with a dog – and a splendid conversation piece of the 3rd Earl and Vice-Admiral of the Blue saying goodbye to his mother (née Molly Lepell) and his two sisters and their husbands before rejoining his ship which lies waiting in the background.

But the *pièce de résistance* is another conversation piece by Hogarth, of the Holland House Group: the Whig *cabal* that ran the Government of the day. Here are John Lord Hervey, the two Fox brothers, and my Lords Ilchester and Holland. A luckless parson, perched on a chair looking at a fat living in the background through a telescope, is oblivious of the fact that Hogarth is having a little joke with him – he is just about to topple into the lake. Evidently he was not preferred after all. The chandelier in this room was added by Lady Theodora in 1908.

As we walk into the Drawing-Room we face, at the other end of it, Augustus John Hervey, the gallant Vice-Admiral whom we have just seen taking leave of his mother. Painted by Gainsborough he assumes a swaggering pose leaning on the fluke of an anchor, standing on a sail, holding a telescope, and in front of a ship, lest there can be any doubt as to his calling. Nearby, on a table, is a Gainsborough of a most charming and sensitive boy, the Vice-Admiral's natural son. Alas he was killed, at the tender age of thirteen, while serving as a midshipman at the Siege of Gibraltar in 1782. There is another Gainsborough of a nephew of the Admiral's,

John Augustus. The Herveys were well served in having Gainsborough as their local portrait painter.

There is a Reynolds of Sir Charles Davers, muzzle-loader on arm and dog leaping up at him, with his seat, Rushbrooke Hall, in the background. It was the sister of this man who married the Earl-Bishop, who apparently did not love her very much as he left her in the old house at Ickworth and seldom saw her. Their daughter, painted by Romney, leans on a harp and looks beautiful, soulful, and very nice. There is a Lawrence of her husband.

There is a most lively portrait of the Earl-Bishop himself by his very close friend Madame Vigée le Brun. There is a gay and summery Lady Elizabeth Foster by Angelica Kauffman. She was the daughter of the Earl-Bishop who later became the Duchess of Devonshire.

But the two really distinguished pieces of furniture are the two eighteenth-century commodes, one each side of the fireplace. The one on the right, which is Louis XV, is a flamboyant piece of work. The overmantel has mosaic work made with marble from all over Italy.

In the Ante-room to the East Corridor is a dinner service made in China (Ch'ien Lung) and decorated with the arms of Augustus Lord Hervey and his wife, née Drummond, made for their marriage in 1779. This is an interesting result of the trade between England and China in the eighteenth century: Chinese potters turning out china to the design of English patrons, with English armorial patterns on them: lease-lend for the Willow Pattern.

In the East Corridor are small family portraits (surely it must have been oppressive to have lived in a house so *covered* with representations of one's relatives?) – one or two of them simple, old, and charming, like that of Isabella Carr Hervey with a bird. There is, on a stand, a 'Boy and Dolphin' by Nollekens. The story goes that Nollekens used to make these and bury them and have them dug up again to sell to English Grand Tourists as unearthed antiques. There is also a copy of Le Sueur's statue of Charles I, such as used to have two removable heads – the correct one, of the Martyr King, for wearing when the Roundheads were not about, another for when they were.

In the Smoking Room, which now contains a state bed of William

IV's time, is a Titian, 'Portrait of a Man', a lovely self-portrait by Madame Vigée le Brun of 1791, the friend, and some say mistress, who painted the Earl-Bishop in the drawing-room (and one admires the Bishop's taste on making friends with such a lady), and there is Benjamin West's hackneyed 'Death of Wolfe'. He reproduced this picture several times; with the faces of the people grouped about the dying hero varying according to whom he intended to sell the picture. There is Sir Robert Davers by Pompeo Battoni, in the full regalia of the Grand Tour, i.e. dressed up like Charles I, or a grown-up Little Lord Fauntleroy, with the various tools of the culture-hunter around him: the eighteenth-century equivalent of mini-camera, guide book, and sun-tan lotion.

At the end of the corridor are children's toys. A doll's school of 1800, with the wooden 'Dutch dolls' that were so soon to be replaced, alas, with those mawkish wax horrors that have offended sensitive Daddies ever since; there is a splendid Victorian grocer's shop; there is the Old Woman who lived in a Shoe; there is a clockwork frog which, wound up, hops every few minutes and which evidently hopped once too often because it bears the teeth-marks of a Victorian dog, and there is a simple doll's house made in 1907 by Mr Marriott who lived in Horringer, nearby.

Back to the Rotunda we go across to the West Corridor. Here is the Bristol silver, one of the most dazzling private collections in the country. Among the serried ranks of sumptuously ornamented ware a quite unadorned but very beautiful silver stewpan of 1716 stands out like an honest man in a group of courtiers. And do not miss the wall cases containing majolica earthenware plates of about 1550.

The Pompeian Room, right at the end, is decorated in *trompe l'œil* style, the 'Pop Art' of the Romans, and later of the Italian Renaissance. Weird clear-cut architectural effects with an almost surrealist feel about them. The basis of these murals is a series of coloured engravings made from late classical frescoes for the Earl-Bishop: the central panels derive from the Villa Negroni on the Esquiline near Rome. John Dibdee Crace (the man incidentally who decorated the staircase of the National Gallery) introduced a nice touch here by using local Suffolk small birds and animals in the dado instead of classical creatures. Within the house is a big

323

portfolio of water-colours of these motifs, peopled principally by voluptuous boys. Beyond the Pompeian Room is a collection of fans accumulated by Geraldine, wife of the 3rd Marquess.

Through the Pompeian Room we come to the Admiral's Room, hung with sea pieces by Dominic Serres of the third Earl's naval engagements. More of Serres' work can be seen at Melford Hall. Serres was a semi-official naval artist in the 1760s. Here are also two French 'love seats' of *c.*1750 and a Louis XV lady's desk of exquisite delicacy and complete impracticability, signed by P. Roussel. Beyond the new exhibition gallery in the old Engine Room is the Orangery, cool and green with semi-hardy trees.

The inside of the Rotunda has never been completed. It was meant to have a u-shaped staircase winding up the centre of the house and into the dome, but this was never built, and the present rectangular staircase by Arthur Blomfield is a compromise of 1908. There is a ceiling of glass on iron grids half-way up the dome – and above this great masses of raw and naked brickwork, reminiscent of Liverpool Street Station, support a huge inverted bowl of timber, built like a wooden ship, and with massive tie-beams to hold it together. An iron spiral ladder leads to the outside on top, and from the lantern above we get a great view over the Ickworth estates and beyond, and from here also we get an impression of the gigantic scale of this house, a scale more fitting for the capital of an American state than for the home of an English family.

CHAPTER 18

North of Bury St Edmunds

East-nor'east of Bury St Edmunds is **Pakenham**, notable for its two mills, one a water and one a windmill, and both working and grinding corn. The windmill is a tower mill (the latest and most developed type to be built before the end of windmills). On its Domesday site the watermill has been completely restored by the Suffolk Preservation Society, equipped with an oil engine and other machinery. It is open to the public Wednesday, weekend and Bank Holiday afternoons at Easter and from May to September.

Near Pakenham is Newe House, nicely Jacobean, and famous for the fact that 'American Reeve' lived here.

Reeve was a married smallholder of Pakenham, but he ran away with a young Pakenham girl to the USA. He went to Dodge City, ran a team of buffalo hunters and flayers (frequently killing a hundred buffalo a day with his own rifle) and made so much money out of the hides of these animals that he came back to England a rich man. Not content, he bought a herd of Aberdeen Angus cattle, shipped them to the States, and drove them himself down the Chisholm Trail to sell to the ranchers to improve the blood of their Spanish longhorns. This proved profitable, and he brought out many another load, once having to jettison a whole flock of sheep in mid-Atlantic because the captain told him that the ship was sinking, and it was either sheep or ship.

He became famous in the West, dressing and acting the part; and it is reported that he would flick his pretty young mistress's ankles with his stock whip if he thought she was lifting her skirts too high while crossing the road and thus providing an unearned treat for the local loungers. When he had made a very big fortune he returned to Pakenham, went to the auction of Newe House,

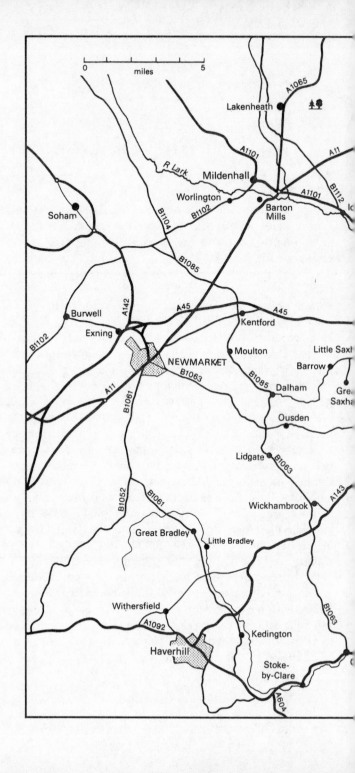

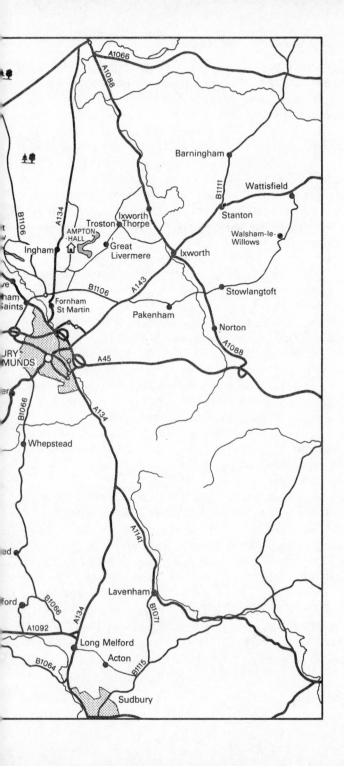

and dropped the first bid of £10,000: far higher than anybody else would have thought of going. He bought a London house also, in which his wife mostly lived (his first smallholding wife having died, he married his mistress), and settled down to being a country squire.

But although he bred pheasants with the best of them, the local gentry would not come and shoot them, and nor would they invite him to go and shoot their own feathered creatures. He was never 'accepted'. But he was extremely popular in the village, and small boys used to pepper the hedgerows with bottles and follow him about to watch him immolate these targets with his six-shooter as he rode about the lanes.

Pakenham rectory has a blocked-up window on which Rex Whistler painted a be-wigged eighteenth-century parson, sitting at his window looking out over the apple trees. Whistler was stationed near here and this was in payment for hospitality.

Not far away, on the main A1088 from Bury to Ixworth, are the Norton Bird Gardens, an alluring four acres of garden with wildfowl and tropical birds, a children's play area and a tea-room. They are open daily all year round.

North we go to **Ixworth**, a visually appealing long street village with oversailing house frontages and some good pargetting. The heavy main road traffic and frequent snarl-ups around the junction with the A143 coated much timber and plaster with dust until by-passed in 1987. Still it is an historic place, with ancient memories going back far beyond its Tudor and Georgian façades, and graced by a priory and a watermill.

Ixworth was a Roman station, later the site of two Anglo-Saxon manors, and at the Conquest was handed over to the Blount family. The Blounts endowed a community of Augustian canons: according to some accounts they started this in about 1100; according to other accounts 1170. At any rate it was a big enough priory to build a cruciform Norman church 220 feet long, very little of which now remains.

At the Dissolution Henry VIII, wishing to give his new wife Anne Boleyn a new toy, built Nonsuch for her; and as he wanted a certain site for this he had to dispossess the existing owners, the Coddington family. So he gave them Ixworth in exchange. As he had got Ixworth for nothing, by stealing it from the canons, he made a pretty good bargain.

After this Ixworth Abbey, as the place came to be known, had many owners. The present house, in a rather agreeable classical style, incorporates the restored fifteenth-century prior's lodging; and the undercroft, dormitory and refectory of the twelfth-century priory are open to the public on Sunday, Tuesday, and Bank Holiday Monday afternoons from early May to the end of August.

Ixworth Thorpe church has a thatched roof and a wooden bell-cote. Inside, its fifteenth-century bench-ends deserve careful inspection, though the same might be said of so many in this region.

South-east to **Stowlangtoft**. Here you must go into the church, for the nine fifteenth-century Flemish carved wooden panels are not to be missed at any price. Bought from a junk shop in Ixworth for an old song by Henry Maitland Wilson, the then owner of the Hall, in 1850, these panels of oak, now set in somewhat reach-me-down frames in front of the altar, are most moving and beautiful. Note such tender details as the footprints of Jesus on the ground behind him, as he leaves the earth in his ascension! These panels repay close study, and time should be set aside for them: they are very remarkable.

The late fifteenth-century carved bench-ends are noteworthy. There are over sixty carved figures in all, most lively and sensitively done. Note especially the 'owl-man', a pig playing a harp, and a man with pen and ink who is supposed to represent 'scandal'; and there are many birds and animals. There is a fine iron-bound door to the belfry. The church outside has chequered flush-work, and is very clean-cut and block-like. It looks good from the west, from the Vicarage garden, with a huge cedar before its tower (map, pp. 326–327).

Church lovers should go north to **Stanton** and south to **Norton**, the former for fourteenth-century tomb canopy, the latter for its font (map, pp. 326–327).

Walsham-le-Willows is as attractive as its name, and does indeed sport a fine fringe of willows along its branch of the Little Ouse. Inside the church hangs a rare example of a 'crant' – a medallion in memory of Mary Boyce, who died young and unmarried in 1685. It was for long the custom to garland the crant with flowers on

329

each anniversary of her death. Under the book-rest of one of the stalls is an old carving of a man with his head trapped under a portcullis; but you need to take a light along to see it. The church tower holds six bells; and the local inn is called the Six Bells.

North is **Wattisfield**, associated with pottery from ancient times. Iron Age pots have been found, and in Calke Wood the traces of a building from the same period were identified from post-holes and a clay floor. In Roman days there were groups of kilns, almost enough to suggest an industrial area, all over this part of Suffolk; and one kiln unearthed at Wattisfield was preserved in the twentieth-century pottery here and copied in order to carry out firing experiments in conjunction with Ipswich Museum.

Barningham church should be visited for its bench-ends, and for its screen.

Troston has a very fine Elizabethan hall. This was the home of Edward Lefft who was an editor of Shakespeare and published a ten-volume edition of the Plays. His nephew, Capel Lefft, helped the poor village poet Bloomfield (see Honington) and also helped Wilberforce put an end to the slave trade. The church has a good Early English chancel, faded but evocative paintings around the wall, and the remains of a rood loft.

The **Livermeres** (Great and Little) were bought by a Baptist who won a state lottery in 1722 and they have a grand park with a fine mere for waterfowl. The rectory was for 44 years the home of M. R. James, renowned writer of ghost stories, who recorded the derivation of the name as being from *laefer*, a flag (or flag-iris) which grows among the bulrushes around the mere.

Ampton Hall, over the water, was the home of Captain Robert Fitzroy, RN, who in 1828 sailed in HMS *Beagle* on the first of his two voyages to explore the Magellan Straits. On the second of these he took Charles Darwin. Fitzroy captured some Tierra del Fuegans and brought them back to England. He became very attached to one girl child, and was heart-broken when she died. The remainder he took back on his second voyage, with some missionaries, but the natives robbed the missionaries and left them destitute and the mission was not a success. Fitzroy was the first weather-forecaster, and a father of meteorology.

There are many fine Calthorpe monuments in the church, and

Chilean pines ('Monkey puzzles'), cork trees and tulip trees among the more ordinary specimens in the fine woods. The village is very pretty.

Ingham has a Roman graveyard, which was brought to light when the railway was cut through it. The railway is now a ghost, too (map, pp. 326–327).

West Stow Hall has a splendid gatehouse of brick, built in the 1500s by Sir John Crofts, Master of Horse to Mary Tudor, in the English style of building the classical style of the Renaissance. In a room above the gateway are murals, including a hunter carrying an enormous hare with the writing 'Thus do I all the day', a man embracing a wench with 'Thus do I while I may', an older man watching him saying 'Thus did I while I might', and a very old man: 'Good Lord, will this world last for ever?' A sequence hardly likely to cheer us up.

The ground around West Stow is almost indecently full of Iron Age, Roman, and Saxon remains. There was a big first-century Roman pottery on the Lark, a mile upstream from West Stow. Traces of a large Anglo-Saxon settlement were so well preserved in the sand that replicas of dwelling houses, made of split tree trunks and roofed with thatch, have been erected on the original foundations. This reconstructed village is open daily from April to October, except Mondays. All year round one can visit the 125-acre country park surrounding it, and stroll along the nature trail with its especially delightful stretch beside the river.

North-west across the heathland is **Icklingham** (all these places the names of which start Ick or Ix are near the Icknield Way), and to this place we must go to look at one of its two churches: All Saints. St James's is dull.

All Saints is thatched, large, and very impressive. On Norman foundations (there are blocked Norman windows to the north) the church is predominantly early fourteenth century with a most beautiful east window to the south aisle and near it a cinquefoiled piscina and two elaborate niches. The south aisle is very wide, the floor of the church is tiled and bare, the few benches are ancient and rude, there are ancient hassocks to kneel on cut out of reed turf from the fen! The church is virtually unrestored (the Victorians let themselves go on St James's) except for the glass in the east window, and the place seems to speak of an older, grander, simpler, and more fundamental religion. This church was not built to the glory of Man. It has fine architecture, uncluttered by trivialities. There are fourteenth-century tiles in the chancel and a sumptuous chest bound with wrought-iron by some master blacksmith of that time. On a smaller scale it has something of the bareness and simplicity of Blythburgh.

We may now take the right fork to Lakenheath, another of the 'shoreline' settlements between Fen and Breckland.

Just north of Lakenheath we find the great modern Cut-off Drain, and across this out towards the Fen a tiny pub called High Bridge – and high the bridge beside it is – all of five feet above sea-level. This pub was once a roistering resort of Fen lightermen, for they brought their floating trains up the Eriswell Lode from the Little Ouse, to Lakenheath which was then a port. Now, since the opening of the Cut-off Drain, the Lode is dry, but the little pub carries on and is a good place to go and have a drink. Farther out into the great sea-bed of the Fens is Burnt Fen, so named because it really did burn, for years. Once the black peat is ignited it is very hard to put it out. Feltwell Anchor, miles out there if you can find it and nowhere near Feltwell, is the loneliest little pub in the world. I have not been to it for several years but hope that it is still there and unchanged.

Lakenheath is next to the biggest American airbase in all East Anglia, and in many ways the little town is transatlantic. Like the other towns and villages of the 'Breckland Shore' it is built of a strange mixture of old brick, chalk 'clunch', flint, carr stone and limestone – the limestone having been carried by water to it down the River Nene and across the Middle Level. Note the wall of the churchyard to the north with its enormous flints: such as we have seen in the 'floor stone' down the flint mines called Grime's Graves. The tower of the church is a fantastic geological mixture: the base limestone – the rest a cocktail. The west end of the nave is topped with that unfortunate Woolpit brown brick (which the Earl-Bishop of Ickworth called 'a brick that looks like a sick, pale, *jaundiced* red brick, that would be red brick if it could . . .' The south aisle has lots of carr stone, and I have read that there is septaria in the chancel. It is as though the builders, over their many centuries, just shoved in whatever came most handy.

As for the church as a building, it is one of the most interesting in Suffolk (map, pp. 326–327).

St Etheldreda owned the church in the seventh century, but the earliest part of the building that we can recognize now is Norman: the chancel arch that was probably the west arch of a crossing tower. The chancel is Early English (thirteenth century), the base of the tower very early Decorated (maybe end of thirteenth century) and so we may assume that the Norman crossing tower fell, or was pulled down, late in the twelve hundreds.

The roof is most famous, and may have been done by the same master carpenter as those other 'shore' churches: Methwold and Mildenhall. There are sixty wooden angels up there, sixteenth century, and stone angels on the corbels which support it. Take field glasses if you have them – it is a sumptuous roof. There is woodwork down below, too: a fifteenth-century pulpit mounted on a stem, most rare bench-ends with acrobats and giant fish, and that silly tiger who gazed into a looking-glass either from the sheer vanity of looking at her own reflection, or thinking she could see her cubs there, while zoo-questers of the ages gone took her real cubs away from her. The font is the choicest thirteenth-century font in England and there is a wall painting of St Edmund, and scenes from the life of Christ – all growing organically out of a tree.

Numerous Kitcheners are buried outside the church; and inside is an inscription to the Lord Kitchener of the First World War.

During the Peasant Rising of 1381 (for which see under North Walsham, p. 158) John of Lakenheath and Chief Justice Cavendish were killed near here by the rebels, together with the Prior of Bury Abbey, and their heads stuck on the ramparts of Bury St Edmunds. Cavendish nearly escaped by jumping into a boat on the Fens, but before he managed to get into the vessel a woman pushed it away from the shore with her feet and he was apprehended. It was Cavendish who was trying with great severity to enforce the Statute of Labourers, which was passed after the Black Death to prevent the surviving peasants from exploiting their scarcity value.

We may now go south to the old river port of **Mildenhall**. But to see one of the glories of this place we will have to go to the

British Museum, for here is exhibited the Mildenhall Treasure, turned up in a field by a ploughman during the war: a collection of late Roman silver dishes, most perfectly preserved. A glory that has not yet been removed to the Museum is the church, an even grander one than that of Lakenheath, 170 feet long, tower 120 feet high, and with a roof of carved timber that beggars description.

The chancel and north chapel are Early English. The east window is Decorated, most strange, and in fact quite unique. It has been much praised, but for me, alas, it does not quite come off. I can imagine it in a Victorian railway station, surrounded by red brick. There is a great north porch with a Lady Chapel over it, as at Fordham. Walk around the church outside to look at the stone carving.

But it is that roof inside that is so marvellous, lavishly carved, and the whole vault above us seemingly filled with angels. The angels are said to be riddled with the shot of the Puritans – what could they have thought they were achieving? The roofs of the aisle, too, are superb: that of the north aisle a surpassing masterpiece of medieval wood carving, and in the south aisle are the swan and antelope of Henry V, saints, birds and beasts galore: the sublime mixing on the happiest of terms with the humorous and the farcical. To me this church far surpasses in interest and beauty many of the far more famous and no doubt more 'perfect' churches of the 'wool villages' in the south of the county.

Under the tower is the altar-tomb of Sir Henry de Barton, Lord Mayor of London in the year after Agincourt. He is said to have been the instigator of London's street lighting, and he fathered this very simply by ordering people to hang lanterns outside their houses after dark. There are other interesting tombs, for Mildenhall was once a great deal more important than it is now. There is still a lively street market, around a market cross said to be sixteenth century.

Down by the River Lark is a great mill, still working although not driven by water, and a gas-works with a certain period charm. Beside it is the old navigable river with a lock pen, now unfortunately and most reprehensibly closed to navigation by having been shut off with a fixed weir. Let us hope that before long the authorities will be found with enough sense to open the river for navigation again as far as Bury St Edmunds. At High Lodge, near Mildenhall, a late Clactonian Palaeolithic site was recently re-excavated by the British Museum.

At **Worlington** (Early English chancel) is the Worlington Herd of pedigree Welsh Pigs (Messrs C. R. Reeder and Son), reminding us that the modern 'Welsh' pig has been much modified by East Anglian breeders, who were the first to cross it judiciously with the Swedish Landrace to give it that extra length beloved of the bacon curer, and to produce that most excellent animal for the outdoor pig keeper: a long white pig, hardy, the ears of which hang over its eyes and prevent it from fence-breaking by obscuring its vision.

Barton Mills has the fine Bull Inn beside its bridge, and the Rev. Tylor Whittle informs me that *Orchis militaris* grows in a wood near here but wild horses will not drag from him which wood.

After the Reformation the Manor of Barton Mills came into the hands of the Steward family, a member of which, Elizabeth, married the corn reeve of Ely to become the mother of Oliver Cromwell. Barton Mills may not seem to be in the centre of world politics now; but in the thirteenth century it had for its rector Jacobus de Scabellis, or Savelli, who became a cardinal, a papal prefect, and ultimately Pope Honorius IV. By then he was so racked with gout that he had to have a mechanical contrivance to raise his hands up at the moment of the Elevation of the Host. The living of Barton Mills is in gift of the Crown and is peculiar in that the rector is not under the bishop of the diocese in which his parish lies.

Back along the main road towards Bury we get **Flempton** which once had a parson named Mr Blastus Godly and still has a west window celebrating the reception of Queen Victoria in Heaven, and then **Hengrave**, with an important house (map, pp. 326–327). Hengrave Hall is now the Convent of the Assumption, and a school for Roman Catholic young ladies whose parents can afford it. By arrangement by telephone it is possible to be shown over the Hall, and its accompanying church, and as the nuns who show visitors around are most charming it can be a very pleasant experience. You approach the Hall through a plantation of fiercely pollarded lime trees, about thirty-five years old, which make an impressive sight and a strange pattern when looked upon from the windows of the Hall above. There is an avenue among the limes called 'The Nuns' Walk', because during the French Revolution the Gages, who lived here, lent the Hall to the refugee canonesses of St Augustine, from Bruges. The superior of this community incidentally was Mother More, a direct descendant of Sir Thomas.

Hengrave Hall was one of the great houses of England held by a recusant family; and Mary Tudor came to it during her flight from Wimpole on her way to Framlingham, before she secured the crown. In Thomas Kytson's time, however, when Elizabeth I stayed at the Hall, she knighted Thomas on condition that he promised to end his recusancy, and accept the Church of England. He promised all right, but back-slid, and his wife even went to prison for recusancy.

Penelope, a daughter of the family who was courted all at the same time by no less than three men, contrived to marry them all: one at a time, of course. They were Sir George Trenchard, Sir John Gage and Sir William Hervey whose picture we saw at Ickworth. Hengrave passed to her second husband's son, thus to the Gage family. Edward Gage was made a baronet by Charles II, and Gages held Hengrave for nine generations and were all Roman Catholics. Their motto was '*Bon temps viendra*'. The Gages ended, the Hall was sold and after passing through the hands of several owners is in Catholic hands again and as we have seen a convent and a girls' school.

The house, of stone and brick, was built by Sir Thomas Kytson between 1525 and 1538 and it cost him £3,000. The south front of the house is magnificent Tudor, with mitred turrets similar to those on top of King's College Chapel, and has a fine bay window over the doorway (dated 1538) on which are painted in florid colour and sumptuously carved the arms of the Kytsons, which include three fish: not, we are told, because the Kytsons, although City merchants, were fishmongers; but because the family held some ancient rights of fishery in the River Lark.

This bay window, as indeed most of the house, is pure Gothic in feeling; but the coming of the Renaissance is felt in the treatment of the coat of arms, and the putti that support it.

Inside the house is an enclosed courtyard surrounded on three sides by cloisters. The courtyard has a pretty wrought-iron Etruscan well-head, with a lady and a unicorn with its head on her lap.

The glory of the house is the Oratory, still used by the nuns, which has one of the most beautiful and complete stained glass windows in East Anglia. The glass is of 1527 and later, Gothic in feeling (we remember again that this was a Roman household – not given to embracing too readily Renaissance ideas) and it does repay close study.

The bedrooms upstairs all have names, and one is named 'Wilbye'. Here lived John Wilbye, the man born in Diss in 1574 who composed madrigals which are still popular today. There is a great room on the north-east side of the house (the occupants call it north) with a rather macabre Elizabethan design around the fireplace, of mysterious origin and unpleasant effect. But the visitor, unless a burglar, is unlikely to enter this house without the escort of one of the charming inmates, so I will describe no more.

The little church, right up against the house, has a Saxon tower. The rest of it was added to the tower towards the end of the fourteenth century by Sir Thomas de Hengrave and his mother, and the Lady Chapel was added in 1540. The little church is notable for its monuments, which remained undesecrated throughout the iconoclastic ages because this was no longer a public church then but a private family one. Now it is the church of the convent. The fine arcades, the miniature clerestory, the slightly skew-whiff appearance of the chancel arch, give the building an unusual and beautiful appearance; as does the fact that it is in use as a Catholic place of worship and therefore richly decorated. There are engaging angels on the capitals of the north arcade, a piscina in the porch, with its own little arch, and the family monuments are noteworthy, but self-explanatory. There is a hopeful poem on the tomb of Thomas Darcy.

On the road to Bury there are **the three Fornhams**: All Saints, St Genevieve, and St Martin. Little remains of St Genevieve, save the memory of the battle between Beaumont, Earl of Leicester, Hugh Bigod, and ten thousand imported Flemish mercenaries on the one hand, and the king's troops under Humphrey Bohun, the King's Constable, on the other. Hugh Bigod got away, of course, but the Flemings perished, it is said to a man. Whether they did

337

or not, bones, weapons and pennies of Henry II's time have certainly been dug up here, and when in 1826 a great pollarded willow was overthrown forty skeletons were unearthed beneath it, lying face upwards in a circle, their feet towards the centre, and their skulls showing traces of violent death. Also found at this time was a gold ring with a ruby in it.

Fornham St Martin has a village hall presented to the village by the Sultan of Johore, who was a great friend of the Squire.

Fornham All Saints has a fine range of flint farm buildings at the cross-roads, with freestone inserts, and some not undistinguished neo-Georgian council houses, another very pretty farmhouse painted Suffolk-pink, and a very workmanlike row of long thatched cottages. There are many things of interest in the church, such as carved heads in the stonework, gargoyles, nice poppyheads, and the comforting thought that on Saturday, the 2nd of June 1927, in 2 hours and 50 minutes, a Peal of Grandsire Doubles of 5,040 changes, being 42 six-scores in ten different callings, was rung on the bells.

CHAPTER 19

South-west Suffolk

West of Bury St Edmunds, past orchards is **Little Saxham** which has a splendid Norman round tower to its church and also a curious modernized house with its lawn running down, fenceless, to the roadside like an American 'yard'. **Great Saxham** has good foreign sixteenth-century glass in its east window, and a memorial to John Eldred, the fabulous merchant adventurer who lived in Nutmeg Hall nearby, and whose adventures we have described under New Buckenham where he was born. Saxham Hall (1779–88) has an Angelica Kauffman ceiling and a Moorish temple.

Heading for Barrow we find ourselves coming into splendid country, hilly and wooded, but a country of large farms and rich men. This is the northern and western edge of the high country of south-west Suffolk.

Barrow has two trackways of some consequence: one the impressive railway embankment, another the 'Shakers Way', which might be supposed to have some connection with the Quakers but in fact was a favourite track with footpads and highwaymen of the Newmarket area. Barrow has Broom's Barn Experimental Station, which is an offshoot of Rothampstead and where research into sugar-beet culture is carried out. The buildings are modern, and of good design, with good big pitched roofs (the flat roof is alien to East Anglia and quite unsuitable to our climate). The original Broom's Farm, incidentally, was used as a small-pox hospital in 1882.

The brick tower standing so forlornly opposite the Weeping Willow is all that remains of a Salvation Army Citadel. The housing estate of tile-hung houses near the village was erected in fifteen weeks flat by T. H. Johnson (Building Systems Ltd) of Doncaster.

Tile-hung walls are a South-of-the-Thames expedient, and have nothing whatever to do with East Anglia, except where introduced by people who ought to know better.

There is a map of Barrow in 1597 in the County Records Office at Bury, often studied by people interested in the Open Field System.

The land was divided into *furlonges* which were approximately 200 yards square, and the furlonges into strips 22 yards wide. The strip was what a team of oxen could plough in a day, and was thus long in order to save the bother of turning the long team too often. The furlonges on this map have names like 'Nether Lightly', 'Wallopes Wentte' and 'Priests Pightel'.

Dalham is a little show village, and now we are getting near Newmarket where are rich people, and show villages abound. Dalham runs along both banks of the River Kennet, there are green strips along the banks with little white footbridges over and the whole place is too pretty for words. There are two mills, neither working, and one is a smock mill.

At **Moulton**, north, and another pretty Surrey-like village, is a famous pack-horse bridge, spanning a stream in which there is hardly any water. The size of the bridge, which is fifteenth century, shows that there was much more water once and is yet another sign of the desiccation of East Anglian streams. There is another fifteenth-century bridge in the village, farther up.

By **Kentford** cross-roads is the melancholy mound of a shepherd boy's grave. Accused of sheep stealing, he hanged himself rather than wait for a public hanging or transportation. Occasionally people tidy the grave and put flowers on it – plastic flowers as often as not – including good-luck offerings on race meeting days.

And so we come, across the famous Heath, to **Newmarket**. The great industry of Newmarket is catering for absentee horse owners. A person buys a race horse (or more often has one bought for him or her by somebody who knows how to do it), and places the horse with a Newmarket trainer. The owner may see his horse several times a year – he may see it more seldom: it is most unlikely that he will ever ride upon its back. The trainer enters the horse for various races up and down the country, and the horse sometimes wins, and sometimes loses; but in the nature of things, there being more than two horses in each race, it most probably loses. If it wins the owner may make some money, if it loses he will certainly lose some; but whether it wins or loses he will certainly be faced with a hefty weekly bill for its training and upkeep.

Newmarket was new, indeed, in 1227, when the old market, down at Exning, was closed up because of a plague. The place rose to great wealth and fame in Charles II's time owing to the passion for racing of that monarch, but James I had come there before him to hunt, hawk, course and race.

The Earl of Bath, writing in 1753, conveys something of the excitement that the sport of horse-racing has for its addicts:

> Now the contention becomes animating; 'tis delightful to see two, or sometimes more, of the most beautiful animals of creation struggling for superiority, stretching every muscle and sinew to obtain the prize and win the goal! To observe the skill and address of the riders, who are all distinguished by different colours of white, blue, green, red, or yellow, sometimes spurring and whipping, sometimes checking and pulling to give fresh breath and courage! And it is sometimes observed that the race is won as much by the dexterity of the rider, as by the vigour and fleetness of the animal.

James I built the King's House here, and conferred no less than ninety-nine knighthoods in the intervals of his sporting activities. Charles II built a great house which was pulled down to make way for the present Congregational Chapel: a notable change of use. The Rutland Arms is still there, a noble coaching inn (this was on the main road between Norwich and London, and Norwich and Cambridge, and so an important staging post). Otherwise there is little of architectural interest, unless we are interested in the great flowering of pseudo-Tudor in the reigns of Edward VII and George V, and in very large and expensive-looking villas put up by sporting gentlemen. Newmarket is a landlocked Cowes. The Jockey Club, by Richardson, is admired.

The Devil's Dyke offers traditionally the only free grandstand view of the racing. Small aeroplanes come and go with great frequency all during race meetings – taking highly-paid jockeys from one meeting to another up and down the country. The juke-box cafés in the town are filled with 'stable lads', who are a race apart, and the Rutland Arms is patronized by tweed-clad trainers and senior jockeys.

If you go early in the morning to the heathland slopes to the west and north-west of the town you will see some hundreds of stable lads, all looking much alike, riding an equivalent number of horses, all looking exactly alike. They are going for their morning training walks. There is a statue of a horse on the Snailwell Road, and one expects to see little votive offerings of oats placed before it. At Tattersalls, the great sale ring over towards the station, if you hear the auctioneer saying 'fifteen' he does not mean fifteen *hundred* guineas. He means *thousand*. This tip may save you a lot of money if you are thinking of buying a horse.

Exning, north-west, is now a very expensive suburb. Here was once one of the palaces of the Wuffinga dynasty; and Queen Etheldreda, later Saint and founder of Ely, was born here, and baptized in St Mindred's Well. The latter was a place of pilgrimage, and is still to be seen, a little spring on land belonging to the Jockey Club.

We can cut back into the main part of Suffolk, via Ashley to **Ousden**, which has a strange little Norman church. The north door could not make up its mind whether to be Norman or Early English (it is half one and half the other). The chancel is under the tower, and the Norman arches are impressive.

Lidgate has a brass in its church to John Lydgate, a poet who followed just after Chaucer and wrote a prodigious number of lines, with some good grain to be found among an unconscionable amount of chaff. He was born at Suffolk House, a fourteenth-century timber and brick building in the village, now nobly restored. At the age of sixteen he became a monk at Bury St Edmunds, and was often referred to as the Monk of Bury.

Wickhambrook is a large parish, scattered over hilly country (hilly for East Anglia, remember) with several large halls and farmhouses. But all of this country is suffering now a little from its proximity to London: the semi-commuters are beginning to move in. But at least they do stop the old thatched cottages from falling down. The cottagers (such as are left of them) move into the council houses, and the Londoners move into the cottages, which they can appreciate. Although one can see the sense of the man who says: 'I would rather live in an ugly house and look out at a pretty one, than live in a pretty one and look out at an ugly one!'

Badmondisfield Hall, two miles to the north of Wickhambrook, is a moated hall, most of it sixteenth century (although some earlier) but ferociously restored. The church is mostly Decorated, with Saxon carving outside the south wall.

Great Bradley should be visited by all brick makers; for the bricks of its south porch are said to have been made by the King's Brick maker in Henry VIII's time. There is a fireplace inside the church, said to be for baking the wafers of the Eucharist. (It may be of interest that the Thomian Christians of South India have had arrangements inside their churches for baking their holy bread since AD 50; but they use leavened bread; and they claim that the yeast that leavens it is the living descendant of yeast handed to St Thomas by Christ himself.) There is a bell at Great Bradley that has rung for 600 years and looks as if it may go on ringing for another 600. There is some *corking* glass in the east window – of a Rupert Brooke-type young soldier in the trenches. It will be a collector's piece in fifty years' time.

Little Bradley has one of the very few predominantly Anglo-Saxon churches left standing in England. It has a round tower, thought to be tenth century, and long-and-short work in the nave and chancel. It is impossible for an Englishman to stand in such a building without awe.

John Daye, the great printer, was buried here; and there is a brass to him, with a wife and six sons and five daughters and two babies under the table. This was nothing – he had as big a tribe by another wife! He still found time for a great deal of printing, however; he published Foxe's *Book of Martyrs* – lodging John Foxe in his house while he wrote it – and printed the works of the Anglo-Saxon Abbot Alfic to please Archbishop Parker, the Master of Corpus Christi who collected the great library of that college. Daye cut an Anglo-Saxon type-face to do the latter work, and he was the first Englishman to cut a face for the printing of music. He was also the first to print the Psalms in English.

> *Here lies the Daye that darkness could not blynd*
> *When Popish fogges had overcast the sunne . . .*

There is a window to him in the church put there by the Stationers'
Company in 1880, and his name is perpetuated by the publishers,
John Day of New York. They still use his emblem: an angel in
front of the sun.

Withersfield has some distinguished and unusual carved benches,
and is a very pretty village. And so we come, if come we must, to
Haverhill. Haverhill is pronounced variously 'aver'il' (we are getting near London where they drop their aitches) 'avvril', 'hayvril'
and 'havvrill''; and most of the present town is late-Victorian, for
the town shot forward at that time, rebuilt after a fire, as a sort of
rural Leeds. It shoots forward again, or at least in some direction,
into the Age of 'Overswill', and is already quite overwhelmed by
factories and council houses. There is a very modern factory,
designed by Messrs E. D. Mills and Partners, for the good old East
Anglian firm of Polak and Schwarz. Nathaniel Ward, a parson
from Haverhill, founded Haverhill in Massachusetts.

Kedington, east-nor'east, called Ketten by the knowing and
Kitten by the even more knowing, has a church of extraordinary
interest. On its east gable is an Anglo-Saxon crucifixion at least
900 years old, which was dug up in 1860; there are Roman bricks
in the church and Roman foundations under it; and it is now the
mausoleum of the Barnardiston family, which has inhabited this
place for twenty-seven generations!

To enter the church, when it is empty of people, is like walking
into some silent dormitory, with stone figures sleeping all about,
or kneeling beside their beds in prayer. Sir Thomas's tomb is
particularly fine, with his two wives and his fine armour. He died
in 1503. There are several later Sir Thomases – one a great fat
Falstaff of a fellow with a lion at his feet; there is Nathaniel who
outdid his fellow Puritans in piety; and a mere stone inscribed to
Sir Samuel, who gave the Puritans their name of 'Roundheads'
(the Queen looked out of her window at a Puritan riot and said:
'See what a handsome round head is there!' looking at the handsome Sam, and the name stuck). He kept his round head well down
in the Civil War, though, so much so that Charles II knighted him

when he got the throne back.

There are finely carved pews in this church, mostly seventeenth century for it was then that the family seems to have flourished the most. There is a most notable Puritan pulpit, from which the famous Fairclough thundered. There is an hour glass and a wig pole, and Addison tells us that John Tilletson, who hung his wig on the latter, was the first parson ever to wear a wig, God bless him.

Sou'east to **Stoke-by-Clare**, which should be visited by all misers, pulpiteers and windmill-lovers. The church has the most beautiful pulpit in England, paid for in 1498, but so small as to be inadequate for a really well-fed incumbent. As for windmills – there is a depiction, in fifteenth-century stained glass, of a post mill in a window of the south transept. There is a Doom on the east wall. Misers will revere this place because John Elwes lived in the priory here in the eighteenth century. His wealthy mother starved herself to death, and John, who incidentally became a Member of Parliament, was so mean that he would not have his boots cleaned lest it wear them out, and when he injured both his legs would only pay the doctor to heal one: he healed the other himself by copying what the doctor did to the first.

Elwes's house had been a college of priests which started at Clare about 1090 but was transferred to Stoke-by-Clare in 1124. Matthew Parker was at one time Dean of it. It is now a college again, or at least a school.

Clare, which Stoke is by, is a fascinating little town and still substantially unspoilt, though there was once great outrage when a large slice of the mound supporting the castle keep was removed to make way for the railway. While these Victorian excavations were going on a reliquary cross of great beauty and value was found, made of gold set with large pearls on a gold chain and bearing a remarkable Christ figure. Thought to have contained a portion of the True Cross, it was presented to Queen Victoria by the loyal railway company, and may well have been her property already, in a way, for later research points to it as having once belonged to Edward III, whose second son Lionel, Duke of Clarence, gave it to his daughter Philippa, who lived in Clare Castle. The intrusive railway has now disappeared but the station platforms remain, and children can shunt happily up and down the grass between them. The site has become the focus of a 25-acre country park, with a nature trail, informal walks, a butterfly garden, and a picnic area; and for the energetic there is a steep, winding climb to the jagged remains of the overgrown castle keep.

In the early Middle Ages Clare was a very important military stronghold. It was the fort that commanded passage along the Icknield Way. It was in a position that could effectually bar passage along that ridge of high well-drained ground that connected East Anglia to the rest of England, and which had the impassable forest-swamps of Essex on one side of it, and the Fens on the other.

It may then be wondered why the castle was not built actually astride the Way. The answer to this is that stone could not have been got to such a site without the almost impossible task of dragging it overland. Clare was the nearest point to the Way on a navigable river (the Stour), up which stone could be carried from Normandy to this stoneless country. The Normans early saw the strategic importance of the site. The first mention of the castle is in 1090, twenty-four years after the Conquest. William had given the Honour of Clare to Richard Fitzgilbert, and by the reign of King John, Gilbert, 7th Earl of Clare, was one of the most important men in England.

But the de Clare that we hear most of was Elizabeth. She was the daughter of yet another Gilbert de Clare, the 9th Earl, and her mother was Joan of Acre, the daughter of Edward I. Joan was born at Acre, when her father was on his crusade; and when Gilbert married her he was three times her age. They had four children: a boy who got killed at Bannockburn, Elizabeth of whom we write, and two daughters who became wards of Edward II who married them off to his two 'creatures', Piers Gaveston and Hugh Despenser.

Elizabeth inherited Clare Castle and other vast estates, for her father had been one of the richest men in England. She married three times, and each time was widowed; by the age of twenty-eight she was a widow for good. There is a story that one of her husbands was killed before her eyes while participating in a joust to celebrate their wedding. She settled down at Clare and there lived in great style, keeping apartments always ready for her cousin Edward III, and entertaining constantly two other cousins and friends: Marie de Valance, Countess of Pembroke, and John, Duke of Lancaster. The former founded Pembroke College, the latter Corpus Christi, and the latter's steward, Edmund Gonville, founded Gonville and Caius: thus this group of friends founded four of Cambridge's colleges.

The massive church of Clare stands bang in the middle of the village. The heavy tower is thirteenth-century Early English, the body of the church remodelled in the fifteenth century (but the chancel later, in the seventeenth). Fortunately the seventeenth-century builders did not despise the style of their ancestors and used good Perpendicular: no worse than that of earlier ages. We may wonder what would have happened had Englishmen not gone whoring off into Italy, but had allowed their architecture and art to go on developing naturally from the Gothic style that they had so triumphantly developed, instead of making that wild jump backwards to the Classical ages again.

There is a very fine 400-year-old brass lectern, an eagle with dogs at foot, probably Flemish and said to be the gift of Queen Elizabeth. There is Tudor heraldic glass in the east window (Dowsing smashed 1,000 'superstitious pictures' in these windows but spared the heraldic glass); good Jacobean stalls; and Roman bricks among the flint of these walls. The church has an ancient look, and seems to crouch down amid the little town around it.

Over the Stour is Clare Priory, the first Augustinian foundation in England. The religious house originally established at Clare was of Benedictines; but we have seen these were removed to Stoke-by-Clare in 1124. They came originally from Bec, in Normandy.

In 1248 Richard de Clare, grandson of Fitzgilbert, brought the Austin Friars from France, the first Augustinians to arrive in England. They spread from here all over the country, and to Ireland where they persisted after the English Reformation, and from where they have since reached out as missionaries to many parts of the world, and now they have come back to Clare, for Clare was again made an Augustinian priory in 1953. There are five or six friars living there now, and their purpose is to teach novices to the order; but when I went there in 1965 they had no novices to teach. In 1298, when we may suppose that the community was at its zenith, there were twenty-nine friars and novices, and it is recorded that Edward I, when he visited the place, gave them one *solidus* each.

The monastery had a large church with cloisters on the south side and infirmary and reredorter on the east. The infirmary building is still standing and in use as an out-house, and extensive remains of the walls of the church are still standing. There is a tomb-recess believed to be that of Joan of Acre, who is known to have been buried at Clare. There is a grave in the chancel thought to be that of Lionel, Duke of Clarence, son of Edward III, who was buried here in 1377. One of the walls of the cloister garth still stands to almost its full height.

The main building still existing, though, is the seventeenth-century dwelling house which was built among the ruins of the Prior's House and Cellarer's Hall. This still has windows and buttresses of the late fifteenth century, and a fine doorway in the west wall of the early fourteenth century. The big house has great charm, and is a jumble of bits of different periods. The priory grounds are almost surrounded by the River Stour, which was diverted by the monks for that purpose, and there are noble trees.

Clare village itself contains many beautiful old houses and cottages, and some of the best *pargetting* in the world. The Ancient House, near the church, has the date 1473 on its pargetting, but undoubtedly this was the date of the house and not of the pargetting, for pargetting was a later art: most of it done in the seventeenth century, about the time of Charles II. Much of this work (the application of moulded plaster) was done to old timber-framed buildings, which probably had to be plastered anyway to cover up the draughts caused by the shrinking of the timbers over the centuries. To see the art at its finest we must go to the Ancient House, Buttermarket, Ipswich.

Following downstream along the Stour we come to **Cavendish**, where is a Sue Ryder Home behind the Old Rectory for victims of Nazi persecution. Here is one of the most attractive village greens in Suffolk. There is a fine church (we are coming now into an area in which fine churches are ten a penny, and so the one at Cavendish may well get disregarded). But observe the noble clerestory of the fifteenth century, Roman bricks in the south aisle and Flemish tiles in the north, a ringing chamber in the tower which was once lived in and has a fireplace, the fourteenth-century door with its original ironwork, the fifteenth-century eagle lectern, the fourteenth-century chest and the seventeenth-century altar table. The chancel was built with money from Sir John Cavendish who had his head cut off by rebels of 1381 because his son had treacherously killed their leader, Wat Tyler, after the king had given the latter amnesty. Sir John's old house is on the green.

Cavendish Manor vineyards, a short step from the church, are among the leading revivalists in the post-war viticultural renaissance. Suffolk is a relatively dry county, and its restricted rainfall is a major factor in restricting the incidence of grape disease. Although East Anglia is north of the apparently richer wine-growing areas, it has in fact more hours of sunshine than many of those regions, and ideal conditions for the leisurely maturing of the fruit. Since the Second World War nearly thirty full-scale commercial vineyards have been established in this part of the world. Basil Ambrose planted Cavendish's first vines in 1972, and now the flourishing estate offers tours of the house and grounds, with a vineyard trail, daily throughout the year.

Glemsford is for some reason or other called 'Little Egypt'. During every war Glemsford has had a flax factory, and Suffolk farmers devote part of their acreage to growing linseed for flax. The factory is turned into a plastics factory now, a sign of the times no doubt; but no doubt again the country will be glad enough to grow and work flax again if there is another 'emergency'. But at the moment West Suffolk farmers seem to grow nothing but barley, owing to the big subsidy on this crop, and the fact that it can be harvested, in the depopulated countryside, with practically no labour whatever.

But as Glemsford has for so long been famous for flax, and as so many people living here have worked in the flax factory, it might be of interest to include a note about it. The flax is cut by reaper-and-binder, stacked, and later sent to the factory. Here it is *rippled*, which consists of combing the seed out of it, and this seed is crushed for the linseed oil which puts such a bloom on fattening cattle. The stems of the plant are then *retted*, which means that they are laid in warm water for a few days. You can see coconut husks being subjected to the same treatment in India and Ceylon. This softens the flesh clinging to the fibres and enables it to be got off, by *scutching* (at Liston, nearby in Essex, there is still a pub called The Scutcher's Arms). The fibre, thus cleaned, goes for linen, the shive as the inferior fibre scutched from it is called, for tow, and the chaff scutched out of the stems goes for cattle food; so that nothing of this most excellent and economical crop is wasted.

Glemsford has been a weaving town for a very long time, and in the Middle Ages had its own peculiar cloth, called Gleynforths. The Angel pub has a fifteenth-century wood carving of the Archangel Michael for its sign, the church is fine, with a notable fifteenth-century font, and George Cavendish, Wolsey's biographer and his faithful servant until his downfall, is buried within the church. Without it is buried James Albion, died 1791, with this on his stone:

> In ringing ever from my youth
> I always took delight.
> My bell is rung and I am gone
> My soul has took its flight.
> To join a choir of heavenly singing
> Which far excel the harmony of ringing.

Let us hope that his bell-ringing was better than the scansion of his commemorator.

Boxted, north-about, has a small church standing behind the gamekeeper's cottage, and there are Poleys everywhere in it. There are Poley windows, Poley slabs, Poley monuments, even a Poley family tree engraved on marble on the wall. Poleys have lived in the nearby Hall for five hundred years, a Poley gave his life for his country on the 15th of September 1942, and Major John Weller-Poley still lives at the Hall.

In the church are two lovely *oak* Poleys, lying down, William and Alice, of 1587, and really sensitively carved: most fine. But the *coup d'œil* is Sir John, who died in 1638 but the statue was later. It is most spirited: Sir John stands in his armour, his hand

350

jauntily on his hip, looking extremely pleased with himself. He has a frog hanging in his ear, said to be a Danish honour, for Sir John served the King of the Danes for twenty years and also fought the Spaniards under Elizabeth. The song *Froggie would a'wooing go* (Roley, Poley, Gammon and Spinach) is thought to refer to Sir John Poley, the Rowleys of Stoke-by-Nayland, the Bacons and the Greenes, all families of this area. There is a little old glass in the Poley chapel; but the east window of the church is in what I can only call the *marzipan* school of glass painting.

Whepstead is of interest if only to the saint-knower. The church is dedicated to St Petronilla, the only one in England so to be. This saint was, of course, long thought to have been the daughter of St Peter; but the opening of her tomb in Rome in 1873 showed that she was in fact the daughter of a Roman nobleman, and suffered martyrdom. There is nothing now, beyond some pretty little villages, to stop us from getting back to Bury St Edmunds.

CHAPTER 20

The West Suffolk
Wool Villages

We now embark on what some people will regard as the most rewarding section of our tour of East Anglia: the inspection of the famous West Suffolk 'wool villages', and we will take the bull by the horns and go straight to Lavenham, the most famous of them all.

It is best to approach **Lavenham** from the west, south-west or south. For thus you drive across the gently rolling Suffolk fields, suddenly to see, very far away, a really large apparently rectangular *block* standing up on the horizon. It is quite alone, there is no other object near it, and at first sight you may take it for a water tower. Almost immediately, though, you notice a slight tapering about its shape and it is borne in upon you that here is no water tower, but significant form. This is Lavenham church tower (map, pp. 326–327).

As you get nearer the tower becomes more distinct and beautiful; until quite suddenly you swing round a corner and there it is, Lavenham church, right in front of you, and from that direction unhindered by any other building. An edifice that, no matter what we may find wrong with its proportions, could not be more beautiful were it studded with diamonds.

But let us keep on past it and have a look at the town first.

This town was built in the period preceding the seventeenth century, when it was a weaving town, and we may suppose that most of the buildings were put up in the fourteen and fifteen hundreds, for it was during a decade or so each side of 1500 that the large amount of money needed to rebuild that splendid church

352

was found, and so that is when Lavenham's prosperity was at its height, and when the greatest amount of rebuilding probably took place. Before 1400 we may suppose the clothiers lived in rude houses. After that they were able to put up houses so substantial, and so well-built and long-lasting, that they are still considered highly desirable, four hundred years old though they may be. After 1600 Lavenham began to decline, and then very few houses were built. The reason why it declined was the development of water power for the laborious business of fulling cloth. The weaving industry moved to the west of England, and the north, where hill streams provided power. The invention then of power looms and spinning-jennies knocked East Anglia out completely, for these machines also depended on water power. The application of coal then to provide the power for them knocked out the west of England too; the north became all supreme and East Anglia was spared the horrors of the Industrial Revolution.

In Lavenham there are streets and streets practically solid with timber-framed building. Whether these houses originally displayed their timber framing to the view is debatable: certainly some of them did not always, as *pecking* on the timber tells us: this pecking was done to form an anchor for plaster. Whether the plaster was put on when the house was built as a protection for the timber, or afterwards to block up draughts, it is hard to say. Now most of the plaster has been stripped off by timber-lovers, so that the attractive black and white pattern results. East Anglian timber framing differs from that of the Midlands and Cheshire in that the verticals are closer together than the horizontals. When these houses were put up timber framing was by far the cheapest method of building a big house. In 1965 when Trust Houses Ltd put up some new timber framing to enlarge their Swan Inn and to incorporate within it the old Wool Hall next door, it cost them £170,000: such is the cost of oak now (they needed 400 tons of it) and the cost of craftsmen. It will be noticed, incidentally, that iron fastenings are not used in good timber framing: the members are held together by wooden pegs, 'dowels' or 'pins'. Thus there is no iron to rust and in so doing split the timber, and the houses do not become 'nail-sick' as do iron-fastened ships; they will last as long as the timber lasts, which appears to be for ever.

353

The Swan, by the way, is a very fine example of Elizabethan timber framing (and some Elizabeth II timber framing as well) and is a big and very good hotel. The incorporated Wool Hall was actually pulled down in 1913, when such buildings were only beginning to be valued; but it was rescued by the Reverend Henry Taylor and the Society for the Preservation of Ancient Buildings and put together again.

It is interesting, and sad, that one of the old weaving families kept on – a family of Huguenot descent, as many of the weaving families were – until a few years ago, when the last weaver (Mr Jarvis) died and his son decided not to carry on the business.

In Shilling Street is Shilling Grange, a very fine house, and in it lived Jane and Anne Taylor who wrote songs for children (Jane wrote 'Twinkle, Twinkle, Little Star'). Their portrait, painted by their dad, hangs in the National Portrait Gallery. Father was an artist and a Dissenter, and his house was attacked once by a mob. When he moved to Lavenham in 1786 his rent was 6s a year. Since then rents have gone up. A secret room was discovered in this house, in modern times, with medieval murals.

De Vere House, in Water Street, is fifteenth century and on a Saxon site, and it was also pulled down once by vandals but re-erected by preservationists. It has new brick-nogging (infilling of bricks in the spaces between the timber framing – the bricks often laid diagonally).

In the Market Place, which has good Georgian building besides Tudor, is the spectacular Guildhall, built by the Corpus Christi Guild soon after this was formed in 1529. At this time John de Vere, 15th Earl of Oxford, gave Lavenham a charter. Notice the splendid porch of this building and its carved corner posts – one with John de Vere holding a distaff and the charter of the Guild – and the oriel windows. When Howard visited it in 1784 the place was a prison – 'dirty and unsafe and lacking straw and water'. The martyr John Taylor was held here on his way to the burning pyre at Hadleigh.

Today the building is in the care of the National Trust and displays Taylor family mementoes, coopers' tools and techniques in its old wine cellars, and a graphic history of the weaving trade. Also connected with that industry are the Priory in Water Street,

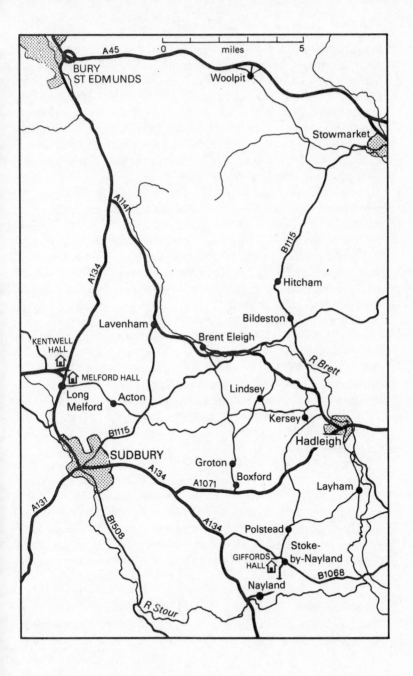

once the home of a rich wool merchant and now, most sumptuously restored, open to the public; and Little Hall, headquarters of the Suffolk Preservation Trust. Note, too, the timbered houses in Church Street with pargetting depicting tools in the wool industry, the Old Grammar School in Barn Street, Mullet House close at hand, and the house called Woolstaplers in Prentice Street. The very names of the old streets echo old occupations. And so back to the church, a shining example of creative collaboration between mercantile interests and the aristocracy.

Lavenham was one of a group of wool towns, and just as mercantile rivalry was intense among them so was rivalry in other things, and particularly in the building of churches. The rivalry, and the prosperity to support it, happened to come in a period of high architectural accomplishment: the period of the Late Perpendicular. Here at Lavenham the landed aristocracy (descendants of William the Conqueror's fellow armed robbers), in the form of John de Vere, 13th Earl of Oxford, combined with the weavers, in the persons principally of Simon Branch and the Spring family, to rebuild the old church on a scale that they hoped would pip Stoke-by-Nayland and Long Melford. They first built a tower that certainly pips the lot: it is 141 feet high and it would have been higher, the story goes, if the master-builder had not fallen from the top of it. They then had the good sense to allow this vast weight of stone to settle before they attached the rest of the church. Meanwhile they were pulling down the ancient nave, and holding their services in the chancel.

Most of the tower was built by 1495, of Barnack limestone and knapped flint – note the unique limestone plinth at the base of it. A rich clothier, Thomas Spring the Second, paid for most of the cost, and it is a little touching that when his son, Thomas Spring the Third, completed the top of the tower he had his coat of arms – which had just been given him – depicted on it no less than thirty-two times! Here was a family of 'base blood' buying itself into the ranks of the gentry by the profits of industry, and enormously proud of its new position!

The new nave was added around 1513, and fortunately the lovely little crocketted sanctus turret, Decorated and of unknapped flint, was left and not pulled down. This church tells us something more about the history of the English cloth trade. The chancel was never rebuilt. It had been intended, once the new nave was complete and services could be held there instead of in the old chancel, to pull the latter down and rebuild it. Not to do so must have been a terrible loss of face. But it was not rebuilt. It can only be because the sands were running out: the weaving industry was dying. Lavenham was eking a precarious living by spinning wool for the looms of Norwich – and even Norwich was beginning to feel the pinch and was soon to dwindle as a cloth town and go over to making shoes. And then, of course the Reformation came and put an end to grandiose church building.

We enter the church through the de Vere Porch, which is most beautiful. The porch was paid for by the 13th Earl, and there are de Vere arms all over it. There are also wild boars – a pun on the name de Vere (*verres* being Latin for boar), and there is the de Vere Star, which was awarded to Albericke de Vere by his fellow crusaders when Albericke had recovered the standard of St George from the Saracens after this had been lost during a battle. 'They gave him a star of silver to beare in the first quarter of his Shield, because a certain star did shine so clerely that the Christian Armye at darke midnight did overcome the Saracens.'

Albericke's father had come to England with the Conqueror (he actually held lands here before the Conquest), and Albericke's son was created 1st Earl of Oxford. The 20th Earl, who was descended in direct male line, died with no heir in 1703, just five hundred years later. Twenty successive Earls of Oxford in half a thousand years! The Oxfords were lords of the manor of Lavenham, and greatly enriched by the cloth trade, and thus they worked with the weavers to build the church; and wonder beyond wonders, Aubrey, the 15th Earl, married the daughter of a clothier – a niece of Thomas Spring the third, who was known as 'the Rich Clothier'! An indication of the standing that the mercantile classes had already achieved by the sixteenth century.

The interior of the church is breath-taking. And yet for me it is lacking in mystery: I feel the cold breath of Reason and the Reformation fast approaching when this church was built. It is all so well-designed, so rational. Those great windows let in so much light.

There is a clean-cut magnificence about it. The decoration, cut in Castleton stone, is so sharp and perfect that it is hard to believe that it is not new; the panels, for example, on the spandrels of the arcades. The piers are slender and most beautiful, with their flowered Tudor capitals. The aisles are wide and spacious: the whole building of lovely proportions. Alas and alas that Dowsing smashed all the glass. These windows need to be a picture gallery to impart colour and warmth, and the Victorian glass that is in a few of them is fairly horrid.

The tower arch is splendid, if not so soaringly moving as the one at Stoke-by-Nayland. And the bells – the eight bells of Lavenham – are famous. The tenor, in particular, which weighs a ton and three hundredweight, is said to be the sweetest bell in all England, and every year a special peal is rung in honour of its birthday, which was the 21st of June 1625. It was cast by Miles Gray of Colchester.

The Spring Chantry, at the east end of the north aisle, has a splendid parclose screen: intricately carved woodwork of Renaissance style, with a lovely dark patina as if smoked by incense. The chantry was built for the souls of Thomas Spring III and his wife Alice. Saint-knowers will scarcely need to be told that the figures of St Blaise are here, together with those of St Catherine to whom the chantry is dedicated, because St Blaise was the patron saint of wool-combers. He was *combed to death* during the Diocletian persecutions.

The Branch Chapel is north of the chancel. It is about 1500. The Oxford Chantry (east end of south aisle) is similar to the Spring Chantry, but slightly different in style, a little earlier, a purer style, perhaps? It is to the 13th Earl, who died in 1513. In the Branch Chapel also are lively fourteenth-century misericords, a Pelican in her piety, a man squeezing a pig under his arm (surely the precursor of the bagpipes?) and other subjects. In front of the altar is a brass to a tiny baby, Clopton d'Ewes, which is bound to wring a tear from any mother. The Dister brass is interesting, mainly for the inscription that is on it.

William Gurnell was Rector here from 1644, and he wrote *The Christian in Complete Armour*, which I have to confess I have not read.

Every year, in May and June, Lavenham runs a modest Festival of Music and the Arts, with lectures, concerts, and exhibitions.

Long Melford, Lavenham's chief rival perhaps, is about five miles to the south-west. It is long, and we should start at the south end of it, and walk northwards. We thus traverse one of the grandest village streets in England, even though it has none of the purity of Lavenham. It is by no means solidly Tudor: there is much eighteenth-century building and, alas, some nineteenth. Since Long Melford was a wool town just as Lavenham was we may well ask ourselves why? And the reason is that Long Melford was a river port and thus shared in Georgian and early Victorian prosperity (map, p. 355).

As we walk northward the street widens and has tree-shaded greens along it, and there is a great mixture of architectural styles until we get to the Bull Inn, very grand, and Melford Green (one of the many 'finest greens in Suffolk'). The Victorian school is fun, with a turret echoing the great Hall over the road. The houses on our left, after the school, stand well back and are a quiet and dignified row. The people who live in them are to be envied, with that great green in front of them and those mighty elm trees.

Standing out in the green is a strange edifice called the Conduit, which had something to do with the conveyance of water to **Melford Hall**, although quite what nobody seems to know. Hard by the Conduit is the gateway to the Hall itself. This is one of the very fine Elizabethan houses in England, and now belongs to the National Trust, although it is lived in by its family. It is open to the public.

Before the Reformation the Hall belonged to the Abbots of Bury St Edmunds, who used it for the strangely secular purpose of a hunting lodge. For these holy men liked to hunt the stag, as well as higher truth. After the monastery was dissolved the Hall fell into the hands of William Cordell (Cordle is still a farming name in Suffolk, and among the Cordle clan are several notable Baptists). William was one of the men of Henry VIII's time who rose from obscurity to affluence by the practice of the Law (at a time of many shipwrecks the sharks flourish) and like hundreds of other smart operators he managed to acquire the sequestrated Hall and lands from the king, firstly for rental, and then for nothing; as

359

King Henry realized that he could not go on drawing rents from a third of England in perpetuity. Cordell became Solicitor-General, Master of the Rolls, and Speaker of the House of Commons. He managed to adapt his faith to the varying changes of religion, and to keep both his job and his head during the reigns of Mary and Elizabeth. In 1578 he entertained the latter queen at a vast banquet, being the first Suffolk man to do so during her Royal Progress; and it is said that he set such an example of lavishness as practically broke the rest of the county, who had to follow suit. '. . . there was in Suffolke suche sumptuous feastinges and bankets as seldom in anie parte of the worlde there hath been seen afore.'

After Cordell various people occupied the Hall, until it came to the present family, the Parkers. Sir Harry Parker, 6th Baronet, bought it in 1786. Sir Harry had come from a family of sailors: Sir Hyde, 5th Baronet, sailed round the world with Anson, became Vice-Admiral of the Blue, and commanded the British fleet at St Lucia on the famous 25th March 1780, and at the Dogger Bank on the 5th of August 1781. On being offered a peerage by George III he gruffly refused it, as he said he was dissatisfied with the way the navy was being run. Unfortunately he was posted to the East Indies, to take command of the fleet there, and went down with HMS *Cate*, which was lost with all hands in 1782.

The second Hyde Parker was knighted for forcing the boom across the Hudson River in the American War while in command of a squadron of frigates, and it was to his signal, later, that Nelson put his telescope to his blind eye – for he commanded the Baltic Fleet at Copenhagen. He was also in command of the West Indies Fleet. Nor were his sons less martial: one of them left a leg at Waterloo – the other was killed at Talavera.

Sir Richard Hyde Parker, 11th Baronet, lives in the Hall today, having restored it after the depredations of the military during the Second World War, farms his large estates on the wheat-and-barley prairie system forced on large farmers by cost of labour, and collects old weapons. He also collects old navigational instruments, and models of farm machinery and has a surpassingly interesting model of the first reaping machine, built by Smith of Deanstone, a Scottish cotton king. It would cut an acre in an hour with its revolving knife, but its manufacture was discontinued owing to the hostility of the Luddites. Sir Richard is pleased to show these collections to visitors to the house.

The Hall itself stands in grand grounds behind a large brick wall (note the nice topiary visible from the road south of it) and is large, early Elizabethan if not indeed pre-Elizabethan, and stands on three sides of a square. There is an old drawing of it when it stood on four sides, forming one of those gloomy and sunless courtyards beloved of the Elizabethans (what could they do in them?) and there are other drawings of it open on one side but with a crazy bridge across the opening which served as a grandstand for the ladies to watch the hunt! Under the present Hall are medieval vaults, indicating that this, indeed, was the hunting lodge of the abbots. The house is of brick made from clay dug up in Melford Green (the hole is still there) and the earlier work is distinguished by the brickwork being in 'English bond' (alternate layers of stretchers and headers) instead of the 'Flemish bond' introduced later.

The classical porch of the house originally led to a Screens passage, like the Screens of Cambridge colleges, with kitchens to the left and Great Hall to the right. The Great Hall remains, although embellished (or not, as the taste might run) with columns put up in 1740 (rather like the ones in the Library at Ickworth) with eighteenth-century moulding, relief painting high up on the walls, and a great fireplace in the style of William Kent. Oh that the eighteenth century could have left well alone! But it is a fine room all the same, and a room in which one could be comfortable and at home.

There are portraits in the Great Hall, of various Parkers, and their predecessors too; for when Sir Harry bought the Hall he surprisingly bought some portraits of former owners with it. There is a set of andirons in the fireplace said to have belonged to Abbot Samson in the eleven hundreds, which have portraits of Samson killing the lion. They have new feet though, with the cockatrice of the Cordells, dated 1559. If 1559 is new.

Most of the glass in the windows is German armorial glass collected by the 9th Baronet; but there is some local glass, including the arms of John Winthrop, first Governor of Massachusetts and a Groton man. There is good and well-fitting furniture in the Great

361

Hall, including some ivory figures carved by Portuguese in Goa: part of the loot from the *Santissima Trinidad* which the 5th Baronet captured while she was sailing from China laden with gifts from the Emperor of China to the King of Spain. There is plenty of loot in Melford Hall, and the house seems to accommodate it quite nicely.

The Hyde Parker Room, into which we next go, used to be the Cordell Room. It was burnt out with the rest of the north wing by the billeted troops during the Second World War. This disaster was not without its benefits to the Parker family, for it enabled them to build new rooms in the north wing, smaller and more convenient for modern living. In the Hyde Parker Room are more family portraits, and fine Regency furniture.

The Blue Drawing-room escaped the fire, and therefore still has Georgian decoration in the style of William Kent. Very nice Dutch paintings: there is much of Low Country origin in the house, for the old admirals traded with the Hollanders, besides fighting them at the Dogger Bank. There is some Chinese porcelain from the *S. Trinidad*.

In the Library is a Romney portrait of the 5th Baronet, every inch a sailor, and a collection of paintings of the various naval battles the 5th Baronet engaged in, including the Dogger Bank, all done by Dominique Serres, the Gascon painter employed by George III as his official war painter and the man who made the similar paintings at Ickworth. Serres was the forerunner of the war-photographers of the present day; and we may be sure his paintings are pretty authentic: it is most unlikely that the 5th Baronet would have tolerated so much as one staysail-halliard in the wrong place!

There are books in the Library, too, which nobody ever reads. If they did they would find that they were a most splendid collection of seventeenth- and eighteenth-century works of topography and exploration; there is a priceless collection of eighteenth-century sea charts, too: the working charts used by the sailing Parkers themselves.

On the staircase is more *Santissima Trinidad* loot, and the 'Miser's Wedding' by Pieter Breughel. In the Gallery is a window depicting Elizabeth I, and a portrait of one of the Hall's owners:

Countess Rivers, who lost it and her other possessions for adhering to the Catholic faith at the wrong moment. Some of her needlework hangs below.

There is a tiny chapel upstairs with an exquisite Goanese Madonna which has twice been looted: once from the *Santissima Trinidad* and once again by a burglar (may we hope not an East Anglian?) who was mean enough to break her fingers and her ears in order to steal the gold rings and earrings.

The grounds are beautiful, with rare trees, topiary, and other delights, including a charming and most uncommon Tudor garden pavilion.

South of the Hall grounds is a river, the Chad Brook; and a pleasant short stroll along it ends at a fish weir. By the river is a round concrete block with a steel bar sticking up from it, which may well puzzle the curious of the younger generation. It is a spigot mortar base. The spigot mortar would fling a bomb as big as a football at unfriendly tanks, and during the Second World War East Anglia was peppered with them. This is one of the few that survives.

Whether it was Melford Hall or one of the other two great houses of this parish, according to George Borrow it was at the 'Great House' of Long Melford that his girl friend Isobel Berners was brought up. A lass of aristocratic origins and heroic proportions, she supported the author on her knee while he rested in between bouts with the Flaming Tinman: that mighty bruiser whom Borrow managed to rout. He lived with the girl in a dell, but we gather platonically.

Over the great and noble Green stands the Trinity Hospital; built by Sir William Cordell in 1573 but since altered. Past it we go (there used to be a branch of Doctor Barnardo's hard by) and suddenly we are confronted by the great church – which many people consider to be the grandest building in all Suffolk. We are too near to it, when we see it, for it to have its fullest impact.

Certainly it is long, large, noble, and Perpendicular. The tower is a bad let-down: the original one fell down, was replaced in 1725, and covered with stone in 1903. At the opposite end is the great Lady Chapel, impeccably enough 1496 but it doesn't fit the rest of the church at all. It is quite the wrong shape, and seems to be (in fact is) a separate building. And yet Long Melford Church would lose a lot of its distinction without it. But the chunk in between: this part is very grand and beautiful indeed: the late-Perpendicular 'glass-house' ideal, superbly carried out. If people say that this is the finest church in Suffolk who is to argue with them?

Unlike most of our churches Long Melford's was built nearly all at one go (except the tower), in the last two or three decades of the fifteenth century. The rich weavers and cloth-finishers were able to sweep away what went before and put up a complete new building. Long Melford is not the product of the slow accretion of the centuries, and this fact gives it purity, its period gives it grandeur and perfection, but – like Lavenham – it lacks the *mystery* of many older churches, and its *ninety-seven* windows let in a vast amount of light. The builders of the modern shrine at Walsingham knew what they were doing when they kept it practically pitch dark.

The interior is staggering. The slenderness of the piers of the arcades, the delicacy of the moulding of the arches, the loftiness of the clerestories which they support, the high proportion of glass to stone: this is most skilful engineering – not just architecture. We are made to feel that reinforced concrete could do no more – nay not as much, than this cut and dressed limestone is doing. Stone building can be carried no further than this.

After recovering from the general effect, walk to the north aisle and look at the glass. The salvaging of the scattered remnants of the old glass was financed by the Pilgrim Trust; and the fragments (some of which had actually been re-inserted paint-to-weather!) have been rearranged, and placed in order. Some time must be devoted to their study, for here is an important collection. Note the lovely *Pietà* over the north door: Our Lady of Pity in the middle, St Peter on her right, St Francis on her left, and three rabbits, sharing the same three ears, and said to be a symbol of the Undivided Trinity. But these windows, painted and fired by Flemish glaziers when the church was built, are a picture-gallery of mayors, judges, citizens, prior and priests.

Let into the north wall, beyond the windows, is an alabaster relief, which do not miss. It is a most sensitive depiction of the Adoration of the Magi. Poor Joseph, looking understandably wronged, sits at the foot of his wife's bed holding a pair of crutches.

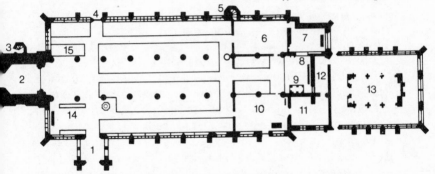

LONG MELFORD CHURCH

1 Porch & South Entrance
2 Tower & West Entrance
3 Belfry Turret
4 North Door
5 Rood Turret
6 Clopton Chapel
7 Clopton Chantry Chapel
  & Lily Crucifix

8 Clopton Tomb (Founder)
9 Cordell Monument
10 Martyn Chapel
11 Choir Vestry
12 Priest's Vestry
13 Lady Chapel
14 British Legion Chapel
15 Children's Chapel

It is a lovely piece and thought to be of *c.* 1350, thus antedating the present church.

In the north aisle too is a carved piscina with ogee arch: the tomb of Sir William Clopton who died in 1446 (thus also before the main part of the church was rebuilt), and was the father of John, who bore the expense of most of the rebuilding. There are many Clopton brasses.

The Clopton Aisle leads to the Clopton Chantry, through a tiny priest's room in which is a fireplace, and which obviously was the cell in which lived the chantry priest whose sole job in life was to chant, for ever, masses for the salvation of the Clopton souls. This room is roofed with solid slabs of stone, carved to make them look like a fan vault, but simply in fact stone beams, like the roof of a Hindu *adyta*, of the times before the introduction of the dome by the Moguls.

The chantry, into which this leads, has an Easter Tomb, delicately carved and with antique paintings on it: one of them of the risen Christ with the text above him: *Omnis qui vivet et credit in me non morietur in aeternum.* The whole chantry was once surrounded by texts and hymns, said to have been written by John Lydgate, the monkish poet of Bury who died in 1450, forty-six years before the chantry was built. But the glory of this chantry is the east window, which contains the tiny but splendidly mystical Lily Crucifix: a depiction of the Lily of the Annunication with the Crucifixion visible within it, the End within the Beginning.

The chancel of the church is completely dominated, so that one feels that the altar itself is about to be edged out, by a monstrous monument to Sir William Cordell, the lawyer, Master of the Rolls, etc, who so lavishly entertained Elizabeth when she made her Royal Progress. It was this man who presumably built Melford Hall, and the hospital by the church gate. The knight rests his feet on a cockatrice, his emblem. His mighty monument is completely classical, vulgarly so to my taste, and it fits ill with the rest of the church. Sir William takes up far more than his fair share of space, in death as he no doubt did in life.

The Lady Chapel, which is quite a separate building, although reached from the body of the church *via* the south-east door of the Martyn Chapel (east end of south aisle), is unique. It has an indoor cloister, or ambulatory, right round it, and going behind the shrine. The cambered roofs are charming, and the whole chapel has an air of sanctity and antiquity. It was for centuries used as a school.

Wandering through the churchyard, the visitor will see to the north a fine avenue of lime trees at the end of which is Kentwell Hall, a red brick Tudor manor not unlike its sister, Melford Hall. Surrounded by a romantic moat, it stages historical pageants and musical events, an open air theatre season, longbow contests, crafts fairs, and a number of educational re-creations of Tudor life. The lime trees were in danger of destruction when the composer and piano manufacturer Clementi bought the entire avenue from a spendthrift owner of Kentwell in order to make piano keys. The mother of the wastrel raised the money to buy the avenue back, at such a vast profit to Clementi that she had to sell a farm at Lavenham to meet his demands.

At the other end of Long Melford's truly long street, which runs upon what excavations have shown to be a former Roman highway, the turnoff towards Foxearth passes the nicely laid out Rodbridge picnic site, from which there is a 2½-mile Valley Walk along the old railway route to Sudbury. At both ends is ample parking space; and between, the most rewarding views across the levels and the upper Stour. In the opposite direction there is the bitty but nevertheless interesting Lavenham Walk.

Acton, two miles east, is an ugly village (that 'bus garage'!) but its church has the most famous military brass in England: that of Sir Robert de Bures. This is one of the five chain-mail effigies of England dated as early as 1302, and is the most perfect of them. Sir Robert is cross-legged (i.e. a crusader), wears reinforced chain-mail common in the period 1250–1325, with knee-pieces made of *cuir-bouilli* (boiled leather), and over his armour he has a long surcoat with a girdle round his waist. His mail hood and hauberk are separate from the body armour, his shield, slung over one shoulder, is charged with the Bures arms. There is an ornamental bawdrick on his hips, and on his thigh the silk pourpoint worn beneath the armour can be seen. He wears pryck spurs. He gives the impression of being very much a warrior and old campaigner, veteran of many camps; and not just a lawyer or a businessman wearing armour to look grand on his monument. Many brasses are best seen from rubbings. This one not. It is most important to see the actual brass (map, p. 355). There is another excellent brass and an important eighteenth-century tomb.

CHAPTER 21

From Sudbury to Woolpit

Described by Dickens in *Pickwick* as Eatanswill, **Sudbury** is a very ancient town, and the biggest of the 'wool towns', or weaving towns, of Suffolk. Weaving is still carried on here, in several factories weaving silk. It does not contain the antique charm and purity of some of the other wool towns, because it continued to be a manufacturing town long after they did, and still is one, making, amongst many other things, and for some extraordinary reason, ship's propellers. (Why here? So far from coal – so far from iron – so far from a ship?) And there are big chalk and lime works. It continued thus in manufacturing importance because it developed as a big river port, and so remained until the railway came.

Thomas Gainsborough was born in Sepulchre Street in 1727, now called Gainsborough Street. The house where he was born, No 46, is a museum.

Gainsborough was the youngest of the nine children of a Nonconformist woollen crêpe maker, and when he was fourteen his father sent him apprentice to the engraver Gravelot in London. He returned to Sudbury and took up portrait painting, and also married a girl of rare beauty, Margaret Burry, who brought with her a dowry of £200 a year.

He moved to Ipswich, and set up there as a portrait painter and landscapist. He was helped by patrons, including Richard Thicknesse, the Governor of Landguard Fort, and the brewing Cobbold family (the latter relationship is described vividly in the novel *Margaret Catchpole*). He moved to Bath, and became the most famous painter of his age.

There is a bronze statue of him on Sudbury Market Hill, clutching a palette and brush in case we should be in any doubt as to what his profession was. It is by Sir Bertram Mackennal.

The other important man in Sudbury was Simon Tybald, who is notable for having had his head cut off by Wat Tyler's men during the Peasants' Revolt. He was Archbishop of Canterbury; but this did not stop him from also holding the office of Chancellor of England. As the former he excommunicated John Ball, the parson who was trying to secure help for the wretched poor; as the latter he imposed a savage poll tax on the labourers, and advised Richard II to keep them in subjection. He urged the utmost severity on the people he called 'barefooted rebels'.

All this led to Wat Tyler leading 10,000 'barefooted rebels' to London in 1381, treating with the king, and dragging the hated Tybald out of the Tower where he was hiding and executing him. His head is now in the vestry of St Gregory's Church, Sudbury, for all to see, or at least his skull is, and St Gregory's is the church that Tybald helped to build.

The church has a marvellous telescopic font cover (over a modern font), very ingenious and lavish. By the tower arch is a picture of a knight booting the Devil. Not applying the toe of his boot to any part of the Devil's person, but confining the Devil in a boot. This is one interpretation: another is that he is conjuring the Devil *out* of the boot – of a person who had the gout.

The other church, St Peter's, is a grand building, standing right up out of the street on Market Hill amid milling traffic, with fine traceried doors, seventeenth-century nave roof panelled in blue and gold, good carved sixteenth-century chairs, a good rood screen with saints and a famous piece of fifteenth-century embroidery still used at the funerals of aldermen; but sadly it has become a 'redundant' church. A third church, All Saints, has a rare oak pulpit, well preserved, and three notable screens.

Thomas Dawes came from Sudbury. It was he who set the lantern in the tower of Old North Church, Boston, Mass., to signal to Paul Revere to make his famous ride: thus a Sudbury man set the first match to the American Revolution.

The town owes much of what it is to the River Stour Navigation. In 1705 (Queen Anne) an Act of Parliament was passed for improving the navigation, the Undertakers to get 5s per chaldron of coals, or ton of other merchandise, between Manningtree and Sudbury.

Millstones, however, and other materials for mills, were to be allowed up free. Sudbury had shot ahead commercially as a port; in 1724 Defoe could say that the Navigation was not paying its operators. By the mid-nineteenth century the proprietors desperately tried to sell out to the all-conquering railway, the offer was refused, and in 1913 the company went into liquidation: in 1930 the last barge went to Dedham.

The barges used are familiar to us by having been so often painted by John Constable – he even painted one being built. They worked in pairs, took fourteen hours to get upstream to Sudbury from the sea-going ships at Mistley, and during this voyage the horse had to cross the river thirty-three times, which he did by being 'boated': i.e. carried across in the boat. The horse also had to be trained to jump the stiles across the tow-path (as did the horses of the Fen lighter trains) and Constable's famous painting 'The Jumping Horse' shows one doing this, with a boy on his back.

The barges were 27 feet long, 9 feet beam and 3 feet draught when carrying 26 tons. In the heyday 12,000 tons of coal a year went to Sudbury in them. Gainsborough held shares in the Navigation, and John Constable Senior, the painter's father, was to have 50s a year in perpetuity in compensation for the closing up of a ford of his, and the Undertakers had to build a bridge instead, which is still there and maintained by the East Suffolk County Council.

Boxford is east, and away from the river. It is a compact and attractive village, once a much larger place, and in 1600 it had four weavers' guilds, eleven clothmakers, thirty-seven weavers, four dyers, two fullers and six shearmen; but these, we presume, were mastermen: there were far more workers. In 1684, in fact, one employer of Boxford is known to have been employing 200 people.

The church is fine. The fourteenth-century north porch of it is of wood, and thus probably the oldest timber porch in England. The south porch is of stone from Caen and is very elaborate. There is a plaque inside the sanctuary that would wring a tear from any mum and not a few dads – to little David Birde, who died in 1606. There he is, a little boy in a great big bed, with his shoes tidily put underneath it. There is also the sad story of Elizabeth Hyams: 'for the fourth time a widow, who by a fall, that brought on mortification, was at last hastened to her End, on the 4th May, 1748, in her 113th year.'

On the pavement opposite the White Hart inn crouches a squat little figure like a cowering dog but meant to represent a lion, once the sidecar partner of a 'wall of death' motor-cyclist who used to stroll through the village with his pet beside him.

Groton produced John Winthrop, who sailed to North America aboard the *Arabella*, 300 tons with a crew of fifty, in the company of three smaller vessels. They carried 200 cows, 60 horses and 700 human beings, and landed at Massachusetts Bay in 1630. Seventy of the animals had died at sea, 200 humans died then or soon after landing, and 100 basely returned to England. But the rest stayed on, Winthrop became Governor of Massachusetts and his son of Connecticut. John Winthrop's *Life and Letters* was recently edited by a descendant, Robert Charles Winthrop. There is a window in Groton Church to him. The church hides behind an old farmhouse, on a hill, and in pretty country. The Fox and Hounds is an attractive country pub (or was when I wrote this – but you never know, these days).

South to **Nayland**, again on the Stour. Most charming. Old weavers' cottages and houses, a willow-shaded loop in the Stour, locks, a watermill which was converted in the early days of electricity to generate it, good pargetting and timber framing, and Alston Court, in the middle, a fine house that it would be an adventure to live in. Its east wing is fifteenth century, the rest Tudor, superb barge-boards. The porch of the church (very fine, but restored in Victorian times) was paid for by Wm. Abel, clothier, in 1525, and he also built the bridge over into Essex. (The word clothier did not mean as it does now a seller of cloth, but a manufacturer of it.)

Stoke-by-Nayland has another mighty church, with a particularly marvellous tower. The little town (a village now, much reduced) is on a hill and the brick tower is 120 feet high and the result is that it is a landmark for many miles around. Thus it was much painted by Constable, who put it in very many of his landscapes (often moving it from one side to the other for better effect). His 'Stoke-by-Nayland Church' is famous, and a painting of great drama: nobody else, save perhaps a Blake or a Palmer, could have got away with that rainbow.

Like all the 'wool churches' this is predominantly fifteenth century; although the south porch is Decorated. Note the bosses in the roof of the latter, and in particular the south door with its fine and original wood carving. The west door is noteworthy too. The setting of the church, in a close of lovely Tudor houses and with green grass and great trees on the little hill, is marvellous. Inside, the glory of this glorious building is the tower arch – a soaring masterpiece. The whole church is beautiful, and undervalued compared with Lavenham and Long Melford. The organ was restored some years ago and has the sweetest tone. There are some good monuments: to the Howards, Tendrings and others.

Of the splendid houses near the church the Guildhall and the old Maltings are the most noteworthy: timber framing and lath and plaster in excellent repair. Outside the village, Thorington Hall, a mile and a half east-south-east, is of the sixteenth and eighteenth centuries: an important house. And Tendring Hall, of which only the park remains, and a fishing lodge, was one of the very mighty houses of England, but was used as a prisoner of war camp during the Second World War and afterwards pulled down. Its history, though, is interesting. It was owned in 1285 by William Tendring, and at the end of the fourteenth century went by marriage into the Howard family. After three generations a Howard, John, was created 1st Duke of Norfolk. Later, when Thomas Howard was beheaded by Queen Elizabeth for trying to marry Mary Queen of Scots and filch the crown (see p. 59), Tendring Hall came into the hands of Sir Joshua Rowley, Vice-Admiral of the White, and he had Sir John Soane design a great new house for him in 1784.

The most interesting thing that remains of all this is *The Household Book of the Duke of Norfolk* (1481), which can be seen in the Library of the Society of Antiquaries, and which gives much day-to-day detail of the life of a great fifteenth-century house. An ox then was worth a pound, a lamb 1s 1d, wheat 6s 8d a quarter, a goose 2d, a chicken a penny, eggs 11d a hundred and it cost 4d to get a horse shod – thus a chicken a leg: what it costs now.

Gifford's Hall, two miles east-north-east of Stoke-by-Nayland, is described by Pevsner as 'one of the loveliest houses of its date in England, neither small nor overwhelming grand; warm and

varied, happy in scale and in the proportions between its materials.'
Its period is Henry VII and Henry VIII but it has alterations of
the early eighteenth and late nineteenth centuries. It is not open
to the public.

Polstead, north, the 'Place of Pools', still has a pool, an artificial
lake in which witches used to be 'swum', and into which once a
coach and four horses, having been bewitched, plunged headlong.
This pool is at the bottom of a hill, and a little green at the top of
the hill (you can walk from the pool at the bottom to the green at
the top by a pleasant village footpath on your left instead of by the
road) would rank high in my list of the prettiest village greens of
East Anglia. It has the Cock public house with its fine inn sign and
the Cock Farm nearby. The Reverend John Whitmore, in the early
nineteenth century (he came to Polstead in 1795) had to exorcize
ghosts. The spirit creation had its own back though, for the reverend gentleman was himself to be seen, after death, driving a horse
and trap down the rectory lane *sans* head.

At Domesday there was a Hall, sixty-two villeins, fifteen cara-
cates (plough teams) and one poor wretched serf. There were 650
souls in the parish. The custom of 'Borough English' prevailed at
Polstead Manor, which meant that the youngest son, and not the
eldest, inherited.

Polstead became nationally famous in that most certain of ways
to achieve fame in England – a good grisly murder. You can still
see the thatched cottage where Maria Marten lived, down Marten
Lane; but the famous Red Barn has since been burnt down, and
it is no good looking for it. But crowds of morbid sightseers –
charabanc loads of them from London and the Midlands – *still* go
and look at where they think it was.

William Corder, the man who brought all this fame to his little
parish, was a rich farmer's son, and he lured Maria, a mole-catcher's
daughter, to the Red Barn to persuade her to don male attire
(Victorian melodrama loved 'male attire') and then run away with
him and get married. Maria was never seen alive again. Corder
went away, writing to the girl's father to say that they were happily
married. But Maria's mother kept having dreams about the Red
Barn. She kept dreaming about one particular spot in it. She finally
persuaded her husband to go and dig there, and dig he did, and

found Maria's body, shot and bashed, in the very position his wife had dreamed about. Corder was found, in Brentford of all places, where he had married a lady of means whom he had discovered through a matrimonial advertisement. They were keeping together, most unsuitably one might think, a school for young ladies. Corder was hanged, in August 1828, in Bury St Edmunds before an estimated 10,000 spectators. The rope used to do it was sold by the hangman for a guinea an inch, a book about his trial was bound in his skin, which the prison doctor thoughtfully took off for the purpose, and is still on display in Bury Museum, while his skeleton is in West Suffolk General Hospital. If his ghost could only draw royalties on all the performances of *Maria Marten and the Red Barn* that have been staged it would buy him a most sumptuous apartment down below.

Polstead church is hidden up a hill behind great trees, west of the road at the bottom of the hill; and it is architecturally most interesting. The church inside is Norman, primitive, and simple. The outside gives no indication of this Norman work inside (compare – and in other ways too – Ickleton in Cambridgeshire). The Norman arches are of *brick*. This is a most pecular circumstance, since the Normans were not supposed to have used brick. These bricks are different size from Tudor bricks (9″ × 4¼″ × 2¼″) and were once thought to be Roman – but then they are a different size from Roman bricks (5¼″ × 2½″ × 1¼″). The inference then is that they were made by the Normans who built the church (at least by the English who built it during the 'Norman' times) and are thus the earliest bricks known to have been made in England since the Romans made bricks: earlier even than the bricks at Coggeshall in Essex. Fibre-glass enthusiasts should examine the font cover, which was made of this material by a nun from the Community of St Clare, in 1964. It has a dove on top of it, a fibre-glass dove. It is believed that under the whitewash of this church are wall paintings. Some good Elizabethan ones were found in the lovely house next door.

In the churchyard is a young oak whose parent was the Gospel Oak, now a mere rotting remnant. The oak was supposed to be 1,000 years old, and Saxon missionaries under St Cedd are said to have preached under it in the seventh century. As old as this or not (as enthusiasts we may believe – as arboriculturalists we may doubt) the oak, before its decline, was 36 feet in girth, so it was a very old tree.

There are cast-iron monuments in the churchyard – a fleeting fashion of the late eighteenth and early nineteenth centuries (although perhaps not so fleeting – there is one as early as 1619 at Burrington in Herefordshire), but Maria Marten's stone has been quite chipped away for souvenirs by the morbid.

At **Layham**, at Holly Lodge Farmhouse, is a small pottery, open to visitors. **Hadleigh** was one of the more important of the wool towns. Its position on the River Brett gave it water power, water for washing wool and fulling cloth, and transport. It has suffered less than others from having all its houses snapped up by wealthy 'old-Tudor' enthusiasts, and is still very much an ordinary country commercial town and you can still hear the birds singing above the clicking of the camera shutters.

The pleasantest part of Hadleigh may well be thought to be down at the old mill weir, near Sun Court, at the north end of the town; but if we walk from there south along the main street we will find pleasant houses to the left and to the right.

The church is surrounded by spectacular houses. The Deanery Tower is very grand indeed, a small edition of the great gate-tower of Oxburgh. It was the grandiose entrance to the ecclesiastical palace built in 1495 by Archdeacon Pykenham, who evidently did not approve the injunction to Christians to embrace poverty like a bride. His palace has since been pulled down, the present Deanery, scarcely less magnificent although much truncated in recent years, was built in mock-Tudor in 1831. But the splendid fifteenth-century gate-tower remains.

The Guildhall, south of the church, is a magnificent timbered building. The church itself is large, but it has none of the architectural purity of the great Perpendicular wool churches. Its tower is too narrow for it, and possibly of Norman origin but of Decorated completion. The walls of the body of the church are of the Decorated period, but the windows in them, and the clerestory above, are Perpendicular. Here was not the wholesale sweeping away of the old and the replacing it with the latest fashion that we find at Long Melford and Lavenham. The result is something of a jumble.

375

The great lead spire of the tower is distinctive, as is the Angelus bell, which is said to be one of the oldest in England. It has Lombardic characters on it: *Ave Maria Gratia Plena Dominus Tecum* – but they were cast in mirror-image by mistake and are therefore backwards! The bell is said to be 600 years old.

Inside is a noble 'ringers' gotch', or bell-ringers' ale jug; for in the olden days, as in ours, bell-ringing was acknowledged to be thirsty work.

Guthrum, King of the Danes, had his headquarters here in the ninth century. Asser records that this king was conquered and converted to Christianity by Alfred the Great and buried in the royal town of Hadleigh. There is a tomb canopy in the south wall of the church, inside, which is still called 'Guthrum's Tomb'. Actually the design of the canopy, which is Decorated, makes it just five hundred years too late; but who is to say that it was not erected in the fourteenth century in place of an older tomb, pulled down? Folk memory, in these matters, is seldom found to be wrong.

The Manor of Hadleigh was given by Brithnoth, the heroic leader of the East Angles killed at the Battle of Maldon, to Canterbury at the end of the tenth century, and such is the tenacity of tradition in England that it was not until 1838 that the practical effects of this were terminated. Until the latter year Hadleigh was a 'peculiar' of Canterbury, and it did not come at all under the spiritual dominion of the bishops of East Anglia. The rectors of Hadleigh had the title 'Dean of Bocking', for Bocking, in Essex, was another Canterbury Peculiar.

In the vestry of the church are many prints and pictures connected with the affair of Dr Rowland Taylor. The most likeable of all Protestant martyrs, Taylor was not an East Anglian but a Northumbrian (much the same stock). He was born at the beginning of the sixteenth century, and thus born a Catholic, but he early heard the preaching of Hugh Latimer, and then became chaplain to Cranmer and a Protestant. Cranmer appointed him to be 'Dean of Bocking', and Taylor became the enormously popular parson of Hadleigh. On the crowning of Mary Tudor, however, Taylor heard the bells ringing in his church, and they were ringing without his consent. He strode into the church, where he found a Catholic priest celebrating Mass. He thrust him forth, and was himself forthwith arrested. He was taken before Bishop Gardiner who badgered him, had him stripped of his garments and re-arrayed as a Catholic priest. Bishop Bonner then came to deprive him of his priestly office. But when Bonner came to strike him in the chest with his crozier, as part of this edifying ceremony, Taylor, who was a huge man physically, warned him that if he did so he would strike him back, and Bonner waived this part of the ceremonial.

Taylor was taken back to Hadleigh (being locked up in Lavenham Guildhall on the way), and amused his guards – the sheriff and other officers – by asserting that he and many others in Hadleigh were to be deceived. When they asked in what way, expecting no doubt another argument about doctrine, he said: 'I am, as you see, a man that hath a very great carcass, which I had thought to have been buried in Hadleigh churchyard, if I had died in my bed, as I well hoped I should have done. But herein I was deceived; and there are a great many worms in Hadleigh churchyard, which should have had a jolly good feeding upon this carrion, which they had looked for many a day.'

He was taken on to Hadleigh, where he arrived at night; but in the darkness he was recognized and his wife and children came out to greet him and the people turned out to cheer him on; even three of the four yeomen who were guarding him were in tears for his sake. He was burnt next morning, on the 9th February 1555, on Aldham Common (then still a common but stolen from the people by the enclosures in 1729). A stone was placed there afterwards with this inscription:

1555
D. TAYLOR. IN DE
FENDING. THAT WAS GOOD
AT THIS PLAS LEFT
HIS BLODE.

In 1819 a new monument was erected, which is still there (we can see it by going about a mile along the main Ipswich road, where there is a sign, and we get to it by walking across a field), and this monument has a poem, very moving I think, written by the Reverend Dr Hay Drummond in 1818.

Kersey is very much on the chara-route. It is so picturesque that it would do, untouched except for wires, for a period film set. The classic view of it is from the church, which is on a steep hill (steep by East Anglian standards) to the south of the village. From here we look down on the roofs of the village (many of them of red tiles or the big Suffolk pantiles but some, alas, of Caernarvon slate), and we see the street running down the hill to the ford at the bottom, and then up again steeply the other side. For Kersey runs down into, and out of again, the valley of a tributary of the Brett.

The church, in this most lovely position, is architecturally very interesting; although much visited by bashers in the seventeenth century and restorers in the nineteenth. The building of the Decorated nave was evidently interrupted by the Black Death. The tower, pure Perpendicular, is all of flint: an intractable material for building such a large edifice, but Kersey is a long way from a water navigation and freestone would have been very expensive if hauled to it overland. The south porch is noteworthy, with a lovely ceiling. There is much in the church to admire, but not the east end of it.

Kersey gave its name to a cloth, and Shakespeare speaks of '. . . russet Yeas and honest Kersey Noes' which contrast with courtly prevarication. **Lindsey**, a village hard-by which washed its wool in the same stream, gave its name to Lindsey-woolsey, another kind of honest cloth. Nearby is St James's Chapel, thirteenth century, full description inside.

In **Brent Eleigh** church is a mural of the greatest interest and importance. On the left of it are two kneeling angels, busily censing a blocked-out figure (Mary?) and with fine wing detail. In the centre is a crucifixion, with John on the right and Mary on the left. To the right is Doubting Thomas, a figure of Christ holding a vexillum (standard), a kneeling figure variously interpreted as being the monkish donor of the church or else Mary Magdalene, and a beautifully painted jug and barrel – most probably a pun on the donor's name. The painting has been dated by Caiger-Smith as 1400, but Dr Tudor-Craig places it earlier: 1290, in fact.

Bildeston, nor'east, has a church stuck out in the fields to the west of it, with a pleasant footpath leading from Chelsworth which certainly offers the best approach. The exterior of the building presents an odd appearance: on Ascension Day in 1975 a corner of the tower collapsed, damaging part of the nave roof and some windows, so that most of the remaining tower had to be pulled down, leaving only a patched-up west end. Inside is a tablet to Captain Edward Rotherham who commanded the *Royal Sovereign*, Head of the Line at Trafalgar. The churchyard has a tombstone to George Whittel, dying in 1884 at the age of eighty-three:

> *These tuneful bells for seventy years*
> *He rang, he tolled, he chimed full well.*
> *Births, weddings, deaths he thus proclaimed*
> *And others now have tolled his knell.*

The village itself is very pretty. The home of a wealthy wool merchant has become the Crown, a timbered inn above a cobbled path near the market square. In the square is a Victorian clock tower built of bricks taken from the old workhouse: the job was completed in four months. Roads leading away from it are lined by terraces of old weavers' cottages, many of them with attics connected right through to form long workshops.

At **Hitcham** is buried John Henslow, who angered local farmers by starting country schools about the country, in which were taught such inflammatory subjects as botany, which of course rendered them unfit for the stations that they had been called to in life; but he later endeared himself to them again by discovering the use of Suffolk Crag: those deposits of fossilized fish dung which provided a rich source of phosphate manure for many years. Henslow was a botanist and a naturalist who had great influence on Charles Darwin. He suffered great fears lest Darwin should develop doubts about the Book of Genesis if he put into his hands Lyall's *Principles*, but nevertheless he was honest enough to do so, trusting in Darwin's piety that the doubts should not prevail. They did, though; and led to *Origin of Species*. Hitcham church has fifteenth-century angels on its screen, in feathered tights, carrying the instruments of the Passion.

Woolpit is supposed to have been named for wolves and not wool, and the last wolves in England are said to have been killed in a pit there: probably, we might suppose, a pit-trap. There are pits still: the remains of vast brick quarries; for here is the source of 'Woolpit brick': the grey-brown bricks from the gault clay of which much of nineteenth-century West Suffolk, and Cambridge-shire too, is built, and it is said the White House, Washington! If the latter piece of information is true then it must be supposed that ships carried the bricks up the Chesapeake and Potomac as ballast for it can scarcely have been economic to ship them over as freight. Certainly they were much in demand, and samples were ordered to be sent to St Petersburg by the Emperor of the Russias, and that was in 1820.

Woolpit church is a very noble one. It has a spectacular Victorian spire, flying buttresses and lettering done in flush-work and all, and perhaps the most sumptuous porch in Suffolk, of 1435–55. Most of the rest of the church is Perpendicular too, except the chancel and south aisle which are earlier, and all is grand within and without. The hammerbeam roof is noteworthy and so is the early sixteenth-century eagle lectern.

There is a legend, fostered in its persistence no doubt by the fact that Camden related it, having read it in the writings of William of Newburgh who lived in the twelfth century, that two green children came out of the ground at Woolpit during harvest time. They were taken to the house of Sir Richard de Calne, where at first they would eat nothing but green food, but at length they took to meat and bread and lost their green colour. They were both baptized but the little boy died soon afterwards. The girl grew up though, and married a Lynn man and had children. After the green children had learned to speak our language (or at least that of our forebears) they told how they had lived in a country called St Martin's Land, where there was perpetual twilight, and it was beyond a great river. They had been attracted by the sound of church bells ringing, and had come up through a hole and found themselves in a harvest field, and could not get back.

CHAPTER 22

Cambridge: the Colleges

The site of **Cambridge** had to be important, for it was the best practicable crossing of the River Cam, or Granta, for many miles. To the north lay the Fens: to the south many miles of riverine swamps; but at the site of Cambridge there was hard ground right to the river on both sides and here a ford could be established, and later a bridge, and a great castle mound to prevent the wrong people from crossing it, and a city grew up. The name may have come from *cam*, crooked, and *rhydd*, ford: both words in the Ancient British language and in the modern Welsh.

As is necessarily often the case in rivers, the head of navigation in the Cam coincided with the lowest ford; and Cambridge was early a port, and a port far inland, which last factor was always of great use in the days of poor land communications. In Roman times Cambridge was thus an important staging post on a trunk road, a river crossing, a port, and a base from which to set out to conquer the denizens of the watery Fens.

To the East Angles, when they came, it was more: it was also a frontier town. For the Kingdom of East Anglia may have met the Kingdom of Middle Anglia and later of Mercia along the Cam, and as Cambridge was the only practicable crossing it followed that it was the most important place of interchange between the two nations. The more powerful state of Mercia occupied the Castle on the western bank, and the East Angles built a settlement on the eastern, of which at least one building survives: St Benet's Church, although this they built under Danish rule.

When the Normans came they used Cambridge as the base for their operations against the English rebels under Hereward the Wake, and in 1068 William built a castle on the Castle Mound, destroying twenty-seven houses to do it. William actually lived here while commanding the long-drawn-out operations against Hereward. At the time of Domesday it was an important place: 400 *masurae*, or homesteads.

And, but nobody knows just when (King John gave a charter in 1211), an annual fair grew up near Cambridge which in its day was the biggest in Europe, surpassing even the Fair of Nijni Novgorod.

Fuller, writing in the sixteenth century, asserted that 'Stourbridge Fair' as it was called was started by Westmorland cloth merchants on their way to Norwich to sell cloth. From Westmorland to Norwich was an enormous journey, but Norwich was one of the wool staples in England, and with its great export trade to the Continent a firm enough market to make such a journey profitable.

But when they reached the bridge over the Cam a great rain storm came on, making it necessary for the merchants to open their packs and spread their merchandise out to dry. And before it was fairly dry they had sold the lot, and so, thereafter, the Westmorland merchants never bothered to go as far as Norwich again.

But it was inevitable that Cambridge should become a centre of trade, for it was the nearest point on the Fenland waterways system to London. We read of wealthy East Anglian families in early Tudor times sending to Stourbridge Fair to buy Continental wine and goods that had been shipped in to London, and no doubt much of the country produce of East Anglia found its way to London in exchange *via* Stourbridge Fair. For anyone who has sailed a motorless boat around the coast of East Anglia it is easy to see that there would be a strong tendency for shippers sending goods from the north of England to London to by-pass the perilous slog round East Anglia by sending their ships straight into the Wash, up the Cam, and then hauling overland to London. It is easy and safe to sail from York to Cambridge, but hazardous and uncertain to sail from York to London.

Carter, the Cambridgeshire historian, writing in 1753, gives a very full description of the Fair. He describes the great procession on St Bartholomew's Day, when the Fair was set out by the Mayor and Corporation of Cambridge, how the site was a cornfield (meaning of course an open field common to all strip-holders, for

382

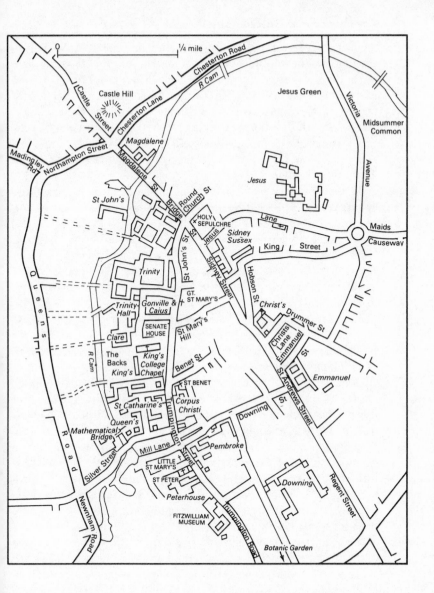

this was before the Enclosures) a field from which, according to ancient custom, all the corn had to be harvested before the date of the Fair otherwise it would be trodden underfoot, and all the Fair tackle had to be removed by the stall-holders, by Michaelmas Day at noon, otherwise the ploughmen could drive their ploughs over it; how the booths were set out in rows with names like Garlick Row, Booksellers' Row, Cooks' Row, Cheese Fair, Hop Fair, Wool Fair, and the Duddery. There is still a street called Garlick Row in Cambridge.

At the Duddery were sold woollen manufactured goods, and within a week £100,000 worth of these might change hands there, and vastly more be sold unseen. One single stall in this Duddery, dealing in Norwich goods only, carried £20,000 worth of stock. Hops were sold in values nearly as great, and it being the East Anglian herring season, then as now, and there being an R in the month vast quantities of oysters from Colchester and fresh herrings from the coast were consumed on the spot.

The 14th of September was the greatest day of all: the Horse Fair. Defoe gives a lively description of the Fair in *Tour Thro' the Whole Island of Great Britain*, and Bunyan parodied it as the 'Vanity Fair' of his *Pilgrim's Progress*.

Quite why or when a university started at Cambridge nobody knows. Alfred the Great is known to have founded a college of priests at Ely, and the monks of Ely certainly established schools at Cambridge: why at Cambridge and not at Ely is hard to understand. Possibly because Cambridge was the bigger place, nearer to London, and they did not wish to have their devotions at Ely disturbed by a lot of undergraduates. An Augustinian abbey was founded at Barnwell, just outside Cambridge, Augustinians came to the Hospital of St John, and Benedictine nuns to the Priory of St Radegund, now Jesus College. This is all fairly conjectural.

It is said that there was a university at Oxford before there was one at Cambridge. There was certainly one at Paris, and in 1229 some students were expelled from it and may have come to Cambridge, and there was certainly some sort of a centre of learning here then. But for a long time there was no kind of university organization: merely halls in which this or that teacher held a school for boys for payment. The boys might lodge with their master, or find private lodgings in the town. A Chancellor was referred to in 1226.

But early in the thirteenth century there was a well-developed university organization; with chancellor, masters, and 'clerks'. The latter were the scholars. The purpose of all education was to train for the priesthood or rather for all the duties, including those of the civil service, then undertaken by clerics. All the members of the university were under clerical law, to be tried for any misdemeanours by 'Courts Christian', and not subject, whatever they did, to the death penalty.

In 1271 the first proper college was founded, Peterhouse, and after this colleges were founded in the following order:

Peterhouse	1281	(received charter in 1284)
Michaelhouse	1324	(since merged into Trinity College);
Clare	1326	(originally called University Hall)
King's Hall	1317	(received charter in 1377 and later merged into Trinity College)
Pembroke	1347	
Gonville Hall	1348	(merged into Gonville and Caius)
Trinity Hall	1350	
Corpus Christi	1352	
King's	1441	
Queens'	1448	
St Catharine's	1473	
Jesus	1496	
Christ's	1439	(charter 1443: refounded in 1505)
St John's	1511	
Magdalene	1428	and 1542
Trinity	1546	
Gonville and Caius	1557	
Emmanuel	1584	
Sidney Sussex	1596	
Downing	1800	(received charter)

Girton	1869	(moved to Girton 1873)
Newnham	1871	
Selwyn	1882	
Fitzwilliam	1887	
St Edmund's House	1896	
New Hall	1954	
Churchill	1961	
Darwin	1964	
Wolfson	1965	
Fitzwilliam	1966	
Robinson	1977	

A guide to the Cambridge colleges would have to be a very long book of its own; so that all we can do here is to give the briefest outline of what there is to see in the most interesting buildings. Most of what is noteworthy is contained in a small space, perhaps half a mile by a mile; but it is not a bit of good trying to see it all in a day. A week would give one a better chance, and indeed in that time a fair idea might be had of the externals of Cambridge, which is certainly one of the most beautiful and interesting cities in the world.

For the student of English architecture Cambridge is a complete education in itself; for it contains monumental buildings of every style from Saxon down to the most 'advanced' of the present day; and nor will it stop here, for the colleges and the university are expanding rapidly and all the time.

Before we embark on a tour of the buildings it might be as well to include a few notes on the more curious customs of the place, most of which have been handed down from the very early Middle Ages.

Fellows are men and women who have been elected by existing fellows to their fellowships. Corporately they are the owners of the college with the Master and Scholars. They can live in rooms in college and are now paid a salary, although in former times it was a 'dividend' and the surplus on the income of the college endowments. Fellows may dine in Hall every evening (scholars may too). The fellows, and others not *in statu pupillari*, eat at the High Table, the rest in the body of the hall. The master lives in his own lodge, which is within the precincts of the college.

The room or rooms of fellows and undergraduates are grouped

behind an outer oak door which is called 'the oak' and over the 'oak' is painted the denizen's name. When this door is shut the inmate is said to be 'sporting his oak' and is not to be disturbed. Undergraduates, and other gentlemen, were traditionally waited upon by men servants called 'gyps', but now many are served by women 'bedders' and are not waited upon much at all.

At night an official of the university called the 'Proctor' prowls the town, accompanied by two men called 'Bulldogs' or 'Bullers'. One of the latter used, in days gone by, to carry a truncheon and the other a stick for measuring butter but now of course they don't. The duty of this triumvirate is to care for, and if necessary apprehend, any undergraduate who is drunk or otherwise disorderly, and try and prevent, if possible, any undergraduate from getting into trouble with the police. Wrong-doers were fined 6s 8d, or multiples of this sum, which was half a mark – monetary denominations both long extinct in England. Or a sinner may be 'gated', meaning that he cannot leave his college at night, or even 'sent down'. 'Up' means towards the university: 'down' means away from it.

The gates are shut at midnight in some colleges, 2 a.m. in many, and after this an undergraduate cannot lawfully get out of his college, although he may lawfully be admitted into it, having his name taken by the porters, and subsequently reported to his 'tutor', the don responsible for directing his studies. No undergraduate has ever, though, been deterred by these circumstances: every college can be 'climbed into' or 'climbed out of', and is every night, despite the elaborate defences erected by the authorities – spikes and *chevaux de frise* and all the rest of it (the more barbarous of these defences recently somewhat mitigated) – to prevent it. There is a story of a kindly policeman who seeing a figure late at night pacing up and down the pavement outside a college wall said: 'Can I give you a leg up, sir?' The figure turned out to be that of the master of the college, having a late night stroll.

The great sporting and social event at Cambridge is called 'May Week'. It is not in May but in June, and not a week but nearly a fortnight.

Entry into colleges by the general public is, by courtesy, at most times free and unhindered. You can wander into any college, go into the chapel if it is open, the hall if a meal is not being served in it (or an examination being held), wander through any court ('court' in Cambridge is the same as 'quad' in Oxford, a space surrounded by college buildings), see the library in some colleges if it is open, but it is better to ask permission. You may not go up any of the stairs leading to living quarters without invitation by somebody who lives there, or into any private rooms.

The master of a college keeps his dwelling in the lodge, and this is, of course, quite private: private, too, his garden and, generally, the Fellows' Garden. In the Porter's Lodge, by the main gate, are always porters (one wonders what they do all the time), and they are extremely courteous men, generally well-informed about their colleges, and very eager to help visitors. Cambridge men are proud of their colleges, and not at all averse to having them looked over by appreciative strangers.

Do not try to see Cambridge by motor car. The traffic congestion is intolerable, parking places full, and the traffic wardens of the city have eagle eyes and stony hearts. Park your car well outside the centre of the town in a multi-storey car park such as Grafton Centre, and resolutely leave it. Walk, bicycle, or take a bus – but do not try to drive.

The perfect way to approach Cambridge, as indeed to approach most English towns and cities, is by water. The voyage up the Great Ouse and Cam from Ely by cabin cruiser hired from one of the many boatyards there is quite delightful. Craft of 100 foot length, 14 foot beam, 4 foot draught and 9 foot briggage can get to Cambridge. This approach to the city avoids the worst of its dismal outskirts: it has to be admitted that Cambridge has allowed herself to become enmeshed in suburbs of a quite exceptional dreariness, and drearily they continue to spread.

Our ship moored, or our car parked, we will take ourselves to Emmanuel College, on St Andrew's Street: Emmanuel because it is at one end of a horse-shoe route which will take us through most of the more interesting colleges of Cambridge. As we can never hope to see even the colleges in one day, I will deal with colleges first, and other buildings afterwards.

Emmanuel was one of the later colleges, founded in 1584 for the same purpose that Sidney Sussex was founded: to combat popery.

It was founded by Sir Thomas Mildmay, a courtier of Queen Elizabeth and her Chancellor of the Exchequer, and it was built on the site of a Dominican friary which Sir Thomas bought for £550. The site must have been healthy, for the first master, Laurence Chaderton, lived to be a hundred and three.

Being so strongly Puritan the college contributed many alumni to the settlements in America. John Harvard was one of them. He sailed, for conscience's sake, in 1636 (the *Mayflower* had sailed in 1620), died of consumption at the age of thirty-one, bequeathing half of his estate (£779 17s 2d) and 320 books to found Harvard College.

So Protestant was Sir Thomas the founder that he turned the old church of the Dominicans into a refectory and their refectory into a chapel, and the latter ran north and south which was so contrary to Catholic practice as almost to constitute black magic. However, another chapel was built later to the design of Sir Christopher Wren, and it is still there, and it runs east and west in the accepted fashion.

Wren's chapel was built between 1668 and 1674, and is less strictly classical than the earlier Wren chapel at Pembroke. The plaster ceiling within is especially fine (by John Grove, who worked under Wren), and there is good woodwork of 1676, organ case of 1686 by Father Schmidt, reredos 1687 which has in it the Return of the Prodigal Son by Jacopo Amigoni and is early eighteenth century. The stained glass is of 1883. The general impression that one gets from the chapel and its furnishings is that it is all very civilized and elegant; but has little to do with the searing religious convictions of former ages.

The rest of the college is architecturally undistinguished; but the gardens are superb. There is an enormous oriental plane tree, a large ornamental pond (and a smaller one, but guarded by fellows – the larger one once the fish-pond of the friars), private swans, a swimming pool and a large and flourishing example of *Metasequoia glyptostoboides*: the 'fossil tree' from that desert-surrounded area of West China in which both plants and animals were protected for so many millennia from outside competition. The tree is a deciduous conifer, and was, until discovered in China, thought to have died out in Cretaceous times.

North-west along St Andrew's Street is **Christ's College**, founded in 1439 by William Bingham and then called God's House but refounded, in 1505, by Lady Margaret Tudor (née Beaufort) the pious mother of Henry VII. This lady used to keep chambers in the college. If Bishop Fisher's sermon preached at her funeral was the truth then she must have been a truly noble noblewoman, at a time when arrogance and insensitiveness were the common qualities of the rich. 'Bounteous she was,' said the Bishop, 'and liberal . . . of singular easiness to be spoken unto . . . of marvellous gentleness to all folk . . . unkind to no creature, nor forgetful of any service done to her (which is no little part of very nobleness) . . . All England for her death have cause for weeping.' It seems consistent with this character that she is supposed to have leant out of the window of her chamber in Christ's College on seeing a boy being beaten by a master and shouted: *'Lente! Lente!'* Students were much younger in those days than undergraduates are now, a tender thirteen or fourteen.

Milton was at Christ's from 1625 to 1632, and there is a venerable mulberry tree in the garden under which he is said to have written *Lycidas*, and which is still called 'Milton's Mulberry Tree'.

The Gateway is a relic of Lady Margaret's time. On the street side there is a brilliant display of heraldic carving supported by beasts called *yales* which have goatish heads. In medieval Indian temples there are animals called *yalis* very similar in feature. The *yalis* have round stones carved out of the rock inside their mouths so that the stones can never be removed without breaking the *yali*: a piece of virtuosity unknown among the *yales* of Cambridge.

The Hall, much altered, alas, by Sir Gilbert Scott but with fine tracery in the two tall windows, has portraits of the pious foundress, Bishop Fisher, Field-Marshal Jan Smuts, Quarles, Paley who wrote *Evidences of Christianity*, Charles Darwin who wrote evidences of quite another sort, and other notables who went to, or were connected with, the college. There is some very good Tudor plate in the Buttery (not normally on view). The Fellows' Building is mid-seventeenth century, vast, idiosyncratically but well and beautifully designed. The chapel, with a brick turret with a pretty eighteenth-century top to it, embodies the original fabric of the former chapel of God's House. There is existing a document dated

12th December 1506, signed by James Stanley, Bishop of Ely, giving permission to the master, fellows and scholars of the college to celebrate divine service. The north vestries are from the original building, as are the moulded beams in the ante-chapel, and some other beams beneath later panelling – some of which have been opened up to the view. The brass eagle lectern is famous: early sixteenth century and very beautiful. The windows of the north side have good fifteenth- and sixteenth-century glass, well worth noticing. In the most easterly window of this north range is Edward the Confessor and the foundress at her prayers. In the Master's Lodge is a fine Tudor bay window.

The gardens of Christ's are famous. There is a fine collection of irises in the Third Court; the Fellows' Garden is a notable winter garden – well furnished with evergreen shrubs and trees; there is a *Stachyrurus praecox* on the west side (so lovely in early spring when its flowers precede its leaves); Milton's mulberry tree supported by its large mound, another *Metasequoia* but a lesser one than that of Emmanuel (ground not wet enough here?) and nine hives for the honey bee. The bees do better here than their sisters of the open countryside owing to the absence of poisonous sprays in the city. These bees seem to confute the commonly held theory that hives must never be placed under trees. The fellows eat the honey and it is held to sweeten their tempers.

Farther along Sidney Street we come to Jesus Lane, on the right, and whatever we do or do not do in Cambridge we should go and look at **Jesus College**. It was founded in 1497 by Bishop Alcock, of Ely, after he had himself, as a visitor, closed the Benedictine nunnery of St Radegund's on the site because there were said to be only two nuns left there and one of these was *infamis*. Persistent legend has it, in fact, that Maids' Causeway, not far distant, was so named in ironical reference to the fact that the nuns of St Radegund's used to go there to meet their gentlemen friends, and in the fellows' garden there is still said to grow a herb with which these naughty nuns anticipated the pill.

The entrance to the college is a long walled paved walk called by undergraduates the 'Chimney' (from *cheminée*) (the church over the road they call 'St Ops' because it is opposite). Going through the chimney we then walk through a building which is basically twelfth century, i.e. very early, but much altered by Bishop Alcock in the fifteenth century. He used white brick – the earliest use of this unfortunate material in Cambridge colleges. We then find ourselves in a biggish courtyard, open to the west which gives a fine sense of air and space and is one of the most fascinating courts in Cambridge. The range of buildings to the north of it is seventeenth century but it fits well with the earlier monastic buildings to the east. In fact this open-sided court is quite impeccable and most attractive.

The beautiful carved doorway in the east range, which gives access to the cloisters, is original, but was moved to its present position in Alcock's time. We pass through it into the cloisters, one of the most magical places in Cambridge.

There are blackbirds in many Cambridge courts, and there are here; they sing most beautifully and the acoustics of the court seem to favour them. The cloister is the original one of the nuns of St Radegund's, altered and enlarged by the founder of the college and it thus has some of the bishop's early white brick in it.

In the north-east of this most charming and peaceful square is an odd alcove – the floor of which has sunk below the level of the present-day cloister (or perhaps remained where it was while the cloister has risen) which was once an entrance to the chapter house of the nunnery. It is a doorway with a window each side of it; about 1230 and Early English in its purest and most lovely form, with stiff-leaf capitals and composite shafts of central pillars surrounded by rings of slender shafts. The latter remind one irresistibly of the 'chiming pillars' of South Indian temples, pillars which when struck emit clear bell-like notes of different pitch. But these at Jesus emit no such notes and are not to be struck. The English, unlike the Indians and the Romans and other peoples, did not build monolithically.

The timber ceilings of the cloisters must be noticed: these again are Bishop Alcock's work. His rebus – the cock – may be seen carved here and there on them: his cockerel, here as at Ely and several parish churches, is carved around with a profusion that is most exhibitionist.

The Combination Room is in what was the chapter house of the nunnery, and has a most noteworthy ceiling. The hall, north of the cloisters, is where the hall of the nuns was, or their refectory; in other words it has been continuously used for eating in for nearly nine hundred years. St Radegund's was founded at the beginning of the eleventh century. St Radegund herself was a queen of the sixth century when the world was filled with saints: daughter of Berthram Prince of Thuringia, queen of Lotharius King of the Franks.

The Hall is a fine one. Particularly note the beautiful bay window, built about 1500 with such delicate carving in its tracery, and also in its walls and vault. The fine massive hammerbeam roof of the hall is original. But St Radegund's Church, which still survives as the chapel of the college, is one of the great things in Cambridge.

We enter this from the south cloister walk – through a door that was once the arch that joined the north aisle of the church to the north transept; for Bishop Alcock lopped the north aisle off the church to enlarge his cloister, and then used the old arch as his door from the outside. The bishop was Comptroller of Works to Henry VIII, and so he knew a thing or two about building.

The chapel inside is Norman in plan: i.e. cruciform with a central tower; but nearly everything in it is very early Early English: in fact the whole building is of this style.

Restored it has been – Pugin went over it about 1850 – but restoration was needed; many thirteenth-century details had been obliterated and had to be replaced. The chapel that we see today is the chancel of the nuns' chapel, and the old nuns' nave and transepts are now an ante-chapel. Perhaps the present ante-chapel has been less restored than the chapel. It was a much bigger church once: Bishop Alcock cut a lump off it to turn into the Master's Lodge.

The chapel is exciting, not only for lovers of the Early English style, but also for admirers of the pre-Raphaelites. Morris designed the ceilings put in between 1864–67, and most of the stained glass in the ante-chapel was made by Morris to the design of Burne-Jones; but there is some glass (the lower scenes in the west window of the south nave and the south window on the east side of the south transept) by Ford Madox Brown. The Burne-Jones windows are brilliant and vivid, utterly unlike medieval glass but strangely fitting very well in this early medieval chapel. There are

393

the nine orders of angels in the south transept, with man in the tenth place; there is a gallery of blessed saints with Bishop Alcock thrown in for good measure, there are the Four Evangelists, each attended by a very pagan sibyl; and in the tower lights are the Incarnation, Passion, Resurrection and Ascension. The south nave windows have patriarchs and prophets, and the north the Virtues, busy trampling underfoot their contrary vices. It is interesting to compare the Ford Madox Brown glass with that of Burne-Jones.

There is much nineteenth- and twentieth-century building round about this medieval nucleus. The big outer court to the east of the cloisters resembles a block of workers' dwellings put up on a bomb-site by an unenlightened town council. There are two angels supporting a coat of arms in the south-east corner, on Morley Horder's building, which immediately strike the eye. They are by Eric Gill. But like his Prospero and Ariel (which he tells us he secretly meant for God the Father and the Son) stuck on the front of London's Broadcasting House the building that supports them does not do them justice.

Cranmer, the archbishop burnt by Bloody Mary because he recanted against his acknowledgment of Catholic doctrine and the supremacy of the Pope, was a Jesus man. Although he prevaricated all his life at least he showed fine hardihood in his death, holding his right hand out into the flames of his pyre to be burnt first because it had offended by signing the wrongful document.

In the library of Jesus there is the autograph copy of the first edition of the first Bible ever printed on the American continent. It is written in the Mohican tongue. The Bible was printed in Cambridge, Mass., in 1663, the Corporation of London paying for this extraordinary enterprise, and the translator was a Jesus man, John Eliot, of Nasing, who took his degree in 1622, joined the Nonconformists nine years later and sailed to the American colonies – to convert untold numbers of Red Indians.

Samuel Taylor Coleridge was also here from 1791 to 1793. He distinguished himself by tracing the words 'Liberty and Equality' on the grass of a court in gunpowder and setting fire to them. This did not endear him to the authorities, who neither endorsed the sentiment nor liked having their lawn branded. The wrought-iron gate of Jesus was recently replaced by an exact copy of the original one by Mr Frank Lewis, of Yelling, on the Huntingdonshire border.

On Jesus Green, the Reverend John Hullier, Vicar of Babraham, was burnt alive in 1556 for being a Protestant. His pyre was made up of Protestant books.

North of Jesus College is that part of the River Cam where the racing eights are housed in large boat-houses, and where the 'bumping races' are held. The latter are a form of race made necessary by the fact that the river is too narrow for eights to navigate two abreast, and therefore have to race in line ahead. If a boat manages to bump the boat ahead she *goes up*, by changing places with it – and if she is bumped by the boat astern she *goes down*. The leading boat is called Head of the River, and may be rowed back to her boat-house with her flag flying.

Magdalene College was founded in 1542, as a hostel to house young monks from the Benedictine abbey of Crowland, in the Fens; and later the monks of Walden, Ramsey and Ely contributed to it money and students. It can be understood that these religious foundations wished their novitiates to benefit by the more sophisticated education that Cambridge afforded, but did not wish them to come into too close a contact with secular students. Thus a separate college, or hostel, was necessary for them. As Henry Stafford, 2nd Duke of Buckingham, contributed to the building of the college it was at first called Buckingham College; but in 1542 Thomas Audley, Lord Chancellor to Henry VIII and some would say his creature, refounded the college on a larger scale with some of the money that he had grabbed from the monasteries at the Dissolution. The nomination of the master of the college is yet within the gift of Audley's descendants.

The most interesting and beautiful thing to see, by far, in this college is the Pepysian Library.

The building was started in the 1670s. Certainly it has somewhat the plan of a Tudor manor house, but with an Italianate colonnade and other seventeenth-century features externally: as a building no doubt it can be faulted and it lacks unity; but nevertheless it is a lovable and beautiful building and attractively idiosyncratic.

The books, the choicest of their day, are as Pepys left them: kept in his own 'book presses', with each book hoisted on a block of wood so that the tops of all the books are level! This system at least has the virtue that, over the centuries, the books have been kept in order. There are some 3,000 books, many of the greatest value and interest; and the famous Diary was discovered among them, written in the short-hand cypher that Pepys invented for himself. It was transcribed into long-hand by a student of St John's College and published in 1825. The range of the other books in the library gives some idea of the catholicity of Pepys's interests, and the lively and enquiring climate of his times.

For the rest, Magdalene is not one of the architecturally great colleges, although it has some comely buildings of clunch.

Charles Kingsley was a Magdalene man, and used to climb out of the college in the small hours of the morning in order to go fishing in the Fen country, about which he wrote so vividly later on in *Hereward the Wake*. Kingsley's portrait is in Hall, so are Pepys's by Lely, T. S. Eliot by Wyndham Lewis, and a copy of Holbein's Lord Audley. While in the hall note the carved bunches of fruit and other flora behind the High Table. These are Tudor, although the rest of the wainscoting is eighteenth century. Sir John Vanbrugh is thought to have designed the stairway and gallery to the Combination Room.

When leaving Magdalene note Benson Court, nearby: a group of charming Tudor houses standing on what was Fisher Row – a medieval staithe. They were very well restored by Sir Edward Lutyens and David Wyn Roberts. The big timber-framed house is sixteenth century and was once the Cross Keys Inn.

St John's College was founded, like Christ's, by Lady Margaret Tudor (or Beaufort). She founded it after she had founded Christ's and it was not built until after her death. The building of it was entrusted to Bishop Fisher, Lady Margaret's confessor and a man in whom she placed great confidence. It was Fisher who had the great gatehouse of red brick and stone built between 1511 and 1516, after the foundress's death. But the college stands on the site of a much earlier foundation: that of the Hospital of St John, which was founded before 1200. The few surviving fragments of the old chapel of the hospital appear to be mid-thirteenth century.

St John's is a vast college, the second largest in Cambridge; and we can here but describe its salient features. The gatehouse, already mentioned, is lofty, turreted, magnificent. On the street side of it is a brilliant and brilliantly painted heraldic display such as that at Christ's College, the arms also supported by yales. The statue of St John was placed there in 1662, replacing an older version.

The first court is much spoiled by Sir Gilbert Scott's monstrous Victorian-Gothic chapel, which rises up on the north side of it, not really joining the other buildings to form part of them – just rearing up its great bulk to be admired, or not admired, as may be the case. The east range of this first court is the hall, kitchen and buttery. The passage that divides hall from kitchens in Cambridge colleges (as in medieval manor houses) is called the Screens. Here the Screens passage is beautiful, with a smaller heraldic group with Lady Margaret presiding over it, carved Tudor screen and original carved beams.

The hall is splendid, with a massive hammerbeam roof, most of it Tudor, and much original linenfold panelling. There is a fine portrait of Lady Margaret, a much smaller one of Bishop Fisher, and a long gallery of famous men including Herrick, Wordsworth, William Cecil, Wilberforce, Herschel the astronomer, Lord Palmerston, and a Romney portrait of Sir Noah Thomas. There is also a portrait of Edward Henry Palmer, orientalist, and Arabic, Persian and Urdu scholar. He taught himself these languages in Cambridge, without visiting the lands where they were spoken, by his friendships with undergraduates who came from them. He became so good that fairly obscure Urdu papers used to commission him to write poems for them. He did eventually spend some time in the East, and was eventually sent to Egypt on a political mission, and was killed by unfriendly Arabs near the Suez Canal.

The Combination Room is the finest in Cambridge, 100 feet long with transomed windows and a plaster ceiling, the latter said to be by the hand of the same Italian craftsmen who made Trinity fountain; the room is contemporary with Trinity Great Court. There are two fine fireplaces: the east one originally where it is – the west one brought here from a house in Cambridge. Its date is 1594. There is a magnificent set of Chippendale chairs.

The library forms the north side of third court, and ends right on the brink of – almost in – the river. It is an interesting building, built 1624 but most unusually for this date very Gothic-looking. Evidently the architect was what we would call a traditionalist, and

397

his building is none the worse-looking for that. The rest of the third court came shortly after the library. The library is best seen from a boat, for there is a splendid oriel window carried right over the water, and the letters J.L.C.S. carved very big and lavishly over the window with the date, the initials being for Johannes Lincolniensis Custos Sigilli, meaning the Dr John Williams, Bishop of Lincoln, who gave the money to build the library. He gave it anonymously, but it leaked out. Lady Mary Cavendish also gave money anonymously, to build the north side of the second court, but that leaked out too.

There are two bridges here across the Cam: one, the more upstream of the two, having been started after the turn of the century by Grumbold, after Christopher Wren's idea; and the other the famous 'Bridge of Sighs', named after the real one in Venice, built 1831. Students of military architecture will be interested to note in all the college bridges the lengths to which the authorities have gone to keep in – or keep out – undergraduates at night. Lengths, it may be said, entirely unavailing: there is not one college that cannot be climbed in and out of by the student of ordinary accomplishment: the present writer, no alpinist, has been in and out of many of them.

What shall we say of St John's new court over the river? It is vast, and a fine Victorian-Gothic cocktail. It might well have been designed as a screen set for a Walt Disney extravaganza and is commonly called 'the Wedding Cake'. By virtue of its size and position it dominates the Backs. The gilded vane at the top of the fantastic flying-buttressed and be-pinnacled lantern in the centre of the great pile was decorated, in the 1880s, with one of the scarlet 'blazers', or flannel sports jackets, of the Lady Margaret Boat Club. In those pre-helicopter days it took the authorities much effort, and several days, to remove the indignity, and one marvels at the virtuosity of the undergraduate – who was probably well primed with beer – who put it there in the first place.

The scarlet jacket of the St John's oarsmen, incidentally, is said to have been the first ever of the genus 'blazer', and it gave its name to all of those egregious garments.

A new range of building, called Cripps, won the RIBA bronze in 1968.

Trinity College is the largest college in Cambridge, bigger than many an entire university and in output of great men it has surpassed many an entire nation. In a short list of poets of Trinity one can include George Herbert, Cowley, Suckling, Marvell, Dryden, Byron, Macaulay, Tennyson, Edward Fitzgerald, Housman, Iqbal. Of public men half a dozen Prime Ministers of Britain, the Earl of Essex, John Winthrop of New England, William Smith O'Brien of Ireland, and the Marquis of Granby, who at the end of the Seven Years' War did not forget the men who had served under him but made himself personally responsible for settling disabled NCOs as landlords of inns, ensuring the perpetuation of his name throughout the land. Of great men of science there is a list many pages long; but Newton, Sedgwick the geologist, Rutherford who split the atom with such unfortunate results, Eddington and Jeans will have to do. Sir James Frazer, Macaulay, G. M. Trevelyan and Lord Acton are among its famous writers of prose, and Vaughan Williams among its writers of music.

Henry VIII founded the College of the Holy and Undivided Trinity in 1546, a year before his death. He did it by knocking together nine existing foundations or hostels, including Michaelhouse and King's Hall, which were two of the biggest colleges in Cambridge. Michaelhouse had been founded in 1324 by Edward II's Chancellor of the Exchequer Hervey de Stanton: King's Hall by Edward III in 1336; so that although Trinity may seem at first sight to be an upstart college only 440 years old, in fact it can claim that, in part at least, it dates from 1324.

The Great Gate, finished 1535, was built to commemorate Edward III, but his statue was removed from it and Henry VIII's put there instead. Edward's was moved to the clock tower by the chapel.

The other buildings that were gobbled up by Henry VIII were: St Catherine's Hostel, Physwick Hostel, Crutched Hostel, Gregory's Hostel, Tyled Hostel, Oving's Inn and St Gerard's Hostel – commonly called 'Garret' Hostel (there is still Garret Hostel Lane nearby). Henry was able to appropriate all of these institutions, including the church of St Michael, because being monastic they fell to the Crown on the Dissolution. He also, of course, appropriated all their endowments, and these, together with the endowments of many other religious houses, were devoted to the great college that was to perpetuate his memory. The Tudor sovereigns looked upon the founding of colleges much as the Pharaohs of Egypt looked upon building pyramids: as imperishable memorials. Henry VIII got his very cheaply.

We enter Trinity through the Great Gate, which was in fact built as the gate for King's Hall between 1519 and 1535, but is on such a scale that it was obviously built with the idea that it should become the gate of a much bigger college. But when Henry VIII died the college had only just been founded, and the Great Court was not conceived until Queen Elizabeth's time. Under Mary was built the chapel and other of the buildings surrounding the court.

But it was Dr Thomas Nevile, Master of Trinity in 1593 and a favourite of Queen Elizabeth, who really built the college as it stands today.

He shifted King Edward's Tower (or the Clock Tower) from its former position due west of the Great Tower and moved it to where it is today – in line with Mary's chapel. He pulled down most of Mary's buildings, and built new ranges to suit his plan: which was to build the biggest and grandest court in either Oxford or Cambridge, and one of the most impressive urban open spaces in the world.

The Great Gate is grand enough, although Henry VIII's statue on one side of it, and James I and his wife and son on the other, seem uninspired. Turn right through the gate and we face the chapel, massive and Marian Gothic, the kind of over-civilized late Gothic of which Mary Tudor was so fond: a Gothic persisted in after the rest of the world had gone over to the styles of the Renaissance. It was built 1555–64, and although individually not a great building it fits in very well indeed with the composition of the Great Court.

Walking into the ante-chapel the breath is taken away by the perfectly white, cold, silent chamber into which one is plunged, in which sit or stand six over-life-sized statues. There is a feeling that these great men have been holding commune with each other, and that one has interrupted their discourse. The famous one is Newton, by Roubiliac, often considered the finest thing in Cambridge and one of the best pieces of stone portraiture since the Greeks. It inspired the lines in Wordsworth's *Prelude*:

> *Newton with the prism and silent face,*
> *The marble index of a mind for ever*
> *Voyaging through strange seas of thought, alone.*

The others are Bacon by Weeks – Bacon in splendid stage Elizabethan costume, but I cannot believe that the original looked quite so miserable; Barrow, the Master who had the library built, by Noble; Whewell, the Master who built Whewell's Court, by Woolner; Macaulay by Woolner; and Tennyson by Thorneycroft, in a fine theatrical pose. There are also a number of busts about the walls.

The lavish screen, holding the organ and dividing the chapel from the ante-chapel, was put up in Bentley's time. Bentley was the most unpopular master any college ever had, even if a great classical scholar. He impoverished his college by putting up grandiose works to embellish the chapel and his own lodge, he used publicly to call his fellows 'asses', 'dogs', 'fools' and 'sots' and even other – yet more scurrilous – names. Masters of Trinity are appointed by the Crown, not elected as in other colleges; and no doubt they are very hard to get rid of. Bentley finally was degraded by orders of the University Senate, was reinstated and died in 1742 after having been master for forty-two most unhappy years. Where a great Perpendicular window was in the east end of the chapel he had a huge reredos raised: gorgeous but somehow the wrong shape.

Tacked on to the west of the chapel is the Clock Tower, or King Edward's Tower, which was originally the gateway to King's Hall and was built 1427–33. The statue of Edward was put in in 1601. Wordsworth mentions the clock in his *Prelude*, and undergraduates try to race the chiming of it at midnight by running right round the Great Court: a feat that can be accomplished by a good athlete.

West of the tower is the Master's Lodge, built by Nevile but enlarged at great expense by Bentley. Then come the hall, kitchens and butteries and all the rest of it. The gate over in the middle of the south range is the Queen Elizabeth Gate with a statue of Elizabeth I in it, and the south-east corner of the Great Court is known as Merton's (or 'Muttonhole') Corner, and is notable for the fact that Lord Byron used to keep his tame bear in it (students being forbidden to keep dogs). When asked by a fellow what he intended to do with the animal, he said that it should sit for a fellowship. There is a story that Byron was finally sent down (expelled) from the college because he would insist on bathing naked in the fountain in the centre of Great Court. This fountain, which is very beautiful, was built by Italian craftsmen in 1602.

The visitor will notice that the Great Court is quite asymmetrical: it is far from being even a perfect rectangle, or even straight sided. Like all really surpassingly beautiful concourses of building it has grown up organically, over the centuries, each new component being fitted into the older ones, and thus has unity in diversity. One cannot help wondering just how well a modern building of any kind we like to think of would fit in to Trinity Great Court. Is ours the first age that could not conceivably contribute?

The steps up into the Hall are, like the chiming of the clock, a challenge to undergraduates. Some of them can, but others cannot, jump down them in a leap: others, but few indeed, can jump up them.

The Hall was built by Nevile, with his own money.

It is one of the finest halls there is, and is modelled on the hall of Middle Temple in London and is 103 feet long. The old hall of Michaelhouse was on the other side of the Screens, i.e. where the kitchen and buttery now are. The kitchens of Trinity are vast and highly organized, like the kitchens of a really great hotel; and in the old kitchen turtle shells, engraved with the dates on which their occupants made soup on great occasions, are hung on the steaming walls.

The screen of the Screens is a most exuberant piece of carved and painted woodwork, reminding one strongly of the decoration of some of the less restrained modern Hindu temples of North India, and obviously the work is influenced by the Elizabethan artists' idea of the Gorgeous East. Awareness of the Orient was coming to England in Tudor times: witness the splendid date palms carved on the west door of King's College Chapel.

The hall, which has a fine hammerbeam roof, is dominated by the famous portrait of that very dominating monarch, Henry VIII, by Holbein. To his right is his unhappy daughter, Mary Tudor,

402

looking crabbed and dissatisfied (compare her portrait as a young girl in Sawston Hall done before all those executions looking innocent and happy). The Mary in Trinity is by Antonio Moro. There is the Duke of Gloucester, in fancy dress, by Sir Joshua Reynolds, Lord Tennyson by Watts, a contemporary painting on wood of Francis Bacon, and a portrait of Nevile, who had it all built, near the entrance. Look up to see the beautiful lantern in the roof, which was originally to let the smoke out, for the hall was heated by a huge centrally-placed open brazier.

Out into the Screens again we turn right and walk out into Nevile's Court. Right opposite is the Wren Library, designed by Sir Christopher and built in 1675, in Isaac Barrow's mastership. Wren was a close friend of Barrow and the latter persuaded him to design the library for nothing. It is a superb building within and without, built of a lovely glowing stone from Ketton in Rutland, and raised above a cloister. To balance the library, on the other side of the court, Wren had a tribune built: a blind and purely ornamental feature with a platform, staircases, columns and niches.

The library itself is a building of fine classical purity and simplicity. The insides of the book cases, designed by Wren, are embellished by busts of Trinity men by famous sculptors, and much enriched by wood carvings of Grinling Gibbons – the greatest master of this art since medieval times. These carvings well repay some study. Some of the busts are pretty run-of-the-mill, but the first Coke (the Lord Chief Justice) by Roubiliac, and also this artist's Cotton, Barrow, Bentley, Newton and Bacon, and each side of the entrance the naturalists Ray and Willoughby, are fine, and so is Woolner's bust of a beardless Tennyson. The great statue by Thorwaldsen of Byron was offered to Westminster Abbey, but the Dean and Chapter refused it because of the poet's morals. It lay in the cellars of the London Customs House before it was rescued by Byron's old college, which apparently had forgiven him for his bear and his bathing. There are other Byron relics in the library. Byron's morals, incidentally, besides leading him into the enormities that we have already spoken of, are also said to have caused him to climb up on the roof of Trinity Library and lewdly embellish the statues up there. (There is a book, incidentally, written in the last century, called, *The Roof-Climber's Guide to*

403

Trinity College. Recently a more comprehensive guide has come out, *Night Climbers of Cambridge*, which is to be bought in any Cambridge bookshop. The sport is still a very popular one.)

In the library also are Newton's death mask and his telescope, some priceless illuminated manuscripts, manuscripts of Milton, Macaulay, Thackeray and Tennyson, and a fifteenth-century Roll of Carols said to be the earliest known manuscript of musical harmony.

Back in Nevile's Court the long cloister on the north side is interesting; for it was in this that Newton worked out his theory of sound. If you stand at the west end and stamp your foot you can hear the clear and very sharp echo which Newton timed to measure, for the first time, the speed of sound.

The New Court is of interest mostly to botanists, or at least gardeners; for it has a distinguished collection of creepers on its walls. Bishop's Hostel is small and very atmospheric. It was paid for in 1667–71 by the Bishop of Lichfield (the man who dammed up Well Creek thus cutting off the navigation between Wisbech and King's Lynn, for which folly he found himself in trouble).

From New Court to the River Cam there was once a mighty avenue of lime trees, planted in 1672. They were all cut down recently because of an heroic decision made by the master and fellows of Trinity. These elderly men preferred that this should be done and new ones planted so that future generations should enjoy them, rather than that they themselves should continue to enjoy the old ones during their lifetimes.

If we like to cross the Cam, and then the traffic-swollen Queen's Road which latter we do at the risk of our lives, we can look through a superb wrought-iron gate down an avenue of mighty elm trees that reminds us of the piers and vaults of a cathedral.

Trinity, besides being the largest of the colleges, is also by far the wealthiest. The agricultural depression which hit England in the 1870s when cheap grain began to flood in from America hit most of the colleges badly, for their investments were mostly in land. Trinity, however, owned much of its property in the industrial north, and thus was enriched rather than impoverished.

Next to Trinity we come to **Gonville and Caius**, generally called 'Caius' which is pronounced Keys.

Gonville Hall was originally founded in some houses in Free School Lane, near the present Corpus Christi, by Edmund Gonville, of Terrington, in Norfolk. He obtained his licence to build it in 1347, but died shortly afterwards, and left his executor, William Bateman, Bishop of Norwich, to finish the job. Bateman also died leaving the college in embryo, and it was not until Dr John Caius came along, in 1557, and refounded the old college as Gonville and Caius, that it really came to much.

Caius was a Norwich man, although of a Yorkshire father. The family name was, in fact, Keys, but was Latinized into Caius in the fashion of the day. He was a great and remarkable man, a student of Latin, Greek and Hebrew at the original Gonville Hall, was made a fellow at the age of twenty-three, studied medicine at Padua, was physician to Edward VI and Mary Tudor and President of the Royal College of Physicans. He was one of the first people in England to put the study of anatomy on a serious footing.

When he was offered the mastership of his new college he accepted reluctantly, refused to accept pay, and himself paid for most of the new building. Unfortunately he had a penchant for collecting Papist objects at a time when Popery was disreputable. A mob of militantly Protestant students collected and – under the eye of the Vice-Chancellor of the University and with his approval – they broke into Dr Caius's lodge, flung his collection of missals and chasubles and other sacred objects into the court, and burnt them; and Caius was forced to retire from the college that he had founded and built and – because he had impoverished himself in the building of it and then had no other means of support – he died destitute. But his grave is in the chapel, and has on it: *Fui Caius* – I was Caius. And also *Vivit post Funera Virtus*.

The court of Caius into which we come from Trinity Street is Victorian and uninspired. We then pass under the great Gate of Virtue.

The Gate of Virtue is one of the first pieces of High Renaissance architecture to be built in England (remember Dr Caius had studied in Padua). It is thus very interesting from an architectural point of view. It is for me curiously unsatisfying, being spoilt, I think, by its windows.

The Gate of Humility, by which in the past students were wont

405

to enter the college, has been removed to the master's garden, where no doubt it reminds the occupant of this important virtue. The Gate of Honour, however, is still there, leading the way towards the Senate House where students receive their degrees.

It is an astonishing little building. It is a splendid miniature – a little fantasia. It is a product, like the Gate of Virtue, of the first impact of classical architecture on England, when anything went: there were no inhibitions about mixing up orders or styles, or about 'purity' or anything else like that. It is really quite absurd. The Greek temple half-way up it should be on the grand scale or not at all, but it is completely dwarfed and dominated by the curious rustic phallic dome on top.

The rest of Caius Court consists of two ranges of chambers put up by Caius, of stone and very medieval-looking, with the chapel on the north. The chapel is fourteenth century (licence to celebrate Divine Office in it was given in 1339), originally of clunch faced with brick; but both are covered up now by stone, put there in 1716. The interior is very eighteenth century, i.e. more fitting for a theatre than for a place of worship. The apse at the east end was added by Waterhouse in 1870, the cross and candles on the altar are by Gerald Benney of 1958 and, for lovers of Victorian sentimentality, there is a corking *Non Angli sed Angeli* in a window, with a roguish bishop eyeing two winsome boys. The original Gonville Court is part fifteenth century.

Caius is noted for producing doctors, and also good food. Its cuisine has always had a reputation for being better than that of other colleges, although certainly the cooks of Peterhouse would dispute this hotly.

Trinity Hall has little to detain us, in its buildings at least, although the principal court is fourteenth century, but ashlared (i.e. covered with dressed stone facing) in the eighteenth. The college was founded in 1350 by the William Bateman, Bishop of Norwich, who took over the care of Gonville from his friend who founded it. Bateman was not only Bishop of Norwich, but one of the great English diplomats of the time: a papal dignitary, and an international lawyer of great renown. He died at the papal court at Avignon; and was buried with great pomp and ceremony in front of the High Altar in the Church of St Mary along with a bevy of previously departed Popes. He gave an impetus towards law in his foundation of Trinity Hall which still persists; and Trinity Hall is to law what Caius is to medicine.

The library is sixteenth century in spite of its Gothic windows, charming and flower-surrounded. There are many old books in it, some of them still chained. In the chapel is a vast painting of the Presentation in the Temple, and the college has one of the best collections of silver in Cambridge.

Clare should really be seen for the first time from over the river. First, then, we come to its perfectly lovely garden, one of the loveliest in the country; with its Perfume Garden, its Sunken Garden in which plays are performed in a most magical setting, and Clare – not to be outdone in this important matter – has a *very* fine *Metasequoia*. In the master's garden is a vast and sumptuous copper beech tree (there is a print by Ackerman showing it six feet high!), and even vaster plane trees. But then Cambridge abounds in mighty trees.

The iron gate that gives on to the bridge is one of the most beautiful in existence – delicate lace-work in iron and in perfect taste. Clare Bridge is beautiful too, with its stone balls. One of these is newer than the others – the reason being that, in an assault by the students of St John's, the balls got thrown into the river before the Clare men counter-attacked and the Johnians were thrown into a rout. All the balls were recovered save one – surely a challenge to modern frogmen? The bridge is 1640, and built by Thomas Grumbold, the great Cambridge mason. The lovely set of gates is by Warren, and is of 1714: there is another like it in the entrance to the college from Trinity Lane.

From the bridge the block of Clare presents to us a massive and most civilized building, which has often been said to look more like a palace than a college. The south side of it, overlooking King's Lawn, is of 1640 or thereabouts, the west side must have at least been influenced by Wren, but the design was by Robert Grumbold – son of Thomas who built the bridge.

The effect of this whole building is urbane and harmonious, and inside the one old court of Clare it is the same. The east range is the oldest part, by John Westley, master mason, of 1638, and showed when it was built a mixture of Gothic and the new styles coming in from Italy and, more especially perhaps, France. Thus there was a Tudor-type Perpendicular fan vault ceiling in the gateway, two oriel windows above, Perpendicular niches to each side, the whole surmounted by a classical gable. When it was built this range (and others to follow) had battlements on top of the walls, hiding the dormer windows, and Tudor-arched windows. The battlements were replaced in the eighteenth century by the present pretty balustrade; and the windows made straight-topped. The building of the whole court took from 1638 to the end of the century – the work being held up for years by the Civil War; but the feeling of unity and harmony in the court is most profound.

The chapel is of the 1760s, again much influenced by Wren. The octagonal ante-chapel is famous for its glazed cupola: it was designed by the Master of Caius, Sir James Burrough, who was an amateur architect and who had a good plasterer. The chapel proper has a barrel vault, with the same delicate plaster work, and an altar painting by Cipriani of the *Annunciation*, but like so many churches of this period absolutely no religious feeling whatever. Pull the stalls and the altar out and it is a ballroom.

Clare College was founded by Lady Elizabeth de Clare, three times widowed, and daughter of Gilbert de Clare. Of this lady more under Clare, the village in Suffolk. Suffice here that she took over the burnt-out University Hall, a college that had been founded in 1326 by Richard Badew, and refounded it as Clare Hall in 1339. She was very friendly with John, Duke of Lancaster, and his steward Edmund Gonville the Rector of Terrington who as we have seen founded his own college of Gonville Hall. Another intimate of Lady Elizabeth was the Countess of Pembroke who founded Pembroke College, so this group of intimates, or little coterie of wealthy friends, did much to build up Cambridge.

There is fine plate at Clare, including many good candlesticks and a 'poison cup' which has a crystal in it which is supposed either to shatter or to discolour at the presence of poison.

There are books in Clare library of the ninth century, made of parchment in which are warble-fly holes. It can be deduced from these that the warble-flies of eleven hundred years ago were much the same as the ones which torment our cattle today, causing them to tear round the fields in panic with their tails in the air.

Over the river is a large block of buildings belonging to Clare designed by Sir Giles Gilbert Scott and built of brick, and it is hard by the university library designed by the same man. The Clare building is inoffensive, although marred by silly bits of vestigial Georgian ornamentation: the university library is very bad. The recently built Castle Hill Hostel, designed by David Roberts, is supposed to be a good piece of modern building and meet for its purpose. But to look at the seventeenth- and eighteenth-century buildings of Clare, and then at those of the twentieth, is to wonder in which direction our civilization is travelling.

King's College is, of course, completely overshadowed by its chapel, which is one of the most famous buildings in the world and the very peak and culmination of the Gothic art.

In our tour of East Anglia so far we have seen much Perpendicular period building: most certainly East Anglia contains more choice building of this period than any other province of England; but here in King's College Chapel we have the *ne plus ultra* of the style: any further change or development could only lead to decadence.

We should, of course, attend at least one choral service in the chapel during our stay in Cambridge, for perhaps nowhere in the world is more joyous music allied to visual surroundings more sublime.

King Henry VI, who would have made a better monk than a king, decided in 1440 to found a college in Cambridge linked with a school at Eton much as William of Wykeham had done seventy years before with Winchester and New College, Oxford.

The first buildings of King's were built north of where the chapel now is, in what is now called the Old Schools. But then Henry became more ambitious; and drew up a grand plan for the greatest college ever built, and he actually swept away a large part of the centre of Cambridge town, the whole of the old parish of St John Zachary – the most central and important commercial parish in Cambridge. Trading hithes on the river, scores of houses and business premises, were ruthlessly flattened, and Milne Street, one of the main streets of the city, was cut in two. During times of drought you can still see the outlines of seventeenth-century paths and walls of the college gardens on the great lawn of King's: for the grass growing over the foundations dries out more quickly than that growing on deeper soil. It was 280 years, though, before any permanent buildings were built on this vast cleared area and the college began to move to the south of its chapel, as King Henry planned that it should.

The foundation stone of the chapel was laid by Henry VI on 25th July 1446. It is believed that the general plan of the chapel was that of his master mason, Reginald Ely.

Henry approved a document in 1448, which is still called his Will, in which he laid down in great detail how both chapel and college were to be built, and alas that later generations did not take more notice of it. In particular the buildings were to eschew 'superfluitie of too great curious werkes of enteille and besy moulding'. But when he died the 'busy moulding' and the 'too great curious works' crept in, and subsequent monarchs sought to glorify themselves on the pretext of glorifying God by adorning the great chapel over with their personal symbols. Thus the buttresses of the east part of the chapel, which were finished in the founder's time, are unadorned and the finer for it: those of later dates are over-embellished with royal emblems. But the grand design of the building could not be altered; and the chapel is great enough to carry these superficial details without detriment.

The work on the chapel was held up twice, the first time by the Wars of the Roses and Henry's deposition in 1461. Before this happened most of the building had been done with a magnesian limestone from Yorkshire.

Yorkshire may seem a long way to go for such a vast amount of stone, until one realizes that a sailing barge, given a fair wind, can go from Hull to the Wash on an ebb and a flood tide, and a modern motor lorry may not do much better. However, after Henry VI's time, when building was resumed by his successors, stone was brought from nearer at hand (although it may have taken just as long to get there) from Weldon in Northants, down the Nene and through the Fen waterways to the Cam.

The join between these two kinds of stone can be seen (more easily on the north side), and it shows almost exactly where the earlier work stopped and the later began. It shows that the whole of the foundation was laid in Henry VI's time and much of the east end of the chapel was completed. Work stopped with unseemly precipitation on Henry's death: so much so that one stone was left half carved in the south-east corner of the Great Court, and it lay there until it was taken to be used as the foundation stone for the 'Gibbs' Building' when this was started in 1724.

One important result of this long break in the building was the fact that the roof inside was built in a different style from that intended. Henry VI and his great master builder planned a lierne vaulted roof, and lierne vaults are indeed to be found in two of the side chapels which were completed before Henry's death. But the actual main roof is fan vaulted.

In order to accommodate the planned lierne vaulting the shafts were given seven components – whereas the fan vaulting substituted only required five. Therefore two of the members or flutings of each shaft were found unnecessary; and they simply stop at the top of the shaft with no upward continuation. Undoubtedly had it not been for Henry VI's deposition the chapel would have been lierne vaulted, and we should not have had that soaring, spreading, delicate lacework in stone which is one of the wonders of the world. The imagination fairly reels when we try to think how that stone was got up there, and fitted, and when we contemplate the utter daring of the people who built that roof soaring up there 80 feet above our heads. There are said to be two miles of stone ribs, the panelling itself is so thin that you may not walk upon it or you would put your foot through, and the bosses which hang at the conjunctions of the fans – alternate Tudor roses with Beaufort portcullises – and which look so ethereal and delicate from the ground – each weigh a ton.

Nor are the walls which support this tent-work of stone any less delicate. By far the greater area of the walls is glass, in fact the chapel is in its way a glorious glass-house. The buttresses which rise up so gracefully between the great windows, and which are, in fact, really all there is of the walling except the windows, do, of course, support all the weight. The twenty-five gargantuan oak trusses, each with a number of beams, were, during the last century, suspected of thrusting the walls apart; hence Sir G. G. Scott's tie-rod inserted in the 1860's above the vaulting which ties the whole thing together. Only Fellows with their guests may ascend

411

into the roof by the stairway in the north-east turrret. Up there the stone vaulting lies beneath one's feet, the lead weather-roof above the head, and the twenty-five mighty beams between.

Simon Clerk, architect in most of this second period, probably intended fan vaulting: he was master mason at King's in 1476; but John Wastell, who was master mason in 1512 when the work was started, actually designed and built the vault. Wastell's master stone-carver was Thomas Stockton. Men were found, from first to last, worthy of the work they were doing: no part of the building shows craftsmanship which lets down the rest: design, masonry, stone-carving, all are perfect.

The glass was made between 1517 and the 1530s. The window over the north-west porch and some others are attributed to the king's glazier, a Fleming named Barnard Flower who lived at Southwark. This man died, and was succeeded by other Flemings, and the style of the glass is essentially Flemish-Renaissance. The study of King's windows can be a life work, rendered difficult by the fact that it is hard, from the ground, to make out the figures and background without close study. An excellent pamphlet can be bought to help one out; and a booklet listing the subjects of the pictures in the windows for a few pence, at the table which sells such things in the north-west corner of the ante-chapel. Sufficient here that the upper tiers of lights in general show scenes from the Old Testament, while the lower scenes from the New which were thought by the artists to show a correspondence in some way; e.g. Job tormented above, Christ scourged below. The glass is glowing and beautiful, made at the peak of the glazier's art. On a sunny day the chapel is flooded with glorious coloured light. It is supposed to be due to Milton that this glass survives. Uncompromising Protestant though he was, Milton loved King's Chapel (he wrote verse about it) and he was a friend of Cromwell and may have interceded with him to let the windows alone. There is a record that the bursar of King's paid William Dowsing his usual fee of 6s 8d. Was Dowsing satisfied with the fee but appalled by the labour? Or had he received orders from Cromwell to spare his hand? The Earl of Manchester, who was in command of the Parliamentary forces, was incidentally a friend of the provost of King's.

There is one window (number XXIII) which has in it the detail of a sailing ship of the early fifteen hundreds. This, depicted in perfect detail, has high fore and stern castles (the high forecastle went out in English ships soon after this period – giving the English ships an advantage to windward of the Spanish ones and enabling us to win the battle with the Armada), three masts, square courses and topsails on main and fore and lateen on the mizzen, running and standing rigging clearly shown and correct, shrouds rattled down, a boat lying alongside and another, very like a modern Yorkshire 'cog boat', pulling off to her in the foreground with white-coated figures. Whichever old Fleming painted that piece of glass knew what a ship looked like.

The quality of the wood carving of the screen and of the choir stalls of the chapel is said to be the best north of the Alps; and Pevsner pronounces it 'the purest work of the Early Renaissance style in England'. The screen and choir stalls are later than the rest of the chapel, and the fact that Anne Boleyn's initials are carved on the screen dates it between 1533 and 1536.

Placed at the east end of the chapel now is the Adoration of the Magi by Peter Paul Rubens, which was painted in 1634 as an altar-piece for the White Nuns of Louvain. This was donated by Major Allnatt in 1961, and is a princely work and very fitting for this position.

Before services candles are lighted at the places of the choristers. Then the choir files in, and – in Wordsworth's words:

> *. . . from the arms of silence – list! O list!*
> *The music bursteth into second life;*
> *The notes luxuriate, every stone is kissed*
> *By sound, or ghost of sound, in mazy strife;*
> *Heart-thrilling strains, that cast, before the eye*
> *Of the devout, a veil of ecstasy!*

For the rest, King's College has its fine Great Court, rendered the greatest in the world by being bounded by the chapel on the north side, but otherwise with the Gibbs' Building on the west (this is actually the Fellows' Building for it contains their rooms; but was designed by James Gibbs in 1723 after plans made by Hawkesmore ten years earlier had been dropped. The Provost had asked

413

Hawkesmore to avoid ornament on the ground that 'something of the nature is in the Founder's Will': thus after 400 years Henry VI's wishes were still being taken into account). The rest of the buildings of King's do not come up to Gibbs' Building: the great range to the south of the court and to the south of the even larger lawn at the Backs is Victorian and later, and so is the stone screen (Wilkins, 1823–8) that fills in the east of the Great Court along King's Parade. The latter has been praised by many competent critics but I must beg to be excused. We can only be thankful that it is no bigger.

The head of King's is entitled 'Provost', and not 'Master' as in other colleges. Until 1851 King's men were not subject to the authority of the university proctors, and they were not allowed to take any footling examinations to get their degrees: these were conferred automatically. Eton men who went to King's and later wished to stay on after having been granted their degrees almost automatically became Fellows, and could 'keep' in fairly luxurious rooms, dine in Hall, and – unless they wanted to do so – perform no visible tasks at all. This gave rise to a splendid race of eccentrics. E. F. Benson, in his most delightful book about Cambridge, *As We Were*, describes several of these gentlemen. One in particular was of the most engaging habits. He 'never emerged except in the evening gloaming. He then shuffled out on to the big lawn, with a stick in his hand, and prodded with it at the worms in the grass, muttering to himself: "Ah, damn ye: ye haven't got me yet!" He said with Dr Faustus, "This feeds my soul," and after this physical refreshment, he returned to his rooms till the same hour the next day.'

But Fellows nowadays have to prove their scholarship in order to get their Fellowships, and thereafter justify themselves in some tangible way; and scholars from Eton do not automatically become Fellows of King's.

After King's, **Queens'**. Some might say that this is the choicest and the most anciently beautiful of the Cambridge colleges. Certainly it contains the greatest mass of Tudor building.

It is interesting to seek a reason for this. There is a very great deal of earlier-than-Tudor and Tudor building in Cambridge colleges, but it was almost all of it ashlared, or covered with dressed stone, in the seventeenth and eighteenth centuries.

The two queens who founded it were Margaret of Anjou and Elizabeth Woodville. While her husband, Henry VI, was founding King's, Margaret of Anjou, not to be outdone, took over Queens', and she was only eighteen when she did it. Elizabeth Woodville, wife of Edward IV, refounded and endowed the college, saying that she should become co-foundress by right of succession. The man who actually did the work was Andrew Doket, Rector of St Botolph's, whose patroness Queen Margaret was, and he named the college after St Bernard.

It was built on the site of a house of Carmelite friars, who came to the place after they had often found themselves going through floods to reach Cambridge from Newnham, the present site of the famous women's college. Doket started St Bernard's in 1446, Queen Margaret took it over two years later, and Queen Elizabeth Woodville in 1465, after Margaret and her husband had been defeated in the Wars of the Roses. Margaret of Anjou wished to found a college 'to laud and honneure of sexe feminine'! What a pity she did not go the whole hog and make it *for* women. It was not until 1869 that the need of the 'sexe feminine' for higher education was realized and Girton was founded.

But if we want to know what a college looked like in the fifteenth century – or a great manor house for that matter – we can find out by going to Queens'. It is as important a monument, in its way, as the medieval warehouses of King's Lynn are in theirs. If we wish to see great dwellings we will have to go to Schleswig Holstein, in the Jutland Peninsula, for there are several (although Gifford's Hall, Stoke-by-Nayland, and Oxburgh Hall, Norfolk, are not dissimilar).

The Principal Court, into which one enters from Queens' Lane through the Great Gatehouse (the latter hardly to be seen entire, because of the narrowness of Queens' Lane) is all fifteenth century, planned and built as one unit by one builder; and he is thought to have been Reginald Ely who was responsible for the beginnings of King's Chapel.

It is of clunch faced with red brick, and it makes you deplore the cold white brick – 'public convenience brick' – used in Trinity Great Gate and Jesus College and used so much, alas, ever since.

The old red Tudor brick is so beautiful and mellow.

The tower in the south-west is still called Erasmus's Tower, for it was at the top of it that he kept his rooms. Erasmus may have been lured to Cambridge by his friend Bishop Fisher, who, as well as Sir Thomas More, wished to broaden the barren and pettifogging teachings of the medieval schoolmen by the introduction of the classical spirit. Erasmus brought the study of Greek to the university, and something of the Greek pagan freedom of mind. Although he lived and died a Catholic his teaching led up to the Protestant Reformation; and in later years Protestants favoured him and the Catholics did not. Even to the extent that, when the Protestants were in power in Cambridge, they enforced the Erasmian pronunciation of Greek (which was quite wrong) and when the Catholics were in power they disallowed it. As the Protestants triumphed in the end the Erasmian pronunciation prevailed.

But standing in this Principal Court, with the Great Gate behind us, we can see what was the plan of many a great country house of medieval times.

On our right is the old chapel, then a passage, then the library, then round the corner – i.e. facing us – the great hall, then the Screens passage, then the kitchens and buttery (facing us but on the left), then the south-west corner with Erasmus's Tower then, round another corner again, the south range which is dwelling chambers.

The old chapel is no longer a chapel; but now a reading and lecture room. It has some good original glass in it still. There is a great and most curious sundial over the old chapel, early seventeenth century, commonly credited to Sir Isaac Newton but actually there before he was born. The present chapel is late Victorian (by Bodley), and for a man in a hurry is not worth going to see.

Above the Screens passage are the Royal Arms of 1557. To enter the hall is to be nearly knocked over by a blinding burst of jolly Victorian colour, supposed to have been done, in part, by William Morris. It is a regular fairground, but very likely the roof was originally painted in much such a fashion. The fireplace was restored in the 1860s and the tiles above it are by Morris – the figures designed by Ford Madox Brown. Elizabeth Woodville – a very pretty girl although she was a queen – is in the painting behind

416

Blickling Hall (*above*), was built in the early 17th century where was once a manor of King Harold of England. The house is much bigger than it looks from this picture, because it is deeper than it is wide. Holkham Hall (*below*), one of the most lavish exercises of the Palladian in England.

A complete absence of building stone (save flint) forced the eastern counties to develop brick to a high art. *Top*, Melford Hall. *Centre*, Oxburgh. *Below*, Hengrave Hall.

the president's chair. The head of Queens', incidentally, is the 'President', not the 'Master'.

Through Screens passage we come to Cloister Court, which takes us right back into the age of the Tudors. In fact it is not a bad idea to come to Queens' for the first time from the river side, so as to enter this court first.

But approached from the Screens we see in front of us the president's lodge, a most spectacular Tudor building with a brick cloister below, and above two stories of typically East Anglian stud timbering – the upper storey is the long and spectacularly beautiful President's Gallery. This gallery, late sixteenth century, is much like the long gallery of many an Elizabethan great house – there is one at Sawston. Quite what the purpose of it was is hard to see (although it is supposed to have been for exercise); it would certainly be a most uncomfortable room to sit in, although this one at Queens' is beautiful within as without.

This block of Tudor buildings is very well seen from outside the Cloister Court: from the college garden to the north. Some of the timbering, especially the curved pieces, was put in during a restoration of 1911; and it is these curved beams that to my eye at least look out of place: a consciously 'rustic' effect in what should have been a highly finished and sophisticated building, and more Midland in feeling than East Anglian anyway. Erasmus's Chair, by the way, a weighty seat for a weighty scholar, is in the President's Gallery.

The brick part of the president's lodge side, which rises straight up from the waters of the River Cam, is older than the timbered, in fact of about 1460. There are filled-in arches at water-level – surely landing bays in the days when the colleges drew their fuel (peat from the Fens), wine, and imported provender, from the Fen lighters? Such arches can be seen in the shops of many a Dutch shop or warehouse leading into tunnels under the canal-side road in such cities as Dordrecht.

But perhaps this Cloister Court of Queens' is one of the most romantic and evocative in Cambridge (although there are so many others that could stake a claim!)

Over the Cam here there is a wooden bridge which is called the Mathematical Bridge and is sometimes attributed, like so much

417

else, to Sir Isaac Newton. It was built in 1749, probably actually to the design of a man named Etheridge, and it was designed so cunningly that it held together with no fastenings: neither bolt, nail, nor dowel, being knitted into one by strange mathematical forces. Alas, some unhappy chap in the Victorian age took it to pieces to see how it worked and was unable to put it together again, and so now it is fastened with ordinary nuts and bolts like other non-mathematical bridges. The bridge upstream of it, Silver Street Bridge, is a very old-established bridge (although not as old as the Great Bridge of Magdalene Street – a modern structure now but on the site of an almost primordial bridge), replaced in 1950. For centuries Silver Street was a toll bridge, and the toll collector was a hermit – fulfilling thus a common office of hermits in early days.

St Catharine's was founded by Robert Woodlarke in 1473. Woodlarke was then 3rd Provost of King's, and responsible for much of the administrative detail of King's Chapel. He came of a wealthy family and spent much of his fortune on St Catharine's (which he named for the Patron Saint of Learning), and he also lent much money to the king to help to build King's and we hear that he did not get it back. None of his original buildings survives at St Catharine's: most of the structure is seventeenth century or later. Robert Grumbold, who did so much of Clare, did much of this – including the chapel, which is well worth seeing for lovers of the Baroque.

Corpus Christi was unfortunately much knocked about in the nineteenth century: Wilkins, who did the stone screen along King's Parade, destroyed a chapel of 1579 to put up his tasteless battlemented 'Gothic' buildings. But thank God he spared the Old Court: perhaps the most perfect ensemble of fourteenth-century collegiate buildings in England.

Corpus is the only college founded by the guilds: the guild of Corpus Christi and that of St Mary combining to start it. Their object was to train clergy to officiate in their own churches; and when the college was founded it had but a master, two scholars, and two servants. These medieval guilds were less trade unions, as many people suppose them to have been, than friendly societies and religious and ceremonial bodies. A guild could be composed of people from many different trades, every member contributed to it and, at real need, could draw from it. Lawsuits between members were not allowed until all the resources of the guild as mediator had failed, prices and conditions of labour were laid down, and elaborate religious ceremonial in the guild's own church was carried out. To see such guild ceremonial today we would have to go to Spain. Corpus Christi was by far the richer of the two guilds founding the college, and therefore the latter retains its name.

The original hall is now kitchens, in the Old Court. The chapel has nice French sixteenth-century glass in the windows with figures and faces of photographic realism, but the east window is Victorian. The chancel, with its blind arcading in the Early English style and its ogee arches, is by Blomfield, 1870.

The two things to see in this college are the Old Court, and the library. The library, castellated like a fortress and with great 'Tudor' windows, contains the best collection of Anglo-Saxon manuscripts in the world, besides an incomparable selection of other very ancient books. The books were collected by Matthew Parker, Master of Corpus from 1544 to 1553 and later Archbishop of Canterbury. As head of the post-Reformation Anglican Church he was much concerned to demonstrate that Christianity was of ancient and venerable foundation in the British Isles, and not just a Roman religion; and to this end he made this astonishing collection of very early books – easy enough to make at that moment in history because of the break-up of the monasteries. He thus saved at least some priceless works from being used for lighting fires. He collected the earliest known version of the Anglo-Saxon Chronicle, the *Canterbury Gospel* – said to have been sent by Pope Gregory to St Augustine when he was coming to England to convert the heathen in AD 597 – and the 'Bury Bible', written and illuminated superbly by the monks of Bury St Edmunds Abbey and said to be the finest English twelfth-century book existing, and very many Celtic manuscripts.

Security in this library is, most rightly, intense. You cannot borrow the original Anglo-Saxon Chronicle and take it back to your hotel. Archbishop Parker laid it down, when he presented the books, that in the event of more than so many of them being lost the remainder should be taken away from Corpus and given to Caius, and in the event of Caius losing any then Trinity Hall should have them. Both these latter colleges, therefore, have the right of inspection in Corpus library.

The Old Court is the prize piece of Corpus Christi. Its six-hundred-year-old walls are of clunch, but plastered, as chalk often is to protect it from the weather. The buttresses and garrets are later, about 1500. The roofs are of small multi-coloured tiles peculiar to Cambridgeshire, and which give them a warm tweedy texture. And, further, the Anglo-Saxon tower of St Benet's church can be seen over the roofs – looking so different from any later architecture that it seems to come from another world, as well as from almost another millennium, and another civilization. The Old Court is connected with St Benet's by a sixteenth-century red-brick corridor – best seen from Free School Lane.

Farther down the street **Pembroke College**. Pembroke was founded by a French girl, Marie, daughter of Guy de Chatillon, Count of St Pol, and widow of Amoryde, or Aymer, de Valence, Earl of Pembroke, in 1346. Aymer de Valence, who was a most important nobleman at the court of the first two Edwards, was about fifty when he married Marie at about seventeen. The legend is that he was killed on their nuptial night before her eyes by a (surely over-zealous) wedding guest in a friendly joust. Gray writes of:

> *Sad Chatillon, on her bridal morn*
> *Who wept beside her bleeding love.*

In fact he died three years after the wedding – probably of apoplexy. After her widowhood she became great friends with another widow of enormous wealth, the Lady de Clare who founded Clare College, and it was perhaps the latter's influence that caused this young French girl to found a college herself.

The earliest parts of the fabric of the college are on the corner of Pembroke Street and Trumpington Street: this is a fourteenth-century building, although encased in sixteenth-century brick in places and nineteenth-century stone in others. At the west end of it is the Old Chapel, now called the Old Library; the oldest collegiate chapel in Cambridge, licensed to celebrate the Office by a Papal Bull of 1354 (of course Jesus Chapel is much older, but started life as a nuns' church). It was re-faced with brick in 1663 and later converted into a library. It has a notable ceiling done in the seventeenth century by Henry Doogood, who did much stucco-work in Wren churches.

The New Chapel of Pembroke is a most important building, being the first essay into architecture by Christopher Wren.

His uncle, Dr Matthew Wren, Bishop of Ely, had for eighteen years been immured in prison by the Puritans for his religious beliefs (at least they didn't burn him up), and when he got out he said to his nephew words to the effect of: 'You're a mathematician – build us a chapel.'

And his nephew did. Then in his thirties, and never an architect, he turned his hand to the job and designed the building we see, and we see it best from across Trumpington Street from the gate of Little St Mary's, where it shows a west end of quiet, well-mannered but decorative Corinthian classicism. The other end of the building is not Wren, for the Victorians had the presumption to add a chancel on to it, the second George G. Scott doing his best with the job in 1880. Wren's part of the interior has a lovely plaster ceiling, and there is a painting of the Deposition after Barocci, with a delicate girlish face of Mary.

Pembroke has the best piece of medieval plate in Cambridge (it was always too easy to melt old silver down and turn it into something more in accord with the latest fashion). This is the Foundress's Cup, which is silver gilt and has written on it on one side 'M.V. help. at. need.' and on the other 'drenk and mak gud cher.' This is not normally on view.

Gray, Edmund Spenser and Pitt the Younger were all at Pembroke. Gray kept his rooms in Peterhouse until, legend says, he was lured out of his window one night by shouts of 'Fire!' from down below. He swarmed down a rope which he always kept in a somehow very Thurberesque way by his window for just such an occasion, for he had a phobia about fire. He 'landed', if that is the right word, in a large tub of water, placed there for his reception by the same undergraduates who had called 'Fire!'. In dudgeon he left Peterhouse, and moved across the road into Pembroke.

421

Peterhouse, whence the poet moved, was the very first of the Cambridge colleges. In 1281 Hugh de Balsham, Bishop of Ely and a Cambridgeshire man, founded a college for secular scholars who were to live alongside the regular canons of the old-established Hospital of St John. This arrangement was not a success – 'the scholars being perhaps too wise, and the brethren possibly over-good', and the college was moved next door to what was St Peter's Church (hence 'Peterhouse') but which has now been altered to the church of St Mary the Less.

De Balsham moulded his college on Merton in Oxford (which had been founded in 1265). Hugh de Balsham died two years after the move was made, but he left 300 marks with which was bought land for the still-existing hall.

This hall, alas, was fallen upon by Sir G. G. Scott, like so much else in Cambridge, in 1868; but it still has good old tables and benches, a lovely Tudor cast-iron fireplace with fireback and tiles by William Morris, the walls are Morris-stencilled and there is Morris glass in the windows (made, at least, by the Morris Company but designed by Burne-Jones and Madox Brown). There is a lovely oak-panelled Combination Room, also with a Morris fireback.

Behind Peterhouse is the Grove, separated from Coe Fen and the Cam by a very ancient wall (a blocked gateway has the arms of Bishop Hotham of 1316 on it), and there is a glorious garden full of fine trees. Coe Fen is beautiful and peaceful and we hope safe from the twentieth century. If you wish to see the old Peterhouse, unfaced with eighteenth-century ashlar, go into the churchyard of St Mary's the Less.

The chapel of Peterhouse is an interesting building half Perpendicular, half classical, completed in 1636 by the Dr Matthew Wren who asked his nephew, Christopher, to make the designs for Pembroke Chapel over the road. Dr Wren made this chapel in fulfilment of a vow which he made during his eighteen years' imprisonment by the Puritans. The chapel was originally brick, but was faced with stone in the 1660s, and much altered then too. The inside is gorgeous: golden suns in the ceiling, old panelling in the walls, vivid coloured glass – galumphing German of the 1850s in most of the windows but Flemish of 1639 in the east window which is said to be from a design by Rubens for his *Crucifixion*.

North of the chapel, abutting the street, is a fine Palladian building by Burrough of 1738–42. The Principal Court is civilized and urbane, without a jarring note in it: nicely carved barge-boards over fifteenth-century building at east end of south range.

Peterhouse was the college of the notorious Dr Perne, who was master through several reigns and changes in religion. He was 'of such accommodating breadth of view' that he was able to switch from one religion to another at the drop of a hat – or at the accession of a sovereign. In Edward VI's reign he was so Protestant that he burned many of the books in the university library because they were too Catholic, in Mary Tudor's reign he was so Catholic that he went to the trouble of digging up the interred bodies of two German Protestant scholars – Bucer and Fagius – and burning them on Market Hill because they were too Protestant, and when Elizabeth came to the throne he was once more convinced of the rightness of Protestantism and preached the sermon at the service in which the two Germans were reinstated in respectability, albeit that their bodies couldn't be buried again having been burned up. He gave rise amongst the undergraduates to the pseudo-Latin verb *pernare*, to change one's opinions; and on a weathercock in Cambridge his initials A.P. were taken to mean 'A Protestant' or 'A Papist' whichever way the wind blew.

Fitzwilliam Street brings us to **Downing College**, if we want to go there, which is Grecian, Grecian, all the way by that versatile man William Wilkins (who died in 1839).

There are even newer colleges. There is **Churchill**, on Madingley Road, by Messrs Richard Sheppard, Robson and Partners (we have gone a long way from the illiterate master mason!) and it is brick and fortress-like, simple and workmanlike, and much praised by good critics.

Fitzwilliam House, of Huntingdon Road, has a hall which, although it might look more at home in Fatehpur Sikri than in East Anglia, is a splendid and exuberant piece of architecture. Nicholas Taylor, in that very good little book *Cambridge New Architecture*, describes it as 'a riot of sculptural invention'.

New Hall, the new college for women, has a hall that looks rather like an atomic reactor pile surrounded by ventilators of the London

Underground. We have come a long way from King's College Chapel.

Darwin, **Wolfson** and **Robinson** may one day settle into the dignified academic ambience; but it will take a few centuries yet.

CHAPTER 23

Cambridge:
University and Town

Having made our circuit of the colleges, we can now make another one of the churches, museums, and other public places, and of the buildings of the university proper.

Of the latter there is the **Senate House**, best seen from the tower of Great St Mary's, from where it looks like a splendid model. From below, as indeed from above, it appears a most accomplished piece of early Georgian Classicism, and was designed by James Gibbs and built in 1722. Here are held the 'Congregations' of the Senate which rules the university. A proposal for new legislation – called a 'grace' – was until recently read aloud by the proctor dressed in his robes. If any member, opposing it, said 'Non placet' the proctor cried 'Ad scrutinum!' and the 'Placets' and 'Non-Placets' then divided and were counted.

Part of the **Old University Library**, rather hidden to the west of the Senate, was built in 1836–42 by the architect C. R. Cockerell in a rather free Grecian style; but the building which stands at right-angles to the Senate, thus forming a rough open-sided quad-rangle with the Senate and King's College Chapel, is pure and pretty Palladian by Burrough, about 1754.

Behind it are the **Old Schools**, for long the only buildings belong-ing to the university and not to a specific college. The most interesting thing about them is the Great Gatehouse which was once the gatehouse of King's College, before its translation to the other side of its chapel. Now, alas, the gatehouse is set in a vast Victorian pile – the university offices. The Great Gatehouse of King's was the second great gateway built in Cambridge, the first of course being the 'Clock Tower', or King Edward III's Tower, of Trinity.

Most of the books of the old library (and its beautiful old book-cases) have gone to the hideous new library over the river; but there is still a thirteenth-century *Life of Edward the Confessor*, the illustrations of which have been used to help with modern coronations; and one of the very earliest manuscripts of the Gospels.

Of museums, the **Fitzwilliam** is one of the best museums in the country. Certainly it is one of the pleasantest and most delightful; and there are not enough hours in the day to spend in it.

It is massive Victorian Greek, or neo-Greek, or neo-neo-Greek, in Trumpington Street. Viscount Fitzwilliam made his bequest in 1816; but the building did not get finished until 1875 and by then it had cost a cool £115,000. Inside it is one of the best collections of works of art that may be seen anywhere. It is far far beyond the scale of any 'provincial museum', and in the scope of this book it would be impossible more than to hint at the contents or list the many bequests made over the years.

There is a noteworthy Egyptian section, a fine collection of Turner watercolours, a wonderful collection of medieval illumi-nated manuscripts from all over Europe (almost too many, one might think). Of things which I feel it would be wrong to miss there is, perhaps first of all, the fifteenth- and sixteenth-century Print Room. Dürers and other German draughtsmen – note the detail of *Christ Carrying the Cross* by Martin Schongauer; the loveliest Renoir of all, *Le Retour des Champs*, in the Impressionist Room, Room No V. In Room VI, the Upper Marley Gallery, the two spirited *Siege of Troy* pictures, all in Renaissance costume, by Biagio de Antonio, fifteenth century (numbers 44 and 45), and the much-reproduced *St Sebastian* by Lorenzo de Credi.

In the Italian Room, Room VII, the lovely bright Canaletto-like *Grand Canal* by Bellotto and the actual Canaletto *Interior of the Doge's Palace*, and do not miss the majolica ware in the side cases. There is also a most moving *Virgin and Child with Saints and Doves* by Marco Basaiti.

In the Flemish Room, Room X, there is a transporting early sixteenth-century reredos, *The Deposition*, and an unforgettable

Village Fête by Breughel the Younger (after the Elder) with the story of the pedlar being enacted on an outdoor stage (where the wronged husband gets carried home inside the pedlar's basket and, while thus hidden catches his wife *flagrante delicto*). In the next room (Room XI No 73) is another *Village Fête* by Jan Steen – note the fellow communing with the pig in the gutter which reminds us of the song which ends: 'And the *pig* got up and walked away.' Above it is a picture of a Dutch frigate seriously taken aback – either the officer of the watch was lax, or very unlucky. And the horrific *Arctic Adventure* by Honduis, nearby.

In Room LX, the Octagon, some lovely small Turner water-colours, a couple of little Cotmans for Norfolkmen, some Constables including a study for *The Lock* which takes you back with a jolt to the Essex–Suffolk border country, a fine, colour-glowing, Samuel Palmer (that most underrated artist), a Blake *Ascension*.

The Spanish Room, No VIII, has a stunning *Road to Calvary* by Antonio and Diego Sanchez, late fifteenth century, with a clean-shaven Christ. There are two large Murillos – the *Vision of Fra Lauterio* particularly notable. In Room II are some good English School: a big Reynolds, *Near Norwich* by James Stark, Constable's *Hampstead Heath*, some Blake manuscripts and water-colours in glass cases, which miss not, and the famous *Last of England* by Ford Madox Brown.

In the Central Gallery are some Hogarths (including some, not to be missed, in a glass case) and there are some more Gainsboroughs. In Room I my eye is always taken by the Sickerts, the Christopher Wood, some Stanley Spencer suburb-scapes, a Graham Sutherland *Deposition*, and *Thomas Hardy* by Augustus John. Also most noteworthy Epsteins – the loveliest being *Oriel Ross*, and there is *Einstein* by Epstein.

These items that I have mentioned are a drop in the ocean in this great museum – idiosyncratic choices of my own. To walk into the Upper Marley Gallery (Room VI) is to plunge into a great bath of golden colour – to run a gauntlet of transcending glowing works of art – it is an almost overwhelming experience. There is so much to see in Cambridge that people are apt to miss the Fitzwilliam on the grounds that, well after all many cities have a museum but how many have a thirteenth-century university? This

427

is a mistake, and perhaps a special journey should be made to Cambridge to see the Fitzwilliam alone.

There is another little museum, the **Folk Museum** in Castle Street over Magdalene Bridge, displaying furniture, tools and domestic articles from several centuries in a building converted in 1936 from the old White Horse Inn. Near it, behind Northampton Street, is the **School of Pythagoras**, never a school, nothing to do with Pythagoras, but late twelfth century and thus perhaps the oldest dwelling house in this country, but now a theatre and part of St John's College. This was bought by Merton to found the first English college in, but unfortunately he thought better of this and went to Oxford instead and founded it there, not realizing at the time that he was founding it in what was to become a vast and suffocating motor-car manufacturing conurbation.

Castle Mound, nearby, is worth climbing for the view.

Of churches there is **St Benet's**, hard by Corpus Christi College, and connected to it, as we may have seen, by a covered passageway. The tower of this is one of the most complete pieces of Anglo-Saxon building in this country, and was possibly the parish church of the East Anglian settlement on the east of the Cam, when the Mercians occupied the castle on the other bank. (There are grounds, though, for dating the existing building to the reign of Canute, the Danish King of England; but this does not make it any less East Anglian, for it would have been built by the Christianized East Anglians and not by the recently pagan Danish invaders.)

The tower is an astonishing Saxon survival. It has the typical long-and-short work in its corners (alternate vertical and horizontal stones which cannot have had much binding-power – a fact which may be one of the reason why there is so little pre-Norman work left standing beyond the round towers which had no corners, apart from the corner of the nave and some walling of the chancel) and it has double sound-holes of a strange shape. The tower arch, inside, is a most barbaric piece of architecture – very reminiscent of medieval Ethiopian cave-sculpture, with the mouldings of the arch springing from the backs of the most strange beasts, and long-and-short work, again, in the jambs. The rest of the church has been altered in various ages; but there are still Saxon components to be seen. The church today is unusual in that it is a parish church, but served by Anglican Franciscans sent from their mother house at Cerne Abbas in Dorset. A former Clerk of this parish was Fabian Stedman, born 1631, who was 'the Father of English change ringing', i.e. he invented the art of ringing bells as we know it today.

Great St Mary's is a big and grand Perpendicular church, which Cambridge people like to compare with the greatest wool churches of Suffolk and Norfolk (it's very fine but it doesn't *really* compare!), and it is well worth while climbing to the top of the tower for the best view that you can get, short of hiring a helicopter, of the city. The church may have been designed by Wastell, who worked on Lavenham church as well as King's Chapel.

Great St Mary's is the university church; and for centuries has been bound up with the life of the university. For years it was used for all sorts of secular uses, as indeed churches all were and churches should still be. Scholars disputed in it to gain their tripos (a B.A. had to sit on a three-legged stool to deliver a satirical speech – hence the name); in the Puritan age a great gallery was built on which the fellows sat at ceremonials with their backs to the east end (in refutation of both *east-worship* and *table-worship*); and there are even now ugly galleries over the aisles, for spectators at university ceremonies. Twice a term, still, the university sermon is preached – by a select preacher invited from afar for his learning. To have 'Select Preacher' after your entry in Crockfords is much desired by prominent divines. When the Assizes are held in Cambridge, an Assize Sermon is preached, with great pomp and ceremony, and, incidentally, the Judge has right of residence in the Master of Trinity's Lodge, the Master having to move out to make way for him.

There is a sensitive wood carving of the Madonna and Child near the south door, and Christ in Majesty in gilded wood by Alan Durst over the altar, splendid and effective, but not as big perhaps, and as commanding, as a Majestas should be. This was done in 1960.

But the things that are really striking to the eye about this church are the great late Perpendicular arcade (although spoilt by the galleries already mentioned), the clerestory, and the wide and generous chancel arch.

St Mary the Less, or **Little St Mary's**, hard by Peterhouse, is a little gem of the Decorated period, a period for which Cambridgeshire is famous.

It has a simple, barn-like plan, and has a fascinating chapel down in a crypt. Richard Crawshaw, the poet, was a parson here in 1639, and there is a monument to Richard Washington who was incumbent here at the beginning of the eighteenth century. His coat of arms was the Stars and Stripes and his crest an eagle, and it was an illustrious member of his family who gave the USA her flag and emblem.

Holy Sepulchre, the Round Church, opposite St John's, might be the most fascinating building in England, but unfortunately the Victorians visited upon it the full wrath of their restoration. They were egged on by the Camden Society; and it seems almost unbelievable that Salvin, their architect, should have chosen to build on to this glorious and purely Norman building a chancel in imitation Decorated!

The church was built about 1130, on the plan of the Holy Sepulchre in Jerusalem. It is probable that the design was influenced by the returning Crusaders. And, restoration or not, it is still a good experience to stand inside 'the Round', as the nave of the church is called, after having put a coin in the little box by the door to switch on the dome lights.

Over Magdalene Bridge is the fascinating little church of **St Peter**. This may well have been the Christianized Mercian answer to the East Anglian St Benet's over the river, and it is said to stand on the site of an earlier fane, a temple to Diana. The door and the font are Norman, the latter wildly barbaric, with mermen with twin tails. There is nothing much *to* this little church, which was practically rebuilt in 1781; but its yard – a slight hill in that flat land – shaded by sycamore and chestnut trees, is a place of such perfect peace and refreshment that it is a good place for the weary sightseer to retire to.

Finally, but not least, **St Mary Magdalene** on the Newmarket Road, just over the railway lines. This is bang in the deplorable suburb of Barnwell, is dumped by the railway tracks, and is in just about the most degrading and slummy position imaginable. This setting simply adds to the wonder of it – the traveller, bounding unwitting in his horseless carriage into Cambridge from the Newmarket direction through the crummy outskirts of the city, is suddenly struck and delighted by this vision of better things.

It is solidly Norman and amazingly unspoiled. The roof and east window are new, but fitting: the rest is original; and the church is not only real Norman but the choicest kind of Norman at that. It is said that it was originally the chapel of a leper hospital at Stourbridge, endowed by King John with money from the mighty Stourbridge Fair.

In hot weather, as the visitor will speedily find, **the 'Backs'** (area between the big colleges and the River Cam) are places of great delight, and furthermore a boat can be hired at any of the boat-hiring staithes and punted, paddled, or sculled gently up and down the river. Surely this must be one of the most civilized strips of water in the world; and the voyage up to Grantchester in the right weather and the right company surpasses all expectations.

Another resort in hot weather, or in very cold for a different reason, is the **university botanic garden**. In cold weather this is fine because of its hot houses – particularly the Tropical House which makes one long for better climes. This latter is the place to resort to when the freezing winds come whistling across the flat Fens from the equally flat steppes of Siberia.

Outside there is a very good rock garden, a scented garden, a terrace garden, a winter garden, a fine collection of trees and shrubs and herbaceous plants, and a chronological bed in which we can see at what date different plants were discovered by explorers.

In going through Trumpington Street towards the botanic garden we will have noticed two little rivers running in the gutters each side, making the newcomer think of burst hydrants. These are the 'Rivers' Pem and Pot, or Pet. They are exactly like the *jubes* in Tehran in Persia, but as you will in Persia you will not in Cambridge notice people washing the baby upstream in them while other people draw water for their tea downstream. If we follow them up, and trace their courses underground, we will eventually come to Hobson's Conduit, a cheerful monument of 1614 to Thomas Hobson the originator of the expression 'Hobson's Choice'. Peterhouse is irreverently called 'Pothouse' because of its nearness to the 'River Pot' as much as because of the fame of its beer.

Hobson, many times Mayor of Cambridge, was also owner of a big carrier's business and livery stable. In the latter he kept no fewer than 'forty good cattle', but if you wanted to hire one you had to take the one he chose for you and not necessarily the one you wanted yourself: hence the immortal expression. He lived from the reign of Henry VIII to that of Charles I, has a street named after him, his portrait is in the Guildhall, and he made possible the scheme (actually thought of by the famous Dr Perne) to bring the waters of a brook into Cambridge, and run them along the street in the 'jubes' we have noticed.

CHAPTER 24

North-east Cambridgeshire

If we leave Cambridge on the Newmarket Road we shortly come to **Stow Cum Quy**, where there is little to see excepting a military brass of John Ansty, 1460.

Bottisham looks good across the flat land from the Newmarket Road, because it is well set back from it, and is seen as a compact village dominated by a lovely and most interesting church.

To understand the series of villages that we are now setting out to see, it must be realized that they are 'shore' villages: they were, when they were built, along the shores of the watery Fens, just as are the Norfolk and Suffolk villages that we have already seen – between Mildenhall and Northwold. And just as the Norfolk and Suffolk 'shore' villages each has a 'hythe', or satellite port village, to which ships or Fen Lighters could come, so each of these Cambridgeshire equivalents has its 'lode'. The lode hamlets are set at the heads of long artificial cuts from the River Cam: their parent villages are built on the drier and firmer chalk uplands and connected to their ports by road. The word 'lode' refers to the watercourse.

Bottisham is a large village, alas being made larger by much very undistinguished modern building; but the centre of the village is still attractive, with good old Cambridgeshire houses. Here is the second of the experimental 'Village Colleges' of Cambridgeshire, architecturally dull but no doubt culturally lively. North of the churchyard is a very attractive group of dwellings called 'The Arch', which was originally a parish rehousing scheme of about 1840. The dwellings are set about a courtyard of mellow brick roofed by Suffolk pantiles and are most distinguished architecturally. This block could well serve as a model for designers of council houses, who, with few exceptions, sorely need a model of some kind.

433

The church is very interesting, as indeed are most of the churches of the old Fenland shore. Being thirteenth and early fourteenth century much of it is transitional between Early English and Decorated. These shoreline churches speak of great prosperity in the Decorated period – before the great cloth export boom which turned trade away from the Wash ports to Norwich and Ipswich. The nave, dated *c.* 1310, is very fine and there is a lovely arcade of the most vigorous period of English Gothic, and there are blind arcades, both inside and out, on the aisle walls. There is a Perpendicular rood screen of stone (the vicar dates it 1474), and two quite lovely Decorated parclose screens. Note the fluting around the clerestory and also the sedilia and piscina. There is a monument to Sir Roger and Lady Jenyns, which depicts them both sitting on the grass apparently just about to have a picnic.

Bottisham has its lode, and this one is just called Lode, *tout simple*.

Lode is an interesting little place, with much thatch (a material right on the doorstep, because it could be floated up from Wicken Fen in punts), and Cambridge white brick. A long straight 'cut', or canal, runs to it, the lode itself, and next to this is a road, and if we drive down this we get a good view, on our right, of the real 'black peat' of the Fens: the soil is nearly as black as soot, soft and friable, and people say that it is worth its weight in gold. At the end of the track is a most lovely Fenland farmhouse with a roof of very small pantiles, and there is an ancient wooden sluice-gate of great interest to sluice-gate lovers.

Lode would be a fine place to lie in a boat if one wishes to visit, or even to work in, Cambridge. The willow-hung canal could be very attractive. South-west of Lode is **Anglesey Abbey**, now National Trust. It is the remains of an Augustinian priory founded in the twelfth century and since made into a private house, and has a grand eighteenth-century type garden stretching to the Fens, with good statuary and ornaments, and 'Emperor's' and 'Warrior's' Avenues started in 1926. It is open to the public and worth a visit.

Swaffham Bulbeck is another big village, and it also has its lode with its port-hamlet called **Commercial End** at the top of it. The size of Commercial End is an indication of its past importance as a port. There is a magnificent tiled warehouse down the most

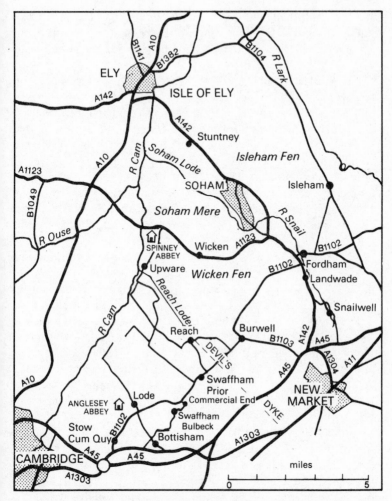

northerly lane leading to it, and several other buildings connected with storing cargoes.

Swaffham Bulbeck has beautiful green and extensive grasslands, willow-bordered, between it and the Cam. The church is mostly built of clunch with an Early English tower and the rest of it mostly fourteenth century, i.e. Decorated. There is a magnificent chest within, or rather a travelling altar: the lid opens to form a reredos and is embellished with good and most interesting carving. This is Italian, probably fifteenth century. There is also good fifteenth-century carved woodwork in the church: arm rests and poppy-heads with weird beasts and fishes.

The vicar of Bulbeck for the greater part of the nineteenth century was Leonard Blomefield, alias Jenyns. He was a close friend of Charles Darwin, and gave up his place in the *Beagle* to let Darwin go instead. He wrote Darwin's book of fishes for him when he got back, and otherwise acted as his amanuensis, and he also edited Gilbert White's writings and is said to have known *Selborne* practically off by heart. He and Darwin used to go for long nature rambles together, and one can imagine that in their days Swaffham Bulbeck would have been a good place for the job, with the Fens on one side, Newmarket Heath on the other, and the Brecklands not far away.

Swaffham Prior has two windmills, alas no longer working, one a tower mill in very good condition but hemmed in between a hideous water tower as high as itself, and a group of council houses. The village also has two churches in the same churchyard.

The churches are most interesting and impressive. Quite why there are two of them nobody seems to know. The lower one of the two, St Mary's, was once in the gift of Ely Abbey, having been granted to it by Brithnoth in the reign of Ethelred the Unready. As we shall discuss later, while dealing with Ely, this East Anglian hero gave Ely many gifts of churches and land as he was on his way to fight the disastrous Battle of Maldon. The church has a square Norman base to its tower with an octagon above it, and on top of that an Early English octagonal top with lancet windows. The lantern which was once at the top of it all was struck by lightning in the eighteenth century.

But by the time of the lightning strike the body of the church had been pulled down, and the church was decayed. But the superstitious parishioners took the lightning as an omen, and they would no longer worship in St Mary's Church. Nothing would do but they must move to the other church, and build a rather undistinguished Georgian nave to it. St Mary's won in the end, however; for its ruins were restored at the end of the nineteenth century, and now it is Saints Cyriac's and Julitta's which is being given over to the bats, swallows, and courting couples. St Cyriac died under the Diocletian persecution as a small boy while his mother, St Julitta, encouraged him to face martyrdom before she was herself immolated: at least that is one version of their story.

St Mary's is very notable for its strange tower, which is grand and impressive from within or without: note the vast thickness of the white clunch walls as seen through the tower arch. There is some early twentieth-century glass of strong period interest (its vogue will come!) with strong scenes from the trenches, the mountains of Switzerland, Wicken Fen, an ammunition factory, and other somewhat unrelated matter.

Baldwin Manor, near the village, is a wonderfully preserved and very beautiful Tudor timber-framed house which can be seen from the road: the goal aimed at, in fact, by every 'Detached Tudor Period Villa' on a hundred bypasses, and so signally missed. It is not open to the public.

Half a mile north-east brings the road to what looks like a long straight abandoned railway embankment. This is in fact the **Devil's Ditch**, which can be seen at this place to perfection. There is nothing to see, beyond what I have described; but, if one knows what it is, this earthwork is romantic, and is well worth going for a walk along.

It is a colossal earthwork. The total length is 7 miles, from the bottom of the ditch to the top of the bank is 60 feet and the width of bank and ditch together is 40 yards. Surely a vast amount of shifted earth, and the product of tremendous labour. Some archaeologists have dated it as pre-Roman, others as Roman and others even as Anglo-Saxon, but post-Roman it most probably was.

If we walk north-east along Devil's Ditch, or else take the road due north from Swaffham Prior (past, incidentally, the site of a Roman villa) we come to the northernmost end of the Ditch at Reach.

The Ditch here comes arbitrarily to an end. At one time it butted on to Reach Lode, a canal certainly dug by the Romans; but it was cut off, for I know not what reason, between 1743 and 1768 (a traveller visited it on both those dates – on the first it was intact, on the second cut).

Reach Lode was dug, one would imagine, for two purposes: for navigation like the other lodes of this old 'coast', and to form a defensive extension to Devil's Ditch.

Now **Reach** is the strangest little place, set around a wide irregular green, all quite unspoiled through not being quite beautiful enough for Cambridge commuters to want to come and live there. It is the remains of a much larger place, and is said to have once had its own fair which rivalled that of Stourbridge.

Roman remains have been dug up from the peat all down Reach Lode, the skull of a wild bull with a flint axe-head embedded in it was found there (my theory is that the wild bull got away with the axe-head in its head and subsequently fell in a swamp – otherwise why would not the hunter have recovered his weapon?); fossil remains of forests have been unearthed – layer upon layer as though forest after forest was destroyed by a new submergence of dry land. Many trunks of 'bog oak' have been dug up; one, discovered in 1909, was 130 feet long. The trees, falling into the swamp, have been perfectly preserved; as have the bones of bears, wolves, wild boars, aurochs, and wild cattle.

Reach was important beyond the other lodes of this inland 'shore', because here the navigable 'cut' runs right into the chalk, and so Reach has a very big quarry where the Romans dug clunch, and whence came the clunch to build the Lady Chapel of Ely and half the Cambridge colleges.

The Church of England church at Reach is so screamingly ugly that it might quite well engender a headache in a moderately sensitive person. It is a product of 1860. In complete contrast is the quiet and well-mannered little Nonconformist chapel: a pleasant building, and most meet for its purpose. Reach is a remote-feeling and self-contained little place, and there is an atmosphere of great antiquity and peace there.

Burwell, hard by, is a big village – nay a small town; and it must have had prosperity after most of the other Cambridgeshire villages had fallen on harder times, for its church is Perpendicular and very grand. It is still prosperous industrially, with a vast factory employing over 400 people making Tillotson's corrugated cardboard cases. In the recreation garden of the factory is a circular pavilion like the Tea House of the August Moon, looking very exotic and charming, and completely un-East Anglian.

Burwell church has a glorious roof, inside, and most of it original; with the liveliest carvings of angels and winged creatures and animals of a kind that we will never recognize as akin to the ones we see in the zoo. Over the altar steps is a fine boss carved as a pelican, from which used to hang the pyx containing the Reserved Sacrament. In the chancel are lavishly carved niches, and a fine roof, with corbels carved as angels playing stringed instruments. There is a brass to John Lawrence de Wardeboys. This divine had his brass made before his death, as many people did; and he had it engraved with a portrait of himself arrayed in a mitre and the fine robes of the Abbot of Ramsey, which at that time he was. However, came the Reformation, and the Dissolution, and de Wardeboys received a pension from Henry VIII for his eagerness in handing over his abbey for dismantling; and so he had the brass cut in half, and half of it turned over and another portrait of himself engraved on it – in humble clerical garb: more fitting for the changed conditions. To add to the confusion the original brass itself was purloined from another use, for the reverse of the canopy shows a much earlier portrait of a deacon.

There was a castle at Burwell: now earthworks only, outside which one of the great rebels or outlaws who took refuge in the Fens was killed by an arrow. This was Geoffrey de Mandeville, who flourished as an outlaw and bandit during the nineteen years' war between King Stephen and Queen Matilda.

Burwell had a great disaster. In 1727 a company of strolling players, on their way to Stourbridge Fair, gave a performance in a Burwell barn. So many people clamoured for admittance that the doors were nailed up to prevent any more getting in, the place caught fire and eighty-two people were burned to death and buried in one pit in Burwell churchyard. In 1774 an old man confessed on his deathbed that it was he who, for some small spite, had started the fire.

Fordham is the next of this series of fine Cambridgeshire 'coastal' villages: the tiny Snail comes down to it from **Snailwell** which has a church with a Norman round tower and some lovely Decorated tracery.

But Fordham itself has its navigation, for it could be reached by Fen lighter from Soham Lode. It has a fine and most unusual

439

church, with a Lady Chapel placed as is the Lady Chapel of Ely Cathedral in relation to the church, with a vaulted, crypt-like, lower storey which acts as a porch for the church, and another chapel above it with very beautiful Decorated windows. There are Norman windows in the west end of the north aisle, a restored Early English chancel, the eastern piers of the arcades are Early English – the rest are splendid Decorated, and the most glorious arcades they are, with painted spandrels. There is a splendid soaring tower-arch, and more painted decoration within it.

Landwade, just south of Fordham, has a most unspoiled church in a semi-private park, full of monuments to departed Cottons. Good screen and glass fragments.

If we take the Soham Road and turn first left we come to Wicken, and, more especially, to Wicken Fen.

Wicken itself is a pretty village with much reed thatch, where – at least until recently – the white poppy was grown in the gardens. The heads of this flower were boiled in days gone by to make an infusion which was drunk for 'Fen ague'. No doubt it had some effect, as it must have been rich in opium.

Wicken Fen is nearly the only piece of primordial Fenland left in approximately its old condition; and so is of first interest to naturalists and ecologists. It is preserved in this state because some of it at least was bought by the National Trust as far back as 1899, and the rest in 1911, and it is still preserved by the Trust as a strict nature reserve. In a building near the entrance is a graphic display showing the Fen's evolution, and the Warden is always ready to help.

The Fen cannot, in fact, be left quite to nature: waterways must be kept clear, water pumped *up* into the Fen because the surrounding cultivated land has shrunk and the Fen has not, alder and buckthorn must be prevented from colonizing the drier land. As far as possible it is kept as sedge and reed growing fenland, and there are giant mare's tail, hart's-tongue fern, flowering water plantain, bog bedstraw, forget-me-not, loosestrife, hemp agrimony, marsh pea, water parsnip, willow-herb, angelica, meadowsweet and many orchids, including the sundew which entraps flies. There are plentiful fish in the waters including the unusual eel-pout, which resembles a catfish.

The *pièce de résistance* of the Fen, though, is the swallowtail butterfly. This disappeared during Hitler's war, when much of the Fen was drained and turned into cultivated land (by Alan Bloom, whom we have met at Bressingham in Norfolk). But the Fen was restocked with swallowtails from the Norfolk Broads, when it was certain that the distinct variety of the Fenlands was completely extinct. There are warblers, water fowl of all sorts, and, on warm summer nights, the moth-collectors make interesting watching. They put up sticky screens and attract the moths into them with lights.

Part of Adventurers' Fen (there are several Fens named like this – 'adventurers' were groups of financiers similar to later joint stock companies who got together to drain the Fens: we also find 'Undertakers' Fen') which was ploughed up during the war was returned afterwards to the Trust, and an old pumping windmill that was on it has been renovated, and removed to Wicken Sedge Fen, and there it still is – probably the only working pumping windmill in Fenland. Incidentally when Adventurers' Fen was ploughed up great numbers of huge bog oaks were found in it, some of them over 100 feet long. They were all lying in a north-easterly direction, as though all felled together in some monstrous south-west gale. Could it have happened that, their roots submerged in the waters by some subsidence of the land, they were all drowned together and then some savage gale – or series of them – laid them low?

Wicken Fen is by now eight feet above the surrounding cultivated land, and this distance will go on increasing until all the surrounding peat has been used up and eroded by cultivation. The pumping windmill, for this reason, is used for pumping water up into the Fen and not out of it.

Apart from the interest of its flora and fauna, Wicken Fen gives some idea of the utter impenetrability of the aboriginal Fenland to all excepting Fenmen. The ditches and lodes are too shallow to swim in, too wide to jump, and too soft-bottomed to wade. To attempt the last would be to court death. To travel by boat, if you were a stranger, would be to get lost and stranded into the bargain. We can here see why William the Conqueror, and other invaders, had such a difficult time in conquering Fenland.

441

Beyond Wicken is **Upware**, for a while a place of memories after the dear old 'Five Miles from Anywhere' or 'No Hurry' Inn burned down.

This was a splendid riverside pub, the resort of both Fen lighter-men and undergraduates who used to row down from Cambridge, where these two diverse breeds of men used to meet on common ground. The undergraduates formed here the 'Upware Republic' in which was done much debating, smoking, and drinking of beer. Samuel Butler was a prominent member. The old pub burned down not many years ago and not a brick remains to show us where it was; but there is an ancient lock nearby, a splendid place to picnic on the river's brink, and the pub has at last been rebuilt.

A mile west of Wicken is Spinney Abbey, a farmhouse to which Henry Cromwell, the Protector's second son, retired from his great offices at the Restoration of the monarchy. Charles II took a notion to visit him in his retirement, and one of Charles's courtiers had a fancy to walk before Cromwell carrying a pitch-fork as he had previously carried a mace when Henry was Lord Deputy of Ireland. Henry Cromwell was a man of high intelligence, and great dignity and integrity.

Back eastwards to **Soham** there is yet another splendid church of the ancient shoreline.

Built upon a promontory of the chalk into the Fens, Soham was one of the earliest places in East Anglia chosen by a monastic community. St Felix, the Burgundian missionary who landed at what is now Felixstowe to convert the East Angles under the reign of Sigebert (or reconvert them, for Redwald, Sigebert's father, as we have seen, at least had a Christian altar in his temple even if it was alongside a pagan one) had his bishopric at Dunwich, but he set up an abbey at Soham, and in this was buried in AD 634. Soham, then, was the farthest flung site of the East Anglian kingdom – for the people west of it were Britons, or Celts, and already Christianized by the Romans.

But Soham Abbey, like Ely, was destroyed in the great Danish raid of 870. Ely rose again: Soham did not, and the remains of St Felix were removed to Ramsey.

Soham's present church has a high Perpendicular nave, window tracery of lovely flowing Decorated, a noble arch to the east of the nave (there is a crossing) with delicious moulding, and a fine hundred-foot tower with East Anglian flush-work at the top of it.

Isleham is somewhat out of our way; but as it is one of the line of 'shore' villages we have been following we might as well look at it now.

If we take the most direct road from Soham we may well come to believe the story that the old East Anglian road-makers liked to work with the wind at their backs, and the wind kept 'a-changing!' This wayward lane, incidentally, takes us past the foundations of a Romano-British villa.

Isleham has some very early Norman remains of a Benedictine priory. Its present church is like all these 'shore' churches: early fourteenth century, high-standing with its lofty clerestory and short in proportion to its great height. The tower is new, and although critics have damned the candle-snuffer roof to it I must admit it comes as a rather pleasant surprise to be greeted by this poking up from the Fen-surrounded island village, taking us in feeling to France.

This is an important as well as an interesting church; but in a land crammed with interesting churches it is likely to go unnoticed. But no-one should miss the brasses and monuments: particularly the brass to Thomas Peyton who died in 1484, with his elaborate and comical-looking plate armour with huge elbow guards, and his pair of wives, most elegant: the one in the lovely flowered dress is Margaret, née Bernard, who brought Isleham into the Peyton family in the first place. Thomas Peyton was a fine fellow: High Sheriff of Cambridgeshire and Huntingdonshire. There are several lush-looking Peyton monuments, and some brasses to the earlier Bernard family. There is a brass to Sir Geoffrey Bernard (probably), who went to the Crusades with Prince Edward – later Edward I. The figure on the brass can be seen to be a Crusader, for his legs are crossed; and he can be dated to about 1275 by the type of tailed surcoat that he is wearing over his armour. Thus this is a very early brass indeed. The moulding of the canopy over the figure on the brass is said to resemble almost exactly the moulding that Edward I had done on the Coronation Chair in Westminster Abbey.

If we wind our way back to Soham now, and embark on the road to Ely, we will be embarking on the causeway built over the flooded

Fens by Hervey, first Bishop of Ely, and its abbot. St Edmund appeared in a dream to a man of Exning telling him to go to this bishop and tell him to build this causeway, and this the man did, and the bishop followed the suggestion. (A parallel of this legend concerns the building of the famous Pont d'Avignon over the Rhône.) Apart from a temporary causeway built by William the Conqueror during his campaign against Hereward, this was the first dry-land communication between Ely and the rest of England.

The Causeway used the little island of **Stuntney** as a stepping-stone. *Stunt* still means *steep* in the Cambridgeshire dialect, and Stuntney is a steep-sided place, and from it can be had a grand view of the goal of our pilgrimage: Ely itself.

The Isle of Ely stands high up above the flat Fenland (I am using 'high' in an East Anglian sense – expect no snow-capped mountains!), and until Bishop Hervey built his causeway it was only to be approached by boat and then only by a boatman who knew the channels. It was thus a refuge for the oppressed; and Celtic Britons lingered on there long after the rest of the country was Anglo-Saxonized; and thus probably kept alive a spark of Christianity before St Felix converted the heathen English.

CHAPTER 25

Ely

First the name. When St Dunstan, who was so insistent on the celibacy of the priesthood, came to Ely he found that many of the monks were married, or at any rate the next best thing. So he miraculously changed all the married monks into eels, and there have been eels in the waters of Ely ever since: hence the name Ely – Eel Island.

The story of the founding of the abbey there is this. Etheldreda was born at Exning, near Newmarket, one of the palaces of the Wuffinga kings of East Anglia – as we have seen, Rendlesham was probably the chief one – and her father was Anna, the king who was slain by the pagan Mercians at Blythburgh, and who was buried there. Anna was blessed with a bevy of saintly daughters. Etheldreda was sent to her aunt at Whitby, Hilda, Abbess of Whitby Abbey, and there she decided to embrace the holy life. Her father, for reasons of state, married her off to a British prince: Tonbert, lord of the wild Girvii, the Celtic tribe that still inhabited the Fens.

But Etheldreda would not let Tonbert consummate the marriage, and Tonbert eventually died, leaving to his somewhat unsatisfactory wife his domains in Fenland, including the Isle of Ely.

In 671 Etheldreda was again forced into marriage, this time with Egfrid, King of Northumberland. From this time onwards, her story is carved, for all to follow if they have a powerful pair of field glasses, on the fourteenth-century corbels halfway up the eight great piers of the Octagon of Ely Cathedral.

King Egfrid was as unlucky as his predecessor had been: consummation was denied him. After twelve years he permitted Etheldreda to go to Coldingham, in Berwickshire, to another aunt there,

Ebba, the Abbess. Bishop Wilfrid of York came and administered the veil of *sanctimonialis femina* to her, and after this it was unthinkable that she would return to her husband. However, Egfrid had other ideas. He gave chase to her, a year later, as she was making the journey back to her dominions in Fenland. He would have caught her too, had he not been miraculously stopped by a high tide at Abb's Head, and Etheldreda got by, a virgin. After this she stuck her staff in the ground and it miraculously took root and put forth branches.

She got to Ely, and there founded a nunnery of which she became Abbess, and it was a monastery too, for there were men as well as women; and Etheldreda ruled them both alike. She practised severe austerities, and eventually died of a tumour in the throat: said to be due to her venal love of wearing necklaces when a girl.

Sexburgha, Etheldreda's sister, took over, and sixteen years after Etheldreda's death her sister had her remains (needless to say uncorrupted) buried in a shrine in the chapel; in a white marble sarcophagus of Roman make which was discovered in what is now the Fellows' Garden at Magdalene College.

Etheldreda was canonized; and became one of the greatest saints of the English, and Ely benefited by the oblations of the pilgrims. And it was not poor in the first place, for Etheldreda, after all, was still Queen of the Girvii. Miracles occurred – not the least when, in 870, the Danes plundered Ely, and a Dane tried to rifle the saint's tomb. His eyes fell out of his head.

Etheldreda's name became shorted to 'St Audrey', and St Audrey's Fairs were held once a year all over England. At them trinkets were sold including 'St Audrey's necklaces'; and our word *tawdry* comes from the fact that much tawdry rubbish came to be sold at these fairs: particularly, as we have seen, the fair at Woodbridge.

In 970, after many vicissitudes and burnings by the Danes, a new Benedictine abbey was founded at Ely by King Edgar, as part of the great revival of monasteries then going on. Then came the Conquest; and Ely held out long after the rest of England; and became the refuge, under Hereward the Wake, of many dispossessed Anglo-Saxons. It might possibly have held out for good, and become a rallying-point for an English counterblast against the

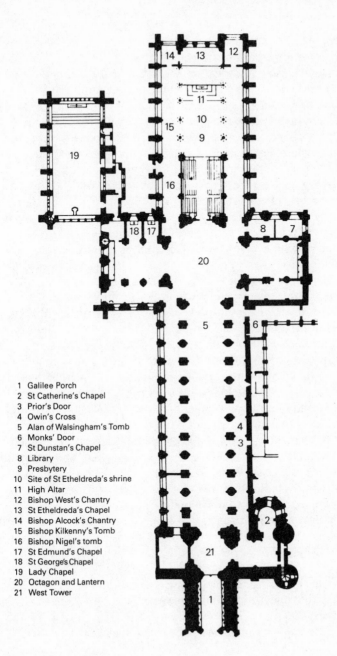

1 Galilee Porch
2 St Catherine's Chapel
3 Prior's Door
4 Owin's Cross
5 Alan of Walsingham's Tomb
6 Monks' Door
7 St Dunstan's Chapel
8 Library
9 Presbytery
10 Site of St Etheldreda's shrine
11 High Altar
12 Bishop West's Chantry
13 St Etheldreda's Chapel
14 Bishop Alcock's Chantry
15 Bishop Kilkenny's Tomb
16 Bishop Nigel's tomb
17 St Edmund's Chapel
18 St George's Chapel
19 Lady Chapel
20 Octagon and Lantern
21 West Tower

Normans. But, alas, the cause was betrayed by the Abbot himself, who secretly made a peace with William and had him shown the way to the island when Hereward was away on a raid. When Hereward got back it was to find the Normans in occupation, and he had to flee for his life.

The monks, if they thought they were going to get off lightly by their treachery, were disappointed. William rode up to the abbey church when they were all at dinner. Without giving them warning he strode up to the shrine of St Etheldreda and flung a small piece of money on it as an offering, and then walked out and rode away. One of his knights strode into the refectory and shouted: 'Ye wretched drivellers! Can ye choose no better time for guzzling than this when the King is here, yea, in your very church?'

But William had gone; and the monks had to run three miles to Witchford (through which place he had built the causeway to attack the isle) to catch him, and he thereupon imposed a huge fine on them for not greeting him in a proper manner, and moreover he billeted on them a great body of knights, one for each monk, to keep an eye on them, and subsequently he doubled the fine because he alleged that some of the coin (they had to set up a mint to cast the treasure of the abbey down into coin to pay their fine) was underweight. William was not a conqueror who wore kid gloves.

Of course it was not long before a Norman was appointed Abbot. Simeon, the brother of Wakelin, Bishop of Winchester, took the job, and with it all the revenue from the old kingdom of the Girvii; and he began to build the mighty church that we see today: the cathedral that ranks among the most glorious and sumptuous buildings of Christendom. The main part of the cathedral took just 268 years to build, and was finished in time for the Black Death which put an end to so much building.

In 1083 Simeon, then an old man, laid the foundations of the north and south transepts which stand to this day, and of the central tower which has since collapsed.

The choir was built, and the remains of St Etheldreda were brought thither from the old Anglo-Saxon church. (The Normans found that they could not do without the Anglo-Saxon saints. Perhaps they did this to consolidate their grip on the conquered race: perhaps because they had so few saints of their own.) Her

Ely Cathedral, looking West along the Choir. Above is the famous Lantern, built by Alan of Walsingham in the 14th century to replace the huge Norman Tower which fell in ruins and smashed the Chancel as it fell. Alan stood amid the ruins on the night when the tower fell and 'knew not whither to turn'. But he recovered his courage, 'set his hand to the work', and produced his masterpiece.

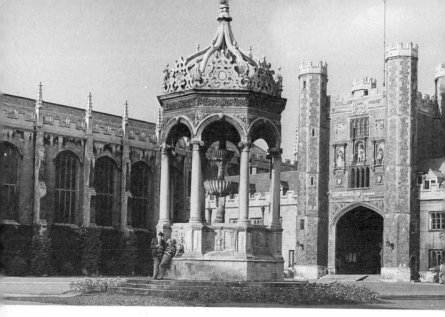

Above, the Great Court of Trinity College, the largest quadrangle in Cambridge. *Right,* the West Front of Peterborough Cathedral, with three recessed arches each 81-ft high.

sister Sexburgha was laid at her feet and on each side of her a second sister and a niece who had both followed her as Abbess. Old King Anna may seem to us to be a semi-legendary figure lost in the pagan past; but in one generation his family had established firmly its immortality and moved from the pre-history of ship-burials at Sutton Hoo into the history of precise dates and carefully documented facts, and of great buildings which are still standing today.

At the request of Henry I the Pope made the Abbot of Ely a bishop, and to this fact we owe the continued existence of the cathedral, for had it not been a cathedral as well as a minster it would have been pulled down at the Dissolution. Hervey, the causeway-builder, was the first bishop, appointed in 1109. This first Norman bishop took over the 'Franchise of Liberty' of the Isle of Ely, which had been handed down from St Etheldreda herself as Queen of the Girvii, and even today the results of Etheldreda's marriage to the wild King of the Girvii remain: the 'Isle of Ely', although part of Greater Cambridgeshire, for long survived as an entity of its own; and while its independence has administratively been wrested from it, its character has not really changed in the least.

When seen from far across the Fens the cathedral stands up enormous, dominating everything; and when no detail can be seen it resembles some vast barn, with turrets, standing up alone in the flat fenny country. As we get nearer, from north or south – i.e. from a side view – we have the impression of a vast ark or ship, riding the hill of the Isle of Ely as a great wave. But it is from the east that the impression of sumptuousness presents itself.

From here the place looks like a gigantic fairy castle, or a magic palace. The foreshortening of the Octagon and the mighty West Tower, the proliferation of pinnacles and Gothic towers, make for a jumbled mass of upward-striving detail. It has been compared by the unsympathetic to 'a great Gothic wedding cake'; but to the more discerning it 'comes off' entirely: an entirely satisfactory *tour de force* of architecture; an attempt of almost inconceivable boldness that completely and brilliantly succeeds.

The building history is briefly thus. Simeon, and the Normans who came after him, built transepts, nave, and a small Norman

449

apsed chancel, and also a huge Norman central tower which fortunately did not have strong enough foundations.

The Norman chancel was, as usual, not big enough for later needs; and the chancel and chancel aisles were lengthened under Bishop Northwold in the thirteenth century, thus in the Early English style, and we see today a glorious and lofty Early English east end. Henry III and his son Prince Edward came to the dedication of this chancel in 1252.

The king and his son came in peace then; but fifteen years later they came in war, for, after the defeat of the barons at the Battle of Evesham and the death of Simon de Montfort, a group of the defeated who called themselves 'The Disinherited' made Ely their refuge; and it was not until the king himself, with Scottish troops, had constructed bridges and causeways and attacked the island, that the rebels yielded.

But the abbey and the minster went on unchanged; and the Benedictine monks continued to rise at two in the morning to say Mattins and Lauds, and say or sing offices at frequent intervals during the day, and sit shivering in the cloisters copying books, and go once every six weeks to the infirmary for the routine blood-letting, and fill any spare time which they may have had with tending the vineyards (for which Ely was noted) and gardens, and draining the marshes.

The minster appeared at that time to be complete. But early in the fourteenth century, that lovely time of English Gothic, it was decided to add a Lady Chapel.

Alan of Walsingham, the Sacrist, discussed the general idea with his assistant, Brother John, who:

> . . . betook himself therefore to prayer, and thereafter called his mates together, some being monks, some, likewise, being seculars. And them he besought to meet at a certain hour, and help him in digging out a square trench which might serve as a foundation for the whole fabric.
>
> At the appointed time, accordingly, they met one night, and began to dig, each separately in the place assigned to him . . .
>
> And when the whole night was well nigh spent, and in the

earliest dawn, a small rain came on, to the annoyance of those digging. Calling then his mates from their work, he said: 'Brethren mine, and fellow labourers, yea, most heartily do I thank you for your long and well-wrought task. And good it is to pause a little after your work. Therefore I commend you to God. And may He pay you a full worthy wage for your labour.'

But Brother John, unknown to the other diggers, had struck a crock of silver in his digging, which he concealed under his bed, and with its contents he subsequently paid for much of the building.

And thus rose up the Lady Chapel, and – with all our tower cranes and bulldozers and pre-stressed reinforced concrete – what can we build today to touch it?

But – disaster. No sooner had the chapel been started than the great central towers of the old cathedral, built two hundred years before by the Normans, collapsed on to the roof of the Norman choir, itself in ruins and bringing ruin as it fell.

Fortunately the Sacrist, Alan of Walsingham, who was then quite a young man, happened to be perhaps the most inspired builder that England has ever possessed. He 'rose up by night and came and stood over the heap of ruins, not knowing whither to turn. But recovering his courage, and confident in the help of God and His kind Mother Mary, and in the merits of the holy virgin Etheldreda, he set his hand to the work.'

Inspiration came to him. In the place of the square tower, with its insufficient foundation, he set up a mighty Octagon, cutting boldly into the fabric of the building to accommodate it, and crowning it with a wooden lantern: the whole piece of work in the Decorated style at its most free and inspired and beautiful. The building took twenty-six years, which is amazingly little; even the removal of the mighty mass of rubble from the ruined tower and choir must have been an enormous work. We read of John Attegrene the Master Mason, John of Burwell the Master Wood-carver, William Shank the Chief Decorator, William Hurle the inspired Carpenter and even Ralph le Goldbeter who beat the gold coin donated by the Sacrist himself for the embellishment of the interior. Their names should be preserved.

451

As for the Lady Chapel, John of Wisbech, who dug during the night, finished it just before he died in the Black Death of 1349.

The West Tower, which soars over everything else – it is 215 feet high – is embellished with tier upon tier of Early English arcading, which gets later in style as it gets higher owing to the time-lag in its construction. The octagon at the top of the tower is a later addition. There is a transept south of the tower, said to be of the finest Norman work in England: the corresponding transept to the north collapsed.

The west porch, or Galilee ('Behold I go before you into Galilee!'), is thus named, some people say, because it is farthest from the altar as the real Galilee is farthest in the Holy Land from Bethlehem; but others have it that it is called Galilee because, in ceremonial circumambulations of the building, the deacon who led the procession would cry out: 'Behold – I am come unto Galilee!' before entering the church. This Galilee, Early English like the west tower, has columns of Purbeck marble, the hard fresh-water limestone from Dorset. Note the slenderness of the shafts on each side supporting their ogee arches. They are much decayed, and some of them have been replaced by a Devonshire marble.

As we walk through the inner door of the Galilee the view that greets us is breath-taking. The more so because Mr Essex, in 1769, simply swept away the whole of the stone screen, or pulpitum, the only Norman stone screen in England, in his 'restoration' work. The eighteenth century could be far more destructive when it came to Gothic buildings than the nineteenth. At least the nineteenth century loved the Gothic – if they often loved it to death. The eighteenth century hated it as the work of barbarians, and said so, and would sweep it away whenever it felt like it.

But the fact that there is no screen means, unlike at Norwich, the whole great vista of the cathedral presents itself. There are the massive Norman arcades of the nave, the equally clean and massive Norman triforia of double arches, with, above them, the treble arched clerestories. The nave roof, 105 feet above our heads, may be a disappointment: it is painted wood. The two Victorians who painted it did their best and one of them, at least, was a Norfolk man: Henry Styleman Le Strange of Hunstanton Hall. He adapted his design from the wooden roof of St Michael's, Hildesheim, in

Germany. The nave and the transepts never got to be roofed in stone: the Black Death intervened.

If we move down the nave and to the right, the south aisle, we come to the Prior's Door, and this we must see from the outside. It presents to us a wealth of strange and barbaric Norman carving: an art more akin to pagan and very early Christian Celtic art than to that of the Middle Ages. There is a primitive but terrifyingly effective Christ on the tympanum above the door. It is worth while to spend some time making out the rest of the carving. Human life is depicted down one side of the door, and the animal creation down the other. The fact that the two men in the rowing boat are pulling against each other would not have been lost on the monks of Ely, for every one of these was perforce a waterman.

Inside again, a little way down the aisle to the east, is Ovin's Cross or, more properly, Owen's Cross. Written on the base of this is: *Lucem tuam ovina da deus et reqvie(m) Amen.*

There is but the base and the shaft left of this: it was smashed at the Reformation; but it takes us back to Saxon times if not, indeed, earlier. Owen, later sainted himself, was Saint Etheldreda's steward, and probably a member of the Girvii tribe, i.e. a Celt, hence his Welsh name. He is mentioned by Bede, who tells us that when Queen Etheldreda no longer required his services he walked to Lichfield monastery, clad in a plain garment and carrying a pick and a billhook to indicate that he had not come to live in idleness, and there became a monk. On down the nave we come to the transepts, the one on the right being the oldest part of the cathedral: Bishop Simeon's work, begun in 1083.

But we may find it hard to contemplate this Norman work because of our pleasure and amazement at what goes on over our heads: Alan of Walsingham's octagonal tower is the wonder of the cathedral, and indeed of medieval building in England. It soars above us: eight lofty pillars branching out into splendid palm leaves, the ribs of which apparently support the eight-sided lantern, the walls of which are offset to the eight walls of the tower below. The effect is momentous. We cannot begin to understand how the mighty lantern (it is said to weight 400 tons) can be held up there by those slender ribs, and yet, somehow, there is no feeling of insecurity by this arrangement. We are not to know, of course,

453

that it is not held up by the ribs at all – but by a cunningly concealed arrangement of mighty beams of oak. For these beams eight trunks had to be found absolutely straight and without a fault, and 64 feet long, 3 feet 4 inches wide by 2 feet 8 inches thick when adzed down (imagine the job of adzing them!). Eight were found – in Bedfordshire, and each one, adzed, weighed 10 tons. We may wonder how they were got to Ely, until we realize that the Great Ouse runs right through Bedfordshire – they *had* to come from Bedfordshire. We may then wonder at the engineering skill, or at least the skill of the riggers who got them up to that height and put them in position. What did the army of monks and labourers sing as they hauled on the falls of the tackles?

Whether Alan intended in the beginning to roof his Octagon with stone we do not know, but this would have involved vaulting a span of 74 feet at a height of 86 feet, something never before achieved. But the solution that he found, or was driven to – the poising of this magnificent wooden lantern at the top of it all – was the happiest that there could have been. The lantern is surrounded with windows, and is full of light; and walking out underneath it after the claustrophobic massiveness of the Norman nave is like moving from a sombre age of militarism and dungeons into a new age of sunshine and wonder and delight.

It is here that we can admire the scenes from the life of St Etheldreda, as imagined by fourteenth-century stone carvers, on the corbels half way up the eight shafts of the Octagon.

The screen is Victorian; but beyond it the choir stalls are fourteenth century, and so are the next three bays of the building: built by Alan of Walsingham to replace the ones smashed by the collapse of the tower. The Bible scenes carved with such a heavy hand (compared, that is, to the hand which carved the delicate woodwork surrounding them) are Belgian, and nineteenth-century insertions. But the rest of the woodwork is medieval, and there are no less than fifty-four miserere seats of the most surprising variety and interest: the strip-cartoons of the Middle Ages. Nor should the 'Ely Imps' be neglected – at the join of the first two arches or the choir on the south side, in stone: the one on the other's back.

We proceed eastwards into the presbytery which was fortunately missed by the tower as it fell and so still stands. It was completed by Hugh de Northwold in 1232. Etheldreda's shrine, the purpose of the whole building, was beneath the two bosses in the vaulted roof: one carved with the Virgin being crowned, the other with the Saint. The shrine was destroyed by Bishop Goodrich in the reign of Henry VIII: the same bishop who desecrated the Lady Chapel. It is interesting that this so zealous Protestant found himself able to turn into an equally zealous Catholic when Mary came to the throne.

There are a number of tombs in the choir aisles, which we have not the space to describe, and in any case they are all clearly labelled. Do not miss the stark effigy of Bishop Kilkenny in the north aisle, and to the north of the choir the weird carving on the monument of a bishop thought to be Nigel – of the Angel Gabriel carrying the bishop's little soul up to Heaven, about 1150, and made of marble by the craftsmen in Tournai in Belgium – like the font of Winchester Cathedral.

In the south-east of the presbytery is Bishop West's Chantry, built in the high Perpendicular style just before the Dissolution of the monastery and built internally of clunch: a stone which lends itself to exuberant carving. There are touches of Renaissance decoration among the lush embellishment: an Italian feel about it, and the whole thing is secular in feeling rather than religious. More sumptuous still is Bishop Alcock's Chantry (1488) in the north-east corner: an absolute fairy palace of clunch, like a cave of ice or of stalactites, with a fan vault of the utmost splendour, a mighty boss in the middle dripping with leaves and grapes. This chapel is best seen through the restrained and dignified Early English arch outside it – the contrast is terrific. Alcock was the man who founded Jesus College, and as we have seen his rebus there – the cockerel – so we see it here too.

Perhaps a harder and more intransigent rock than chalk would have led to more restrained carving than we see in these two chantries, but all the same they are nothing if not *fun*.

The chapel in between the two chantries of the merry bishops is dedicated to St Etheldreda herself, and is a memorial to the 'men of Grantabryggeshire' who stood firm in 1939–45, as their ancestors did nine hundred years before on Ringmere Heath.

In Bishop West's Chantry, incidentally, lie the bodies of seven

East Anglians who were dug up from various parts of the cathedral and moved here. They include the heroic Brithnoth, Alderman of East Anglia under Ethelred the Unready; who met and at least withstood the Danes at the Battle of Maldon, when he was killed.

> *Then drave from each hand*
> *Full starkly the spear,*
> *Showered the sharp arrows,*
> *Busy were bows,*
> *Shield met shaft,*
> *Bitter the Battle.*

Brithnoth's headless body (the Danes got away with his head) was brought back to Ely by the monks and buried here. The story is that, on his way to the battle, Brithnoth put in to the Abbey of Ramsey and asked for food. The monks said that they could entertain him and a few picked companions, but not his whole force. He replied: 'Tell my Lord Abbot that I cannot fight without my men, neither will I feed without them!' and he proceeded to Ely, where men and leader were alike entertained, and to require this hospitality he bestowed upon the Abbey, there and then, no less than nine manors only stipulating that his body should be buried there, which it still is.

The next great thing to see is the Lady Chapel, the foundations of which were laid out by Brother John and his mates in that night which ended in 'a small rain'. To find this we have to search for a small door in the north-east corner of the north transept.

We walk into the chapel as into a bath of light. It is Late Decorated work of the most splendid, although a tracery of the east window is just beginning to verge on the coming Perpendicular discipline. The span of the vaulted roof is 46 feet – the widest in England. The interior is lined on all sides with the most exquisite carving in clunch (all this chalk was brought down the river from the great quarry at Reach), but unfortunately the statues that were held by these seemingly innumerable niches were ravaged by the iconoclasts, and only one small example remains out of hundreds. Thomas Goodrich made it his business to destroy this great heritage of medieval art because he considered them 'works of Mariolatry', and as we look around the chapel now we may well feel that the strong and simple faith that kept Brother John and his mates digging through the night until that small rain came has gone from the building just as surely as have the statues which embellished those empty niches.

But there is still enough splendour to keep us entranced for days. The white rock has been carved with inconceivable intricacy and great delicacy; with none of the vulgarity which we may feel compromises the chantries of those two jolly bishops; the lovely lierne vaulting soars above our heads, the generous clear windows, bereft of their original coloured glass, dazzle us with the flowing brilliance of their tracery.

It now remains for us to do one last thing, and that the most strenuous. We must climb the 215 feet of the West Tower. On the journey upwards we receive a conception of the almost inconceivable amount of stone that went into a great cathedral: a vast volume of massive masonry, all hidden away behind the scenes. From the top we look down at the tweedy-textured tiled Georgian roofs, the careful flower gardens and fruitful vegetable plots of the clergy, all professional gardener-tended, the playing fields of King's School, the jumbled old houses of the city and beyond it all the far-stretching Fens, the Great Ouse winding through it, and if it is clear enough the spires of Cambridge to the south and the hazy waters of the Wash to the northward.

Of monastic buildings, there are the cloisters – nothing like so complete as those at Norwich – the Prior's House and the Bishop's House built in what was the monks' refectory, Prior Cauden's Chapel, now the chapel of King's School, which was built by Alan of Walsingham and is therefore very unusual and beautiful and not to be missed on any account at all – it is one of the choicest pieces of building at Ely – the Ely Porta, or great gate of the monastery, and beyond it the tithe barn, now a gymnasium for King's School.

King's School (despite the placing of the apostrophe, two kings were involved in it) was founded before the reign of Edward the Confessor, for he was a scholar at it. It was, in fact, founded by Alfred the Great after his defeat of the Danes at Ethaldune, as the 'College', and to this day what would be called 'the Close' in other cathedral cities is here called 'the College'.

> *These things are of note at Ely, the Lantern and Chapel of*
>   *Mary,*
> *A windmill too, and a vineyard that yieldeth wine in*
>   *abundance.*
> *Know that the Choir before ye exceedeth all others in beauty,*
> *Made by Alan our brother, Alan the wise Master Builder;*
> *Alan the Prior, forget not, here facing the Choir lyeth buried.*
> *He, for that older Tower which fell one night in the darkness,*
> *Were erected, well-founded, the Tower that ye now are*
>   *beholding.*

(Latin inscription on the brass over Alan of Walsingham's grave, translation by Conybeare.)

As for the city of Ely itself, it is an unspoilt little market town and river port which has escaped industrialization and remains predominantly Georgian in character. The maltings built in 1868 for the local brewery were burnt out in 1967 but put to good use in the 1970s, when a public hall was established in the premises, containing a conference room, a well-equipped stage, and other leisure facilities. The Cutter inn, down by the river, is a good place by which to tie up in a boat, and the local council has laid out a delightful riverside walk linking various quays. There is also a nature trail, opened in European Conservation Year, 1970, starting at Springhead Lane and offering superb views of the cathedral across Roswell Pits and a variety of birdlife such as godwits, redshank, greenshank and plovers.

Oliver Cromwell's grandfather was Steward, or tythe-farmer, for the Dean and Chapter of Ely; responsible for collecting every tenth sheaf in the harvest fields of the Isle of Ely and far beyond and storing, some of it at least, in the great tythe barn now used as a school gymnasium. Oliver, born at St Ives, succeeded his grandfather in this office and accordingly came to live in Ely, in the Steward's House. When the Civil War broke out Cromwell came to drill his Ironsides on St Mary's Green. He sent a message to Canon Hitch, who was then responsible for the services in the cathedral, telling him to give up his popish practices; and when the message had no effect led a body of troopers into the cathedral during Holy Communion and 'drave out' both priest and communicants. He must have had a soft spot for the building, though, for he did not allow it to be pulled down during the Commonwealth.

At **Prickwillow**, a tiny village north-east of Ely, is a pumping station that lifts the waters of the River Lark a great height so that they can flow in the Great Ouse. The Engine Museum in Main Street is open dawn to dusk daily from the beginning of April to the end of October, with a working diesel unit. The most note-worthy object in the otherwise quite unprepossessing little church in this tiny and undistinguished Fen village (not that the *people* are undistinguished – far from it, they are famous men) is the font. This is a marble bowl of urbane and sophisticated eighteenth-century workmanship, quite incongruous in its bucolic surroundings.

From here we can circle through the black Fens, where celery and onions grow in endless weedless rows down hedgeless billiard-table fields, to **Littleport**, remembered for its martyrs. In 1816 there was widespread hunger in the Fens owing largely to the Enclosure of common land. When their children were starving the unemployed farm workers of Littleport were obliged to watch trains of Fen Lighters being loaded in their village with the grain that would have kept them alive – grain grown in their own parish and being sent away to London to make profits for the already extremely wealthy farmers. Wages, for the few that had any, were 9s a week: wheat was £5 5s 0d a quarter.

They rioted. They marched to Ely armed with billhooks and scythes, and covered by a predecessor of the tank: a farm wagon on which were mounted four great punt-guns. They fired no shot, killed nobody, and after some window-breaking and lawlessness retired home.

The military were sent for, and invested the district, and after weeks of searching and interrogating eighty men were arrested and taken to Ely to be made an example of.

They were tried by judges selected by the Bishop of Ely, for in this 'Liberty and Franchise' he had this power. Five men were publicly hanged (with great difficulty, for the Bishop could not for a long time get anybody to lend him a cart for the job), five were transported for life, and the rest all put in prison for long periods. The bishop then marched into the cathedral in a great procession with fifty men of Ely carrying white wands, his sword being borne before him by his butler, and everybody singing 'Why Do the Heathen Rage?'

This miserable exhibition was the last exercise of temporal power by the Bishops of Ely: a power handed down to them in direct line from the ancient British tribe of the Girvii, in the Fens 1,146 years before.

CHAPTER 26

North-west Cambridgeshire

We now embark into the drained Fens north of Cambridge, first coming to the two villages of their ancient shore, Landbeach and Waterbeach.

At **Waterbeach** Car Dyke is to be seen south of the village, a Roman canal. This navigation of the Romans is traceable all the way to Lincoln, where it joined the Foss Dyke, another Roman canal, at Breyford Pool. Vessels were thus able to go from just north of Cambridge to York, to carry Fenland grain to the Military Zone in the North of England, via Car Dyke, Foss Dyke, down Trent, and up the Yorkshire Ouse. The Car Dyke, incidentally, is mostly obliterated by later Fenland draining: the Foss Dyke is still easily navigable, and much used by motor keels carrying grain from Hull to Lincoln.

North of Waterbeach is the site of Denny Priory, where the widowed Countess of Pembroke, who founded Pembroke College, Cambridge, founded a nunnery. Parts of the refectory and fragments of the chapel are left.

Landbeach is notable for its angel lectern, seventeenth century and very dashing, supposed to have been the support to a Dutch pulpit.

Stretham is across the Old West River. The Old West is the original course of the Great Ouse, before Vermuyden cut his two Bedford rivers thus cutting off the great corner, much as Bishop Morton dug his Leam to cut off the corners of the River Nene centuries before. The Old West is still navigable, although somewhat weeded up in summer time, and it has a great charm of its own: a natural winding watercourse in a land of straight artificial ones. It joins the Cam at Pope's Corner, where is the Fish and

461

Duck Inn, a hostelry only approachable by water or by land over a track over the Fens: a marvellous place to moor a boat, or to stay ashore for a holiday of complete retirement.

But Stretham is remarkable for its Old Engine. This was installed by the Waterbeach Level Draining Commissioners in 1831, and is a 60 HP Boulton and Watt beam engine, erected by the Butterley Company of Derbyshire. It cost £400, and when first installed drained 5,600 acres, taking over from a great many windmills. That is, it lifted the water from the lower Fens into the higher Old West River between its banks. The engine originally drove a scoop wheel of just over 30 feet in diameter, which had to be increased to 33 feet in diameter in 1849 owing to further shrinking of the peat and consequent subsidence of the land, and again to 37 feet 2 inches in 1896, which it is now.

The engine is still in perfect working order, having worked for a hundred years and stood mostly idle for another thirty, for a diesel has now taken over its task. It is in the care of the Stretham Engine Preservation Trust, by which the above details were supplied, and is open to the public daily, with a collection of items found in the Fens. The engine looks most impressive and beautiful in its lofty house, and can be appreciated as much for its beauty by laymen as for its technical and historical interest by engineers.

West from Stretham we rise into a spur of the Isle of Ely to **Wilburton**, the church of which is interesting to saint-knowers, for there is a faded mural, besides the usual Saint Christopher, of Saint Blaise, who was of course Bishop of Sebaste, martyred in 316, and the patron saint of wool combers, and of Saint Leodegar, Bishop of Autun in France during the seventh century. Wilburton also has a lovely red-brick manor house of 1600 called the Burystead.

Haddenham is a large village, and we are now becoming aware that we are no longer really in East Anglia at all. Although built on a spur of the Isle of Ely this place has a Midland air about it: we might be in Leicestershire or Bedfordshire. The church has been severely dealt with by the Victorians, who rebuilt the tower in its original style of transitional between Decorated and Perpendicular. This church was founded by our old friend Owen, Latinized to Ovin, whose cross is in Ely Cathedral. The cross was set up here as an object of veneration until the Reformation, when it was

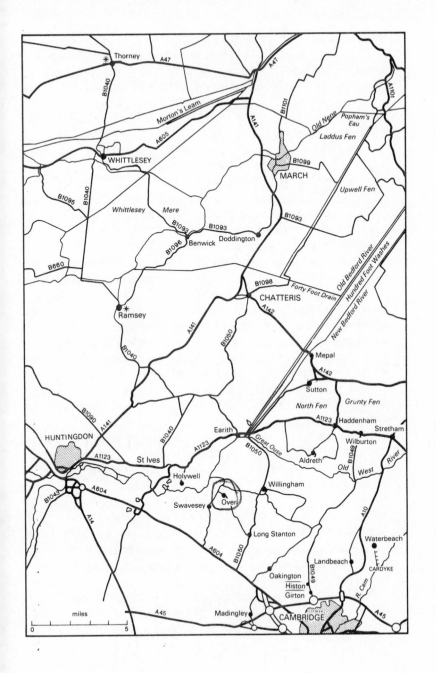

smashed and made into a mounting-block.

South-west of Haddenham is the hamlet of **Aldreth**, which is historically interesting because from here to Willingham runs the first ever Fen causeway to Ely, set up by William the Conqueror.

But north from Haddenham we drop sharply down into the Fen again, to below sea level in fact – North Fen on our left and Grunty Fen on our right. In Grunty Fen were dug up a bronze sickle and ornaments of twisted gold, on the other side of Haddenham spur a great hoard of bronze weapons was found, as though tipped out of a canoe, also gold money, a Celtic urn and the bones of an aurochs.

We traverse only a narrow strip of Fenland here, though, to rise again to another spur of the Isle on which stands Sutton.

Sutton has an unforgettable church, all Decorated, with a tower which soars so high on its hill that on a misty day travellers from afar have taken it for Ely. The church was started by Bishop Barnet of Ely in 1366, thus after the Black Death, and the tower was obviously inspired by Ely Octagon. It is in fact one octagon perched on top of another and the lower perched on a square tower. The whole church is interesting and beautiful: the last lovely flourish of the Decorated before the Perpendicular came in, and a product of the great wealth of Ely in the fourteenth century before it suffered the eclipse that lasted until the Great Drainings of the seventeenth century. Note the ceiling in the tower, the tower arch, the corbels south of the nave, the lovely Decorated window tracery.

Mepal has long been noted for its Three Pickerels Inn, backed by a group of attractive but faded riverside buildings, keeping themselves to themselves on the water's edge. The inn now stands by a bridge leading nowhere, since the introduction of a bypass has cut off part of the old road which, beyond the two Bedford Rivers, runs along Ireton's Way, a causeway built by the great Roundhead general Ireton, during the Civil War. From the Three Pickerels there is a footpath to Mepal church; and an Outdoor Centre offers sailing, surfboarding and canoeing on flooded gravel pits.

Doddington was once the site of a palace of the Bishops of Ely (they had many, including Ely Palace in the City of London, where the Liberty and Franchise of Ely extended so that the city authorities could not enter without permission, and where is still to be seen St Etheldreda's Chapel) and here Christopher Tye was rector. He was a man who composed much music, including the air to 'While Shepherds Watch their Flocks by Night', an anthem which has been much paraphrased by small boys. When rebuked by Queen Elizabeth for playing music out of tune he told Her Majesty that it was her ears that were out of tune. The east window in the north aisle of the church is early William Morris.

Benwick, to the west, has a pub called The Five Alls. The spirited sign depicts a lawyer: 'I Plead for All', a parson: 'I Pray for All', a soldier: 'I Fight for All', Queen Victoria: 'I Rule All', and underneath them all a man at the tail of a plough and the legend in larger letters: 'I PAY FOR ALL'.

There is a funny little Victorian church built of Norfolk carr stone – a long way to bring this rather unsuitable building material but presumably done to make the church look 'rustic'. Rustic it looks. The Old Nene, hard beside the church, is navigable, and below the level of the land (most Fenland rivers are above it) and has a pleasant natural appearance.

The road from Benwick to **Whittlesey** takes us across the drained bed of Whittlesey Mere, which was the biggest of the open waters of Fenland. Big sailing vessels once sailed its waters: one of them which had sunk with a freight of stone was discovered when the Mere was drained in 1850 – and the draining extinguished the last of the Great Copper butterflies of this country. In the woodland near Holme Fen is the iron column described on p. 282.

Whittlesey Museum in the Town Hall, Market Street, has a large collection of local photographs and an even larger one of the tools of brickmaking, along with the Sir Harry Smith exhibition of 'A Brickmaker's Living Room' – all very appropriate when one considers that all around are the creators of a substantially large part of the material which makes up London; for here are England's biggest brick-works, with sky-raking 'shafts' (chimneys) and vertical-sided pits deep down into the gault clay. It is from here and from Fletton near Peterborough that the cheap red moulded bricks that make up so much of modern England come in such prodigious quantities. Whittlesey's St Mary's Church has one of the finest spires in Cambridgeshire – we are getting very near to

Northamptonshire, the county of squires and spires.

North we cross **Morton's Leam**, which was dug by the order of Bishop Morton, Abbot of Ely, in 1480, the first of the really radical Fen drainage works. It cut off a great corner of the River Nene from Peterborough to Wisbech thus allowing the river to precipitate its water more quickly into the sea. The Bishop's plan was quite sound, although in later centuries the work itself proved inadequate and another great cut was made, and this we cross shortly after having crossed Morton's Leam, and which simply parallels it. This is navigable as far as Peterborough for quite large vessels: until quite recent years two sailing barges still regularly carried foreign grain along here from Hull. In fact you can go up this river, past Peterborough and right up to Northampton and thereafter by a flight of narrow locks into the Grand Union Canal and the whole waterways system of England. Just downstream of where we cross is the 'Dog in a Doublet Sluice': the big modern lock which keeps the tide from going any higher, just as Denver Sluice does on the Great Ouse. This sluice is named after the very fine inn nearby.

North again and we come to **Thorney Abbey**. After King Wulfhere of Mercia (who, incidentally, was married to one of St Etheldreda's sisters – the seed of old King Anna had Christianized even the pagan Mercians who killed him) had endowed the Abbey of Peterborough with great possessions 'the Abbot prayed of him that he would give him whatsoever he should ask. And the King granted him. Then said the Abbot: "Here have I God-fearing monks, who would fain live as hermits, knew they but where. And there is an island which is called Ancarig"' (modern Thorney). 'And my boon is that we might there build a Minster, to the glory of St Mary, so that they who would lead a life of peace and rest may dwell therein.' The king acceded to his request and Thorney was founded in 657, when a small abbey was built, not much more than the abode of anchorites. In the devastating Danish raid of 870, described so vividly in the 'Crowland Chronicle', the much greater foundations of Crowland and Peterborough were utterly destroyed – every building burnt and every monk who could be captured tortured and killed – all except one, a young boy 'fair in form and face', who was taken on by a Danish chief as a pet but who later escaped to tell the tale. Thorney was used as a refuge for the few who fled from Crowland, but the probability is that it later suffered in its turn.

Thorney Abbey was refounded by the Benedictines in 972, by Ethelwold, Bishop of Winchester. It became important, and William of Malmesbury wrote of it, about 1135: '. . . a little paradise, delightsome as Heaven itself may be deemed, fen-circled, yet rich in loftiest trees, where water-meadows delight the eye with rich green, where streamlets glide unchecked through each field. Scarce a spot of ground lies there waste: here are orchards, there vineyards. Nature vies with culture, and what is unknown to the one is produced by the other. And what of the glorious buildings, whose very size it is a wonder that the ground can support amid such marshes? A vast solitude is here the monks' lot, that they may the more closely cling to things above. If a woman is there seen she is counted a monster, but strangers, if men, are greeted as angels unawares. Yet here none speaketh, save for a moment; all is holy silence . . . From its dense thickets it is called Thorney.'

The Abbey Church was spared by Henry VIII on condition that it became a parish church, and its remains are still parochial. All that still stands is 117 feet of its nave with the aisles shorn off it and the east end cut away too. The west end still has a certain grandeur (the 'Perpendicular' inserts, such as the west window, were Perpendicular revival of 1638) and there is a ravaged beauty about the Norman arcades and triforia within.

The village around it is quite un-Fenlike, owing to the fact that this countryside fell to the Earls of Bedford in the great Fen Drainings of Vermuyden's day, and still remains in the Bedford family, and they have made of Thorney a model estate village. There are pretty estate houses and the country is planted with trees in a most un-Fenlike manner: your true Fenman only has one reaction when he sees a tree – he reaches for his axe.

A strange thing is that the Bedfords allowed Huguenot refugees to settle at Thorney in the seventeenth century, and right until 1715 French pastors were ministering in the church. In the churchyard are many French graves; and there is much French blood in the people of Thorney.

We might cut back to Cambridge by way of Ramsey and St Ives, both of them once in the lost county of Huntingdonshire.

Ramsey is approachable by boat from the Forty Foot Drain, and we can see by its main street that the canal once ran straight through it but has now been filled in. How delightful the place would look if it were once again main-streeted by a waterway like a Dutch village, and yachts lay alongside its quays! Of its old abbey only the ruined gatehouse is authentically fifteenth century. Behind it, the early seventeenth-century house built on the original monastic ruins was altered in the nineteenth century by Sir John Soane and Edward Blore, and is now a girls' school; but it can be visited on Sunday afternoons between Easter and the end of October. The gatehouse (National Trust) is open daily from July until mid-September, and most spring and autumn weekends. Ramsey Rural Museum with exhibits of local agricultural life is open the first and third Sunday afternoons each month from April to September.

St Ives is a charming place, but let us not stop now: we can study it in more detail in Chapter 28. Just downstream at **Holywell** the thatched Ferry Boat Inn was recorded as selling beer in 1068 and may thus dispute with the Trip to Jerusalem in Nottingham the claim to be the oldest licensed house in England. Its age is in fact pre-Conquest, for documents mention it as early as AD 980. It is said to be haunted by a wraith of a later decade: poor Juliet Tewsley hanged herself from a tree by the river on 17th March 1050 because a woodcutter named Thomas Zoul spurned her as she waited for him with a bunch of flowers on his way home from work. Ghost-lovers visiting the pub on St Patrick's Day may, if they drink enough, hope to see her walk.

Earith is at a great meeting place of the waters. Here the Old and the New Bedford Rivers take off from the Great Ouse, to cut as straight as two rulers across the Fenland to Denver Sluice. The Old was cut in 1630: the New in 1650. The Old is tideless, being cut off from the tidal Great Ouse below Denver Sluice by a sluice of its own. The New is tidal, and, at High Springs, the tide may even get up it as far as Earith.

It was here, on the Old Bedford, that a bizarre experiment was conducted to prove to an incorrigible Flat-Earther that our planet is, indeed, round. The Flat-Earther was a man who went about lecturing under the *nom-de-plume* Parallax, proving to one and all that the earth was flat. He supported his claim by offering to lay a heavy wager with anybody who was willing to prove otherwise. A man took him up, and an experiment was carried out on the Old Bedford River, this being the longest straight stretch of perfectly calm water in the kingdom (the Victoria Canal on the Coast of Coromandel would have done better, this being 300 miles longer than the Old Bedford). Three vessels were moored, having their cross-trees at the same level above the water. These Victorian gentlemen then clambered to the cross-trees of one of them and aimed a telescope at the cross-trees of the other two. If the earth was flat – then these should be in line. If round then they should not. Perhaps not unexpectedly the Flat-Earther found they were but everyone else found they were not, and Parallax lost his money.

Over has a grand and lavish church with the most engaging gargoyles this side of Notre Dame de Paris: they should certainly be visited on a rainy day to see them in full gush. But everything about this church is beautiful. It is lavishly built of Barnack stone, Early English tower and chancel (although the latter has Perpendicular windows inserted), Decorated the lovely south porch, which has a weathered sculpture believed by most people to be Christ in Glory but in fact Our Lady in Glory, a much rarer subject. There is a sanctus bell in its turret over the eastern gable of the nave – again a rare survival as nearly all these bells and turrets were especially obnoxious to Protestants since they tolled at the moment of the Elevation of the Host. There is lovely woodwork within, old misericords from Ramsey Abbey, a Decorated roof and most of the window tracery; this is a fine church, full of quality and good workmanship.

Willingham is a big village, and to the east of it rises the prehistoric fortification known as Belsar's Hill. Belsar was the general of William the Conqueror who built the causeway to the Isle of Ely to give access for the final attack of that place. The church at Willingham again is a superb one (we are again here on that magic line – the ancient shoreline of the Fens: the villages of which were all prosperous, having extensive common rights on the drier parts of the Fen for summer grazing) with a massive hammerbeam roof almost as glorious as the one at March and the most fascinating chapel off the chancel with a lovely stone roof of very unusual

469

design: Decorated as is most of the rest of the church. Can it have been a rising in the waters of the Fens in the fifteenth century, making it impossible to graze sheep, that accounts for the existence of so much Decorated in these 'shoreline' churches? The resulting impoverishment would have prevented the rebuilding that went on in the rest of East Anglia during the Perpendicular period that followed. Or can it be another explanation: the build-up of liver-fluke, inevitable in marshy grazing overstocked with sheep?

Swavesey, south of Over, had a Benedictine priory founded by Alan de la Zouche just after the Conquest, and it later turned Carthusian, but there is nothing to see of it. The church, like that of Over, is another of this magnificent group on the south side of the Great Ouse Valley. With its splendid cedars and larches it looks fine when approached from the village, with something very clean-cut and blocky about it like a good modern building. It has lovely Decorated tracery in its windows, sumptuous south doorway inside its Perpendicular porch and the nave has a notable array of bench-ends, some of them very good Victorian copies. Some of the benches are tiny, evidently for children.

Long Stanton has not one, but two interesting churches. St Michael, mostly Early English although the chancel is Victorian-rebuilt, has a notable double piscina and a twelfth-century oak chest. All Saints is cruciform, mostly Decorated and has monuments to the Hatton family which bought the manor from Queen Elizabeth after that monarch had filched it from the Bishop of Ely. When he protested she said: 'Obey my pleasure or I will forthwith unfrock you!'

On a former occasion Elizabeth was entertained by the same bishop at his palace at Long Stanton, and an embarrassing event occurred. Some Cambrige undergraduates, wishing to show the queen their Protestant zeal, performed a masque before her in which a dog, presumably a Protestant one, danced before Her Majesty with a consecrated Host in its mouth. When the Queen saw what was going forward she swept from the room in disgust – ordering all the lights to be put out and leaving the wretched undergraduates to find their properties in the pitch dark as best they could and make their way back to Cambridge.

Oakington would be a place of pilgrimage to Nonconformists, if, indeed, Nonconformists were given to making pilgrimage. Here is a graveyard in which are buried the bodies of Francis Holcroft, Joseph Oddy, and Henry Oasland. These three were leaders of the Nonconformist movement that survived the Restoration of Charles II, losing their Anglican livings for it under the Act of Uniformity of 1662, and thereafter preaching clandestinely up and down the land.

Histon is more a town than a village, with many modern factories including one which makes Chivers' Jam. The place is not attractive, although it has a church very interesting to lovers of the Early English – very similar to St Radegund's, in Jesus College.

Girton is famous for its women's college, which moved here from Hitchin in 1873. Except for the lovely grounds, and many pretty girls, there is nothing to go and see.

Madingley has a huge and very beautiful Tudor mansion, set in a great park in which Herefords fatten in summer. The house was built by Mr Justice Hinde in Henry VIII's time, partly with material he took from the church of St Etheldreda in Histon when he pulled this down. He filched the fine Norman font when he did so, but this has now been removed from the house and placed in Madingley Church. Edward VII lived at Madingley when he was an undergraduate at Trinity, and Charles I is supposed to have hidden there when he had escaped from the army at nearby Childerley Hall. The army had captured him in order to exert pressure on Parliament to meet its demands, but he escaped, and Madingley was owned by Sir John Coton, a Royalist. King Charles is said to have banged on his door in the middle of the night, disguised as a peasant, but the troopers soon came after him, and the whole incident was hushed up. The Hall now belongs to Cambridge University.

Nearby is a very pretty little post mill, brought here and set up as an ornament, and well looked after. There is also the American War Cemetery, in which are buried thousands of American dead.

CHAPTER 27

South-west Cambridgeshire

Cambridgeshire has shown us one of the loveliest cities in the world, the most sumptuous of all English cathedrals, and the magnificent line of great churches along the old Fenland shores. Surely it can be excused from not having so very much more to offer, and indeed the south of the county, although in odd corners quietly pretty, has little to show to equal the great Suffolk wool villages.

Grantchester is traditionally approached from Cambridge in a punt, with a pretty girl reclining on the cushions, but it may be achieved by other means. And however one gets there the place has its enchantment, a fact that Byron, Tennyson and Rupert Brooke alike acknowledged, and even Chaucer mentioned the place. There are several large pubs here now; and the village itself has got itself the stigma of a 'beauty spot'; but surprisingly the lovely riverside is seldom overcrowded for long. On a sunny day beneath one of those enormous willow trees watching the punts being slowly poled up from Cambridge, one is convinced that Grantchester is all that Rupert Brooke cracked it up to be. There is a most pleasant walk, too, to Cambridge along the river.

The mill . . .

> *And laughs the immortal river still*
> *Under the mill, under the mill.*

. . . is a mill, alas, no longer; having been burned down in 1928. If the church clock still does not stand at ten to three somebody ought to be shot, the church has Roman bricks in its walls, there is a window that may be a Saxon one, and one of the most lovely chancels of the Decorated style in the country.

The rector of **Hardwick** in 1644 being a man blessed with a wife and seven children was accused of being a man devoted to 'many superstitious ceremonies, and commonly useth altar-worship, east-worship, and dropping-worship, and after the sermon came out of the pulpit and there made an end of his ill-worship'. He was ejected and sequestrated. He might have taken a tip or two from the celebrated Dr Perne (see p. 423) or from the Vicar of Bray for that matter.

Toft has some alabaster fragments in its church of sculptures which were smashed by Dowsing in 1663 for which service, with other destruction, he was paid 6s 8d. St Hubert is recognizable among these fragments, the patron saint of hunters. He was, of course, converted to Christianity by meeting a hart with golden antlers in the forest and was given a key by St Peter which has the power of curing hydrophobia. The fragment here shows him, headless, thanks to Dowsing, but with the key, a hound, and the golden hart, all very sensitively carved.

Bourn is a pretty little place, with the River Bourn flowing through it, and what is supposed to be the oldest windmill in England. This is a post mill with an appearance rather of a sentry-box set up on wooden legs, and it was built in 1636. It was bought and repaired and presented to the Cambridge Preservation Society with funds raised at an exhibition, in Cambridge, of Epstein's *Genesis*!

There is an Elizabethan mansion at Bourn, built on the site of a former castle which itself was built by Picot, Sheriff of Cambridge-shire under the Conqueror. The church is noteworthy, cruciform, Norman and Early English, with noble arches inside and on the floor of the tower there is a maze, most rare in England now although there is a recently-made one in Ely Cathedral. At one time, like maypoles, they were widespread and had a mystical significance.

Eltisley, where the higher greensand ridge from Cambridge begins to peter out into the Valley of the Great Ouse, is of interest to the saint-knower. Here are buried two blessed saints of great obscurity: St Pandiana, who, Leland tells us, was a Scots princess (meaning at the time that she lived in Ireland, where the Scots

473

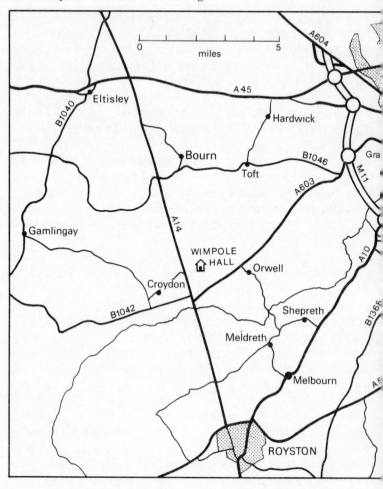

came from) and that she fled all the way to Eltisley to escape the importunities of her suitors and there founded a nunnery which perished at the Conquest. The other is St Wendreda, who has a well near Newmarket and the great church of March.

At Eltisley in 1234, according to Roger of Wendover, there was a great famine; and it caused the poor of the parish to invade the fields and devour the crops. The farmers 'who ever from their

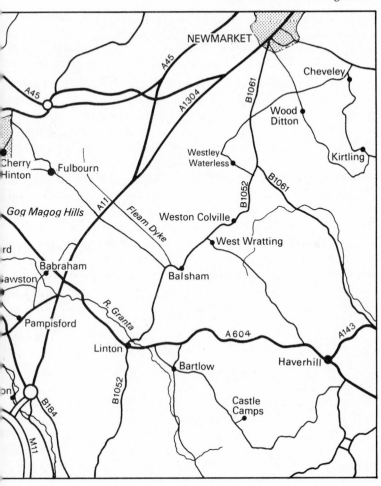

avarice look upon the poor with an evil eye' went to the parson and asked that the poor should be excommunicated; but one farmer 'adjured him in God's name to pronounce such sentence for *his* crops'. A great gale blew up, which blew down every man's corn excepting that of the good man who did not grudge the starving poor.

From here we might cut south through foreign (Bedfordshire)

475

territory to **Gamlingay**. This has a grand and very big cruciform church, built of red ironstone, and about as un-East Anglian looking as a church could be. There are daunting gargoyles below battlements, a fine and individual west tower, and from the outside the church reminds one of a fortress. In a field nearby are several thatched barns being allowed to fall down in the name of Profit, there is a range of two-storied seventeenth-century almshouses, unusual in being of a size big enough to live in and very good-looking, there is a good modern school, and, east of the village, a noteworthy timber-framed farmhouse, really well restored, and with no obnoxious 'olde-Tudor' knick-knacks slung about it.

By **Croydon**, south-east, we are in lovely and atypically Cambridgeshire country: rolling uplands with extensive woods in places. Truth to tell South Cambridgeshire is scenically uninspiring for the most part, and in these days being brought very much under the bulldozer; but there are the delicious corners to be come upon unexpectedly well away from the main roads. Croydon is a little hamlet near an actual *hill* that anybody would recognize as a hill; and there are woods and trees about, and the Queen Adelaide was a noble little pub until it was all done up inside with plastic tiles and wallpaper printed to make it look like Cotswold oolitic stonework.

At Croydon lived the Downing family. The first of the name was a sort of James Bond of the Commonwealth and Restoration period. His mother was a sister of John Winthrop, the Governor of Massachusetts, and George spent his childhood in the American colonies, returned to England to act as head spy for Cromwell, became Ambassador to France and Holland, while at the Hague managed to ingratiate himself with Charles Stuart by giving away Commonwealth secrets to him and thus stayed in favour at the Restoration. He doubled-crossed everybody, forced England into a war with Holland for his personal profit, starved his aged mother and built Downing Street. His grandson founded Downing College in Cambridge, with the money left by his grandsire's childless cousin.

Orwell has orchards around it, embellishing the chalk downland. The church has a clunch tower, originally Early English, a light and airy Perpendicular chancel, also of clunch and really lovely;

476

there is what looks like a Celtic cross inside the porch and the great treasure is the early fourteenth-century Calvary, now in the south chapel, with Christ nailed to a tree-trunk. This was hidden by being embedded in the south-east spandrel of the north arcade at the Reformation to save it from destruction, and was not re-discovered until 300 years later.

Archæological excavations have revealed traces of a Neolithic settlement at **Shepreth**, and later there was an Anglo-Saxon one. Although hemmed in today by small clusters of light industry, the village's scattered thatched cottages by leafy, twisting roads about the village green utterly refuse to be overwhelmed. One of two trout farms on the outskirts, Willers Mills Farm, houses what is virtually a small zoo, and there is a country walk about the property including a stroll on the embankment above the railway. Beside the road to **Meldreth**, which begins almost as soon as Shepreth leaves off, are the spacious premises of the Spastics Society, with a special riding school. On Meldreth's village green stand the old stocks and whipping post, and the base of a wayside cross.

Melbourn is much cut through by the London–Cambridge A10 It has a very new-looking church which is in fact not new as some of it is thirteenth century, there are fourteenth-century arcades and a fifteenth-century clerestory and roof and there is said to be one of Bishop Alcock's many cockerels on a tie-beam up there. There are saint niches in the south transept, the tower arch is strangely asymmetrical with the west window behind it, the east window is most distinguished Perpendicular. It is over the road from a most genteel licensed restaurant where you can get a very good steak, and can sip your sherry first in a pretty garden.

To the east, stretching between Fowlmere and Heydon is the Bran Ditch, one of the several defensive works athwart the Icknield Way. Skeletons of Romano-British soldiers have been unearthed here, with their bones broken as if in war. The whole district is rich in Iron Age, Roman, Saxon and other pre-Conquest remains. The chalk ridge between Essex forests and Fens was well inhabited in ancient times. Bran, in Welsh, means crow or raven.

Ickleton, one of the many villages with names influenced by the Icknield Way, has a church which is really worth going far to see.

477

Do not be put off by the undistinguished exterior, for this is just a shell over a Norman church the equal of which it would be hard to find. There are very stark and simple arcades, very early Norman with some of their arches resting on monolithic Roman pillars. Traces of colour show that there was once painted decoration on this otherwise quite undecorated stonework.

Some people assign these arcades to earlier-than-Norman times. They have a very strange, almost Byzantine, look about them. Without doubt the piers are Roman: monoliths of Barnack stone which must have been brought to this locality with enormous trouble. They could have been floated up the River Granta for some way but the river is very small for some distance below Ickleton. Some authorities believe that the piers were brought to the church from nearby Chesterford, in Essex, where there was certainly a Roman station. Others, though, believe that the Romans set them up where they are now, and that there was a Roman villa where the church now is. The plan of the church suggests that this might have been so – the pillars having stood each side of the Roman central open court, and having been roofed over by the Saxons, not the Normans, who built the existing clerestory (which indeed looks very Saxon) to admit light. The Saxons did not take over many Romano-British buildings for their own uses, being as a rule more concerned with burning them down: but there is no reason why this should not be the exception that proves the rule. It is a strange experience to stand within this church.

North to **Duxford**, where are three sacred buildings, one the old chapel of St John's Hospital, for long employed as a barn. These 'hospitals' were not institutions for the care of the sick but rest-houses put up for travellers and pilgrims. At Duxford Airfield is a branch of the Imperial War Museum, displaying First World War hangars, military vehicles, and over 90 historic military and civil aircraft. The prototype of the supersonic Concorde arrived here to take its place in the collection and can never fly out again, the runway having been truncated by a motorway. The museum is open daily from mid-March until the end of October, except for Good Friday and May Day Bank Holiday.

Pampisford has some of the biggest maple trees, Norway and

Common, in the British Isles. There is a Norman tympanum over the west door of the church, and beside the church is a lovely row of thatched, whitewashed cottages, one of them the Chequers Inn with the date 1599 on its wall.

And so we come to **Sawston** and its famous Hall, which was lived in by the Huddlestons for almost five hundred years, until very recent times. The family is a long-established Catholic one and it is this fact – this adherence to the old faith – that explains why the Hall has remained virtually unchanged since Elizabethan times when it was built. The family, constantly impoverished by the heavy fines that it had to pay for being of the wrong religion, and denied all chances of office, never had the money to carry out 'improvements' as all other country magnates were doing in later centuries. Thus instead of having some concoction of the Renaissance, more Italian or pseudo-Italian than true English, we have this lovely Elizabethan mansion in its four-square simplicity and good sense and lack of pretension.

The house is built of clunch, or chalk, and demonstrates the endurance of this soft rock so long as 'you keep its head and its feet dry'. In any case it has stood there since 1584, when the house was finished, and it looks as good as new, and some of it is earlier than 1584, for the present house was built within the walls of a much earlier mansion.

When the first settlers came from Angeln, in the Jutland peninsula, after the withdrawal of the Romans from Britain, they sailed into the land via the Wash, made their ways up the Wash rivers, and settled along their banks. These settlers turned their backs on the sea, burned their boats metaphorically if not physically, and it was not until the Wuffinga kings came over, probably from Uppsala in Sweden, that, as we have seen, East Anglia became united into a single kingdom.

Sawston, then called Salsingetune, or the town of Salsa, was one of the scattered settlements of these early settlers, and thus Sawston Hall has a very early antecedent.

Sir Edmund de la Pole, Captain of Calais and Sheriff of Cambridgeshire and Huntingdonshire, became owner of the manor of Sawston in 1377, and it was a great great great grand-daughter of his who married a Huddleston shortly after 1500, and thus the Hall came into the Huddleston family. William Huddleston, the man she married, had a great grandfather who fought at Agincourt.

The great crisis in the life of the Hall was when Edward VI died and Mary Tudor, his half-sister, was sent for from where she had been more or less a prisoner at Hunsdon, to go to London. On the way she was warned that her summons was a plot by the Duke of Northumberland, who had every intention of having her executed so that his daughter-in-law, Lady Jane Grey, should be queen instead of her. She fled to East Anglia, towards her own house in Kenninghall in Norfolk, and as we have seen while discussing Framlingham she eventually reached the latter place and there rallied a sufficient force to secure the Crown for herself.

But while on her way she arrived at Sawston Hall, on the 7th June 1553, and was entertained for the night by John Huddleston. Early the next day some of Northumberland's troops, under Lord Robert Dudley, another of his sons, and a Cambridge mob, came and attacked the Hall. Princess Mary left by a back door disguised as a dairymaid, riding pillion behind a servant and escorted by her host. Without doubt John Huddleston saved her life, and thus assured the present royal line of England.

They fled to the Gog Magog Hills, and looking back saw the sky smudged with flames: the mob, balked of their quarry, had set fire to Sawston House. Princess Mary said to John Huddleston: 'Let it blaze! When I am Queen I will build Huddleston a better house.' And when she was queen she knighted him, and made him Captain of the King of Spain's (her husband's) guard, and allowed him to take away the stone from Cambridge Castle to build a new house. And it is the new house which we see now.

The house was built between 1557 and 1584, taking so long because the family had to go into hiding during part of Elizabeth I's reign, on account of its recusancy. Things looked up with Charles I, for the Huddlestons of course were staunch Royalists, but they looked very gravely down during the Commonwealth when most of the Huddleston lands were sequestrated. Better with the Restoration, for it was a Huddleston who hid Charles II when he hid in the Boscobel Oak after the Battle of Worcester, but rough after Charles's death, when heavy fines were imposed on recusants.

The house today is little changed despite the ravages of the

Second World War, when this unspoilt Elizabethan treasure was unbelievably seized by the army for billeting troops. Photographs kept by the Huddlestons in the butler's pantry showed what devastation was caused. But there had so often been threats of violence here. A tower which probably antedates the rest of the house leads to one of the most famous priest-holes in the country, hollowed out of solid masonry in such a way that it could never be discovered from ordinary observation. It has an air vent into the central courtyard, most cunningly disguised, and a cover which fits in perfectly with the floor of the chamber above, fastened from within so that it could withstand not only close inspection but assault from a battering-ram. It was designed by that most skilful of all priest-hole contrivers, Nicholas Owen or 'Little John', a Jesuit who made such hiding places all over England. Finally captured, he was tortured in the Tower to make him reveal the whereabouts of his work. When asked by Cecil what information had been extracted from him, the Governor of the Tower had to admit none at all, and added: 'The man is dead, he died in our hands.'

In the attic is a hidden chapel, the paten and chalice of which are now on loan to the Victoria and Albert Museum. The present chapel is an elegant one, used by local Catholics as a parish church until a new church was built in the village.

In Sawston is the first of the Cambridge village colleges, designed by Dunn and built in 1930. Although neo-Georgian may be regarded by some as a dirty word, it is very good-looking and excellent for its purpose, making one wonder if we ought not to have gone on developing our architecture step by step, as we had done for the previous few thousand years, rather than taking wild leaps into the ugly dark.

Sawston church is very high; the Sacrament is reserved. There is a fascinating squint from the south aisle to the chancel; the piers are of very hard clunch; and on Monday 15th November 1948 a peal of 5040 chimes in Bob Minor was rung by the campanologists of the parish in 2 hours 47 minutes.

Sawston Hall was for many years open on certain days to the public, but has now become a School of Language and no longer encourages visitors. Another great house which was once private *is* now open, thanks to the wishes of its late owner and the sterling work of the National Trust. This is **Wimpole Hall**, a few miles to the west near Royston.

The mansion in its enormous park was begun in the middle of the seventeenth century by Sir Thomas Chicheley, probably to his own design: he was a talented man, and a great friend of Wren. Later it was sold off to a city merchant and then passed through several hands before becoming the home of the Earls of Hardwicke. The first of these, Philip Yorke, rose from being an obscure lawyer to the post of Lord Chancellor and in this office amassed a great fortune. He condemned the Highland rebels of the '45 to death, and enacted a law forbidding the Scots to wear the kilt or tartan. In 1938, after further changes of ownership and of architectural fashions, it was bought by Captain George Bambridge and his wife Elsie, daughter of Rudyard Kipling. Mrs Bambridge set about removing a number of Victorian excrescences and collecting furniture and pictures to suit the various rooms. During the Second World War Wimpole, like Sawston, suffered under military requisitioning, and a large American hospital was built in the park. Nevertheless Mrs Bambridge, after her husband's death, continued to work for the preservation and restoration of all that was best in Wimpole and the elimination of anything out of character. When she died in 1976 she was able not merely to leave a worthy monument to her endeavours but also to offer a generous endowment, including remaining copyrights on her father's work (which expired in 1986) and all his papers, which have since been lent to the University of Sussex (in which county the author spent so many creative years) for the benefit of scholars.

Like many family houses taken over by the National Trust, this one is being maintained with a 'lived-in' atmosphere rather than that of an informative but over-austere musuem. There are any number of friendly rather than fossilized memories of the Rudyard Kipling connection, while at the same time, in keeping with Mrs Bambridge's own long-term planning, the histories of her predecessors and of painting and architecture over the whole period of the house's existence are clearly displayed. What was used as a family dining-room until 1939 and then as a store-room for the Kipling papers is now laid out with drawings by most of the architects and landscape gardeners who have contributed to

Wimpole, including Gibbs, Soane, Repton and – but who else? – 'Capability' Brown. In the Saloon is a longcase clock with a movement by one William Kipling of 'Broad Street near Ratcliff Cross'.

This Saloon was remodelled in 1745 for that Earl of Hardwicke so bloodily associated with events of that year. The architect, Henry Flitcroft, added a bay window to command a vista of the great avenue to the north, enhanced in 1772 by a Gothic tower and ruins. The path to the folly crosses a Chinese bridge which may well have been a nineteenth-century replica of 'Capability' Brown's original. Another fine view, that from the superb Library, tends to negate the purpose of that vast room: sitting at the round table in the bay window, one might feel little inclination to read or write when the beautiful landscape offered such tempting prospects.

One equally alluring prospect was destroyed when the famous double avenue of elms was killed off by Dutch Elm disease. To replace it, the first lime tree of a new avenue was planted by Lord Hailsham (another Lord Chancellor!) in February 1982.

A model farm designed by Sir John Soane had become virtually derelict by 1976, but a comprehensive scheme for restoring it is being steadily carried through by the National Trust. Some less common, threatened breeds of sheep, pigs and cattle are being reintroduced for the benefit of students and future breeders, and the farm will become a vigorous museum of agricultural history.

Hall and garden are open afternoons except Monday and Friday from the end of March to the end of October; the farm on the same days 10.30 am–5 pm; the park daily all year round, sunrise to sunset.

Babraham has a fine park in the Granta valley at the foot of the Gog Magogs in which is an ugly great Victorian mansion and a church with Saxon work in its walls. The predecessor of the present hall was built by a fine swashbuckling character, Horation Palavazene, a Genoese sailor who came to England and commanded a ship against the Armada. In Queen Mary's reign he had the job of collecting 'Peter's Pence', the penny a year that every householder had to contribute to the Vatican. He collected a vast amount but, providentially, he had not actually sent any of it to the Vatican when Queen Mary died and he didn't have to. Instead he lent it to Queen Elizabeth, who certainly wasn't going to send it to any

Pope, and this gave rise to his epitaph, which goes:

> *Here lies Horation Palavazene,*
> *Who robbed the Pope to lend the Queen.*
> *'He was a Thiefe.' 'A Thiefe? Thou liest;*
> *For why? He robbed but Antichrist.*
> *Him Death with besom swept from Babram*
> *Into the Bosom of old Abram.*
> *But then came Hercules with his Club,*
> *And struck him down to Beelzebub.*

We might perhaps be tempted to think that the last two lines were added by a Roman Catholic: we are, after all, next door to Sawston Hall. A vicar, John Hullier, was burnt as a Protestant.

The **Shelfords**, **Great** and **Little**, have fine and interesting churches but all this country between Sawston and Cambridge has been so smothered with dreary twentieth-century building that I cannot imagine any traveller wishing to go there. But go he should to Trumpington.

To **Trumpington** if only to see the Trumpington brass, to Sir Roger, who died in 1289, and the second oldest brass in England. He is splendidly attired in chain-mail, with a dog biting the scabbard of his great sword, his shield slung on his shoulder, his mailed hands pressed together in prayer and his rugged soldierly face forced into what one might suspect was a rather unwonted expression of piety although he did sail to the Crusades with Edward I.

The church is very noble, and nearly all in the best Early English style. There is an inscription by Eric Gill to an officer killed in 1914, and the village war memorial is also by Gill. In the village, The Green Man is a magnificent timbered pub.

East of Cambridge, **Cherry Hinton**, now swallowed up, has an Early English chancel to its church of the greatest beauty – if only somebody hadn't knocked a late Perpendicular window in its east end! It is important to go inside this chancel for the inside is better than the out, and note the piscina and sedilia, and in the body of the church the arcading, the priest door, and the carved coffin lid in the west wall of the tower.

The road from Cherry Hinton to Fulbourn is dead straight, but is not, as one might suppose, a Roman road. It is a 'furrow-drawn' road. When the common lands were enclosed in various ages before the eighteenth century new roads were often made across the common fields, and these were generally drawn out by the best ploughman of the parish with his plough.

Fulbourn has a (very restored) church of interest to saint-knowers, for it is dedicated to St Vigor, the only church in England to be so excepting the one at Stratton on the Fosse, in Somerset. Needless to say St Vigor was Bishop of Bayeux in AD 514, but only a real saint-knower will know how he came to be patron of Fulbourn in Cambridgeshire, and I do not.

There are five brasses in the church and several lavish tombs: the one to John Careway, 1433, grisly indeed and not to be shown to the children. The brass to Canon William Fulburne, 1380, is said to be the earliest known brass of a priest vested in a cope. There is a fine fourteenth-century oak pulpit with painted panels.

South-east of Fulbourn we hit the A11, the main London–Norwich road, and if we turn left along it soon come to where it traverses **Fleam Dike**. The road is historically interesting (if dull) in that it follows the course of the Icknield Way. This was an ancient trackway running, roughly, from the Wiltshire downlands to the uplands of West Norfolk. These two comparatively well drained and treeless areas were ideal for settlement by people without iron axes and ploughs: it was not until the Belgians came, shortly before Julius Caesar, bringing their heavy iron wheeled ploughs, that men began to conquer the heavy clay lands of Suffolk and Essex.

The Way, which is supposed to be 8,000 years old, was not a road but a wide droving-way, like the overland routes that preceded diesel road-trains of cattle trailers in the Australian Outback. Anyone who has driven cattle along established droveways in roadless countries (such as parts of South-west Africa) will know that a narrow track is impracticable. The cattle, or small-stock such as sheep and goats, must forage as they go; and to do this each flock of herd must spread out beyond ground tramped over by its predecessors – and spread widely itself as it grazes along at from eight to ten miles a day (at eight miles a day in good bush cattle will fatten). The Icknield Way runs along the dry well-drained chalk ridge between the Essex clay, which was densely forested, and the impassable Fens, and was thus the only possible route for men to drive their animals between East Anglia and the rest of England.

If we stand on top of Fleam Dike, near the A11, we have a most impressive view of the Way, which was in constant use for cattle droving from these very early times to the Enclosures at the beginning of the nineteenth century. Over the rolling hedgeless Cambridgeshire fields, whose only crop nowadays is barley, we can see the soil changed in texture, the underlying chalk churned up in it, the very crops themselves modified in tone by this broad belt trodden and kicked up by the hooves of countless animals over thousands upon thousands of years.

And Fleam Dike, on which we stand, was the Maginot Line of the Celts living in East Anglia against incursions of hostile tribes along the Icknield Way; but like the Maginot Line and other linear defence works it succumbed to attack by a superior force.

When the Romans invaded Britain AD 55 the ruling people in East Anglia were the Iceni, who were traitors to the extent that they co-operated with the Romans in order to free themselves from the domination of Cymbeline who called himself King of Britain. As the English discovered later on when they drove the Celts from England and afterwards conquered Scotland Ireland and Wales, it was always possible to persuade half the Celts to fight against the other half. But, after the Roman victory, when the Romans asked the Iceni to hand over their arms, the Iceni refused, and manned their Fleam Dike, on which we now stand. The Roman general Ostorius came upon them suddenly with his light auxiliary troops only. Not waiting for his regulars to arrive he attacked the Dike along the whole of its length – flung the Iceni back – and slaughtered them as they tried vainly to clamber up their second line of defence: Devil's Dyke across Newmarket Heath.

It must be remembered that these great earthworks were crowned by wooden palisades.

The survivors of the tribe were disarmed, and accepted the Roman yoke. But twelve years afterwards, goaded beyond endurance by the legions, they made their heroic stand under Boudicca and slaughtered a vast number of Romans – but unfortunately not enough, for the Romans counter-attacked and would have wiped the Iceni off the face of the earth had clemency not been exercised by, of all people, the Emperor Nero.

But Fleam Dike today is much more peaceful, and the last resort in Cambridgeshire of many chalk-loving plants that the selective weed killers have wiped out elsewhere, such as the rare Pasque Flower (*Anemone pulsatilla*) – that grand anemone that is supposed to flower at Easter time.

Linton is an outstandingly pretty village straggling along each side of the Granta, home of another Cambridgeshire village college and of a small zoo open daily all year round except Christmas Day.

Bartlow has four great tumuli, alas excavated in 1835 when excavating wasn't what it is now – on top of which the finds were kept in a house which burnt to the ground; but there were walled graves with enamel-ware, bronze and glass. Bartlow church has a round tower, certainly Norman and perhaps earlier as to its base. It has been conjectured, in fact, that this tower was the 'minster of stone and lime' raised by Canute to celebrate his victory over the English at Assundon, which has been identified with the modern Ashdon in Essex. The English, in this battle, were betrayed by one of their nobles: Edric, who had been promised by Canute that if he did this he would be raised up higher than any of the other of the English nobility. He was: after the battle his head was cut off and raised to the highest turret of the Tower of London.

Castle Camps, where is little to see, had a castle, now earthworks. It was built by de Vere, Earl of Oxford, soon after the Conquest.

Balsham, the highest place in Cambridgeshire, all of 400 feet up in the clouds, has an important and interesting church. The tower is Early English but so shored up with massive buttresses that the west door and old pointed windows have been obscured. Inside is that rare thing – not only a rood screen, but a rood loft. How this escaped the Reformation, and the Puritans, is hard to understand. John de Sleford added the nave and aisles to the earlier tower and chancel, and he died in 1401, and his sumptuous brass is still in the church for all to see – nine foot long and with saints embroidered all down his cope. This man was Master of the Wardrobe to Edward III, Canon of Ripon, Archdeacon of Wells, Chaplain to the Queen as well as Rector of Balsham. There is another fine brass to another

487

barefaced pluralist: John Blodwell, Rector here in 1439 besides being Dean of St Asaph, Canon of St David's, Prebendary of Hereford and Prebendary of Lichfield. It is to be feared that, in those days of slow travel, he could not have discharged all these duties very conscientiously, particularly as among his activities he numbered assisting at the prosecution of Joan of Arc.

Dr Sleford paid for the excellent carvings of the chancel stalls, which none should miss; and a recent rector carved, with his own hands, the font cover, altar rails and alms box, and taught wood carving to his parishioners.

There is a simply corking east window by A. K. Nicholson, and a possibly even more sentimental chancel window by Christopher Webb. As an antidote to this seek out the Anglo-Saxon coffin lid which was dug up in the graveyard.

In Anglo-Saxon times the entire population of Balsham was wiped out, save one man, by the Danes after the terrible battle of Ringmere Heath when Svend Forkbeard overthrew the English hero Ulfcytel so that 'all England did quake before him like a reed bed rustling in the wind'. The men of Balsham put up a stiff resistance and so were made an example of; but one man took refuge in the doorway to the tower of the church and defended himself to such good effect that the Danes retired and left him alone. This may well be the same doorway that we can stand in today.

Hugh de Balsham, who founded Peterhouse, comes, as his name suggests, from Balsham.

At **West Wratting**, in 1877, a man named Frost built a flying machine powered by steam, but it did not fly. At **Weston Colville** are two good brasses: Robert Leverer of 1427 in armour amid flowers, wife in flowing headdress and son between them; and Abraham Gates, 1636, with wife at a *prie-dieu*, cherubs, skulls, angel flying away with a trumpet to announce his arrival to St Peter, the lot.

Westley Waterless also has a brass, and a good one, to Sir John and Lady Alyne de Creke. He is in chain-mail with a surcoat known as a cyclas, she in a lovely dress. Their faces remind one of many a young well-bred couple at a Hunt Ball. The brass, being 1324, is a very early one.

Kirtling has Kirtling Tower, of which only the gateway is old, the mansion having been pulled down in the last century. The gatehouse is 1530, brick, and pretty grand with turrets – more for show than for defence. The house was built by the first Lord North, Chancellor to Henry VIII. His son entertained Queen Elizabeth at Kirtling Towers and it is even rumoured that she was hid there during part of Mary Tudor's reign. Both father and son have lavish tombs in Kirtling church. The 3rd Lord died in the Fire of London. He is credited with the startling discovery of the health springs of Tunbridge Wells, and was a close friend of Charles II. The church has a really fine south doorway, well carved, with Norman ironwork on the door, Norman arches in the south arcade, and it is, though small, very interesting and evocative (map, pp. 474–475).

Kirtling's 'Beehive' is a delicious country pub, although corrugated iron replaces thatch on the roof. Here, in a Sunday lunchtime session, you will hear the liveliest conversation, full of East Anglian pithiness and wit (if you can understand it), and the young men sit in too with the good and natural relationship that existed between the age-groups in pre-juke-box days. We are really back in East Anglia now, after our excursion across the Cam. This is a good place to savour, besides good beer, the rich East Cambridgeshire dialect.

Cheveley has a cruciform church with a crossing-tower and a fine Decorated oak screen and a very beautiful Early English chancel. Noble arches support the crossing-tower: their piers said each to have been the property of a trade guild, and on which that guild kept its light burning (map, pp. 474–475).

Wood Ditton is so named for having been at the 'wood', i.e. the forest, end of Devil's Dyke. There is a rather defaced brass in the church of a knight wearing *camail* armour: steel discs sewn to boiled leather. This is to Henry Englissh and his wife, 1393.

We have missed one place out in Cambridgeshire. The **Gog Magog Hills**. These do not need crampons and ice-axes to ascend, being no more than 220 feet of very gentle chalk slope; but they make a good walk out of Cambridge, and from them a good view of the city can be had, and, on a clear day, the Fens as far as Ely. There are several theories as to the derivation of the name – the most intriguing being that the Emperor Probus quartered gigantic

Vandal auxiliaries there, and the much shorter Celts gave to them the names of giants – Gog and Magog. Hence, also, the name Wandlebury, which is still used for the great earthwork on the summit of these tiny mountains. Lethbridge believed that this was a sacred Iron Age site, and that great figures of gods were cut in the chalk (now no longer visible).

CHAPTER 28

Huntingdonshire and Peterborough

by John Burke

The small but far from insignificant county of Huntingdonshire and its close ally the Soke of Peterborough ('Soke' being an Anglo-Saxon area with specific privileges) have owed a great deal through the centuries to two thoroughfares: the Great North Road and the Great Ouse. The road brought prosperity – and near-suffocation – to little towns and villages, then took much of it away when bypasses relieved congestion but left the shops and coaching inns to a drowsy decline. Beside the river grew up snug little communities which today profit from the activities of leisure craft rather than any brisk freight traffic.

St Neots stands at what was once a key junction of road and river, and also a junction with the cross-country A45. The Great North Road, or A1, now avoids it, but the A45 still cuts through its spacious market square and over its sturdy bridge. Such river crossings were of importance from earliest times, and the town itself is known to have existed here since the tenth century. Its fifteenth-century church has a finely carved tower rising above the cluster of old inns whose great stableyard entrances recall past glories. The Cross Keys is still distinguished both outside and in, though in this homeland of Oliver Cromwell one doubts the social implications of a Cromwell *bar* and a Royalist *lounge*. It was not far from here that the legendary coachman Tom Henesey, 'the adored of barmaids, the idol of schoolboys', nearly came to grief on the river bank. Making a detour around a papermill he found himself on a track so waterlogged that water was beginning to seep into the interior of the coach and drag it towards the deeper course

491

of the Ouse. It was only by the most desperate efforts that he was able to get his horses to haul it free.

Across the river in **Eaton Socon** is another worthy relic, the thirteenth-century White Horse inn, refaced in mellow brick and with a glowing interior of polished woodwork, low beams, and inviting window alcoves. Early in the nineteenth century it was run by a Charles James Fox – not the politician but a mail guard from St Neots. When he died the premises were taken over by his sister-in-law and her husband, who also took on the orphaned Fox children to bring the total of children in the house up to seven. As they also boasted two coachmen and three servants, one wonders how they ever managed to squeeze in any paying guests.

A few miles north and we can once again slip off the newer A1 on to the old road and find ourselves in **Buckden**, one of whose large inns has had different names and functions in the past. Originally the refectory of the nearby episcopal palace, it became the Lamb Inn; then the Old Lion and Lamb remembered in a huge carved wooden boss in the lounge ceiling depicting those two creatures; and today trades simply as the Lion.

The neighbouring tower and Tudor gatehouse, now sheltering also a modern Roman Catholic church and children's holiday centre, formed part of a palace belonging to the Bishops of Lincoln from the twelfth to the nineteenth centuries. Seven of them died here. Two other distinguished men also met their end here while believing that they were avoiding it: two uncles of Lady Jane Grey, arriving from Cambridge to escape a 'sweating plague' in 1551, found they had brought it with them and died within half an hour of each other. They are buried in the parish churchyard. In this church Laurence Sterne, author of *Tristram Shandy*, was ordained in 1736.

Another name forever associated with Buckden is that of Catherine of Aragon, imprisoned in the palace after Henry VIII had cast her aside. Later he tried to have her removed to a lonelier place, and although at first she shut herself away in her room and refused to come out, in due course he had her transferred to Kimbolton.

Kimbolton today is a charming little place, largely Georgian in character, with a wide main street of fine brick and plaster frontages, no two the same, and wavy tiled roofs. Unfortunately that

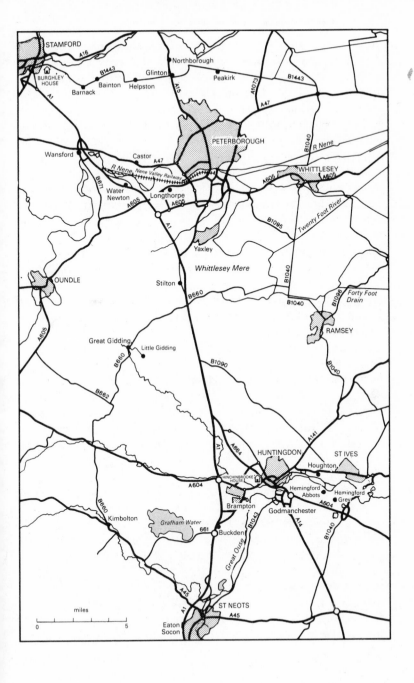

main street is the A45, entering from one end around a cramped double bend which jams lorries against the walls and builds up traffic to either side. Beside that bend stands Kimbolton Castle. In 1066 King Harold had a hunting estate here, in what was then thick woodland. Around 1200 a fortified manor house stood on the site, but completely vanished under Tudor and Jacobean alterations. The whole place was rebuilt after 1522 by Sir Richard Wingfield, a confidant of Henry VIII, and it was here that Catherine was lodged from 1534 until her death two years later. She breathed her last in what is now known as the Queen's Room, and her ghost is said to haunt the main staircase; but as this did not come into existence until about 1690, the story is rather implausible. Among the architects called in during the seventeenth century to carry out major reconstructions was Vanbrugh, who was most insistent that throughout all alterations the 'castle air' should be retained. Behind its Adam gatehouse, the resulting mansion is now a school. State rooms and the extensive grounds are open to the public between Easter and late August certain weekend and Bank Holiday afternoons.

From the road between Buckden and Kimbolton, or alternatively from byroads off the A604 west of Huntingdon, one can drive to picnic sites beside **Grafham Water**. This reservoir covers an area of 1570 acres at top water level and offers fishing and sailing, a nature trail, and a number of public footpaths including one right across the dam between the parking spaces of Plummer Park and Marlow Park. A nature reserve with a hide overlooking the sanctuary area of Littless and Dudney Creeks is open every Sunday from September to February. Permits to visit this, and for fishing, are obtainable from the fishing lodge. There are plenty of seats, benches and tables along the pleasantly landscaped banks, providing a relaxing view across the wide, rippling lake.

Brampton has become a rather smug residential dormitory outpost of Huntingdon, but retains much of its old village character in the neighbourhood of the green, with houses in agreeable mixtures of styles and materials, and streets where old red brick and tile mingle with modern walls of various hues from the brickworks of Fletton and Whittlesey to the north. The pub on the edge of the green became known as the New Inn some time early in this century, but in 1973 changed its name to The Harrier – not because of any local tradition of hare coursing, but in honour of nearby RAF Brampton. Its sign makes this clear, as do coloured pictures of the aircraft in the bar. If they are still here a hundred years from now, what will they mean to visitors of that time?

A certain Mr John Pepys inherited a small farmhouse near the church and spent some years there until his daughter married and took him away to live with herself and her husband. John's son Samuel lived in the house while attending Huntingdon Grammar School and later revisited it frequently, both when at Cambridge and when at the Admiralty in London. During the Plague he sought refuge here and, fearing a possible Dutch invasion, buried his money in the garden. An iron pot of silver coins discovered near the garden wall in 1842 is thought to have been part of the cache.

The story of a ghostly drummer boy in R. H. Barham's *Ingoldsby Legends* is based on a murder which took place in Brampton in 1780. The murderer was hanged from a gibbet near the Brampton Hut, now part of a large modern hotel at the crossroads of the A1 and the main Huntingdon–Kettering road.

Beside the short stretch of road between Brampton and Huntingdon is **Hinchingbrooke House**, once a Benedictine nunnery around whose remains Sir Richard Cromwell, Oliver's great-grandfather, built a mansion. The sculpted gatehouse is thought to have been brought from Ramsey Abbey in the sixteenth century. Many alterations took place over the years: after the Restoration the 1st Earl of Sandwich added to the west side of the court, and restoration of a different kind was needed after a fire in 1839 had done a great deal of damage. Today the house is a school, but is open to the public on Sunday afternoons from April to the end of August, with some enjoyable walks through the extensive grounds, part of whose layout has been ascribed to Samuel Pepys.

We meet both Pepys and Oliver Cromwell again in **Huntingdon** – if, that is, we can find our way into the town. Of all the ring roads, one-way systems and parking arrangements one has to cope with nowadays, those of Huntingdon are surely the most baffling, infuriating and frustrating. Yet in spite of all the presumably well-meant protection of the inner town, the most recent innovations have still allowed for a continual flow of traffic upon the far from indestructible bridge over the Ouse, installed in the thirteenth century, renovated some centuries later, and now in grievous peril.

Once in and parked, and capable of drawing breath again, one can hardly escape the lingering presence of Cromwell. His grandfather was proprietor of the splendidly galleried George Hotel. Oliver was born in 1599 in a house close to the ancient highway of Ermine Street, its site marked by a plaque on the Huntingdon Research Centre. He was baptized in All Saints' Church, where his father is buried. Some three decades before that baptism a London alderman, Sir Anthony Bartholomew, acquired the twelfth-century Hospital of St John on Market Hill and converted it into a grammar school, retaining only two bays of the original Norman great hall and dividing the new premises into two floors. Oliver came to school here, as did Samuel Pepys some years later. The building is now a Cromwell Museum, with relics including hs sword, water-bottle and a copy of *The Soldier's Catechism* of 1644. Oliver represented the town as its MP for several years, though after 1631 he chose not to live in it: following a quarrel with the town council he moved to St Neots. During the Civil War he was responsible for rallying most of East Anglia to the Parliamentary cause, and remains one of the most contentious figures in English history: however just that cause may have been in so many respects, the destructiveness of his soldiers and above all the vindictive iconoclasm of William Dowsing have left grievous wounds which still scar the churches of East Anglia to this day.

A seventeenth-century causeway links Huntingdon to **Godmanchester** beyond that graceful bridge referred to earlier. In Roman times this was an important settlement at a crossroads of Ermine Street, on its route between London and York, and the road running from Colchester to Chester which was later named the Via Devana by an eighteenth-century pseudo-classicist basing it on the Roman name for Chester – Deva. The original fort guarding a ford across the Ouse was ravaged by Boudicca's rebellion, but then was renewed and converted into a residential and agricultural centre on the supply highways to the north and west, using not just the roads but the river Ouse and its links with other waterways.

The Ouse swirls into a number of little offshoots between The

Causeway and the water meadows known as Portholme, criss-crossed with footpaths. These paths are reached from the street over a Chinese Bridge, gracefully arching over one tranquil water-course to another bridge over a less tranquil, foaming weir. The Chinese Bridge was erected in 1827, rebuilt in 1869, and then replaced by a replica in 1979. The river frontage has what might be regarded as a textbook display of small town house architecture. Two 'long houses', each with a central chimney stack, are joined so that from the meadows they appear almost one, with an expanse of half-timbered upper storey. One has an end gable oversailing its lower storey. Their near neighbours are eighteenth-century, with chimneys at each end instead of in the middle; and one has a mansard roof – quite a common feature in this region.

Other little settlements along the Ouse have charms of their own, best seen from a boat but very rewarding from the banks. Lying snug and secretive off the main road to St Ives is **Houghton**, a stylish little assemblage of black and white timber and plaster, neat brickwork, and amiable little shops. The low-slung Three Horseshoes Inn, with dormer windows peering out almost low enough to be touched, is too pretty to be true: but it *is* true. A thatched market cross facing it looks just as traditional, but in fact was erected only in 1902 in memory of a local worthy named Brown; and there is another of that name, Potto Brown, whose marble memorial on the corner of the square complements the village pump and market cross – which is used mainly as a bus shelter. Potto Brown was one of two millers and philanthropists who operated the watermill at the end of Mill Lane, a towering edifice of brick and black weatherboard with a high tiled roof, parts of the fabric being held together by massive bolts and beams. This is now cared for by the National Trust, who keep the machinery in working order and set it to grind corn at some weekends. It is open most afternoons from Easter until mid-October except Thursday and Friday. Even when it is closed, there is a footbridge right through the building and out across the water to a footpath leading on to another little complex of swirling tendrils of the Ouse, another bridge to meadows beyond, and yet another footpath to yet another footbridge into the secluded byways of the Hemingfords.

Hemingford Abbots, once a possession of Ramsey Abbey, looks

497

smart and complacent and well-to-do; and keeps itself that way. Its modern houses are thatched in keeping with the rest of the village, and there is an especially appealing cluster of older dwellings about the church, whose soaring spire makes up for the amputation of its neighbour a little way along the river. The parish church of St James in **Hemingford Grey** carries a mere stump crowned with eight stone balls, all that remains of a spire blown down during a hurricane in 1741 which also destroyed the spire of St Ives and left 'hardly a windmill standing in the district'. The pieces are believed to be still lying in the mud of the river bed. Dignified old buildings crowd together along the river bank and watch over the traffic of houseboats, skiffs and cruisers. Beside the church is a Queen Anne house whose gardens, also bordering the Ouse, sport one of the mightiest plane trees in the land. For long the home of the family who held the advowson of the church, it has now become a study and conference centre. Among other fine buildings stands a Norman manor claiming to be the oldest inhabited house in England, set within a square moat whose fourth side is the river itself. The original entrance was on the first floor, whose door must have been reached by an external stairway.

There was once a direct road from the outskirts of Hemingford Grey over the beautifully arched fifteenth-century bridge into **St Ives**. This road in fact still exists, but the bridge has been closed to all traffic save, for some weird reason, buses and taxis. A well-laden bus will surely cause more strains upon the fabric than a number of smaller cars; and lorry drivers delivering in the neighbourhood seem blandly to ignore the restriction, which can hardly improve the bridge's chances of survival. From whichever bank one starts, it is well worth walking over. The Quay below the town itself presents an engaging prospect of the river and the symmetry of the bridge, with the admirably designed modern Dolphin Hotel to enhance the far bank. From the riverside courtyard of the hotel one looks back on the whole waterfront of the town. And in the middle of the bridge is one of the three surviving medieval bridge chapels in England. In the nineteenth century it was converted into a house with the provision of an absurd upper storey, but this has now been removed. Renovation of the chantry chapel is planned for the late 1980s, with regular opening to visitors, who at the time of writing have to go in search of the key.

The centre of St Ives was never meant to cope with modern vehicles, and its long market place is now a mixture of car park and traffic jam, watched over by a statue of, inevitably, its most famous resident – Oliver Cromwell, with a remarkably rakish hat. In addition to farming just outside the town he was a churchwarden at All Saints' church whose spire, as we have noted, came down in the 1741 hurricane; and it had to be repaired yet again in our own century after an aeroplane had crashed into it. A monastery under the aegis of Ramsey Abbey not merely built the bridge chapel but, much earlier than that, provided the town with its name: when the monastery was founded in the eleventh century, remains were found and claimed to be those of an obscure Persian missionary, St Ivo de Slepe.

Roads this eastern side of the A1 lead us unavoidably back into the Fens. To the west the land rises, and although it is not to any great height there is an impression of being in what one might call the Huntingdonshire Highlands – an undulating countryside from which so many hedges have been grubbed up that one can foresee a repetition of the dust storms and uncontrollably drifting snow which have plagued Norfolk farmlands since greed for an immediate profit took over from old-fashioned notions of long-term husbandry.

On a windy slope beside a minor road out of Great Gidding stands a little huddle of buildings at whose heart is the tiny church of **Little Gidding**. The site was chosen in the seventeenth century for its remoteness, and even today it remains remote and calm – though that calm can be ruffled by wind howling across the low hills and through the treetops. The founder of the church and community was Nicholas Ferrar, born in London in 1592 into a wealthy merchant family. He became Deputy Treasurer of the Virginia Company and an MP, but gradually was persuaded that his real vocation was a religious one. Ordained a deacon in 1626, he invited his mother, elder brother and sister to join him in setting up a contemplative group around the derelict manor house and church of Little Gidding. They were joined by others, established a school for their children, and practised a routine of prayer and meditation. In spite of the predictable malicious rumours abut heresy and secret immorality in what one pamphlet denounced as an 'Arminian Nunnery', devout visitors began to come and were always made welcome. Most distinguished of these was King Charles I, two of whose visits resulted in some misfortune for the community. He had spent a day here a short time before the outbreak of the Civil War; and in May 1646 came seeking refuge after his defeat. Hard on his heels were the Roundheads, who ransacked the church, burnt the pulpit, and threw much of the contents into the pond.

After Nicholas's death his brother John and sister Susanna went on with the good work. Susanna had been an only daughter, but when she married John Collet she presented him with more than just one girl: eight daughters, plus eight sons.

Interest in the history of the community was reawakened after publication of a book about Nicholas Ferrar in 1938, followed by T. S. Eliot's poem *Little Gidding*, in the *Four Quartets* sequence. It was not until 1969, however, that members of the fellowship were able to buy the farmhouse nearby and provide accommodation for conferences and retreats. In 1976 a charitable trust was set up, new houses were built, and members of Anglican, Roman Catholic and Free Churches now come regularly to pray, work on the land, and achieve a balance of privacy and shared disciplines in what now calls itself the Community of Christ the Sower. Visitors are made welcome, and the atmosphere of the diminutive church, with Nicholas Ferrar's tabletop tomb on the path up to its door, is soothing and equally welcoming.

Back on to the dual carriageway of the main northbound road, we can make a brief diversion along what was once itself the main highway through **Stilton**. The coaching inns here have lost much of their trade and two of them threatened to disappear altogether not so many years ago – one gutted by fire, the other left derelict. Now things are looking healthier. The Bell, with its huge sign restored, is open again and once more serves the cheese which made the name of the place famous. That cheese has never in fact been made in or near the village itself: it is a Leicestershire product from the neighbourhood of Melton Mowbray which was sold to travellers up and down the Great North Road as they halted for sustenance. Its reputation grew so great that Stilton became also a main collection point for dealers in London and elsewhere. The stonework of the restored Bell is still a great joy, and the interior has everything to commend it apart from the inescapable churning out not of high quality cheese but of sour quality pop music and the frantic radio gabble of morons whose campaign to destroy the whole leisurely, talkative atmosphere of English pubs seems only too likely to succeed. This remark is aimed not only at the otherwise delightful Bell: it applies to almost every other similar establishment these days, so many of them enchanting to the eyes and taste buds but wantonly offending the ears.

After another stretch of the A1, another turning takes us on to its old course through **Wansford**, around whose incomparable medieval bridge has grown up a flawless village of limestone the colour of light rye bread. The name of one inn, the Paper Mill, recalls a past industry by the river Nene. Its mightier companion, the Haycock, is another of those great coaching inns which acted as the bus stations of their day, serving a countrywide network of routes. The name is associated with the legend of a seventeenth-century drunkard who fell asleep on a haycock and woke to find himself being carried down the Nene on a flood. When people along the banks laughingly asked where he had come from, he replied he was 'from Wansford Brigs in England'; and to this day the place is still referred to locally as Wansford-in-England.

Just over a mile away on the other side of the A1 is Wansford station, terminus of the flourishing Nene Valley Railway, which runs steam services at weekends and on public holidays from Easter until October, with a midweek timetable through most of the summer and special pre-Christmas events for enthusiasts, using part of what was once the rail route between Northampton and Peterborough. Built to an international loading gauge, it has the capability, unique in this country, to run Continental locomotives and rolling stock along the same track as British engines and coaches. The revivified railway operated between Wansford and an eastern terminus at Orton Mere in the Nene Park leisure area, until allowed to run right into Peterborough upon the opening of a city terminus by H.R.H. Prince Edward on 30th June 1986.

The **Nene Valley** has offered up many an archaeological bounty over many decades. At Flag Fen the well-preserved wooden piles and platforms of a Bronze Age lake village were found in 1982, and opened to the public in 1987 under the auspices of English Heritage and the Fenland Archaeological Trust. Also along the banks of the Nene are fragments of Roman building, and traces of old drainage ditches. Near the children's boating lake at Ferry Meadows are the outlines and postholes of an aisled barn. Longthorpe Tower, a fourteenth-century fortified manor house decorated with lavish wall paintings of religious and secular subjects, stands close to the site of a Roman marching camp, expanded during the rebellion of Boudicca and her Iceni but abandoned when the Ninth Legion left for new quarters in Lincoln. Today its sketchy remains are buried beneath Thorpe Wood golf course.

Castor, a most inviting village beside the A47, produced some of the finest indigenous pottery in this Roman province: grey or with a touch of blue, it imitated the then fashionable Samian ware in its animal figures and basic shapes, but instead of being moulded on, its relief patterns were piped on like whorls of icing on a wedding cake. Castor was an industrial centre of some consequence then, with its central trade hall, warehouses, and a bath block which must have had much in common with a modern pit-head shower building. Quays beside the Nene supplied a steady barge traffic, just as in later centuries the Midland canals shipped the products of Josiah Wedgwood's Etruria factory smoothly away. Travellers through modern Castor should not regard the stone houses and inns of the main road as all that the place has to offer: the village green, Church Hill, and narrow High Street are all tucked away to one side. A Romano-British tessellated pavement was discovered in 1820 near St Kyneburga's church and relaid in the dairy of Milton Hall. St Kyneburga was the founder of a nunnery on ground where this church stands today, while her brother Peada, first Christian king of Mercia, established a monastery at what was then called Medehamstede but later, in his honour, became Peterborough. The present church is cruciform, with an elaborate central tower topped by a fourteenth-century spire, and an interior which is stepped up in four shallow stages towards the altar. The nave roof bristles with the outspread gilded wings of colourful angels, while on the north wall is a rare medieval fresco of the martyrdom of St Catherine of Alexandria, patron saint of wheelwrights: decayed because of incompetent attempts at preservation, the mural is in process of more skilful restoration during the late 1980s.

Castor was in Roman times merely an industrial suburb of *Durobrivae*, a sizeable settlement between here and **Water Newton**. The original earthworks of the encampment were strengthened by a stone wall and, in the fourth century, stone bastions. It grew into a major military, residential and commercial centre, with shops and what has been identified as a large market hall or senate house. The most remarkable treasure yielded up in the region was the Water Newton silver hoard, one of the earliest known collections of objects marked with Christian symbols so far found in the Roman world. A large silver dish bearing the *Chi-rho* Christian monogram had been loaded with a goblet, a flagon, votive plaques, and a golden disc on which the symbol was accompanied by Alpha and Omega, the Beginning and the End. It is possible that this family treasure had been buried to hide it from religious persecutors; but nobody knows why it was not later retrieved – unless by then the Saxon invaders had driven the local Romano-Britons away in disarray. At some risk of repetition, one has to classify Water Newton as yet another of those villages and hamlets once on the Great North Road which have been granted a reprieve on what is now a little side road; though the thunder of the A1, a few yards away, reverberates unceasingly through the ragged, half-forgotten churchyard.

Both the A47 and the A605 offer attractive glimpses of the many delights of **Nene Park**, with the Nene Valley Railway threading through it. Absence of common land and open spaces for public use in the city of Peterborough and its immediate vicinity led to the development of this country park, always open for walking, sauntering, and watching birdlife. From Easter onwards a number of more specialized facilities build up towards the height of the summer holiday season: board and dinghy sailing, pony and pony-and-trap rides, river cruises, and a miniature railway linking various play areas and lakes. As well as a garden specially designed as a habitat for birds and other creatures there is a bird reserve which provides a passage site of great interest to ornithologists, particu-

503

larly in the study of waders; though it may be permissible to wonder whether such a reserve is really needed, since the wildfowl make themselves so blithely free of the lakes, islands and banks in and about the Nene. The wildlife of the park is explained in a permanent display in the Visitor Centre at Ferry Meadows. Although Nene Park can be entered at several points, this is the centrepiece and probably the most suitable introduction for a newcomer. Ferry Meadows is well signposted from the A605 down Ham Lane, over the Nene Valley Railway, and past a pitch-and-putt course and Orton Meadows public golf course.

For the energetic the Nene Way offers a seven-mile country walk from the outskirts of Peterborough to Wansford station, and this may in due course be extended beyond the A1. It takes in Orton Mere, a nine-acre picnic site created around what were once British Sugar Corporation settling ponds, Thorpe Park public golf course, Bluebell Woods (within which there is a separate waymarked path, worth a walk in itself, through woodland managed until 1973 by Earl Fitzwilliam), osier plantations, and Castor watermill and its roofless windmill. Generous provision is made for the handicapped: those arriving at Ferry Meadows car park without their own wheelchairs will find Batricars on loan – though at the height of the season it is as well to check in advance that they are not already commandeered.

This consideration for the disabled is echoed in the city which rises above the eastern end of Nene Park. **Peterborough** might be described as a flat city without being a dull one. Its level pavements are ideal for walks of any age, and developments since 1968 have made due allowance for those in need of special help: Queensgate, for example, the largest of the central car parks, houses a 'Shop-mobility' voluntary service which allows the disabled to park easily and, if not accompanied by their own wheelchair, to hire a hand-propelled or battery-operated one without fee, though donations by users towards the cost of the service are appreciated.

There were settlements in the Peterborough region from Neo-lithic times onwards. The Romans had their legionary fort at Longthorpe, their potteries along the valley, and their villas dotted about the neighbourhood. But it was during the Saxon era that the town really began to take shape around King Peada's monastery.

Today's urban street layout is still basically Saxon. Unfortunately the wealth of the monastic foundation attracted the attention of the Vikings, who sacked it in 870, slaughtering the monks and a large part of the populace. In Norman times the restored monastery regained its old importance, and again was attacked – by the recalcitrant Hereward the Wake from his base at Ely. Later prosperity derived mainly from Peterborough's position as a market town serving the whole locality and from its acquisition of an important station on the railway line from London up the north-eastern side of Britain.

Random development in the early 1960s permitted the erection of the hideous Hereward Centre concrete block and other grisly errors. When the place was scheduled as a New Town in 1967, Peterborough Development Corporation planned work more conscientiously, and by 1970 had put in hand a far-ranging scheme for expansion conceived not to spoil the city's true character. Within the next fifteen years the population rose from 86,000 to almost 130,000, without ever overloading the facilities. Bridge Street, which had once carried the main north-south road right through the very heart of Peterborough and was widened in the 1920s to accommodate a new Town Hall, provided a focus for a four-acre pedestrian precinct with trees, seats, and cycle stands. At night the clusters of lights are most attractive, especially upon the old Guildhall, where imaginative angling has given the distinguished building a mellow glow, best contemplated from within the gateway of the cathedral. The huge Queensgate enclosed shopping centre was evolved in a series of rising storeys so that, although lofty within, there is no aspect of it from outside which overpowers neighbouring structures or the pedestrians and shoppers themselves. As in many a town nowadays, the most pleasing architectural features are the older upper storeys surviving above modern shop fronts; but in Peterborough there is the difference that one can stand well back to view these without fear of being mown down by cars or lorries.

On the river's edge is the Key Theatre (surely it ought to have been the Quay Theatre?) opened in 1973. Its bar, glazed in along three sides, offers a view across the Nene – best at night, when the lights in the water are romantic and the shoddy tangle of the far bank is shrouded in mystery. The footpath leading eventually across Nene Park runs below the theatre. An audience of some four hundred is accommodated in well-raked rows of seats, with a perfect view of the stage from anywhere in the auditorium. For those in search of less sedentary pastimes, the East of England Ice Rink is the largest of its kind in the country, and in 1984 played host to the World Indoor Speed Skating Championships.

Some of the most attractive survivors of past generations are the stone houses which, looking as if they had been shifted bodily from the streets of Stamford, are woven into sequences of ancient arches and monastic remains under the shadow of the cathedral.

The Cathedral of St Peter, St Paul and St Andrew, whose statues look down from the gables above the rose windows, was begun in Norman times, with the deeply recessed west front in Early English style. The first thing to catch the eye on entering is a large hanging crucifixion above the nave, presented by the Reverend William Elborne in 1975. But one of the cathedral's greater glories is to be found high above that, in the actual roof of the nave. Here is a breath-taking sequence of panels painted with colourful lozenges in the early thirteenth century – the earliest such wooden ceiling in England, and one of only four of its kind in the whole of Europe. It is all the more breath-taking if one peers dizzily up rather than using the mobile mirror provided. The chancel roof is even more elaborate, with painted vaulting and a great flourish of cross-ribbed panels and bosses.

Two queens have been laid to rest within these walls. Catherine of Aragon's body was brought here from Kimbolton in 1536, though even after her miseries were ended she was not allowed to rest: in 1643 Cromwell's men destroyed her tomb. The present black marble slab was paid for in the 1890s after an appeal for sixpences from anyone named Catherine. Another memorial tablet on a nearby pillar was subscribed to by the people of Peterborough and installed in January 1986, the 450th anniversary of her death. Nor did the decapitated Mary, Queen of Scots, lie undisturbed. Her body, brought from Fotheringhay after her execution in 1587, was removed to Westminster Abbey in 1612, some years after her son James VI of Scotland had become James I of England.

A lesser mortal is commemorated in a wall painting and portrait

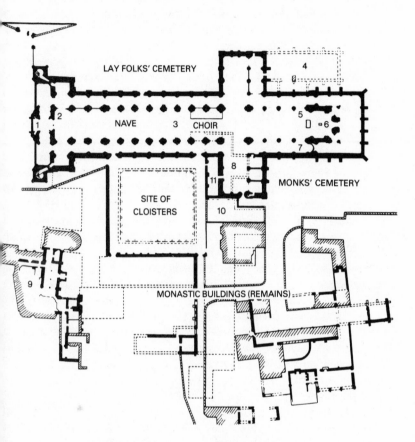

LAY FOLKS' CEMETERY

NAVE 3 CHOIR

4

5

6

7

8

11

SITE OF
CLOISTERS

10

MONKS' CEMETERY

9

MONASTIC BUILDINGS (REMAINS)

1 Trinity Chapel (Now Library)
2 Robert Scarlett's Portrait
3 Nave Crucifix
4 Site of Lady Chapel
5 Catherine of Aragon's Tomb
6 Monk's Stone
7 Mary, Queen of Scots' Tomb
8 Saxon church foundations
9 Bishop's Palace
10 Site of Chapter House
11 Sacristy

just inside the west door. Robert Scarlett, parish sexton in the sixteenth century, dug the graves or both queens and of many other folk. His own gravestone is in the floor below his memorial.

The cathedral bells were the work of Henry Penn, a bellfounder thought to have been a relative of William Penn, founder if not of bells at any rate of Pennsylvania. Because of their deteriorating condition it had been found unsafe to ring them during more than fifty years, until in 1986 an offer was made for their transfer to the United States, the purchase price going towards the manufacture of a new peal.

In the precincts is a crocketed cone suggesting some strange war memorial. It is in fact a spirelet which was blown by a hurricane against the south-west spire in January 1976. The Dean enlisted the help of twelve good men and true to lower it down into the garden, where it has been erected near the gates of The Vineyard.

North of Peterborough lies a string of superb stone villages which once belonged to Northamptonshire and clearly display their kinship to that county's characteristic limestone belt. One of the most famous quarries was at **Barnack**, which supplied much of the material for Ely and Peterborough cathedrals and several Cambridge colleges. The village itself is a gem of drystone walls, grey and buff-coloured cottages and houses, barns, and two old inns. The Hills and Holes Nature Reserve provides a landscape of irregular grassy hummocks above what were once busy workings, now rich in flowers associated with limestone soils: Barnack is one of the two most valued sites in England for the endangered species of the purplish, bell-shaped Pasque Flower.

Charles Kingsley, author of *The Water Babies*, was brought here at the age of five by his clergyman father, whose rectory has since been renamed Kingsley House. During a childhood illness the boy was kept isolated in a room where he suffered frightening intimations of a presence believed by locals to be the ghost of a former rector who had cheated a widow and orphan of the parish, and who was condemned to haunt the room known as Button Cap in his dressing gown and a nightcap with a button on it.

One of the village inns is The Fox, very appropriate when one considers that Barnack stone went to the building of vast **Burghley House** between here and Stamford, home of Elizabeth I's favourite counsellor William Cecil, whose cunning earned him the nickname of 'The Fox'. This colossal building, once described as more like a town than a dwelling-house, has a splendour of painted ceilings, state apartments, a bedroom for the Queen, the dazzling Heaven Room painted by Verrio, carvings by Grinling Gibbons, and a matchless collection of Italian old masters. The Burghley Horse Trials are held in the park every September. House and grounds are open to the public on weekdays and Sunday afternoons from April until the first week in October.

Humbler than the great Lord Treasurer was the 'Northamptonshire Peasant Poet', John Clare, who hated change and would surely have been particularly incensed by the shifting of his birthplace from Northamptonshire into Huntingdonshire and now into Greater Cambridgeshire. The thatched cottage in **Helpston** where he was born in 1793 still stands beside the Blue Bell Inn, on whose premises he worked for a time as a servant. Of limited education but an ardent, erudite naturalist, Clare lived most of his life in poverty, and failed in most of his farming enterprises. One early job was that of ploughboy at nearby Woodcroft Castle, where during the Civil War Cromwell's troops besieged Royalists under the command of Charles I's chaplain and ruthlessly slaughtered them. Sounds of battle and cries for mercy are still said to resound through the moated manor house into which the castle has been transformed.

Marrying and fathering eight children, Clare moved a few miles away to Northborough, where his wife Patty is now buried. He was twice committed to lunatic asylums, the second time for the twenty-three years until his death in 1864, when his body was brought to Helpston churchyard and a memorial set at the crossroads. In spite of his anguish, Clare never lost his poetic gift. 'A peasant in his daily cares, a poet in his joy,' he said of himself, though even in his verses there was often much gloom: he lamented the field enclosures and the passing of old rural ways, and records with dismay the arrival of railway planners bent on spoiling some of his favourite countryside with their main line from King's Cross to the North.

The meandering road from Barnack through Helpston towards Thorney has many delights, passing as it does through a succession of stone villages until all at once we are back in the drab brickwork

509

of Fenland. **Bainton**, a little huddle of houses around a heavily
restored church with some strangely carved stone, has some other
stone worthy of note: the huge steps at the foot of what must once
have been a mighty village cross. **Glinton** has a seventeenth-century
manor house with mullioned windows, and some laudably preserved cottages of the same period. Its church, whose tall, slender
spire has an alarming bulge in it, contains a Norman font and, in
the porch, two stone figures whose features have been much worn
away and who must once, one supposes, have lain more sedately
upon a tomb.

At **Northborough**, a little way north on the road to Sleaford, as
we have noted, Clare's wife is buried. The manor house was the
last home of Oliver Cromwell's widow, whose son-in-law John
Claypole was lord of the manor and has a chapel and monument
in his honour in the church.

Peakirk has the only church in England dedicated to St Pega, a
sister of St Guthlac who lived here in the early eighth century.
Close at hand is a hermitage chapel dedicated to St Bartholomew,
with a chancel dating from about 1280. The most celebrated local
feature, however, is the seventeen-acre spread of the Waterfowl
Gardens, a branch of the Wildfowl Trust founded by Sir Peter
Scott. There are more than a hundred kinds of ducks, geese, swans,
and flamingoes – some seven hundred birds in all. The collection
includes rarities such as Hawaiian and Andean geese, a breeding
flock of Chilean Flamingoes, and Trumpeter Swans descended from
a group presented by Queen Elizabeth II. Many are tame enough to
feed from the hands of visitors, who will in any case find the whole
area of woodland and lakes inviting and relaxing. The Roman waterway of the Car Dyke ran through an osier bed here, though it is
doubtful if the bargees of those times found such comforts in the
way of shop and refreshments as are offered today. The gardens
are now open daily except for Christmas Eve and Christmas Day.

Peakirk may not be one of the great historic sites of Britain, but
with its ambience of migratory birds, happily domesticated birds,
and its vast skies above the Fens and stretching away to the eastern
coastline, it is as good a place as any for summing up one's
impressions of East Anglia and then, like the wildfowl, choosing
either to move on or to settle here.

The East Anglian Voyage

By far the most rewarding way to see the East Anglian coast is to approach it, as the first East Anglians did, by water. The present writer has cruised the Suffolk and Norfolk coasts in everything from a fourteen-foot dinghy to a 175-ton sailing barge loaded with wheat, and entered every enterable harbour in his own thirty-four ton Dutch *hoogaerse* (when he had one), and landed on nearly every beach with what Yorkshiremen call a coble, whose equivalent in East Anglia is known as a shannock. Such craft can be beached, a big advantage over larger vessels.

The coast of East Anglia is not for the inattentive navigator. Between Harwich and the Wash, harbours are not only few but extremely difficult, and in some cases impossible, to enter. If anyone has ever tried sailing into Lowestoft in an on-shore gale they will know what I mean. If you cannot enter these harbours (and sometimes you cannot) there is *no shelter*, anywhere, and there are dangerous off-shore shoals like the Haisborough, the Scroby and the Whiting. The North Norfolk coast is ferocious in a north-easterly gale, and admittance into its tiny unmarked harbours difficult at any time and impossible at low water. The Wash is a refuge, but only to the good navigator: it is a death trap to the unwary. The next stop north is the Humber, and that is an inhospitable place for the small boat if ever there was one.

I am not trying to put the mariner off the East Anglian Voyage. I am merely warning him that he must know what he is doing before he makes it. Some rely on good sails and gear; others disagree and prefer the steerage and power of an engine to fight against sudden gusts of wind. Either way, this coastline can provide cruising as good as any in the world. You do not get the lofty mountain or fiord scenery that you do in the Highlands or Norway, but the company you meet ashore in the little fishing or old barging places is superb, and where else can the sailor moor his vessel in the shadow of buildings like King's College Chapel or Norwich or Ely Cathedrals? The rewards of the East Anglian voyage are enormous. And the Londoner, pressed for time, can leave his boat at a railhead in a dozen places, catch a train back to London, and come back again when the chains are loosened to fare farther on.

In providing a few notes on the East Anglian Voyage I do not intend to offer a Pilot's Guide. Plenty of these are available, and I trust that nobody will venture along this coast without an Admiralty chart, or at best one of those coloured yachtsmen's charts made for people who cannot afford a pair of parallel rulers.

By starting the Voyage in the south I am not making the bland assumption that nobody exists north of the Wash. But I have got to start at one end or the other, and I do recognize that more people live in London and all those even more foreign places across the Channel than in the North of England and Scotland, and therefore we shall begin our voyage at Harwich: its harbour being the first one on the East Anglian coast that we can enter on any tide and in any weather.

Harwich itself is a historic old English town, somewhat altered by Second World War bombs and commercial expansion since Nelson was based here. But it still has its mariners' taverns by the quayside, including the imposing Angel and fine neighbour, the Globe; and do not neglect the Alma – round the corner from the Angel and inland a bit. There is a depot of the Brethren of Trinity House here, with a yard full of huge sea buoys lying awaiting painting themselves and also painting by artists, and out in the river you sometimes see light vessels with such evocative names as 'Shipwash' or 'Galloper' painted on their sides: resting for a spell from their stormy stations.

The trouble with Harwich is that it is a very uncomfortable place for the yachtsman to lie. The harbour itself is exposed; if he moves round into the Stour he is in the way of the fast Parkeston ferries to the Continent, and if he tries to get into that tiny harbour enclosed by wooden jetties just in front of the Angel he is moved constantly by Trinity House or other working boats. The only thing for him to do is to anchor in a couple of fathoms of water inside the Guard Buoy (Heaven help him if he anchors outside, or to the north of it: he will be run down by a ferry rushing back from the Hook of Holland) and go ashore in his dinghy. He will find nowhere to leave the latter and may well get his rowlocks pinched.

If he wants a quiet night he had better go on up-Orwell and anchor at **Stone Heaps**. This is an anchorage perhaps a few hundred yards up-stream from Shotley Point, on the Shotley side. There is deep water there, good holding ground, it is sheltered from all winds, and for centuries barges used to lie there waiting for a fair wind for London or 'down North' (all East Coast seafaring men talk of 'down North' and 'Up South' – the tides run that way). Stone Heaps is so named because in the days of the 'cement stone' trade – when septaria was dredged up from the seabed to be taken to the cement factories – it was dumped ashore here by the 'stone drudgers' (sailing smacks used for the job) before being loaded into barges.

The shore delights of Stone Heaps are negligible (it's a long walk to the Bristol Arms, down at **Shotley Ferry**) so soon the voyager will decide to go up-river to **Pin Mill**.

Just round Collimer Point comes Butterman's Bay, where the ocean-faring windjammers used to lie while lightering their cargoes into the sailing barges. The voyager should here think seriously of finding an anchorage, for the nearer he gets to Pin Mill the more difficult that will be. As we have noted earlier, though (see p. 79), Pin Mill merits a visit. Here for twenty-one years lived the legendary Bob Roberts, who owned the mulie barge *Cambria*, last working sailing vessel under the Red Ensign. He first went to sea at the age of fifteen in the barquentine *Waterwitch*, and during the Second World War was twice sunk. His book *Breeze for a Bargeman* will tell you more than any other writer on the subject could hope to do.

The Pin Mill Sailing club is most hospitable, and the chandlery one of the most comprehensive along these shores. There was even a spate of bookselling in 1982, when E. Arnot Robertson's novel *Ordinary Families* was reissued in Virago Modern Classics. The story is set in Pin Mill, with references to the Butt and Oyster inn. Retired literary agent and publisher, James MacGibbon, set to work with a will to promote it, so that within a short time the pub and chandlery between them had sold over 500 copies.

There is a footpath from here to **Woolverstone**, or one can choose to take to the water again and head for its famous Cat-house (not the kind of establishment that usually goes under that name) and the Royal Harwich Yacht Club, all apparently lost in the forests. Farther up again, through lovely sylvan reaches, **Ipswich** heaves into view, and we come to **Lavender Bay**, one of the few places in the world where we can navigate by *nose* (it is here that Ipswich discharges her unwanted material) past a very hospitable and vigorous sailing club to port near Bourne Bridge – the Orwell Yacht Club – with a fair but drying-out anchorage in not very salubrious water, and then we can lock into Ipswich Wet Dock (for a fee), where we can take on fresh water or anything else. It is a very busy commercial harbour but there is plenty of room still alongside its wharfs. The centre of Ipswich is not far away, and how better to see it than from your own floating hotel? Whitmores, near the Custom House, is a fine yacht and ship chandler and a sail maker of the first class.

Down-river again there is always Felixstowe Dock, to port, enterable at any stage of the tide but not the quietest place in the world since the huge expansion of its freight trade, which also necessitated the widening of the main road to the Midlands and the construction of the Orwell Bridge for lorries feeding the port and carrying goods away from it.

Around Landguard Fort, where the Ipswich Fencibles drove off the Dutch, stand well out if you don't want to hit a submerged Roman castle, and head for the **Deben**. Here pull out your pilot's guide or signal for a real live pilot to flag you in or come out in a boat and lead you. Inside you will find a lovely anchorage in all weathers and a good steep clean landing place for a dinghy on the Felixstowe side (better than all that mud at Pin Mill). The happily untidy little settlement of **Felixstowe Ferry** has two good pubs, the Victoria and the Ferry Boat.

The Deben upstream is as lovely a river in its way as the Orwell but much shallower, so beware the griping mud. To starboard, **Ramsholt** has a wonderfully situated waterside inn, privately leased on private land below a church-crowned hill, and a very beautiful

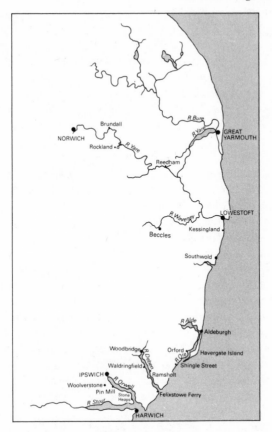

anchorage and landing. And let no one dispute your right either to anchor or to land. **Waldringfield**, farther up and to port, is another Pin Mill-type place, yacht club, boat builder, splendid pub, miles from anywhere. The owner of a large yacht might be advised to anchor or moor there and go farther by tender: **Woodbridge** is accessible to deep-keeled craft at high tide but it is very crowded and dries right out at low – unless you pay to enter the new yacht harbour built in the old pound of the tidal mill. Woodbridge is a lovely place to lie for a long period though, and to winter in: good facilities ashore, civilized company, and fast trains to London.

The stretch farther up, as far as **Melton**, I think we may leave to the dyed-in-the-wool mud-crawler. The river is not navigable above the bridge, but there is a number of flourishing yacht builders and repairers between Woodbridge and Melton.

The next estuary north, the **Ore**, is easier to get into than the Deben (in both rivers there is a buoy outside and leading marks ashore, but in both rivers I disclaim all responsibility). There is a part-time coastguard at **Shingle Street**, just by the entrance, whom the Felixstowe Coastguard will put you on to, and he will sometimes flag you in or come out in a small boat. Scenically the Ore is a boring anchorage below the old oysterage at Ferry Cottage where the Pinney family established their oyster beds quite some years ago to supply their admirable little shop and restaurant in nearby Orford. A dash in the dinghy up to Butley Mill is delightful, with reed-covered marshes, saltings, huge rafts of widgeon in winter, pheasants galore ashore (and gamekeepers!), and wild loneliness. But beware of mud.

Havergate Island, which we can circumnavigate if we wish, is an RSPB reserve and the meeting-place of avocets, which can be seen sometimes winging their way up and down on their occasions.

At **Orford** you can anchor either above or below the jetty, land on the jetty for temporary reasons, or drag your dinghy up the clean shingle beach just upstream from the jetty for longer trips ashore (to the Jolly Sailor or the Butley Oysterage in the square!) but not on the concrete slipway, still government administered in spite of the dismantling of much material once here. As well as a centre of secret research, the Ness also served as an underground storage dump and bomb disposal area. For a few years local fishermen were warned not to come in too close when an experimental early warning system was in operation, since it was liable to blow up their radar and other equipment. The strange cat's cradle of masts and cables is gone now, to be replaced by the transmitters of the BBC World Service; but in 1986 there were disturbing rumours of possibly using the shifting ground of 'the Island' as a dump for old reactor components from atomic submarines.

A long straight boring run takes you to **Aldeburgh**, where you will be a hundred yards from the sea as the mariner spits but ten miles as his boat sails. Here is good anchorage above the yacht club and, hard over the other side of the river, easy dinghy landing. A fine small but rather exclusive yacht club (you have to be the child of a member to become a member – rather like the London dockers), a short walk to a splendid little seaside town with a great lifeboat record and the Cables and Burrells and Wards continuing, as they have done for generations, to dominate the local fishing community. Everything can be found in Aldeburgh that a reasonable man's heart could desire.

Higher up the river is for mud-crawlers only, and if you even get as far as **Iken** I admire your pertinacity. This is a beautiful sylvan and deserted place, with a tiny river beach and an anchorage that you will never forget afterwards (even if you can forget getting stuck on the mud getting to it). **Snape Maltings** has a very good wharf to tie up (with permission ashore), a drying out berth of course, and incidentally it's fun to paddle in your dinghy under the horrible new bridge and a mile or so up up into fresh-water river (the Alde here of course); a thing very few people have thought of.

Downstream and out at sea again we round Orfordness, and the mariner should heed the old bargeman's saw:

Wind from the West
One foot on deck – one on the Ness,

the significance of which is that there is deep water right up to the point and it behoves you to stay up-wind so that you do not have to fall away from the coast too far on rounding the Ness.

We sail by Aldeburgh, which looks lovely from the sea, and Thorpeness, and along a beautiful deserted coast which for many miles is spoiled only by that bloody power station at Sizewell. Past Dunwich – where the superstitious claim at night to hear the bells of drowned churches ringing under the sea – and then in at **Southwold Harbour**. Again be warned. It is a difficult harbour to enter, with a strong cross-current and a sand bar which certain winds push straight across the entrance, so that one has to come in or out at an angle towards Sizewell. There is some fierce-looking concrete to either side of the channel. If in doubt, it is advisable to contact the harbour-master.

I have sailed into Southwold in my 34-ton Dutch barge (when I had one) with a strong on-shore wind, at low tide, with a huge sea running into the entrance and the harbour master waving frantically to me from the pier-head not to come in because he couldn't believe that such a big boat could only draw three feet (she was flat bottomed). It was a most exhilarating experience and the sense of quiet when I got inside reminded me of Mrs Patrick Campbell's commendation of 'the peace of the marriage bed after the hurly-burly of the *chaise-longue*!' I had all sail set and only just managed to scramble it off and get an anchor down before colliding with the Bailey bridge. This brought me up just opposite the Harbour Inn and it couldn't have brought me up at a better place. I would be hard put to think of a nicer pub, in the world, than the Harbour Inn at Southwold. It's a long walk from here to the town, and stores, but if you can't find a lift in the Harbour something has gone wrong somewhere as Southwold has a vigorous little long-shore fishing fleet and the nicest lot of fishermen imaginable.

To sea again, north again, along a deserted and wooded coast – endless deserted beaches – past Covehithe (non-existent), **Kessingland**, where there are no longer any full-time professional fishermen but which offers a good place to beach if you are in a beaching boat. Then on to the grand harbour of **Lowestoft**.

Entry to this harbour has been controlled since the 1970s by a system of lights introduced after a number of collisions. If the light is not flashing, it is safe to go in; if it is flashing, you must wait. On exit, you leave when the light if flashing; wait if it is not. Yachts and dinghies are not allowed in the trawl basin. If you are lucky, there will be space in the yacht basin of the Royal Norfolk and Suffolk Yacht Club immediately to port as you enter the harbour. If not, it is necessary to go through the bridge and on to Lake Lothing. There is a story that when Queen Victoria sent her consent for the Yacht Club to be dubbed royal the Secretary forgot to reply, and it took years of lobbying by the Prince of Wales to get her to renew the favour.

Great Yarmouth is easier to get into although here again is a narrow entrance and fierce cross-currents and many ships have come to grief trying to make it. Large sailing vessels that have to run in before a gale can bring themselves up by rounding to starboard inside and putting themselves ashore on the Spending

Ground, a beach of sand hard round the corner.

The **Yare** is long, busy with big shipping but there is plenty of room to tie up to the long quays on either side and ashore every delight and every facility for the ship's husband. Great Yarmouth is a magnificent place to be, and it is, of course, the gateway to the Broads. Without even lowering your mast you can get to **Norwich**, tying up at **Reedham** and **Brundall** on the way and seeing a typical broad at **Rockland** (where is the New Inn with a shelter with rings to which horses were once tied, and a good gathering of knowledgeable locals who can tell you everything there is to know about the wildlife and navigational features of Broadland). You could well instead of going up-Yare, go up-**Waveney** instead, to **Beccles**, taking in **Burgh Castle** *en route*. If you can get your mast down, and don't draw more than six feet, you can enter the 'North River' from Great Yarmouth and thread your way into the classic Broadland country: but that is another story.

When you put to sea from Yarmouth, northward bound, you want a good weather forecast; for you have eighty miles of coast before you which is to all intents and purposes harbourless. For forty-five miles it is completely harbourless – there is not a hole or cranny into which you can get. Then comes **Blakeney Harbour**, for which you need high water, fine weather, and a knowledge of what you are doing. There is a fine big anchorage in **The Pit**, inside Blakeney Harbour, but a very long pull up to the village. It is here that you feel the need either for a sail on your dinghy and a fair wind, or else one of those new-fangled outboard motors. If you know it, or can find it, there is a footpath leading across some miles of saltings to **Morston**, whose marshes, greens and quay are now in the keeping of the National Trust. The Warden operates next door to the Anchor inn, and sells tickets for the ferry to the bird reserve of **Blakeney Point**. If you make a landing on the point, beware treading on terns' nests. It is of special interest in the winter. There is splendid bird-watching on this coast, good fishing, and wild-fowling in winter, and Blakeney village is almost impossibly pretty. If you do take your yacht up there you will find the river terribly crowded and much opposition to your taking a big boat there at all, and the only thing to do is to plonk yourself down and say 'shift me!' which nobody can legally do. But, after all, the

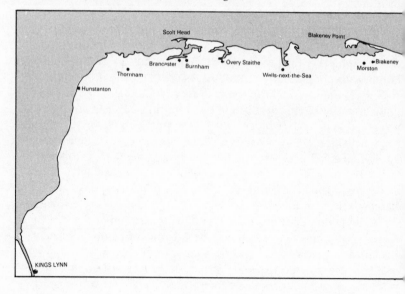

people who live there should have priority. Blakeney is inhabited by very nice people, and well served by its yacht chandlery.

Wells-next-the-Sea is hard to get into (if you get there in an on-shore gale and see the buoy marking the harbour entrance *high up on a sand bank*, it inspires no confidence), but once in it is fine and you can tie up within a few yards of a pub, or a shop for that matter. You will soon be asked to move on though, by the harbour master, for this is a busy little fishing port and there are some Dutch coasters. You may be allowed to lie awhile tied up to the quay, or you can go over the river and anchor by the saltings, or farther up, to the whelk boiling sheds, and throw yourself on the mercy of the Cox family, one of whom will tell you where to lie. The Shipwright's Arms is a splendid pub, but like most waterside pubs better in the winter than in the summer.

Burnham Harbour is even trickier than Wells, but **Overy Staithe** is charming when you get there. A pub, not many facilities, but interesting walking to the seven Burnhams, in Nelson country.

Brancaster, around **Scolt Head** (another bird-watcher's paradise) is another fiendish place to get into (although there is more water over the bar there than there is at Wells). The village is not attractive, but the Jolly Sailor is famous for its food and, for those who like them, there is a golf course.

Thornham Harbour I have never been into.

These harbours were all busy shipping harbours once, and within living memory there was a busy trade of Billyboys, which sailed from the Humber loaded with coal, selling the coal to farmers and merchants who came with carts to the ship-side to get it, then loading gravel from the banks outside and sailing that back to Yorkshire.

You now have nowhere to run, really, until you get right round into the **Wash** and up-river to King's Lynn. You could of course anchor for a while off **Hunstanton**, but if a northerly gale springs up you might wish you hadn't. The **Lynn Channel** is well marked, but tortuous, and remember that the Wash is for the competent mariner. If you are not – get a pilot.

At **King's Lynn** really the only sensible thing to do is to lock into the Wet Dock. The gates only open at high tide, so tie up alongside a lighter if you can, by the mouth. If you make friends with the fishermen they may allow you to tie up to the staging inside their **Fisher Fleet**, where the mud dries out steep at low tide – it's a most interesting place to lie but you will be *very* privileged if you are allowed to lie there – though you will be safer, and more comfortable, inside the Wet Dock, where you must pay up like a man, and where you will be afloat all the time, can step ashore dry-shod, and be right near the centre of one of the most interesting towns in England. The two Wet Docks are not pretty places (unless you like ships, cranes, and piles of Baltic timber) but they are convenient. I cannot understand why yachtsmen flock to the South Coast in such numbers, to all those crowded, commercialized and basically very uninteresting places, and ignore a coast that has King's Lynn. Here is something *worth* sailing a few hundred miles to see.

Up-Ouse you must have a lowering mast and a good sense of rivermanship. The tidal **Great Ouse** is really a horrid river. If you anchor you have to land from your dinghy in steep and sticky mud – and when you want to go aboard again your dinghy will either be high and dry or else upside down or carried right away. There

521

is a sluicing tide – it can be seven knots – so you need good ground tackle. But anchor just the same – to see the **Wiggenhalls**, which are dealt with in the text of this book.

Beware **Denver** Bridge. I once wrote that the builder of this bridge should be put in a sack and chucked off it – but then I *met* the builder, who was a most charming man named Charles Slade (alas dead now) who lived in a house at Hammersmith Mall which was hung all over inside with portraits of himself done by Augustus John, and so I hereby retract my statement. It is a fine bridge, no doubt, for the landsmen who have to go over it, but not for the boatman who has to go *under* it. My advice is to go up on the flood tide but turn round to face the flood and let this drop you slowly astern through the bridge (the most westerly opening is the one to choose) while your engine goes slow ahead to give you steerage. Like this, if you hit anything, at least you won't hit it hard.

At **Salter's Lode** you can, if you wait for the exact moment when there is a tidal level, pen through into the **Old Bedford River**, or else **Well Creek**, newly opened up again by the Fen Waterman's Association, headquarters **March**. Either of these waters give you access to the whole intricate network of the Fenland **Middle Level Navigations**. These are not to everybody's taste. They are for the most part dead straight, very weeded up, with the water well below the banks so you can't see anything without getting out of the boat. To the initiated they are quite fascinating because they lead through the country of the Fenmen who are such fascinating people. It is the people here who are everything, and to enjoy this country you must meet them.

But, if you by-pass these labyrinths and keep up-Ouse, you almost immediately come to **Denver Sluice** (you could, if you had the hardihood, carry on up the tidal **New Bedford River** to **Earith**: I have never done it). Pen through the great double locks and you enter placid, clean, non-tidal water; the river is a natural one and slightly winding, you *can* see over the banks, and there is marvellous coarse fishing (and it's complete nonsense that coarse fish taste 'muddy' – they taste delicious, and it would improve river fishing enormously if more of them were eaten: all our rivers suffer from over fish-population) and you can, if you draw not more than three foot six inches, turn up the **Wissey** as far as **Stoke Ferry**, which has been a crossing point ever since Roman times. **Hilgay**, on the way, is a fine big Fenland village, well worth a Saturday evening visit. Farther up-Ouse and one can penetrate the **Little Ouse** as far as **Brandon Staunch** but no further, just below the town's flinty bridge. But stay on the Great Ouse and you will get to **Ely**. This is one of the nicest places to lie. You are within not many yards of the cathedral, there are good wharves to tie up to, good shops within spitting distance, the excellent Cutter Inn, and any number of boat yards to repair your vessel, build you a brand new one, or else charter you one.

Up-stream at the confluence of the Great Ouse (here called the **Old West**) and the **Cam** is the **Fish and Duck Inn** – and what a marvellous place! Just the Fish and Duck Inn and absolutely nothing else. Not even a road. If you take the right fork you can get right up (along an increasingly beautiful and un-fenlike river) through **St Ives** and **St Neots**, and the locks are being repaired as far as **Bedford**. But if you turn left at the Fish and Duck you will come to **Upware**, where the old 'Five Miles from Anywhere – No Hurry Inn', was burnt down but has mercifully been restored. It is a short walk to **Wicken Fen**, a National Trust Nature Reserve and one of the last pieces of unchanged Fenland. This was what it was like in Hereward the Wake's day. Up-stream very light-draught boats can get to lovely villages like **Wicken**, **Burwell**, **Reach** or **Swaffham Bulbeck** (I have never tried it) or you can keep on up to Cambridge.

There are three locks to **Cambridge** and they have lock keepers, and these gentlemen will tell you how far upwards to the middle of the city you can decently go without getting in everybody's way and where to tie up. Much depends on how many boats are already there. There are fees.

The sea voyage from the Great Ouse to the **Nene** is very difficult, for there are tortuous sands and channels to navigate. You might well go 'overland' through the Middle Levels achieved through Salter's Lode. If you go by sea and want a pilot you might telephone the Lineham family, who have been here a long time and can be relied on to supply good advice, even if they themselves are too busy to help: which they frequently are – out fishing. If you go through the Middle Level you will come out at **Standground**, near **Peterborough**. If you take the sea way you will run up-stream to **Sutton Bridge** (if you haven't run aground outside at Big Annie) and there the only thing to do is to tie up to Mr Lineham's jetty. You cannot lie to anchor because of the big ships going up to Wisbech.

You can get up to **Wisbech** with your mast up. Here you can tie to the long quays on either side of the river, but remember you will dry right out at low tide, there is a terrible rise and fall, so you must have long warps out and look to them. Or, if you can get permission to do so, hang on to one of the floating pontoons various people have moored in the river, or else to the side of a coasting vessel. Wisbech is a fine place to see from a boat, although a difficult place to lie (the fools filled in their canal – which would have made such a good yacht harbour. But how were people of limited imagination to know the yachts would ever want to go there anyway? As time goes on they will go there more and more).

Mast down, you can run up-stream to **Dog in a Doublet**, where there is a pub of that name, and a huge lock. The lock is manned, and electric, and you can pen through into non-tidal Nene, and to Peterborough, and on, if you want to go to **Oundle** and then **Northampton** (it's a lovely river), and *then* – but only if you are under seven feet wide – up the locks into the Grand Union and the narrow waterways of England.

The East Anglian Dialect

In Norfolk, Suffolk, North Essex and Cambridgeshire east of the River Cam a dialect is spoken which is recognizably East Anglian and quite distinct from the language spoken anywhere else. An East Anglian can notice a great difference between, say, a North Norfolk man and one from South Suffolk, but they speak basically the same dialect and one can understand the other perfectly well. Perhaps nowhere in England is there a sharper dividing line between two dialects than there is between King's Lynn, in Norfolk, and Sutton Bridge in Lincolnshire. The former is pure Norfolk – the latter strong Midland without an East Anglian element in it. The Essex men are recognizably East Anglian until you come near to the Thames, where they become abruptly and completely Cockney (people from both sides of the Thames Estuary can be recognized by their use of the word 'fur' for *far*).

The East Anglian does not drop his aitches. He talks with a singsong intonation that is very difficult to copy. No 'foreign' (i.e. non-East Anglian) actor has ever been able to master the tongue: as witness all the performances of Arnold Wesker's play *Roots*. Few educated East Anglians indeed can do it. The true East Anglian countryman can talk the Queen's English as well as anybody (although he can never hide the fact from a fellow countryman that he comes from East Anglia) but also, if he wants to, he can talk in such a way that the Londoner or other 'foreigner' will never understand him.

I list here, with Mrs Claxton's very kind permission, some of the many hundreds of words and phrases included in *The Suffolk Dialect of the Twentieth Century*, by the late A. O. D. Claxton, published by Norman Adlard and Co. of Ipswich. I have only taken

526

words which I have heard used myself (and many of which I have, unconsciously, used). Many of the words are received English words: it is their use by the Suffolk person that is peculiar. Although these words were collected in Suffolk most of them will be recognizable to the Norfolk 'Dumpling' too: and to the man from East Cambridgeshire. West Cambridgeshire tends more to the South Midland dialect and intonation. I have not always stuck to Claxton's interpretations of examples.

Abroad. Out of doors. Seamen use it for 'out at sea'. Said by an old man on his last legs: 'Oi'll sune be sleeping abroad.'

Addle. To thrive, flourish.

A'doin'. Same as addle. 'He's a'doin'!' means he's getting on not too badly. It also might mean he's doing a piece of work well.

A-huh. Lop-sided. 'Whoi, missus, yar hat's all of a-huh.'

Airy-wiggle. Earwig.

Annind. On end. Of a horse – 'he reared right up annind.'

Antic. Play the fool.

Arse-uppards. Regularly used for upside down – even in polite society!

Arternune – getting into the . . . Getting old. Of an old dog – 'Oi doubt he's a'gittin' into the arternune.'

Babbing. Catching eels or crabs with a bunch of worms or a piece of meat but no hook.

Bachelors' Buttons. White campion.

Back-us. The scullery at the back of a farmhouse. Every farmhouse once had its 'back-us boy'.

Bagging iron. Instrument like a sickle but with a smooth edge – not serrated.

Bait. Food. To 'bait the hosses' – to feed them. Commonly used for a snack in the fields.

Barley Bird. Nightingale.

Bawk. Balk. Ridge left in ploughing. (Old English – *balca* – a ridge.)

Becket. A knife sheath. A man who keeps his hands in his pocket is called 'Beckets'.

Beevers. Afternoon snack in the fields. (Also 'fourses'.)

Betsy. Tea kettle.

Betty. A womanish man – one who bustles about the house. 'Stop you a'bettyin' about!' Stop fussing.

Bezzle. Booze.

Bibble. Ducks bibble in the mud. Babies bibble (dribble). To tipple.

Billy-buster. A bluster – or a large dumpling.

Billywitch. Cockchafer.

Binger. 'Tha's a binger' – that is finished. A goner.

Bishop Barnabee. Ladybird.

Blare. To cry – to shout. 'He was a'blarin' away there!'

Blood Olp. Bullfinch.

Blowbroth. Busybody.

Bodge. Mend clumsily.

Bolsom. Humbug. 'Oi don't want to listen to yar owd bolsom!'

Bonka. Fine, strapping, when applied to kids.

Bop. To curtsey.

Bor. An extremely common term of familiar address in East Anglia. Not to be confused with 'boy' which is used too, but quite differently. Bor has been derived from *neighbour* – Old English *neahgebur* – and Low German – *bur* – countryman. I favour the latter.

Botsy. Rabbit.

Browne. To wind-dry fish. Done to small 'butts' or flounders to prepare them for lobster bait, as well as sprats for human consumption.

Brackly. Brittle.

Braft. Work.

Brand. Smut in wheat – a fungus disease.

Brawtch. Pointed flexible twig for holding down thatch.

Bread-and-pull-it. A piece of dry bread with a smaller piece a'top of it. Of a poor person – 'all he's got to eat is bread-and-pull-it.'

Breeder. A whitlow, or any sore without visible cause.

Brew. Claxton just gives 'the edge of a ditch away from the hedge' but I've heard it also as 'the brew of a hill' – the *brow* of a hill. 'Just over the brew there.'

Brawk. To belch.

Brung. Past tense of 'to bring'. East Anglians have a lot of these special past tenses! 'She brung me some bread and cheese.'

Brush. To beat coverts to drive out game. To trim nettles, etc.

Buck. The body of a wagon or tumbril.

Bullfice. (I've heard it *bullfist*.) Puff ball. Powder stops wounds bleeding.

Bulley. Man who stands half-way up a stack to pass on hay or sheaves passed from below.

Bulley-hole. Hole in which the above stands.

Bush. A thorn. A Suffolker never has 'a thorn in his finger' – always 'a bush'. I knew a man who got a 'bush' in his eye whereat the 'jelly' inside ran down his face. He cycled six miles into Ipswich hospital, had his eye out, and cycled back again in time to milk his cows.

Butt. Dab or flounder.

Butterwitch. Cockchafer.

Buzzhawk. Nightjar.

Cade. Measure of herrings.

Cadman. Smallest pig in litter.

Cankers. Hips of the dog rose.

Carnser – carnsey. Causeway over wet ground.

Chaits. Scraps or leavings. (Also called 'mungey' – there's a horrible story about the skipper of a yacht who went below to eat his dinner, it was dark in the fo'c's'le, and when he remarked on the toughness of the steak the Third Hand shouted out: 'Blas bor – you're eatin' the Mate's mungey!')

Chance one. The odd one. When asked if he had docks in his field a farmer might say: 'Well – chance one.'

Chance time. Occasionally.

Charley. Toad.

Chice. A small quantity – a taste.

Cis (pronounced sis). A poor attempt. 'Oi've made a rare cis o' that, Sir!' (I've made a mess of it.)

Cley. A narrow draining spade.

Clip. A hit. 'I'll give you a clip o' the lug do you don't stop a'blarin'!'

Clung. Shrunken, shrivelled, of fruit or roots.

Clunk. To whet a blade on a stone.

Cob. Wicker basket to carry on arm for baiting animals.

Cob. Chaff from threshing clover for seed.

Cobble. A fruit stone.

Cock Ulf. Cock bullfinch.

Come-backs. Guinea-fowl (from their cry).

Conjuration. A weird contrivance. Claxton doesn't give this but he gives 'combustibles' for 'a bundle of sundry things'.

Coop-wee. Cry to a horse to make it go to the left (*see* 'Wardee').

Cow mumble. Cow parsley.

Crab. A capstan on a boat.

Crank. A heron (*see harnser*).

Cringle. To shrivel up.

Crome or croom. Any crook or hook.

Cruddle. To nestle – to lie close.

Cuckoo Barley. Barley planted too late.

Cuckoo Flower. Early purple orchis.

Cuckoo's Mate. Wryneck.

Dag. Dew.

Dan. A yearling lamb.

Dawzled. Stupid. Confused.

Dead. Death in the sense of: 'Oi'm worrit to dead!' (i.e. worried to death).

Debble (according to Claxton – I think it's 'dibble'). Wooden tool for making holes for putting in plants.

Deek (Claxton – I've always heard 'Dick'). A ditch. (Old English – *dic*.)

Delf. Claxton gives 'A dug drain or small hole'. I've heard it only used for the ditch behind all sea and river walls. (Dutch – *delft*. All sea-wall makers' tools are still called by Dutch names.)

Dickey. Donkey.

Didall (long *I* – as 'dide-al'). Spade for digging out ditch. Also a huge shovel used on Broads – hauled·up by tackle – for dredging channels. I have seen the same thing – with nearly the same name – used in Randstat Holland.

Diddle. Duck.

Dills. Tears.

Dilly. Small cart on two wheels used as trailer.

Ding. To throw – hurl. The past tense is *dung*. 'He hully dung that at me!' Or hit. 'He give him a ding about the lug-hole!'

Dinger. An even larger 'ding'.

Do. Now this is the most overworked word in the East Anglian dialect. It can have all the meanings it has in received English, but it can also mean: *if* ('do that rain we's'll get wet'), *a command*: ('do you come along o' me!), *prosper*: ('That ol owd sow do well on that grub'. 'You'll do boy!' 'He's a'doin'!'), *or*: ('You come with me do you'll get lost!').

Don't. Used like 'do' but negatively. Thus: 'Do you hurry up don't you'll miss the bus.' But sometimes you also hear: 'Do you hurry up do you'll miss the bus.' Learning the various ramifications of the word 'do' is halfway to understanding East Anglian.

Dodman. Snail (*see* hodmedod).

Dog in a Blanket. Roly-poly pudding.

Dog weed. Wild cornel.

Dorhawk. Nightjar.

Dow (rhymes with cow). Wood pigeon.

Dreening. Very wet.

Drift. Rough private roadway.

Drindle. To trickle. A tiny stream (*see* grindle).

Drug. A 'timber drug' – vehicle for carrying timber.

Dudder. Shake.

Dun billy. Crow.

Dunk. House sparrow.

Dunt. Wallop on the head.

Dussn't. Dare not.

Dutfin. Bridle of a cart horse.

Duzzy. Euphemism for damned.

Dwile. Wiping-up flannel. (Dutch *dweyle*.)

Eel pritch. Spear with several barbed prongs. (Also *butt pritch*.)

Elevenses. Mid-morning snack in fields.

Fang. To grab.

Fare. (Very common) – to seem – to appear. 'That fare to be going to rain.' 'That don't fare very hot to me.' Also used as 'do' – 'How do you fare today bor?' Claxton quotes an old man who has been on a switchback as saying: 'That fare t' make me fare hully duzzified.'

Fare thee well. Or farewell. Commonly used for 'good-bye' still. In other cases the second person (thou, thee, thine) is seldom used in East Anglia, in contrast to the North of England.

Fetched. Reached. 'Oi fetched the pub a'fore closing toime.'

Few (good). Not a few.

Fillia (or thriller). Shaft horse.

Fist. Claxton gives 'to make a fist of a job is to do it awkwardly'. But I have always heard: 'He made a good fist o' that' or 'he didn't make much of a fist of it!'

Five fingers. The ox-lip. Also the star fish.

Flash. To trim the side of a hedge or a bank.

Flee. To skin. 'My missus allus flee a teal afore she cook it. Thass quicker'n featherin' of it.'

Fleet. Shallow. 'Plough that a bit fleet' (don't plough too deep). East Anglian sailors also say: 'Fleet the cable round the drum', meaning: let the cable run out slowly checking itself on a windlass drum.

Fleet. To skim cream off milk. A cream skimmer is called 'a fleeter'.

Floaters. Dumplings. I've also heard them called 'sinkers'.

Fog nightingale. Frog.

Fold pritch. A heavy iron bar for making holes in ground for stakes of sheep hurdles.

Frawn. Frozen. ('Oi be hully frawn!')

Fulfer. Fieldfare.

Funny. Very. ('That do funny rain.')

Gainer. Cleverer or better.

Gambrel (I've heard gambel). The steel or wooden cross-piece you hang a pig up with.

Gay. Picture. Still commonly used. 'Gimme the paper – I just want to look at the gays.'

Gnew. Past tense of gnaw. Claxton quotes: 'That duzzy owd hog gnew a hole in th' stye.'

Gon. Past tense of to give. 'He gon me a pint.'

Goslins. Willow catkins.

Grindle. Same as drindle – a tiny stream. (Also called a *purl*.)

Grunt. 'What a lot o' grunt they put in the papers nowdays!' Rubbish.

Guler. Yellow bunting.

Gull. A deep channel in the saltings.

Hake. Kettle-crane in fireplace. Or iron in front of plough on which whipple-tree is hooked.

Happen. Haps. Perhaps. 'Happen he will – happen he won't.'

Harnser. Heron. ('I know a hawk from a handsaw' – Shakespeare.) It is said that when a harnser swallows an eel the eel wriggles right through. Therefore the harnser backs up against a gatepost before swallowing it.

Hayjack. Reedwarbler.

Haysel. Hay harvest.

Hew. Past tense of to hoe.

Hewd (pronounced *howd*) past tense of to hold. 'Oi hewd on hud!'

Hin. Yonder.

Hob gob. Nasty short sea.

Hodman or *Hodmedod.* Snail.

Hopnetot. Frog.

Horkey. Harvest home supper. Once a great thing – now no more.

Hornpie. Lapwing.

Hoss needle. Dragonfly.

How: hud. Or howd yew hud. 'Hold hard' – stop talking.

Housen. Plural of house. (I have heard *cown* as plural cow.)

Hulk. To gut a rabbit.

Hully (rhymes with fully). Means *wholely* and is a very much used word. Claxton gives: 'Oi felt hully ill.' 'That fare to be hully cowd (cold).' 'That hully rained last night.' 'Tha's hully a nice dawg.' 'Oi wuz hully stammed (confounded).'

Hulver. Holly.

Hurdle (pronounced huddle). To thread one leg of a rabbit or hare through the hamstring of another to carry it (*hock* in received English).

Jacob. A toad.

Jasper. Wasp.

Jereboam. Chamber pot. ('Oi hully drunk some beer las' night – that was 'thumbs awash!')

533

Jowlies. Young herring.

Kedgy. Alert.
Kiddle. To cuddle, embrace.
King Harry. Goldfinch.
Knap Kneed. Knock kneed. (The opposite is: 'He couldn't stop a pig in a passage!')

Largesse. Gifts to harvesters for their harvest beer. An old custom.
Larn. To teach.
Leece. Plural of louse.
Leet. Crossroads.
Lijahs. Or Elijahs. Leggings.

Mardle. To gossip.
Mash. Marsh.
Master. Very. Claxton gives: 'Owd Rubbud ha' got a master grut hog.' 'Yow take a master long time a'dewin' that job.' 'Tha's a master rummun!' (rummum = rum one – i.e. peculiar).
Maw. Term of address for young girl.
Mawkin. Scarecrow.
Mawther. A girl, either ready for courting or else a little girl. 'She's a rare dear little mawther.'
Meetiner. A Nonconformist. (One who attends the meeting house.)
Mew. Past tense of to mow.
Moithered Up. Claxton gives 'cluttered up' but I've heard 'Do you stop a'moitherin' me!' meaning stop worrying me.
Mockbeggar's Hall. A poor, or mean, household. (There are several Mockbeggar's Hills about – one just before Orford. There is a 'Drag-Arse Hill' just west of Wickham Market. It is down this hill condemned men used to be led to the gallows.)
Mort. Can be *dead*, or can be *plenty*. (Old Norse – *morgt* =much.)

Nab Nannies. Lice.
Neezen. Plural of nest.

Olp. Bullfinch.
Onsensed. Stunned.

534

Owd. Old, but used as a diminutive or endearment. 'Good owd boy!' a very common term of approbation, or 'Good owl gal!' 'My little owd dawg.' Used for nearly everything you like or are used to, including very *young* things: 'Moi little owd babby.'

Owd Sarah. Hare. 'My little old larcher hully hustled owd Sarah about!' (larcher = lurcher = a hunting dog).

Paigle. Cowslip. 'Paigle wine' is very common.

Pea-make. A hook for harvesting (i.e. *making*) peas.

Phoebe. Very often used for the sun. 'Owd Phoebe begin to show!'

Pipman. Like *pitman* – runt. Smallest pig in litter.

Polliwog. Tadpole.

Pritch. A pointed instrument.

Pudden-e-poke. Long-tailed tit.

Railing. Trolling for mackerel. (Now surplanted by 'the feathers'.)

Ringle. Ring in pig's snout (to stop it *grunnying*). To insert such ring.

Roker. Skate.

Rug. Past tense of to rig.

Rum. Peculiar. 'He's a rummun' means he's strange – possibly untrustworthy. 'Thass a rummun!' constantly used for any peculiar circumstance. 'That fare a bit rum to me!'

Sarnick. To loiter. Claxton gives: 'Whoi, bor, how yow dew go a'sarnickin' along!'

Sew (rhymes with few). Past tense of to sew or to sow.

Shotten herring. Herring that's spawned (and 'in't na good').

Shruk. Past tense of to shriek. 'Oi hully shruk!'

Shug. To shake. 'I shug this har cask and I could hear that a'swugglin'.'

Silly. Excessively. 'You don't want that silly tight.'

Snew. Past tense of to snow. 'That snew!'

Solomon Grundy. Pickled herrings.

Sowja (soldier). A red herring.

Sparling. Sprat.

Spreed. Always used for *spread*. 'Oi've bin a'spreedin' o' muck.'

Squit. Nonsense. 'Thass a lot o' squit what he talk.'

Stam. To astonish. (Old English *stamm*.)

Staunch (pronounced starnch). To dam a river. (Launch is pronounced larnch.)

Sukey. Tea kettle.

Swift. Newt.

Swounded. Swooned.

Tewk. Redshank. (Claxton didn't get *that* one!).

That. Always used for *it*.

Thow. To thaw. (Past tense *thew*, past participate *thowed*).

Togither. Claxton says this is the plural of 'bor'. It is constantly used when addressing several people. 'Come along yew togither!' 'How are yew togither?' 'Oi hully enjoyed myself – how did yow enjoy yourselves togither?' 'Oi don't know about you togither but Oi'm a'gooin' hoom!'

Wurr-de. Command to a horse to go right.

Published in 1830, and now reprinted by David and Charles, *The Vocabulary of East Anglia* is another useful book dealing with this subject.

Bird-Watching

East Anglia is still one of the best places for the birdwatcher. The large Suffolk estuaries, cut off from humanity by miles of roadless marshes, the Suffolk beaches too, shingle or sand, also well insulated from the roads (try even *reaching* the sea in most parts of Suffolk!), the unique North Norfolk coast with its many deserted inlets from the sea, its sand dunes and its saltings, the Wash, still, thank God, unenclosed and un-'improved' in any way, one of the great wild goose habitats in Britain, the Broads and the Fens, the Sandlings and the Breckland. All attracting their own bird populations, and providing miles of quiet sanctuary – for bird and birdwatcher alike. The Great Bustard may have been slaughtered to extinction by pre-Victorian 'sportsmen' – but the stone curlew still haunts the Breckland, the avocet which came back to Havergate Island has been protected by the RSPB, the goldcrest and the crossbill are discovering new habitat among the Forestry Commission pine forests, and the bittern still booms away in the eastern marshes.

Mr R. S. R. Fitter has very kindly allowed us to quote the relevant passages from his book *Collins Guide to Bird Watching*. This is certainly one of the most useful and practical books for the bird lover in the British Isles that there is: by relating birds strictly to where they live it is of far more interest and use than a mere list of birds jumbled in together. In fact with this and *Collins Pocket Guide to British Birds*, (by the same author and Mr R. A. Richardson), in his pocket and a pair of binoculars, the birdwatcher is splendidly equipped.

P   = Permit needed
PF = Permit needed away from footpath
NP = No permit needed

CAMBRIDGESHIRE

Woodland (B/1): Borley Wood, Linton; Ditton Park Wood, Wood
   Ditton: Eltisley Wood; Gamlingay Wood; Hall Yard Wood,
   Fordham; Hayley Wood, Long Stowe; Wandlebury; Chippen-
   ham Fen; Wicken Fen.
Heaths and Downs: Gog Magog Hills, Newmarket Heath.
Marshes: Chippenham Fen; Ely Beet Factory; Fulbourn Fen; Nene
   Washes, Peterborough to Guyhirn; Ouse Washes, Earith to
   Denver; Quy Fen, Stow-cum-Quy; Teversham and Wilbraham
   Fens; Wicken Fen.
Fresh Water: Nene Washes; Ouse Washes; Gravel pits at Fen
   Drayton, Hauxton, Landbeach, Mepal, Milton, Waterbeach and
   Wimblington, Wicken Fen.
Heronries: Chettisham, Guyhirn.
Gull roosts: Cambridge sewage farm, Ouse Washes.
Museum: Cambridge.

SPECIAL BIRDS

Long-eared owl: breeds at Wicken Fen and several isolated fen
   woods.
Heronries: Chettisham, Guyhirn.
Bewick's swan: regular on Nene and Ouse Washes, the latter its
   main haunt in England.
Pink-footed goose: Fens.
Pintail: Ouse Washes are most important winter haunt in eastern
   England.
Little ringed plover: breeds at several gravel pits.
Dotterel: still one fairly regular migration halt, at Melbourn, and
   less regular ones on chalk in S.E.
Stone curlew: breeds on the chalk.

Gull roosts: Cambridge sewage farm, Ouse Washes.
Black-headed gullery: Ely sugar beet factory.
Quail: breeds on the chalk.
Red-legged partridge: common.

RESERVES AND SANCTUARIES

Chippenham Fen (Nature Conservancy; P).
Fulbourn Fen (Cambridgeshire and Isle of Ely Naturalists' Trust).
Hall Yard Wood (CIENT).
Hayley Wood (CIENT).
Peakirk (Wildfowl Trust).
Ouse Washes (Royal Society for the Protection of Birds; P).
Welches Dam (CIENT).
Welney (Wildfowl Trust).
Wicken Fen (National Trust; NP).

SOCIETIES, ETC.

Cambridgeshire and Isle of Ely Naturalists' Trust.
Cambridge Bird Club.
Madingley Ornithological Field Station, Cambridge University.

LITERATURE

Cambridge Bird Report, annually (Cambridge B.C.).
The Birds of Cambridgeshire, by David Lack (1934).
Adventurer's Fen, by E.A.R. Ennion (1942), is about Wicken Fen.
The Birds of the Letchworth Region, by A. R. Jenkins (1958).

NORFOLK

HABITATS

Woodland (B/1): Blickling Woods; Fellbrigg Great Wood; North-repps Hall Woods; Thursford Woods; Westwick Woods.
Woodland (conifer): Breckland; sep. Thetford Chase.
Heaths: Breckland, inc. Cockley Cley Warren, Croxton Heath, E. Harling Heath, E. Wretham Heath, Garboldisham Heath, Gooderstone Warren, Santon Warren, Thetford Heath, Weeting

Heath, Buxton Heath, Hevingham; Dersingham Heath; Holt Lowes; Kelling Heath and Warren, with Salthouse Heath; Roydon Common, with Grimston Warren, King's Lynn.

Marshes: Barton Broad, Bure Marshes, Hickling Broad, Horsey Mere, Ranworth Road, Hoveton Broad, Alderfen Broad; Waveney Valley; Yare Valley; Surlingham Broad; sewage farm at Wisbech; Welney Washes.

Fresh Water: Breckland: Didlington Park, Fowlmere, Langmere, Micklemere, Ringmere, Shadwell Park, Standford Water, Thompson Water; *Broads:* Alderfen, Barton, Ranworth, Cockshoot, Decoy, Hoveton, S. Walsham, Upton, Ormesby, Rollesby, Filby, Hickling, Martham, Heigham, Horsey, Rockland, Surlingham, Bayfield, Park, Holt; Blickling; Gunton; Holkham Park; Narford, Swaffham; Scoulton Mere; Sea Mere, Hingham; gravel pits at Snettisham and Welney; Welney Washes.

Estuaries: Blakeney Harbour, with Morston and Stiffkey Marshes; Brancaster Harbour; Breydon Water, with Halvergate Marshes; Cley and Salthouse Marshes; the Wash, esp. Heacham, Snettisham, Ouse Mouth and Terrington Marsh; Burnham Overy Marsh; Wells Harbour, with Warham Marshes; Holme next the Sea; Thornham Harbour.

Seashore: Hunstanton, Blakeney Point; Scolt Head Is.; Holkham; Palling to Gt. Yarmouth, inc. Winterton Dunes.

Migration Watch Points: Blakeney Point, Cley East Bank, Hunstanton, Scolt Head Is.

Heronries: Buckenham, Denver Sluice, Earsham, Holkham Park, Islington Kimberley Park, Mautby Hall, Melton Constable, Snettisham, Wickhampton.

Gull roosts: Breydon Water, Blakeney Harbour, Hickling Broad, Thompson Water, Wroxham Broad, The Wash, Ouse Washes (Welney).

Bird Collections: Cromer, Kelling, Great Witchingham.

Museums: King's Lynn, Norwich, Thetford.

SPECIAL BIRDS

Crossbill: breeds in Breckland.
Snow bunting: regular in winter on north and east coasts.

Lapland bunting: fairly regular in winter on north coast.

Shore lark: regular in winter between Scolt Head and Salthouse.

Bearded tit: breeds in Broads area and on Cley Marshes.

Spoonbill: fairly regular on migration at Breydon Water and Cley.

Heronries: Buckingham Carrs, Denver Sluice, Earsham, Holkham Park, Islington, Kimberley Park, Mautby Hall, Melton Constable, Snettisham, Wickhampton.

Bittern: breeds Broads and Cley Marshes.

Greylag goose: feral flocks from Woodbastwick and Rackheath visit Breydon Water, Broads and north coast.

Canada goose: breeds in Broads, Breckland and Holkham Park.

Brent goose: Blakeney Harbour, Scolt Head Is., the Wash.

Egyptian goose: feral breeding colony in Holkham Park, often seen on nearby marshes.

Shelduck: breeds inland, Wisbech sewage farm.

Gadwall: breeds (originally introduced) in Breckland; has recently spread to the Broads and Cley Marshes.

Garganey: breeds regularly, the Broads and Cley Marshes.

Eider: winter flocks at Heacham and Hunstanton; summering increasingly along north coast.

Fulmar: breeds on cliffs near Sheringham.

Collared dove: original British breeding colony still exists near Cromer.

Stone curlew: breeds fairly commonly in Breckland.

Ringed plover: breeds sparsely inland in Breckland.

Knot: up to 50,000 winter in the Wash; a flock of *c.* 30,000 feeds off Snettisham and roosts at Thornham.

Purple sandpiper: regular on South Hunstanton mussel beds in winter and on front at high tide.

Terneries: Blakeney Point, Scolt Head Is., Scroby Sands.

Gull roosts: Breydon Water, Blakeney Harbour, Hickling Broad, Thompson Water, Wroxham Broad, the Wash.

Black-headed gulleries: 14, mainly on North coast, but large ones inland at Cantley and Wissington sugar beet factories and Alderfen Broad.

Arctic skua: regular on migration in the Wash and along north coast.

Golden pheasant: frequent in Breckland.

Red-legged partridge: common.

RESERVES AND SANCTUARIES

Breckland: East Wretham Heath (Norfolk Naturalists' Trust, NP).
  Weeting Heath (N.N.T. and Nature Conservancy; P).
Broads:
Alderfen Broad (N.N.T.; P).
Barton Broad and Barton Turf Marshes (N.N.T.).
Bure Marshes (Ranworth, Cockshoot and Decoy Broads) (Nature
  Conservancy and N.N.T.; P).
Hickling Broad (Nature Conservancy and N.N.T.; P).
Horsey Mere (National Trust; PF).
Martham Marshes (N.N.T.).
Surlingham Broad and Bargate Fen (N.N.T.).

COAST

Blakeney Point (National Trust: NP).
Cley and Arnold's Marshes (N.N.T. and National Trust; PF).
Holkham (Nature Conservancy; PAF).
Home-next-the-Sea (N.N.T.).
Scolt Head Island (Nature Conservancy, N.N.T. and National
  Trust; NP).
Winterton Dunes (Nature Conservancy; PF).

ELSEWHERE

Blickling Woods (National Trust).
Blo Norton Wood (N.N.T.).
Bulfer Grove (N.N.T.).
Thursford woodlands (N.N.T.).

SOCIETIES, ETC.

Norfolk Naturalists' Trust.
Norfolk and Norwich Naturalists' Society.
Norfolk Wildlife Park (Ornamental Pheasant Trust), Great Witch-
  ingham (collection of pheasants, waterfowl, etc.).

LITERATURE

The Norfolk Bird and Mammal Report, published annually by

Norfolk and Norwich Nat. Soc.; and notes on the Wash and Fen areas in *Cambridge Bird Report*.

A History of the Birds of Norfolk, by B. B. Riviere (1930).
A Check List of the Birds of Cley, by R. A. Richardson (1961).
In Breckland Wilds, by W. G. Clarke (1925).
Broadland Birds, by E. L. Turner (1924).
Bird Watching on Scolt Head, by Miss E. L. Turner (1928).
Birds of Norfolk, by M. J. Seago (1968).

SUFFOLK

HABITATS

Woodland (B/1): Combs Wood; Fakenham Wood, Euston; Staverton Forest and the Thicks, Butley; woods around Bentley; Redgrave and Lopham Fens.
Woodland (conifer): Breckland.
Heaths: Breckland, inc. Cavenham Heath, Horn and Weather Heaths, Lakenheath Warren, Thetford Heath and Tuddenham Heath; coastal heaths, inc. Aldringham Common; Black Heath, Wenhaston; Blaxhall Common; Hollesley Common; Knodishall Common; N. Warren and Hazelwood Common, Aldeburgh; Rushmere Heath, Ipswich; Sutton Common; Tunstall Common; Walberswick Common; Westleton Heath.
Marshes: Benacre Broad, Easton Broad, Dunwich to Walberswick, Minsmere Level, Redgrave and Lopham Fens, Thorpeness, Tuddenham Fen.
Fresh Water: Benacre Broad, Covehithe Broad, Easton Broad, Fritton Decoy, Livermere, Culton Broad, gravel pits at Benacre Ness.
Estuaries: Alde–Ore, inc. Havergate Is.; Blyth, Deben, Breydon Water, Butley River, Orwell, Stour.
Seashore: Orfordness, Benacre Ness, Shingle Street, Lowestoft Ness.
Migration Watch Points: Lowestoft, Walberswick.
Heronries: Benham, Livermere, Methersgate Hall, N. Cove, Snape.

Gull roosts: Breydon Water, Orewell estuary.
Bird Observatory: Walberswick.
Bird Collection: Bury St Edmunds, Lowestoft.
Museums: Bury St Edmunds, Ipswich.

SPECIAL BIRDS

Hawfinch: at least as common in any other county.
Crossbill: breeds in Breckland.
Bearded tit: breeds coastal marshes, esp. Minsmere.
Long-eared owl: Herringfleet area.
Short-eared owl: coast, breeds Havergate Island.
Marsh and Montagu's harriers: coastal marshes, esp. Minsmere.
Spoonbill: fairly regular on migration, Breydon Water.
Heronries: Livermere, Methersgate Hall, North Cove, Snape, Walberswick.
Bittern: breeds coastal marshes, esp. Minsmere.
Canada goose: breeds Breckland.
Shelduck: breeds inland, Butley Thicks.
Gadwall: breeds coastal marshes.
Stone curlew: breeds Breckland and coastal heaths.
Ringed plover: breeds inland, Breckland heaths.
Avocet: Havergate Island and Minsmere are the only breeding places in British Isles.
Sandwich tern: Havergate Island; North Weir Point, Orfordness.
Gull roost: R. Orwell, Breydon Water.
Black-headed gull: large gullery on Havergate Island; three smaller ones, two on coast, one at Bury St Edmunds.
Kittiwake: nests on South Pier Pavilion, Lowestoft.
Golden pheasant: frequent in Breckland.
Red-legged partridge: common.

RESERVE AND SANCTUARIES

Cavenham and Tuddenham Heaths (Breckland) (Nature Conservancy; P for part only).
Havergate Island (Royal Society for the Protection of Birds; P).
Horn and Weather Heaths (Royal Society for the Protection of Birds; P).
Minsmere (RSPB; P).

544

North Warren, Thorpeness (RSPB; NP).
Orfordness–Havergate (RSPB and Nature Conservancy; P for part only).
Redgrave and Lopham Fens (Suffolk Naturalists' Trust).
Thetford Heath (Norfolk Naturalists' Trust and Nature Conservancy; P).
Westleton Heath (Nature Conservancy; PF).

SOCIETIES, ETC.

Dingle Bird Club.
Flatford Mill Field Centre, East Bergholt (Field Studies Council).
Suffolk Naturalists' Society, Ornithological Section.
Suffolk Naturalists' Trust.
Walberswick Ringing Station (Dingle Bird Club).

LITERATURE

Annual bird report in *Transactions* of Suffolk Nat. Soc.
The Birds of Suffolk, by C. B. Ticehurst (1932).
RSPB pamphlets on Minsmere and Havergate.
In Breckland Wilds, by W. G. Clarke (1925).
The Birds of Suffolk, by W. H. Pain (1962).

Index

Principal references are in **bold** type

Certain specialist interests are listed in the Index for the enthusiast. These lists are not necessarily complete. The subjects thus listed are:

Castles
Cathedrals, Pro-cathedrals and great
  churches
Churches, outstanding
Fen Lighters
Fisheries
Fonts, Font covers and Baptistries,
  outstanding
Houses, outstanding
Mills, Tidal
Mills, Water
Mills, Wind
Monastic Buildings and Remains

Museums
Porches, church, outstanding
Romans
Royal National Lifeboat Institute
Sailing Barges
Screens and Retables, outstanding
Thatch
Tombs and Brasses, outstanding
Towers and Spires, outstanding
Wherries, Norfolk
Wildfowling
Wood-carving, outstanding
Wool and Weaving Industries

Abel, Clarke, 106
Acle, **115**
Acle Bridge, **149**
Acton, **367**
Adam, Robert, 317
Addison, Joseph, 345
Adeliza, Queen, 214
Adnam's beer, 50
Adventurers' Fen, 441
Aethelberg, 44
Aethelbert, St, 63
Aethelhere, 24, 44
Aethelthryth, *see* Etheldreda, St
Alan of Walsingham, 450
Albemarle, Lord, 307
Albini, William d', 184, 190, 214
Albion, John, 350
Alcock, Bishop, 391 *et seq*, 455
Alde, River, 26, 30, 34
Aldeburgh, **33**, 516
Aldeburgh Festival, 32, 34
Aldeby, **126**
Aldreth, **464**
Alfic, Abbot, 343
Almar, Bishop of East Anglia, 134
Alnoth, 30, 58, 136
Alnwich, Bishop, 104
Ampton Hall, **330**
Ancient House, Ipswich, **73**
Ancient House Museum, Thetford, 293, 298
Anderson, Elizabeth Garrett, 36
Anderson, M. D., 66
Angel Corner, Bury St Edmunds, 315
Anglesey Abbey, **434**
Anglo-Saxons, 22 *et seqq*
Anna, King, 44, 445, 449

Appleby, John, 313
Arfast, 294
Arlington, Lord, 306
Arminghall, 130
Aspall, **88**
Assembly House, Norwich, 97
Astley family, 178
Attleborough, **188**
Audley, Thomas, 395
Augustinians, 347
Aylsham, **167**

B. X. Plastic Works, 82
Babraham, **483**
Backs, the, Cambridge, **431**
Bacon, Edward, 89
Bacon, Revd Nicholas, 89
Bacon, Sir Roger, 110, 158
Baconsthorpe Castle, **178**
Bacton, **155**
Badmondisfield Hall, 343
Bainton, **510**
Baldwin, Abbot, 312
Baldwin Manor, 437
Bale, John, 72
Ball, John, 369
Ball, Parson, 262
Balsham, **487**
Balsham, Hugh de, Bishop of Ely, 422, 488
Bambridge family, 482
Bardolph, Lord, 60
Barefoot, Peter, 68
Barham Manor, 90
Barham, R. H., 495
Barnack, 508
Barnardiston family, 344

Barnham Broom, 181
Barningham, **330**
Barrow, **339**
Barry, Sir Charles, 89
Barry, Sir Thomas, 109
Barsham, **140**
Bartlow, **487**
Barton, Bernard, 21
Barton Broad, **154**
Barton, Sir Henry de, 334
Barton Mills, **335**
Barton Turf, **154**
Bateman, William, Bishop of Norwich, 405 *et seq*
Bath, Earl of, 341
'Battle Area', **292**
Bawburgh, **181**
Bawdsey, **25**, 78
BBC, 110
'Beach yawls', 47
Beagle, HMS, 330
Beaufon, Ralph de, 126
Beaufort *see* Tudor
Beccles, 140, **141**, 519
Bede, 44
Bedford, 525
Bedford Drains, 265
Bedford family, 467
Bedingfield family, 257
Bedingfield, Sir Edmund, 256
Bell, Adrian, 142
Bell, Henry, 201
Bell, William, 305
Benwick, **465**
Beowulf, 22–3
Berners family, 79
Bicknell, Maria, 84
Bigod family, 57 *et seq*, 95
Bigod, Hugh, 126, 337
Bigod, Matilda, 214
Bigod, Roger, 52, 136 *et seq*, 295
Bildeston, **378**
Billingford, **186**
Bingham, William, 390
Binham, **239**
Bird-watching, 537–545
Black Prince, 214
Blackborough Priory, 248
Blackston, W., 98
Blaise, St, 358, 462
Blakeney, **237**
Blakeney Harbour, **519**
Blakeney Point, **237**, 519
Blandevyle, Thomas, 131
Blaxhall, 32b
Blickling Hall, **168** *et seqq*
Blodwell, John, 488
Blogg, Henry, 174
Blomefield, Leonard alias Jenyns, 436
Blomfield, Arthur, 324
Bloomfield, Robert, 306, 330
Blore, Edward, 468
Blount family, 328
Blyth, River, 41 *et seq*
Blythburgh, 43b

Blythe, Ronald, 32
Boleyn, Amata, 82
Boleyn, Anne, 82, 172
Boleyn family, 165
Boleyn, Geoffrey, 165, 168
Boleyn, Sir William, 106
Boleyn, Thomas, 165
Bonhote, Mrs, 137
Bonner, Bishop, 180, 377
Bonomi, Joseph, 173
Borrow, George, 91, 101, 105, 137, 143, 179, 363
Boston, 197
Botanical garden, university, Cambridge, **431**
Bottisham, **433**
Boudicca, 486
Boulge, 20
Bourn, **473**
Boxford, **370**
Boxted, **350**
Boyton, 27
Braine, John, 248
Brampton, **494**
Bran Ditch, 477
Brancaster, **222**, 521
Brancaster Staithe, **222**
Branch, Simon, 356
Brandeston, 51b
Brandon, **301**
Brandon, Charles, Duke of Suffolk, 28
Brandon Park, 302
Brandon Staunch, 523
Brantham, **82b**
Braunche, Robert and wives, 203
Breccles Hall, **189b**
Brecklands, 187, **289** *et seqq*, 300
Brent Eleigh, **378**
Bressingham, **186**
Brettingham, Matthew, 228
Breydon Water, **116**, 123, 125
Bridewell Museum, Norwich, **97**, 187
Bridgham, **305**
Brigg, Thomas, 166
Brightly, John, 137
Bristol, Earls of, 316, 319
Brithnoth, 376, 436, 456
Britten, Benjamin, (Lord), 31 *et seqq*
Broadland Conservation Centre, 148
Broads, the, 115, 118, 124, 135, 141 *et seq*, **145** *et seqq*
Broke Hall, 76
Broke, Sir Philip, 76
Bromholm Priory, **155**
Brooke, Rupert, 472
Broom's Barn Experimental Station, 339
Brotherton, Thomas de, 52
Brown, Basil, 23 *et seq*, 74
Brown, 'Capability', 61, 229, 483
Brown, Ford Madox, 393
Brown, Potto, 497
Browne, Sir Thomas, 99, 106
Bruisyard, **51**
Brundall, **111**, 519
Bryans, H., 165
Buckden, **492**

Buckland, H. T., 82
Bulcamp Hill, 44
Bungay, **135**
Bure, River, 111, 145
Bures, Sir Robert de, 367
Burgh Castle, 44, 118, **123**, 519
Burgh, Hubert de, 30, 95
Burgh St Peter, **126**
Burghley House, **508** *et seq*
Burke, Edmund, 298
Burne-Jones, Sir Edward, 393
Burney, Charles, 203
Burney, Fanny, 168, 204
Burnham Deepdale, **223**
Burnham Harbour, 520
Burnham Market, **224**
Burnham Norton, **223**
Burnham Overy, **223**
Burnham Thorpe, **224**
Burnt Fen, 332
Burwell, **438** *et seq*, 525
'Bury Bible', 317
Bury Museum, 317
Bury St Edmunds, **309**
Buss, 45
Butley, **27**
Buttermans Bay, 80, 513
Buttley Priory, Register or Chronicle, 27
Buxton, **161**
Byron, Lord, 402

Caister, 118
Caister Castle, **150**
Caister-on-Sea, 123, 149, **150**
Caistor St Edmunds, 130
Caius College, *see* Gonville and Caius
Caius, Dr John, 405
Cam, River, 431, 461, 524
Cambridge, **381** *et seqq*, 524
Cambridge University, **384** *et seqq*
Campbell, Colin, 227
Camperdown, Battle of, 119
Canaries, Norwich, 98
Cantley, **114**
Canute or Knut, King, 285, 294, 309, 311, 487
Car Dyke, 461
Carleton Rode, **183**
Carlyle, Thomas, 311
Carrow Works, Norwich, **107**
Castle Acre, **249** *et seqq*
Castle Camps, **487**
Castle, Norwich, **94**
Castle Rising, **210**
CASTLES AND CASTLE MOUNDS (Castles worth going to see are in *italics*)
    Baconsthorpe, 178
    Bungay, 135
    Burgh, 23
    Burwell, 439
    Caister, 150
    Cambridge, 428
    Castle Acre, 249
    Castle Camps, 487
    Clare, 345

Eye, 66
Framlingham, 56
Haughley, 87
Kimbolton, 494
Little Wenham, 85
New Buckenham, 184
Norwich, 94
Orford, 29–30
Thetford, 293
Wingfield, 63
Castles and Castle Mounds,
Castor, **502**
Catchpole, Margaret, 31, 75
Cathedral Church, Norwich, **102** *et seqq*
CATHEDRALS, PRO-CATHEDRALS AND GREAT CHURCHES
    Ely, 448, 508
    King's College Chapel, Cambridge, 409
    Norwich, 102
    St Edmundbury, Bury St Edmunds, 313
    St Peter, St Paul and St Andrew, Peterborough, 506–508
    Wymondham Abbey, 390
Catherine of Aragon, 492, 506
Catherine of Braganza, 306
Cattawade Bridge, **83**
Cautley, Munro, 67, 86
Cavell, Nurse Edith, 104
Cavendish, **348**
Cavendish, Chief Justice, 333
Cavendish, George, 350
Cavendish Manor vineyards, 349
Cawston, **162**
Chamberlain, Sir William, 341
Châteaubriánd, vicomte de, 139
Chaucer, Alice, Countess of Salisbury, 64
Chaucer, Geoffrey, 62, 85
Chaucer, Thomas, 64
Cherry Hinton, **484**
Chet, River, 126
Chevallier, Anne Francis, 88
Cheveley, **489**
Chicheley, Sir Thomas, 482
Childs, J. R., 137
Chillesford, 27, **29**
Christ's College, **390**
Christchurch Mansion Museum, Ipswich, 21, 31, **75**
CHURCHES, outstanding,
    Blythburgh, 43
    Cawston, 162
    Cley-next-the-Sea, 239
    Dennington, 59
    Fordham, 440
    Ickleton, 477
    Icklingham All Saints, 331
    Lakenheath, 332
    Lavenham, 352
    Little Gidding, 499
    Long Melford, 363
    Over, 469
    St Benet's, Cambridge, 428
    St Margaret's, King's Lynn, 202
    St Mary Magdalen, Cambridge, 430
    St Mary's, Bury St Edmunds, 313

St Peter Mancroft, Norwich, 98
Sall, 164
Soham, 442
Southwold, 45
Stoke-by-Nayland, 371
Sutton, 464
Terrington, 268
Walpole St Peter, 274
Walsoken, 276
Wiggenhalls, 266
Wymondham, 190
Churchill College, **423**
Churchill, Randolph, 83
Churchyard, Thomas, 21
City Hall, Norwich, **109**
City Library, Norwich, **109**
Clare, **345** *et seqq*
Clare College, **407** *et seqq*
Clare, de, family, 346 *et seq*, 408, 420
Clare Priory, 347
Clare, John, 509
Clare, Lady Elizabeth de, 347, 408
Clark, J. M., 74
Clarke, Joseph, 74
Clay, Richard, 138
Clere family, 169
Cleverly, James, 76
Cley-next-the-Sea, **239**
Clifton, Adam de, 261
Clifton, Sir John de, 190
Cloister, Norwich cathedral, **104** ,
Clopton family, 365
Coates, Francis, 171
Cobbett, William, 76, 299, 309
Cobbold family, **75**
Cobbold, Revd James, **31**
Cocley Cley, **256**
Cod, Thomas, 193 *et seq*
Coddenham, 90b
Coddington family, 328
Coke family, 228 *et seq*, 252
'Coke of Norfolk', 230, 249
Coke, Sir Edward, Lord Justice, 105, 108, 228
Coke, Thomas, 229
Cole, Margaret, 17
Coleridge, Samuel Taylor, 394
Collet, John, 500
Colman's mustard, 107
Coltishall, **160**
Commercial End, **434**
Comper, Sir Ninian, 99, 191
Constable, Golding, 84
Constable, John, 83, 370, 371
Cooper, Major E. R., 120
Coralline Crag, Chillesford, 29
Cordell, William, 359 *et seqq*
Corder, William, 373 *et seq*
Corpus Christi College, 418 *et seqq*
Costessey Woods, 181
Costin, Robert, 215
Cotman, J. J., 111
Cotman, John Sell, 96, 111
Cowper, William, 180
Cox, Harry, 153

Coypu, 126
Crabbe, George, 34 *et seq*, 139 *et seq*, 305
Crabs, 175
Cranmer, Thomas, 394
Cranwich, **304**
Crashaw, Richard, 430
Creake Abbey, **226**
Cretingham, 51
Crofts, Sir John, 331
Crome, John, 94 *et seq*
Cromer, 174
Cromwell Museum, Huntingdon, 496
Cromwell, Oliver, 99, 204, 458, 495, **496**, 499
Cromwell, Sir Richard, 495
Crow's Hall, Debenham, 88
Croydon, **476**
Cubitt, Thomas, 161
Cunningham, Revd Francis, 144
Cut-off Channel *and see* Great Ouse, 209, 263
Cut-off Drain, 332
Cymbeline, 486

Dalham, **340**
Dallinghoo, 51
Darwin, Charles, 379, 436
Darwin College, **424**
Dawes, Thomas, 369
Daye, John, 40, 343 *et seq*
Deben Estuary, 25
Deben, River, 15, 78, 514
Debenham, **88**
Deering, J. P. Gandy, 89
Defoe, Daniel, 71, 72, 115, 189, 152, 306
Dennington, **58**
Denny Priory, Waterbeach, 461
Denver, **264**, 282
Denver Bridge, 522
Denver Sluices, 264, 523
Dersingham, **217**
Despencer, Henry, Bishop of Norwich, 158, 179
Devil's Dike or Ditch, Cambs, 437–8
Devil's Ditch, Norfolk, 305
Devil's Dyke, 248
Dialect, East Anglian, 526–36
Dickens, A. G., 27
Dickens, Charles, 122, 368
Didron, 262
Diss, **185**
Ditchingham, **140**
Docks, Ipswich, 73b
Doddington, **464**
Dog in a Doublet, 466, 525
Dokets, Andrew, 415
Doubleday family, 284
Doughty, Charles Montagu, 38
Downham Market, **265**
Downing College, **423**
Downing family, **476**
Downing, William, 'Smasher', 21, 41, 60 *et seq*, 347, 412, 473
Drake, Sir Francis, 108
Drayton, **161**
Drudge, 80

Duleep Singh, Maharajah, 293, 307
Duncan, Admiral, 119
Dunn, architect, 481
Dunwich, **39** *et seqq*
Dunwich Heath, 38
Duxford, **478**

Earith, **468**, 523
Earl Stonham, **87**
Earlham Hall, 101
East Anglian Daily Times, 68–9
East Anglian Life Museum, Stowmarket, 86
East Anglians, 25
East Barsham, **246**
East Bergholt, **83b**
East Dereham, **179** *et seq*
East Harling, **187**
East Lexham, **254**
East Raynham, 255
East Wretham, **305**
Eastbridge, **38**
Eastern Daily Press, 69
Easton Farm Park, 36
Eaton Socon, **492**
Edgar, King, 15, 446
Edge, William, 255
Edmund, King and St, 22, 52, 62, 179, 294, 309
Edward the Elder, 63
Edward the Sixth School, Norwich, **105**
Edwards, Edwin, 40
Egelmar, Bishop, 294
Egfrid, King of Northumberland, 445
Eldred, John, 184, 339
Eliot, T. S., 500
Ellis, E. A., 129
Ellis, George Wilfrid, 67
Elm Hill, Norwich, **108**
Elmhams, the, **134**
Elmhurst, Mrs Sheila, 21
Elsing, **180**
Eltisley, **473** *et seqq*
Elveden, 307b
Elwes, John, 345
Ely Cathedral, **445** *et seqq*
Ely, city, **458** *et seqq*, 523
Emmanuel College, **388**
Emneth, **284**
Engine Museum, Prickwillow, 459
Eni, 44
Eorpwald, 40
Erasmus, 244, 416
Erpingham, **174**
Erpingham Gate, Norwich, **106**
Erpingham, Sir Thomas, 100, 106, 169
Erwarton, 81b
Erwarton Hall, 81
Erwarton, **81**
Etheldreda or Aethelfryth, St, 44, 180, 333, 342, 445 *et seq*
Ethelwold, Bishop of Winchester, 467
Eurosports Village, 81
Euston, **305**
Euston, Battle of, 294
Euston Hall, **305** *et seq*

Evans, George Ewart, 32
Evelyn, John, 289, 306
Everard, Bishop, 169
Exning, **342**
Eye, **65** *et seq*

Fakenham, **247**
Farmar, Hugh, 28
Fastolf, (Fastolfe, Falstaff), Sir John, 143, 150, 161, 165, 169
Felbrigg Hall, **174**
Felix, St, 40
Felixstowe, 30, **78**
Felixstowe Ferry, 26, 78, 514
Feltwell, **262**
Fen Lighters, 201, 208, 264, 282, 285, 297, 332, 417
Fens, the, 207 *et seqq*, 264, **279** *et seqq*, 499
Ferrar, Nicholas, 499
Ferry Meadows, 504
Filby Broad, **149**
Fisher Fleet, **198**, 521
Fisheries, 47 *et seq*, 118, 143, 152, 175, 198, 235, 240, 266
Fitz Osbert, Roger, 124
Fitz Walter, Robert, 241
Fitzgerald, Edward, 17, 20, 40, 138, 305, 399
Fitzgilbert, Richard, 346
Fitzobern, William, 94
Fitzroy, Captain Robert, 330
Fitzroy, Henry, Duke of Grafton, 306
Fitzroy, Henry, Duke of Richmond, 55
Fitzwilliam House, (college), **423**
Fitzwilliam Museum, Cambridge, **426** *et seq*
Flatford Mill, 84b
Flax, 349
Fleam Dike, **485** *et seq*
Flempton, **335**
Flint knapping, 302
Flixton, **133**
Flush-work, 27
Folk Museum, Cambridge, **428**
Fonnereau, Zachary, 75
FONTS, FONT COVERS AND BAPTISTRIES, outstanding
   Burnham Deepdale, 223
   Castle Rising, 215
   Little Snoring, 246
   Melton, 21
   Norton, 329
   St Peter Mancroft, Norwich, 98
   Sudbury, 369
   Trunch, 157
   Ufford, 21
   Walpole St Peter, 275
   Walsoken, 276
   Worlingsworth, 62
Fordham, **439**
Forestry Commission, 24, 291, 300
Forncett St Peter, **182**
Fornham All Saints, 337, **338**
Fornham St Genevieve, **337b**
Fornham St Martin, 337, **338**
Foss Dyke, 461
Fountaine, Sir Andrew, 249

Index

Fountaine, William and Margaret, 165
Fox, Charles James, 492
Fox, John, 16 *et seq*
Foxe, John, 215, 343
Framlingham, **51** *et seqq*
Framlingham castle, 56
Francis, Clement and Charlotte, 168
Frere, John, 63
Fressingfield, **62**
Freston Hill, **79**
Freston Park, 79
Frettenham, **160**
Fritton, 124 *et seq*
Fry, Elizabeth, 101
Fulbourn, **485**
Fursey, St, 44, 124

Gage family, 336
Gahan, Revd Stirling, 104
Gainsborough, Thomas, 368
Galgagus, 295
Gamlingay, **476**
Ganges, HMS, 81
Garboldisham, **305**
Gardiner, Alderman, 100
Gardiner, Bishop, 377
Gardner, Mrs Rodney, 15
Gaunt, *see* John of Gaunt
Geldeston Lock, **141**
German, St, 267
Gibbons, Grinling, 74, 403, 509
Gibbs, James, 425, 483
Gifford's Hall, **372**
Gill, Eric, 82, 394, 484
Gipping, **87**
Gipping River, 86
Girton College, **471**
Girvii, the, 445 *et seqq*, 453, 460
Glemsford, **349**
Glinton, **510**
Godly, Bastus, 335
Godmanchester, **496**
Godwin, William, 279
Godwinsson, Gyrth, Earl of the East
    Anglians, 94
Gog Magog Hills, **489** *et seq*
Gomme, Sir L., 257
Gonville and Caius College, 347, **404** *et seqq*
Gonville, Edmund, 347, 405
Gooding *see* Latimer
Gorleston, **123**
Goseford, 15 *et seq*
Grafham Water, **494**
Grafton, Duke of, 306
Grantchester, **472**
Gray, Miles, 358
Gray, Thomas, 421
Great Bradley, **343**
Great Cressingham, **304**
Great Dunham, **254**
Great Livermere, **330**
Great Ouse River, 200, **207** *et seqq*, 264 *et
    seqq*, 468, 491, 496, 521
Great St Mary's, Cambridge, **429**
Great Saxham, **339**

Great Shelford, **484**
Great Snoring, **246**
Great Walsingham, **241**
Great Witchingham, **167**
Great Yarmouth, **117** *et seqq*, 518
Green children, 380
Gresham, 156
Gresham, Sir John, 178
Gressenhall, 180
Grey, de, family, 304
Grey, Lady Jane, 492
Grime's Graves, **302** *et seq*
Groton, **371**
Grumbold, Thomas, 407
Guader, Ralph, Earl of Norfolk and Suffolk,
    94, 167
Guert or 'Gurth', Earl of East Anglia, 167
Guildhall, King's Lynn, **204**
Guildhall, Norwich, **109**
Gundreda de Glanville, 138
Gundreda de Warenne, 250
Gurnell, William, 358
Gurney family, 101, 279
Guthrum, King of the Danes, 376

Haddenham, **462**
Haddiscoe, **125**
Hadleigh, **375**
Haegelisdun, 310
Hakluyt, Richard, 67
Halesworth, 42
Halesworth-Southwold Railway, 42
Hall Farm, 134
Halvergate, **115**
Happisburgh, **152**
Hardwick, Bess of, 260
Hardwick, Rector of, **473**
Hardwicke, Earls of, 482
Harleston, **132**
Harling, Anne, 187
Harling, Sir Robert, 187
Harold, King, 94, 167
Harvard, John, 389
Harwich, **512**
Hastings, Sir Hugh, 180
Haughley, **87**
Havergate Island, 516
Haverhill, **344**
Hayward, W., 82
Heacham, **220**
Helpston, **509**
Hemingford Abbots, **497** *et seq*
Hemingford Grey, **498**
Hemsby Gap, **151**
Henesey, Tom, 491
Hengrave, **335**
Hengrave Hall, 335 *et seqq*
Hengrave, Sir Thomas de, 337
Henslow, John, 379
Hereford family, 75
Hereward the Wake, 381, 446 *et seq*, 505
Heritage Centre, King's Lynn, 206
Herringfleet, **124**
Herrings, 118
Hervey family, 318, 324

Heveningham Hall, **61**
Heydon, Sir Henry, 178
Hickling Broad, 128, **154**
Hilborough, **304**
Hilgay, **264**, 523
Hinchingbrooke House, **495**
Hinde, Mr Justice, 471
Hingham, **188**
Hintlesham, **85**
Hinvar, 52, 63
Histon, **471**
Hitcham, **379**
Hitches, Sir Robert, 54
Hobart, Sir Henry, 164, 169, 172
Hobart, Sir James, 127
Hobbs, Jack, 185
Hobson, Thomas, 431 *et seq*
Hockwold cum Wilton, 263b
Holbrook, 82b
Holkham Hall, **228** *et seqq*
Hollesley, **26**
Holme-next-the-Sea, **221**
Holt, **178**
Holy Sepulchre, Cambridge, **430**
Holywell, **468**
Honey Hill, **286**
Honington, **306**
Hoo, 51
Hooker, Sir William Jackson, 105
Horning, **145**
Horringer, **318**
Horsey, **152**
Houghton, **497**
Houghton Hall, **227**
Houghton St Giles, **244**
HOUSES, outstanding,
   Baldwin Manor, 437
   Blickling, 168
   Bourn, 473
   Burghley House, 508
   Burystead, 462
   Christchurch Mansion, Ipswich, 75
   East Barham Manor, 246
   Euston Hall, 305
   Gifford's Hall, 372
   Hemingford Grey, 498
   Hengrave Hall, 335
   Heveningham Hall, 61
   Hinchinbrooke, 495
   Holkham Hall, 228
   Houghton Hall, 227
   Ickworth, 318
   Longthorpe Tower, 502
   Maddingley, 471
   Melford Hall, 359
   Music House, Norwich, 107
   Narborough Hall, 249
   Oxburgh Hall, 257
   Peckover, 278
   Raveningham, 126
   Raynham Hall, 255
   School of Pythagoras, Cambridge, 428
   Seckford Hall, 18
   Strangers' Hall, Norwich, 97
   Sawston Hall, 479

Thorrington Hall, 372
Thorpland Hall, 246
Tolhouse, Great Yarmouth, 121
Troston, 330
Howard, Henrietta *see* Suffolk, Countess of,
Howard, Henry, Earl of Surrey, 54
Howard, Lady Mary, 55
Howard, Philip, Earl of Arundel, 243
Howard, Theophilus, 54
Howard, Thomas, 214
Howard, Thomas, 3rd Duke of Norfolk, 54, 214, 252
Howards, Dukes of Norfolk, 52, 137
Hoxne, **62**, 310
Hubba, 294
Hubert, St, 473
Huddleston family, 479
Humbert, Bishop, 63
Hunstanton, **221**, 521
Huntingdon, **495**
Huntingdon, Samuel, 195
Huntingdon, Simon, 195
Hutton, John, 68
Hyde Parker *see* Parker

Iceni, the, 130, 486
Ickleton, **477** *et seq*
Icklingham, 331b
Icknield Way, 221, 346, **485**
Ickworth, **318** *et seqq*
Ignatius, Father, 108
Iken, **32**, 517
Imperial War Museum, branch of, 478
Ingham, **331**
Ingua, 294
Ipswich, **68** *et seqq*, 514
Ipswich Museum, **74**
Isabella, Queen, 214
Isleham, **443**
Iveagh, Lord, 307
Ives, Charlotte, 139
Ivory, John, 97, 101, 168
Ivory, Thomas, 171
Ivory, William, 173
Ixworth, **328**
Ixworth Thorpe, **329**

Jesus College, **391** *et seqq*
Jodrell, Sir Alfred, 165
John 2nd earl of Bucks, 170
John of Gaunt, 167, 296 *et seq*
John of Lakenheath, 333
John, King, 203, 273, 312
Johnson, Dr, 204
Joice, Dick, 255
Jones, Inigo, 255
Julian, St, Mother Juliana, 107

Keane, Charles, 40
Kedington, **344**
Kempe, Margery, 207
Kent, William, 228, 255, 305
Kentwell Hall, 366
Keppel, Admiral Lord, 307
Kerdiston, Sir Roger de, 161

Kerr, Philip, 11th Marquis Lothian, 170
Kersey, **377** *et seq*
Kessingland, 518
'Kett's Castle', 216
Kett, Robert, 110, 191 *et seqq*
Kett, William, 191 *et seqq*
Kettleburgh, 51
Killigrew family, 66
Kimbolton, **492** *et seqq*
Kimbolton Castle, 494
King Street, King's Lynn, **200**
King Street, Norwich, **107**
King, Thomas, 205
King's College, **409** *et seqq*
King's Lynn, **196**, 521
King's Staithe Square, King's Lynn, **201**
Kingsley, Charles, 396, 508
Kipling, Rudyard, 482
Kirtling, **489**
Kitchener family, 333
Kitchener, Lord, 88
Knapton, **157**
Knut *see* Canute
Knyvett, Thomas, 165
Kodak Museum, 278
Kyneburga, St, 502
Kytson, Sir Thomas, 336

Lakenheath, **332**
Landbeach, **461**
Landguard Fort, 78, 514
Landwade, **440**
Langley, **128**
Lark, River, 331
Larner, Sam, 151
Latimer (or Gooding) family, 79
Laud, Will, 31
Lavender Bay, 514
Lavenham, 70, **352** *et seqq*
Lawrence, James, 78
Laxfield, **60**
Layham, **375**
Le Strange, Sir Hamon, 220
Le Strange, Sir Roger, 220
Leather industry, 139
Lefft, Capel, 330
Lefft, Edward, 330
Leicester, Earls of, 252
Leiston, **36**
Leiston Abbey, **37**
Leodegar, St, 462
Lepell, Molly, 318
Letheringham, 36
Levington, **78**
Lidgate, **342**
Lifeboats *see* Royal National Lifeboat
    Institute,
Lincoln, Abraham, 188
Lincoln, Earl of, 62
Lincoln, Samuel, 188
Lindley, John, 105
Lindsey, **378**
Lineham family, 272, 524
Linton, **487**
Lister, Geoffrey, 110, 158

Litcham, **254**
Little Bradley, 343
Little Cressingham, **304**
Little Gidding, **499**
Little Livermere, **330**
Little Ouse River, 187, 296, 523
Little St Mary's, Cambridge, **430**
Little Saxham, **339**
Little Shelford, **484**
Little Snoring, **246**
Little Walsingham, **241**
Little Wenham, and Hall, **85b**
Littleport, **459**
Livermeres, the, 330
Loddon, **126**
Lode, **434**
Long Melford, **359**
Long Melford Church, 364
Long Stanton, **470**
Long Stratton, **131**
Long, Stratton, Mr, 238
Longthorpe Tower, 502
Losinga, Herbert de, Bishop, 102, 121, 134,
    169, 202, 295
Lothbroc, 52, 115
Lothian, 8th Marquis, 170
Lothing Lake, 125, 518
Lovell, Sir Thomas, 187
Lowestoft, **143**, 518
Ludham, **153**
Lydgate, John, 342, 365
Lyhart, Bishop, 102
Lyminge, Robert, 171
Lynn Channel, 521
Lynn Museum, King's Lynn, 206

MacGibbon, James, 513
Maddermarket Theatre, Norwich, **108**
Madingley, **471**
Magdalen Street, Norwich, **107**
Magdalene College, **395**
Maldon, Battle of, 70, 376, 456
Mallet, William, of Graville, 66
Malling, Thomas, 252
Manby, George William, 264
Manea, **286**
March, **286**, 523
Margaret Catchpole, see also Catchpole, 368
Margaret of Anjou, Queen, 415
Market Place, Norwich, **108**
'Marshland Series', 276
Marshlands, the, **277** *et seqq*
Marten, Maria, 373
Martin, Sarah, 122
Martineau, Harriet, 101
Mary Tudor, Henry VIII's sister, 314
Mary Tudor, Queen, 59, 400, 402, 480
Mary, Queen of Scots, 55, 260, 506
May, Samuel Charles, 46
McLaren, 185
Melbourn, **455**
Meldreth, **477**
Melford Hall, **359**
Melton, **21**, 515
Melton Constable, **178**

Mepal, **464**
Merton, **304**
Methwold, 250, **261**
Mettingham, **140**
Middle Level Navigations *and see* Fen
  Waterways, 201, 208, 523
Middleton, William Fowle, 89
Mildenhall, **333** *et seq*
Mildmay, Sir Thomas, 389
Mills, tidal, 15, 83
Mills, water, 84, 126, 141, 167, 178, 324, 504
Mills, wind, 60, 114, 157, 264, 281, 325, 345,
  436, 441, 473, 504
Milton, John, 390, 412
Minsmere, bird sanctuary, **37**
Moeran, E. J., 155
MONASTIC BUILDINGS OR REMAINS,
  outstanding,
  Anglesey Abbey, 434
  Binham, 240
  Blackborough, 248
  Bromholm, 155
  Bury St Edmunds, 311
  Butley, 27
  Carrow Works, Norwich, 107
  Castle Acre, 250
  Clare Priory, 347
  Creake, 226
  Denny Priory, 461
  Ely, 445
  Hengrave, 335
  Ixworth, 328
  Jesus College, Cambridge, 391
  Leiston, 37
  Mendham, 250
  Normansburgh, 250
  Norwich Cathedral, 102
  Old Barge Inn, Norwich, 107
  Orford, 30
  Peterborough, 504
  Ramsey, 468 •
  Red Mount Chapel, King's Lynn, 206
  Slevesholm, 250
  Soham, 442
  South Elmham, 134
  St Andrew's Hall, Norwich, 99
  St Benet's, Ludham, 153
  St Olave's Priory, 124
  Swavesey, 470
  Thorney Abbey, 467
  Walsingham, 241
  West Acre, 248
  Wymondham, 190
Monewden, 51
Monk, Nugent, 108
Montalt, Robert de, 214
Montalt, Roger de, 214
Monuments *see* Tombs,
Moor Hall, **167**
Moore, Robert, 17
More, Sir Thomas, 416
Morley, Lord, 188
Morris, William, 393
Morston, **237**, 519
Mortimer, Sir Robert, 189

Morton's Leam, 466
Morton, John, Archbishop, 132
Moulton, **340**
Mount, Lady Elizabeth, or Talbois, 55
Mousehold Heath, **110**, 193
Mowbray family, 58
Mowbray, Dukes of Norfolk, 58
Mowbray, John, 52, 295
Moyse's Hall, Bury St Edmunds, 317
Mulbarton, **182**
Mundesley, **157**
Mundford, **304**
MUSEUMS,
  Ancient House, Thetford, 293
  Bridewell, Norwich, 462
  Christchurch Mansion, Ipswich, 75
  Clock Museum, Bury St Edmunds, 315
  Cromwell Museum, Huntingdon, 496
  East Anglian Life, Museum of,
    Stowmarket, 86
  Fitzwilliam Museum, Cambridge, 426
  Folk Museum, Cambridge, 428
Maritime Museum, Great Yarmouth, 122
  Moyse's Hall, Bury St Edmunds, 317
  Norwich Museum, Norwich, 95
  Old Engine House, Stretham, 462
  Social History Museum, King's Lynn, 206
  Stranger's Hall, Norwich, 97
  Tolhouse, Great Yarmouth, 121
Music House, Norwich, **107**
Mytens, Daniel, 169, 173

Nacton, **76**
Nar, River, 248
Narborough, **248**
Narborough Hall, **249**
Nash, John, 168
Nashe, Thomas, 122
Nayland, **371**
Needham Market, 86b
Neill, A. S., 36, 82
Nelson Hall, Burnham Thorpe, 225
Nelson, Horatio, 99, 109, 140, 142, 158, 224,
  256
Nene Park, **503**
Nene, River, 525
Nene Valley, **501** *et seq*
Nevile, Dr Thomas, 400
New Bedford River, 523
New Bells Farm, 87
New Buckenham, **182** *et seq*
New Hall College, **423**
Newark Castle, 203
Newe House, 325
Newmarket, **340** *et seqq*
Newnham College, 415
Newton-by-Castleacre, **254**
Newton Flotman, **131**
Nicholson, A. K., 488
Nix, Bishop, 102
Noble, Vera, 29
Nordelph, **287**
Norfolk and Suffolk Aviation Museum, 133
Norfolk, Dukes of, *see* Howard,
Norfolk, Dukes of, *see* Mowbray,

Norfolk Rural Life Museum, 180
Norfolk Wherry, 116
Norfolk Wildlife Park, 167
North Creake, **226**
North Elmham, **179**
North Lopham, 187
North Tuddenham, **180**
North Walsham, **158**
North Wootton, **210**
Northampton, 526
Northampton, Earl of, 215
Northborough, **510**
Northwold, **261**
Norton, **329**
Norton Bird Gardens, 328
Norton, John, 307
Norton Staithe, **114**
Norwich, **91** *et seqq*, 519
Norwich Castle, 95, 195
Norwich Cathedral, 102 *et seq*
Norwich Cattle Market, 108
Norwich, Sir John de, 140
Noyers, William de, 135
Noyes, John, 60

Oakington, **470**
Octagon Chapel, Norwich, **100**
Odo, Bishop, 214
Offa's daughter, 63
Ogard, Sir Andrew, 190
Olaf, 70
Old Bedford River, 523
Old Buckenham, **184**
Old Hunstanton, **221**
Old Meeting House, Ipswich, 74b
Old Meeting House, Norwich, **100**
Old Merchant's House, Great Yarmouth, 121
Old Schools, Cambridge, **425**
Old University Library, Cambridge, **425**
Old West (Great Ouse), 524
Onslow, 119
Ore, River, 26, 30, 51, 56, 516
Orford, **29**, 516
Orford, Lord, 284
Orfordness, 517
Ormesby Broad, 149
Orton Mere, 504
Orwell Bridge, Ipswich, 76
Orwell, Cambs, 476
Orwell, River, 70, 78
Otter Trust, 140
Oulton Broad, **142**
Oundle, 526
Ousden, **342**
Outwell, **285**
Over, **469**
Overy Staithe, **224**, 520
Owen, St or Ovin, 453, 462
Oxburgh Hall, **257** *et seqq*
Oxford, Earl of, *see* also Vere de, 487
Oxnead Hall, 173

Paine, James, 89
Paine, Thomas, 298

Pakefield, **144**
Pakenham, **325**
Palavazene, Horation, 483
Pampisford, **478**
Pandania, St, 473
Parallax, (Flat-Earther), 468
Parco, Richard de, 241
Parker family, 360
Parker, Matthew, Archbishop, 343, 345, 419
Parkington, Frederick Gershom, 315
Paston family, 106 *et seqq*, 150
Paston Grammar School, 158
Paston Letters, 106, 156 *et seq*, 159, 161
Paston, Bridget, 108
Paston, Sir John, 106
Paston, William, 159
Patten, Revd Hope, 244
Peada, King of Mercia, 502
Peakirk, **510**
Pears, Peter, Sir, 32, 34
Peck, Robert, 188
Peckover House, 278
Peckover, Jonathan, 279
Peddar's Way, 222, 250
Pembroke College, 54, 347, 420 *et seq*
Pembroke, Countess of, Marie de Valance, 420
Penda, King of Mercia, 44
Pepys, John, 495
Pepys, Samuel, 395, 495 *et seq*
Pepysian Library, Magdalene College, 395
Perne, Dr, 423, 473
Peterborough, **504** *et seq*, 524
Peterborough Cathedral, **506** *et seqq*
Peterhouse College, **422**
Peto, Samuel, 125
Petronilla, St, 351
Pett, Peter, 17
Phillips, C. W., 22
Picot, Sheriff, 473
Piers, Jan, 125
Pin Mill, **79**, **513**
Pitman, Jeoffrey, 18
Platt, Roger, 255
Pocahontas, 220
Pole, Alice de la, 62
Pole, de la, family, 64, 132
Pole, Sir Edmund de la, 479
Pole, Michael de la, 28, 162
Poley family, 350
Poley, Sir John, 351
Polstead, **373**
Pool, Michael atte, Earl of Suffolk, 64
Pool, William atte, 64
Pope, Alexander, 484
Pope, Sir Thomas, 75
'Poppy Line' Railway, 176
PORCHES, CHURCH, outstanding
    Beccles, 142
    Cley-next-the-Sea, 239
    Ely Cathedral, 452
    Lavenham, 357
    Terrington St Clements, 268
    Walpole St Peter, 274
    Woolpit, 380

Potter Heigham, **153**
Pounder, Thomas, 75
Powell, Edgar, 193
Powle, Adam, 41
Pretty, Mrs E. M., 23
Prickwillow, **459**
Pulham Market, **132**
Pulham St.Mary, **132**
Purl's Bridge, **287**
Pykenham, Archdeacon, 375

Queens' College, 414 *et seqq*

Radegund, St, 391
Raedwald, King, 23, 25, 40, 44
Ralph of Coggeshall, 30
Ramsey, **468**
Ramsholt, **25**, 514
Ranworth, **148**
Raveningham, **126**
Raynham Hall, **255**
Raynhams, the, **255**
Reach, 438, 525
Reach Lode, 437 *et seq*
Reade, Gifford Sherman, 82
Redenhall, 132b
Redwald, *see* Raedwald,
Reedham, **114**, 519
Reeds, 128
Reepham, **161**
'Reeve, American', 325
Reffley Wood, **210**
Rendlesham, 22b
Rennie, Sir John, 264, 272
Repton, Humphry, 168, 483
Reveningham, **126**
Reynolds, Sir Joshua, 204
Rhudde, Dr, 84
Richardson, Anne, 85
Richardson, Samuel, 85
Richeldis, Lady, 241 *et seq*
Richmond, Duke of, *see* Fitzroy
Riley Channel *see* Great Ouse,
Ringmere Heath, 70, 294, 488
Risby, **318**
Roberts, Bob, 513
Robertson, E. Arnot, 513
Robinson College, **424**
Robinson, Lionel, 185
Robinson, William, 89
Rochefoucauld, duc de La, 306
Rockland Broad, 128, 519
Rockland St Mary, **128**
Rolfe, John, 220
ROMANS,
    Branodum, Brancaster, 222
    Burgh Castle, 123
    Caister St Edmunds, 131
    Castor, 502
    Car Dyke, 510
    Fens, 281
    Fleam Dike, 486–7
    Holme-next-the-Sea, 221
    Honey Hill, 286
    Ickleton, 478
    Ingham, 331
    Ixworth, 328
    Kedington, 344
    Longthorpe, 504
    Methwold, 262
    Nene, River, 502
    Swaffham Prior, 437
    Terrington, 270
    Water Newton, 503
    Waterbeach, 461
    West Stow, 331
Romans, the, 24
Rose, Thomas, 166
Rossem, Meneer Ru van, 121
Rowley, Sir Joshua, 372
Royal Harwich Yacht Club, 79
Royal Hospital School, 82
Royal National Lifeboat Institute, 34, 151, 175, 236
Rubaiyat of Omar Khayyám, 20
Russel, Richard, 41

Sailing barges, 72, 80, 83, 175, 466
Sainsbury Centre for Visual Arts, 101
Saints' Country, **133**
Salisbury, Countess of, *see* Chaucer,
Sall or Salle, **164**
Salle, Sir Robert de, 158
Salters Lode, 208, 265, 523
Salthouse, 239
Salvin, architect, 94
Sampson, Abbot, 312
Sandemanians, 185
Sandlings, the, **24**
Sandringham, **217**
Sandwich, Earl of, 49, 495
Sandys, Francis, 142, 315, 319
Santon, **299**
Santon Downham, **299**
Sarawak, Rajah of, 105
Saturday Market, King's Lynn, **204**
Sawston Hall, **479**
Sawston, village college, 481
Saxham Hall, 339
Saxons, the, 24
Saxtead Green, **60**
Sayers, Dorothy L., 268
Scabellis, Jacobus de or Savelli, 335
Scarfe, Norman, 26, 142, 315
Scargill, Daniel, 182
School of Pythagoras, Cambridge, **428**
Scolt Head, **222**, 521
Scott, Sir Gilbert, 202, 390, 397, 409
Scott, Sir Peter, 272, 510
SCREENS AND RETABLES, outstanding,
    Attleborough, 189
    Balsham, 487
    Barton Turf, 154
    Castle Acre, 253
    Loddon, 127
    Peterborough Cathedral, 506
    Ranworth, 148
    Southwold, 45
    Thornton Parva, 67
Seckford Hall, **18**

556

Seckford, Henry, 18
Seckford Library, Woodbridge, 27
Seckford, Thomas, 18
Senate House, Cambridge, **425**
Septaria, 30, 80, 82
Sewell, Anna, 122
Sexburgha, 44, 446
Shannon, Lady *née* Killigrew, 66
Shelfanger, **185**
Shelland, **87**
Shelley, Percy Bysshe, 279
Shepreth, **477**
Sheringham, **176**
Sheringham and Cromer crab boat, 175
Sheringham Park, 178
Shingle Street, **26**, 516
Shipdam, **188**
Shotley, **80**
Shotley Ferry, **513**
Shotley Gate, **80**
Shrewsbury, Countess of, *see* Hardwick,
Shrublands, **89**
Shuck, Black or Old, Black Dog of East
    Anglia, 138
Sigebert, King, 40, 124, 309
Singh, *see* Duleep,
Sizewell, **37**
Skelton, John, 186
Sleford, John de, 487
Smith, Samuel, 278
Snailwell, **439**
Snape, 33
Snape Maltings, **32**, 517
Snettisham, 219
Snetzler, John, organ by, 202
Soane, Sir John, 372, 483, 468
Social History, Museum of, King's Lynn, 206
Soham, **442**
Soil Association, 87
Sole Bay, 40 *et seq*
Sole Bay, Battle of, 49
Somerleyton, **125**
Somerleyton hall, 125
Sotherton, Nicholas, 97
South Creake, **226**
South Elmham Minster, 134
South Lopham, **186**
South Walsham, 149
South Walsham Broad, **146**
South Wootton, **210**
Southwold, **45** *et seqq*
Southwold Harbour, 517
Sparke, Revd Edward Bower, 262
Sparrowe family, 73
Spinney Abbey, **442**
Spring family, 356
St Andrew's Church, Norwich, **100**
St Andrew's Hall, Norwich, 99b
St Benet's Abbey, 153
St Benet's Church, Cambridge, **428**
St Catharine's College, **418**
St Ethelbert's Gate, Norwich, **106**
St Gregory's, Pottergate, Norwich, **99**
St Gregory's, Sudbury, 369
St Ives, **468**, **498**, 524

St John the Baptist, Norwich, **102**
St John the Baptist, Timberhill, Norwich, **100**
St John's College, **396** *et seqq*
St Margaret's Church, King's Lynn, **202**
St Mary Magdalene, Cambridge, **430**
St Mary the Less, Cambridge, **430**
St Neots, **491**, 524
St Nicholas Chapel, King's Lynn, **198**
St Nicholas, Great Yarmouth, **121**
St Olave's Priory, **124**
St Peter Hungate, Norwich, **98**
St Peter Mancroft, Norwich, **98**
St Peter, Cambridge, **430**
Stafford, Henry, 2nd Duke of Buckingham,
    395
Stalham, **155**
Standground, 524
Stannard, Joseph, 111
Stanton, **329**
Staverton Thicks, 28
Steward, Austen, 193
Steward family, 335
Steward, Elizabeth, 335
Stiffkey, **237**
Stigand, Archbishop, 211
Stilton, **500**
Stockholm, Dirck Lowensen van, 44
Stoke Ferry, **264**, 523
Stoke-by-Clare, **345**
Stoke-by-Nayland, **371**
Stokes, Anthony, 85
Stone Heaps, **513**
Stonea Camp, **286**
Stour Gardens, 83
Stour, River, 82, 369
'Stourbridge Fair', Cambridge, 382
Stow Bedon, **187**
Stow Cum Quy, **433**
Stowlangtoft, **329**
Stowmarket, **86**
Stradbroke, **62**
Strange, Le *see* Le Strange,
Strangers' Hall, Norwich, **97**
Stratford Saint Mary, **84**
Stretham, **461**
Strickland, Agnes, 143
Strumpshaw, **111**
Stuntney, **444**
Suckling, Catherine, 142
Sudbourne Hall, 29
Sudbury, **368** *et seqq*
Suffolk, Countess of, 170 *et seq*
Suffolk, Countess of, *see* Howard,
Suffolk, Earl of, 64
Suffolk, 1st Duke of, 85
Suffolk House, Lidgate, 342
Suffolk Preservation Trust, 356
Suffolk Regiment, 75, 314
Suffolk Sea Phrases, 20
Sugar beet, 114
Summerhill School, 36, 82
Surlingham, **128**
Surrey, Countess of, Frances de Vere, 55
Surrey, 2nd Earl of, 250
Surrey, Earl of, *see* Howard,

557

Sutton, **464**
Sutton Bridge, **270** *et seqq*, 525
Sutton Hoo, **22**
Svend Forkbeard, 488
Swaffham, **256** *et seq*
Swaffham Bulbeck, **434** *et seqq*, 525
Swaffham Prior, **436** *et seq*
Swainsthorpe, **182**
Swallowtail butterfly, 441
Swardeston, **104**
Swavesey, **470**
Sweyn Forkbeard, 311
Sweyne, King of all the Danes, 294

Tas, River, 130
Tattingstone, **82**
'Tawdry', 18
Taylor and Green, architects, 127
Taylor, Jane and Anne, 354
Taylor, Sir Robert, 61
Taylor, Dr Rowland, 376
Tendring Hall, 372
Tendring, William, 372
Tennyson, Alfred Lord, 17
Tennyson, Julian, 32, 63, 115, 310
Terrington St Clement, **267** *et seqq*
Terrington St John, **267**
Textile Conservation Workshop, 170
Thatch, 27, 128, 434, 509
Theberton, **38**
Theberton Hall, 38
Theme Park at Pleasurewood Hills, 144
Thetford, 289, **293**
Thomas, Brian, 121
Thompson, **187**
Thoresby, Thomas, 201
Thorham Harbour, 521
Thorington Hall, 372
Thorney Abbey, 466 *et seq*
Thornham, **222**
Thornham Magna, **66**
Thornham Parva, **67**
Thorpe, Mackenzie, 272
Thorpe St Andrew, **111**
Thorpland Hall, **246**
Thursford, **247**
Thursford Steam Museum, King's Lynn, 207
Tilney All Saints, 277
Timber frames, 353
Timperley, Captayne John, 86
Tivetshall St Margaret, **132**
Toft, **473**
Tolhouse, Great Yarmouth, 121
Tombland, Norwich, **106**
TOMBS AND BRASSES, outstanding,
    Acton, 367
    Ely, 455
    Framlingham, 52
    Fulbourn, 485
    Isleham, 443
    Kedington, 344
    Orford, 31
    Oxborough, 260
    Methwold, 261
    Raynham, 255

Stanton, 329
Stow Cum Quy, 433
Trumpington, 484
Westley Waterless, 488
Weston Colville, 488
TOWERS AND SPIRES, outstanding,
    Beccles, 141
    Cromer, 174
    Eye, 65
    Great Dunham, 254
    North Walsham, 158
    Redenhall, 132
    St Neots, 491
    Snettisham, 219
    Stoke-by-Nayland, 371
    Walsoken, 276
    West Walton, 275
    Whittlesey, 465
    Worstead, 159
Townsend family, 255
Townsend, Sir Roger, 255
Trinity College, **399** *et seqq*
Trinity Hall College, **406**
Troston, **330**
Trowse, **130**
Trumpington, **484**
Trunch, **157**
Tuck, William, 205
Tudor, *see* Mary Tudor,
Tudor, (or Beaufort), Lady Margaret, 390,
    396
Tuesday Market, King's Lynn, **200**
'Turnip' Townsend, 255
Tusser, Thomas, 76, 83
Tybald, Simon, Archbishop, 369
Tydd St Giles, 277
Tydd St Mary, 277
Tyler, Wat, 369
Tyrell family, 87
Tyrell, Sir James, 87
Tyttla, King, 23

Ubba, 52, 63
Uffingas, *see* Wuffingas
Ufford, **21**
Ulfketle, Earl of East Anglia, 134
Uncumber, St, 159
University of East Anglia, 101
Upton, **149**
Upware, **442**, 525
Upwell, **285**

Vaillant, John de or de Montford, 214
Valance, Marie de, *see* Pembroke
Vanbrugh, Sir John, 494
Vancouver, George, 207
Vanneck, Sir Gerald, 61
Venta Icenorum, 130
Vere, de, family, 487, 354, 365
Vermuyden, Cornelius, 264, 281, 287
Vernon, Admiral, 76
Vigor, St, 485
Vikings, the, 70, 505

Walberswick, **41**

Waldringfield, 515
Waldy, 248
'walks', 25
Walpole family, 275
Walpole, Horace, 227
Walpole, Sir Robert, Earl of Oxford, 171, 227
Walpole St Andrew, **273**
Walpole St Peter, **274**
Walsham-le-Willows, **329**
Walsingham, 241
Walsingham, Lord, 304
Walsoken, **276**
Walsokne, Adam and Margaret, 203
Walstan, St, 181
Walton Castle, 78
Wanamaker, Mr, 217
Wandlebury, 490
Wansford, **501**
Warenne, William de, 250
Warlock, Peter, 155
Wash, the, **219** *et seq*, 521
Wastell, John, 313, 412, 429
Waterbeach, **461**
Waterfowl Trust, 510
Water Newton, **503**
Wattisfield, **330**
Watton, **188**
Watts, G. F., 170
Waveney, 519
Waveney River, 111, 133, 139, 141, 187, 319
Waveney Valley, **133**
Wayland (or Wailing) Wood, 188
Wayre, Philip, 167
Weavers' Way, 173
Weaving *see* wool,
Webb, Christopher, 488
Webb family, 80
Weeting, **304**
Wehha, King, 23
Weir, 47
Welches Dam, **286**
Well Creek, 208, 284, 523
Wells-next-the-Sea, **234** *et seqq*, 520
Welney nature reserve, **265**
Wenhaston, **42**
West Acre, **248**
West Lexham, **254**
West Lynn, **268**
West Raynam, 254
West Stow Hall, **331**
West Walton, 275 *et seq*
West Wratting, **488**
Westleton, 39b
Westley Waterless, **488**
Weston Colville, **488**
Weston Longville, 120
Wetheringsett, **67**
Wheatacre, 126
Wheeler, Charles, PRA, 299
Whepstead, **351**
Wherries, Norfolk, 98, 116, 141, 153
White, Gilbert, 436
Whitmore, Revd John, 373
Whittle, Tyler, 105

Whittlesey, **465**
Whittlesey Museum, 465
Wicken, 282, **440**, 524
Wicken Fen, **440** *et seq*, 524
Wickey, William, 17
Wickham Market, **36**
Wickhambrook, **342**
Wiggenhall St German, **266**
Wiggenhall St Mary Magdalen, **266**
Wiggenhall St Mary the Virgin, 267
Wiggenhall St Peter, **266**
Wiggenhalls, the, 522
Wilburton, **462**
Wilbye, John, 186
Wildfowling, 218
Wilkins, William, 316
Willers Mills Farm, 477
William of Norwich, St, 127, 159, 317
William of Wykeham, 132
Willingham, **469**
Wilson, Henry Maitland, 329
Wilton church, **263**
Wimpole Hall, **482**
Winfarthing, (Winefarthine), **185**
Wingfield, **63**
Wingfield College, 65
Wingfield, Katherine, 64
Wingfield, Sir Richard, 494
Wingfield, Sir Robert, 187
Winterton, **152**
Winthrop, John, 371, 476
Winthrop, Robert Charles, 371
Winthyusen, Admiral, 109
Winwaed, Battle of the, 24, 44
Wisbech, **277** *et seqq*, 524
Wissey, River, 523
Withburga, St, 179 *et seq*
Withersfield, **344**
Withipoll, Edmund, 75
Withipoll, Paul, 75
Wiveton Downs, **238**
Wolferton, **216**
Wolfson College, **424**
Wollstonecraft, Mary, 279
Wolsey, Thomas, 71, 83
Wood Ditton, **489**
Woodbridge, **15** *et seqq*, 515
WOODCARVING, outstanding,
  Burwell, 439
  Dennington, 60
  Ely, 455
  Lakenheath, 333
  March, 286
  Mildenhall, 334
  Norwich Cathedral, 104
  Over, 469
  Stowlangtoft, 329
  Swavesey, 470
  Trinity College, Cambridge, 403
  Walsoken, 276
  Wiggenhall St German, 267
  Wiggenhall St Mary the Virgin, 267
  Willingham, 469
  Withersfield, 344
Woodforde, Parson, 120

559

Woodget, Captain Richard, 224
Woodlarke, Robert, 418
Woodville, Elizabeth, 415
Wool and weaving industries, 159, 164, 187,
    197, 263, 350, 353, 356
Woolpit, **379** *et seq*
Woolverstone, 514
Woolverstone hall, 79
Worlingham, **142**
Worlington, **335**
Worlingworth, **62**
Worstead, **159**
Worsted cloth, 159
Wren, Sir Christopher, 389, 403
Wrethams, the, 292

Wroxham, **145**
Wuffa, King, 23, 23, 309
Wuffingas or Uffingas, 21, 309, 445, 479
Wulfhere, King of Mercia, 466
Wyatt, James, 61
Wymondham, 189 *et seq*

Yare, River, 111, 519
Yarmouth, *see* Great Yarmouth
Yorke, Philip, 482
Young String Players, National Association,
    37
Young, William, 307

Zouche, Alan de la, 470